Cambridge Studies in Medieval L

CW01496329

MONEY AND POW
ANGLO-SAXON ENGLAND

This groundbreaking study of coinage in early medieval England is the first to take account of the very significant additions to the corpus of southern English coins discovered in recent years, and to situate this evidence within the wider historical context of Anglo-Saxon England and its continental neighbours. Its nine chapters integrate historical and numismatic research to explore who made early medieval coinage, who used it and why. The currency emerges as a significant resource accessible across society, and, through analysis of its production, circulation and use, the author shows that control over coinage could be a major asset. This control was guided as much by ideology as by economics and embraced several levels of power, from kings down to individual craftsmen. Thematic in approach, this innovative book offers an engaging, wide-ranging account of Anglo-Saxon coinage as a unique and revealing gauge for the interaction of society, economy and government.

RORY NAISMITH is a Junior Research Fellow at Clare College, Cambridge, working in the Department of Anglo-Saxon, Norse and Celtic at the University of Cambridge, and the Department of Coins and Medals at the Fitzwilliam Museum, Cambridge.

Cambridge Studies in Medieval Life and Thought
Fourth Series

General Editor:
ROSAMOND MCKITTERICK
Professor of Medieval History, University of Cambridge, and Fellow of Sidney Sussex College

Advisory Editors:
CHRISTINE CARPENTER
Professor of Medieval English History, University of Cambridge

JONATHAN SHEPARD

The series *Cambridge Studies in Medieval Life and Thought* was inaugurated by G.G. Coulton in 1921; Professor Rosamond McKitterick now acts as General Editor of the Fourth Series, with Professor Christine Carpenter and Dr Jonathan Shepard as Advisory Editors. The series brings together outstanding work by medieval scholars over a wide range of human endeavour extending from political economy to the history of ideas.

A list of titles in the series can be found at:
www.cambridge.org/medievallifeandthought

MONEY AND POWER IN ANGLO-SAXON ENGLAND

The Southern English Kingdoms 757–865

RORY NAISMITH

Clare College, Cambridge

CAMBRIDGE
UNIVERSITY PRESS

CAMBRIDGE
UNIVERSITY PRESS

The Edinburgh Building, Cambridge CB2 8RU, UK

Published in the United States of America by Cambridge University Press, New York

Cambridge University Press is part of the University of Cambridge.

It furthers the University's mission by disseminating knowledge in the pursuit of education, learning and research at the highest international levels of excellence.

www.cambridge.org
Information on this title: www.cambridge.org/9781107669697

First published 2012
First paperback edition 2013

A catalogue record for this publication is available from the British Library

Library of Congress Cataloguing in Publication data
Naismith, Rory.
Money and power in Anglo-Saxon England : the southern English kingdoms, 757–865 / Rory Naismith.
p.   cm. – (Cambridge studies in medieval life and thought : fourth series ; 80)
Includes bibliographical references and index.
ISBN 978-1-107-00662-1 (hardback)
1. Coins, Anglo-Saxon–England, Southern.   2. Coinage–England, Southern–History–To 1500.   3. Great Britain–History–Anglo-Saxon period, 449–1066.
4. Anglo-Saxons–Kings and rulers.   5. Coins, Anglo-Saxon.
6. Mints–England–History–To 1500.   7. Numismatics–England.   I. Title.
CJ2490.N35 2011
737.4942–dc23
2011026076

ISBN 978-1-107-00662-1 Hardback
ISBN 978-1-107-66969-7 Paperback

CONTENTS

List of figures	*page* viii	
List of maps	xii	
List of tables	xiii	
Acknowledgements	xiv	
List of abbreviations	xvi	

I	INTRODUCTION	I
	Coinage in southern England and its neighbours 757–865	4
	The historical setting: Mercia, Wessex and the vikings	9

2	MONEY IN ITS POLITICAL CONTEXT	13
	Kings, states and power in England and its neighbours	16
	Royal resources	23
	Land and warriors	29
	Towns and trade	32
	Conclusion	36
	Coinage as a royal resource: the Roman legacy	37
	Emperors, kings and minting	39
	Minting profits	41

3	LOOKING AT COINAGE: ICONOGRAPHY AND INSCRIPTIONS	47
	Coins, kings and propaganda	47
	'Portraits'	53
	Offa, *novus Constantinus*?	54
	After Offa	64
	Archiepiscopal portraits	67
	Crosses and other religious iconography	69
	Inscriptions	72
	Numismatic titulature	79
	Conclusion	84

Contents

4 AUTHORITY AND MINTING I: THE KING   87
   Royal coinage in England before *c.* 740   90
   The establishment of royal coinages in northwest
        Europe *c.* 740–*c.* 770   96
   The development of royal coinage: the Mercian
        regime 757–*c.* 825   100
   The development of royal coinage: the West Saxon
        regime *c.* 825–65   106
   Case studies in royal coinage I: gold coinage   112
   Case studies in royal coinage II: the interstices of royal coinage   117

5 AUTHORITY AND MINTING II: MINTS,
   DIE-CUTTERS AND MONEYERS   128
   Mint-towns   128
   Moneyers and die-cutters   132
   The moneyers of Anglo-Saxon England   142
        Origins and parallels   142
        Connections and positions   146
   Case studies in the role of moneyers I: favoured moneyers   150
   Case studies in the role of moneyers II: the
        Anonymous coinage   153
   Kings, mints and moneyers   154

6 VALUE JUDGEMENTS: WEIGHT AND FINENESS   156
   Metal standards   157
        Silver sources   157
        Fineness   161
   Weight standards   168
        Offa's weight standards   171
        Offa, Charlemagne and the coin reforms of 792–4   175
        Metrology after 792/3   178

7 PRODUCTION OF COINAGE   181
   Coinage and recoinage   181
   The scale of minting   184
        The productivity of moneyers   192
        Contexts and comparisons   194
   Conclusion   196

8 THE CIRCULATION OF COINAGE   199
   English money, foreign money   203
   Global trends within southern England: 'monetary recession,
        without geographical retreat'   209

Contents

A tale of two mints: Canterbury and Ipswich compared   211

London   214

Rochester and Southampton: the minor mints   216

Coin-circulation and kings, moneyers and clergy   218

The rate of loss: monetization and production compared   224

The forces behind circulation   229

     The monetary economy of southern England   229

     Changes in the monetary economy   231

     Contexts of circulation: pottery and metalwork   239

     Contexts of circulation: Francia, Northumbria and Italy   244

Conclusion   251

9   THE NATURE OF COIN-USE IN THE EARLY MIDDLE AGES   252

   Background: Mauss, Pirenne, Grierson and after   252

   Coins and commerce?   259

     Gifts and coins   260

     Case study: payments in Anglo-Saxon charters   267

     Coinage and exchange in context   273

   Coinage, markets and peasants   276

   The problem of small change   284

   Conclusion: coinage in the economy   291

10   CONCLUSION   293

Bibliography   296

Index   340

FIGURES

Permission to reproduce the images in this volume was kindly given by the Trustees of the British Museum, the Trustees of the Fitzwilliam Museum, the Classical Numismatic Group (Lancaster, PA, and London), Dr Stewart Lyon and by another private collector, who wishes to remain anonymous. Figures are reproduced at ×2 life size.

2.1 *Tremissis* of Grimoald III, with Charlemagne (*MEC*, no. 1098
(Fitzwilliam Museum)) *page* 14
3.1 Examples of Offa's and Constantine's busts with diadem and
bareheaded (Chick 8a (British Museum); Chick 31c
(British Museum); and Fitzwilliam Museum) 56
3.2 Curly-haired busts of Offa and Lucius Verus (Chick 32a
(Fitzwilliam Museum); and Fitzwilliam Museum) 57
3.3 Offa and Constantine with 'eyes to God' (Chick 51a
(British Museum); and British Museum) 59
3.4 Offa's Constantinian bust with vision of the cross (?)
(Chick 25b (Fitzwilliam Museum)) 59
3.5 Busts of Cynethryth, Faustina Senior and Irene (Chick 140d
(Classical Numismatic Group); Fitzwilliam Museum; and
Fitzwilliam Museum) 63
3.6 Cross-and-Wedges busts of Coenwulf and Cuthred (Naismith
C28f (British Museum); and Naismith C31k (British Museum)) 65
3.7 Portrait coins of Coenwulf and Æthelberht (Naismith C44.1a
(Fitzwilliam Museum); Naismith C203b (Lyon collection);
and Naismith C212b (Lyon collection)) 66
3.8 Facing busts of Pope Hadrian I and Archbishops Wulfred
and Ceolnoth (*MEC*, no. 1032 (Fitzwilliam Museum);
Naismith C46.2j (Lyon collection); and Naismith C154a
(Fitzwilliam Museum)) 67

List of figures

3.9 Examples of the crosses on Offa's Light coinage (Chick 102a
(Fitzwilliam Museum); Chick 10p (Fitzwilliam Museum); Chick
17b (British Museum); Chick 38b (British Museum); Chick 47b
(Lyon collection); and Chick 117a (British Museum)) 71

3.10 Mint-name monograms from ninth-century England (Naismith
C46.2j (Lyon collection); Naismith C85a (Fitzwilliam Museum);
Naismith C105a (Fitzwilliam Museum); and Naismith R36a
(Fitzwilliam Museum)) 74

4.1 Coins of Eadbald of Kent and Aldfrith of Northumbria and
of the Church (Fitzwilliam Museum; Fitzwilliam Museum;
and Fitzwilliam Museum) 92

4.2 Imagery of selected early pennies or *sceattas* (Fitzwilliam
Museum; and Fitzwilliam Museum) 93

4.3 The first regular royal coinages of Eadberht of Northumbria,
Beonna of East Anglia, Pippin of Francia, Heaberht of Kent and
Offa (Fitzwilliam Museum; *MEC*, no. 1121B (Fitzwilliam
Museum); Fitzwilliam Museum; Chick 84a (British Museum);
and Chick 102a (Fitzwilliam Museum)) 98

4.4 Offa's Light coinage, showing specimens from Canterbury,
London and East Anglia (Chick 10p (Fitzwilliam Museum);
Chick 91a (Fitzwilliam Museum); and Chick 177b
(Fitzwilliam Museum)) 101

4.5 Offa's Heavy coinage, showing specimens from Canterbury,
London and East Anglia (Chick 212f (private collection);
Chick 220a (Fitzwilliam Museum); and Chick 258a
(Fitzwilliam Museum)) 102

4.6 The three-line coinages of 796–8 (Naismith L2b
(Fitzwilliam Museum); Naismith C4a (Fitzwilliam Museum);
and Naismith E2.1a (Fitzwilliam Museum)) 103

4.7 Coins of Ceolwulf I with extended titulature and three-line
design (Naismith C49.3a (Fitzwilliam Museum); Naismith
R7.3a (British Museum); and Naismith E20.2j
(Fitzwilliam Museum)) 105

4.8 The DOROB-C type of Ecgberht, and the Inscribed Cross
type of Æthelwulf and Æthelberht (Naismith C85a
(Fitzwilliam Museum); Naismith C146a (Fitzwilliam Museum);
Naismith C154a (Fitzwilliam Museum); and Naismith C167a
(Fitzwilliam Museum)) 108

4.9 The Offa dinar and the Coenwulf mancus (Chick 1a
(British Museum); and Naismith G2a (British Museum)) 113

List of figures

4.10 Pennies of Æthelberht II, Eanred and Beorhtric (Chick 186a
(British Museum); Naismith U1a (British Museum); and
Naismith W2a (British Museum)) 119

4.11 Ecclesiastical coins of Archbishops Iænberht and Æthelheard,
and of Eadberht, bishop of London, and Beornmod, bishop of
Rochester (Chick 154a (Fitzwilliam Museum); Chick 248a
(British Museum); Chick 81c (Fitzwilliam Museum); and
Naismith R14.3a (Fitzwilliam Museum)) 122

5.1 *Thrymsas* and *sceattas* in the names of probable moneyers
(British Museum; British Museum; Fitzwilliam Museum;
Fitzwilliam Museum; Fitzwilliam Museum; and
British Museum) 135

5.2 Specimens of the royal and archiepiscopal Anonymous
coinage (Naismith C56.2a (Fitzwilliam Museum); and
Naismith C57.2a (Fitzwilliam Museum)) 136

5.3 Royal moneyer continuity at Canterbury 136

5.4 Archiepiscopal moneyer continuity at Canterbury 137

5.5 Moneyer continuity at Rochester 137

5.6 Moneyer continuity at London 137

5.7 Moneyer continuity at Ipswich 138

5.8 Moneyer continuity at Southampton/Winchester 138

6.1 Weights of all Offa's Light coinage 172

6.2 Weights of all Offa's Heavy coinage 172

6.3 Weights of all coins struck 792/3–*c.* 840 (to Offa's
Heavy standard) 173

6.4 Weights of Carolingian *denarii* of Pippin II, Carloman and
Charlemagne, struck *c.* 755–93/4 175

6.5 Weights of Carolingian *denarii* of Charlemagne, struck 793/4–814 177

6.6 Weights of the Inscribed Cross coinage *c.* 854–*c.* 864 179

7.1 Estimated output in dies per annum at Canterbury 188

7.2 Estimated output in dies per annum at London 189

7.3 Estimated output in dies per annum at Rochester 189

7.4 Estimated output in dies per annum at Ipswich 190

8.1 Regional representation of finds of pennies minted at Ipswich 212

8.2 Representation of different mints within all finds
from East Anglia 212

8.3 Regional representation of finds of pennies minted
at Canterbury 213

8.4 Representation of different mints within all finds from Kent 213

8.5 Regional representation of finds of pennies minted at London 215

8.6 Regional representation of finds of pennies minted at Rochester 216

List of figures

8.7 Regional representation of finds of pennies minted at
    Southampton/Winchester   217
8.8 Losses per annum based on date of production   227
8.9 Single-finds per annum adjusted for probable time in circulation   228
8.10 Approximate number of known southern English
    hoards per decade   233
8.11 Loss rate of single-finds of Northumbrian coins   248
9.1 Rate of loss per decade in later Anglo-Saxon England   257

MAPS

1.1   Mints probably active in England 757–865   *page* 8
8.1   Monetary regions of England   203

TABLES

7.1 Output of individual moneyers   *page* 193
8.1 Representation of local or friendly mints within
    independent kingdoms   205
8.2 Finds of Carolingian and related silver coins in England   206
8.3 Southern English finds of Northumbrian coins   207
8.4 Number and percentage of finds per region per period   211
8.5 Finds of the coinage of Cynethryth arranged by region   219
8.6 Regional distribution of finds of coins of certain moneyers   221
8.7 Regional distribution of finds of ecclesiastical coins   224
8.8 Totals of single- and stray-finds   226
8.9 Estimated rate of loss after production   227

ACKNOWLEDGEMENTS

It has been a privilege and a pleasure to work with so many kind, learned and congenial colleagues in the studies of which this book and its companion volume *The Coinage of Southern England 796–865* (British Numismatic Society Special Publication 8) are the culmination. Medieval coinage and its interpretation have fascinated me since childhood, but my interest in them became serious only as a student at the University of Cambridge, where since 2002 I have split my time between the Department of Anglo-Saxon, Norse and Celtic, and the Fitzwilliam Museum's Department of Coins and Medals. Simon Keynes from the former and Mark Blackburn from the latter have been models of all that supervisors should be: guides, supporters and counsellors as well as fast friends. I also owe a collective debt of thanks to the members of both departments. In particular, Martin Allen at the Fitzwilliam generously shared his expertise on the Corpus of Early Medieval Coin Finds and later medieval English numismatics; Jonathan Jarrett, Adi Popescu and Elina Screen also stand out for help in a range of ways. In Anglo-Saxon, Norse and Celtic, Richard Dance read and commented on parts of the draft, and Rosalind Love and Paul Russell helped me with other specific points.

The doctoral research which lies behind this book was conducted at Trinity College, Cambridge, with the financial support of the Arts and Humanities Research Council. I would like to thank Michael Metcalf and Fiona Edmonds for their role as examiners of the Ph.D. which resulted from it. Both provided valuable comments which have helped pave the way towards publication. I am also grateful to Gareth Williams for many years of helpful discussion and assistance at the British Museum. A Junior Research Fellowship at Clare College, Cambridge, has given me the opportunity to update and complete this volume for publication while working in a supportive and stimulating environment. Thanks are also due to Rosamond McKitterick for her efficiency, suggestions and general advice as series editor, and to the team assembled by Cambridge University Press to see this volume through to completion, particularly Jo Bottrill, Christopher Feeney, Elizabeth Friend-Smith and Chloe Howell. Their thoroughness and expertise have improved the work immensely. I was lucky enough at various times to discuss this work as it developed with many others, some of whom kindly read portions of successive drafts or allowed me access to unpublished work of their own; these include Alex Burghart, Fiona Edmonds, Anna Gannon, Stewart Lyon, Neil Middleton, George Molyneaux, Hugh Pagan, Levi Roach, Elina Screen, Ben Snook, Lord Stewartby and Gareth Williams. Any errors which remain are, of course, my own.

Tres digiti scribunt et totum corpus laborat ('three fingers write but the whole body labours') were the words used by at least one medieval scribe to bemoan the toll which writing took on him. Advances in technology have spread the burden to more than three fingers, but the labour which goes into preparing a book remains considerable. This work has been made into a pleasure through the encouragement and companionship of my wife Brittany and my family; for this I owe them special thanks.

ABBREVIATIONS

ASC	*Anglo-Saxon Chronicle*, cited from C. Plummer, ed., *Two of the Saxon Chronicles Parallel*, 2 vols. (Oxford, 1892–9), and *The Anglo-Saxon Chronicle: A Revised Translation*, trans. D. Whitelock, with D. C. Douglas and S. I. Tucker (London, 1961) (which provides a corrected chronology)
ASE	*Anglo-Saxon England*
ASPR	*The Anglo-Saxon Poetic Records*, ed. G. P. Krapp and E. van K. Dobbie, 6 vols. (New York, 1931–42)
ASSAH	*Anglo-Saxon Studies in Archaeology and History*
BCS	*Cartilarium Saxonicum: A Collection of Charters Relating to Anglo-Saxon History*, ed. W. de G. Birch, 3 vols. (London, 1885–99)
BEASE	M. Lapidge, J. Blair, S. Keynes and D. Scragg, eds., *The Blackwell Encyclopaedia of Anglo-Saxon England* (Oxford, 1999)
BMC	C. F. Keary and H. A. Grueber, *A Catalogue of English Coins in the British Museum. Anglo-Saxon Series*, 2 vols. (London, 1887–93)
BNJ	*British Numismatic Journal*
BSFN	*Bulletin de la Société française de numismatique*
CCSL	Corpus Christianorum, Series Latina
Chick	D. Chick, *The Coinage of Offa and His Contemporaries* (London, 2010)
DOC	P. Grierson and M. Hendy, *Byzantine Coins in the Dumbarton Oaks Collection and in the Whittemore Collection*, 5 vols. in 9 (Washington, DC, 1966–99)
EcHR	*Economic History Review*
EHD	D. Whitelock (trans.), *English Historical Documents*, vol. I, *c. 500–1042*, 2nd edn (London, 1979) [cited by document number]
EHR	*English Historical Review*

EMC	Corpus of Early Medieval Coin Finds, Fitzwilliam Museum, Cambridge (www-cm.fitzmuseum.cam. ac.uk/emc/)
EME	*Early Medieval Europe*
FEMA	C. Wickham, *Framing the Early Middle Ages: Europe and the Mediterranean, 400–800* (Oxford, 2005)
HE	Bede, *Historia ecclesiastica gentis Anglorum*, ed. B. Colgrave and R. A. B. Mynors (Oxford, 1969)
JEcH	*Journal of Economic History*
MEC	P. Grierson and M. Blackburn, *Medieval European Coinage I: The Early Middle Ages (5th–10th Centuries)* (Cambridge, 1986)
MGH Capit.	*Monumenta Germaniae Historica, Capitularia. Legum sectio II, Capitularia regum Francorum*, ed. A. Boretius and V. Krause, 2 vols. (Hanover, 1883–98)
Conc.	*Concilia. Legum sectio III, Concilia II.i–ii (Concilia aevi Karolini)*, ed. A. Werminghoff (Hanover and Leipzig, 1906–8)
Epist.	*Epistolae III–VIII (Epistolae Merovingici et Karolini aevi I–VI)* (Hanover, 1892–1939)
Epp. sel.	*Epistolae selectae I (Die Briefe des heiligen Bonifatius und Lullus)*, ed. M. Tangl (Berlin, 1916)
Poet.	*Poetae Latini Aevi Carolini*, ed. E. Dümmler, L. Traube, P. von Winterfeld and K. Strecker, 4 vols. (Hanover, 1881–99)
Naismith	R. Naismith, *The Coinage of Southern England 796–865* (London, 2011)
NC	*Numismatic Chronicle*
NCAH XIV	A. Cameron, B. Ward-Perkins and M. Whitby, eds., *The New Cambridge Ancient History XIV: Late Antiquity: Empire and Successors, A.D. 425–600* (Cambridge, 2000)
NCMH I	P. Fouracre, ed., *The New Cambridge Medieval History I, c. 500–c. 700* (Cambridge, 2005)
NCMH II	R. McKitterick, ed., *The New Cambridge Medieval History II, c. 700–c. 900* (Cambridge, 1995)
NCMH III	T. Reuter, ed., *The New Cambridge Medieval History III, c. 900–c. 1024* (Cambridge, 1999)
NUMIS	Numismatic Information System, Geldmuseum, Utrecht (www.geldmuseum.nl/museum/content/dutch-coin-finds)
OLD	P. G. W. Glare *et al.*, eds., *Oxford Latin Dictionary* (Oxford, 1968–82)

PAS   Portable Antiquities Scheme, British Museum (www.finds. org.uk)

PASE   Prosopography of Anglo-Saxon England (www.pase. ac.uk/)

P&P   *Past and Present*

PL   *Patrologiae cursus completus. Series (Latina) prima*, ed. J. P. Migne, 221 vols. (Paris, 1844–64)

S   P. Sawyer, *Anglo-Saxon Charters: An Annotated List and Bibliography* (London, 1968)

SEHD   F. Harmer, ed., *Select English Historical Documents of the Ninth and Tenth Centuries* (Cambridge, 1914)

Settimane   *Settimane di studio del centro italiano di studi sull'alto medioevo*

T&S   D. M. Metcalf, *Thrymsas and Sceattas in the Ashmolean Museum, Oxford*, 3 vols. (London, 1993–4)

TRHS   *Transactions of the Royal Historical Society*

Chapter 1

INTRODUCTION

At every turn in the four or five hundred years before 1066 historical
questions arise which are illustrated and sometimes, perhaps, are hap-
pily brought nearer solution when they are brought into connection
with the numismatic evidence.[1]

Such was the opinion of Sir Frank Stenton on the evening of 23 April
1958, when he addressed the British Numismatic Society and brought the
best of pre-Conquest historical research into contact with the numismatic
community. Since then coinage has remained close to the forefront of
historical assessments of Anglo-Saxon England, and the special relationship between numismatists and historians continues to flourish.[2] It is as
a result of this relationship that this book came to be written: it presents
not a numismatic study as such, but an exercise in the use of numismatic
and monetary material in order to draw conclusions of wider historical
significance. This approach has few precedents, in that although coinage
is widely recognized for its significance as a historical source, rarely has it
been the primary focus of historical research. More commonly coins have
been drawn on by historians and archaeologists as a supplement to other
material, with less focus on the potential advantages or insights that coinage has to offer on its own terms. These studies have tended to approach
the coinage from one of two perspectives: that of trade, exchange and the
activity of the economy; or that of government and administration. Only
occasionally have the two themes been broached side by side.

To a large extent such a break is justifiable, and is grounded in the different aims, agendas and experiences of those involved in the patronage
of minting, the production of coinage and in its subsequent use as currency. Yet separating the functions of coinage in this way, and divorcing

---

[1] F. M. Stenton, *Preparatory to Anglo-Saxon England*, ed. D. M. Stenton (Oxford, 1970), p. 371.
[2] M. Blackburn, 'Stenton and Anglo-Saxon Numismatics', in *Anglo-Saxon England Fifty Years On*, ed.
D. Matthew (Reading, 1994), pp. 61–81.

them from the specifics of numismatic detail, can conceal some of the coinage's most interesting contributions. The central aim of this book is to bring these traditions together and combine them with conclusions drawn from exhaustive and up-to-date study of the raw numismatic material – above all a complete catalogue of all 4,000 surviving specimens of gold and silver English coinage produced outside Northumbria in the period 757–865.[3] More than half of this total has come to light only within the last four decades, making a renewed investigation of the coinage long overdue. This large corpus can be used to home in on important aspects of the coinage, such as how many sets of minting stamps (dies) were used and hence (after some statistical acrobatics) the probable productivity of different mints at different times, as well as the contributions of individual moneyers and the distribution of single-finds and hoards. Results drawn from this corpus lie, implicitly or explicitly, behind all of the conclusions presented here.

From this blend of numismatic and historical analysis emerges a more well-rounded understanding of one segment of Anglo-Saxon coinage in its proper context – a context that begins to provide answers to a host of questions on how money's symbolic, administrative and economic roles converged.[4] What, for example, do the volume of production and networks of circulation indicate about kings' wealth and control over the monetary economy? How much power did the makers of coinage wield, and in what ways did they relate to other authorities? In what ways could (or would) kings manipulate or profit from minting within their kingdoms? Can coinage, in short, be examined in the same critical way as charters, law-codes and other written and archaeological sources?

Of necessity the several separate traditions which this study brings under consideration must often be approached in different ways. It thus makes most sense to impose chapter divisions according to aspects of governmental and cultural background (Chapters 2–5), production (Chapters 6 and 7) and circulation (Chapters 8 and 9). This structure takes as its starting point the conceptual and organizational framework within which coinage operated. It grew to become an important trapping of kingship, but there were major limitations on the nature of kings' involvement, and considerable power lay with the die-cutters, who made the dies used for minting within each town, and the moneyers, who oversaw day-to-day aspects of minting and exchange from individual workshops. The subsequent treatment of production and circulation

---

[3] Published as Chick; and Naismith.
[4] Cf. the challenge recently laid down by Matthew Innes ('Framing the Carolingian Economy', *Journal of Agrarian Change* 9 (2009), 42–58, at pp. 6–7).

begins from this more nuanced view of 'control' over minting. These chapters demonstrate how much there was to play for, and how the power structure behind coin production affected its monetary role (and vice versa). Economy, society and government found one of their most revealing intersections in the making and use of coinage.

The separation of the numismatic, administrative and economic aspects of coinage is of course a simplification – arguably an oversimplification. These divisions are themselves vague agglomerations dictated by long-established disciplinary norms: the users, makers and patrons of early medieval coins saw the world through different eyes. Pennies did not, in the first place, constitute all money in circulation or play a part in every exchange. Other forms of money existed, of both high and low value, only some of which can now be traced.[5] Many exchanges did not need money at all, but were negotiated through barter or systems of gift, trust and favour. Study of the coinage is simply not synonymous with study of the entire economy, or even all media of exchange. Nevertheless, the silver currency of southern England played an important role: it was purpose-made for exchanges and versatile in its uses and users. A silver penny might have passed from a moneyer to a merchant, to a nobleman, to a peasant, to a clergyman and then to a king before finally coming, by chance, to rest in the ground for 1,200 years. To some users a coin might have represented a store of considerable wealth to be treasured, and to others a potential medium of exchange for large or small purchases. Some might have dealt with coinage very rarely, others on a daily basis. Just as with modern money, the details of these events are largely lost, save as a daydream with which to conjure. But its comparatively wide social and geographical remit and capacity for survival, retrieval and recording makes coinage a very apt vantage point from which to survey the numerous strands that have come together to create modern perceptions of early medieval history. Ambitious and politically aware rulers, educated and idealistic churchmen and a bustling and dynamic economy could all be found in Europe in the first millennium. Although it may be a cliché often repeated in recent decades, only latter-day barbarians still harbour views of this period as the 'Dark Ages'. A wealth of high-calibre scholarship on the early Middle Ages has done away with images of too benighted and poverty-stricken a society.

One crucially important aspect of this ongoing research is a broadened geographical perspective. Southern England in the eighth and ninth centuries was far from being as isolated as its island setting might suggest, and it was an important cultural, political and economic player in

---

[5] Below, pp. 289–90.

Christian Europe as a whole. Wilhelm Levison's classic study of *England and the Continent in the Eighth Century* explained how much was gained by cross-Channel contacts in the early Middle Ages, above all from a religious and intellectual point of view, and his attempt to downplay the insularity of England has been followed up successfully many times since. Glances, and extended forays, across the Channel (or the North Sea or the Irish Sea) are now accepted as integral to a full understanding of Anglo-Saxon history. Here, frequent comparisons will be made between what can be said about the coinage of southern England and about that of other parts of contemporary Europe, highlighting similarities as well as contrasts. Francia in particular but also Northumbria, Ireland, Italy, Spain, Scandinavia and other areas offer important alternative backgrounds and historiographical traditions; these add pieces to the puzzle in southern England, underscore its special features and can (when used judiciously) plug some of the holes in its often scarce sources.

Comparisons of this sort must be used with care, as must methodologies and conclusions borrowed from multiple disciplines. To some extent a multi-faceted approach is inherent in coinage as a source: it is a category of artefact of great importance to archaeologists and historians as well as numismatists, which combines an economic function with a physical manifestation of political, cultural, artistic and administrative activity. Numismatics as such provides one of several possible points of departure from which to approach the surviving remnants of the currency, but this ultimately remains a historical study based on the central theme of the coinage. Numismatic data and analysis are vital to its foundations, but will not be discussed in detail save when they are necessary for understanding more general conclusions.

COINAGE IN SOUTHERN ENGLAND AND ITS
NEIGHBOURS 757–865

The period from the appearance of the broad penny to the height of the 'first Viking Age'[6] in the 860s is an attractive one in terms of the connections between coinage and other historical developments, both in the short and the long term.[7] Its opening is clear from a numismatic point of view, and lies with the emergence of the broad silver penny in the middle of the eighth century. However, this did not spring *ex nihilo*. There

---

[6] For this periodization see P. Sawyer, 'The Two Viking Ages of Britain', *Mediaeval Scandinavia* 2 (1969), 163–207.

[7] For overviews, see *MEC*, pp. 155–89 and 267–325; I. Stewart, 'The English and Norman Mints, c. 600–1158', in *A New History of the Royal Mint*, ed. C. Challis (Cambridge, 1992), pp. 1–82.

was already a tradition, over a century old, of minting in Anglo-Saxon England, going back to an early seventh-century currency of high-value gold *scillingas* modelled on Merovingian Frankish *tremisses*, which in turn grew out of late Roman currency. Close connections between England and the Frankish kingdoms were to be a hallmark of the coinage down to the eighth century and beyond, and at this early stage England generally seems to have followed the monetary developments of its most powerful continental neighbour very closely. The designs of Anglo-Saxon *scillingas* imitated those of Frankish and older Roman coins, but while the Frankish prototypes normally bore the name of the moneyer and mint responsible for production (and only rarely that of the king),[8] English coins were for the most part uninscribed.

In the early 670s these Frankish *tremisses*, which had become very debased, gave way to a new coinage of small silver *denarii*, a process repeated almost simultaneously in England.[9] There, the new silver coins – which, like their gold predecessors, were largely uninscribed – apparently came to be known as *pæningas* or pennies, although it is still common for them to be referred to as *sceattas*.[10] The age of the early pennies or *sceattas* lasted until approximately the middle of the eighth century, and increased use of metal-detectors and reportage of finds since the 1970s has revealed that at their height the early pennies were probably the most plentiful currency England had between the fourth and late twelfth centuries. Over 2,800 single-finds were recorded as of October 2010.[11]

The seventy-five or so years of the early pennies' currency can be divided into a 'primary' phase lasting until *c.* 710/15, which was dominated by a smaller number of types concentrated in the southeast of the country, and a subsequent 'secondary' phase in which the number of minting-places and types expanded substantially. Coinages produced in Frisia and Jutland also circulated freely in England, and are powerful witnesses to the vibrancy of North Sea exchange at this time.[12] Over 200 different types of early pennies can be traced in all, some very common, others known from only a handful of specimens. Again, English moneyers only occasionally used the Frankish custom of placing their name or the name of their mint on the coins, making the early pennies difficult to date or localize precisely, or attribute to any specific authority. Yet the avoidance of inscriptions seems to have fostered an

---

[8] *MEC*, pp. 81–154.   [9] See in general *T&S*.   [10] *MEC*, p. 157.

[11] M. Blackburn, '"Productive" Sites and the Pattern of Coin Loss in England, 600–1180', in *Markets in Early Medieval Europe: Trading and 'Productive' Sites, 650–850*, ed. T. Pestell and K. Ulmschneider (Macclesfield, 2003), pp. 20–36. Find totals are derived from EMC and PAS.

[12] Cf. S. Lebecq, *Marchands et navigateurs frisons du haut moyen âge*, 2 vols. (Lille, 1983) and 'The Northern Seas (Fifth to Eighth Centuries)', in *NCMH* I, pp. 639–59.

unusually subtle and diverse use of iconography among the patrons and makers of early pennies, and this phase was noteworthy for the artistic and intellectual sophistication of coin design, which reveals much about the religious and cultural background of English society in the age of Bede.[13]

But, repeating the cycle of the gold coinage in the seventh century, the early pennies fell into decline in the 730s and 740s. Issues became scarcer, lighter and more debased, presumably signalling a shortage of silver, though the reasons for the shortage – and indeed for the profusion of bullion earlier in the eighth century – are obscure.[14] As a result of this decline new coinages of different organization and format were eventually adopted in several kingdoms of northwest Europe, on all of which the king's name was inscribed as standard for the first time.[15] The tight chronology of these reforms reveals the integration of the kingdoms around the North Sea, and also that the initiative originated in a perhaps unexpected locale: Northumbria, which was probably the first kingdom to make the change, in the reign of Eadberht (737–58). Eadberht's new coinage stuck with the small, thick format of the early pennies, establishing a precedent that would be followed in Northumbria until the 860s, despite serious debasement in its later stages.[16] As a result, the Northumbrian coinage remained quite distinct from that of southern England: only a very limited number of southern coins have been found north of the Humber, while debased Northumbrian coins found a niche in the mid ninth century as small change in parts of Southumbrian England. Apart from occasional comparisons, Northumbria's complex and intriguing monetary history will largely be left to one side in this volume.

New coinages from south of the Humber began with that of Beonna, king of the East Angles (c. 749–c. 760),[17] and were followed soon afterwards by a related reform in the Frankish kingdom under Pippin III (751–68).[18] This and the earlier English reforms influenced the new coinages of the southeast, which appeared in the 760s in the names of Offa

---

[13] A. Gannon, *The Iconography of Early Anglo-Saxon Coinage: Sixth to Eighth Centuries* (Oxford, 2003).

[14] Below, pp. 96–7 and 161–8.

[15] R. Naismith, 'Kings, Crisis and Coinage Reforms in Northwest Europe *c.* 740–70', *EME* (forthcoming).

[16] J. Booth, '*Sceattas* in Northumbria', in *Sceattas in England and on the Continent*, ed. D. H. Hill and D. M. Metcalf, BAR British Series 128 (Oxford, 1984), pp. 71–111.

[17] M. Archibald, 'The Coinage of Beonna in the Light of the Middle Harling Hoard', *BNJ* 55 (1985), 10–54, and 'A Sceat of Ethelbert I of East Anglia and Recent Finds of Coins of Beonna', *BNJ* 65 (1995), 1–19.

[18] See J. Lafaurie, 'Des Mérovingiens aux Carolingiens. Les monnaies de Pépin le Bref', *Francia* 2 (1974), 26–48.

of Mercia (757–96) and (probably) Heaberht (*fl. c.* 765), an obscure local ruler of Kent.[19]

By approximately 770 five kingdoms bordering on the North Sea had adopted new royal coinages: Northumbria, East Anglia, Francia, Kent and Mercia. In England this change had been accompanied by a significant contraction in the number of mints. While up to twenty or so locations had produced early pennies,[20] just six can be identified with confidence in the period 757–865: York, Ipswich, London, Canterbury, Rochester and Southampton or Winchester (Map 1.1). The first four were all active at the outset of this period, while the last two only opened (or, quite probably, reopened) *c.* 797/8 and *c.* 810 respectively. The identification of these and the attribution of coins to them is complicated by the general lack of mint signatures, although their number, location and organization can be gleaned with more or less confidence by other means. All six locations were important settlements in their own right, and their concentration in the eastern part of England was a reflection of the importance to Anglo-Saxon minting of incoming foreign bullion. Patterns of political control over these mints were complex. At various times, however, one or more mints lay under the control of Mercian, Northumbrian, West Saxon, Kentish and East Anglian kings. There was also a small quantity of ecclesiastical coinage – again probably the outgrowth of an earlier tradition – produced simultaneously.[21] Archbishops of Canterbury were named on coins until the early tenth century (and the archbishops of York until the mid ninth); one bishop of London was named on pennies under Offa; and at Rochester there are some coins which, although not naming the local bishop, should probably be assigned to ecclesiastical patronage.

Within the southern mints it was almost universal for coins to carry the names of the man responsible for production, and of the king whose authority and patronage underwrote the moneyer's activity. Very little is known about these moneyers, although their importance is undeniable.[22] In many ways it is a misnomer to speak of mints as specific institutions in England at this time: moneyers shared the services of a small number of die-making craftsmen – die-cutters – within each town, but physically and administratively each moneyer's operation was a separate entity. For the sake of convenience, however, 'mint' will be used as shorthand for each location at which one or more moneyers were active.

[19] Below, pp. 97–100.   [20] *T&S* III, 300.
[21] R. Naismith, 'Money of the Saints: Church and Coinage in Early Anglo-Saxon England', *Anglo-Saxon* 2 (forthcoming). Also below pp. 92–4 and 121–3.
[22] Below, pp. 132–49.

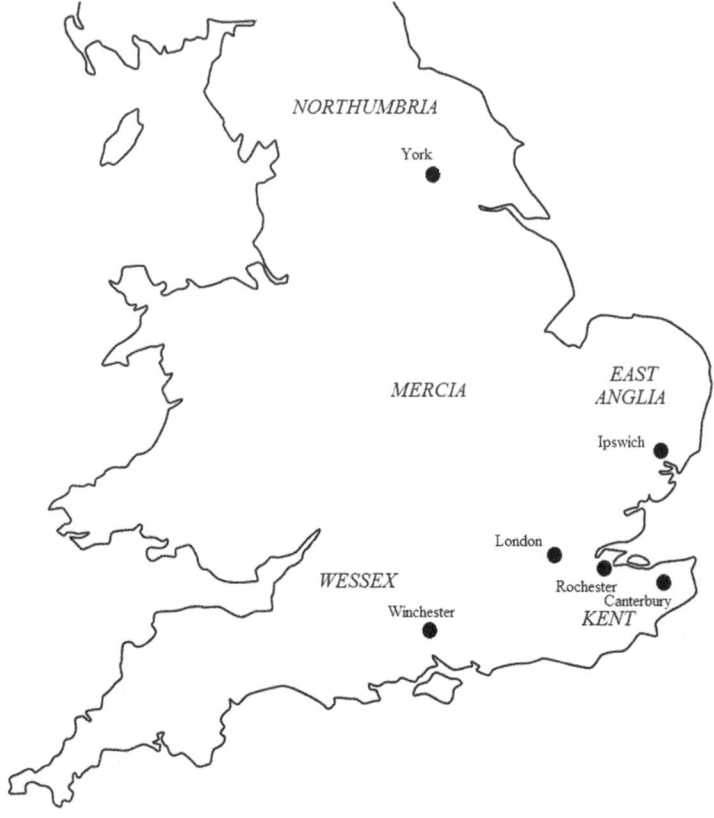

Map 1.1 Mints probably active in England 757–865.

The long-term importance of these eighth-century reforms can hardly be overestimated. Silver coins of approximately the same format as these broad, thin reformed pennies were to be the mainstay of western European currency until the thirteenth century, and in England and the Carolingian empire they established a tradition of explicit royal patronage that survives to this day. In the 760s, however, there could be no guarantee that these new coinages would achieve such an impact. One might have thought that gold would enjoy more of a resurgence in the west, as significant quantities of it were apparently available in the form of Arabic dinars and Roman-inspired *solidi*. In Northumbria the small debased coins of the ninth century, which eventually came to contain no silver at all, arguably presented a coinage of greater economic versatility, more akin to the base-metal coinages of the ancient or modern worlds. Elsewhere, in Jutland, the early pennies characteristic of the earlier eighth

8

century in England seem to have persisted in use and production until about the early ninth century, while in southern Italy debased gold coinage remained current. Much of Europe beyond the Rhine and England was not using or minting coin to any substantial degree in the mid eighth century. The origins of the success of northwest Europe's new silver currency lie in its contemporary circumstances; in its links to government, administration and economic developments.

THE HISTORICAL SETTING: WESSEX, MERCIA AND THE VIKINGS

The important changes in the currency which occurred in the middle of the eighth century did not, in England, accompany any major political watershed, as was the case in Francia. Rather, in southern England the reforms of the coinage coincide with the high point of the 'Mercian supremacy' under Æthelbald (716–57), king of the Mercians, who did not apparently take any action with the coinage of his kingdom, and his successors Offa and Coenwulf (796–821). This was the era in which the midlands-based kingdom of Mercia exercised dominance over England south of the Humber.[23] The decline of its hegemony was marked most vividly by a series of battles and conquests in 825–30 in which Ecgberht, king of the West Saxons (802–39), established his kingdom's premier position and laid the foundations for his dynasty's future. Wessex's survival and prosperity were secured by Ecgberht's heirs, most notably Alfred the Great (871–99). Knowledge of the eventual fates of Mercia and Wessex naturally endows these events with special significance, but such a barebones narrative of Mercian decline and fall, followed by West Saxon rise and rise over the course of the ninth century, neglects important details that flesh out these developments.[24]

Most of historians' knowledge of this period is derived from the material recorded in the West Saxon Anglo-Saxon Chronicle and associated sources such as Asser's *Life of King Alfred*, leading unavoidably to an emphasis on the subjects of most interest to chroniclers in Wessex in the late ninth century, especially in the reign of Alfred the Great. Coinage is an important alternative category of evidence that can help redress this imbalance, shedding light on political developments in so far as they impinged on the mints of southern and eastern England, and also on one

---

[23] See Stenton, *Preparatory*, pp. 48–66; and S. Keynes, 'The Kingdom of the Mercians in the Eighth Century', in *Æthelbald and Offa: Two Eighth-Century Kings of Mercia*, ed. D. Hill and M. Worthington, BAR British Series 383 (Oxford, 2005), pp. 1–26.

[24] Below, pp. 18–22.

dimension of how kings' power was exerted. Nevertheless, important developments are forced to the sidelines by the agendas of several crucial sources. Mercia's heyday down to the 820s must be reconstructed largely on the basis of non-narrative sources such as charters and letters from the circle of Alcuin of York (d. 804). The calamities of the 820s did not signal the total eclipse of Mercia: it remained a major power, and relationships with Wessex even recovered to the point where the two kingdoms could ally with one another against the Welsh and the vikings in 854 and 868 respectively. The rise of Wessex was by no means a foregone conclusion in 825.

Although they were undoubtedly the leading powers of the ninth century, Mercia and Wessex were not the only Anglo-Saxon kingdoms. The period down to the late eighth century had seen the number of independent kingdoms in England whittled down, eventually to just four by the 860s. Kent, Essex and Sussex – the other members of the traditional 'heptarchy' of English kingdoms[25] – had maintained sporadic and often precarious independence down to the late eighth or early ninth century. Of the other survivors besides Wessex and Mercia, Northumbria is left almost completely in the dark by southern sources and must be approached through (often problematic) local sources. East Anglia fares even worse than Northumbria, in that it is not only neglected by the Anglo-Saxon Chronicle and other southern texts, but did not preserve any native historiographical or documentary tradition.

To contemporary observers, therefore, England in the eighth and ninth centuries may have looked very different from what is presented in the dominant written accounts, and it is crucial to bear such alternative perspectives in mind. The Mercian supremacy and the rise of Wessex are not to be discarded as frameworks on which to build an understanding of the period, but they certainly do not tell the whole story. They also risk downplaying the administrative and economic backgrounds that made the successive hegemonies of Mercia and Wessex possible, the features which allowed these kingdoms to become so successful, and which contributed to the latter's ultimate success.

The other key development usually emphasized in this period is the one which eventually led to the extinction of the Anglo-Saxon kingdoms with the exception of Wessex: the viking invasions. These grew out of small raids which can be traced back to the late eighth century, and in the ninth graduated into extended sojourns that culminated in

---

[25] D. Kirby, *The Earliest English Kings*, 2nd edn (London, 2000), pp. 4–9; S. Keynes, 'Heptarchy', in *BEASE*, p. 233.

the Scandinavians' first wintering in England in 851/2. Another step-up came in 865 when, in the words of the Anglo-Saxon Chronicle, 'cuom micel here on Angel cynnes lond'.[26] This 'great army' was to enjoy a successful career of violence and conquest. In 867 the last two known native kings of Northumbria were slain, and in 869 Edmund, king of the East Angles, was also defeated and killed. It was Mercia's turn in 874, when King Burgred was forced into exile and half the kingdom was taken over by the vikings. Only Wessex was left by this stage, under the rule of Alfred, and its survival was imperilled by repeated attacks throughout the 870s.

These conquests and defeats paved the way for important changes – in the cultural life, administration and military organization of Wessex, and of course in the evolution of a dynamic new Anglo-Scandinavian society in East Anglia, east Mercia and Northumbria. In both peace and war, the vikings served the important purpose of forging long-distance connections and galvanizing military, administrative and economic activity.[27] It is in 865, at the dawn of this new era and its epoch-making developments, that this study closes. It examines the last century of the 'heptarchy' and the first of the broad penny, until the effects of the 'first Viking Age' began to make themselves most keenly felt. From this point onwards English coinage and its relationship to political authority took a different turn, of which there were signs in the decades immediately before 865. The relationship between royal power and minting changed, most visibly in Wessex.[28] It is therefore also from events in this kingdom that the end-date of 865 has been selected: this year saw the death of Æthelberht, king of the West Saxons, and the accession of his brother, Æthelred I. The latter took the important step of adopting a new coin-type based not on local tradition, but on the Lunettes-type current in contemporary Mercia. The year 865 thus saw not only the arrival of the viking great army that would dismantle most of the Anglo-Saxon kingdoms, but also the beginning of the end for separate coinages in separate kingdoms.

'Coins', wrote Peter Sawyer in 1989, 'pose a problem for the historian. It is a commonplace that the purpose of a source must be understood if its evidence is to be interpreted correctly. That is true of coins as well as of charters or chronicles.'[29] Coinage, that is to say, is a source which should be

---

[26] 'The great army came to England.' *ASC* s.a. 865.
[27] Below, pp. 234–5. [28] Below, pp. 106–12.
[29] P. Sawyer, 'Coins and Commerce', in *Sigtuna Papers. Proceedings of the Sigtuna Symposium on Viking Age Coinage 1–4 June 1989*, ed. K. Jonsson and B. Malmer (Stockholm, 1990), pp. 283–8, at 283.

read critically and on multiple levels, in the same way as charters, literary texts, artefacts or archaeological remains. Attention should be paid to the interaction of patrons, producers and users, and also to the different backgrounds and scholarly discourses which have grown up in relation to the sources. This must begin with the broader setting within which minting operated: what constituted the exercise of power for kings such as Offa, Coenwulf and Ecgberht, and the part coinage played in it.

Chapter 2

MONEY IN ITS POLITICAL CONTEXT

Far away from Anglo-Saxon England, at the same time as Offa of Mercia's rule was at its height in 787, one of the few other rulers in western Europe to have largely escaped Charlemagne's conquests met his death. Arichis II (758–87), duke of Benevento, had begun his political career as the protégé and son-in-law of Desiderius (757–74), last king of the Lombards. After Desiderius' defeat and deposition by Charlemagne in 774 Arichis assumed the title prince (*princeps*) of the Lombards, and spent the rest of his reign conspiring to expand his large south Italian duchy and resist the king of the Franks. Eventually, however, he was backed into a corner and forced to make concessions when Charlemagne himself came south into Italy in 786. In the last year of his life Arichis managed to stave off the Frankish army by sending money and offering up his two sons as hostages. A magnanimous Charlemagne accepted only the younger son and even Arichis' one condition of submission to Carolingian overlordship: that the Frankish king should not return to impose his authority in person.

The months after this agreement proved extremely unfortunate for the Beneventans. Arichis' death was shortly preceded by that of his eldest son, Romuald, which left Grimoald, now heir to the throne, in Charlemagne's hands. When a Beneventan delegation arrived at his court pleading for Grimoald's return, the king took full advantage of the hand dealt him by fate to reinforce his superiority over the stubbornly independent principality. In the words of Erchempert, a monk of Montecassino later in the ninth century:

quorum petitionibus rex annuens, illic continuo predictum contulit virum, simulque ius regendi principatus largitus est. Set prius cum sacramento huiusmodi vinxit, ut Langobardorum mentum tonderi faceret, cartas vero nummosque sui nominis caracteribus superscribi semper iuberet.[1]

---

[1] 'The king agreed to their requests, and there and then gave them [Grimoald], and at the same time bestowed on him the right to rule the principality. But first he subdued him with this oath: that the

Figure 2.1 *Tremissis* of Grimoald III, with Charlemagne.

Erchempert immediately went on to note that Grimoald did indeed place Charlemagne's name on his coins and charters for a while, 'reliqua autem pro nihilo duxit observanda; mox rebellionis iurgium initiavit'.[2]

Whether Erchempert had direct knowledge of the numismatic and documentary traditions of eighth-century Benevento is unclear, but his mention of the prominence of charters and coins finds corroboration in surviving documents and gold pieces from the 780s (Figure 2.1). These media were formal statements of Charlemagne's recognition as overlord, a recognition by which Grimoald was sufficiently irked to break the custom after a short time. Benevento may have been a long way from Offa's England, but Carolingian interests touched on both regions, and all three realms shared important common features such as, by this time, a coinage issued in the name of the ruling monarch. Charlemagne's insistence on monetary recognition and Grimoald's eagerness to shrug off this imposition show the significance attached to minting, and how far its usurpation could undermine royal authority. The coinage's significance to the king is, however, not necessarily as transparent as the coins' appearance might suggest. Modern preconceptions derived from contemporary or ancient currency cannot be mapped easily onto early medieval coinages, above all because control over the making of money is one of the functions which is now closely associated with the administrative machinery and often sovereignty of government, links which first evolved in the classical world.[3]

---

prince would have the Lombards shave their chins, and command that charters and coins should forever be inscribed with the letters of [Charlemagne's] name.' Erchempert, *Historia Langobardorum Beneventanorum*, c. 4 (ed. Waitz, p. 236).

[2] 'But for the rest of the time he commanded that they should not be observed at all, and soon he began to rise up in rebellion.' See also Einhard, *Vita Karoli*, c. 10 (ed. Holder-Egger, p. 13). Cf. R. Poupardin, 'Études sur la diplomatique des Princes Lombards de Bénévent, de Capoue et de Salerne', *Mélanges d'histoire et d'archéologie. École française de Rome* 21 (1901), 117–80, at p. 134.

[3] P. Grierson, *Numismatics* (Oxford, 1975), pp. 9–29.

For this reason coinage has often been used as a barometer of the rise and fall of states and statehood in the early medieval West. The decline and fall of the late Roman monetary system, which was nowhere more complete than in Britain, is one of the clearest threads in the complex tapestry of the end of the western Roman empire. Although elements of this edifice survived and were adapted elsewhere in the kingdoms that succeeded the western empire (and persisted intact in the eastern empire), minting and coin-use in Britain had to be rebuilt from the ground up, just like many other aspects of government. Whatever administrative machinery was available for these purposes in Anglo-Saxon England was embryonic compared to that of the modern world, or even the late Roman world, and drew inspiration from the methods of the latter and from contemporary kingdoms elsewhere in Europe.

By the 780s major changes were afoot. Mercia, long the dominant power in southern England, was entrenching its position, while across the Channel Charlemagne was busily legislating and refining the governance of his expanding domains. Much more than coinage was affected by these developments, and indeed it is from the perspective of charters, letters, capitularies and other documents that kingship and government in the eighth and ninth centuries are best known. Yet coins, as Charlemagne's dealings with Benevento reveal, were an important symbol of power at this time.[4] They also have the virtue, especially in England, of surviving in large numbers as a comparatively random representation of the currency, produced in areas which are sometimes all but a blank in other sources. In short, they mattered, both to rulers in the early Middle Ages and to modern historians.

But coinage should not be seen in isolation, and its testimony cannot be used outside its proper context. Two major preliminary topics therefore must be broached concerning coinage in the context of eighth- and ninth-century England: the background of 'state' exploitation of related resources, and the extent to which minting and coin-use fell within, or came back into, the remit of the early medieval state. Determining how this link developed is the subject of several chapters: the king's role (Chapter 4) and that of the moneyers and others (Chapter 5). Here, the focus will be on the setting of these questions: how rulers in England at this time approached the resources of their kingdoms, both in theory and in practice, and the general background of coinage as a royal resource in the post-Roman world.

---

[4] For recent development see I. Garipzanov, *The Symbolic Language of Authority in the Carolingian World (c. 751–877)* (Leiden and Boston, MA, 2008). See also P. Grierson, 'Symbolism in Early Medieval Charters and Coins', *Settimane* 23 (1976), 601–40.

KINGS, STATES AND POWER IN ENGLAND
AND ITS NEIGHBOURS

The history of 'the state' in the early Middle Ages is by and large synonymous with the complex interaction of kings and other powerful agencies and institutions.[5] In the words of Matthew Innes, 'early medieval polities were emphatically not bundles of administrative structures claiming sovereign power',[6] while Gerd Althoff characterized this period as one of *Königsherrschaft ohne Staat*.[7] Power and political organization were founded principally on control of agricultural resources, especially land, and on the social relationships of those with land.[8] Kings wielded superiority as major landholders and as the focal point in this hierarchy of social relationships. Maintaining a kingdom in the early Middle Ages was a highly personal business, and kings ruled over peoples first and territories second. As a result personal matters lay at the heart of politics. The proper ruling of both the royal household and the court or palace was stressed by contemporary commentators as a microcosm of ruling the whole kingdom: kingship was intimately associated with family and household management, and the king occupied a central place in his realm as a *paterfamilias* writ large with special duties, powers and properties.[9] These could be characterized as public, and were underpinned by sanctity and spiritual authority as long as kings kept their people on the straight and narrow as defined by established customs and Christian teaching.[10] Common Christian identity – the kingdom as

---

[5] See in general S. Reynolds, 'The Historiography of the Medieval State', in *Companion to Historiography*, ed. M. Bentley (London, 1997), pp. 117–38; M. Innes, *State and Society in the Early Middle Ages: The Middle Rhine Valley, 400–1000* (Cambridge, 2000), esp. pp. 4–12; P. Wormald, 'Pre-Modern "State" and "Nation": Definite or Indefinite?', in *Staat im frühen Mittelalter*, ed. S. Airlie, W. Pohl and H. Reimitz (Vienna, 2006), pp. 179–89.

[6] Innes, *State and Society*, p. 255.

[7] G. Althoff, *Die Ottonen. Königsherrschaft ohne Staat*, 2nd edn (Stuttgart, 2005). Cf. H.-W. Goetz, 'Die Wahrnehmung von "Staat" und "Herrschaft" im frühen Mittelalter', in *Staat im frühen Mittelalter*, ed. Airlie, Pohl and Reimitz, pp. 39–58, esp. 55–8.

[8] For the development of this socially conceived view, see H. Keller, *Ottonische Königsherrschaft. Organisation und Legitimation königlicher Macht* (Darmstadt, 2002), pp. 22–33. For further discussion and a case study see B. Rosenwein, *Negotiating Space: Power, Restraint, and Privileges of Immunity in Early Medieval Europe* (Manchester, 1999), pp. 6–9 and 137–55.

[9] J. L. Nelson, 'Kingship and Empire in the Carolingian World', in *Carolingian Culture: Emulation and Innovation*, ed. R. McKitterick (Cambridge, 1994), pp. 52–87, at 61–5. Cf. J. Fried, 'Das karolingische Herrschaftsverband im 9. Jh. zwischen "Kirche" und "Köngishaus"', *Historische Zeitschrift* 235 (1982), 1–43.

[10] This element of royal government was ever-present in England and Francia, though more prominent under certain rulers, especially Louis the Pious: see M. de Jong, *The Penitential State. Authority and Atonement in the Age of Louis the Pious, 814–840* (Cambridge, 2009), esp. pp. 22–4; K.-F. Werner, 'Hludowicus Augustus. Gouverner l'empire chrétien: idées et réalités', in *Charlemagne's Heir: New Perspectives on the Reign of Louis the Pious, 814–840*, ed. P. Godman and R. Collins (Oxford, 1990), pp. 3–123, at 69–79.

ecclesia in the wider sense of 'congregation' – could be built upon as a major prop of royal power that helped make early medieval kingdoms more than the sum of their parts.[11] To do this the king had to maintain the moral high ground for himself: his conduct was thought to affect the fortunes of his entire kingdom.[12] According to the tract *De duodecim abusivis saeculi*, a king could be defined as a *corrector iniquorum* – 'corrector of the unjust'. 'Sed qualiter', it went on, 'alios corrigere poterit qui proprios mores ne iniqui sint corrigit?'[13] These *alii* theoretically encompassed the entire populace within the king's charge, but on a practical level the group over whom he watched most closely and depended on most heavily was the secular and ecclesiastical elite. Management of legal process, military organization and other responsibilities of government was vested in local elites as a matter of course, and ruling depended on the king's relationship with those elites.[14]

These conclusions derive principally from investigation of the Carolingian empire in the century *c.* 770–*c.* 870 – a land and an era characterized not only by ambitious and enterprising kings, but also by an outpouring of rich source materials for the historian. There are, of course, still important blanks. The enormous empire ruled by Charlemagne and his heirs is not evenly covered by this wealth of surviving sources, and was by no means a homogeneous entity. There were important differences between Aquitaine, northern Italy, the Paris basin, the middle Rhine, Bavaria, Brittany and all the other larger and smaller building blocks of the Carolingian realm. England, however, in terms of source coverage comes off substantially worse than many regions of its continental neighbour in

[11] M. de Jong, 'Ecclesia and the Early Medieval Polity', in *Staat im frühen Mittelalter*, ed. Airlie, Pohl and Reimitz, pp. 113–32, and 'The State of the Church: *Ecclesia* and Early Medieval State Formation', in *Der frühmittelalterliche Staat: europäische Perspektiven*, ed. W. Pöhl and V. Wieser (Vienna, 2009), pp. 241–54.

[12] M. Blattmann, '"Ein Unglück für sein Volk". Der Zusammenhang zwischen Fehlverhalten des Königs und Volkswohl in Quellen des 7.–12. Jahrhunderts', *Frühmittelalterliche Studien* 30 (1996), 80–102.

[13] 'But how is he to correct others when he cannot keep his own morals from wickedness?' Pseudo-Cyprian, *De duodecim abusivis saeculi* (ed. Hellmann, p. 51). For the popularity of this text in England and Francia, see H. Anton, 'Pseudo-Cyprian: *De duodecimo abusivis saeculi* und sein Einfluß auf den Kontinent, insbesondere auf die karolingischen Fürstenspiegel', in *Die Iren und Europa im früheren Mittelalter*, ed. H. Löwe, 2 vols. (Stuttgart, 1982) II, 568–617; R. Meens, 'Politics, Mirrors of Princes and the Bible: Sins, Kings and the Well-Being of the Kingdom', *EME* 7 (1998), 345–57.

[14] See inter alia S. Airlie, 'The Aristocracy in the Service of the State in the Carolingian Period', in *Staat im frühen Mittelalter*, ed. Airlie, Pohl and Reimitz, pp. 93–111; K.-F. Werner, '*Missus – Marchio – Comes*: entre l'administration centrale et l'administration locale de l'empire carolingienne', in *Vom Frankenreich zur Entfaltung Deutschlands und Frankreichs: Ursprünge, Strukturen, Beziehungen: ausgewählte Beiträge: Festgabe zu seinem sechzigsten Geburtstag* (Sigmaringen, 1984), pp. 121–61; F.-L. Ganshof, *Frankish Institutions under Charlemagne*, trans. B. and M. Lyon (Providence, RI, 1968), esp. pp. 26–34.

the eighth and ninth centuries: its charters are scarce, its narratives few and late, while the rich seventh-century tradition of Anglo-Saxon legislation dried to a trickle until the reign of Alfred the Great.

Determining how the Anglo-Saxon kingdoms of this period operated is therefore more problematic.[15] Certainly there were important similarities with contemporary Frankish government and society – more, arguably, than has often been recognized[16] – and so there is much to be learned from close comparison. Yet it should not be taken for granted that the relationship between kings, regions, elites and other groups always functioned in the same way on either side of the Channel. More searching comparisons have highlighted the smaller scale and generally weaker grip of early Anglo-Saxon kings, at least in comparison with their Frankish contemporaries.[17] The difficulty comes in reconciling this with the administrative strength and coherence of the late Anglo-Saxon kingdom, which by the later tenth century compares much more favourably with realms elsewhere in western Europe.[18] Key points of transition have been highlighted in the times of Offa and Coenwulf, under Alfred and later under Edgar (959–75).[19] Yet these rulers (and others) built to a large degree on the regimes they inherited, warts and all.[20] The longer-term trends of Anglo-Saxon political development were marked, for example, by the malleability of larger kingdoms, which were made up from smaller, relatively well-established building blocks.[21] The afterlife of these territories, usually referred to as *regiones* or *provinciae* in Latin sources, lay within larger political entities, among which Mercia and Wessex were the most prominent in eighth- and ninth-century southern England. Their rulers took different approaches towards these component parts, and towards other aspects of government and political culture. There may

---

[15] General discussions include A. Williams, *Kingship and Government in Pre-Conquest England, c. 500–1066* (Basingstoke, 1999); H. Loyn, *The Governance of Anglo-Saxon England, 500–1087* (Stanford, CA, 1984).

[16] D. Bates, 'England and the "Feudal Revolution"', *Settimane* 61 (2000), 1–49.

[17] *FEMA*, pp. 339–51, and C. Wickham, *The Inheritance of Rome. A History of Europe from 400 to 1000* (London, 2009), pp. 158–64; J. L. Nelson, 'Carolingian Contacts', in *Mercia: An Anglo-Saxon Kingdom in Europe*, ed. M. Brown and C. A. Farr (London, 2001), pp. 126–43, at p. 143.

[18] For this view, and the role the coinage played in shaping it, see below, pp. 87–8.

[19] *FEMA*, pp. 345–51, and Wickham, *Inheritance of Rome*, pp. 455–7.

[20] B. Yorke, 'The Anglo-Saxon Kingdoms 600–900 and the Beginnings of the Old English State', in *Der frühmittelalterliche Staat*, ed. Pöhl and Wieser, pp. 73–86, at 75–6; N. Brooks, 'Alfredian Government', in *Alfred the Great. Papers from the Eleventh-Centenary Conferences*, ed. T. Reuter (Aldershot, 2003), pp. 153–73.

[21] Yorke, 'Anglo-Saxon Kingdoms', pp. 77–85; D. Dumville, 'Essex, Middle Anglia and the Expansion of Mercia in the South-East Midlands', in *Britons and Anglo-Saxons in the Early Middle Ages* (Aldershot, 1993), no. IX, and 'Terminology of Overkingship in Early Anglo-Saxon England', in *The Anglo-Saxons from the Migration Period to the Eighth Century: An Ethnographic Perspective*, ed. J. Hines (Woodbridge, 1997), pp. 345–65.

have been important unifying factors which brought the Anglo-Saxon kingdoms together into a single cultural community, but it is nevertheless instructive to examine Mercia and Wessex separately.

An interesting test case for these different approaches to overlordship can be found in the small former kingdom of Kent, which is uniquely well known thanks to its comparatively rich archive of eighth- and early ninth-century charters, and as the location of two of the five southern English mints.[22] In the period *c*. 765–825 Kent seems to have functioned as a distinct regional unit in the greater Mercian kingdom with ties to distant kings passing at various times through sub-kings, ealdormen and archbishops of Canterbury. A discrete body of local worthies repeatedly attested local charters, sometimes explicitly as a group separate from their Mercian counterparts. Kent had its share of royal estates and other trappings of kingship inherited from its time as a separate kingdom,[23] but on the whole it seems to have functioned in a manner analogous to regions within the Carolingian empire which had limited direct contact with the royal centre of authority. The nexus between Kent and Mercia (as probably was also the case for Sussex and East Anglia) lay with a few members of the local aristocracy and clergy.[24] Offa and Coenwulf in particular went a long way towards formalizing what had previously been quite a loose form of overlordship over these local potentates, often by means of demoting local rulers but allowing them to retain many of their powers as Mercian subordinates.[25]

Arrangements such as these were characteristic of the recently incorporated eastern and southern additions to the Mercian kingdom: Kent, East Anglia, Essex, Sussex and Surrey. As far as they were concerned, the Mercians were threatening but absent landlords, and several rebellions against Mercian rule took place.[26] Yet the Mercian heartland between (roughly) the Thames and the Humber seems to have functioned as a more cohesive unit, within which it is more difficult to identify fissile regional

---

[22] S. Keynes, 'The Control of Kent in the Ninth Century', *EME* 2 (1993), 111–31; J. Crick, 'Church, Land and Local Nobility in Early Ninth-Century Kent: The Case of Ealdorman Oswulf', *Bulletin of the Institute of Historical Research* 61 (1988), 251–69; S. Kelly, ed., *Charters of St Augustine's Abbey, Canterbury, and Minster-in-Thanet* (Oxford, 1995), pp. xci–xcii.

[23] For example, the *oppida regis* mentioned at Faversham and Rainham (S 168; cf. J. Blair, *The Church in Anglo-Saxon Society* (Oxford, 2005), p. 287) and the *praefectus* Aldhun in 805 (S 1259).

[24] For Sussex, see S. Kelly, ed., *Charters of Selsey* (Oxford, 1998), pp. lxxx–lxxxiv.

[25] Keynes, 'Kingdom of the Mercians', pp. 10–14; P. Wormald, 'Bede, the *Bretwaldas* and the Origins of the *Gens Anglorum*', in *Ideal and Reality in Frankish and Anglo-Saxon Society: Studies Presented to J. M. Wallace-Hadrill*, ed. P. Wormald *et al.* (Oxford, 1983), pp. 99–129, at 112–13 and 115–17; H. Finberg, *The Early Charters of the West Midlands* (Leicester, 1961), pp. 167–80; P. Sims-Williams, *Religion and Literature in Western England, 600–800* (Cambridge, 1990), pp. 29–39; B. Yorke, 'The Kingdom of the East Saxons', *ASE* 14 (1985), 1–36, at pp. 31–6.

[26] In Kent 776–*c*. 785 and again 796–8, and in East Anglia *c*. 792, 796–*c*. 800 and 825–6.

divisions as the eighth and, especially, ninth centuries progressed.[27] This may simply be a result of the relatively scarce source material preserved from most of the kingdom outside Kent and the diocese of Worcester. Nonetheless, as far as one can tell the Hwicce, Magonsætan, Lindsætan, Middle Angles and other midland peoples never tried to break away from Mercian rule. By the time of Offa and Coenwulf Mercia had come a long way from the diverse confederation of peoples illustrated by the Tribal Hidage.[28] It was in this midlands area – above all at places such as Tamworth and Lichfield, though also stretching south to London – that the power bases of the Mercian supremacy were to be found, from which successive overlords managed most of their affairs, and within which a number of leading kin-factions vied for supremacy.[29] These groups and the ealdormen who headed them were sometimes associated with specific peoples or regions, but there is also evidence for landholdings and connections (particularly based on strategically sited monasteries) among the aspiring royal kindreds which spanned the kingdom and helped weld it together.[30]

Many of these leading families had, or at least asserted, royal blood, and so could produce equally valid claims to the throne. Kings from up to five dynasties held power between 757 and 880.[31] Internal competition bred external aggression, and Mercia was conspicuous for the scale and success of its military activity.[32] But this was hardly a recipe for stability: the predatory nature of Mercian kingship often left the kingdom prone to periods of dissension, and may have hampered the long-term development of governmental institutions. Efforts by Offa and Coenwulf to establish dynastic succession came to nothing, and it was seemingly by dint of military might, victory in war and a delicate balance of consensus, generosity and vigilance at home that successive rulers held on to the throne. Kings who lost these credentials, or by chance succeeded to the throne without them, inevitably fell from power, as was the fate of Æthelbald and Coenwulf's brother, Ceolwulf I, to name just two.

[27] M. A. Burghart, 'The Mercian Polity, 716–918' (unpublished Ph.D. dissertation, King's College London, 2007), pp. 226–56; C. Hart, 'The Kingdom of Mercia', in *Mercian Studies*, ed. A. Dornier (Leicester, 1977), pp. 43–61; Dumville, 'Essex, Middle Anglia', pp. 123–40.

[28] D. Dumville, 'The Tribal Hidage: An Introduction to Its Texts and Their History', in *The Origins of Anglo-Saxon Kingdoms*, ed. S. Bassett (Leicester, 1989), pp. 225–30.

[29] This is most revealingly illustrated by the Mercian royal itinerary: D. Hill, *An Atlas of Anglo-Saxon England* (Oxford, 1981), p. 83.

[30] Burghart, 'Mercian Polity', pp. 230–49; for monastic networks spanning the kingdom see Stenton, *Preparatory*, pp. 179–92; S. Keynes, *The Councils of Clofesho* (Leicester, 1993), pp. 33–48.

[31] S. Keynes, 'Mercia and Wessex in the Ninth Century', in *Mercia*, ed. Brown and Farr, pp. 310–28, at 314–23.

[32] Below, pp. 29–32.

Wessex, on the other hand, reaped considerable benefits from the stability brought by Ecgberht and his successors after 802, who were unusually fortunate in their long string of eligible and vigorous male heirs. The rise of Wessex in the ninth century thus owed much simply to good genes and biological accident, but the kingdom had many other advantages, which shone through most dazzlingly in the outburst of literary activity during the reign of Alfred the Great.[33] These writings stress a view of royal responsibility for good governance by a team which, while captained and coached by the king, was drawn from all levels of the political establishment – ealdormen, reeves, bishops and others.[34]

Yet while the expression of this view comes only at the end of the ninth century and may owe something to the personal convictions of Alfred himself, it was founded on important pre-existing developments.[35] By recourse to other sources such as charters, historians can penetrate the workings of Wessex before Alfred and even Ecgberht's time.[36] These seem to show precocious developments quite distinct from those of Mercia. Witness-lists illustrate integration of the elites from different segments of the kingdom, including the territories in the southeast, not least Kent,[37] acquired from Mercia only in 825. A greater emphasis may have been placed on royal appointment of aristocrats than on succession to defined hereditary positions. Charter production, too, seems to have become centralized and associated with the royal court in the course of the ninth century,[38] while in Mercia it appears that several episcopal scriptoria retained responsibility for the writing of local charters.[39] Some of these trends can be traced back into

---

[33] See most recently D. Pratt, *The Political Thought of King Alfred the Great* (Cambridge, 2007), esp. pp. 338–45. On the authorship of these texts, M. Godden, 'Did King Alfred Write Anything?', *Medium Aevum* 76 (2007), 1–23, and 'The Alfredian Project and Its Aftermath: Rethinking the Literary History of the Ninth and Tenth Centuries', *Proceedings of the British Academy* 162 (2009), 93–122; D. Pratt, 'Problems of Authorship and Audience in the Writings of King Alfred the Great', in *Lay Intellectuals in the Carolingian World*, ed. P. Wormald and J. L. Nelson (Cambridge, 2007), pp. 162–91; J. Bately, 'Did King Alfred Actually Translate Anything? The Integrity of the Alfredian Canon Revisited', *Medium Aevum* 78 (2009), 189–215.

[34] For the international dimension of this outlook, see J. L. Nelson, 'West Frankia and Wessex in the Ninth Century Compared', in *Der frühmittelalterliche Staat*, ed. Pöhl and Wieser, pp. 99–112.

[35] Brooks, 'Alfredian Government'.

[36] Keynes, 'Mercia and Wessex', pp. 323–8; B. Yorke, *Wessex in the Early Middle Ages* (Leicester, 1995), esp. pp. 94–103.

[37] Keynes, 'Control of Kent', pp. 121–2 and 125–6.

[38] S. Keynes, 'The West Saxon Charters of King Æthelwulf and His Sons', *EHR* 109 (1994), 1109–49.

[39] P. Chaplais, 'The Origin and Authenticity of the Royal Anglo Saxon Diploma', *Journal of the Society of Archivists* 3.2 (1965–9), 48–61, at pp. 39–40; N. Brooks, *The Early History of the Church of Canterbury. Christ Church from 597 to 1066* (Leicester, 1984), pp. 168–70 and 327–30; Kelly,

the eighth century, though they are most strongly associated with the dynasty of Ecgberht after 802.[40]

One other important feature of government which has often been discussed in the context of both Wessex and Mercia in the eighth and ninth centuries as well as later Anglo-Saxon England is the existence of royal reeves, agents apparently answering directly to the king and responsible for the management of his estates and the enforcement of his prerogatives.[41] Some of the *ministri* and especially *thelonarii* and *praefecti* who received lands in charters from eighth- and ninth-century kings may have been reeves, and men called *portgerefan* or *wicgerefan* ('town-reeves') are mentioned in law-codes from the seventh century onwards.[42] This group of officials worked alongside but largely separately from the ealdormen, who were tasked with military and judicial responsibilities.[43] The bilateral framework of ealdormen and reeves working in different capacities directly under the king seems to have been characteristic of the smaller Anglo-Saxon kingdoms, and was exploited most fully by the West Saxon dynasty.[44]

Differences between the two leading kingdoms of ninth-century England were thus significant, but did not spring into being fully formed. Many of the features that were to be of benefit to ninth-century Wessex were in an early stage of development when Ecgberht took the throne in 802. Similarly, Mercia was by no means a second-rate kingdom as a result of the more fragile nature of its power: with a strong and long-lived king holding the reins, it was a force to be reckoned with.

St Augustine's, pp. lxxi–xcvi; S. Keynes, 'Angelsächsische Urkunden (7.–9. Jahrhundert)/Anglo-Saxon Charters (7th–9th Century)', in *Mensch und Schrift im frühen Mittelalter*, ed. P. Erhart and L. Hollenstein (St Gallen, 2006), pp. 97–109, at 101 (who leaves the issue open to further debate).

[40] H. M. Chadwick, *Studies on Anglo-Saxon Institutions* (Cambridge, 1905), pp. 282–92; Yorke, *Wessex*, pp. 197–203.

[41] C. Cubitt, '"As the Lawbook Teaches": Reeves, Lawbooks and Urban Life in the Anonymous Old English Legend of the Seven Sleepers', *EHR* 124 (2009), 1021–49, esp. pp. 1034–42. See also P. Stafford, 'Reeve', in *BEASE*, pp. 386–7; A. Williams, *Kingship*, pp. 51–2; Chadwick, *Studies*, pp. 228–39.

[42] Cf. the law-code of Hlothere, c. 16 (ed. Liebermann, *Die Gesetze der Angelsachsen*, I, 11). For discussion see N. Middleton, 'Early Medieval Port Customs, Tolls and Controls on Foreign Trade', *EME* 13 (2005), 313–58, at pp. 334–6 and 351; A. Williams, *Kingship*, pp. 51–2; Thacker, 'Some Terms for Noblemen', pp. 211–12; Keynes, 'Mercia and Wessex', pp. 235–6.

[43] A. Williams, *Kingship*, pp. 52–6; N. Banton, 'Ealdormen and Earls in England from the Reign of King Alfred to the Reign of King Æthelred II' (unpublished D.Phil. thesis, University of Oxford, 1981), pp. 4–62.

[44] Banton, 'Ealdormen and Earls'; Pratt, *Political Thought*, pp. 28–34 and 345–50; P. Stafford, *Unification and Conquest: A Political and Social History of England in the Tenth and Eleventh Centuries* (London, 1989), pp. 134–49. For possible similarity between later Anglo-Saxon shire-reeves and Carolingian *comites*, see C. Hammer, '"Pipinus rex": Pippin's Plot of 792 and Bavaria', *Traditio* 63 (2008), 235–72, at p. 239.

ROYAL RESOURCES

This general background of government presupposes some means of actually making things happen – of turning land, its products and its inhabitants into a kingdom. On one level this meant the maintenance of kings, ealdormen and high-ranking clergy in appropriate comfort, but servants, dependants, hospitality, gifts and wealth in general were also necessary for furthering the agendas of rulers and demonstrating their authority.[45] It was not for nothing that from Bede's time onwards Latin and Old English words denoting power gradually converged with those signifying wealth.[46]

Resources and their effective use were, on a fundamental level, bound to power and its exercise, and encompassed relationships and manpower as well as material assets.[47] One unusually explicit statement of this basic requirement of successful rulership can be found in the Old English rendition of Boethius' *De consolatione philosophiae* (possibly associated with Alfred the Great), which discusses the *cræft* of a king and the *andweorc and ... tol* ('resources and tools') that were necessary to carry it out: the three *geferscipas* of *gebedmen and fyrdmen and weorcmen* ('praying men and fighting men and workmen'), as well as 'land to bugianne and gifta and wæpnu and mete and ealo and claþas, and gehwæt þæs ðe þa þre geferscipas behofiað'.[48] Likewise Asser described how Alfred, *antecessorum morem transcendere volens* ('wishing to surpass the practice of his predecessors'), devoted half his annual income (*divitiae*) to religion, and 'quod Deo libenter devoverat quomodo recte divider posset, cogitavit, et, ut dixit Salomon, "Cor regis in manu Domini"';[49] his plan for a three-way

---

[45] That is, maintaining what Pierre Bourdieu has described as 'social capital'. Cf. P. Bourdieu, *The Logic of Practice*, trans. R. Nice (Cambridge, 1990), pp. 108–21, and *Distinction. A Social Critique of the Judgement of Taste*, trans. R. Nice (London, 1984), esp. p. 291. See also P. B. Roscoe, 'Practice and Political Centralisation. A New Approach to Political Evolution', *Current Anthropology* 34 (1993), 111–40; J. Smith, *Europe after Rome: A New Cultural History 500–1000* (Oxford, 2005), pp. 183–214.

[46] M. Godden, 'Money, Power and Morality in Late Anglo-Saxon England', *ASE* 19 (1990), 41–65, at pp. 42–8.

[47] J.-P. Devroey, *Puissants et misérables. Système social et monde paysan dans l'Europe des Francs (VIe–IXe siècles)* (Brussels, 2006), esp. pp. 242–5 and 257–8; R. Faith, *The English Peasantry and the Growth of Lordship* (Leicester, 1997).

[48] 'Land to inhabit, and gifts, and weapons, and food, and ale, and clothes, and everything that the three communities need.' Boethius/Alfred (?), *De consolatione philosophiae*, c. 17 (ed. and trans. Godden and Irvine, *Old English Boethius* I, 277–8, and II, 26, with comment at II, 318). For selected discussion Pratt, *Political Thought*, pp. 287–95; R. Hodges, 'Society, Power and the First English Industrial Revolution', *Settimane* 38 (1991), 125–50, at pp. 146–9; J. R. Maddicott, 'Trade, Industry and the Wealth of King Alfred: A Reply', *P&P* 125 (1991), 164–88, at pp. 165–7. On authorship, see also ed. and trans. Godden and Irvine, *Old English Boethius* I, 140–6.

[49] 'He considered how he might justly divide what he had generously promised to God; and, as Solomon says, "the heart of the king is in the hand of the Lord".' Asser, *Life of King Alfred*, cc. 99–102 (ed. Stevenson, pp. 85–9; and trans. S. Keynes and M. Lapidge, *Alfred the Great: Asser's Life of King Alfred and Other Contemporary Sources* (London, 1983), pp. 105–7).

division of secular expenditure and a four-way division of religious expenditure is thereafter laid out in detail.

Evidence of early medieval rulers actually viewing the resources of their kingdoms in such frank terms is unusual. Alfred's sophisticated conception of a king's duties, and the intersection of those duties with material and spiritual resources, should not necessarily be accepted for all early medieval rulers: as Asser noted, his views and involvement with writing were exceptional, his devotions and sensitivities sharpened by the ravages of (probably) Crohn's disease.[50] Alfred's views can be contrasted with other contemporary manuals of rulership, which are mostly concerned with moral and religious guidance,[51] and with literature on secular aspects of rulership such as *Beowulf*, which emphasizes martial prowess, courtly interaction and vaguely defined success as a landowner.[52] When economic acumen appears to be highlighted in early medieval sources, it does not always conform to modern expectations,[53] and care should be taken in assuming that all early medieval rulers viewed their kingdoms' resources in the same way as King Alfred, let alone their modern-day counterparts.

Kings in the early Middle Ages thus needed wealth, but it is unclear whether economic resources of different kinds were seen as an end in themselves developed into 'a differentiated sub-system of society',[54] or rather as a means of attaining status and power – the socially conceived *Realpolitik* of the early Middle Ages – which, while important, did not necessarily foster exploitation beyond a certain baseline needed to maintain stability. Even this was not necessarily an easy thing to accomplish. A king's need for an adequate reserve of authority, land and other forms of wealth conflicted with the need to redistribute those resources in order to shore up support. According to one Old English maxim, 'cyning biþ anwealdes georn; lað se þe londes monað, leof se þe mare beodeð'.[55] At the same time, however, a king had to dig deep into

---

[50] D. Pratt, 'The Illnesses of King Alfred the Great', *ASE* 30 (2001), 39–90, esp. pp. 81–90.

[51] T. F. X. Noble, 'Secular Sanctity: Forging an Ethos for the Carolingian Nobility', in *Lay Intellectuals*, ed. Wormald and Nelson, pp. 8–36, at 10–17; R. Balzaretti and J. L. Nelson, 'Trade, Industry and the Wealth of King Alfred', *P&P* 135 (1992), 142–63, at pp. 144–7; H. Anton, *Fürstenspiegel und Herrscherethos in der Karolingerzeit*, Bonner Historische Forschungen 32 (Bonn, 1968).

[52] P. Wormald, 'Bede, *Beowulf* and the Conversion of the Anglo-Saxon Aristocracy', in *Bede and Anglo-Saxon England: Papers in Honour of the 1300th Anniversary of the Birth of Bede*, ed. R. T. Farrell (Oxford, 1978), pp. 32–95, at 34–8. See also below pp. 260–1.

[53] M. Hendy, 'East and West: Divergent Models of Coinage and Its Use', *Settimane* 38 (1991), 637–74, at pp. 640–7.

[54] M. Finley, *The Ancient Economy*, 2nd edn (Berkeley, CA, 1999), p. 21.

[55] 'A king is eager for sovereignty; he hates anyone who claims land, loves anyone who offers him more.' *Maxims IA*, lines 59b–60, in T. Shippey (ed. and trans.), *Poems of Wisdom and Learning in Old English* (Cambridge, 1976), pp. 66–7.

his pockets to buy – quite literally (*gebicgan*) – his queen 'with goblets and rings' (*bunum ond beagum*), and thus established, both king and queen 'sceolon ærest geofum god wesan'.[56]

Debate on this very same question of how the early medieval political community viewed and used material resources has been going on for several decades among Anglo-Saxonists,[57] and also historians of the early Middle Ages elsewhere in western Europe.[58] They have built on an even longer-running polemic going back to the roots of economic anthropology in the 1950s and 1960s, when formalist and substantivist schools of thought emerged and clashed. The former saw economic processes as largely governed by universal economic rationality – as conscious attempts to maximize restricted resources and produce profit – whereas the latter placed the emphasis on economics as an embedded function of wider social relationships, in which profit and maximization of resources were not leading motivations.[59]

More recent reassessments have stressed a middle road between these two extremes.[60] Economic rationality might have governed some

---

[56] 'Shall first of all be free with gifts.' *Maxims IB*, lines 12b–13a, in Shippey (ed. and trans.), *Poems of Wisdom and Learning*, pp. 68–9.

[57] J. R. Maddicott, 'Trade, Industry and the Wealth of King Alfred', *P&P* 123 (1989), 3–51, 'Trade, Industry and the Wealth of King Alfred: A Reply', *P&P* 125 (1991), 164–88, and 'Prosperity and Power in the Age of Bede and Beowulf', *Proceedings of the British Academy* 117 (2002), 49–71; Balzaretti and Nelson, 'Trade, Industry and the Wealth of King Alfred'; R. Hodges and D. Whitehouse, *Mohammed, Charlemagne and the Origins of Europe: Archaeology and the Pirenne Thesis* (London, 1983), pp. 104–8; A. Williams, *Kingship*, pp. 32–64; Pratt, *Political Thought*, pp. 17–27; Wickham, *Inheritance of Rome*, pp. 160–1; N. Brooks, *Church, State and Access to Resources in Early Anglo-Saxon England*, Brixworth Lecture, 2nd ser, 2 (Brixworth, 2003).

[58] J. L. Nelson, 'Kingship and Royal Government', in *NCMH* II, pp. 383–430, esp. 383–98; D. Harrison, 'Structures and Resources of Power in Early Medieval Europe', in *The Construction of Communities in the Early Middle Ages: Texts, Resources and Artefacts*, ed. R. Corradini, M. Diesenberger and H. Reimitz (Leiden, 2003), pp. 17–37; P. Fouracre, 'Comparing the Resources of the Merovingian and Carolingian States: Problems and Perspectives', in *Der frühmittelalterliche Staat*, ed. Pöhl and Wieser, pp. 287–98; M. McCormick, 'Um 808. Was der frühmittelalterliche König mit der Wirtschaft zu tun hatte', in *Die Macht des Königs. Herrschaft in Europa vom Frühmittelalter bis in die Neuzeit*, ed. B. Jussen (Konstanz, 2005), pp. 55–71; Ganshof, *Frankish Institutions*, pp. 34–45; R. McKitterick, *The Frankish Kingdoms under the Carolingians, 751–987* (London, 1983), pp. 77–105; Innes, *State and Society*, pp. 141–64; E. Goldberg, *Struggle for Empire: Kingship and Conflict under Louis the German, 817–876* (Ithaca, NY, and London, 2006), pp. 186–230; *FEMA*, pp. 56–150 and 303–79, C. Wickham, 'The Fall of Rome Will Not Take Place', in *Debating the Middle Ages: Issues and Readings*, ed. B. H. Rosenwein and L. K. Little (Oxford, 1998), pp. 45–57; J.-P. Devroey, *Économie rurale et société dans l'Europe franque (VIe–IXe siècles)*, vol. I, *Fondements matériels, échanges et lien social* (Paris, 2003), pp. 227–55.

[59] On this debate see R. Wilk and L. Cliggett, *Economies and Cultures: Foundations of Economic Anthropology*, 2nd edn (Boulder, CO, and London, 2007), pp. 3–14. The seminal text for substantivist methods is K. Polanyi, *The Great Transformation* (Boston, MA, 1957); cf. his *Primitive, Archaic and Modern Economies: The Essays of Karl Polanyi*, ed. G. Dalton (New York, 1968). The terms go back to M. Weber, *Economy and Society: An Outline of Interpretive Sociology*, trans. G. Roth and C. Wittich, 2 vols. (Berkeley, CA, and London, 1979) I, 85–6.

[60] For example, J. Lie, 'Sociology of Markets', *Annual Review of Sociology* 23 (1997), 341–60, at pp. 347–51; Wilk and Cliggett, *Economies and Cultures*, pp. 12–14.

situations and aspects of life, but not others.[61] Even modern capitalistic commerce of the sort associated with Wall Street and the Square Mile is governed in part by non-economic customs and forces, while in deepest New Guinea hunter-gatherers living in small tribes dominated by gift-exchange between friends and family will follow economic rationality when they set out to hunt in areas they know to be richest in prey. Likewise in the early Middle Ages kings might block movement of traders and travellers over a personal dispute with a neighbour,[62] while monks and abbots, whose lives were dedicated to maintaining a strict rule of religious devotion, could bring their intensely rational numerical skills to bear on estate and community management as well as intellectual questions.[63] In short, no society was ever entirely substantivist or formalist in its outlook. All occupied middle ground between the two – middle ground which could, even in the same society, shift substantially under different circumstances.

To a large extent the matter turns on definitions of rationality. Many seemingly economically unsound actions were responses to pressing forces and needs, often political in that they were concerned with the maintenance of power and all its appurtenances and symbols.[64] In the context of the early Middle Ages this often meant cultivating relations with a host of institutions and individuals which were essential props of royal authority. Doling out lands, immunities and other gifts thus served to demonstrate the king's primacy as master of 'public' jurisdiction and arbiter of space, and would help him make friends and influence people in future.[65] Redistribution of wealth to the Church or to the poor fulfilled injunctions such as Matthew 6:19–20, which strongly encouraged the storing up of heavenly rather than earthly treasures.[66] A gift of land from a ruler or aristocrat to a monastery thus brought no monetary recompense, for example, and alienated a valuable piece of property; yet that gift might kindle a mutually beneficial friendship with the receiving institution in life, and prayers for the soul of the donor in death.[67] For the ruling elite in the early medieval period, building relationships and

---

[61] A. Robben, *Sons of the Sea Goddess: Economic Practice and Discursive Conflict in Brazil* (New York, 1989), pp. 2–29.

[62] Below, pp. 36–7.

[63] Devroey, *Puissants et misérables*, pp. 591–600.

[64] For an insightful comparison from the ancient world, see Finley, *Ancient Economy*, pp. 150–76.

[65] Rosenwein, *Negotiating Space*, pp. 3–9.

[66] T. D. Hill, 'The Falling Leaf and Buried Treasure: Two Notes on the Imagery of *Solomon and Saturn*', *Neuphilologische Mitteilungen* 71 (1970), 571–6, at pp. 573–6.

[67] See in particular I. F. Silber, 'Gift-Giving in the Great Traditions: The Case of Donations to Monasteries in the Medieval West', *European Journal of Sociology* 36 (1995), 209–43.

reinforcing social ties was an eminently rational thing to do, and advancing their social position had knock-on effects for their political standing. Giving, to put it bluntly, entailed an expectation of getting, even if the end result was a gain in regard or prestige rather than material wealth: the two were closely enmeshed.[68]

Focusing on resources, including coinage, in purely material terms thus risks distorting the ways in which power was viewed and exercised in the early Middle Ages. It was often conceived socially and ideologically rather than economically, and much of the importance of resources like land, tolls and coinage lay in facilitating the manipulation of interpersonal relationships. There was, of course, much flexibility within this generalization. Different groups had different outlooks, although the focus here will be on the king, as in England it was he rather than the aristocracy or (usually) the Church who patronized minting.[69] In addition, although rulers were strongly guided by tradition,[70] each king was an individual at the heart of a small and fluctuating body of clergy and magnates with influence of the sort German medievalists have termed *Königsnähe*. Consequently, different concerns came to the fore under successive monarchs. Alfred, for example, is known in great detail as a king with strong views on wisdom, duty and all manner of other activities within his kingdom. In terms of coinage, Offa, Charlemagne and Æthelwulf all presided over relatively numerous and important reforms, and might thus be seen as having a deeper involvement with minting.

Most Anglo-Saxon kings before Alfred cannot, unfortunately, be approached in anything like as much detail. Loss of sources can explain some, but not all, of this gap. Legislation and literary endeavour simply seem to have been unusual among the rulers of eighth- and ninth-century England, and most kings' interests probably lay outside the scriptorium and away from detailed consideration of how best to maximize the means at their disposal. But on a fundamental level kings had a right to receive, and subjects had a duty to give.[71] In other words, kingship itself was defined by jurisdiction over resources, not necessarily by shrewd exploitation of them. Hence there was a strong onus on rulers to keep things the way they were, or rather as they and their subjects thought they should be, even if sustained interest in trade, production and coinage was

---

[68] Cf. P. Bourdieu, *Outline of a Theory of Practice*, trans. R. Nice (Cambridge, 1977), pp. 177–8. For further discussion of reciprocity and gift-giving, see below, pp. 260–70.

[69] On these other groups and their possible contribution, see pp. 92–4 and 218–24.

[70] G. Althoff, *Otto III*, trans. P. G. Jestice (University Park, PA, 2003), pp. 24–6 and 146–7.

[71] Fouracre, 'Comparing the Resources', p. 294. The context here is that of the Carolingians and their eagerness to codify and enforce such rights, particularly in contrast with the Merovingians. But the same expectation applied in (for example) Alfred the Great's Wessex (above, n. 48).

unusual.[72] When kings did engage in what historians would call management of resources or economic intervention, it was frequently in response to specific or passing needs and crises, such as the various rebellions and natural disasters of the 790s or the civil war in the Frankish empire after 840,[73] or can be directly related to products and activities of a prestigious and highly symbolic nature. The famous and mysterious *petras nigras* ('black stones') which Offa at one point requested from Charlemagne as a gift are a case in point:[74] they should probably be identified with the rare and precious black marble extracted from quarries in northern Francia and used for the most prestigious of projects, such as the inscribed epitaph of Pope Hadrian I (772–95).[75]

It is therefore debatable whether conscious and rational exploitation of resources for material gain dominated 'economic policy' in the early medieval period, at least outside times of crisis; the perpetuation of stability and tradition was generally more prominent.[76] Kings were concerned to maintain the status quo as it related to themselves and their establishment. Within this remit they could attempt to answer problems that affected not only themselves but other groups within the kingdom:[77] the Church and the aristocracy most prominently, but also in some circumstances even merchants and the peasantry.[78] Care for orphans and widows and distribution of alms to the poor were among the virtues advocated for kings in *De duodecim abusivis saeculi*.[79] This view of kingship was

---

[72] M. McCormick, *Origins of the European Economy: Communications and Commerce A.D. 300–900* (Cambridge, 2001), pp. 573–80; for an early observation to this effect, H. Pirenne, *Medieval Cities: Their Origin and the Revival of Trade*, trans. F. D. Halsey (Princeton, NJ, 1925), p. 39.

[73] Balzaretti and Nelson, 'Trade, Industry and the Wealth of King Alfred', pp. 140–52; challenged by Maddicott, 'Trade, Industry and the Wealth of King Alfred: A Reply', pp. 165–71. Cf. A. Verhulst, *The Carolingian Economy* (Cambridge, 2002), pp. 126–31; O. Bruand, *Voyageurs et marchandises aux temps carolingiens* (Brussels, 2002), pp. 31–2; McKitterick, *Frankish Kingdoms*, p. 86; Wickham, 'Fall of Rome', pp. 55–6; R. Samson, 'Fighting with Silver: Re-thinking Trading, Raiding and Hoarding', in *Social Approaches to Viking Studies*, ed. R. Samson (Glasgow, 1991), pp. 123–33, at 124–5.

[74] MGH Epist. IV, no. 100, p. 145 (trans. *EHD*, p. 849).

[75] J. Story, *Carolingian Connections: Anglo-Saxon England and Carolingian Francia, c. 750–870* (Aldershot, 2003), pp. 106–9; J. Story et al., 'Charlemagne's Black Marble: The Origins of the Epitaph of Pope Hadrian I', *Papers of the British School at Rome* 73 (2005), 157–90.

[76] J.-P. Devroey, 'Réflections sur l'économie des premiers temps carolingiens (768–877): grands domaines et action politique entre Seine et Rhin', *Francia* 13 (1986), 475–88, at pp. 477–81; F. Vercauteren, 'Monnaie et circulation monétaire en Belgique et dans le Nord de la France du VIe au XIe siècle', *Settimane* 8 (1961), 279–311, at p. 294.

[77] S. Reynolds, 'Compulsory Purchase in the Earlier Middle Ages', in *Frankland. The Franks and the World of the Early Middle Ages. Essays in Honour of Dame Jinty Nelson*, ed. P. Fouracre and D. Ganz (Manchester, 2008), pp. 28–43, at 31–40; Nelson, 'Kingship and Empire', pp. 61–7, and 'Kingship and Royal Government', pp. 405–6, 409–10 and 417–30; Devroey, *Puissants et misérables*, pp. 318–35; H. Loyn, *Anglo-Saxon England and the Norman Conquest*, 2nd edn (London, 1991), pp. 311–25.

[78] P. Sawyer, 'Kings and Merchants', in *Early Medieval Kingship*, ed. P. H. Sawyer and I. N. Wood (Leeds, 1977), pp. 139–58; Devroey, *Puissants et misérables*, pp. 328–44.

[79] Pseudo-Cyprian, *De duodecim abusivis saeculi* (ed. Hellmann, p. 52).

most highly developed in the case of earlier Carolingian rulers, above all Charlemagne and Louis the Pious, who worked closely with the Church to promote themselves as its protectors and in so doing built an ethos of kings and their delegated subordinates as secular equivalents of bishops or abbots, divinely appointed to look after their flock.[80] How they and their Anglo-Saxon counterparts maintained the balance of power and society, and how effectively they responded to various needs and developments, requires more specific treatment of the different resources available in eighth- and ninth-century England – in other words, of what resources power consisted.

Land and warriors

Land – and by extension the services and dues that pertained to landowner-ship – lay at the very heart of kingship and most other forms of power in the early Middle Ages.[81] Possession of a significant quantity of it was one of the defining characteristics of elite status (*gesith*, *nobilis* or similar).[82] As a result, land was by far the most important and best-recorded resource of the period. In southern England, prevalent tenurial systems seem to have emphasized dispersed and specialized production spread over very large estates.[83] These could provide a wide range and large quantity of agricul-tural goods: a famous passage from the law-code of Ine, king of the West Saxons (688–726), lists the food-rent expected from 10 hides as 10 vats of honey, 300 loaves of bread, 12 'ambers' of Welsh ale, 30 of clear ale, 2 full-grown cows or 10 wethers, 10 geese, 20 hens, 10 cheeses, an 'amber' of butter, 5 salmon, 20 pounds of fodder and 100 eels.[84]

This rich yield would have required the owner, king or otherwise, to be on or near the spot in order to make use of it.[85] Later in the

---

[80] P. Fouracre, 'Carolingian Justice: The Rhetoric of Improvement and Contexts of Abuse', *Settimane* 42 (1995), 771–803; R. McKitterick, *Charlemagne: The Formation of a European Identity* (Cambridge, 2008), esp. pp. 292–380; Devroey, *Puissants et misérables*, pp. 606–7.

[81] *FEMA*, pp. 58–9.

[82] Devroey, *Puissants et misérables*, pp. 242–5; T. Charles-Edwards, 'Kinship, Status and the Origin of the Hide', *P&P* 56 (1972), 3–33; but cf. H. Loyn, 'Gesiths and Thegns in Anglo-Saxon England from the Seventh to the Tenth Century', *EHR* 70 (1955), 529–49, on the changing status of these terms in relation to service and landownership.

[83] F. W. Maitland, *Domesday Book and Beyond: Three Essays in the Early History of England* (Cambridge, 1897), pp. 272–90; G. Jones, 'Multiple Estates and Early Settlement', in *Medieval Settlement: Continuity and Change*, ed. P. H. Sawyer (London, 1976), pp. 15–40; F. M. Stenton, *Anglo-Saxon England*, 3rd edn (Oxford, 1971), pp. 302–5; Faith, *English Peasantry*, pp. 7–14; *FEMA*, pp. 320–4; contra N. Gregson, 'The Multiple Estate Model: Some Critical Questions', *Journal of Historical Geography* 11 (1985), 339–51; Verhulst, *Carolingian Economy*, pp. 31–60.

[84] Ine, law-code, c. 70.1 (ed. Liebermann I, 118–20).

[85] P. Wormald, 'The Emergence of Anglo-Saxon Kingdoms', in *The Making of Britain: The Dark Ages*, ed. L. M. Smith (Basingstoke, 1984), pp. 49–62, at 58; J. Smith, *Europe after Rome*, pp. 175–7; R. Hodges, *The Anglo-Saxon Achievement* (London, 1989), p. 112.

Anglo-Saxon period it is clear that many royal estates were run by designated reeves, who collected the rent from the land on behalf of the king, and already by the eighth and ninth centuries some of the traditional food rents were being commuted for cash, which was of more direct use to an often absent king or landlord.[86] The existence of large food-rents in part explains why kings moved between estates. By doing so they avoided exhausting their provisions, though the entourage with which kings travelled was not always large, and movements between estates could meet social as well as economic needs.[87]

There is some evidence for an increase in the demands placed on landed possessions at large by the king during the time of Æthelbald and after, particularly in the form of the *trimoda necessitas* of military service, bridgework and road maintenance.[88] There are also signs of more intense exploitation of agricultural land in England in the eighth century,[89] continuing processes begun in the seventh and known as the 'Middle Saxon shuffle'.[90] More detail can be discerned of the process of manorial expansion in the contemporary Carolingian realms. There, recent studies by Jean-Pierre Devroey and Pierre Toubert in particular have emphasized examples of land clearance for new settlement as well as large-scale movement of surpluses for sale by tenants and landlords alike.[91] Some landlords, especially ecclesiastical institutions, thus seem to have overseen

---

[86] This development is discussed on pp. 277–80.

[87] McKitterick, *Charlemagne*, pp. 176–7.

[88] N. Brooks, 'The Development of Military Obligations in Eighth- and Ninth-Century England', in *England before the Conquest: Studies in Primary Sources Presented to Dorothy Whitelock*, ed. P. Clemoes and K. Hughes (Cambridge, 1971), pp. 69–84, and 'Rochester Bridge, A.D. 43–1381', in *Traffic and Politics: The Construction and Management of Rochester Bridge, A.D. 43–1993*, ed. N. Yates and J. M. Gibson (Woodbridge, 1994), pp. 3–40; S. Keynes, 'The Reconstruction of a Burnt Cottonian Manuscript: The Case of Cotton MS. Otho A. I', *British Library Journal* 22 (1996), 113–60; R. Abels, *Lordship and Military Obligation in Anglo-Saxon England* (Berkeley, CA, 1988), pp. 52–7; G. Williams, 'Military Obligations and Mercian Supremacy in the Eighth Century', in *Æthelbald and Offa*, ed. Hill and Worthington, pp. 103–9; W. H. Stevenson, '*Trinoda necessitas*', *EHR* 29 (1914), 689–703; P. Blinkhorn, 'Of Cabbages and Kings: Production, Trade and Consumption in Middle-Saxon England', in *Anglo-Saxon Trading Centres: Beyond the Emporia*, ed. M. Anderton (Glasgow, 1999), pp. 4–23, at 11–13; Chadwick, *Studies*, pp. 100–2.

[89] J. Moreland, 'The Significance of Production in Eighth-Century England', in *The Long Eighth Century*, ed. I. L. Hansen and C. Wickham (Leiden, 2000), pp. 69–104, at 82–96; R. Faith, 'Forces and Relations of Production in Early Medieval England', *Journal of Agrarian Change* 9 (2009), 23–41, at pp. 38–9; S. Rippon, *Beyond the Medieval Village: The Diversification of Landscape Character in Southern Britain* (Oxford, 2008), esp. pp. 265–6; R. Fleming, *Britain after Rome. The Fall and Rise, 400–1070* (London, 2010), pp. 276–84; H. Hamerow, *Early Medieval Settlements: The Archaeology of Rural Communities in Northwest Europe, 400–900* (Oxford, 2002), esp. pp. 121–4.

[90] C. Arnold and P. Wardle, 'Early Medieval Settlement Patterns in England', *Medieval Archaeology* 25 (1981), 145–9; Hodges, *Anglo-Saxon Achievement*, pp. 58–65.

[91] J.-P. Devroey, *Études sur le grand domaine carolingien* (Aldershot, 1993) and *Économie rurale et société*, pp. 65–77; P. Toubert, *L'Europe dans sa première croissance: de Charlemagne à l'an mil* (Paris, 2004), esp. pp. 84–99.

quite dynamic development of the rural economy around this time.[92] There may well have been significant differences in the methods of running estates used by kings, bishops, aristocrats and others – though all are now largely invisible.

The prominence of hunting and military services in the context of charters concerning landholdings highlights one of the central royal concerns of the age: warfare.[93] The ability to raise an army and exert deadly force on one's enemies has, under the influence of Max Weber, often been read as a – or even the – *raison d'être* of political authority.[94] It is debatable how far this was always recognized or accepted by contemporaries, although the basic point was set down by at least one Anglo-Saxon poet: 'þrym sceal mid wlenco, þriste mid cenum, sceolon bu recene beadwe fremman'.[95] Certainly he was right that the martial ethos of the ruling class in early medieval Europe was strong. Military exploits exerted a very powerful hold over contemporary thought and literature, above all that produced for, in or about secular society. The training and hunting that were part of everyday aristocratic life were not just for entertainment, however. Prowess at arms, tactical ability and control of an experienced and well-motivated army could be just as politically decisive as superior cultural, religious or economic resources, especially in the short term.[96] Moreover, although warfare was expensive and dangerous, it served the very important purpose of providing an occasion on which the *crème de la crème* of lay society could unite in common purpose. Military gatherings, such as those which took place every year under the Carolingians for much of the eighth century, could thus provide the setting for hunting, feasting and spectacle, during which gifts passed both ways and important social bonds were cemented.[97] If

---

[92] For example, McCormick, *Origins*, pp. 702–3.

[93] T. Reuter, 'The Recruitment of Armies in the Early Middle Ages: What Can We Know?', in *Military Aspects of Scandinavian Society in a European Perspective, A.D. 1–1300*, ed. A. Nørgård Jørgensen and B. L. Clausen (Copenhagen, 1997), pp. 32–7; B. Bachrach, *Early Carolingian Warfare: Prelude to Empire* (Philadelphia, PA, 2000); Abels, *Lordship*; G. Halsall, *Warfare and Society in the Barbarian West, 450–900* (London, 2003), esp. pp. 27–8.

[94] For example, C. Wickham, 'Conclusion', in *The Byzantine and Early Islamic Near East 3: States, Resources and Armies*, ed. A. Cameron (Princeton, NJ, 1995), pp. 461–8, at 463; Reynolds, 'Historiography of the Medieval State', pp. 118–19; for a more critical view R. Davies, 'The Medieval State: The Tyranny of a Concept?', *Journal of Historical Sociology* 16 (2003), 280–300, at p. 291.

[95] 'Power goes with pride, bold men with brave ones; both must be quick to make war.' *Maxims IA*, lines 61–2 (ed. and trans. Shippey, *Poems of Wisdom and Learning*, pp. 66–7).

[96] T. Reuter, 'Plunder and Tribute in the Carolingian Empire', *TRHS* 35 (1985), 75–94, at pp. 92–3; Goldberg, *Struggle for Empire*, pp. 11–13 and 195–6.

[97] F. Curta, 'Merovingian and Carolingian Gift Giving', *Speculum* 81 (2006), 671–99; Reuter, 'Plunder and Tribute', p. 81.

campaigns were successful, they might also provide the ruler with a substantial supply of plunder or tribute. Regular successful offensives could come to provide a significant stream of royal income.[98]

Even before the viking attacks of the ninth century, conflict between English kings and their foreign neighbours was common, if not yet on the scale of the 860s and 870s. Mercian kings of the eighth century were noteworthy for the organization which they combined with their belligerence, and directed their efforts against the Welsh, South Saxons, West Saxons and men of Kent, among others.[99] The most famous manifestation of this is Offa's Dyke.[100] Wessex, however, took the initiative against the vikings later in the ninth century, especially under Alfred, when *burh* construction was adopted as a key strategy alongside a number of other refinements and innovations to the military system.[101] Although fortifications such as *byrg* could serve a range of interests, the military underpinning of early medieval political thought cannot be forgotten.

Towns and trade

Food, goods and services (military and otherwise) derived from land dominated the background of royal resources in early medieval Europe. They are, however, in many respects divorced from royal involvement with coinage. Minting was associated with towns in the later eighth and ninth centuries, which were foci of lesser but still important royal interests.

Indeed, when the scale of new urban developments in the seventh, eighth and ninth centuries first became apparent thanks to archaeological excavations in the second half of the twentieth century, the archaeologist Richard Hodges postulated a major role for kings in their

---

[98] T. Reuter, '"You Can't Take It with You": Testaments, Hoards and Moveable Wealth in Europe 600–1100', in *Treasure in the Medieval West*, ed. E. M. Tyler (York, 2000), pp. 11–24, and 'Plunder and Tribute'; M. Hardt, 'Royal Treasures and Representation in the Early Middle Ages', in *Strategies of Distinction: The Construction of Ethnic Communities, 300–800*, ed. W. Pohl and H. Reimitz (Leiden, 1998), pp. 255–80; J. Durliat, *Les finances publiques de Dioclétien aux Carolingiens (284–889)* (Sigmaringen, 1990), pp. 286–7; D. Tyler, 'Orchestrated Violence and the "Supremacy" of the Mercian Kings', in *Æthelbald and Offa*, ed. Hill and Worthington, pp. 27–33; K. Leyser, 'Early Medieval Warfare', in *The Battle of Maldon: Fiction and Fact*, ed. J. Cooper (London, 1993), pp. 87–108, at 92–3.

[99] Above, pp. 9–10 and 18–20.

[100] D. Hill and M. Worthington, *Offa's Dyke: History and Guide* (Stroud, 2003). Cf. S. Bassett, 'Divide and Rule? The Military Infrastructure of Eighth- and Ninth-Century Mercia', *EME* 15 (2007), 53–85.

[101] See in general the papers in D. Hill and A. Rumble, *The Defence of Wessex: The Burghal Hidage and Anglo-Saxon Fortifications* (Manchester, 1996).

establishment.[102] Also thanks to Hodges, it is now common practice to refer to these important new commercial centres as *wic*, a term which originates in early medieval texts, or *emporia*, a label applied by Karl Polanyi to highlight commercial as opposed to more generally urban functions.[103] Hodges' use of these terms emphasized the functions he saw for these settlements: they were not centres of secular or ecclesiastical government, but essentially large, semi-permanent markets through which rulers could funnel imports for their own benefit.

Several elements of this interpretation have been challenged and revised subsequently, including the prominence of the king in all aspects of the origin and development of the new towns.[104] The foundation of a *wic* or *emporium* could be the responsibility of a larger body of craftsmen and traders, whose role remained significant for a long time thereafter.[105] Likewise the *wic* should probably no longer be seen as artificial markets pure and simple, standing in splendid isolation from their surrounding hinterlands and dedicated solely to serving the expensive tastes of the elite through long-distance trade.[106] Rather, they lay at the centre of networks of increasingly elaborate local and regional economies. These existed alongside a relatively tight-knit world of international

---

[102] R. Hodges, *Dark Age Economics: The Origins of Towns and Trade A.D. 600–1000*, 2nd edn (London, 1989) and *Anglo-Saxon Achievement*. For further general discussion of these settlements, see Anderton, ed., *Anglo-Saxon Trading Centres*, pp. 44–67.

[103] Polanyi, *Primitive, Archaic and Modern*, pp. 238–60.

[104] *FEMA*, p. 684; McCormick, 'Um 808'; J. Henning, 'Early European Towns: The Way of the Economy in the Frankish Area between Dynamism and Deceleration 500–1000 AD', in *Post-Roman Towns. Trade and Settlement in Europe and Byzantium*, ed. J. Henning, 2 vols. (Berlin and New York, 2007) I, 3–40, at pp. 20–1 and 27–9; J. Newman, '*Wics*, Trade and the Hinterlands – the Ipswich Region', in *Anglo-Saxon Trading Centres*, ed. Anderton, pp. 32–47; Moreland, 'Significance of Production', pp. 72–6.

[105] H. Hamerow, 'Agrarian Production and the *Emporia* of Mid Saxon England, ca. AD 650–850', in *Post-Roman Towns*, ed. Henning, I, 219–32, at pp. 226–30; S. Brookes, *Economics and Social Change in Anglo-Saxon Kent AD 400–900: Landscapes, Communities and Exchange*, BAR British Series 431 (Oxford, 2007), pp. 30–1; Samson, 'Fighting', pp. 124–5; S. Sindbæk, 'Networks and Nodal Points: The Emergence of Towns in Early Viking Age Scandinavia', *Antiquity* 81 (2007), 119–32, at pp. 128–9; J. Henning, 'Early European Towns: The Way of the Economy in the Frankish Area between Dynamism and Deceleration 500–1000 AD', in *Post-Roman Towns*, ed. Henning, I, 3–40, at pp. 27–9; M. Mitterauer, *Markt und Stadt im Mittelalter. Beiträge zur historischen Zentralitätsforschung* (Stuttgart, 1980), pp. 174–5; M. McCormick, 'Where Do Trading Towns Come From? Early Medieval Venice and the Northern *Emporia*', in *Post-Roman Towns*, ed. Henning, I, 41–68, at pp. 44–7, and 'Um 808'.

[106] J. Naylor, 'Access to International Trade in Middle Saxon England: A Case of Urban Over-Emphasis?', in *Close Encounters: Sea- and Riverborne Trade, Ports and Hinterlands, Ship Construction and Navigation in Antiquity, the Middle Ages and in Modern Time*, ed. M. Pasquinucci and T. Weski, BAR British Series 1283 (Oxford, 2004), pp. 139–48, at 140–5; E. Lorans, 'Les élites et l'espace urbain: approches archéologique et morphologique (France du Nord et Angleterre, VIIe–Xe siècles)', in *Les élites et leurs espaces: mobilité, rayonnement, domination (VIe–XIe s.)*, ed. P. Depreux, F. Bougard and R. Le Jan (Turnhout, 2007), pp. 67–97, esp. 72–83; J. Bourdillon, 'The Animal Provisioning of Saxon Southampton', in *Environment and Economy in Anglo-Saxon England*, ed. J. Rackham (York, 1994), pp. 120–5. See below p. 279.

exchange based on a small number of traders moving between only a few major centres.[107]

The kings' part in founding and fostering towns and trade in the seventh and eighth centuries was therefore far from all-encompassing. What it did extend to was taking a cut of the proceeds of towns once they were up and running. These fiscal benefits and the symbolic patronage and protection associated with them were arguably the key interest that trade and towns held for early medieval kings.[108] An important example of this can be found in tolls, which were already being charged by agents of Æthelbald on ships entering London in the early eighth century.[109] Much about these tolls is unclear: the rate at which they were charged; the form in which they were taken; and also the overall contribution they made to royal income. Later in the ninth century one *wægnscilling* and one *seampending* were charged on each wagon of salt at Droitwich,[110] while a tenth (*decima*) was common on the Continent.[111] Kings did not, it should be noted, always hold a monopoly over tolls, and in some cases they delegated their collection to high-ranking local potentates.[112] In England, the cessation of toll charters after only a brief period is somewhat mysterious, but as they record only the alienation of toll rights away from the king, it may be presumed that ships carried on coming to London, and agents of the king carried on charging tolls from them.

Later medieval evidence reveals tolls to have been just one of the prerogatives enjoyed by rulers within towns. Kings' agents, for example, may also have had first choice of incoming goods.[113] This presupposes that they would have been on hand whenever a trading ship appeared, ready to enforce the king's due before anyone else got a look-in. One such

---

[107] For the Scandanavian branch of this especially, see S. Sindbæk, 'The Small World of the Vikings: Networks in Early Medieval Communication and Exchange', *Norwegian Archaeological Review* 40 (2007), 59–74, and 'Networks'. Cf. McCormick, *Origins*, esp. pp. 151–73.

[108] Brookes, *Economics*, pp. 30–2; D. Hinton, *Southampton Finds*, vol. II, *The Gold, Silver and Other Non-Ferrous Alloy Objects from Hamwic, and the Non-Ferrous Metalworking Evidence* (Stroud, 1996), pp. 98–102; Naylor, 'Access', p. 147; C. Scull, 'Urban Centres in Pre-Viking England?', in *The Anglo-Saxons*, ed. Hines, pp. 269–98, at 284–9.

[109] S. Kelly, 'Trading Privileges from Eighth-Century England', *EME* 1 (1992), 3–28; Middleton, 'Early Medieval Port Customs'; J. Stoclet, *'Immunes ab omni teloneo': étude de diplomatique, de philologie et d'histoire sur l'exemption de tonlieux au haut moyen âge et spécialement sur la 'Praeceptio de navibus'* (Brussels, 1999); Verhulst, *Carolingian Economy*, pp. 105–6 and 130; F.-L. Ganshof, 'À propos du tonlieu à l'époque carolingienne', *Settimane* 6 (1959), 485–508.

[110] S 223 (*SEHD* no. 13): J. R. Maddicott, 'London and Droitwich, c. 650–750: Trade, Industry and the Rise of Mercia', *ASE* 34 (2005), 7–58, at p. 41; D. Hooke, 'The Droitwich Salt Industry: The West Midlands Charter Evidence', *ASSAH* 2 (1981), 123–69, at pp. 134 and 149.

[111] Middleton, 'Early Medieval Port Customs', pp. 324–30; and Kelly, 'Trading Privileges', p. 20.

[112] S 86 and 208: Middleton, 'Early Medieval Port Customs', pp. 336–40; Kelly, 'Trading Privileges', p. 19; Hodges, *Anglo-Saxon Achievement*, p. 96.

[113] Middleton, 'Early Medieval Port Customs', pp. 333–5.

official met his end through his perhaps over-zealous application of the king's preferential access to incoming goods. Beaduheard, a reeve under Beorhtric, king of the West Saxons (786–802), was killed by vikings landing at Portland in Dorset when he approached and asked them to come, like other traders, to the king's estate: a demand which met with deadly disapproval.[114]

As the unfortunate example of Beaduheard illustrates, trade- and town-related duties, as well as the witnessing of purchases, fell to the king's reeve, who was already a standard part of the machinery of government in the seventh century. Town-reeves occupied and oversaw the king's hall or estate in or near the town where they worked.[115] These were mentioned already in the seventh century, and traces of royal estates or *villae/vici* can be found at several other towns.[116] Southampton as a whole was described as a *villa regalis* in 840,[117] and lay relatively close to the royal and ecclesiastical centre of Winchester.[118] To the east, London, too, was host to a royal *vicus*,[119] and royal gatherings and ecclesiastical synods were often held in the vicinity of London.[120]

The strength of the king's ties varied considerably from town to town, often in line with more general fluctuations in the strength and nature of royal government. London and Southampton, for example, both seem to have featured quite prominently in their respective kingdoms, and possessed relatively strong links to the king and his entourage. So little is known of kingship in contemporary East Anglia that Ipswich's relationship to the crown is highly obscure. Canterbury, however, in common with the rest of Kent under Mercian overlordship, displayed much less direct evidence of royal interests. Kentish officials, clergy and aristocrats were tied together, but to a large extent moved in separate circles from

---

[114] *ASC* s.a. 789; Æthelweard, *Chronicon* iii.1 (ed. and trans. Campbell, pp. 26–7).

[115] Above, n. 42.

[116] On *vicus/wic*, see Sawyer, 'Kings and Merchants', pp. 152–3; J. Campbell, 'Bede's Words for Places', in *Names, Words and Graves: Early Medieval Settlement*, ed. P. H. Sawyer (Leeds, 1979), pp. 34–54, at 43–5; A. Rumble, 'Notes on the Linguistic and Onomastic Characteristics of Old English *wic*', in *Wics: The Early Medieval Trading Centres of Northern Europe*, ed. D. Hill and R. Cowie (Sheffield, 2001), pp. 1–2; H. Clarke and B. Ambrosiani, *Towns in the Viking Age* (Leicester, 1991), pp. 15–16; A. H. Smith, *English Place-Name Elements*, 2 vols. (Cambridge, 1956) II, 257–64; E. Ekwall, *Old English Wic in Place-Names*, Acta Universitatis Upsaliensis: Nomina Germanica 13 (Uppsala, 1964).

[117] S 288 (BCS 431).

[118] J. Smith, *Europe after Rome*, pp. 188–9; and *FEMA*, pp. 684–6 and 809–10.

[119] S 170. See also Maddicott, 'London and Droitwich', pp. 16–22; R. Cowie, 'Mercian London', in *Mercia*, ed. Brown and Farr, pp. 194–209, and 'The Evidence for Royal Sites in Middle Anglo-Saxon London', *Medieval Archaeology* 48 (2004), 201–9; D. Keene, 'Alfred and London', in *Alfred the Great*, ed. Reuter, pp. 235–49. See also below pp. 114–16.

[120] S 132, 168, 170, 318 and 1436.

those of Mercia proper, and tended to remain in place despite violent changes in king and dynasty.[121]

Conclusion

The selection of royal resources discussed here is by no means exhaustive, but it serves to illustrate some of the primary concerns of early medieval rulers, and the context of royal interest in matters related to coinage. To take a broader view, it might be noted that early Anglo-Saxon rulers enjoyed somewhat less power to exploit their kingdoms than contemporaries in Francia or Italy, and much less than late Roman emperors.[122] Eighth- and ninth-century rulers, most famously Æthelbald, Offa and Alfred, took steps that strengthened their position, above all increasing exploitation of rights over land and subordinates.

The place of towns and trade in their regimes was significant, but overall not outstandingly prominent. A glance at what can be gleaned about royal itineraries reveals that the kings' presence was concentrated in western Mercia and Wessex: regions which were markedly less economically sophisticated than the southern and eastern reaches of England.[123] The rich pickings they offered of towns, trade and money have sometimes been cited as one of the key motivating factors behind Mercian and (later) West Saxon expansion.[124] But such encroachments were not unique to the southeast: the Welsh, the Hwicce, Cornwall, Sussex and other areas were targeted as well. The lands, manpower, plunder and prestige these conquests provided may have been just as attractive as the fleshpots of the southeast.[125] For most kings, economic advantages were just one of several factors to be weighed against the symbolic, social and military benefits of ruling.

A particularly vivid illustration of the way in which rulers thought about economic resources in their kingdoms came – tellingly – when Offa and Charlemagne apparently entered negotiations over the marriage of their children in the early 790s.[126] Offa would accept the wedding of his daughter to Charlemagne's son only on condition that his son could also marry one of Charlemagne's daughters; consequently the

---

[121] Above, n. 24.
[122] Brooks, *Church, State*, pp. 3–7; *FEMA*, pp. 303–4.
[123] *FEMA*, pp. 813–14; Hodges, *Anglo-Saxon Achievement*, pp. 96–7. Cf. below, p. 229.
[124] Keynes, 'Control of Kent', p. 112.
[125] H.-W. Goetz, 'Social and Military Institutions', in *NCMH* II, pp. 451–80, at 471–3 and 479–80; Reuter, 'Plunder and Tribute'.
[126] For the primary sources, see *Gesta sanctorum patrum Fontanellensis coenobii* xii.2 (ed. Lohier and Laporte, pp. 86–7; trans. *EHD*, p. 341); MGH Epist. IV, nos. 7, 9 and 82 (trans. Allott, nos. 31, 10 and 39).

Frankish king ordered an embargo on all English shipping, which Offa countered with a similar embargo on Frankish trade in England. It says much that both kings could do this, and that they expected it to work as a sting to their adversary.[127] Yet at the same time, trade was clearly a tool, which played second fiddle to the power politics and personal vendettas of rulers.

COINAGE AS A ROYAL RESOURCE:
THE ROMAN LEGACY

If royal views on the exploitation of resources were comparatively circumscribed, wherein lay the attraction of coinage, and how did it come to be associated with royal power?

The clash of Charlemagne and Grimoald highlighted at the beginning of this chapter came only as the conclusion to long and complex developments. In the context of Anglo-Saxon England, coinage was a creation of the seventh century, based most immediately on the issues of Merovingian Francia, and ultimately on the currency of the later Roman empire.[128] The function of precious-metal coinage in the latter became closely tied to the emperor's taxation of land across the empire, as part of a process known as *adaeratio*.[129] Taxation in gold became more prevalent from late in the fourth century as the demands of paying barbarian soldiers grew more acute.[130] However, then, as later, gold was very precious, and only the wealthier members of society were able or required to pay in *solidi*, *semisses* and *tremisses*: there probably always existed a second tier of taxation in kind which embraced a much larger number of poorer tax payers.[131]

But by the time Anglo-Saxon England saw minting reappear in the first half of the seventh century this system was being replaced in Gaul and elsewhere with one in which royal income derived principally from land

---

[127] For discussion see Keynes, 'Kingdom of the Mercians', pp. 16–17; Story, *Carolingian Connections*, pp. 184–7; Nelson, 'Carolingian Contacts', pp. 132–5; for a more cautious reading, McKitterick, *Charlemagne*, pp. 282–4.

[128] *T&S* I, 29–62; and G. Williams, 'The Circulation and Function of Coinage in Conversion-Period England, *c*. AD 580–675', in *Coinage and History in the North Sea World c. 500–1250. Essays in Honour of Marion Archibald*, ed. B. Cook and G. Williams (Leiden and Boston, MA, 2006), pp. 145–92.

[129] S. Barnish, A. D. Lee and M. Whitby, 'Government and Administration', in *NCAH* XIV, pp. 164–206, at 194–8; A. Cerati, *Caractère annonaire et assiette de l'impôt foncier au Bas-Empire* (Paris, 1975), pp. 57–183; J. Banaji, *Agrarian Change in Late Antiquity: Gold, Labour, and Aristocratic Dominance*, 2nd edn (Oxford, 2007), pp. 39–88 and 264–7.

[130] J.-M. Carrié, 'L'état à la recherche de nouveaux modes de financement des armées (Rome et Byzance, IVe–VIIIe siècles)', in *Byzantine and Early Near East*, ed. Cameron, pp. 27–60, at 35–59.

[131] W. Goffart, *Barbarians and Romans A.D. 418–584: The Techniques of Accommodation* (Princeton, NJ, 1980), esp. pp. 78–9.

rents rather than general taxation, and came predominantly in kind.[132] Coinage became a vehicle for paying rents and tributes which passed through the hands of private customers, not a specifically tax-orientated mechanism run by the imperial or latterly royal administration for its own benefit.[133] The transition between these systems could be painful. When, in 366/7, Emperor Valentinian I (364–75) heard that private persons had been using the imperial mints to have their own gold struck into coin or melted into ingots, he proclaimed that all such gold was to be forfeit to the state, though he mitigated this harsh judgement some years later.[134]

Each different region and polity in the post-Roman west underwent these changes at a different pace, to a different degree and with different end results: to suggest otherwise would be a gross oversimplification, and often the link between minting and taxation did not evaporate entirely or overnight. It survived in an attenuated form in Merovingian Gaul and Visigothic Spain, and continued to be a significant if obscure force behind minting.[135] But in Gaul the large, state-run imperial mints disappeared and scattered, while in Spain they had never existed at all.[136] Instead of coin being brought to and from a few major mints either by tax-collectors or private individuals, minting spread out across the kingdoms to answer smaller and more localized needs.

With the atrophy of monetary taxation in western Europe, coin-use was maintained on a comparatively small scale for other purposes, especially those of relatively high value in which custom and prestige played a part: legal fees, rents, occasional tributes, perhaps some gifts and certain kinds of purchase, as well as general commerce.[137] These practices ensured

---

[132] *MEC*, pp. 2–6; W. Goffart, 'Old and New in Merovingian Taxation', *P&P* 96 (1982), 3–21, at pp. 18–19; C. Wickham, *Land and Power: Studies in Italian and European Social History 400–1200* (London, 1994), pp. 7–42, and *FEMA*, pp. 56–150; A. Dopsch, *The Economic and Social Foundations of European Civilization*, trans. M. G. Beard and N. Marshall (London, 1937), pp. 359–83; P. Spufford, *Money and Its Use in Medieval Europe* (Cambridge, 1987), pp. 7–73; M. Hendy, 'From Public to Private: The Western Barbarian Coinages as a Mirror of the Disintegration of Late Roman State Structure', *Viator* 19 (1988), 29–78.

[133] A. Stahl, *Zecca: The Mint of Venice in the Middle Ages* (Baltimore, MD, 2000), p. 99; Bruand, *Voyageurs et marchandises*, pp. 156–65. A contrary view stressing continuity of royal taxation has been developed in Durliat, *Les finances publiques*; criticized in Wickham, 'Fall of Rome'.

[134] *Codex Theodosianus* ix.21.7–8 (ed. Mommsen and Meyer I, 473–4). M. Hendy, *Studies in the Byzantine Monetary Economy c. 300–1450* (Cambridge, 1985), pp. 386–94, and 'Public to Private', pp. 34–5.

[135] I. Garipzanov, 'The Coinage of Tours in the Merovingian Period and the Pirenne Thesis', *Revue belge de numismatique et de sigillographie* 147 (2001), 79–118, at pp. 98–104; Hendy, 'Public to Private', pp. 59–70; *FEMA*, pp. 102–15; Goffart, 'Old and New'; A. Stahl, *The Merovingian Coinage of the Region of Metz* (Louvain-la-neuve, 1982), pp. 115–18.

[136] On Visigothic coinage in this context see *MEC*, pp. 49–54; Hendy, 'Public to Private', pp. 49–59; R. Pliego, *La Moneda Visigoda*, 2 vols. (Seville, 2009) I, 187–98.

[137] Below, pp. 252–4.

that coin-use survived, albeit on a reduced scale in both volume and variety. Gold persisted most strongly after the end of the western empire thanks to its preferred status in official payments and consequent prestige, but silver and low-value base-metal coinages largely disappeared after the first half of the sixth century, one of the starkest demonstrations of the impact of the end of the Roman empire.[138]

Emperors, kings and minting

Much of the economic and administrative impetus behind minting thus fell away in the period after the end of the western Roman empire. Under these circumstances, the symbolic aspect of coinage, inherited from Rome, came to play a very significant part in both the use and issue of currency. In the late Roman period this was closely associated with the figure of the emperor. The writers of the *Historia Augusta* cited coinage as one of the prime credentials for emperors,[139] and distribution of money was an important feature of processions and ceremonies.[140] The images on coins drew on a widely held but idealized view of the emperor: they showed what an emperor should look like, not how the emperor actually looked.[141]

If anything, the explanation for the rarity of explicitly regal coinage in the post-Roman west lies in the strength of the imperial associations of gold coinage – the one part of the currency which persisted on any scale through to the later seventh century. During the fifth and sixth centuries especially, even though no more emperors were actually recognized, most 'barbarian' mints still toed the line and used the name and image of the current emperor or one of his recent predecessors on gold. The Byzantine writer Procopius recorded how Constantinople was up in arms when Theudebert I, king of the Franks (548–55), decided to thumb his nose at the traditional imperial prerogative of gold and placed his name and image on *solidi*.[142] His short-lived coinage proved exceptional: in Frankish Gaul, the overwhelming majority of the gold coinage retained a Roman appearance, including a pseudo-imperial bust and (until later in the sixth century) the name of an emperor. Issues in the names of Merovingian kings were always a rarity, probably produced on

---

[138] B. Ward-Perkins, *The Fall of Rome and the End of Civilization* (Oxford, 2005), pp. 110–17.

[139] *Historia Augusta: Tyranni Triginta* xxvi.3, xxxi.3, *Divus Claudius* xiv.2 and *Firmus, Saturninus, Proculus et Bonosus* ii.1 (ed. Ballou, Peter and Magie III, 128, 144, 182 and 388).

[140] Hendy, *Studies*, pp. 192–201.

[141] Below, pp. 53–69.

[142] Procopius, *History of the Wars*, 7.33.5–6 (ed. and trans. Dewing IV, 438–9). For discussion R. Collins, 'Theodebert I: *Rex Magnus Francorum*', in *Ideal and Reality*, ed. Wormald *et al.*, pp. 7–33.

a small scale for specific occasions in a similar way to other batches of coin made for individual customers.[143] Naming the mint and (in Francia) moneyer brought a degree of accountability and authentication for the coinage in order to supplement the unverbalized bond between king and coinage.[144] Minting thus retained a link to the fiscal system in the Merovingian kingdom, but not to the king himself.

This broad-based demand for minting across the kingdom eventually resulted in a very large network of mints and moneyers who issued money under peripheral royal authority. In Francia the process culminated in the establishment of mints where the ruler's interests were explicitly shared with those of local magnates and churches in the early Carolingian era.[145] Exactly how the numerous moneyers of the seventh century made this transition is an important yet so far largely unanswered question; but it was the strongly moneyer-based organization of the early seventh century, adopted in England in imitation of Merovingian Gaul, which provided the point of departure for future developments on that side of the Channel.

Although the link between coinage and contemporary rulers only re-emerged on an explicit and substantial level in the middle of the eighth century – and then inheriting several influences in addition to the late Roman, as will be seen in due course – coin design from the fifth century onwards was heavily based, directly or indirectly, on Roman models. Most prominent of all, for a combination of chronological and religious reasons, were the written and numismatic remains of the fourth and fifth centuries: Christian emperors of this era such as Constantine the Great (307–37) were seen as exemplary in numerous ways.[146] When early medieval manuscript illuminators called on coin-inspired roundels they were modelled almost universally on Roman rather than current issues.[147] Texts discussing early medieval coinage also viewed it in the mould of late Roman legislation. A prime example is the extensive dependence of Charles the Bald's (840–77) Edict of Pîtres on the Theodosian Code.[148]

Southern England from the time of Offa's reform onwards was thus just one of several western European successors to the Roman monetary

[143] *MEC*, pp. 81–154.
[144] On Merovingian moneyers see A. Dieudonné, 'Les monétaires mérovingiens', *Bibliothèque de l'École des chartes* 103 (1942), 20–51; *MEC*, pp. 97–102.
[145] See p. 145.
[146] For the influence of Constantine in particular, see pp. 58–62.
[147] H. Maguire, 'Magic and Money in the Early Middle Ages', *Speculum* 72 (1997), 1037–54, at pp. 1050–3 and plate 32–7.
[148] J. L. Nelson, 'Translating Images of Authority: The Christian Roman Emperors in the Carolingian World', in *Images of Authority. Papers Presented to Joyce Reynolds on the Occasion of Her 70th Birthday*, ed. M. M. Mackenzie and C. Roueché (Cambridge, 1989), pp. 194–205, at 196–7.

legacy. Different aspects of this rich background had loomed large at different times and in different places. In England the Roman monetary heritage was mediated through Merovingian Gaul. Overall there had been a considerable breakdown in the centralization of minting as imperial authority crumbled away. Western kings, at least outside Italy and north Africa, for a long period exercised relatively limited authority over the former imperial coinage. Michael Hendy characterized this as the transition from public to private, mirroring a general fragmentation of institutions and powers. Yet the boundaries between public and private, indeed the very basis of this division in the early Middle Ages, have come under sustained fire.[149] Important changes certainly took place in the management of minting, but these might also be seen as a realignment of one aspect of public power rather than a usurpation of it by private persons, the better to serve the changing needs to which coinage answered.

MINTING PROFITS

The eighth-century reassertion of explicit royal involvement with the coinage took place against a background of coin production that had departed substantially from its late Roman roots. The fiscal role of coinage had declined, and minting had become less centralized. Its use and volume also decreased, particularly as the range of denominations came to be restricted more or less to gold alone. What profit, if any, kings made from coinage around this time is unclear.

The late seventh-century move from gold to silver had, however, been followed by a considerable upsurge in the scale of coin being manufactured and entering circulation. In both England and Francia this coinage, like its gold predecessor, remained largely non-royal, at least as far as can be deduced from the great diversity of designs and (in Francia) inscriptions.[150] But the temporary slump of the new silver coinage in the mid eighth century and the implementation of royal oversight thereafter begs the important question of how far rulers could, or desired to, establish the coinage as a source of revenue. Later silver coinages from the ninth century onwards, which derived ultimately from the reforms of this era, have sometimes been cited as significant money-spinners for medieval kings.[151]

---

[149] Cf. Barnish, Lee and Whitby, 'Government and Administration', pp. 170–1; J. L. Nelson, 'The Problematic in the Private', *Social History* 15 (1990), 355–64; Innes, *State and Society*, esp. pp. 254–9; de Jong, *Penitential State*.

[150] Below, pp. 90–6.

[151] For example, H. R. Loyn, 'Currency and Freedom: Some Problems in the Social History of the Early Middle Ages', in *Studies in Medieval History Presented to R. H. C. Davis*, ed. H. Mayr-Harting and R. I. Moore (1985), pp. 7–19, at 11–12.

There were many ways of deriving income from the coinage, and it is possible that the largest source of royal profit was not minting per se, but rather the facilitation of renders and fees in cash, and concomitant manipulation of the discrepancy between the face value of coinage and its actual metal content. This could be changed by raising and lowering the weight of coinage and the fineness of its silver. When these were altered, established payments presumably remained fixed, and coin-users had to pay the same number of pennies to the king. If he was in a position to have coins and bullion reminted at preferential rates, then a tidy profit would have resulted.

Although this would have been an elegant and potentially lucrative method of extracting income from coinage, there were only a couple of points in the century of southern English coinage 757–865 when the weight and metal standards were changed substantially. Times of such major exploitation generally came at crisis points, as in the 850s, when Æthelwulf of Wessex faced a situation in which normally auxiliary sources of income such as coinage had to be tapped.[152] In the normal course of things, it is thus unlikely that this method provided a major monetary contribution to royal coffers, and it depends on a number of unknown quantities: on the king's treasury containing a large element of coinage,[153] on some of that treasury being put at the disposal of one or more moneyers[154] and on cash rents and other monetary income already being very substantial and reliable.

Creaming off profits from minting thus remained the most obvious and tangible way in which a medieval king could benefit materially from coinage in his kingdom. How this actually functioned in England 757–865 is very obscure. On the one hand, contemporary Carolingian legislation and tenth-century English law-codes are, despite their several entries on minting, remarkably reticent about how or if any profit should be derived from the coinage.[155] On the other, fees on minting could be high from the point of view of the customer, and it has been argued that they reached up to 33 per cent in late Anglo-Saxon England.[156]

---

[152] Below, pp. 107–12.

[153] M. Hardt, 'Royal Treasures', and *Gold und Herrschaft. Die Schätze europäischer Könige und Fürsten im ersten Jahrtausend* (Berlin, 2004).

[154] Thus, for example, the moneyers at Hereford were enjoined (according to Domesday Book) to strike coins from the king's silver when he visited, and also to accompany the earl on campaign: P. Grierson, 'Domesday Book, the *Geld de moneta* and *Monetagium*: A Forgotten Minting Reform', *BNJ* 55 (1985), 84–94, at pp. 85–6.

[155] E. Screen, 'Anglo-Saxon Law and Numismatics: A Reassessment in the Light of Patrick Wormald's *The Making of English Law*', *BNJ* 77 (2007), 148–72.

[156] H. B. A. Petersson, *Anglo-Saxon Currency* (Lund, 1969), p. 101; for reservations, see C. S. S. Lyon, 'Variations in Currency in Late Anglo-Saxon England', in *Mints, Dies and Currency: Essays Dedicated to the Memory of Albert Baldwin*, ed. R. Carson (London, 1971), pp. 101–20.

There were two standard ways in which minting could be turned to the benefit of the patron. The first was simply to take a proportion of the profits based on output. At London's Tower mint in the thirteenth century, 16*d.* was charged per pound (by weight), of which 6*d.* went to the king and the earl (i.e., 2.5 per cent) and 10*d.* to the makers.[157] These shares of the profits for patrons and moneyers were known as seigniorage and brassage respectively. Evidence for proportional fees like these already survives from the time of Pippin III, in a capitulary of 754/5.[158] This states that no more than twenty-two *solidi* of coin should be produced from a pound by weight (i.e., a pound and two *solidi* by tale) and that one of those *solidi* was to be taken by the moneyer. If the king was profiting from the coinage at this time, it is not clear how.

The second way of taking seigniorage from minting was for the king's agents to demand flat fees from moneyers or customers at certain times, such as when the coinage was changed or new dies had to be obtained. Domesday Book shows that payments like these were common by 1066, though the details of their implementation varied across the kingdom.[159] Payments on new dies were presumably, like proportional fees, useful as a constant if relatively small source of cash income for the king, while payments extracted from coin-owners and moneyers at the time of a general recoinage could have been much more substantial if also more occasional.

There were other means of profiting from coinage used by medieval rulers which do not seem to have been adopted in Anglo-Saxon England. From the twelfth century, kings and other patrons of coinage sometimes pledged to maintain the currency at a certain standard in return for levying a tribute.[160] In England, however, it is likely that proportional fees, flat fees and perhaps occasional exploitation of new weight or metal standards provided the bulk of income which kings could expect from the coinage. It is worth reiterating that there is no hard evidence from any point in the history of Anglo-Saxon England for how much income the coinage would generate, or how it compared with other sources of income. But later comparanda suggest that minting normally provided a relatively small element of royal income and

[157] C. Johnson, ed. and trans., *The De Moneta of Nicholas Oresme and English Mint Documents* (London, 1956), pp. 51 and 95.

[158] MGH Capit. I, no. 13, c. 5, p. 32.

[159] Grierson, 'Domesday Book', pp. 85–7; and D. M. Metcalf, 'The Taxation of Moneyers under Edward the Confessor and in 1086', in *Domesday Studies: Papers Read at the Novocentenary Conference of the Royal Historical Society and the Institute of British Geographers*, ed. J. C. Holt (Woodbridge, 1987), pp. 279–93.

[160] T. N. Bisson, *Conservation of Coinage: Monetary Exploitation and Its Restraint in France, Catalonia and Aragon (c. 1000–c. 1125)* (Oxford, 1979), esp. pp. 14–28.

that, like other resources, its exploitation was governed by other motives besides profit.[161]

The closest one can get to data on this subject from Anglo-Saxon England comes from Domesday Book. It contains several references to moneyers each paying around £2 for new dies *quando moneta vertebatur* ('when the coinage was changed'):[162] theoretically, this should have produced several hundred pounds each time the coinage was reformed, in addition to any (unmentioned) proportional fees which went to the king. The precise total figure from the fixed fees cannot be calculated, as among the twenty-five mints mentioned in Domesday there are several different methods of paying, sometimes by moneyer, sometimes by town and sometimes as part of the town's general payment. One might tentatively allow — for argument's sake — that an average of two moneyers at the seventy or so mints active under Edward would produce around £200–£250 at a reform of the coinage, some of which was probably siphoned off in the earl's third penny.[163] It should be noted that dies would presumably have had to be bought in subsequent years outside reforms, and so the stream of income would have continued at a lower level throughout the reign. Unfortunately, the overall size of Edward the Confessor's income is also a hotly debated subject. Estimates of land revenue range from around £5,000 per annum up to £18,000 per annum, and two recent studies have arrived at about £8,100.[164] Most of this would have come from payments made by tenants of the king's lands, with contributions (perhaps including a higher proportion of cash) from legal fees, tolls and minting.[165] The approximately £200–£250 which may have derived from recoinages at this time would have been 2.5–3.1 per cent of the king's total £8,100 and an uncertain (though probably still small) proportion of the king's income that came in the form of cash.

More concrete figures from slightly later periods lead to similar conclusions, and suggest that the existence of a royal fee as an expression of dominance was just as important as the actual size of the fee.[166] In the first

---

[161] G. G. Astill, 'Archaeology, Economics and Early Medieval Europe', *Oxford Journal of Archaeology* 4 (1985), 215–31, at pp. 223–5; Harrison, 'Structures and Resources', p. 28.

[162] Grierson, 'Domesday Book', pp. 85–7. Grierson also highlights changes instituted between 1066 and 1086.

[163] S. Baxter, *The Earls of Mercia. Lordship and Power in Late Anglo-Saxon England* (Oxford, 2007), pp. 89–97.

[164] J. L. Grassi, 'The Lands and Revenues of Edward the Confessor', *EHR* 117 (2002), 251–83, at pp. 251–2; and Baxter, *Earls of Mercia*, pp. 125–51. A high estimate can be found in F. Barlow, *Edward the Confessor*, 2nd edn (New Haven, CT, and London, 1997), pp. 153–7.

[165] Baxter, *Earls of Mercia*, p. 134; Grassi, 'Lands and Revenue', pp. 253–4; D. M. Metcalf, 'Continuity and Change in English Monetary History *c.* 973–1086. Part I', *BNJ* 50 (1980), 20–49, at pp. 23–4.

[166] Cf. A. de Barthélemy, 'Note sur la classification des monnaies carolingiens', *Revue numismatique*³ 13 (1895), 79–87, at pp. 80–1.

decades of the reign of Henry II (1154–89), the income from the coinage probably constituted only £100 per annum: less than 1 per cent of total annual royal revenue.[167] Similarly, in medieval Durham the bishops fiercely protected their right to minting even though the proceeds never represented even 1 per cent of their annual income,[168] and Hohenstaufen emperors of the twelfth and thirteenth centuries drew massively varying revenues from mints under their control (though often paltry in relation to their overall output).[169] At the internationally important mint of Venice between the thirteenth and fifteenth centuries profits to the state were often slim or non-existent.[170]

It is of course not necessarily for modern commentators to decide what profit margin a medieval ruler could afford to sneeze at. Income was still income, and if Edward the Confessor got up to £250 from the coinage in a year, that was still a very considerable sum in itself by eleventh-century standards – more than even wealthy thegns would have made over the same period.[171] Nevertheless, minting – even of a substantial coinage – was probably not a major source of early medieval royal income under normal circumstances: it was first and foremost a money-making scheme, not a profit-making scheme.

The restoration of the king's name on silver pennies in the middle of the eighth century therefore should not be assumed to have heralded the rise of coinage as a major element in regular fiscal administration – in spite, it should be noted, of the monetary developments which seem to have precipitated these sudden and widespread changes.[172] The new coinages were not rationalized economic ventures implemented on a grand scale: they were responses to a general monetary slump, influenced by measures taken in successive kingdoms as much as by a resurgence of Roman tradition.

But there were other ways in which coinage could be exploited by eighth- and ninth-century kings and those who worked in their name. Rulers probably saw the greatest benefits of coinage as symbolic: it was their name and, sometimes, image that graced the currency. When Charlemagne imposed his name on the currency of Benevento, there is

---

[167] D. F. Allen, *A Catalogue of English Coins in the British Museum: The Cross-and-Crosslets ('Tealby') Type of Henry II* (London, 1951), p. lxxxviii. On English royal income at this time see R. Bartlett, *England under the Norman and Angevin Kings* (Oxford, 2000), pp. 159–77; J. Ramsay, *History of the Revenues of the Kings of England, 1066–1399*, 2 vols. (Oxford, 1925).

[168] M. Allen, *The Durham Mint* (London, 2003), pp. 47–8.

[169] N. Kamp, *Moneta regis: Königliche Münzstätten und königliche Münzpolitik in der Stauferzeit* (Hanover, 2006), pp. 389–97.

[170] Stahl, *Zecca*, pp. 168–200.

[171] P. A. Clarke, *The English Nobility under Edward the Confessor* (Oxford, 1994), pp. 32–4.

[172] Below, pp. 96–100.

no indication that he demanded the profits of this coinage; for him, the key point was to force his sovereignty on Benevento in the best way he knew how. Symbolic this gesture may have been, but it was no token: kings had to be seen to do what was appropriate for a king, and by taking over the coinage Charlemagne was undercutting Grimoald's authority and legitimacy. This blow was surely at least as damaging as loss of the profits of minting.

Thus early medieval kings in England and neighbouring realms from the eighth century onwards revitalized and adapted the tradition of Roman emperors' association with minting, as revealed above all through the iconography and titulature of coinage. This symbolic aspect of money provided not only prestige to the king. It guaranteed the authority of the coinage just as the royal name legitimized charters – the other manifestation of royal power which Charlemagne specified in his oath of submission from Grimoald of Benevento – and so was presumably appreciated by the makers and users of coinage as well. Their stake in the issue of coin was also highly significant, and at different times these interests worked in parallel and co-operation with, or in opposition to, those of the king himself. These differing interests and varied manifestations of royal involvement will be at the heart of the next three chapters.

Chapter 3

LOOKING AT COINAGE: ICONOGRAPHY AND INSCRIPTIONS

COINS, KINGS AND PROPAGANDA

The symbolic role of the currency as a statement of legitimacy and authority depended on its ability to answer to preconceived notions of how such qualities should be portrayed.[1] It was the appearance of coinage that therefore secured its status as currency rather than as small pieces of bullion. Coin-users could and frequently did test the weight and purity of their money, but if the appearance of coinage satisfied their expectations these qualities were normally taken for granted. This was the point at which the visual demonstration of power intersected with the economic realities of day-to-day life.

Determining what these expectations were in eighth- and ninth-century England, however, depends solely on the extant coins and on examination of their iconographic and ideological background. There are no surviving statements about the appearance of money in England at this time in any written source: in discussing coin both Bede and the Anglo-Saxon Chronicle focused only on ancient and exotic gold pieces.[2] Neither can it be assumed that all parties involved in the patronage, manufacture and use of coinage shared the same views and expectations of money and its appearance, or that these expectations remained static.[3] Reconstructing the features of coinage Offa, Coenwulf, Æthelwulf and other rulers may have specified, and those which they were content to leave to the taste of the die-cutter, rests on the coins which happen to have been found in modern times.

---

[1] I. Garipzanov, 'The Image of Authority in Carolingian Coinage: The Image of a Ruler and Roman Imperial Tradition', *EME* 8 (1999), 197–218; Grierson, 'Symbolism'; E. A. Arslan, 'Emmissioni monetarie e segni del potere', *Settimane* 39 (1992), 791–854.

[2] *ASC* s.a. 418; Bede, *HE* iii.8 (ed. and trans. Colgrave and Mynors, pp. 238–9).

[3] Cf. the different 'horizons of expectations' as applied to early medieval coinage and other sources in Garipzanov, *Symbolic Language*, pp. 24–5.

This question of how far design, titulature and other visual features were standardized within and between mints is key to understanding the significance of numismatic iconography. The nature and especially the coherence of iconography underpinned the coinage's potential role as royal propaganda.[4] There is no question that coinage was potentially a very effective form of propaganda, in the sense of material propagated for the manipulation of the opinions of the populace.[5] Even early medieval coin-issues existed in comparative bulk, and were surely by far the most numerous manifestations of royal names and titles in circulation. Despite uncertainties over the exact scale of production, there is no question that a huge number of coins bearing the names of Anglo-Saxon kings were made in the eighth and ninth centuries and circulated among a broader swathe of the population than that reached by charters, manuscripts and other media favoured by early medieval rulers and magnates. The Roman imperial coinage on which Anglo-Saxon issues drew so heavily included many clear examples of propaganda. The gold, silver and copper-alloy currency of the empire portrayed emperors with realistic portraits subtly incorporating allusions to imperial or divine status, and combined these with references to recent victories, political events or favoured deities.[6] Modern coinage has to some extent inherited this function. Yet coin-issues tied to specific events in this way were extremely unusual in Anglo-Saxon England and early medieval Europe as a whole. One probable example survives in the unique penny of Ecgberht as king of the Mercians which names the mint of London rather than the moneyer:[7] an arresting example of emphasis on Ecgberht's newly won status in Mercia, and on his control of a new minting centre, one with possibly strong symbolic importance.[8] Some of the coins of Offa probably also made very specific links between the current ruler and favoured models of kingship from scripture and history.

These cases highlight the limits to which the propagandist role of early medieval coinage may be taken. Full appreciation of the statements made on coins depended on the user's ability to read their inscriptions and to understand the detailed significance of the images they carried: a

---

[4] For example, Stenton, *Preparatory*, pp. 379–80. This approach to medieval material remains was most fully articulated in P. E. Schramm, *Die deutschen Kaiser und Könige in Bildern ihrer Zeit: I. Teil, bis zur Mitte des 12. Jahrhunderts (751–1152)*, 2 vols. (Leipzig, 1928) and *Herrschaftszeichen und Staatssymbolik: Beiträge zu ihrer Geschichte vom dritten bis zum sechzehnten Jahrhundert*, 3 vols. (Stuttgart, 1954–6); J. M. Bak, 'Medieval Symbology of the State: Percy E. Schramm's Contribution', *Viator* 4 (1973), 33–64.

[5] For a sophisticated theoretical reading of the symbolic exercise of power through coins and other media (avoiding the term propaganda altogether), see now Garipzanov, *Symbolic Language*, pp. 1–41.

[6] P. Bastien, *Le buste monétaire des empereurs romains*, 3 vols. (Wetteren, 1992).

[7] Naismith L30–1.   [8] Below, pp. 83 and 128–9.

perennial obstacle to their appreciation by the uneducated. Yet expectation of these skills seems to have been standard among those responsible for producing coins in Anglo-Saxon England. Many of the surviving designs are detailed and intellectually demanding, not least of and presuppose contact with the age-old tradition of Roman coinage. This still seems to have been the point of departure for many early medieval observers. Coins which were copied for nummular brooches,[9] or provided the inspiration for manuscript illustrations, were much more often Roman than contemporary.[10] A certain amount of Latin literacy was also needed to appreciate the legends on the coins. No vernacular terminology was ever employed on eighth- and ninth-century coinage beyond personal names; as in most contemporary charters, Latin was still seen as the most suitably solemn medium for expression.[11] Evidence for how − even if − most coin-users appreciated all these layers of meaning is scant. The distribution of surviving finds and the make-up of hoards suggest that in the kingdoms south of the Humber any English coin of broadly correct metal and weight was acceptable regardless of its age or origin.[12] Designs commonly remained identical despite changes of king and even of dynasty.

The likelihood therefore is that the details of coin design were not primarily intended to appeal to as large an audience as possible. Rather, coins were a specialized continuation of the sophisticated and often explicitly literate developments in royal representation that can be traced elsewhere in charters, literary compositions and other pieces of artwork. The small size and established customs of coin design obviously limited the extent and novelty of such messages, but they are better seen as an abbreviation rather than an adumbration of royal representation. The visual symbolism of coinage was, in other words, aimed at an audience which was rated in quality, not quantity.

It is dangerous to assume, however, that such symbolism always emanated directly from the king and his immediate circle, or that it was part of an internally consistent programme of centralized and elaborate royal image-making. Coins present as much a bottom-up as a top-down view of kingship, combining the expectations of the makers and other

---

[9] K. Leahy, 'Anglo-Saxon Coin Brooches', in *Coinage and History*, ed. Cook and Williams, pp. 267–85. However, it should be noted that most of the specimens listed here date to the ninth century or after.

[10] Above, p. 40.

[11] On expanding use of the vernacular see S. Kelly, 'Early Anglo-Saxon Society and the Written Word', in *The Uses of Literacy in Early Mediaeval Europe*, ed. R. C. McKitterick (Cambridge, 1990), pp. 36–62; K. Lowe, 'Lay Literacy in Anglo-Saxon England and the Development of the Chirograph', in *Anglo-Saxon Manuscripts and Their Heritage*, ed. P. Pulsiano and E. M. Treharne (Aldershot, 1998), pp. 161–204.

[12] Below, pp. 203–9.

audiences with (sometimes) the specific wishes of the king. To achieve this goal elements of established tradition were blended with innovations or borrowings; a pattern which was repeated in other media that could be linked with early medieval authority. The personnel behind book production and sculpture,[13] for example, had their own visual vocabularies and were not always in direct contact with one another, the king or with moneyers and die-cutters. Divergent developments could therefore be followed at one and the same time; a unified front in terms of royal representation, such as that associated with Æthelstan in the early tenth century,[14] was rare.

The numerous surviving coins show again and again that the level of royal input into design varied substantially both in scale and in intensity.[15] On some occasions there can be no denying that significant elements of design were being decided at a level well below that of the king. Continuity of design, for example, could be deep-rooted, spanning long periods of several reigns or dynastic changes. This in itself could work to the king's advantage, demonstrating visually that it was business as usual despite a change in ruler. But there were also strong precedents for kings taking a direct interest in the visual arts in general, often in a very focused fashion.[16] Manuscript production in particular – which has traditionally taken centre stage in studies of early medieval art – epitomizes many of the issues which bedevil the relationship between powerful individuals and objects associated with them.[17] Books and their illuminations

---

[13] For manuscript representations of royal and other power, see below, n. 18. On eighth- and ninth-century sculpture, see R. Jewell, 'Classicism of Southumbrian Sculpture', in *Mercia*, ed. Brown and Farr, pp. 246–62, 'The Anglo-Saxon Friezes at Breedon-on-the-Hill, Leicestershire', *Archaeologia* 108 (1986), 95–115; S. Plunkett, 'The Mercian Perspective', in *The St Andrews Sarcophagus: A Pictish Masterpiece and Its International Connection*, ed. S. Foster (Dublin, 1998), pp. 202–26; for a recent addition to the corpus M. Brown, 'The Lichfield Angel and the Middle Saxon Context: Lichfield as a Centre for Insular Art', *Journal of the British Archaeological Association* 160 (2007), 8–19.

[14] C. Karkov, *The Ruler Portraits of Anglo-Saxon England* (Woodbridge, 2003), pp. 53–118; S. Keynes, 'King Athelstan's Books', in *Learning and Literature in Anglo-Saxon England*, ed. M. Lapidge and H. Gneuss (Cambridge, 1985), pp. 143–201.

[15] For further discussion see R. Naismith, 'An Offa You Can't Refuse? Eighth-Century Mercian Titulature on Coins and in Charters', *Quaestio Insularis* 7 (2006), 71–100, and 'Kingship and Learning on the Broad Penny Coinage of the "Mercian Supremacy"', in *Studies in Early Medieval Coinage 2: New Perspectives*, ed. T. Abramson (Woodbridge, 2011), pp. 70–87.

[16] Cf. H. Mayr-Harting, 'Charlemagne as a Patron of Art', *Studies in Church History* 28 (1992), 43–77.

[17] Cf., for a few outstanding examples, Karkov, *Ruler Portraits*; D. Bullough, 'Imagines regum and Their Significance in the Early Medieval West', in *Carolingian Renewal: Sources and Heritage* (Manchester, 1991), pp. 39–96; I. Garipzanov, 'David, imperator augustus, gratia dei rex: Communication and Propaganda in Carolingian Royal Iconography', in *Monotheistic Kingship: The Medieval Variants*, ed. A. Al-Azmeh and J. M. Bak (Budapest and New York, 2005), pp. 89–117; N. Staubach, *Herrscherbild Karls des Kahlen: Formen und Funktionen monarchischer Repräsentation im früheren Mittelalter* (Münster, 1982) and *Rex christianus: Hofkultur und Herrschaftspropaganda im Reich Karls des Kahlen* (Cologne, 1993).

can reveal the association of kings with production and patronage of manuscripts,[18] the motivations for which were as much devotional as political.[19] It is also possible that manuscripts could have been made for a royal recipient without any direct input on his or her part until the point of presentation.[20] Such cases do not necessarily show what Æthelstan, Edgar, Charles the Bald, Otto III or any ruler thought of themselves, but what others thought might suit their sensibilities and perhaps subtly pass some sort of message from the maker to the monarch. Partly because of their high value and the personalized nature of production, manuscripts were very specifically directed in manufacture and in reception: only a portion of manuscript illustrations would have circulated widely, and most were created for the benefit of a tiny audience of the intended recipient and their immediate household.[21]

Following the conjunctures of patronage and power in other media is even more problematic. Very few surviving pieces of metalwork or sculpture, for example, can be confidently associated with a specific individual or occasion.[22] Seals provide an exception, though on a substantial scale only in the late Anglo-Saxon period:[23] just one pre-viking royal seal, in the name of Coenwulf, is known, and it has only slight affinities with contemporary coinage.[24] But Asser wrote that Alfred the Great, for one, used to *agere … aurifices et artifices suos* ('urge on … his goldsmiths and craftsmen'), and have them make new *aedificia* ('objects') with *illo edocente* ('him acting as guide').[25] Alfred may have included die-cutters among his *artifices*,[26] and he may also have been exceptional for the interest he

---

[18] H. Mayr-Harting, *Ottonian Book Illumination: An Historical Survey*, 2nd edn, 2 vols., (London, 1999), esp. I, 36–8 and 51, 'Herrschaftsrepräsentation der ottonischen Familie', in *Otto der Grosse. Magdeburg und Europa*, ed. M. Puhle, 2 vols. (Mainz, 2001) I, 133–48; R. McKitterick, *Charlemagne*, pp. 345–72, and, more widely, *Frankish Kings and Culture in the Early Middle Ages* (Aldershot, 1995). Artistic patronage more generally is discussed in M. Lapidge, 'Artistic and Literary Patronage in Anglo-Saxon England', *Settimane* 39 (1992), 137–91; R. McKitterick, 'Royal Patronage of Culture in the Frankish Kingdoms under the Carolingians: Motives and Consequences', *Settimane* 39 (1992), 93–129, and other papers in the same volume of the *Settimane*.

[19] L. Körntgen, *Königsherrschaft und Gottes Gnade: zu Kontext und Funktion sakraler Vorstellungen in Historiographie und Bildzeugnissen der ottonisch-frühsalischen Zeit* (Berlin, 2001), esp. pp. 435–45.

[20] Garipzanov, *Symbolic Language*, pp. 235–6.   [21] *Ibid*.

[22] Lapidge, 'Artistic and Literary Patronage', pp. 40–59.

[23] R. Deshman, '*Christus rex et magi reges*: Kingship and Christology in Ottonian and Anglo-Saxon Art', *Frühmittelalterliche Studien* 10 (1976), 367–406; B. Bedos Rezak, 'The King Enthroned: A New Theme in Anglo-Saxon Royal Iconography. The Seal of Edward the Confessor and Its Political Implications', in *Kings and Kingship*, ed. J. Rosenthal (Binghampton, NY, 1986), pp. 53–88.

[24] P. Chaplais, 'The Anglo-Saxon Chancery: From the Diploma to the Writ', *Journal of the Society of Archivists* 3.4 (1966), 160–76, at pp. 52–3.

[25] 'Direct … his goldsmiths and craftsmen.' Asser, *Life of King Alfred*, cc. 76, 91 and 101 (ed. Stevenson, pp. 59, 76 and 87; and trans. Keynes and Lapidge, *Alfred the Great*, pp. 91, 101 and 106).

[26] Karkov, *Ruler Portraits*, pp. 25–7; S. Keynes, 'King Alfred and the Mercians', in *Kings, Currency and Alliances: History and Coinage of Southern England in the Ninth Century*, ed. M. A. S. Blackburn and

showed in the activities of craftsmen; certainly the array of exquisite objects probably associated with Alfred's patronage – including the Alfred jewel, the other related objects and probably the Fuller Brooch – has no clear parallels.[27] Asser did not see fit to mention in what way the king encouraged his craftsmen, leaving any hint of the king's own wishes and ideas to be worked out from surviving objects. In the case of coins, certain kings may have played a more direct part in the selection of design, but often only by interaction with specific moneyers. In other cases, kings' interests could have been restricted to just one or two aspects of design, and there were also occasional instances of more wide-reaching involvement, most clearly when a number of mints simultaneously adopted the same design or feature(s). Some agency with power in all locations involved must be behind this, and it is difficult to identify this agency as anyone other than the king.

Coinage thus enjoyed an on–off and frequently indirect relationship with royal representation. Nevertheless, the bond – however distant – between coinage and kingship quickly became engrained at a visceral level in the decades after *c.* 760. On one level this meant that continuity in general format and design became fixed. Practically and ideologically, it seems to have been the norm for rulers to stick with tried and tested means of legitimization and representation known from previous rulers: a proper coinage signified a proper king.[28] The most valuable propaganda coup royal coinage could provide was its own existence and conformity to expectations. For this reason the royal name and title *rex* were the most ubiquitous element of coin design, while 'portraits' showed an idealized Roman-derived impression of royal authority. The set of ideas which gave rise to this imagery did not necessarily apply in other settings: it was particular to coinage, and to some extent to England. Emergent visual norms were also not exclusively bound to the royal interest in minting: episcopal coinages were issued at York, Canterbury, London and Rochester; the name of the ruler was always joined by the moneyer's name; and there was also a strong religious aspect to coin design, within which crosses were especially prominent.

This examination of selected developments in the iconography of coinage in the later eighth and ninth centuries rests therefore on critical

---

D. N. Dumville (Woodbridge, 1998), pp. 1–45, at 14–16; M. Blackburn, 'The London Mint in the Reign of Alfred', in *Kings, Currency and Alliances*, ed. Blackburn and Dumville, pp. 105–23, esp. 116–20.

[27] D. Pratt, *Political Thought*, pp. 179–92, 'Persuasion and Invention at the Court of King Alfred', in *Court Culture in the Early Middle Ages. Proceedings of the First Alcuin Conference*, ed. C. Cubitt (Turnhout, 2003), pp. 189–221; Nelson, 'West Francia and Wessex', pp. 107–9; L. Webster, '*Ædificia nova*: Treasures of Alfred's Reign', in *Alfred the Great*, ed. Reuter, pp. 79–103.

[28] Cf. Garipzanov, *Symbolic Language*, p. 207.

assessment of the likely administrative and intellectual background; specifically those which were manifested in images of rulers, religious iconography and inscriptions, including titulature. Questions of purpose, audience and agency will be to the fore, as will the wider artistic context. For all that coinage evolved its own idiomatic modes of expression, these were by no means divorced from the rich background of metalwork, sculpture in wood and stone, illumination of manuscripts, textiles and other media, only a minute fraction of which survives to inform modern scholars.

'PORTRAITS'

There were no portraits as such in eighth- or ninth-century England, at least in so far as the images associated with royal or archiepiscopal names on coinage actually bore any resemblance to the individual in question.[29] In the west this had not been the case with coinage since approximately the fourth century: late Roman emperors' numismatic busts were almost as interchangeable as those of Anglo-Saxon kings and conformed to an ideal of stability associated with the ruling authority.[30] Busts of, for instance, Coenwulf and Cuthred, Coenwulf and Ceolwulf I, and Æthelwulf and Æthelberht were identical, and there even exists one portrait die of Coenwulf with the name recut from Cuthred.[31] Similarly, portraits could be used without any indication that they represented a specific ruler: they were a badge of kingship that had come to be expected on coins.[32] Examples include the coins minted when royal and archiepiscopal titles were temporarily removed from the coinage at Canterbury in the 820s, on which portraits of a 'king' type and an 'archbishop' type were retained,[33] and two of the scarce gold coins minted in southern England in the time of Offa and Coenwulf, which show portraits lifted from Roman originals but without any king's name or other indication that they relate to a contemporary ruler or to contemporary numismatic portraiture.

---

[29] Schramm, *Die deutschen Kaiser* I, 4–11. That said, some concessions could be made to particularly striking individual features, such as moustaches or beards: Garipzanov, 'Image of Authority', p. 211.

[30] R. Bianchi Bandinelli, *Rome, the Late Empire. Roman Art, A.D. 200–400*, trans. P. Green (London, 1971), pp. 23–38; J. Elsner, *Imperial Rome and Christian Triumph: The Art of the Roman Empire A.D. 100–450* (Oxford, 1998), pp. 159–89.

[31] Naismith C25b and c.

[32] For a ninth-century Frankish medallion with a generalized late Roman-style bust and the legend CAPVT IMPERATOR see C. Stiegemann and M. Wemhoff (eds.), *799: Kunst und Kultur der Karolingerzeit: Karl der Grosse und Papst Leo III. in Paderborn: Katalog der Ausstellung, Paderborn 1999*, 3 vols. (Mainz, 1999) II, no. 35.

[33] Below, pp. 153–4.

The 'portraits' on Anglo-Saxon coins should thus be seen as generalized *imagines* of a ruler rather than of the current king: they show an ideal of a king moulded in the Roman imperial tradition.[34] When looking at images on coins, coin-users were presumably expected to equate their contemporary ruler with the emperors of Rome, and the authority they had wielded. This was the dominant visual association which numismatic images of rulers sought to convey, though it should be stressed that it was not the only influence on contemporary representations of rulers. The Repton Stone, for example, displays a figure – possibly to be identified as Æthelbald, king of the Mercians – in a martial role, combining native Anglo-Saxon features with military symbols and imagery from late antiquity.[35] Manuscript illuminations showing Anglo-Saxon rulers in the tenth and eleventh centuries, on the other hand, stress the ruler's role as a literate, Christian – sometimes even Christ-like – king acting in support of the Church; similar attributes were applied to representations of ninth-century Carolingian rulers.[36]

Offa, novus Constantinus?

The portrait coinage of Offa, which probably began simultaneously at Canterbury and London in the mid 780s, was the first substantive issue in England to bear the explicitly labelled image of a contemporary ruler. It substantially predates the celebrated portrait coinages of Charlemagne and Louis the Pious (issued *c.* 812/13–816/19),[37] and has come to be arguably the most celebrated series among the entire Anglo-Saxon coinage. All serious works on Anglo-Saxon coinage have made reference to the artistic qualities of Offa's portrait pennies,[38] and so too have most historians writing on the period of Offa's rule.[39] Yet detailed study from a specifically art-historical perspective had been lacking

---

[34] For a history of such ruler representations, see Bullough, '*Imagines regum*'.

[35] M. Biddle and B. Kjølbye-Biddle, 'The Repton Stone', *ASE* 14 (1985), 233–92, at pp. 271–2 and 289–90. An alternative interpretation (Anna Gannon *pers. comm.*) sees the figure as St Michael.

[36] Above, p. 50.

[37] J. M. Wallace-Hadrill (*Early Medieval History* (Oxford, 1975), p. 160) suggested that Offa's portrait coinage was inspired by Carolingian seals, but there is little evidence for this: see Story, *Carolingian Connections*, p. 195; (for surviving seals) Schramm, *Die deutschen Kaiser*. On the dating, see S. Coupland, 'Carolingian Single Finds and the Economy of the Early Ninth Century', *NC* 170 (2010), 287–319, at pp. 297–300.

[38] R. C. Lockett, 'The Coinage of Offa', *NC* 20 (1920), 57–89, at pp. 62–5; C. E. Blunt, 'The Anglo-Saxon Coinage and the Historian', *Medieval Archaeology* 4 (1960), 1–15, at pp. 2–3, 'The Coinage of Offa', in *Anglo-Saxon Coins: Studies Presented to Sir Frank Stenton on the Occasion of His 80th Birthday*, ed. R. H. M. Dolley (London, 1961), pp. 39–62, at 41–3; R. H. M. Dolley, *Anglo-Saxon Pennies* (London, 1964), p. 15

[39] For just a few examples, see Stenton, *Preparatory*, pp. 378–82, and *Anglo-Saxon England*, pp. 222–3; Keynes, 'Kingdom of the Mercians', p. 13.

until Anna Gannon's recent study of the iconography of early Anglo-Saxon coinage.[40]

Offa's pennies were the last real heir to the combination of artistic flair and bewildering diversity which had been the hallmark of the early eighth-century silver pennies or *sceattas*, and present a veritable embarrassment of riches in terms of beauty and symbolism. This extended beyond portraiture to the complex array of inscriptions, crosses, creatures and other imagery of the coinage. The iconographical diversity of Offa's coinage in itself militates against close management, with important implications when considering the source of some of the sophisticated messages conveyed by the images on the coinage. If these did emanate from the king and his circle then royal patronage must have worked in a very directed fashion, and focused on specific moneyers and short issues, perhaps for particular occasions or purposes.[41]

Offa's coinage established norms for numismatic portraiture in England which would be followed for much of the ninth century. The crucial feature was adaptation of Roman models, though not in a slavish fashion. Portraits on the coins of Offa drew parts of their design from several different sources and occasionally added new features that do not relate to ancient coinage. Decisions on what to select, reject and add can betray the visual idiom of rulership which the die-cutters drew upon. In selection of headgear, for example, there was a strong emphasis on diadems and on bareheaded busts (Figure 3.1a–c).

In origin, the diadem was associated with victorious athletes and (by extension) supreme rulers.[42] Its associations with absolute dictatorship were such that even emperors were rarely depicted with the diadem during the first centuries of the Roman empire, and it became common only in and after the time of Constantine I the Great (Figure 3.1c).[43] It remained an important part of imperial iconography in the Byzantine empire, featuring prominently on coins, mosaics and elsewhere throughout this period, even though on Byzantine coins it is not always easy to distinguish from the crown.[44] In written sources that would have been accessible in eighth-century England, the diadem was firmly associated with kingship. Bede, in commenting on II (IV) Kings 11:12 ('And he brought forth the king's son, and put the crown (*diadema*) upon him, and gave him the testimony (*testimonium*)'), wrote that 'in diademate insigne capitis regium, in testimonio designat decreta legis Dei, quibus quid agere rex debeat, qualiter vivere

---

[40] Gannon, *Iconography*, pp. 31–3, 40–1, 51, 59–61, 142–4 and 168–71.
[41] Below, pp. 150–3.   [42] Bastien, *Buste monétaire* I, 143–4.   [43] *Ibid.*, I, 156–64.
[44] P. Grierson, *Byzantine Coins* (London, 1982), p. 32.

(a)   (b)

(c)

Figure 3.1 Examples of Offa's and Constantine's busts with
diadem and bareheaded.

praecipitur'.[45] This regal aura can be detected in other depictions and
survivals of the diadem.[46] The Repton Stone appears to show a rider
(either a king or a saint) wearing a diadem.[47] Glosses translate *diadema*
into Old English as *cynehelm* ('noble helmet') and also make it clear
that the distinctions between different forms of classical headgear were
becoming blurred: the *diadema* and the *corona* were so closely associated
that they could be seen as synonymous,[48] though the crown's original
connection with victory was still sometimes emphasized.[49]

---

[45] 'With the diadem he indicates the headgear of kings, and with the affirmation he indicates the decrees of God's law; from these the king knows what he must do and how it has been commanded he should live.' Bede, *In libros regum quaestiones xxx*, 19 (*PL* 91, col. 0730A).
[46] For general remarks see J. L. Nelson, 'Inauguration Rituals', in *Early Medieval Kingship*, ed. P. H. Sawyer and I. N. Wood (Leeds, 1977), pp. 50–71, at 54; for crowns and diadems specifically Schramm, *Herrschaftszeichen* II, 379–89.
[47] Biddle and Kjølbye-Biddle, 'Repton Stone', p. 263.
[48] Thus a gloss to Aldhelm's prose *De laude virginitatis* reads 'diadema, id est corona: cynehelm' (ed. A. S. Napier, *Old English Glosses, Chiefly Unpublished* (Oxford, 1900), no. 2208). For detailed discussion, see J. Kirschner, *Die Bezeichnungen für Kranz und Krone im Altenglischen* (Munich, 1975); M. Gretsch, *Intellectual Foundations of the English Benedictine Reform* (Cambridge, 1999), pp. 98–104 and 297–304.
[49] C. Erdmann, *Forschungen zur politischen Ideenwelt des Frühmittelalters* (Berlin, 1951), pp. 31–43.

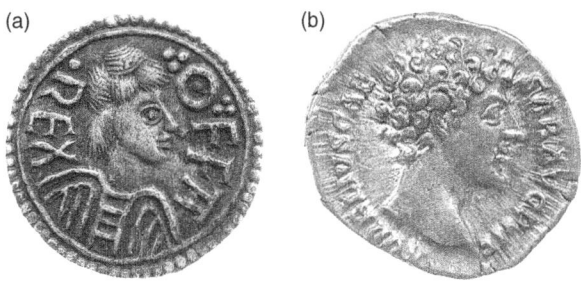

Figure 3.2 Curly-haired busts of Offa and Lucius Verus.

Most busts associated with Offa drew on this and related post-Roman traditions of imperial portraiture, and do not appear to have had any more specific association, but two particular groups among the pennies of Offa stand out as possible candidates for special manipulation. The first group is distinguished by the elaborate, curled hair of the bust (Figure 3.2a).[50] This had extensive classical precedents, when it was used to suggest the movement skywards of divine figures and was adopted as a sign of godhood by some Roman emperors (Figure 3.2b).[51] These supernatural connotations remained after conversion, so that representations of Christ, angels and saints might also be given a curled hairstyle.[52] In the context of early Anglo-Saxon England it can be found on the Breedon angel,[53] on angels on the cover of two Insular ivories and a number of Carolingian parallels,[54] on St John in the Lindisfarne Gospels[55] and on a (probable) apostle on the Reculver Cross.[56] A Roman jewel depicting an emperor with such a hairstyle was selected as the basis for one of Charlemagne's seals.[57]

But the association Offa's coins probably aimed at was more specific: the biblical King David, who was often shown with such hair and who was a favourite paradigm of kingship in the early Middle Ages, especially

[50] Chick 22, 31–3, 43 and 126–7.
[51] Bastien, *Buste monétaire* I, 21 and 25; H. P. l'Orange, 'Le Néron constitutionnel et le Néron apothéosé', *Collections of the Ny Carlsberg Glyptothek* 3 (1942), 247–67, at pp. 283–90.
[52] L. Webster and J. Backhouse, *The Making of England: Anglo-Saxon Art and Culture A.D. 600–900* (London, 1991), no. 141; R. Kozodoy, 'The Reculver Cross', *Archaeologia* 108 (1986), 67–94, at pp. 76–7; Schramm, *Deutschen Kaiser*, pp. 34–5 and 148–9. See also G. Peers, *Subtle Bodies: Representing Angels in Byzantium* (Berkeley, CA, and London, 2001), pp. 24–8; T. F. Mathews, *The Clash of Gods: A Reinterpretation of Early Christian Art*, 2nd edn (Princeton, NJ, and Chichester, 1999), pp. 123–8.
[53] Jewell, 'Classicism', p. 257.
[54] Webster and Backhouse, *Making of England*, no. 141, for details.
[55] London, BL, Cotton Nero D.IV, f. 209r.
[56] Kozodoy, 'Reculver Cross', pp. 76–7.
[57] Schramm, *Die deutschen Kaiser*, pp. 34–5 and 148–9.

in an iconographical context.[58] Images of David could highlight his role as eloquent musician, repentant singer, young warrior or wise priest-king.[59] As a ruler closely connected to God and a prefiguration of Christ himself, David was a natural touchstone for Roman and Byzantine emperors who claimed power over Church as well as state.[60] Acclamations of a ruler as a new David had been common since the council of Chalcedon in 451, when the emperor Marcian had been called both *novus David* and *novus Constantinus*;[61] acclamations which were repeated for, among others, Æthelberht I of Kent (d. 616)[62] and Charlemagne.[63]

References to David's counterpart at Chalcedon, the emperor Constantine I, also seem to be reflected in the iconography of certain coins of Offa. The first relevant group consists of a very few coins of the London moneyer Ibba, on which the bust is shown gazing heavenwards, as on the famous 'eyes to God' coins of Constantine, which were thought (erroneously) to hark back to his famous vision of the cross at the battle of the Milvian Bridge in 312 (Figure 3.3a–b).[64] These circulated widely and were influential in later ages, for instance being copied at Tours in the tenth century and probably inspiring a series of roundels on the tenth-century Byzantine Veroli Casket.[65]

The same incident is probably referenced in another series of coins by the London moneyer, Dud (Figure 3.4). These show Offa in *paludamentum*

---

[58] For discussion and examples see Gannon, *Iconography*, pp. 31–3; I. Henderson, 'The "David Cycle" in Pictish Art', in *Early Medieval Sculpture in Britain and Ireland*, ed. J. Higgitt (Oxford, 1986), pp. 87–123, and '"Primus inter pares": The St Andrews Sarcophagus and Pictish Sculpture', in *St Andrews Sarcophagus*, ed. Foster, pp. 97–167, at 119–34; Webster and Backhouse, *Making of England*, no. 89; M. Archibald, M. Brown and L. Webster, 'The Heirs of Rome: The Shaping of Britain A.D. 400–900', in *The Transformation of the Roman World, A.D. 400–900*, ed. L. Webster and M. Brown (London, 1997), pp. 208–48, at 226–30.

[59] H. Steger, *David Rex et Propheta: König David als vorbildliche Verkörperung des Herrschers und Dichters im Mittelalter, nach Bilddarstellungen des achten bis zwölften Jahrhunderts* (Nuremberg, 1961); Garipzanov, 'David, *imperator augustus*'; Bullough, '*Imagines regum*', pp. 54–6.

[60] Garipzanov, 'David, *imperator augustus*', pp. 92–3.

[61] *Concilium Chalcedonense* i.2 (ed. Schwartz II.ii, 351). E. Ewig, 'Das Bild Constantins des Großen in den ersten Jahrhunderten des abendländischen Mittelalters', *Historisches Jahrbuch* 75 (1956), 1–46, at pp. 3–5; H. Fuhrmann, 'Das frühmittelalterliche Papsttum und die Konstantinische Schenkung', *Settimane* 20 (1973), 257–92, at pp. 282–3; U. Zahnd, 'Novus David – Νεος Δαυιδ. Zur Frage nach byzantinische Vorläuen eines abendlandischen Topos', *Frühmittelalterliche Studien* 42 (2008), 71–88.

[62] Bede, *HE* i.32 (ed. Colgrave and Mynors, pp. 112–13).

[63] *Codex Carolinus*, ep. 60 (ed. Gundlach, p. 587). Cf. Anton, *Fürstenspiegel*, pp. 436–46.

[64] P. Grierson, *Coins of Medieval Europe* (London, 1991), pp. 52–3 (figure 110); Maguire, 'Magic and Money', p. 1048 (figure 20). Cf. Bastien, *Buste monétaire* I, 55–9. For descriptions of the vision, see Eusebius/Rufinus, *Historia ecclesiastica* IX.viii.15 (ed. Schwartz and Mommsen I, 827); *Elene* 88b–94a (*ASPR* II, 68). For Cynewulf's view of Constantine, see E. R. Anderson, *Cynewulf: Structure, Style and Theme in His Poetry* (Rutherford, NJ, and London, 1983), pp. 126–33.

[65] For the Tours coin see Grierson, *Coins of Medieval European*, pp. 52–3 (with figure 110); for the Veroli Casket, Maguire, 'Magic and Money', p. 1048 (and figure 20).

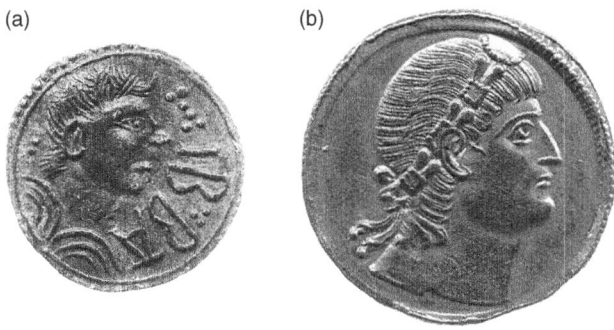

Figure 3.3 Offa and Constantine with 'eyes to God'.

Figure 3.4 Offa's Constantinian bust with vision of the cross (?).

and brooch, but the most striking feature is a prominent Latin cross immediately before the bust in a space normally left blank.[66] Crosses before busts were uncommon if not in themselves unusual, and occurred on *sceattas* and Merovingian coins;[67] but they were never found on the Roman coins which provided the inspiration for most of Offa's portraits and do not occur elsewhere in the coinage of Offa.

Constantine the Great, like David, loomed large in the imagination of early medieval Europe as a model for exemplary Christian kingship. Charlemagne patterned himself on Constantine in a number of respects, possibly including coinage,[68] and the eighth century probably

---

[66] Chick 25.

[67] *MEC*, nos. 430A, 444–5, 551, 694 and 697–9; and *T&S*, nos. 267–74, 301–2, 306–8, 318, 326 and 331–3.

[68] For the difficulties in dating the portrait issue and determining its prototype, see P. Grierson, 'Money and Coinage under Charlemagne', in *Karl der Grosse. Lebenswerk und Nachleben*, ed. W. Braunfels, 2 vols. (Düsseldorf, 1965) I, 501–36, at pp. 518–27; J. Lafaurie, 'Les monnaies impériales de Charlemagne', *Comptes-rendus de l'académie des inscriptions et belles-lettres* (1978), 154–72. For the Constantinian link, see B. Kluge, '*Nomen imperatoris* und *Christiana religio*', in *Kunst und Kultur*, ed. Stiegemann and Wemhoff, III, 82–90, at p. 82; with a more sceptical view taken in Grierson,

saw the creation of the (in)famous *Constitutum Constantini*, the 'Donation of Constantine', predicated on that emperor's reputation in the eyes of Roman clergy.[69] The increasingly popular and widespread cult of the cross was moreover closely linked to legends of Constantine and his mother Helena: the former because of his famous vision of the cross (or *labarum*) in the sky before the battle of the Milvian Bridge; the latter for her finding of the remains of the true cross in Jerusalem.[70] These two legends formed the basis of the Old English poem *Elene*, written by Cynewulf (possibly) in Mercia in the ninth century.[71]

Artistic representations of Constantine from this period in England, Francia and elsewhere were rare, but traces of them can be found, often including reference to the defining moment of his vision. Constantine and the cross were depicted in at least one ninth-century Byzantine manuscript illumination,[72] and were also included in a suite of early medieval mosaics at the Lateran in Rome and in a string of lost frescoes adorning the Carolingian palace at Ingelheim.[73] The famous equestrian bronze statue of Marcus Aurelius (161–80) at Rome only survived the early Middle Ages because it was believed to represent Constantine.[74] By the eighth century his reputation in England seems to have been considerable.[75] Aldhelm of Malmesbury wrote a passage on Sylvester and Constantine in his *De virginitate*,[76] and an inscription preserved at Jarrow

---

'Symbolism', pp. 633–4. For Constantine's numismatic influence in general see Maguire, 'Magic and Money', pp. 1040 and 1044.

[69] *Constitutum Constantini*, ed. Fuhrmann. For discussion, see Fuhrmann, 'Das frühmittelalterliche Papsttum'; an alternative view is found in J. Fried, *Donation of Constantine and Constitutum Constantini: The Misinterpretation of a Fiction and Its Original Meaning* (Berlin, 2007); challenged by C. L. Goodson and J. L. Nelson, 'The Roman Contexts of the "Donation of Constantine"', *EME* 18 (2010), 446–67. At the coronation of Louis the Pious in 825, it was believed that the crown placed on his head had previously belonged to Constantine (Ermoldus Nigellus, *In honorem Hludowici*, ii.425–6 (MGH Poet. II, p. 36)).

[70] Ewig, 'Das Bild Constantins', pp. 74–5 and 90–1. Cf. McKitterick, *History and Memory*, pp. 259–60.

[71] Anderson, *Cynewulf*, pp. 126–33.

[72] See Paris, Bibliothèque nationale, MS Grec 510, f. 440r (comment and illustration in S. C. Novelli, 'Scritture e immagini Insulari', *Settimane* 41 (1994), 463–504, at plate 27).

[73] Bullough, '*Imagines regum*', pp. 60–2 and 64–5. For the Lateran mosaics see Schramm, *Die deutschen Kaiser* II, figure 4; and T. F. X. Noble, *The Republic of St Peter: The Birth of the Papal State, 680–825* (Philadelphia, PA, 1984), pp. 323–4. For the famous account of Constantine's depiction in Ingelheim, see Ermoldus Nigellus, *In honorem Hludowici carmen*, iv.267–82 (MGH Poet. II, pp. 65–6); for comments and parallels W. Lammers, 'Ein karolingisches Bildprogramm in der Aula Regia von Ingelheim', in *Festschrift für Hermann Heimpel*, 3 vols. (Göttingen, 1971–2) III, 226–89.

[74] M. McCormick, 'Textes, images et iconoclasme dans le cadre des relations entre Byzance et l'occident carolingien', *Settimane* 41 (1994), 95–158, at pp. 102–3. It is not exactly clear when or how this identification came to be made.

[75] J. Hawkes, 'The Legacy of Constantine in Anglo-Saxon England', in *Constantine the Great: York's Roman Emperor*, ed. E. Hartley *et al.* (York, 2006), pp. 104–14.

[76] Aldhelm, *De virginitate prosa*, xxv (ed. Ehwald, pp. 257–60; trans. Herren and Lapidge, pp. 82–4).

from around the early eighth century reveals awareness of Constantine's part in the developing cult of the cross.[77] The letter copied by Bede likening Æthelberht of Kent to Constantine would also have been well known in Offa's time, and there is evidence that a copy of Bede's *Historia* was available at Offa's court.[78] From this source Offa could also have heard of St Oswald's victory at Heavenfield under the sign of the cross in 634, which has been noted for its marked similarities to Constantine's victory at the Milvian Bridge three centuries earlier.[79] In this connection, it may be significant that Offa patronized the resting place of St Oswald at Bardney in Lincolnshire,[80] and he could also have imitated the model kings of Bede's *Historia* when he proposed a marriage between his son and a daughter of Charlemagne named Bertha, evoking the Frankish wife of the first Christian king of Kent.[81]

What were the particular attractions of Constantinian (and indeed Davidian) iconography in the reign of Offa? The virtue which most commended Constantine to early medieval rulers and clergy was support of the Church. The written evidence from Offa's reign is notoriously patchy, but he was remembered in some quarters as an important patron of learning and the Church.[82] Alcuin's correspondence with Offa mentions that the latter's promotion of learning attracted widespread admiration,[83] and he was probably the donor of one of the sumptuous Monkwearmouth-Jarrow pandects to Worcester.[84] There is also a general mention in one of Alcuin's letters of the 'mores bonos et modestos et castos ... quos beatae memoriae Offa instituit',[85] probably alluding to the decrees of the legatine synod held under Offa's auspices in 786.[86] Despite the discomfiture it

---

[77] W. Levison, 'The Inscription on the Jarrow Cross', *Archaeologia Aeliana*[4] 21 (1943), 121–6; J. Higgitt, 'The Dedication Inscription at Jarrow and Its Context', *Antiquaries Journal* 59 (1979), 343–74, at p. 364.

[78] W. Levison, *England and the Continent in the Eighth Century* (Oxford, 1946), pp. 245–6.

[79] Bede, *HE*, iii.2 (ed. Colgrave and Mynors, pp. 214–19). For comment, see J. M. Wallace-Hadrill, *Bede's Ecclesiastical History of the English People: A Historical Commentary* (Oxford, 1988), pp. 88–9.

[80] Alcuin, *Versus de patribus, regibus et sanctis Euboricensis ecclesiae*, lines 388–91 (ed. Godman, pp. 34–5).

[81] Story, *Carolingian Connections*, p. 186. See also above, pp. 36–7.

[82] S. Matthews, 'Good King Offa: Legends of a Pious King', *Transactions of the Lancashire and Cheshire Antiquarian Society* 98 (2002), 1–14.

[83] MGH Epist. IV, no. 64, p. 107 (trans. *EHD*, no. 195).

[84] See S 118. Sims-Williams, *Religion and Literature*, pp. 182–3; P. Meyvaert, 'Bede, Cassiodorus and the Codex Amiatinus', *Speculum* 71 (1996), 827–83, at pp. 878–80.

[85] 'Good, moderate and chaste customs which Offa of blessed memory established.' MGH Epist. IV, no. 122, p. 180 (trans. *EHD*, no. 202).

[86] P. Wormald, 'In Search of King Offa's "Law-Code"', in *People and Places in Northern Europe, 500–1600: Studies Presented to P. H. Sawyer*, ed. I. Wood and N. Lund (Woodbridge, 1991), pp. 25–45, and *The Making of English Law: King Alfred to the Twelfth Century*, vol. I, *Legislation and Its Limits* (Oxford, 1999), pp. 106–8; C. Cubitt, *Anglo-Saxon Church Councils c. 650–c. 850* (London, 1995), pp. 169–70. It was probably these decrees to which Alfred referred when, in the preface to his law-code, he

caused to the see of Canterbury, it is also possible that from Offa's – and Mercia's – perspective the institution of a new archbishopric at Lichfield in 787 could have been another act of benefit to the Church.[87]

This programme of royal representation on the coinage of Offa, while exceptional in its specificity, invites the question of how royal patronage influenced the process of production. The pennies with Davidian and Constantinian references constitute only a very small proportion of Offa's currency, and are restricted to a select few moneyers. They must have been minted for only a short period and on a very restricted scale, probably in the early part of the substantive Light coinage in the mid 780s.[88] While it would be naïve to assume that a complete record of all the coin-types struck under Offa's authority survives today, the limited use of Davidian and Constantinian designs contrasts sharply with the more uniform coin designs current from the early 790s. This demonstrated in no uncertain terms that Offa could exert a firm grip over design of the coinage. It also suggests that the earlier instances of symbolically charged iconography represent a different phenomenon: potentially the interaction of the king with individual moneyers, either directly or indirectly. The Constantinian and Davidian types of Offa cluster among a small group of moneyers who can all be attributed to London. London was a prominent centre of the Mercian royal regime, and certainly would have provided an apt setting for royal interaction with local die-cutters and moneyers. But it was also home around this time to Eadberht, bishop of London (772×782–787×789), the only bishop of that see ever named on coins. The Anglo-Saxon see of London is obscure, and was not particularly prominent in relation to other contemporary Mercian bishoprics,[89] but it was nevertheless an appreciable centre of wealth and learning.[90] As an educated figure with interests in coinage based in London who must also have had access to the royal court, Bishop Eadberht might have been responsible for communicating a special programme of royal imagery to the die-cutters and moneyers of London.

Offa's Light coinage, almost uniquely for early medieval western currency, presents an instance of another eminently Roman custom: coinage with the image of a female consort (Figure 3.5a). Like the equally accomplished portrait coins of her husband, the pennies of Cynethryth

cited Offa as a legislative predecessor: Alfred, *Law-Code*, introduction 49.9 (ed. Liebermann I, 46; trans. *EHD*, no. 33, p. 208).

[87] The story of the institution of the archbishopric of Lichfield is best told in Brooks, *Early History*, pp. 117–27.

[88] R. Naismith, 'The Coinage of Offa Revisited', *BNJ* 80 (2010), 76–106, at pp. 89–93.

[89] Keynes, *Councils of Clofesho*, pp. 24–5.

[90] D. Whitelock, *Some Anglo-Saxon Bishops of London* (London, 1975).

Figure 3.5 Busts of Cynethryth, Faustina Senior and Irene.

have attracted much comment from both numismatists and historians.[91]
They were the work of a single, particularly favoured moneyer, implying
special circumstances of production.

Over forty specimens of Cynethryth's coinage are now known, probably produced at Canterbury on a substantial scale during the earlier stages
of the Light coinage in the 780s.[92] It is possible that some conceptual
inspiration for Cynethryth's coinage was taken from the distant example
of the Byzantine empress Irene, who in the 780s placed her own portrait
on the coins of her son Constantine VI and later (797–802) was the first
empress ever to rule in her own right (Figure 3.5c).[93] However, if Offa,
Cynethryth and their die-cutters did have these coins in mind, they had
no actual iconographic impact, and Irene's coinage probably began too
late to be the direct model of Cynethryth's:[94] the design used for most of

---

[91] See, for example, G. Williams, 'Mercian Coinage and Authority', in *Mercia*, ed. Brown and Farr,
  pp. 210–28, at 216; Gannon, *Iconography*, pp. 39–41; *MEC*, pp. 279–80; Blunt, 'Coinage of Offa',
  pp. 46–7; Lockett, 'Coinage of Offa', pp. 70–1.
[92] D. Chick, *The Coinage of Offa and His Contemporaries* (London, 2010), p. 15.
[93] *MEC*, p. 280. For Irene's coinage, see *DOC* II.i, 336–46 (with Constantine 780–97) and 347–51
  (sole coinage 797–802).
[94] S. Zipperer, 'Coins and Currency – Offa of Mercia and His Frankish Neighbours', in *Völker
  an Nord- und Ostsee und die Franken: Akten des 48. Sachsensymposiums in Mannheim vom 7. bis 11.
  September 1997*, ed. U. von Freeden, U. Koch and A. Wieczorek (Bonn, 1999), pp. 121–7. See also
  Gannon, *Iconography*, p. 40.

the portraits of her coinage was strongly influenced by Roman models, particularly those of Faustina, wife of Antoninus Pius (Figure 3.5b).[95] Coins of Helena, mother of Constantine and finder of the cross, were available and sometimes copied in Anglo-Saxon England,[96] but do not seem to have provided the direct model for Cynethryth's portraits.

After Offa

Anglo-Saxon numismatic portraiture in the seventy or so years after Offa was never again quite so sophisticated, diverse or pleasing to modern tastes. The basic diademed bust used on much of the Light coinage of Offa was revived for the Cross-and-Wedges coinage of Coenwulf and Cuthred around 805, in a slightly adapted form: although the diadem and hair were of similar design, the drapery was somewhat different (Figure 3.6a–b). It gives the impression of a facing, symmetrical bust, which contrasts with the profile head to create a somewhat artificial effect.

The design of bust used on the Cross-and-Wedges pennies (and the related Coenwulf 'mancus') was probably inspired by the cuirassed bust found on some Roman coins, particularly from the later third century onwards; again, roughly the age of Constantine.[97] Certain busts by the moneyer Sigeberht of an anomalous style seem to have been inspired by the two-lobed form of drapery on some of Offa's portrait pence. These coins apart, the portraits of Cuthred, Coenwulf and Ceolwulf I followed broadly the same pattern, with the introduction of a slightly different 'bonneted' bust in the Anonymous coinage of *c.* 822–3. Thereafter busts on Canterbury coins were to remain relatively homogeneous, as the work of a succession of die-cutters or groups of die-cutters who supplied all the moneyers at this large mint.

By this time, English numismatic busts were becoming more stylized and divorced from ancient models: sometimes they assumed a keyhole-like shape,[98] with highly simplified drapery, and the diadem was frequently represented as only a line (if it was represented at all). This was largely true at all the mints which produced portrait coinage in this period (London, Canterbury, Rochester and Ipswich), though there were stylistic variations by mint and die-cutter. London in particular

---

[95] Bastien, *Buste monétaire* III, plate 60 nos. 2 and 6–7. The hairpiece on these coins is almost identical to that on the coins of Cynethryth.

[96] Gannon (*Iconography*, pp. 39–40) cites an early Anglo-Saxon gold *solidus* modelled on a coin of Helena.

[97] Bastien, *Buste monétaire* I, 259–78. For particular examples, see *ibid.*, III, plate 148 no. 9 and plate 173 no. 11.

[98] This is already apparent to a certain extent even under Offa: see Chick 136.

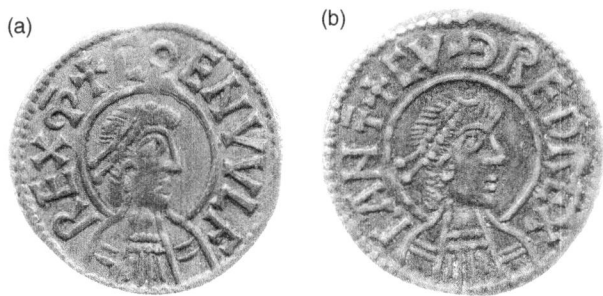

Figure 3.6 Cross-and-Wedges busts of Coenwulf and Cuthred.

was marked by wide diversity in style, presumably reflecting the work of different die-cutters. Some of them were much more able than others, and there could occasionally be room for marked differences in design as well as style. In the latter part of Coenwulf's reign and under Ceolwulf I, for example, London portraits include many which follow the format established by the Cross-and-Wedges and subsequent coinages from Canterbury, with varying degrees of competence. But there were also portraits that did away with the inner circle, or which were unusually small and delicate, without the drapery or diadem more characteristic of regular issues. One surprising aberration at London under Coenwulf was a brief flirtation with contemporary Carolingian models – specifically with the laureate and moustache-bearing busts of Charlemagne's portrait coinage and Louis the Pious' *solidi*.[99] This short-lived experiment reveals that further models could and did come to hand, but that the prevailing tradition remained very strong and resistant to change.

Actual alteration of the basic elements of the portrait was thus very rare in the ninth century. Though implemented in different ways, the format established in the first decade of the ninth century exerted a powerful influence for over fifty years. The bust had become a standard part of the repertoire of coinage design, modelled on an increasingly idiosyncratic native tradition rather than ancient models.

Towards the end of Æthelwulf's reign the Inscribed Cross type saw a revival in the quality and consistency of the busts and legends (Figure 3.7b). These and the rare coins of the succeeding Floreate Cross type of Æthelberht do not seem to have been modelled directly on Roman coins (Figure 3.7c); the closest affinities are with English

---

[99] Naismith L18.1 and L19.2.

Figure 3.7 Portrait coins of Coenwulf and Æthelberht.

coins from earlier in the ninth century, such as those from later in the reigns of Coenwulf and Ceolwulf I (Figure 3.7a), and there are also some similarities with the busts of the immediately preceding part of Æthelwulf's coinage.

This strong native tradition is an important warning against looking for complex expression of royal ideology in numismatic iconography. Busts remained popular, and certainly must have served to link the king with both ancient and recent predecessors, but display very little innovation or imagination except in matters of detail. When 'portraits' were used – and they were by no means the only or even the most popular design for Anglo-Saxon pennies in this period – they did not follow any new agenda, and represented a general appeal to the authority of established tradition. Stability was surely the primary message. Direct recourse to ancient models did, however, revive about a decade after Æthelberht's death in 865 during the reign of Alfred the Great.[100]

---

[100] The most pertinent recent discussion of the relevant Two Emperors and London Monogram issues can be found in Blackburn, 'London Mint'.

Figure 3.8 Facing busts of Pope Hadrian I and Archbishops
Wulfred and Ceolnoth.

Archiepiscopal portraits

Alongside the busts on royal coinage, there was a parallel series of quite
different busts placed on the pennies of two archbishops of Canterbury:
Wulfred (805–32) and Ceolnoth (833–70).[101] These coinages, which
began at the time of Wulfred's election in 805, diverged sharply from
the earlier tradition of recognizing the king's name and coin-types on
archiepiscopal issues (Figure 3.8b). Instead, the reverse carried the mint-
name, stressing the archbishop's affiliation with his see, and initially also
dispensing with the moneyer's name. On the obverse, a facing bust
appeared, inspired by the independent papal coinage instituted under
Hadrian I (Figure 3.8a).[102] The facing bust of papal coinage owed its

---

[101] There is also a unique gold solidus of Wigmund, archbishop of York (837–54), which uses the
facing bust characteristic of Canterbury (M. Blackburn, 'Gold in England during the "Age of
Silver" (Eighth–Eleventh Centuries)', in *Silver Economy in the Viking Age*, ed. J. Graham-Campbell
and G. Williams (Walnut Creek, CA, 2007), pp. 55–98, no. B5).

[102] *MEC*, pp. 259–66 and 638.

origins to the facing busts of emperor and Christ found on Byzantine coinage, which had been made and used in Rome until the time of Hadrian.[103] It was perceived as carrying an air of serene disconnection that was thought especially proper for Christ and the saints, and by extension the emperor.[104] By Wulfred's time, it should be noted, portrait coins of this sort were no longer being produced in Rome. Epigraphic types associating the pope with the current reigning emperor had been the norm since 800. Revival of the older type thus represents a significant statement on the part of those responsible for the design of archiepiscopal coinage at Canterbury, which is most reasonably associated with the initiative of Wulfred himself. What he intended to stress was the pseudo-papal dignity and importance of his see. Wulfred's archiepiscopate saw many associated developments in Canterbury: attempts to increase the wealth and influence of the cathedral community, a reform of its discipline and eventually a challenge to Coenwulf over control of certain Kentish monasteries. It should be noted that even the apparent suspension of Wulfred as archbishop for six years in the 810s had no discernible effect on either his or Coenwulf's coinage.[105]

The connection with the royal coinage was not abandoned altogether, however, as 805 also saw the adoption in Canterbury of new portrait designs for Coenwulf and his brother Cuthred. Moving to a portrait on the archiepiscopal coinage was therefore entirely in keeping with the development of the royal coinage, and should not be read as a rejection of royal authority by the archbishop. Moreover, the personnel responsible for producing Wulfred's coinage were the same as those behind the royal coinage: the moneyers (who were named on archiepiscopal issues from *c.* 810) also worked for the king, and the dies – though different in design – came from the same source. Wulfred's new design of coinage should probably be perceived as a virtue salvaged from necessity.

The parallel archiepiscopal coinage of Canterbury persisted into the tenth century, and the archbishop's rights to profit from minting survived even longer without any formal recognition in the design of

---

[103] T. F. X. Noble, 'Topography, Celebration, and Power: The Making of a Papal Rome in the Eighth and Ninth Centuries', in *Topographies of Power in the Early Middle Ages*, ed. M. de Jong and F. Theuws (Leiden and Boston, MA, 2001), pp. 45–91, at 72–5.

[104] Cf. the facing bust on the so-called 'Hexham Plate' (Webster and Backhouse, *Making of England*, no. 104). For discussion see Gannon, *Iconography*, pp. 25–30; Bastien, *Buste monétaire* I, 305–20; Grierson, *Byzantine Coins*, pp. 29 and 36–7.

[105] See in general Brooks, *Early History*, pp. 132–42 and 175–206. On the reform of the Christ Church community see also B. Langefeld, '*Regula canonicorum* or *Regula monasterialis uitae*? The Rule of Chrodegang and Archbishop Wulfred's Reforms at Canterbury', *ASE* 25 (1996), 21–36; on the concoction of forged charters to support Wulfred's case against Coenwulf, C. Cubitt, 'Finding the Forger: An Alleged Decree of the 679 Council of Hatfield', *EHR* 114 (1999), 1217–48.

coinage. However, the separate designs established under Wulfred did not outlast even his own archiepiscopate. His later coinages used the same reverse designs as those of Baldred, king of Kent, and – after an apparent hiatus in archiepiscopal minting *c.* 825–8 – Ecgberht of Wessex. The better relations built up between his successor, Ceolnoth, and the West Saxon dynasty following the Kingston agreement of 838 seem to be reflected in the coinage of subsequent decades,[106] which saw distinction in the design of archiepiscopal coinage, though type-changes coincided with those of the royal coinage (Figure 3.8c). The earliest issue of Ceolnoth employed the same reverse monogram as contemporary pennies of Ecgberht, but those of *c.* 839–54 adopted different designs. Finally, in the late 850s and early 860s, Ceolnoth's coinage followed the king's in using the Inscribed Cross and Floreate Cross reverse designs before, in the Lunettes coinage of *c.* 865 and after, adopting the same profile obverse bust as well.

CROSSES AND OTHER RELIGIOUS ICONOGRAPHY

It is easy to forget the most ubiquitous iconography of late eighth- and ninth-century pennies: variations on the cross. A cross introduced most obverse and reverse legends, just as in contemporary charters and many inscriptions, and imparted spiritual authority to what came after. The cross's prominence stemmed from a rich theological and iconographic tradition, which had taken hold across the early medieval west with the spread of Christianity and the cult of the cross.[107] It was a recollection of the crucifixion, a powerful symbol of salvation and a sign of victory for figures like Constantine the Great and St Oswald, which was free of any controversy.[108] The theological contention over the value and purpose of images most notably associated with eighth- and ninth-century Byzantium had only a limited effect on artistic production in the contemporary west,[109] including coin design in Anglo-Saxon England. No compunction seems to have been felt about using human

---

[106] Brooks, *Early History*, pp. 145–7.
[107] K. L. Jolly, C. Karkov and S. L. Keefer, eds., *Cross and Culture in Anglo-Saxon England: Studies in Honor of George Hardin Brown* (Morgantown, WV, 2008); Novelli, 'Scritture e immagini'; M. Werner, 'The Cross-Carpet Page in the Book of Durrow: The Cult of the True Cross, Adomnan and Iona', *Art Bulletin* 72 (1990), 174–223, at pp. 190–4; and Blair, *Church*, pp. 137–40. For the wider context, see F. Cabrol, ed., *Dictionnaire de l'archéologie chrétienne et de liturgie*, 15 vols. (Paris, 1907–53) IV, col. 3045–131; E. Dinkler and E. Dinkler-von Schubert, 'Kreuz', in *Lexikon der christlichen Ikonographie*, ed. E. Kirschbaum, 8 vols. (Freiburg, 1968–76) II, 562–90.
[108] T. F. X. Noble, *Images, Iconoclasm, and the Carolingians* (Philadelphia, PA, 2009), pp. 336–7; for a detailed case study of the crucifixion see C. Chazelle, *The Crucified God in the Carolingian Era. Theology and Art of Christ's Passion* (Cambridge, 2001).
[109] For the most recent exploration of the topic see Noble, *Images, Iconoclasm*.

and other images. But one result of the debate as it unfolded in the writings of eighth- and ninth-century scholars was an ever stronger sense of the cross's special status in Christian thought and iconography: it transcended all other images to occupy a unique place at the heart of Christian belief.

The sophistication with which the basic emblem of the cross could be elaborated was almost endless (Figure 3.9a–f). In the context of coinage in the late eighth and ninth centuries there were strong precedents for sophisticated cruciform designs inherited from the *sceattas*,[110] and also from sculpture, metalwork and manuscript art.[111] The parallels could sometimes be extremely close, for instance between the Floreate Cross coinage and the seal of Æthelweald, bishop of Dunwich (acc. 845×870).[112] Interpretation of crosses could be very specific: a floreate cross could, for example, recall the tree of life, the *crux florida* of the crucifixion or the description of Christ as the true vine.[113] A cross–crosslet could have originated as a 'patriarchal cross' with a double bar, symbolizing the panel attached to the true cross at Christ's crucifixion, which was later expanded in the Insular context into a cross with each arm itself crossed.[114] There are further layers of meaning: four crosses were placed at the corners of a newly consecrated altar *mensa*,[115] and the five crosses on a cross–crosslet might also be thought to relate to the five wounds of Christ – hence the five jewels on the cross in the *Dream of the Rood* and the five larger roundels on the Rupertus Cross.[116]

Other religious imagery, such as the alpha and omega, was also sometimes used on coins of this period. Signifying that God was the beginning and the end, based on the words of Revelation 1:8, 21:6 and 22:13, this emblem was also part of the standard repertoire of western Christian iconography in the early Middle Ages. In the English numismatic context, it first appears on a unique penny of Beorhtric of Wessex. In this case the monogram was probably suggested by the

---

[110] Gannon, *Iconography*, pp. 160–5.

[111] Jewell, 'Anglo-Saxon Friezes'; M. Brown, *The Lindisfarne Gospels: Society, Spirituality and the Scribe* (London, 2003), pp. 326–7

[112] D. M. Wilson, *Anglo-Saxon Ornamental Metalwork 700–1100 in the British Museum* (London, 1964), no. 18.

[113] M. Werner, 'Cross-Carpet Page', pp. 182–3 and 195; J. Flemming, 'Baum, Baüme', in *Lexikon der christliche Ikonographie*, ed. Kirschbaum, I, 258–68.

[114] One instance of this is the cross on folio 1v of the Book of Durrow (Dublin, Trinity College, A.4.5): M. Werner, 'Cross Carpet-Page', pp. 179–80.

[115] M. Werner, 'Cross-Carpet Page', pp. 208–9.

[116] *Ibid.*, p. 209 n. 177. Cf. *Dream of the Rood* 7a–9b (*ASPR* II, 61); and, for the Rupertus Cross, Webster and Backhouse, *Making of England*, no. 133; A. Scharer, 'Duke Tassilo of Bavaria and the Origins of the Rupertus Cross', in *Belief and Culture in the Middle Ages: Studies Presented to Henry Mayr-Harting*, ed. R. Gameson and H. Leyser (Oxford, 2001), pp. 69–75.

Figure 3.9 Examples of the crosses on Offa's Light coinage.

Tribrach type issued at London and Canterbury from 797/8 which prominently featured an ⋒, signifying *Merciorum*, as part of its obverse design. At a stroke, the West Saxon die-cutter was cleverly able to transform an ethnic device with strongly political overtones into a politically neutral religious emblem, yet still retain a general overall similarity that may have helped keep his coins economically viable.[117] An almost identical alpha–omega monogram was used a few years later in an unambiguously religious context as one of the first designs on Archbishop Wulfred's independent coinage.[118]

---

[117] Cf. Grierson, 'Symbolism', p. 609.   [118] Naismith C36.2.

INSCRIPTIONS

Also often neglected are the letters of numismatic legends, which frequently constituted all or most of the design. Busts and other figural emblems were not integral to Anglo-Saxon coinage, but reference to the issuing authority or authorities quickly became the *sine qua non* of coin design in the centuries after *c.* 760. Changes from portrait to inscriptional designs should not be seen as a step down, but as a shift in emphasis intended to highlight the ideological and conceptual features of a ruler's *nomen* rather than his Roman credentials expressed through a portrait.

Words, like crosses, occupied a prominent place in Christian iconography. Indeed, other kinds of images were accepted largely as a substitute for the superior medium of writing:[119] to the unlettered they could, in the words of Bede, 'quasi uiuam dominicae historiae pandere lectionem'.[120] It was this veneration for writing which had in part led to the famous ornamentation of script as a complement to or replacement for figural decoration;[121] to the common emphasis on books, scrolls and other literary paraphernalia in representations of prophets, evangelists and other holy figures;[122] and in the ninth century to a revival of the genre of *carmina figurata*: Latin verses which traced out images with letters and words with images.[123]

The small size and consequent brevity of numismatic inscriptions naturally militated against some of the more extravagant trends of other contemporary media, but nevertheless they are witnesses to the same imaginative treatment of the written word. There are several examples from across the eighth and ninth centuries of coin designs in which the inscription is disposed in such complex fashion that it must have been laid out by a die-cutter who was comfortable with the meaning and rendering of letters, and who might be compared with the makers of contemporary inscribed metalwork.

Monograms provide a particularly vivid expression of the die-cutter's abilities in manipulation of the written word. Although monograms for personal- and place-names had a long pedigree extending back into classical antiquity and continued to be popular in Carolingian Francia and

[119] Mayr-Harting, 'Charlemagne as a Patron', p. 50.
[120] 'Make available a sort of living narrative of the story of the Lord.' Bede, *De templo* II.19 (ed. Hurst, p. 223). For discussion of Bede's views, see Noble, *Images, Iconoclasm*, pp. 112–16.
[121] Cf. R. McKitterick, 'Text and Image in the Carolingian World', in *Uses of Literacy*, ed. McKitterick, pp. 297–318; McCormick, 'Textes, images et iconoclasme'; W. Diebold, *Word and Image: An Introduction to Early Medieval Art* (Boulder, CO, and Oxford, 2000), pp. 99–126.
[122] Mayr-Harting, 'Charlemagne as a Patron', p. 53, with reference to the 'Ada' or court school under Charlemagne.
[123] M. C. Ferrari, *Il 'Liber sanctae crucis' di Rabano Mauro: testo, immagine, contesto* (Berne and New York, 1999), pp. 359–410.

Italy,[124] in contemporary England they seem to have been an exclusively numismatic phenomenon save for standard religious invocations such as Christograms. There is no evidence that Anglo-Saxon rulers ever used monograms in charters or other documentary contexts. On coins, however, monograms were used quite extensively in the ninth century. The earliest, simplest and most widespread examples were religious: alpha and omega, Christogram and staurogram. All of these were employed by the southern English mints at different times.

The six other known monograms are all variants on the kingdom- or mint-name. At Canterbury, beginning with the coinage of Archbishop Wulfred *c*. 810, a monogram for *Dorovernia* was employed as the centrepiece for the reverse design of the archiepiscopal coinage (Figure 3.10a). It was later revived in a simpler form in the 840s under Archbishop Ceolnoth (Figure 3.10b), and another mint-name monogram was created for the royal and archiepiscopal DOROB-C coinage of *c*. 828 and after (Figure 3.10c).[125] Meanwhile, at the West Saxon mint in the reign of Ecgberht, a monogram of *Saxon* was used, which was expanded in full on a few rare specimens into a three-line inscription spelling out *Saxoniorum*. In the late 840s or early 850s the so-called DORB/CANT coinage of Rochester and Canterbury arranged the letters of *Cant* into a monogram (Figure 3.10d).

In palaeographical terms the lettering of the inscriptions placed on eighth- and ninth-century coins of southern England might be described as capitals, with some use of letter forms drawn from other display scripts such as uncial and occasionally Insular half-uncial or 'mixed' majuscules.[126] The latter script, with a variable mixture of majuscule forms, was widely used in contemporary inscriptions on stone and metalwork,[127] and for some display scripts in manuscripts.[128] Further inspiration could have come from Roman coins, or from visits to

[124] For the most recent and detailed discussion of late antique and early medieval monograms (though excluding the ninth-century English examples) see I. Garipzanov, 'Metamorphoses of the Early Medieval *signum* of a Ruler in the Carolingian World', *EME* 14 (2006), 419–64.

[125] This monogram may have been influenced by contemporary papal–imperial coinage: *MEC*, p. 289; and Garipzanov, 'Metamorphoses', p. 445.

[126] Cf. B. Bischoff, *Latin Palaeography: Antiquity and the Middle Ages*, trans. D. Ó Cróinín and D. Ganz (Cambridge, 1990), pp. 54–61 and 66–80.

[127] E. Okasha, 'The Non-Runic Scripts of Anglo-Saxon Inscriptions', *Transactions of the Cambridge Bibliographical Society* 4 (1968), 321–38.

[128] M. Brown, *The Book of Cerne: Prayer, Patronage and Power in Ninth-Century England* (London, 1996), pp. 63–4 and 125–6, and *Lindisfarne Gospels*, pp. 230–44; J. Higgitt, 'The Display Script of the Book of Kells and the Tradition of Insular Decorative Capitals', in *The Book of Kells: Proceedings of a Conference at Trinity College, Dublin 6–9 September 1992*, ed. F. O'Mahony (Aldershot, 1994), pp. 209–33; for Monkwearmouth-Jarrow in particular see E. A. Lowe, *Palaeographical Papers, 1907–1965*, 2 vols. (Oxford, 1972) II, 441–58.

(a)   (b)

(c)   (d)

Figure 3.10 Mint-name monograms from ninth-century England.

contemporary Gaul or Italy, both substantially richer in surviving inscriptions using similar capital script.[129] Unfortunately, precious little research has been carried out on the numismatic epigraphy of early medieval Europe.[130]

Variant forms which commonly occur on Anglo-Saxon coins across the period alongside the capital norm include top-barred and chevron-barred A (Ⱥ and Ⱥ), angular C (Ⅽ), uncial E (Ɛ), uncial G (Ɠ) and uncial M (ⅿ). Other, more diverse forms are particular to specific mints and

---

[129] S. Morison, *Politics and Script: Aspects of Authority and Freedom in the Development of Graeco-Latin Script from the Sixth Century B.C. to the Twentieth Century A.D.* (Oxford, 1972), pp. 87–100; N. Gray, 'The Palaeography of Latin Inscriptions in the Eighth, Ninth and Tenth Centuries in Italy', *Papers of the British School at Rome* 16 (1948), 38–171; E. Le Blant, 'Paléographie des inscriptions latines du IIIe siècle à la fin du VIIIe', *Revue archéologique*³ 29 (1896), 177–97, 345–55; 30 (1897), 30–40, 171–84; 31 (1897), 172–84; P. Deschamps, 'Étude sur la paléographie des inscriptions lapidaires de la fin de l'époque mérovingienne aux dernières années du XIIe siècle', *Bulletin monumental* 88 (1929), 5–86.

[130] Visigothic coinage presents an important exception: see, for the most recent treatment, Pliego, *Moneda Visigoda* I, 182–6.

periods. As in so many other regards, Offa's coinage presents considerably more variation in its letter forms than the coinage of subsequent decades. Lozenge-shaped O, uncial D (Ꝺ), uncial A (ᴀ) and uncial U (ᴜ) occurred frequently. Thereafter numismatic inscriptions are less diverse – probably in substantial part because, from at least the time of the Large Portrait coinage of Coenwulf (*c.* 810 and after), letters were more often made up with punches for specific strokes, which limited the range of the die-cutter. Nevertheless, there were aberrations, particularly outside the mints of Canterbury and Rochester. Products of the London mint from later in Coenwulf's reign and under Ceolwulf I retained some letter forms that had more or less disappeared in Kent, such as chevron-barred A (Ꜳ), curved C (Ϲ), uncial D (Ꝺ) and uncial H (ʜ). Winn (ᚹ) competed with V and VV for representation of the phoneme /w/ throughout this period, and only began to appear in Canterbury under Coenwulf. Runic legends were particularly popular at Ipswich under Offa,[131] presumably indicating more widespread runic literacy in the region.[132] However, Offa's name and title were never spelt out in runes, despite their frequent use for the moneyers' names on the reverse: different strictures and concerns seem to have governed the two inscriptions, and may be a result of the king's stipulations on the form of the coinage. Outside East Anglia runes were used much more rarely. Exceptions include one probably London-based moneyer of Offa who used a runic 'g', and occasional runic letters in Northumbria.[133] Runes aside, there were many other unusual letter forms in common use at Ipswich: uncial D (Ꝺ) and lozenge-shaped O survived until the mid 820s, and other unusual forms developed under the independent East Anglian kings, most notably uncial T (ꞇ) and two different forms of M (ᛗ and another characteristically Insular form resembling two capital Hs back to back).[134] There is, in short, strong evidence that the composers of coin legends in southern England worked in the same general

[131] R. Page, *An Introduction to English Runes*, 2nd edn (Woodbridge, 1999), esp. pp. 127–9; M. Blackburn, 'A Survey of Anglo-Saxon and Frisian Coins with Runic Inscriptions', in *Old English Runes and Their Continental Background*, ed. A. Bammesberger (Heidelberg, 1991), pp. 137–89.

[132] D. M. Metcalf, 'Runes and Literacy: Pondering the Evidence of Anglo-Saxon Coins of the Eighth and Ninth Centuries', in *Runeninschriften als Quellen interdisziplinärer Forschung*, ed. K. Düwel (Berlin and New York, 1998), pp. 434–8, at 435–6; Page, *English Runes*, pp. 212–25; Kelly, 'Lay Society', pp. 37–8; R. Derolez, 'Runic Literacy among the Anglo-Saxons', in *Britain 400–600: Language and History*, ed. A. Bammesberger and A. Wollmann (Heidelberg, 1990), pp. 397–436; for an opposing view E. Okasha, 'Script-Mixing in Anglo-Saxon Inscriptions', in *Writing and Texts in Anglo-Saxon England*, ed. A. R. Rumble (Woodbridge, 2006), pp. 62–70, at 67–8.

[133] Blackburn, 'Survey', pp. 158–62.

[134] On the latter see J. Higgitt, 'The Pictish Latin Inscription at Tarbat in Ross-shire', *Proceedings of the Society of Antiquaries of Scotland* 112 (1982), 300–21, at p. 312; N. Gray, *A History of Lettering. Creative Experiment and Letter Identity* (Oxford, 1986), p. 62.

tradition of display scripts as those responsible for inscriptions and for some manuscript headings.

On the other hand, one must be wary of assuming that the die-cutter was actually responsible for composing the legend, or even aware of its meaning. Much has been written on the interaction of craftsmen, composers and patrons of various levels of education in the context of inscriptions on stone and metal, and no consensus or common practice can be pinned down. The famous epitaph of Pope Hadrian I was ordered by Charlemagne but probably composed by Alcuin and made by professional craftsmen with a high degree of expertise;[135] other Frankish and Lombard inscribed epitaphs were made at the request of family or friends, though only in a few cases is detailed information on patronage and composition available.[136] Model books might be used, for instance at Jouarre in the seventh century,[137] although the orthographic cacophony presented by early medieval inscriptions on the Continent suggests widespread literacy on the part of makers and presumed literacy, or at least respect for the written word, among potential readers.[138] Within England the closeness between scribes and those responsible for lapidary inscriptions apparently varied from place to place, and there were often notable correspondences between the display capitals preferred for inscriptions and used occasionally for headings in manuscripts.[139] Certainly it is clear that artisans, clergy and sometimes laymen and women worked together in different capacities to bring an inscription into being. Die-cutting should not necessarily be seen as directly related to stone-carving or placing inscriptions onto other objects, which were all distinct from the act of writing on vellum,[140] but these analogies act as a reminder that nothing can be taken for granted.

[135] C. Treffort, *Mémoires carolingiennes. L'épitaphe entre célébration mémorielle, genre littéraire et manifeste politique: milieu VIIIe–début XIe siècle* (Rennes, 2007), pp. 9–12; Story *et al.*, 'Charlemagne's Black Marble'.

[136] See in general R. Favreau, 'Les commanditaires dans les inscriptions du haut moyen âge occidental', *Settimane* 39 (1992), 681–722; M. Handley, *Death, Society, and Culture. Inscriptions and Epitaphs in Gaul and Spain, AD 300–750*, BAR International Series 1135 (Oxford, 2003), pp. 23–34; Treffort, *Mémoires carolingiennes*, esp. pp. 100–17; N. Everett, *Literacy in Lombard Italy, c. 568–774* (Cambridge, 2003), pp. 235–76.

[137] B. Bischoff, *Anecdota novissima: Texte des vierten bis sechzehnten Jahrhunderts* (Stuttgart, 1984), pp. 142–9; Handley, *Death, Society and Culture*, p. 26.

[138] Handley, *Death, Society and Culture*, pp. 168–9 and 174–5. For the expectation of inscriptions being read aloud, see J. Higgitt, '*Legentes quoque vel audientes*. Early Medieval Inscriptions in Britain and Ireland and Their Audiences', in *The Worm, the Germ and the Thorn. Pictish and Related Studies Presented to Isabel Henderson*, ed. D. Henry (Balgavies, 1997), pp. 67–78.

[139] W. Koch, *Inschriftenpaläographie des abendländischen Mittelalters und der frühen Neuzeit. Teil 1: Früh- und Hochmittelalter* (Munich, 2006), pp. 88–95; J. Higgitt, 'The Stone-Cutter and the Scriptorium: Early Medieval Inscriptions in Britain and Ireland', in *Epigraphik 1988: Fachtagung für mittelalterliche und neuzeitliche Epigraphik, Graz, 10.–14. Mai 1988: Referate und Round-Table-Gespräche*, ed. W. Koch (Vienna, 1990), pp. 149–62, 'Display Script', p. 217, and 'Dedication Inscription', pp. 358–9.

[140] Handley, *Death, Society and Culture*, p. 171.

Letter forms and orthography nevertheless betray some hints about how the craftsmen who made the dies interacted with the other parties involved in the making of the coins. Sometimes this encompassed the highest levels of organization. Specific written forms were occasionally circulated to multiple mints or die-cutters, generally governing the obverse inscription which gave the names and titles of rulers. The preference for Roman rather than runic **OFFA REX** in East Anglia was noted above, and at all mints under Offa a standardized title – along with a standardized obverse layout – was adopted after 792/3. Distribution of some sort of model dies, coins or some other form of representation must have accompanied the institution of this coinage. Under Coenwulf, the remarkable consistency of the royal name and title – down to the same letter forms – must have resulted from a standard form laid down at all mints. Distribution of, or at least close acquaintance with, written models probably also accounts for occasional specific crossovers between coin-dies and the bookhands used in Anglo-Saxon charters and manuscripts. Perhaps the most striking of these is the range of ligatures and abbreviations for *episcopus* and *archiepiscopus*, which find close parallels in the work of contemporary scribes.[141]

The key level of responsibility for composing and engraving the legend seems to have rested with the die-cutter, not the moneyer.[142] Moneyers and patron usually seem to have given a non-specific description of the legend to be used, presumably giving oral rather than written instructions, implying literacy on the part of the die-cutter. One orthographic slip made by a die-cutter responsible for the archiepiscopal coinage at Canterbury 805–10 is particularly revealing, as it is difficult to reconcile with the legend being based on a model supplied by the archbishop or the Christ Church community. On no fewer than three reverse dies for Archbishop Wulfred (which, unusually, include the mint-name), the word **CIVITATIS** was rendered as **CIFITATIS**. This aberration was not a characteristic of charters and other pieces of writing produced at Canterbury in the early ninth century,[143] and the error is probably best explained as a result of a die-cutter who was literate but more accustomed to the phonemic properties of letters in the vernacular. In Old English, *f* signified a

---

[141] See the similarity between the **ЄP** used on the coinage of Eadberht, bishop of London (Chick 78–83) and those in S 139, preserved as an apparently original single sheet (Webster and Backhouse, *Making of England*, no. 158).

[142] See further below, pp. 139–42.

[143] On degrees of literacy in Canterbury in the ninth century see Brooks, *Early History*, pp. 171–4; M. Lapidge, *Anglo-Latin Literature 600–899* (London and Rio Grande, OH, 1996), pp. 409–54. For an alternative view, see J. Morrish, 'King Alfred's Letter as a Source on Learning in England in the Ninth Century', in *Studies in Earlier Old English Prose*, ed. P. Szarmach (Albany, NY, 1986), pp. 87–107.

voiced labiodental spirant when used medially,[144] much like consonantal *v* (/v/) in Latin.[145] In other words, the die-cutter – not a member of the scribal community of early ninth-century Canterbury – was either composing the legend personally or, more probably, spelling out what had been explained to him orally.

There are many further examples of coin legends which are not compatible with composition by an agency other than the die-cutter. In particular, probable occasions of die-cutters working from a specific model are actually quite few, and variation was the norm. There were quite consistent orthographic differences in the king's name between Canterbury and Rochester in the time of Ceolwulf I and Ecgberht, for instance.[146] On a more general level, the quantity of dies used for the minting of coinage would surely have presented a major demand on any agency other than the die-cutters if a fresh composition was required for every new die. Variations of spelling rather than palaeography therefore point strongly towards the legend being the responsibility of the die-cutter: they indicate that he was actively composing the legend for one or both faces of a coin on each separate occasion, with awareness of the values and meanings of letters. One moneyer of Offa, Ealhmund, received some dies from a die-cutter who favoured the forms **EALHMVND** or **ALHMVND**, whereas a different contemporary die-cutter preferred the form **EALMVND**.[147] In the Inscribed Cross coinage of the 850s and 860s the quite stable West Saxon dialectal form of the archbishop's name (**CEOLNOÐ**) contrasts with the more varied Kentish forms of his moneyers' names.[148] Fluctuation in moneyers' names can be difficult to perceive, as many moneyers only ever drew on the services of one die-cutter. But when a moneyer got his dies from more than one source there is often a recurring difference in orthography, suggesting that the moneyers were not responsible for composition.

The growth of lay literacy in the early Middle Ages has been a topic of considerable interest among historians,[149] but has so far been based primarily on the evidence of documents. Coins provide important evidence for vernacular and (albeit more slight) Latin literacy among at least one small and specialized segment of society. The extent of their skills is difficult to gauge. The ability to sign one's name, however, has commonly been taken as a key benchmark of literacy, and on this basis all die-cutters and possibly some moneyers must have been literate. Coinage

---

[144] A. Campbell, *Old English Grammar* (Oxford, 1959), § 57(1) and 444.
[145] D. Norberg, *Manuel pratique de latin médiéval* (Paris, 1968), pp. 21, 48 and 143.
[146] Naismith C48–51, C70–90, R3.1–7.5 and R11.1–17.
[147] Cf. Chick 36–7 and 38–42, and for the second die-cutter 37A and 43–50.
[148] Naismith C149–59.
[149] For example, K. Lowe, 'Lay Literacy'; Kelly, 'Early Anglo-Saxon Society', pp. 46–61; R. McKitterick, *The Carolingians and the Written Word* (Cambridge, 1989), pp. 211–70.

may not be able to reveal how many coin-users could read numismatic inscriptions,[150] but it can speak volumes about the learning available to those producing the coinage.

The letters placed on coins functioned as a verbal as well as a visual manifestation of authority. Names and titles provide a window on how rulers and their subjects conceived of power, and can shed light on religious, social, historical and geographical affiliations in a succinct yet powerful way.[151] Great importance lay in developments such as the use of religious formulae like *Dei gratia*,[152] or the changing emphasis on people(s) over whom mastery was claimed: thus kings of Mercia and the Franks respectively remained *rex Merciorum* and *rex Francorum* even after campaigns of conquest had expanded their geographical and ethnic domains considerably.[153] The link to the original, dominant people from whom the royal stock claimed their descent remained crucial, and interactions with subordinated groups and their rulers can reveal the underlying complexities of political authority,[154] especially in areas where dominance by another king was a recent development.[155] In the Anglo-Saxon context,[156] study of royal titulature has generally focused on issues of

---

[150] P. Wormald, 'The Uses of Literacy in Anglo-Saxon England and Its Neighbours', *TRHS* 27 (1977), 95–114, at p. 95.

[151] H. Wolfram, *Intitulatio I: Lateinische Königs- und Fürstentitel bis zum Ende des 8. Jahrhunderts* (Graz, 1967), esp. pp. 24–9.

[152] J. M. Wallace-Hadrill, *Early Germanic Kingship in England and on the Continent: The Ford Lectures Delivered in the University of Oxford in Hilary Term 1970* (Oxford, 1971), pp. 107 and 111–14; Deshman, '*Christus rex*', pp. 401–2; A. Scharer, 'Die Intitulationes der angelsächsischen Könige im 7. und 8. Jahrhundert', in *Intitulatio III. Lateinische Herrschertitel und Herrschertitulaturen vom 7. bis zum 13. Jahrhundert*, ed. H. Wolfram and A. Scharer (Vienna, Cologne and Graz, 1988), pp. 9–74, at 48–63; J. A. Dabbs, *Dei gratia in Royal Titles* (The Hague, 1971); K. Schmitz, *Ursprung und Geschichte der Devotionsformeln bis zu ihrer Aufnahme in die fränkische Königsurkunde* (Amsterdam, 1965), pp. 141–53; J. L. Nelson, 'The Lord's Anointed and the People's Choice: Carolingian Royal Ritual', in *Rituals of Royalty: Power and Ceremonial in Traditional Societies*, ed. D. Cannadine and S. Price (Cambridge, 1987), pp. 137–80; Wolfram, *Intitulatio I*, pp. 213–17; I. Garipzanov, 'Communication of Authority in Carolingian Titles', *Viator* 36 (2005), 41–82, at pp. 55–6.

[153] Dumville, 'Terminology of Overkingship' and 'Essex, Middle Anglia'; P. Fouracre and R. A. Gerberding, *Late Merovingian France: History and Historiography, 640–720* (Manchester, 1996), pp. 340–3; Goldberg, *Struggle for Empire*, pp. 39 and 188–9; H. Mayr-Harting, 'Charlemagne, the Saxons and the Imperial Coronation of 800', *EHR* 111 (1996), 1113–33.

[154] For a recent survey of the topic and its literature, see Garipzanov, *Symbolic Language*, pp. 19–23, 122–3 and 273–6.

[155] Wormald, 'Bede, the *Bretwaldas*', pp. 112–13 and 115–17; Kelly, *Charters of Selsey*, pp. lxxx–lxxxiv; Sims-Williams, *Religion and Literature*, pp. 29–39.

[156] For general discussion see B. Yorke, 'The Vocabulary of Anglo-Saxon Overkingship', *ASSAH* 2 (1981), 171–200; A. Scharer, 'Intitulationes', and *Die angelsächsische Königsurkunde im 7. und 8. Jahrhundert* (Cologne and Vienna, 1982). On Francia see especially Wolfram, *Intitulatio I*, pp. 206–44, and H. Wolfram, 'Lateinische Herrschertitel im neunten und zehnten Jahrhundert',

overlordship, particularly labels such as *imperium*, *bretwalda* and similar.[157] These were theoretically reserved for kings with mastery over multiple peoples or kingdoms (*gentes* or *provinciae* in the preferred contemporary terminology), yet despite occasional flourishes, the large majority of royal titles surviving from the eighth and ninth centuries are not grandiose or especially elaborate.[158]

In Anglo-Saxon England charters are the most important single source of royal titulature, but cannot be taken unreservedly as direct manifestations of views emanating from the king and his circle. Unlike contemporary Carolingian royal diplomas, Anglo-Saxon royal charters were probably not drawn up by a centralized agency, and production is tentatively thought to have been in the hands of episcopal scriptoria (except perhaps in ninth-century Wessex).[159] The ramifications of this for the study of royal titulature – especially for any attempt to get back to the 'official' form, if such a thing ever existed – are considerable. Agreement on royal style at multiple charter-producing centres presumably indicates a widely known form, probably promulgated at the meetings where grants were made. Differences particular to various locations might be taken as evidence of varying local tastes and perceptions. Examples include a tendency towards hyperbole at Worcester under Æthelbald, and perhaps a stronger sense of Offa as an 'Anglian' ruler at South Saxon Selsey.[160]

Numismatic forms of titulature were quite different in nature from those found in written documents. Space was obviously limited, though

in *Intitulatio II: Lateinische Herrscher- und Fürstentitel im neunten und zehnten Jahrhundert*, ed. H. Wolfram (Graz, 1973), pp. 19–178.

[157] Stenton, *Anglo-Saxon England*, pp. 34–5 and 202–3, and *Preparatory*, p. 48; E. John, *Orbis Britanniae and Other Studies* (Leicester, 1966), pp. 1–63; R. Drögereit, 'Kaiseridee und Kaisertitel bei den Angelsachsen', *Zeitschrift der Savigny-Stiftung für Rechtsgeschichte: Germanistische Abteilung* 69 (1952), 24–73; E. Stengel, *Abhandlungen und Untersuchungen zur Geschichte des Kaisergedankens im Mittelalter* (Cologne and Graz, 1965), pp. 325–38; H. Vollrath-Reichelt, *Königsgedanke und Königtum bei den Angelsachsen bis zur Mitte des 9. Jahrhunderts* (Cologne, 1971), pp. 79–121; Erdmann, *Forschungen*, pp. 31–43; R. Folz, *The Concept of Empire in Western Europe from the Vth to the XIVth Century*, trans. S. A. Ogilvie (London, 1969), pp. 16–25; R. Collins, *Charlemagne* (Basingstoke, 1998), pp. 147–53; Nelson, 'Kingship and Empire', pp. 69–73; Yorke, 'Vocabulary', esp. pp. 171–80; W. Pohl, 'Ethnic Names and Identities in the British Isles: A Comparative Perspective', in *The Anglo-Saxons*, ed. Hines, pp. 7–32; S. Keynes, 'Rædwald the *Bretwalda*', in *Voyage to the Other World: The Legacy of Sutton Hoo*, ed. C. B. Kendall and P. S. Wells (Minneapolis, 1992), pp. 103–23; S. Fanning, 'Bede, *Imperium* and the Bretwaldas', *Speculum* 66 (1991), 1–26.

[158] Yorke, 'Vocabulary', p. 183.

[159] Above, p. 21. For the Carolingian chancery, see G. Tessier, *Diplomatique royale française* (Paris, 1962), pp. 39–57; R. H. Bautier, 'La chancellerie et les actes royaux dans les royaumes carolingiens', *Bibliothèque de l'École des chartes* 142 (1984), 5–80; Garipzanov, 'Communication of Authority', pp. 52–66.

[160] Above, n. 155.

the use of iconography could make up for some of the lost detail. Royal titulature on coinage was heavily grounded in tradition and a boiled-down version of charter styles: what was left on the restricted space of coinage might give some indication of what the die-cutter considered or had been told to be most important. As a rule, this was very simple and straightforward: the majority of royal titles 757–865 consist simply of the king's name and the title *rex*. As in contemporary charters this is preceded by a cross, and the title also often surrounds a cruciform design, placing emphasis on the sacral element of royal authority. In all the coin-producing realms of England the majority of coins followed this pattern. Indeed, there are many occasions when changes of king or even dynasty were not marked by any alteration in the design of coinage or in the title accorded to the king: it was only the name itself that changed. Having one's name on money therefore seems to have been the most basic and important statement that a king could make through coins.

Not surprisingly, some of the most diverse titulature appears on the coinage of Offa.[161] Everything from OF[*fa*] R[*ex*] M[*erciorum*], +OFFA REX M[*erciorum*], OFFA and (+)OFFA REX to +OFFA REX MERCIORVM can be found. The diversity of royal styles reflects the general fluidity of Offa's coinage in the period before 792/3. Abbreviated styles such as OF[*fa*] R[*ex*] M[*erciorum*] are associated with the earliest phase of the coinage, and were influenced by the abbreviated royal titulature of Pippin III,[162] particularly in the use of the distinctive abbreviation R[*ex*]. This, along with the broad, thin format of the coinage, had probably been adopted from Visigothic and Lombard custom.[163]

Despite their beauty, the large majority of the portrait and related coinages bear quite basic royal styles: either (+)OFFA or (+)OFFA REX. Those with an extended ethnic are extremely rare, but the most chal-lenging from the historical point of view are a few early specimens that read OFRA. The likeliest interpretation of this inscription is OF[*fa*] R[*ex*] A[*nglorum*]. An alternative reading is OF[*f*]A R[*ex*], but Ofa (or Oba) was a distinct Old English name, normally kept quite separate from Offa,[164] and this interpretation also goes against the order suggested by the alignment

---

[161] For further details see Naismith, 'Offa You Can't Refuse'.

[162] *MEC*, p. 204.

[163] For its appearance in Visigothic Spain see Pliego, *Moneda Visigoda* I, 178 (where its introduction came in the reign of Chindaswinth (642–53)); for Lombard examples *MEC*, nos. 320–31. In Italy it was used from the time of the earliest Lombard royal *tremisses* under Cunincpert (688–700) and possibly earlier on silver coins under Perctarit (661–2 and 671–88); for the date of the latter coins, see recently Garipzanov, 'Metamorphoses', p. 437.

[164] M. A. Redin, *Studies on Uncompounded Personal Names in Old English* (Uppsala, 1919), pp. 101–2 and 103–5.

of the letters and by analogy with the **OFRM** issues. A series of charters of Offa also accords him the title *rex Anglorum*, although many of these have now been diagnosed as forgeries.[165] The coins therefore assume considerable importance as an instance of the use of the title *rex Anglorum*. Some commentators have seen this development as evidence of a move towards a pan-English kingdom,[166] though more recent interpretations view the title as a reference to rule over one or more 'Anglian' peoples.[167]

A potentially more significant point in relation to Offa's royal titulature emerges from the mint-context of these coins. Before the reform of 792/3, and with the exception of the early abbreviated royal style **OFRM**, all royal titulature beyond **(+)OFFA** and **(+)OFFA REX** seems to have been confined to the coins of London moneyers. These include all the **OFRA** coins and the slightly later portrait coins with direct and lengthy reference to the Mercians. In the same way as Worcester charter scribes often engaged in the elaboration of royal titles, so London diecutters were especially ambitious in the development of iconography and titulature. Yet, for all that, London's place in the eighth-century Mercian polity was significant, royal interest or involvement in these developments was probably indirect and occasional, and there was a general lack of standardization between mints or even between different moneyers at London. While Offa presumably approved of the initiative of his coin-producers in London, there is no direct evidence that London's titulature stood any closer to the 'official' norm: both **(+)OFFA REX MERCIORVM** and **OF**[*fa*] **R**[*ex*] **A**[*nglorum*] only ever appeared on a small proportion of London's output. It is likely that quite vague instructions (if any) stipulating the form of his *nomen* were issued by Offa, which were interpreted in various ways.

Offa's last years witnessed a break from the simple tradition of just the king's name and *rex*. The reform of 792/3 saw the Heavy coinage adopt a common design at all three southern mints, involving a standardized title: **+OFFA REX M**[*erciorum*]. This reflects the most common appellation given to Offa in charters from throughout his reign. The standardization established in 792/3 did not end with Offa: almost all the coins of Coenwulf from London, Canterbury, Rochester and East Anglia used the very same form of title throughout the reign: **+COENVVLF REX M**[*erciorum*]. Even

---

[165] P. Sawyer, *From Roman Britain to Norman England*, 2nd edn (London, 1998), p. 101; Keynes, 'Kingdom of the Mercians', pp. 3–7; Scharer, *Angelsächsische Königsurkunde*, pp. 159–278.

[166] Stenton, *Preparatory*, pp. 60–4, and *Anglo-Saxon England*, pp. 211–12. For more recent general comments on this topic cf. S. Foot, 'The Making of *Angelcynn*: English Identity before the Norman Conquest', *TRHS* 6 (1996), 25–49; N. Brooks, *Bede and the English* (Jarrow, 1999) and 'English Identity from Bede to the Millennium', *Haskins Society Journal* 14 (2005), 33–51, at pp. 35–46.

[167] Wormald, 'Bede, the *Bretwaldas*', pp. 122–9; Fanning, 'Bede, *Imperium*', pp. 20–2; M. Richter, 'Bede's *Angli*: Angles or English?', *Peritia* 3 (1984), 99–114.

details such as the uncial ꟿ and square Ꞇ were maintained, presumably as a result of some sort of visual model being distributed and adhered to. Other aspects of the design showed much more variation around the basic concept of (first) the tribrach and subsequently and more vaguely a bust and cross. The form of title need not have been promulgated often, as it remained static over the whole reign; but it nonetheless constitutes an important manifestation of royal interest in standardization and control over at least one detail. Presumably emanating from the king and his circle, this form of title has a good claim to represent some sort of 'approved' form, and corresponds with the title *Coenwulf rex Merciorum* that is found most commonly in Coenwulf's charters.[168]

Subsequent Mercian rulers did not maintain the same level of unity in numismatic titulature as Coenwulf. Ethnic references in particular appeared more sporadically, and their inclusion was probably left to individual die-cutters. It survived long enough to be used on Ecgberht's rare London coinage as **REX ꟿ**[*erciorum*]: another exceptional case where direct royal influence can be posited. By the time of Berhtwulf it was used only occasionally. The standardized spelling of Coenwulf's name, too, had quickly given way to variation under his brother Ceolwulf I, suggesting that close control over features of the royal title was an unusual step that other kings did not necessarily feel the need to emulate.

Rulers elsewhere in southern England used expanded royal titles much more rarely than their Mercian counterparts. Among kings of Kent expanded titles were confined to some coins of Cuthred and Baldred. The latter's reign includes an interesting group from Rochester which bears the enigmatic title **REX H**. Only one known example survives of a penny of Baldred from Rochester with the royal style **REX CANT**[*iae*]. **REX H** should probably be read as *rex Hrofesceastir* (Rochester):[169] a unique local alternative to *rex Cantiae*, possibly preserving a relic of the long-established western division of the kingdom of Kent.[170] Nothing, however, marks out the **REX H** pennies as being any earlier than those with the title **REX CANT**: they should not necessarily be seen as an early coinage of Baldred before his power was extended to include east Kent.

The first extended ethnic reference on the West Saxon coinage took the form of a monogram and three-line central inscription, both spelling out *Saxonum*, completing the circumscriptional legend **ECGBEORHT REX**. These coins were produced at Southampton or Winchester in the kingdom of Wessex itself in 802 or soon after, but the three-line variant was

---

[168] See S 152–85.

[169] C. E. Blunt, C. S. S. Lyon and I. Stewart, 'The Coinage of Southern England, 796–840', *BNJ* 32 (1963), 1–74, at pp. 24 and 41–2.

[170] B. Yorke, 'Joint Kingship in Kent *c.* 560 to 785', *Archaeologia Cantiana* 99 (1983), 1–19.

transplanted from there to Kent at the outset of the reign of Ecgberht's son Æthelwulf in 839. They should probably be seen as a special attempt to mark the accession of a new ruler by adding more detail to the royal title.[171] At Rochester a small group of (possibly episcopal) pennies associated with this inaugural coinage of Æthelwulf replaced the moneyer's name with the even more extended **OCCIDENTALIVM SAXONVM**, the longest title ever to appear on a West Saxon coin. In independent East Anglia, it was again a non-moneyer signed issue that provided the fullest title on coins of Æthelstan: **REX ANG**[*lorum*]. A truncated form of this same title occurs on some coins of Edmund (**REX AN**[*glorum*]), and the popular obverse design of a large central **A** (originally an alpha, occasionally coupled with an omega) probably alluded to this ethnic element of the royal title. Charters and letters showing what other titles East Anglian rulers used are virtually non-existent, leaving these coins as the only evidence to draw upon.[172]

CONCLUSION

The watchwords of numismatic iconography in the late eighth and ninth centuries were symbolism and standardization. Here, the focus has fallen primarily on the former, on the ways in which coinage conveyed the thoughts, insights and perceptions of the period. These were numerous and often highly sophisticated. The individuals who came up with the designs for coinage effectively combined imagination and education with respect for tradition. The key question is who these agencies were. Coin inscriptions provide important clues to their identity. After the string of reforms associated with the mid eighth century the authorities behind the coinage were the king and the moneyer. A new emphasis fell on the invocation of their names and (in the case of the king) titles. There can be little doubt that this initiative started with the king, whose role was the major new factor in the broad penny and associated coinages.[173] Words thus lay at the core of the new iconography of the later eighth century, and thereafter constituted the most ubiquitous and fundamental element of coin design. This is a point worth reiterating, as the coinage of southern England frequently switched back and forth between figural and aniconic designs, with the inscription alone remaining constant.

---

[171] H. Pagan, 'Coinage in Southern England, 796–874', in *Anglo-Saxon Monetary History*, ed. M. Blackburn (Leicester, 1986), pp. 45–66, at 50.

[172] Felix, *Vita sancti Guthlaci*, prologue (ed. Colgrave, p. 60), addressed King Ælfwald as *rex orientalium Anglorum*; and Bede in *HE* referred to the East Angles as *orientales Angli* (ed. Colgrave and Mynors, p. 596).

[173] Below, pp. 96–100.

Developments of these basic principles were grounded in three major interconnected traditions: those of Roman coinage; early medieval art, especially that derived from the Insular world and from immediately preceding coinages; and contemporary royal and religious ideology. It was the last which commended inscriptions and extensive use of crosses to die-cutters of both secular and ecclesiastical coinage, and which was the most constant and concrete element in coin design. Roman models, sometimes mediated through earlier Anglo-Saxon adaptation, provided the inspiration for busts and a few other figural pieces of imagery, and deeply influenced views of kingship and its representation. In only a few respects, however, was the rich vein of diverse iconography which had flourished in the early eighth-century coinage maintained after the mid-eighth-century reforms. Just a small proportion of the formerly diverse figural elements of coin design persisted. Coiled serpents were used as the reverse design by several moneyers of Offa,[174] while under Æthelstan of East Anglia one moneyer made a totally new departure for Anglo-Saxon coinage when he struck coins with the obverse design of a ship.[175] Also in East Anglia, the emblem of the wolf and twins was famously used on the coinage of Æthelberht II (d. 794).[176] Offa's reign saw the most successful union of artistic flair and varied design with the changing emphasis and structure of coin production; subsequent issues retained the latter but for the most part abandoned the former.

What was the basic meaning of the array of images and ideas which characterized the coinage of late eighth- and ninth-century England? Regularization and decline in aesthetic merit did not necessarily go hand in hand with royal micro-management. In terms of organization and administration, numismatic iconography of this period illustrates the multi-layered complexity with which all the components of coin design were controlled. Standardization, within and between mints, is crucial to tracing the extent of royal control, and will be revisited in the next chapters, but it is important to note at this point that variation itself could take many forms and work on different levels: titulature, orthography, iconography and other features did not always march in step, and could change substantially over just a short period. At times there could be close standardization between mints, or at least among all the moneyers

---

[174] Chick 18, 26, 37, 37A, 68–9 and 172. Gannon, *Iconography*, pp. 136–40; D. M. Metcalf, 'Offa's Pence Reconsidered', *Cunobelin* 9 (1963), 37–52, at p. 41; G. Speake, *Anglo-Saxon Animal Art and Its Germanic Background* (Oxford, 1980), pp. 85–92.

[175] Naismith E29.3–4. Cf. M. Archibald, 'A Ship Type of Athelstan I of East Anglia', *BNJ* 52 (1982), 34–40; G. Williams, 'The Influence of Dorestad Coinage on Coin Design in England and Scandinavia', in *Dorestad in an International Framework. New Research on Centres of Trade and Coinage in Carolingian Times*, ed. A. Willemsen and H. Kik (Turnhout, 2010), pp. 105–11.

[176] Chick 172 and 186. Below, pp. 118–20.

of a mint-town, while at other times die-cutters seem to have been given *carte blanche.* The development of tight control over the design of coinage was not smooth or linear, and was not solely the domain of kings. A significant say in the implementation of coin design always lay in the hands of die-cutters, moneyers and perhaps other intermediaries. All coins may have been royal in the sense of representing the king's name, title and possibly associated imagery, but some were more royal than others in terms of whose perception of royal power they actually showed.

Yet the changeable relationship between coinage and royal power did not hamper the emergence of a distinct idiom of numismatic iconography in southern England under Offa and his successors. This remained very distinct from developments in the contemporary Carolingian realms.[177] There, for example, an even greater emphasis was placed on the verbal aspects of coin design – inscriptions and monograms – and on religious emblems such as the cross and the temple. This reached its peak in Louis the Pious' *Christiana Religio* coinage, which formed part of an ambitious empire-wide reassertion of responsibilities and duties, secular and spiritual alike, under the aegis of the emperor in the early 820s.[178] Conversely, figural designs and busts were substantially rarer in the Carolingian world: busts were prevalent for only a brief period in the 810s, otherwise being restricted to sporadic local issues. As in England, the level of standardization could also fluctuate under different kings and in different areas, though on the whole there was a stronger tendency towards unity in design across broad swathes of territory and numerous mints. Generally the Carolingian currency, which shared many physical and economic affinities with contemporary issues from across the Channel, followed a quite different iconographic path that reflected local ideological priorities and only partially coincided with those current in England. There were also pragmatic reasons for the difference. Offa's coinage created a strong precedent for figural coin design which persisted on and off across the ninth century, while the need to be able to distinguish English from Frankish coins at a glance acted as a strong incentive for clear differences in appearance between coins on both sides of the Channel. The differing nature of minting organization was also an important factor, contributing significantly to the level and manner in which designs and other features were selected. It is to that organization that the next two chapters turn.

---

[177] See in general Garipzanov, *Symbolic Language.* Much interest has surrounded Charlemagne's famous portrait issue (above, p. 59), despite its brevity and rarity.

[178] De Jong, *Penitential State*, pp. 36–7 and 131–3; S. Patzold, *Episcopus. Wissen über Bischöfe im Frankenreich des späten 8. bis 10. Jahrhunderts* (Ostfildern, 2008), pp. 135–84.

Chapter 4

AUTHORITY AND
MINTING I: THE KING

'A special, but very solid, demonstration of the English state is the coinage.'[1] Thus wrote James Campbell, one of several historians in recent times who have quite rightly emphasized the remarkable unity and sophistication of the late Anglo-Saxon monetary system.[2] It stands in stark contrast to the currency of late Carolingian and early Capetian France, or that of Ottonian and Salian Germany, where in both cases power over minting had passed into the hands of a plethora of secular and ecclesiastical magnates. Almost every mint had its own distinct coinage.[3] In the whole kingdom of England, there was only one. As Campbell observed, this contrast in monetary history has been used as one benchmark of royal authority in a more general sense. The frequent reforms and nation-wide standardization instituted by Edgar towards the end of his reign brought into being the 'gold standard' of early medieval royal coinages, at the same time as other – though often less clearly traceable – developments in government and kingly representation were building momentum.[4]

In essence there is no disputing this special place which coinage occupies in the armoury of sources available to the early medieval historian. It survives in relative quantity and consistency from diverse parts of the kingdom, and gives an important insight into one sphere of society and government which usually operated separately from that responsible for chronicles, charters and most other raw materials of early medieval history. At the same time, numismatists should be under no illusions about

---

[1] J. Campbell, 'The United Kingdom of England: The Anglo-Saxon Achievement', in *Uniting the Kingdom? The Making of British History*, ed. A. Grant and K. Stringer (London, 1995), pp. 31–47, at 32.

[2] Further selected examples include S. Keynes, *The Diplomas of King Æthelred 'the Unready' 978–1016: A Study in Their Use as Historical Evidence* (Cambridge, 1980), p. 196; Loyn, *Governance of Anglo-Saxon England*, p. 122; Stafford, *Unification and Conquest*, pp. 213–15.

[3] F. Dumas, 'La monnaie au Xe siècle', *Settimane* 38 (1991), 565–609.

[4] For a survey see D. Scragg, ed., *Edgar, King of the English, 959–975: New Interpretations* (Woodbridge, 2007).

the importance of coinage. In the grand scheme of things coinage was a relatively minor part of a kingdom's administration, at least as long as it was broadly meeting expectations.[5] Insignificance is in one sense, however, a virtue. Substantive changes in the coinage are unlikely to have been isolated phenomena and hint at more general enterprises which once touched on many other, now lost, media.[6] If this is what could be accomplished with coins, the argument goes, how far could the same arrangements have extended into other areas?[7]

Answers to this question in the context of the tenth and eleventh centuries have been explored in considerable depth, thanks to the high level of detail with which the English coinage of that period has been scrutinized.[8] Its connections with royal government are comparatively well understood. Other periods have not been neglected, although the coinage has usually been highlighted as a tool of royal government even when many of the elements of the later system – not least its nation-wide unity in design and physical features – were still absent. In the context of the earlier part of the tenth century, for example, historians and numismatists have had to be more flexible, and more generous, in their expectations of a royal English coinage which was marked by substantially greater diversity.[9] What made a coinage royal, and to what degree, remains a very malleable judgement.

The formative period of explicitly royal silver broad pennies – Offa's reform and the decades thereafter – has remained even more enigmatic. The complex coin-issues of this time differ dramatically from the bench-mark 'royal coinage' of the late tenth century and after. As with the earlier tenth century, most historians seem to have accepted that these issues were essentially a fully fledged royal coinage comparable to that of Edgar and Æthelred the Unready.[10] A royal coinage, once established in the his-toriography, leaves very little room for shades of grey.

Characteristics which made a coinage royal, however, are difficult to define. In the most basic sense it meant a coinage directly managed by

---

[5] Astill, 'Archaeology, Economics', pp. 223–5; Harrison, 'Structures and Resources', p. 28.

[6] Cf. S. Keynes, 'England, 900–1016', in *NCMH* III, pp. 456–84, at 481.

[7] J. Campbell, 'The Late Anglo-Saxon State: A Maximum View', *Proceedings of the British Academy* 87 (1995), 39–65.

[8] See A. Freeman, *The Moneyer and the Mint in the Reign of Edward the Confessor, 1042–1066*, 2 vols., BAR British Series 145 (Oxford, 1985); P. Stafford, 'Historical Implications of the Regional Production of Dies under Æthelred II', *BNJ* 48 (1978), 35–51; I. Stewart, 'Coinage and Recoinage after Edgar's Reform', in *Late Anglo-Saxon Coinage*, ed. Jonsson, pp. 455–85.

[9] For example, S. Keynes, 'England, 900–1016', pp. 459 and 465, 'Edgar, *rex admirabilis*', in *Edgar, King of the English*, ed. Scragg, pp. 3–59, at 24; D. N. Dumville, *Wessex and England from Alfred to Edgar* (Woodbridge, 1992), p. 170.

[10] For examples see P. Wormald, 'The Age of Offa and Alcuin', in *The Anglo-Saxons*, ed. J. Campbell (London, 1982), pp. 101–28, at 118; Stenton, *Anglo-Saxon England*, p. 223.

the king, or by agents whose position was directly dependent on his authority. This management could take many different forms, and areas which have been picked out in the past include imposition of the royal name and title; enforcement of explicitly royal iconography; standardization in design; manipulation of the locations and materials of production; regulation of weight and alloy; restriction of the types of coin which may be used for some or all purposes; extraction of royal seigniorage at the point of production; and power of appointment over the agencies of production. Even at the peak of the late Anglo-Saxon coinage, it must be stressed, not all of these characteristics applied consistently. Weight and die-distribution in particular were only sporadically regularized on a national level.[11] A coinage which was manifestly linked to the king in terms of appearance could thus contain elements of diversity and divergence in its physical aspects; conversely, a coinage without any form of overtly royal title or iconography could be regulated in its circulation, weight and fineness. The danger with any and all such analyses is the temptation to apply false expectations of what constituted a royal coinage – or an ecclesiastical, mercantile or other form of coinage. Disunity did not always mean the lack of interest of royal government, although sudden changes encompassing multiple mints smack of decisions from above. On the other hand, standards, customs, iconography and personnel, once set up, could prove highly resilient in the face of dynastic turmoil or changing political circumstances, and might be maintained for decades without active reform on the part of the king.[12] The essential point is that it is not enough simply to assert the existence of a royal coinage just because one criterion potentially indicative of it is met: all of its other features must be considered before the relationship to royal government can be established.

An important corollary of this is that one cannot focus on the king alone. Interest in the growth of royal coinage, by leaps, bounds or crawls, has tended to overshadow these non-royal elements in its management: the individuals and institutions through which the king manipulated the currency to a greater or lesser degree. Understanding how and to whom he delegated power over the coinage is crucial to contextualizing its historical significance.

The ways in which a king regulated a coinage and its makers varied considerably and must be approached with attention to what contemporaries may have considered most or least necessary to an acceptable currency. This is not a matter easily broached on the evidence of written

---

[11] Below, p. 177.
[12] Cf. the case of weight standards in southern England from 796: below, pp. 171–80.

testimony alone. In so far as it might be taken as a guide to the priorities of kings with regard to the coinage,[13] late Anglo-Saxon and especially Carolingian legislation on monetary issues focused heavily on unity; on the general maintenance of a standardized coinage which would be acceptable to everyone and which excluded all competitors.[14] Weight, fineness and a ban on foreign and especially counterfeit currency were therefore stressed frequently, but this public face of royal currency control leaves to one side many of the details on which modern enquiry has concentrated – design and the delegation of authority, for example, are discussed only incidentally if at all. Orderly management of these and other details underpinned the more general uniformity of the currency and so cannot have been completely neglected; but deduction of what kings, producers and coin-users saw as royal control rests largely on analysis of the coins themselves.

ROYAL COINAGE IN ENGLAND BEFORE *c.* 740

By the middle of the eighth century coinage in England and its coin-producing neighbours stood in a somewhat anomalous position. By classical, late antique and ongoing Byzantine, Arabic, Lombard and Visigothic custom, minting was jealously guarded as a regalian right. The name and (often) representation of the ruler were features of fundamental importance. It was out of this tradition that Frankish and, later, Anglo-Saxon coinage had developed, although in the process the close link between ruling authority and the coinage became lost, or at least obscured, such that in outward appearance there was very little to associate most seventh- and early eighth-century coins with the king.

The rarity of explicitly royal coinage in early England and Francia does not necessarily preclude royal involvement; nor is it always clear what other agencies might have taken a hand in the production and regulation of coinage. But both matters are severely complicated by the anepigraphic nature of most early Anglo-Saxon coins. Scholars have taken a range of views, some seeing royal control over most production;[15] others have laid greater emphasis on the role of moneyers or,[16] alternatively, the Church.[17]

---

[13] Although it should be noted that the composition of extant Anglo-Saxon law-codes and Carolingian capitularies often owed as much to their audiences as it did to issuing kings: Wormald, *Making of English Law*, pp. 477–82; C. Pössel, 'Authors and Recipients of Carolingian Capitularies, 779–829', in *Texts and Identities in the Early Middle Ages*, ed. R. Corradini, R. Meens, C. Pössel and P. Shaw (Vienna, 2006), pp. 253–74.
[14] Above, pp. 40 and 42.   [15] *T&S* I, 10–25.   [16] *MEC*, pp. 158–9.
[17] Gannon, *Iconography*, pp. 189–91.

Inscriptions occur on a small minority of early pennies or *sceattas* and are for the most part explicable as moneyers' names, though there are also two definite cases of royal names on early coins: Eadbald of Kent (616–40) and Aldfrith of Northumbria (685–704) (Figure 4.1a–b).[18] There are also a few small series of coins with legends that strongly associate them with the Church (Figure 4.1c).[19] The most natural reading of this evidence is that, at various times and places, a range of different agencies took responsibility for the production, value and issue of coinage. The rub comes in determining how representative these legends might be for the uninscribed issues; whether the exceptional presence of an inscription is a sign that these coins were exceptional in their circumstances of production as well.

One is forced to turn elsewhere for conclusions, and the most obvious potential answer lies in the diverse imagery of the *sceattas*. However, it is difficult to know how much should be read into seemingly 'royal' iconographic affiliations.[20] Various types and emblems have been advanced as possible examples of royal imagery associated with specific kings or kingdoms.[21] The standing figure flanked by two crosses on Series U, for example, was once construed as a representation of Æthelbald of Mercia wearing a *cynehelm* (Figure 4.2a).[22] Further analysis of the chronology of the *sceattas* and of the art-historical background now suggests that this coinage began at too early a date to be associated with Æthelbald's expanding control, and that it builds on a strong tradition of devotional imagery that could be associated with a range of figures.[23] Determining what constituted royal iconography in the eighth century is therefore highly problematic and depends on matching date and origin with specifically royal imagery, which in many cases is still open to debate. Moreover, even after Offa's reform and the imposition of more obvious association with the king, many elements of coin design remained highly flexible both in content and level of unity. When royal control was exerted over the design of coinage, it was more frequently

---

[18] M. Blackburn, 'Two New Types of Anglo-Saxon Gold Shillings', in *Coinage and History*, ed. Cook and Williams, pp. 127–40, at 127–35; D. M. Metcalf, 'The Coinage of King Aldfrith of Northumbria (685–704) and Some Contemporary Imitations', *BNJ* 76 (2006), 147–58.

[19] Naismith, 'Money of the Saints'.

[20] M. J. Morehart, 'Female Centaur or Sphinx? On Naming *Sceat* Types: The Case of *BMC* Type 47', *BNJ* 55 (1985), 1–9, at pp. 4–6.

[21] For the relatively clear example of the lion (or possibly another quadruped) in Northumbria, see Gannon, *Iconography*, pp. 125–7. Even in this case, however, the same emblem – at least when used outside Northumbria – may not always have been intended to convey the same meaning.

[22] D. M. Metcalf, 'Monetary Affairs in Mercia in the Time of Æthelbald (716–57)', in *Mercian Studies*, ed. A. Dornier (Leicester, 1977), pp. 87–106, pp. 88–90, and 'The "Bird and Branch" Sceattas in the Light of a Find from Abingdon', *Oxoniensia* 37 (1972), 51–65. On headgear see above, pp. 55–6.

[23] Gannon, *Iconography*, pp. 87–93.

Figure 4.1 Coins of Eadbald of Kent and Aldfrith of Northumbria
and of the Church.

expressed through standardization than through use of imagery which
in isolation could be interpreted as unambiguously royal.

Similar difficulties apply to identification of the ecclesiastical contribution to the coinage. Religious numismatic iconography is generally much more clearly identifiable than royal, and was sometimes
of a very sophisticated, polyvalent nature. The bird and branch motif
characteristic of several series of *sceattas* (and indeed of stone sculpture) should probably not be read as a political badge, but as a reference
to the *vitis vera* ('true vine') of John 15:1–8.[24] Similarly the rare and
intriguing archer series appealed on one level to the secular world of
hunting, and possibly also to the story of Egil the archer,[25] but was probably also intended to recall a Christian metaphor of the preacher as an
archer shooting forth God's word (Figure 4.2b).[26] Other emblems, such

[24] *Ibid.*, pp. 117–20.
[25] M. J. Morehart, 'Anglo-Saxon Art and the "Archer" *Sceat*', in *Sceattas*, ed. Hill and Metcalf, pp.
181–92.
[26] Gannon, *Iconography*, pp. 105–6.

Figure 4.2 Imagery of selected early pennies or *sceattas*.

as variations on the cross, could be much less intellectually demanding in their basic meaning.

Christian symbolism on the coinage drew both openly and metaphorically on long and varied traditions, many of which are not preserved in other Anglo-Saxon media,[27] implying a learned and religious background to their production. But the reach of Christian faith into Anglo-Saxon society was deep. It did not stop at the gates of *oratoria* or minsters, and pervaded all levels of lay society, not least through the presence of religious art among the laity.[28] Conversely, the minsters of pre-viking England were flexible in their attitudes towards secular culture, sometimes to the point of accepting dress and artwork associated with lay society.[29] Religious content, even of a sophisticated nature, does not necessarily imply ecclesiastical patronage, and vice versa. A test case can again be found in the inscribed coinages of the mid eighth century and after, on which crosses and other religious symbols remained very prominent, even on those which were not in any way associated with an ecclesiastical institution. Similarly, coins with inscriptions indicating ecclesiastical production, such as the episcopal issues of the mid eighth century and after or the **MONITA S[an]C[t]ORVM** *sceattas*, did not

---

[27] *Ibid.*, pp. 185–6.
[28] C. R. Dodwell, *Anglo-Saxon Art: A New Perspective* (Manchester, 1982), pp. 20–3 and 66–82. Cf. Blair, *Church*, pp. 166–81; H. Mayr-Harting, *The Coming of Christianity to Anglo-Saxon England*, 3rd edn (London, 1991), pp. 254–61.
[29] S. Foot, 'The Role of the Minster in Earlier Anglo-Saxon Society', in *Monasteries and Society in Medieval Britain*, ed. B. Thompson (Stamford, 1999), pp. 35–58; Wormald, 'Bede, *Beowulf*, and the Conversion'; Blair, *Church*, pp. 106–7 and 135–41.

necessarily carry iconography which would otherwise mark them out as ecclesiastical. Christian art and the Church, in short, cannot be assumed to have gone hand in hand, and Christian iconography could just as easily have been deployed on coinages of kings or other laymen.[30]

Diagnosis of the patron of a coinage from its iconography is therefore highly uncertain, especially in the context of the decades leading up to Offa's reform, when there was much diversity in the design of coinage. Yet appearance was only one possible manifestation of a ruler's grip over a coinage.[31] There were many other ways in which a coinage could be associated with or controlled by the king, as listed above.

The early pennies or *sceattas* fall down on many of these criteria. Diversity of imagery, even within the same stylistically associated series, suggests that designs were probably selected well below the level of the king. There is no evidence of centralized die-production for multiple mints, or for anything beyond sporadic and partial sharing of designs.[32] As with broad pennies under Offa and his successors, circulation was not normally hampered by known political borders, while weight and alloy have to be considered on a type-by-type basis, many presenting a picture of considerable internal diversity.[33]

It should be noted that some types of early pennies seem to have been regal in volume if not in form. Michael Metcalf has highlighted the fact that several series of early penny are now known from hundreds of specimens, with comparatively few die-links to be found among them. Some major centres, such as Southampton and (in Jutland) Ribe, seem to have been largely dominated by just one local type: Series H and X respectively.[34] These particular types were large and stable coinages, with relatively little variation in design, alloy or weight as a long series of dies was used.[35] Metcalf's extrapolation is that these series can only have been the product of a large and powerful agency, presumably one working under the aegis and patronage of a king or other major potentate.

This is an important point, but it should first be noted that by no means all *sceattas* formed part of such large undertakings. There could also be important divisions within these series: for example, data from Series H suggest that type 49 – the largest type within the series – was probably produced from 150–240 obverse and 350–400 or 500 reverse

---

[30] Naismith, 'Money of the Saints'.   [31] *T&S* I, 10–25.

[32] *Ibid.* III, 554–69.

[33] *Ibid.* III, 660–79; Archibald, 'Coinage of Beonna'.

[34] D. M. Metcalf, 'Variations in the Composition of the Currency at Different Places in England', in *Markets*, ed. Pestell and Ulmschneider, pp. 37–47. In the case of Southampton it should be noted that this was not true of all Wessex, or even all modern Hampshire.

[35] *T&S* I, 12–17.

dies.[36] If this coinage lasted for many years, then it was broadly comparable to what one productive moneyer of Offa's reign or after could produce.[37] Moreover, just as major centres like London and Canterbury later boasted numerous moneyers, so the greatest minting centres could be home to multiple types of *sceat* issued simultaneously by different sources.[38] Some of the smallest types – including one of the few mint-signed issues from London[39] – are known from only a few specimens, in the same way as the products of some of Offa's moneyers. The larger types presumably represent the product of bigger operations, based either on favoured individual moneyers (like Eoba under Offa) or multiple moneyers using similar designs (such as Wigræd and Tilbeorht late in Series R).[40] Royal patronage could have brought a larger, even exclusive, share of bullion to these moneyers within a given area and also guaranteed long-term stability, but there were many alternative arrangements, even within a large and organized coinage.[41] The Anonymous coinage of Canterbury in the early 820s provides an interesting, if short-lived, example of common standards and large-scale production being maintained in the absence of a king. It is also clear that the quantity of silver available in early eighth-century England must have been very large indeed, and its relative value was therefore possibly lower than in later years of the century.[42] Under these circumstances, even a substantial coinage was not necessarily as major an undertaking as it would be in later times, and so a successful moneyer or group of moneyers could have found scope to work on a large scale without special royal intervention.[43] Even if there was royal patronage and regulation behind a coinage, the evidence of Offa's coinage and after suggests that many of the practicalities were left in the hands of moneyers working under limited oversight.

The anonymity of the early pennies thus conceals how kings may have interacted with those responsible for their production, though the likelihood is that the relationship differed from one coinage to the next. The rare inscribed royal issues explicitly reveal close but sporadic involvement

---

[36] D. M. Metcalf, 'The Coins', in *The Coins and Pottery from Hamwic*, ed. P. Andrews (Southampton, 1988), pp. 17–59, at 31, *T&S* III, 321, and 'Coins from *Wics*', in *Wics*, ed. Hill and Cowie, pp. 50–3, at 51. On the Frisian Series D in this context see D. M. Metcalf and W. Op den Velde, 'The Monetary Economy of the Netherlands, *c.* 690–*c.* 715 and the Trade with England: A Study of the *Sceattas* of Series D', *Jaarboek vor Munt en Penningkunde* 90 (2007 for 2003), 1–211, esp. pp. 74–5.

[37] Below, pp. 198–200.   [38] *T&S* III, 368–83.

[39] Naismith, 'Money of the Saints' (the *Monitascorum/Lundonia* group).

[40] Below, p. 100.

[41] Metcalf and Op Den Velde, 'Monetary Economy', p. 115; *T&S* II, 175, 180 and 222 (though based on Frisian series).

[42] Blackburn, '"Productive" Sites', pp. 34–5.

[43] Below, pp. 192–4.

in Kent and Northumbria. Other series may have been patronized by the king when it came to manufacture and use in specific locations but not the entirety of Wessex, East Anglia, Mercia or any other large kingdom. In other cases there are no traces of royal involvement whatsoever, implying that if there were links between the king and the minting agency they must have been of so vague a nature that the coins were royal only in name. The existence of such links is conjectural and rests on the assumption that kings simply must have played a direct role in all that went on in their territories, which is far from clear in the context of the raw, patchwork kingdoms which constituted early Anglo-Saxon England.[44] In sum, if kings were concerned with the production of coinage at large in the seventh and early eighth centuries, their interest was not enforced in a strict or uniform manner.

A more productive view of early Anglo-Saxon coinage requires a more nuanced approach than royal versus non-royal coinage. Probably the best scheme to accommodate their variation in scale and organization is one which allows for the involvement of a broad spectrum of authorities and individuals. Patrons behind coinage may have included kings, bishops, abbots and secular aristocrats, and it was these figures who could provide the authority and perhaps the personal wealth needed to support the scale and localized use of certain coinages.[45] These magnates do not seem to have had any expectation of exclusive or general control over coinage, and all of them must have worked – often quite loosely – through subordinate moneyers, many more of whom might have operated on their own account.[46] It was probably in the role of these moneyers that the coinages of southern England saw most continuity across the eighth century. The extent of the king's role was the key new feature introduced in the middle of the century.

THE ESTABLISHMENT OF ROYAL COINAGES IN NORTHWEST EUROPE *c.* 740–*c.* 770

It might be contended that the basic continuity of Anglo-Saxon government over the eighth century suggests underlying stability in minting management, and that Offa's reform merely revealed what had already been going on behind a curtain of anonymity for many decades.[47] But the wider international context of the coinage tells a different story. Offa's reform was part of a larger process in which kings in northwest Europe

---

[44] Above, pp. 19–21, and Bassett, ed., *Origins of Anglo-Saxon Kingdoms*. For Frankish parallels I. N. Wood, *The Merovingian Kingdoms 450–751* (Harlow, 1994), pp. 301–3.

[45] On treasure, see above, pp. 32 and 42.

[46] See also Maddicott, 'Prosperity, Power', p. 64.   [47] *T&S* I, 12–13.

began to involve themselves closely and consistently with the coinage during a widespread monetary decline.[48] Shortage of bullion was probably the principal factor leading up to this, and its effects were strongest and most easily traced in the Anglo-Saxon kingdoms, where the volume and precious-metal content of *sceattas* declined substantially from around the 730s. By the 740s and 750s most series of *sceat* had come to an end and the survivors were rare, debased and of low weight.[49]

The response to this downturn began in Northumbria. There, around 740, Eadberht instituted a new coinage of more reliable weight and metal standard, which was modelled in design on the earlier issues of Aldfrith and included an inscription naming the king (Figure 4.3a). Eadberht's new coinage seems to have been based on a general recoinage of older currency, and thereafter all other issues were excluded from use within Northumbria:[50] a powerful statement of the efficacy of Northumbrian government at this time, even after the heyday chronicled by Bede.[51] Beonna, king of the East Angles (749–c. 760), followed suit about a decade later. His new coinage likewise utilized an improved silver alloy and a more consistent weight, as well as an aniconic obverse design based on the king's name and title (Figure 4.3b).[52] One local practice which Beonna's coinage inherited was the use of the moneyer's name as a reverse design. This had emerged during the last stages of the East Anglian Series R *sceattas*, presumably as a measure to help foster the acceptance of an increasingly debased coinage.[53]

These two reforms seem to have exerted some influence on the next major kingdom to undertake a similar move, which was that of the Franks. There the new coinage was instituted at some point 751×755, very soon after the establishment of the new Carolingian dynasty under Pippin III (Figure 4.3c).[54] The new Frankish coinage was broader, thinner and finer than the reformed issues of Eadberht and Beonna, though the aniconic design and general principle of explicitly royal silver coinage probably stemmed from current English practice (Figure 4.3).

---

[48] For more detail on this important series of reforms, see Naismith, 'Kings, Crisis and Coinage Reforms'.

[49] Blackburn, '"Productive" Sites', pp. 34–5; D. M. Metcalf, 'Monetary Expansion and Recession: Interpreting the Distribution-Patterns of Seventh- and Eighth-Century Coins', in *Coins and the Archaeologist*, 2nd edn, ed. J. Casey and R. Reece (London, 1988), pp. 230–53, at 236–9, and 'Betwixt Sceattas and Offa's Pence. Mint Attributions, and the Chronology of a Recession', *BNJ* 79 (2009), 1–33, esp. pp. 12–22.

[50] J. Booth, '*Sceattas*', 'Northumbrian Coinage and the Productive Site at South Newbald ("Sancton")', *ASSAH* 11 (2000), 83–97.

[51] D. W. Rollason, *Northumbria, 500–1100: Creation and Destruction of a Kingdom* (Cambridge, 2003), pp. 171–208.

[52] Archibald, 'Coinage of Beonna', 'Beonna and Alberht'.   [53] *T&S* III, 518–22.

[54] Lafaurie, 'Des Mérovingiens aux Carolingiens'; *MEC*, pp. 203–4.

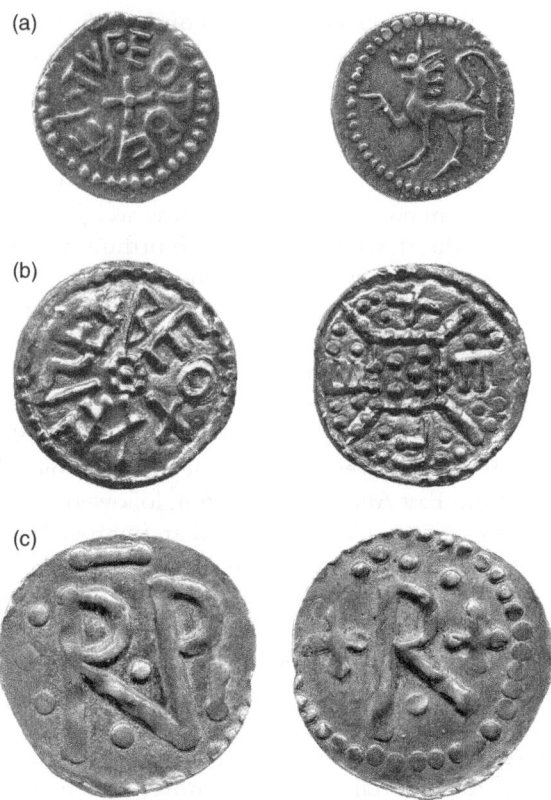

Figure 4.3 The first regular royal coinages of Eadberht of Northumbria,
Beonna of East Anglia, Pippin of Francia, Heaberht of Kent and Offa.

Other inspirations came from elsewhere. The different format of the
Frankish coinage and elements of its epigraphy seem to have been
modelled on Visigothic, Lombard and possibly Islamic precedents,[55] for
example, while the new weight standard of approximately 1.30g was
inherited from practice in northern Gaul in earlier times. Moreover, it
is not clear whether there had been the same extent of decline in volume or quality of silver coinage in the 730s and 740s as there had been
in England.[56]

The reforms of Offa, which probably occurred contemporaneously with those of the native ruler Heaberht in Kent in the 760s

[55] M. Blackburn, 'Money and Coinage', in *NCMH* II, pp. 538–59, at 545. Also above p. 81.
[56] Below, p. 161.

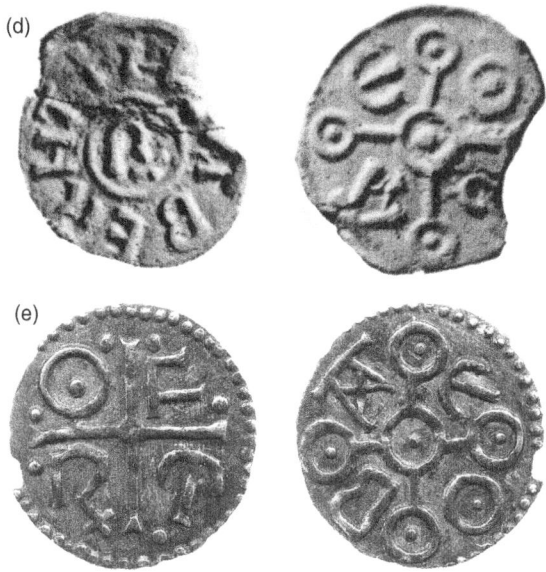

Figure 4.3 *(cont.)*

(Figure 4.3d–e),[57] followed the precedent of Pippin's coinage in most outward respects, suggesting that by then these coins constituted the most highly regarded and probably the largest element of silver which was being brought to England. They used the same broad, thin format, the same high and consistent purity of silver and the same form of abbreviated royal title. However, they placed the moneyer's name on the reverse, like Beonna's coinage, not the mint-name as on Pippin's *denarii*.[58]

No fewer than five kingdoms in total undertook reforms of the silver coinage in the period *c.* 740–70, driven by a combination of encroaching monetary problems and, in Francia, a major political adjustment. All preserved some local traditions, yet were also marked by important common features. The most prominent of these was the universal imposition of the royal name and title, which carried with it connotations of oversight and responsibility for the standards of a new, improved coinage.[59] These efforts at reform were grounded more in ideals than in economic realities, and all of the new coinages either quickly succumbed to debasement or went through a phase of very small-scale production. The key

[57] Chick, *Coinage of Offa*, pp. 1–15; Naismith, 'Coinage of Offa Revisited', pp. 89–92.
[58] For the significance of this, see below, p. 145.   [59] Above, pp. 41–6.

point, however, is that this is the context from which Offa's reform sprang. It did not emerge from a vacuum, but was part of a broader and quite recent burst of royal initiative. This was precipitated, and surely in large part facilitated, by the contraction in minting and coin-circulation in mid-eighth-century England. Whatever royal involvement with the coinage there had been before, Offa's reform was part of a general change in the nature and durability of royal input: the imposition of the king's name, in short, was not simply a recognition of existing practice but a genuine innovation that evolved out of a specific set of circumstances. These steps established a new baseline of royal recognition and oversight, although in many respects the homage paid to the king on the coinage would prove to be only skin-deep.

THE DEVELOPMENT OF ROYAL COINAGE: THE MERCIAN REGIME 757–*c*. 825

The early part of Offa's reign was highly auspicious from the point of view of the coinage. Theoretically most of the characteristics which defined royal coinage throughout the Middle Ages had emerged to some degree: a common design based on the royal title prevailed at multiple mints, which all used common weight and metal standards. It was the first time a single coinage had been produced on this geographical scale in Anglo-Saxon England. This level of uniformity was not sustained, however. The bulk of Offa's coinage in the period down to the second reform of 792/3 displayed great diversity in terms of style, design and titulature (see Figure 4.4a–c). The breakdown of the coinage's typological unity coincided with its expansion onto a much larger scale in the 780s.[60] It should be stressed that weight and fineness remained more uniform, and so in an important sense Offa's coinage retained greater coherence than earlier Anglo-Saxon coinages. But in terms of appearance and the distribution of dies, great complexity prevailed. Both portrait and non-portrait coins with a variety of royal styles were issued simultaneously. Die-cutting was generally carried out within each mint-town,[61] though there were often multiple die-cutters available, and some Canterbury moneyers apparently had access to London-made dies. Explaining all of these permutations is impossible, but they are easier to grasp if it is accepted that the moneyer – not the mint-town – was the basic unit of production.

The coinage of Offa's last three or four years – the Heavy coinage – re-established a common obverse design and, with it, form of royal title

---

[60] Naismith, 'Coinage of Offa Revisited', pp. 94–5.   [61] Below, pp. 138–42.

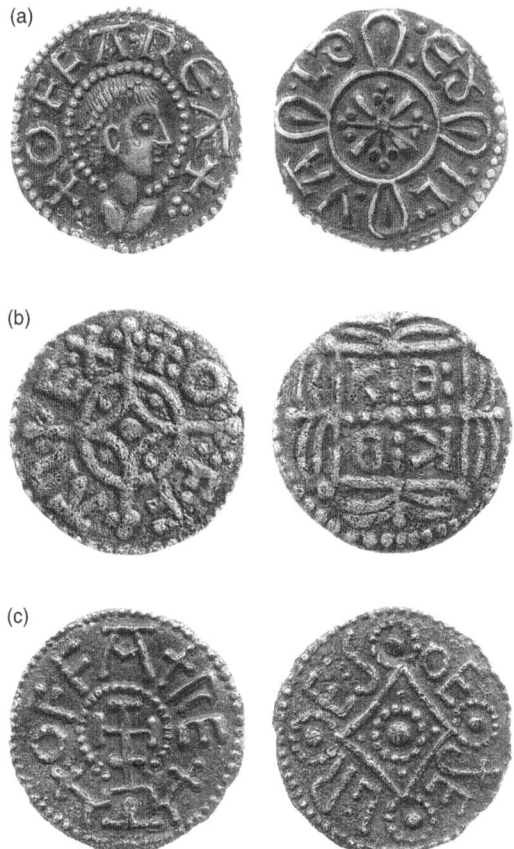

Figure 4.4 Offa's Light coinage, showing specimens from Canterbury, London and East Anglia.

which was used by all moneyers at all mints (see Figure 4.5a–c). This new design coincided with the imposition of a new weight standard.

In many ways Offa's Heavy coinage represents just as important a development as the introduction of the broad penny thirty years earlier. Although unity between mints was to prove elusive for much of the ninth century, after 792/3 die-production and often design generally became more unified within each mint-town. In terms of metrology and monetary circulation, Offa's Heavy coinage also established a benchmark that would be maintained for the better part of a century across Southumbrian England until the viking conquests of the 870s. The three-line obverse design of the Heavy coinage even persisted in separate mints and kingdoms

(a)

(b)

(c)

Figure 4.5 Offa's Heavy coinage, showing specimens from Canterbury, London and East Anglia.

for some time after 796. In the aftermath of Offa's death the three main mints set up coinages naming the new local kings – Coenwulf at London, Eadberht 'Præn' at Canterbury and Eadwald at Ipswich (796–*c*. 800) – all following the same basic design as Offa's last coinage (Figure 4.6a–c).

This monetary harmony in the teeth of political turmoil persisted for several years, even a little beyond the lifespan of the immediately post-Offa issues. In late 797 or early 798 a new design of coinage was instituted at

Figure 4.6 The three-line coinages of 796–8.

London. Its most prominent features were a large uncial M in the centre of the obverse, which formed the final part of the royal title *rex Merciorum*, and a tribrach device on the reverse around which the moneyer's name was arranged. Yet despite the overt reference to Mercia this design was copied by contemporary die-cutters for a few moneyers at Canterbury and Ipswich striking in the name of Eadberht 'Præn' and Eadwald. One finds it difficult to believe that the local rulers would have knowingly endorsed this coinage, and it is telling that although it strongly influenced the first issues of the West Saxon mint under Beorhtric around this time, there the uncial ꟿ for *Merciorum* was joined by an Ⱥ. Thus the design was subtly reinterpreted as an alpha and omega monogram, transforming the political overtones of the design into a religious emblem. The Tribrach coinage illustrates how firm the recently established precedent of unity in design (based, it seems, on Mercian or London practice) had become, and how details of design were not always determined by the king.[62]

By approximately 800 Kent and East Anglia had been brought back under Mercian rule. The coinage struck in Coenwulf's name over the next two decades presents a complex picture of surprisingly close management in some respects and considerable diversity in others, even within each mint. The most striking feature is the rigid and universal standardization at all mints of the royal name and title. In all coinages from 797/8, Coenwulf was recognized as **COENVVLF REX ꟿ**[*erciorum*].[63] This uniformity contrasts sharply with the Light coinage of Offa's reign, and even with the later coinages of West Saxon rulers, under whom greater variation in name and title suggests no attempt at a single form.

Yet stipulation of a prescribed form of title, and the now traditional maintenance of established weight and metal standards, was as far as standardization went in Coenwulf's reign. London, Canterbury and (after *c.* 810) Rochester retained only general coherence of design. The next substantive change in the coinage of these centres came at approximately the time of Archbishop Wulfred's accession in 805, when both London and Canterbury moved over to portrait designs. But there was no attempt to co-ordinate the reverse designs used at the two mints, and within Canterbury a wide variety of devices was used. Rochester followed a similar pattern of portrait obverses with diverse reverse designs following its establishment in about 810. All three southeastern mints were responsible for their own production of dies. The Ipswich mint followed a divergent path. It used the standard form of royal style, but seems to have adopted a portrait design immediately after being retaken from Eadwald *c.* 800,[64] at the time when the Tribrach design had just been extended from London to Canterbury. No attempt seems to have been made to regularize the reverse designs of the East Anglian moneyers, who stuck with the portrait obverse and a variety of (usually personalized) reverse designs over the rest of Coenwulf's reign.

Despite his short and troubled reign, Coenwulf's brother Ceolwulf I left a surprisingly rich numismatic legacy. His coinages were more unified in design than those of previous years, and followed those of

---

[62] For further discussion see R. Naismith, 'Tribrach Pennies of Eadberht "Præn" and Eadwald', *BNJ* 78 (2008), 216–22; and, pp. 71–3 and 125.

[63] Above, p. 82–3.   [64] Naismith, *Coinage of Southern England*.

Figure 4.7 Coins of Ceolwulf I with extended titulature and three-line design.

his brother in maintaining some regulation of the royal name and title. Two major standardized types are known, one from London and Canterbury and featuring an unusual non-portrait design with the royal title given in extended form (**REX MERCIORVM**) around a standing cross (Figure 4.7a–c); the other with a portrait obverse like that of

Coenwulf's later years combined with a three-line reverse.[65] This type was produced at Canterbury, Rochester and Ipswich; no specimens survive from London, though coins of this mint are so rare that the possibility of its production there cannot be ruled out. It was the last and only type after the 790s to be struck in East Anglia in addition to the southeastern mints.

For a short time, therefore, a policy of greater standardization was implemented in southern England. But the keynote of these decades of Mercian dominance was one of diversity within the parameters allowed by established weight, fineness and exclusion of foreign coin. Unity of design and die-cutting within mints was common by the end of the eighth century, but wider unification of title and design was sporadic and depended on the priorities of individual rulers.

THE DEVELOPMENT OF ROYAL COINAGE: THE WEST
SAXON REGIME *c.* 825–65

Prior to Ecgberht's conquest of Kent, Essex, Sussex and Surrey in 825, West Saxon coinage and its relationship to the king had not, it seems, differed very markedly from that of contemporary Mercia. Minting seems to have taken place at one location, probably Southampton,[66] and the pennies from it used the same format and weight standard as contemporary Mercian issues. As at the mints under Mercian control, the various moneyers within Wessex by and large used the same couple of coin designs. This mint was probably the same one that had been responsible for early pennies or *sceattas* of Series H earlier in the eighth century. After a hiatus it reopened under Beorhtric, probably in the wake of Offa's death in 796, and remained active – albeit on a small scale – until approximately 870.[67]

It was the establishment of Ecgberht and his heirs in the southeast which began more substantive changes in the relationship between the king and the currency. At the core of these developments was a firmer grip over the position and work of the moneyers. Eventually this would lead to expansion in the number of mints and moneyers and the increased prevalence of common types, limited circulation and

---

[65] The dates of these issues are unclear, but analogy with the full (OCCIDENTALIVM) SAXONIORVM title of Æthelwulf's earliest coins might suggest that Ceolwulf I's issue with extended title came first as an inauguration type (Pagan, 'Coinage in Southern England', p. 50).

[66] R. H. M. Dolley, 'The Location of the Pre-Ælfredian Mint(s) of Wessex', *Proceedings of the Hampshire Field Club and Archaeology Society* 27 (1970), 57–61.

[67] M. Blackburn, 'Alfred's Coinage Reforms in Context', in *Alfred the Great*, ed. Reuter, pp. 199–217, at 208–12; R. Naismith, 'A New Moneyer for Ecgberht of Wessex's West Saxon Mint', *Numismatic Circular* 106 (2008), 192–4.

centralized die-production.[68] Initially, however, there was nothing to indicate that Ecgberht's handling of the mints he inherited in Kent was to be any different from that of his Mercian predecessors. Weights and metal standards were maintained as they had been for decades. The same cohort of long-established moneyers remained in place and there was no effort to standardize the designs used at Rochester and Canterbury. But soon the moneyers at Canterbury adopted the new DOROB-C type, probably *c.* 828 (Figure 4.8a). Although unremarkable in its iconography and adhering to customary weight and fineness, it did present important organizational changes, most notably of design standardization for an extended period and an increase in the number of moneyers, with twelve known in total. Presumably these did not all work simultaneously, and the increase can largely be explained by the replacement of outgoing moneyers in the course of this relatively long coinage. There was probably no deliberate attempt to muscle out the long-established moneyers; yet even so, by 839 none of the moneyers who had been active before Ecgberht's reign survived, and several others had been and gone: an era of generally shorter moneyers' careers had been ushered in. A further indication that the king's hand weighed heavily on the DOROB-C coinage was the imposition of this type on the archiepiscopal coinage. This was the first time the archiepiscopal coinage had followed the designs of royal issues in thirty years, and it came after an apparent hiatus in the archiepiscopal coinage during Ecgberht's early years – perhaps a punitive measure incurred after Wulfred developed a close relationship with King Beornwulf.[69] The coinage thus provides a valuable complement to other shreds of evidence for a shake-up in the relationship between Kent and its overlord after the West Saxon takeover of the 820s.[70]

Yet the DOROB-C coinage does not mark the start of a smooth or linear process towards firmer royal manipulation of minting. Ecgberht did not, for instance, extend the new style of managing the Canterbury coinage to other mints; Rochester, and presumably also Southampton, operated just as they had before. In the first part of his son Æthelwulf's reign the number of moneyers and the degree of standardization within each mint dropped back to the level seen in earlier times.

One important development which originated under Æthelwulf, however, was debasement of the coinage: a process which must have begun with the king's permission and perhaps encouragement, even if its actual

---

[68] M. Blackburn, 'Mints, Burhs and the Grateley Code, cap. 14.2', in *The Defence of Wessex: The Burghal Hidage and Anglo-Saxon Fortifications*, ed. D. H. Hill and A. R. Rumble (Manchester, 1996), pp. 160–75, and 'Alfred's Coinage Reforms'.

[69] Blunt, Lyon and Stewart, 'Coinage', p. 22; Brooks, *Early History*, pp. 136–7.

[70] Keynes, 'Control of Kent', pp. 120–8; Cubitt, *Church Councils*, pp. 236–8.

Figure 4.8 The DOROB-C type of Ecgberht, and the Inscribed Cross type of Æthelwulf and Æthelberht.

progress is difficult to chart and seems not to have followed any kingdom-wide policy.[71] It implies that in many particulars the initiative still lay with the moneyers, whose input – again probably with royal agreement if not guidance – can probably be seen in the links between Rochester and London in the 840s. But *c.* 849 Æthelwulf's third coinage (DORB/CANT) saw a return to the more interventionist policy of his father. A common design was introduced at Rochester and Canterbury, and it was followed a few years later by even further-reaching changes in the Inscribed Cross type (Figure 4.8b–d). Although the consequences of these developments were to be important in the long term and are demonstrative of changing attitudes towards the coinage, it is probable that they were not part of a specific plan, and instead evolved in the short-term crisis of 854–6, when Æthelwulf was deprived of part of his kingdom.

This chain of events began in 854 with measures taken in advance of the king's departure on pilgrimage to Rome, including the decimation of royal lands.[72] The institution of a new coin-type at both Canterbury and Rochester, apparently with a higher, restored level of metallic purity in its initial stages,[73] would be consistent with an effort to achieve stability in all aspects of running the kingdom before departing. Æthelwulf left for Rome, and on both his outward and return trip he was fêted by Charles the Bald, and even married the latter's daughter Judith at the royal palace of Verberie on 1 October 856.[74] But when he returned home to Wessex he was met with rebellion on the part of his eldest son Æthelbald, who had probably been entrusted with the kingdom of Wessex on his father's departure.[75] Whether this revolt was precipitated by Æthelwulf's marriage – which risked invalidating the succession rights of his four older sons – or preceded the marriage and forced Æthelwulf to cast about for allies is not clear.[76] In either case, the situation was defused after Æthelwulf

---

[71] Below, pp. 163–5.

[72] *ASC* s.a. 855; and Asser, *Life of King Alfred*, c. 11 (ed. Stevenson, pp. 8–9; trans. Keynes and Lapidge, *Alfred the Great*, pp. 69–70). See also S 302–4, 307–8 and 315 and, for the more contentious 'first decimation' charters allegedly from 844, S 294 and 294a–b. For discussion see H. Finberg, *The Early Charters of Wessex* (Leicester, 1964), pp. 187–213; S. Keynes and M. Lapidge, *Alfred the Great: Asser's Life of King Alfred and Other Contemporary Sources* (London, 1983), pp. 232–4; S. Keynes, 'West Saxon Charters', pp. 1115–16 and 1119–23, and 'King Æthelred's Charter for Eynsham Abbey (1005)', in *Early Medieval Studies in Memory of Patrick Wormald*, ed. S. Baxter, C. Karkov, J. L. Nelson and D. Pelteret (Aldershot, 2009), pp. 451–73, at 464–8; S. Kelly, *Charters of Malmesbury Abbey* (Oxford, 2005), pp. 65–91, and 'King Æthelwulf's Decimations', *Anglo-Saxon* 1 (2007), 285–317.

[73] Below, p. 164.

[74] *Annales Bertiniani* s.a. 855 and 856 (ed. Grat, Vielliard and Clémencet, pp. 70–3; trans. Nelson, pp. 80 and 83).

[75] Asser, *Life of King Alfred*, c. 12 (ed. Stevenson, pp. 9–10; trans. Keynes and Lapidge, *Alfred the Great*, p. 70, with discussion on pp. 234–5).

[76] On the motives behind the marriage and the 856 rebellion see M. Enright, 'Charles the Bald and Æthelwulf of Wessex', *Journal of Medieval History* 5 (1979), 291–302; J. L. Nelson, *Charles the Bald*

ceded part of the kingdom to Æthelbald. According to Asser, Æthelwulf took the eastern *plagae* of the kingdom, and Æthelbald the western and *principalior* part of the kingdom.[77] It may have been Wessex itself that was split,[78] with the southeastern territories remaining under Æthelberht, who had been appointed sub-king sometime around 851×853/5;[79] or, more probably, Æthelwulf lost all Wessex to Æthelbald, ruling the southeast alone or in conjunction with his younger son.[80]

Either way, in the last years of his reign Æthelwulf must have been operating in straitened circumstances without access to key royal estates in Wessex. It was probably under these exceptional conditions that the normally ancillary royal resource of the mints, which were concentrated in Kent, began to be exploited more intensively. The monetary separation of east and west during the period 856–60 can only be assumed rather than proven, as only two pennies of Æthelwulf from the West Saxon mint survive, none in the name of Æthelbald or Æthelberht, and just one of Æthelred I. Its activity must have been minimal, and had probably faded to nothing by about 870. At the uncertain point in Æthelwulf's reign when these coins were minted a different design was being used in Wessex, but by the time of Æthelred I the West Saxon mint was using the same design as mints in the southeast. Unless further coins come to light there is no way of telling how the division of the kingdom in 856 affected the West Saxon mint.

In Kent, however, the rare early Inscribed Cross coins gave way to a much-expanded series in Æthelwulf's last few years, which continued under his son Æthelberht (who was likewise ruler only of the southeast until 860). Die-cutting came to be focused in Canterbury for both Kentish mints, while the number of moneyers rose considerably after a dip *c.* 854. Seven moneyers from the previous phase were among the ten known at Canterbury in Æthelwulf's DORB/CANT type, but just two of these ten

---

(London and New York, 1992), p. 182; Kirby, *Earliest English Kings*, pp. 164–7; P. Stafford, 'Charles the Bald, Judith and England', in *Charles the Bald: Court and Kingdom*, 2nd edn, ed. M. Gibson and J. L. Nelson (Aldershot, 1990), pp. 139–53. The broader context of West Saxon–West Frankish relations under Æthelwulf is treated in Story, *Carolingian Connections*, pp. 224–43. For further traces of Æthelwulf's journey in Brescia's *liber vitae* see S. Keynes, 'Anglo-Saxon Entries in the *Liber Vitae* of Brescia', in *Alfred the Wise. Studies in Honour of Janet Bately on the Occasion of Her Sixty-Fifth Birthday*, ed. M. Godden, J. Robert and J. L. Nelson (Cambridge, 1997), pp. 99–119.

[77] For *principalior* meaning 'more important' see S. Keynes, 'The Power of the Written Word: Alfredian England 871–899', in *Alfred the Great*, ed. Reuter, pp. 175–97 at 186; for 'more royal', Balzaretti and Nelson, 'Trade, Industry', p. 163; Nelson, 'Kingship and Royal Government', p. 385.

[78] Stafford, 'Charles the Bald', pp. 149–50.

[79] S 315–17; Keynes, 'West Saxon Charters', p. 1122 n. 1.

[80] Stenton, *Anglo-Saxon England*, p. 245; Keynes and Lapidge, *Alfred the Great*, p. 235; A. Smyth, *King Alfred the Great* (Oxford, 1995), pp. 191–3; D. N. Dumville, 'The Ætheling: A Study in Anglo-Saxon Constitutional History', *ASE* 8 (1979), 1–33, at pp. 21–4; J. L. Nelson, 'England and the Continent in the Ninth Century: III, Rights and Rituals', *TRHS* 14 (2004), 1–24, at pp. 14–24.

persisted into the Inscribed Cross phase. At Rochester six moneyers were known in the DORB/CANT phase, all of them attested in previous coinages, but only a couple of them were among the four known in the next type. Twelve moneyers struck Inscribed Cross coins at Canterbury under Æthelwulf, but only six survived to produce coins for Æthelberht – among the total of fifty moneyers known for the type in his reign. Presumably not all of these operated simultaneously, and just ten continued into later coinages, none of whom had worked before the Inscribed Cross coinage. Not only, it seems, did the number of moneyers active at one time rise, but the turnover of moneyer activity increased as well.

Fluctuations on this scale could have been brought about by a breakdown in control thanks to viking depredations, also manifested in the debasement of the Inscribed Cross coinage.[81] But a more persuasive explanation lies in administrative changes; specifically the division of the kingdom and intensified exploitation of southeastern resources. If royal income was being extracted on a per-moneyer basis, a removal of limits on the number and turnover of moneyers would have provided a larger contribution.[82] Yet to have enticed so many new moneyers there must also have been an expectation of benefit for each individual. This need not have been wholly pecuniary: if the position of moneyer was a desirable one denoting status and responsibility it may have been an end in itself. But the likelihood is that all these moneyers expected at least to break even, and any additional monetary advantage for so many of them depended on a very substantial increase in output – sufficient to outweigh any payments made to the king as well as other production costs. Unfortunately, the surviving sample of Inscribed Cross pennies is insufficient to indicate reliably the scale of production, and overall it may not have been much greater than earlier coinages. A brief but large-scale recoinage or *renovatio* part-way through the coinage, beginning late in Æthelwulf's reign and continuing into the first years of his son's, is the most probable explanation.[83] It would accord well with the circumstances and policies of the late 850s, such as debasement, but is difficult to confirm. Even if the data were more reliable, a brief burst of recoinage would not be detectable from estimates of output for the whole type. Hoard evidence from the 850s and 860s, moreover, is too sparse to confirm a recoinage: the only pertinent hoards from within Wessex and the southeast are those from Croydon (*c.* 1906), which probably belongs to

[81] Pagan, 'Coinage in Southern England', pp. 57–8; D. N. Dumville, 'Textual Archaeology and Northumbrian History Subsequent to Bede', in *Coinage in Ninth-Century Northumbria*, ed. D. M. Metcalf (Oxford, 1987), pp. 43–55, at 55.

[82] Blackburn, 'Alfred's Coinage Reforms', p. 204.

[83] Pagan, 'Coinage in Southern England', pp. 58–60.

the early years of the new coinage before *renovatio* began, and Dorking (1817), which was a large hoard probably representing some element of savings rather than currency; even so, approximately half of its 700 or so coins were of the Inscribed Cross type, alongside only four post-*c.* 854 Mercian or East Anglian coins. Some sort of major change clearly came with the Inscribed Cross coinage. It may or may not have been a success, and may or may not have been a recoinage, although the evidence of the Dorking hoard and the persistence of similar policies in decades thereafter hint that it was so on both counts. The logical conclusion to this process and the ultimate move in standardization (which obviated the problem of dealing with coin from other English kingdoms at a stroke) came after Æthelberht's death, when the West Saxon mints adopted the same Lunettes coinage as the Mercian mints.[84]

Thus, through fits and starts, Ecgberht's dynasty exerted a higher degree of royal control over the coinage. This was of a primarily administrative nature, with little innovation in terms of 'propaganda' in imagery or titulature, but while moneyers remained prominent as the basis of minting organization, surges in their number along with the demise of long-established personnel resulted in the dilution of their role. Equally, the emphasis on mint-wide and eventually inter-mint and inter-kingdom standardization grew considerably, and was soon followed by expansion of the minting network itself in both Wessex and Mercia: a development which favoured the interests of king and kingdom, but not of the old, tightly focused moneyers of eastern England. The middle decades of the ninth century thus saw the foundation of the stronger royal grip on currency and minting, albeit still in partnership with the moneyers rather than any other administrative agency, that would be characteristic of later Anglo-Saxon England.

CASE STUDIES IN ROYAL COINAGE I: GOLD COINAGE

Two exceptional coins of the Mercian regime which buck a number of trends in the contemporary silver coinage are the so-called Offa dinar and Coenwulf mancus. Gold coins such as these worked very differently from silver at this time, and so their position should not be taken as representative of the currency at large. They belonged to a sphere of high-value and high-prestige exchange, and were seemingly made on an ad hoc, case-by-case basis with few restrictions on production and design; thus there could be a sharper emphasis on the structure of authority behind their manufacture, closely connected with the symbolic value of the more precious

---

[84] Blackburn, 'Alfred's Coinage Reforms', pp. 204–5; *MEC*, pp. 310–13.

Figure 4.9 The Offa dinar and the Coenwulf mancus.

metal.[85] If there were coinages produced directly under royal auspices, these special, high-profile issues were probably among them.

In the case of the Offa dinar (Figure 4.9a), there is a good case to be made that it is one of the 365 mancuses which Offa promised to send to Rome every year in 786.[86] 'Mancus' was at this time a relatively new term, probably derived from Arabic and introduced to describe Islamic gold dinars (such as the model of this coin) circulating in Italy, which would have been familiar and acceptable currency in Rome.[87] These were valuable and prestigious objects, closely associated with high-status purchases and gifts: eminently suitable for a donation to St Peter.[88] Their religious

---

[85] Above, pp. 37–41 and below pp. 272–3.

[86] As mentioned in a famous letter from Pope Leo III (795–816) to Coenwulf, written in 798 (MGH Epist. IV, no. 127, pp. 188–9; trans. *EHD*, no. 205). Cf. Blackburn, 'Gold in England', pp. 61–2.

[87] For surveys of the extensive literature see McCormick, *Origins*, pp. 323–42; *MEC*, p. 327; Blackburn, 'Gold in England', pp. 57–9. For a different and more cautious reading of the Italian evidence, see P. Delogu, 'Il mancuso è ancora un mito', in *774: ipotesi su una transizione. Atti del seminario di Poggibonsi, 16–18 febbraio 2006*, ed. S. Gasparri (Turnhout, 2008), pp. 141–59.

[88] Below, pp. 272.

significance was concealed by the unintelligibility of their legends. If the Offa dinar was indeed made from royal gold as part of Offa's gift (and perhaps for other, similar expenses) then its production surely lies close to the king and the ruling elite's expectation of high-value coinage. In appearance, it replicated the legends of a dinar, which served to guarantee the model's acceptability to Christian as well as Muslim users; the only debt it owes to contemporary Anglo-Saxon numismatic iconography is the legend **OFFA REX** inserted (upside down) into the Arabic. What made the coin royal was not its design as such, but rather its inscription and its probable use in the king's affairs.

Unlike the Offa dinar, the Coenwulf mancus (Figure 4.9b) is closely comparable to the contemporary silver coinage in its design.[89] The obverse replicates almost exactly the appearance of the dies used to strike the Cross-and-Wedges penny coinage at Canterbury in the period *c.* 805–10; the one departure is the omission of the inner circle separating the inscription from the bust. This small difference may have been intended as a safeguard against the misuse of regular silver dies for striking gold, or vice versa. The central floral device of the reverse is also paralleled in the silver issues of Canterbury, though only on coins probably issued several years later.[90] In this case the likelihood is that the mancus inspired the design of the later pennies. The reverse inscription of the mancus is its most exceptional feature: **DE VICO LVNDONIAE**. Mint signatures are rare enough in the eighth and ninth centuries, and this is doubly surprising given the Canterbury origin of the dies. There is no other evidence for Canterbury dies being used at London under Coenwulf, which in itself suggests special circumstances for this coin's production.

It is conceivable that the mancus was actually struck at Canterbury and the reverse inscription refers to the gold from which the coin was struck, or to the place of issue, which might also explain the unusual use of a preposition; a more likely explanation, paralleled by the inter-mint movement of dies under Offa, is that for certain purposes and individuals there was greater flexibility in the supply of dies, which could be sought from the most accomplished of artisans.[91] At this time obtaining dies from outside the home mint-town was highly unusual, and suggests that it was, in the words of Mark Blackburn, 'the product of a carefully considered policy decision implemented by the royal administration'[92] – in

---

[89] Blackburn, 'Gold in England', pp. 62–4. [90] Naismith C41.3.
[91] London portrait dies of this period were of highly variable workmanship compared to those from Canterbury: Naismith, *Coinage of Southern England*. Cf. C. R. Dodwell, *Anglo-Saxon Art*, pp. 44–7.
[92] Blackburn, 'Gold in England', p. 64.

other words, a direct product of the king for his own purposes, commissioned and executed in suitably exceptional fashion.

If the mancus was specifically associated with the king's use its reverse legend should perhaps not be interpreted as 'from *Lundenwic*', but rather as 'from the (royal) estate of London'. *Vicus* was a word of highly variable meaning, which in the Roman period signified a neighbourhood within a large city or an informal settlement of any kind, typically one set up adjacent to a military centre.[93] In Anglo-Saxon England, *vicus* and its Old English cognate *wic* retained this semantic breadth.[94] They could denote a rural estate or village, an old Roman town, a tenement within such a town or a substantial settlement with major economic importance and no Roman past.[95] The latter meaning has come to prominence in recent years, and, at London, the large extramural settlement uncovered to the west of the Roman city in the 1980s and after has become known as *Lundenwic*, on the authority of references in charters and law-codes.[96] But it is not clear to what extent the extramural settlement was viewed or administered as a separate entity to the Roman city.[97]

There is, on the other hand, strong evidence that *vicus* in the context of eighth- and ninth-century London might also have been used of an estate near or within the city, specifically one held by the king. This is referred to a number of times in contemporary documents,[98] and may or may not have been the same as the alleged palaces of Offa and Æthelberht of Kent mentioned in London at various times.[99] Another possibility is that the whole of the extramural settlement at London was in some sense a royal estate, as may have been the case at Southampton.[100] But there were also many other royal estates, without any pretensions to

---

[93] *OLD*, s.v. *vicus*.

[94] Ekwall, *Old English Wīc*; A. H. Smith, *Place-Name Elements* II, 257–64.

[95] See S 125 (BCS 248) for *vicus* as a tenement within Canterbury, and S 141 (BCS 248) and 171 (BCS 351) for *vicus* as a royal estate. In S 148 (BCS 278), even the Roman city of Bath was referred to as a *vicus*. For views on the connotations of *vicus*, see J. Campbell, 'Bede's Words', pp. 108–11; Rumble, 'Notes'; Clarke and Ambrosiani, *Towns*, pp. 15–16.

[96] The term *Lundenwic* first occurs in the law-code of Kings Hlothhere and Eadric of Kent (673–85?), c. 16 (ed. Liebermann I, 11), and subsequently in S 29 (763/4), 133 (790) and 318 (857): see Ekwall, *Old English Wīc*, p. 16.

[97] Cf. Keene, 'Alfred and London', pp. 236–9. There was also a (possibly separate) *portus Lundoniae*, for which see S 86, 88, 133 and 1165, and G. Milne, *The Port of Medieval London* (Stroud, 2003), pp. 29–40.

[98] S 168 (BCS 335) (*oppidum regalis Lundaniae vicus*) and 170 (BCS 340) (*vicus regis*). Cf. *villa regalis Lundoniae* in S 1436 (BCS 384).

[99] Cowie, 'Evidence for Royal Sites'; Keene, 'Alfred and London', pp. 240–1; T. Dyson and J. Schofield, 'Saxon London', in *Anglo-Saxon Towns in Southern England*, ed. J. Haslam (Chichester, 1984), pp. 285–313, at 294 and 306–8; D. Russo, *Town Origins and Development in Early England, c. 450–950 A.D.* (Westport, CT, and London, 1998), pp. 118–19.

[100] A. Rumble, 'HAMTVN alias HAMWIC (Saxon Southampton): The Place-Name Traditions and Their Significance', in *Excavations at Melbourne Street, Southampton, 1971–6*, ed. P. Holdsworth

urban status, described as *vici* elsewhere in the kingdom,[101] and within London, Canterbury and Rochester there are a number of references to closed-off estates or quarters (*hagan*).[102]

Minting at a royal estate would explain many of the unusual features of the Coenwulf mancus. It fits within the extant minting organization while at the same time remaining subtly distinct from the bulk of the silver currency, and was presumably the product of an authority able to command these resources in unusual ways. In this respect it might be compared with, for example, the rare gold *solidi* of Louis the Pious, issued perhaps at the imperial palace of Aachen in 816 and after,[103] or more tentatively with the rarer and less regular gold issues of Charlemagne.[104]

Two points must be highlighted in conclusion. One is that these royal gold coins provide a sharpened insight into how kings could manifest their special position relative to coinage: how they might have a tranche of gold minted to send to Rome, or implement unusual movements of dies and bullion for the minting of gold. The second point is that, just as the looser traditions surrounding high-profile gold coinage could strengthen the emphasis accorded to royal input, so in other cases could they highlight the role of other agencies. Royal gold coins account for only two of the five intelligible English specimens of the eighth and ninth centuries. Among the other three, two are in the names solely of moneyers and one is in the name of an archbishop of York.[105] Like the

(London, 1980), pp. 7–20, at 19. For further discussion, see Lorans, 'Élites et l'espace urbain', pp. 79–81.

[101] S 121, 155, 163, 171 (all Tamworth, Staffordshire), 177 (Barrow, Leicestershire (?)), 178 (Wychbold, Worcestershire). The latter was an important estate linked to salt production: Maddicott, 'London and Droitwich', p. 32.

[102] S 168 (BCS 335), 208 (BCS 492) (*Ceolmundingchaga*) and 331 (ed. Campbell, *Rochester*, no. 25) (*Cregsetna haga*) for *hagan* belonging to specific families. Cf. S 175 (BCS 346) (in which a *haga* at Bexley, Kent is equated in a boundary clause with a *cyninges healh*), 315 (ed. Campbell, *Rochester*, no. 23) (for a *haga* within Rochester described as a *villa*) and 1617 (in which *hagae* in Canterbury are described as *mansiones*). *Tun* was another term sometimes used for urban enclosures or estates (Brooks, *Early History*, pp. 26–7).

[103] P. Grierson, 'The Gold Solidus of Louis the Pious and Its Imitations', *Jaarboek voor Munt- en Penningkunde* 38 (1951), 1–41, at p. 5. See also R. Naismith, 'Six English Finds of Carolingian-Era Gold Coins', *NC* 170 (2010), 215–25. The Coenwulf mancus predates Louis' *solidi* by approximately a decade.

[104] G. Williams, *Early Anglo-Saxon Coins* (Oxford, 2008), pp. 40–5. The date of the equivalent coins of Charlemagne (one each in the British Museum (Dolley and Morrison, *Carolingian Coins*, no. 98) and in the State Museum, Berlin (Morrison and Grunthal, *Carolingian Coinage*, no. 643)) is debatable: *vicus* in Carolingian coin inscriptions is otherwise associated with the mid ninth century, and while the form of title is associated with Charlemagne, the workmanship of the coins is very different from that of his seals or the famous portrait issue of *c.* 812–14. Cf. Blackburn, 'Gold in England', p. 64; *MEC*, p. 328. For another gold coin of Charlemagne, of very different style, see P.-H. Martin, 'Eine Goldmünze Karls des Großen', in *Karl der Große in Ingelheim, Bauherr der Pfalz und europäischer Staatsmann*, ed. K. H. Henn and E. Kähler (Ingelheim, 1998), pp. 37–47.

[105] These are listed and illustrated in Blackburn, 'Gold in England', pp. 85–7.

royal coins, these draw on diverse iconographic influences and were presumably designed and issued on an ad hoc basis. The Coenwulf mancus, which is the only one of the group to approach the silver in appearance and also the latest specimen from south of the Humber, may herald a more general encroachment of royal control over the minting of gold which was getting up steam in the 800s.[106] But on the basis of so few surviving coins the status of gold currency must remain highly uncertain.

CASE STUDIES IN ROYAL COINAGE II: THE INTERSTICES OF ROYAL COINAGE

The number of mints in the late eighth and ninth centuries was small and relatively static.[107] Their locations and output were determined largely by non-political forces, above all by where bullion and trade were most concentrated. Rulers superimposed themselves on these centres, and thus had little direct say over the scale of production. Yet there are exceptions which probably represent issues driven more by political than economic factors. Probable examples include the rare surviving coinages of rulers such as Heaberht of Kent, Æthelberht II of East Anglia, Beorhtric of Wessex and (possibly) Eanred of Northumbria. All of their issues survive in such small numbers – three specimens or fewer in every case – that they can never have been very substantial. Naturally more must initially have been produced, but the absence of new specimens among the thousands discovered in recent decades remains telling. These minor coinages underscore the fact that not only did kings come to stamp their authority on minting, but minting quickly became an important demonstration of status for an aspiring king – even if the economic basis for a substantial coinage was lacking.

Usually these minor coinages were achieved only when a ruler took control over an existing mint for a brief time; opening a new mint altogether was much rarer. Further, for all that small and peripheral royal issues were effectively exercises in propaganda, they usually did not exploit unusual iconography or titulature, let alone alter recognized weight or metal standards. Rather, the strongest statement they made was their placement of the new ruler's name on a coin alongside the title *rex*. Even among more substantive coinages, changing the name of the king was the paramount priority at the start of a new reign. Haste is suggested by an obverse die on which the king's name was recut from Cuthred to Coenwulf in 807[108] – surely evidence for concern over whose name was

---

[106] *Ibid.*, p. 64.   [107] Below, pp. 128–32.   [108] Naismith C24a and C25b.

on the die – and inter-reign mules (i.e., rare transitional coins which were struck from dies of two chronological periods) of only an older reverse die (naming the moneyer) occur in this period.[109]

Unfortunately the historical background of these small and obscure coinages is often equally enigmatic. The one known broad penny of Eanred (Figure 4.10b) may not even be in the name of a known king.[110] All that can be said is that its stylistic and typological affinities are with Kentish coins minted in the mid 850s and before, but that the only known king named Eanred ruled in Northumbria and may have been dead for some years by this time. A number of ingenious hypotheses have been put forward to explain the origins of this anomalous penny, including an otherwise unknown ruler in Kent.[111] But it should also be noted that the reverse inscription is highly unusual (ÐES MONETA, 'his coin'(?)), implying not only an obscure king but an unusual context. A batch of southern-style coin struck at Canterbury, Rochester or London for a specific purpose on behalf of the Northumbrian king, possibly posthumously, is one conceivable scenario.[112]

The addition of a clearer historical context does not necessarily dispel the obscurity surrounding some of the other marginal coinages of the period. Heaberht, king of Kent, for example, is known from one surviving coin (Figure 4.3d) and from two references in charters of the 760s, which do not add up to a particularly informative whole.[113] It is likely that his coins were among the earliest broad pennies struck in southern England, though uncertainty surrounds their chronology and relationship to Offa's issues. Either may have come first, and the confused political situation of Kent in the 760s allows for other possibilities, such as sharing of minting rights at Canterbury.[114]

Similar uncertainties plague the coinage of Æthelberht II of East Anglia (Figure 4.10a). His extremely rare pennies may have been one manifestation of an attempt by the East Anglian king to assert independent rule. Certainly Æthelberht was executed by Offa in 794, presumably as a result of bad blood between the two rulers, to which Æthelberht's issue of coinage could have contributed. The sole moneyer responsible for these coins, Lul, is also known from a recent find bearing exactly the same

---

[109] For an example of such a mule, see Naismith C55.3a.

[110] Naismith U1a.

[111] E. Hawkins, *The Silver Coins of England Arranged and Described with Remarks on British Money Previous to the Saxon Dynasties* (London, 1841), pp. 41–2; Dumville, 'Textual Archaeology'. Cf. E. Pirie, 'Eanred's Penny: A Northumbrian Enigma', *Yorkshire Numismatist* 3 (1997), 65–8.

[112] C. S. S. Lyon, 'Ninth-Century Northumbrian Chronology', in *Coinage in Ninth-Century Northumbria*, ed. Metcalf, pp. 27–41, at 34.

[113] S 34 and 105. Cf. Kelly, *St Augustine's*, p. 201.

[114] Naismith, 'Kings, Crisis and Coin Reforms'.

Figure 4.10 Pennies of Æthelberht II, Eanred and Beorhtric.

reverse design in combination with Offa's name on the obverse.[115] This famous image of the wolf suckling Romulus and Remus was a popular Roman motif used on coins and elsewhere. In Anglo-Saxon England it was probably used first and foremost as an appeal to Roman power and culture,[116] while its reappearance in eighth-century East Anglia in

---

[115] Chick 171 and 186. On his role in this coinage see below, pp. 151–2.
[116] Gannon, *Iconography*, pp. 144–7.

particular has been read as an allusion to the dynasty of the Wuffingas – 'wolf-ings' – who ruled the kingdom in the seventh and eighth century.[117] On such a small, politically charged series as Æthelberht II's this unusual symbolism is all the more striking, suggesting that it did indeed serve a special local function. The wolf and twins penny of Offa probably fulfilled a symbolic role, marking the transfer of power from one dynasty to another through the output of an especially favoured moneyer.

Beorhtric's coinage was in many ways very similar (Figure 4.10c). It stands out for its production at a newly established (or re-established) West Saxon minting-place. Southampton is the more likely location, though an economically minor issue such as this also presents a greater chance of being linked to a political rather than economic centre, such as Winchester.[118] Only three specimens of Beorhtric's coinage survive, all influenced by the design of the Tribrach coinage of Coenwulf. The lack of earlier coins could simply be a matter of poor survival, but on present evidence it appears that Beorhtric waited until the death of Offa before striking coinage.[119] Offa probably enjoyed a position of overlordship over Wessex under Beorhtric, which would imply a restriction of minting rights to authorities keen to stress either overlordship or independence from overlordship, like Æthelberht II of East Anglia. Minting does not seem to have been usual for rulers who accepted subordination. Beorhtric's charters likewise hint that this subordinate position was shrugged off after Offa's death,[120] when coinage as well as documents may have been used to reinforce the king's new powers, though this coin-issue surely was of a token nature: it is difficult to explain the scale or date of production without resorting to largely political motives.

These and other cases reveal the part that kings could sometimes play in initiating the production of coinage for symbolic reasons, although the minting system was flexible only up to a point: there are several cases in which the assertion of kingship through minting seems to have broken down. For example, if Beorhtric used coinage to demonstrate his independence after 796, why did his predecessor in Wessex not do the same, at a time when kings of Kent were already producing royal coinage, and a much stronger case can be made both for the prosperity of Southampton and for West Saxon resistance to Mercia?[121]

---

[117] Bede, *HE* ii.15 (ed. Colgrave and Mynors, pp. 190–1).
[118] Dolley, 'Location of the Pre-Ælfredian Mint(s)'.
[119] M. Archibald in Webster and Backhouse, *Making of England*, no. 223.
[120] S. Kelly, *Charters of Abingdon Abbey*, 2 vols. (Oxford, 2000–1) I, 29–30; Abels, *Lordship*, pp. 55–6.
[121] S. Keynes, 'England, 700–900', in *NCMH* II, pp. 18–42, at 33–6, and 'Kingdom of the Mercians', pp. 10–12. The existence of such a coinage was suggested (P. Andrews and D. M. Metcalf, 'A Coinage for King Cynewulf of Wessex?', in *Sceattas*, ed. Hill and Metcalf, pp. 175–9), but subsequently retracted (*T&S* III, 331).

Another intriguing gap in the evidence is the reign of Ecgfrith of Mercia (July–December 796). It is possible that five months simply was not enough time to implement a new coinage,[122] or that coins were struck for Ecgfrith but do not survive, although this is looking increasingly unlikely after three decades of metal-detecting. Moreover, other short reigns could produce coins, such as that of Harold II in 1066, or Ecgberht's brief spell as king of the Mercians in 829–30. In general, the concept of all coins being linked to a king apparently took hold quickly and effectively, but that is not to say that all kings thought it was necessary to have a coinage.

A further complicating factor for the basic equation of independent kingship with coinage is the occasional delegation of minting rights to sub- or co-rulers. This phenomenon was rare in the early Middle Ages, and in England most overlords' rights were scrupulously maintained. Alfred the Great's overlordship of Mercia was recognized through the production of coins in his name at London, Oxford, Gloucester and possibly Chester, while no coins were issued in the name of the Mercian rulers Æthelred (d. 911) or his widow Æthelflæd (d. 918).[123] The split of the expanded West Saxon kingdom in 957 between Eadwig (955–9) and Edgar (959–75) was not reflected in the coinage.[124] Carolingian examples of shared minting rights are also rare and mostly associated with Aquitaine, where Louis the Pious minted under his father Charlemagne in the period 781–93/4, and Pippin I (817–38) did so in the time of his father Louis,[125] and with Rome, where the popes enjoyed recognition on the coinage alongside the emperor from 800 onwards.[126]

In eighth- and ninth-century England there are only a few examples of certainly or possibly delegated rather than usurped minting authority. One of these is the special case of ecclesiastical coinage,[127] which was for the most part restricted to the archbishops of Canterbury (Figure 4.11a–b). Their names began to be inscribed on coins only shortly after the earliest royal broad pennies from Kent, probably *c.* 776,[128] and persisted until the

---

[122] Blunt, Lyon and Stewart, 'Coinage', p. 40.

[123] Keynes, 'King Alfred and the Mercians', pp. 29–31.

[124] Blunt, Stewart and Lyon, *Coinage*, p. 272.

[125] Coupland, 'Money and Coinage', pp. 24–5; and, for a 1992 hoard composed largely of these coins of Louis, G. de Benedittis and J. Lafaurie, 'Trésor de monnaies carolingiennes du VIIIe siècle trouvé à Larino (Italie, Molise): les monnaies de Louis, roi d'Aquitaine (781–94)', *Revue numismatique* 153 (1998), 217–43. For the coinage of Pippin, see Coupland, 'Coinages of Pippin', esp. pp. 195–9.

[126] *MEC*, pp. 259–66.

[127] For general discussion see Naismith, 'Money of the Saints'.

[128] Chick, *Coinage of Offa*, pp. 8–9.

Figure 4.11 Ecclesiastical coins of Archbishops Iænberht and Æthelheard, and of Eadberht, bishop of London, and Beornmod, bishop of Rochester.

920s, though the archbishops continued to enjoy profits from minting in Canterbury down to the time of Henry VIII. Canterbury's minting privileges were in part a recognition of its unique prominence among the churches of England, and significantly the only other bishopric to enjoy such long-lasting minting rights was the archbishopric of York (*c.* 737–*c.* 870). It has been suggested that the origins of archiepiscopal coinage in Canterbury may go back even further than the inscribed coins of the 770s, and that some specimens of Series K early pennies or *sceattas* should be attributed to ecclesiastical authority.[129] But the complex power struggle of Kent in the 760s and 770s also presents a persuasive context for the extension of special dispensation to the archbishop by one of the successive kings who vied for dominance.[130]

Canterbury was not the only Southumbrian bishopric to be recognized on coins, but it was the only one where the privilege seems to have been institutional rather than personal. Two other examples of episcopal coinage are known, both restricted to the tenure of a single individual, suggesting *ad hominem* concessions under Offa to Eadberht, bishop of London (772×782–787×789) (Figure 4.11c),[131] and, less certainly, under Ceolwulf I, Ecgberht and Æthelwulf to Beornmod, bishop of Rochester (803×805–842×844) (Figure 4.11d).[132] No documentary evidence for either privilege survives, and both incumbents are unfortunately very obscure. Neither, indeed, comes across as particularly prominent in other contemporary sources,[133] whereas other leading bishops – not least Hygeberht, the sole archbishop of Lichfield (787–803) – never enjoyed any minting privilege. The episcopal coinages of Rochester and London were probably due not to the special status of those bishoprics, but to a combination of royal permission and the pre-existence within them of minting. As with contemporary royal coinages, taking advantage of a pre-existing mint was the norm, and the opening of new mints was a very different matter.

---

[129] D. M. Metcalf, 'A *Sceat* of Series K Minted by Archbishop Berhtwald of Canterbury (693–731)', *BNJ* 58 (1988), 124–6.

[130] Naismith, 'Money of the Saints'.

[131] Chick 78–83. For further discussion see Naismith, 'Coinage of Offa Revisited', pp. 78–9.

[132] Naismith R3.1–3, R14.1–5 and R18.1–2. Beornmod is never named on these coins: the feature they have in common is absence of reference to a moneyer, and the invocation of St Andrew on R14.1–5 suggests a link to Rochester cathedral. On the debatable status of R18.1–2, see Booth, 'Monetary Alliance', pp. 69–70; and C. S. S. Lyon, 'Historical Problems of the Anglo-Saxon Coinage (2): The Ninth Century – Offa to Alfred', *BNJ* 37 (1968), 216–38, at p. 224. The bishop continued to enjoy rights to the profits of one moneyer until at least the early tenth century, when this was recognized in Æthelstan's Grately Code (II Æthelstan c. 14.2 (ed. Liebermann I, 158–9)).

[133] On the low rank of London and Rochester see S. Keynes, *An Atlas of Attestations in Anglo-Saxon Charters, c. 670–1066* (Cambridge, 2002), table VIII.

The other instances of delegated rights over coinage were to members of the immediate royal family; to figures very close to the king with important roles to play in the kingdom at large. Cynethryth, Offa's queen, is the most unexpected of these. She was the sole living queen portrayed on coinage anywhere in the early medieval west. The significance of her coinage is, however, difficult to gauge: it was produced on a large scale, but at only one mint by a single (albeit unusually prominent) moneyer. Cynethryth's coinage may represent a formal delegation of minting rights, in the form of the services of a specific moneyer, just as the archbishop of Canterbury enjoyed at the same time.[134] Offa's queen was certainly a force to be reckoned with in her own right,[135] but no other grants of land or privilege to her as a separate entity from the king are known; rather, Cynethryth's power stemmed from an unusually strong dynastic identification with Offa and their son Ecgfrith. All three often attested charters as a group.[136] The very point of the coinage was a royal couple in harmony; whether Cynethryth herself enjoyed formal title to the privilege is of secondary importance, and the fact that her separate coinage did not survive into the last phase of Offa's coinage after 792/3 suggests that it only ever functioned as a branch of the royal coinage. Cynethryth's exceptional issue should thus probably be viewed as a Roman-style representation of familial power, one which could have functioned under the auspices of either king or queen (probably both) but which made a special statement about the importance of Cynethryth in the ruling regime.

More clear-cut cases of delegation of minting came in the early ninth century. Particularly intriguing are the coinages of Coenwulf and his brother Cuthred (d. 807), who both issued coins from the mint of Canterbury in the nine years after its reconquest from Eadberht 'Præn' in 798. Various observers have suggested that these issues could have been either consecutive or simultaneous.[137] Stylistic and typological evidence is inconclusive, and does not reveal any obvious lacuna in the run of either king's coinage (either in the non-portrait Tribrach coinage issued before *c.* 805, or in the portrait Cross-and-Wedges coinage of *c.* 805–10). Important evidence for concurrent production in the

---

[134] G. Williams, 'Mercian Coinage', p. 216. For further numismatic discussion see *MEC*, pp. 279–80; Blunt, 'Coinage of Offa', pp. 46–7.

[135] P. Stafford, 'Political Women in Mercia, Eighth to Early Tenth Centuries', in *Mercia*, ed. Brown and Farr, pp. 35–49, at 37–40; Keynes, 'Kingdom of the Mercians', p. 14.

[136] Keynes, *Atlas of Attestations*, table X. For Offa's dynastic ambitions, see Keynes, 'Kingdom of the Mercians', pp. 15–16; Story, *Carolingian Connections*, pp. 178–80; Brooks, *Early History*, pp. 117–20; Nelson, 'Inauguration Rituals', p. 52; Stenton, *Anglo-Saxon England*, pp. 218–19; Wallace-Hadrill, *Early Germanic Kingship*, pp. 113–15.

[137] For example, Blunt, Lyon and Stewart, 'Coinage', p. 40; *pace MEC*, p. 288.

names of both kings comes from the archiepiscopal coinage, which (until the abolition of the king's name from archiepiscopal issues *c.* 805) was exclusively struck in Coenwulf's name. That is to say, whenever the Tribrach pennies of Cuthred were issued, there were at least some coins in Coenwulf's name being issued elsewhere in Canterbury at the same time. Examination of the moneyers' affiliations further suggests a pattern of contemporaneous minting. Some struck exclusively for Cuthred, some exclusively for Coenwulf and some mixed their loyalties either throughout the years 798–807 or only during one part of the coinage.[138] Just as with Cynethryth's coinage, the best way to understand the complexities of the relationship between Coenwulf's and Cuthred's coinages is to focus on the affiliations of moneyers rather than of the mint as a whole.

Further certain or probable occasions when ninth-century kings delegated minting rights to others are also associated with the rule of Kent, control over which seems to have been closely tied to possession of its mints of Canterbury and Rochester.[139] Under Beornwulf of Mercia, minting at the Kentish mints seems to have been delegated to Baldred, who was probably some sort of subordinate Mercian ruler in Kent.[140] Power-sharing of coinage under the West Saxon dynasty was more unusual. It was at one point suggested that Æthelwulf began issuing coins at Rochester before his father's death in 839, but the evidence for this is debatable.[141] Finally, in 858 the Inscribed Cross coinage of Canterbury and Rochester seems to have switched immediately from recognition of Æthelwulf to his younger son Æthelberht, apparently bypassing the older Æthelbald, who held power in Wessex. All alleged Inscribed Cross pennies of Æthelbald have been identified as forgeries.[142] Given the general rarity of delegating minting rights away from the overall ruler, especially in the case of the West Saxon dynasty, the transfer from Æthelwulf to Æthelberht should be read as an important manifestation of the planned separation of the east and west components of the West Saxon kingdom: an arrangement discussed by Asser though still left murky in many details.[143] If Æthelbald had enjoyed

---

[138] Naismith, *Coinage of Southumbrian England.*

[139] Keynes, 'Control of Kent', p. 112.

[140] Stenton, *Anglo-Saxon England*, p. 231; Brooks, *Early History*, p. 136; Keynes, 'Control of Kent', p. 120; *MEC*, p. 283; B. Yorke, *Kings and Kingdoms of Early Anglo-Saxon England* (London, 1990), pp. 32, 119 and 122.

[141] Pagan, 'Coinage in Southern England', p. 54; answering Lyon, 'Historical Problems (2)', pp. 219–25.

[142] Naismith, *Coinage of Southern England.*

[143] Asser, *Life of King Alfred*, cc. 12–18 (ed. Stevenson, pp. 9–18; trans. Keynes and Lapidge, *Alfred the Great*, pp. 70–4). Above, n. 80, and also Keynes, 'West Saxon Charters', pp. 1123–31; Keynes

overlordship over the southeast there can be little doubt that this would have been recognized on the coinage, as (for example) Alfred's power was in Mercia some twenty years later.[144]

The interstices of royal coinage serve several important purposes. On the one hand, they throw the mainstream of coinage into relief, and force the question of why some coinages were less successful than others. The basic answer seems to have been that the quantity in which coins were produced and used depended primarily on economic forces, which imposed significant limits on the manifestation of political and ideological power through coinage. Coinages produced without (for whatever reason) the full and sustained economic strength of one of the main mints were doomed to insignificance. Consequently kings had to work within the pre-existing framework of minting, and also within the parameters established by earlier coinage.

Yet the minor coin-issues of the period also highlight what royal control and power actually meant. They demonstrate a swift development of the principle that patronage of minting was a royal prerogative and a significant statement of authority. Being named on coins became an important credential of kingship within years of the reforms of the 760s. However, this is not to say that kings exerted equal or consistent levels of influence over the coinage. The majority were content to leave most features intact and allow the coinage to persist in laissez-faire fashion. Often this extended to the design of the coins, and it was exceptional for kings to set up new minting towns or – after the formative reign of Offa – alter the weight or pattern of circulation of the coinage. The greatest advantage royal coinage afforded a king was its very existence: a demonstration that the ruler in question was recognized by the moneyers, and by extension the kingdom as a whole. Any exploitation or manipulation beyond this was at the discretion of individual kings, and might fluctuate substantially within and between reigns. A high level of continuity, to demonstrate that the ruler was following in the tried and tested methods of showing authority, was therefore both a virtue and a necessity of the system of coinage in southern England.

This continuity depended on a well-established minting organization which could function effectively without frequent royal intervention. Due attention has not always been paid to this aspect of the coinage, in contrast to the careful scrutiny which has been applied to the interaction

and Lapidge, *Alfred the Great*, pp. 314–15; John, *Orbis Britanniae*, pp. 40–4; Dumville, 'Ætheling', pp. 21–4; A. Williams, 'Some Notes and Considerations on Problems Connected with the English Royal Succession, 860–1066', *Anglo-Norman Studies* 1 (1979), 144–67 and 225–33, at pp. 145–9.
[144] Above, n. 123.

of kings both in England and on the Continent with other agencies in the administration of justice or the production of charters.[145] Yet the coinage was founded on the smooth operation of three interlocking levels of organization below the king: those of the mint, the die-cutter and above all, the moneyer.

[145] See, e.g., M. Mersiowsky, 'Towards a Reappraisal of Carolingian Sovereign Charters', in *Charters and the Use of the Written Word in Medieval Society*, ed. K. Heidecker (Turnhout, 2000), pp. 15–25, at 20–5; Keynes, 'Angelsächsische Urkunden', p. 101.

Chapter 5

AUTHORITY AND MINTING II: MINTS, DIE-CUTTERS AND MONEYERS

MINT-TOWNS

The production of coinage in the eighth and ninth centuries was intimately associated with the basic superstructure of mint-towns. Yet the custom of naming just the king and the moneyer on most issues obscures the exact number and location of minting-places. On one level this emphasizes that, to all intents and purposes, each moneyer was his own mint. However, patterns of political affiliation, typology and die-cutting style among the moneyers indicate that there was a relatively small number of groups into which they can be divided. Five main groups can be distinguished south of the Humber, and these are usually taken to represent five mint-towns: London, Canterbury, Rochester, Ipswich and Southampton or Winchester.

Minting at the first three of these locations is confirmed by occasional episcopal and mint-signed coins. At London these include the issues of Bishop Eadberht in the 770s and 780s, and two famous mint-signed coins from the early ninth century: the Coenwulf mancus and a unique penny produced during Ecgberht's short spell as king of Mercia.[1] Certain pennies of Ecgberht carry on the reverse an invocation of St Andrew, patron saint of Rochester cathedral, and other pennies of similar style under Ceolwulf I explicitly name the mint: *Dorobrebia*.[2] The archbishops of Canterbury were named on coins from the 770s onwards, and from *c.* 805 and after four royal and seven archiepiscopal coin-types were issued which expressly referred to the location of the mint at *Dorobernia*.[3] The two other recognizable mints in East Anglia and Wessex are never named on coins, nor were they ever the source of episcopal issues. Identification

---

[1] Chick 78–83; Naismith G2a and L30a.
[2] Naismith R3.1–3 and R14.1–5.
[3] Chick 149–59 and 240–9; Naismith C36.1–2, C46.1–C47.2, C49.3, C50.3, C52.1–60, C61.1–2, C62.1, C63.1, C64.1, C65.1, C67.1–69, C78.1–95, C103.1–105, C120–31 and C134–5.

of them rests on careful analysis of coin-circulation and on the wider historical and archaeological context.

Ipswich seems to have been a major hub of coin production in the earlier eighth century, and was an urban settlement of some size and importance;[4] a leading example of the so-called *emporia* or *wic* which grew up between the seventh and ninth centuries.[5] The West Saxon mint is more enigmatic, but the two leading possible locations are Southampton and Winchester; that is, either a town in gradual decline,[6] or a royal and episcopal power base which did not apparently develop into a substantial urban centre until the time of Alfred.[7] On the model of the other known mints, all of which were associated with significant towns on or near the coast, Southampton is the more likely candidate, but the West Saxon coinage was so small that the whole issue may have had a more symbolic than economic function.[8]

Rochester stands out as the only place which is not known to have been a substantial town among the named minting-places of the eighth and ninth centuries. It was also the only new mint opened – or more likely reopened – between *c.* 760 and *c.* 870 in a kingdom where other mints were already active, possibly in response to the deepening decline of London as a mint in the years after *c.* 800.[9] Rochester was in addition the only mint to be completely closed within this period, when (around 860) local production of dies ceased, probably followed soon after by all minting. It seems to have been a subsidiary mint, usually overshadowed by its rival in east Kent. But like Canterbury and London it was an important episcopal centre, and there are some archaeological and documentary hints that further excavation might yield important rewards.[10]

---

[4] K. Wade, 'Ipswich', in *The Rebirth of the Town in the West, AD 700–1050*, ed. R. Hodges and B. Hobley (London, 1988), pp. 93–100, 'The Urbanisation of East Anglia: The Ipswich Perspective', in *Flatlands and Wetlands: Current Themes in East Anglian Archaeology*, ed. J. Gardiner (Norwich, 1993), pp. 142–51 and 'Gipeswic – East Anglia's First Economic Capital', in *Ipswich from the First to the Third Millennium*, ed. N. Salmon and R. Malster (Ipswich, 2001), pp. 1–6; C. Scull, 'Ipswich: Development and Contexts of an Urban Precursor in the Seventh Century', in *Central Places in the Migration and the Merovingian Periods. Papers from the 52nd Sachsensymposium, Lund, August 2001*, ed. B. Hårdh and L. Larsson (Stockholm, 2002), pp. 303–16. Publication of the important reports on excavations in Ipswich is still pending.

[5] Above, pp. 32–6.

[6] Cf. R. Hall, 'The Decline of the *Wic*?', in *Towns in Decline AD 100–1600*, ed. T. R. Slater (Aldershot, 2000), pp. 120–36.

[7] Dolley, 'Location of the Pre-Alfredian Mint(s)' rehearses all the principal arguments.

[8] Cf. *MEC*, p. 169.

[9] Below, pp. 189–91 and 196–7. It is possible that Rochester remained the leading town of west Kent, which had been a separate entity until quite late in the eighth century: Yorke, 'Joint Kingship'.

[10] Russo, *Town Origins*, pp. 200–1; T. Tatton-Brown, 'The Towns of Kent', in *Anglo-Saxon Towns in Southern England*, ed. J. Haslam (Chichester, 1984), pp. 1–36, at 12–16; Yorke, 'Joint Kingship'. S 88 (ed. Campbell, *Rochester*, no. 2) provides one tantalizing hint of the town's commercial activities in the ninth century.

Smaller it might have been, but Rochester may nevertheless have represented a commercial settlement of some importance.

Common features of these five places hint at what drove minting in this period – in particular, all stood on or near the east or south coast and all could make a claim to significant commercial status.[11] Minting, trade and urbanization were not always inseparable, and examples can be lined up, even just from Anglo-Saxon England, of important places and possible towns which apparently did not issue coinage, and of inconsequential places, at least in economic terms, which did.[12] A large number of mints is not a prerequisite for a successful monetary economy, and later medieval England usually made do with just two or three mints in close proximity in the southeast.[13] Conversely, the creation of new mints could be driven by many factors besides commercial demand.[14] Yet at this time the five mints were marked by an eastern, coastal and urban setting, which corroborates the evidence for an important commercial element behind minting and coin-use in this period.[15]

It would be misleading, however, to speak of these five mints as a coherently planned whole. If anything, their location and prolonged dominance are better explained as the husk of a once more extensive system frozen after colliding with economic, political and administrative change. The contraction of minting to these few locations was in the first place a result of the monetary decline of the mid eighth century. It is surely significant that the five minting-places of the ninth century were probably among the leading minting-places in the early eighth century,[16] when there may have been twenty or more minting-places active.[17] Yet even as the broad pennies expanded in volume and circulation the network of mints did not return to what it had been in the early eighth century. With the exception of Rochester, expansion was within the small

---

[11] D. Hinton, 'The Large Towns 600–1300', in *The Cambridge Urban History of Britain I, 600–1540*, ed. D. M. Palliser (Cambridge, 2000), pp. 217–43, at 217–25.

[12] D. M. Metcalf, 'Geographical Patterns of Minting in Medieval England', *Seaby's Coin and Medal Bulletin* (1977), 314–17, 353–7 and 390–1; D. Hinton, 'Coins and Commercial Centres in Anglo-Saxon England', in *Anglo-Saxon Monetary History*, ed. Blackburn, pp. 11–26; G. G. Astill, 'Community, Identity and the Later Anglo-Saxon Town: The Case of Southern England', in *People and Space in the Middle Ages*, ed. A. Reynolds, W. Davies and G. Halsall (Turnhout, 2006), pp. 233–54, at 240–50 (for the later example of the *byrg*).

[13] For movement towards this paradigm in the twelfth century and after, see N. Mayhew, 'From Regional to Central Minting, 1158–1464', in *History of the Royal Mint*, ed. Challis, pp. 83–178.

[14] Below, n. 26.

[15] Below, pp. 252–84.

[16] Metcalf, 'Betwixt Sceattas and Offa's Pence', p. 4. This is, admittedly, only clearly true of London, Canterbury, Ipswich and Southampton; Rochester is rather more obscure.

[17] *T&S* III, 300. It should be noted that this estimate preceded many of Professor Metcalf's subsequent studies of the early pennies, which have indicated that there may have been even more minting-places, sometimes of a small or temporary character.

number of existing mint-towns, not to new mint-towns. This was one element of the king's regulatory role in the partnership that was established with the moneyers in the middle of the eighth century: limitation of the number of places where moneyers could be based, and seemingly of the number of moneyers within those places. The roots of this restriction can probably be traced back to an effort in the middle of the eighth century to limit minting to one location within each kingdom. In practice these locations were already long-established economic and monetary centres, responsible for earlier minting and probably the only places where there was continuity of minting across the mid eighth century. Thus Canterbury served Kent, Ipswich served East Anglia and London served Mercia,[18] and in the same way York served Northumbria.[19] All three southern mints fell under the control of Offa almost immediately, although the principle of restriction to these centres persisted for much of the ninth century. It would only be substantively adapted a century later when Alfred the Great and his successors expanded the network of mints to new locations elsewhere in Wessex and Mercia (generally *byrg*); Æthelstan's Grately code and mint-signed coins reveal the system most clearly.[20] This arrangement of restricting the locations of minting provided benefits to both the king and the moneyers. For the latter, it combined effectively with the restrictions on foreign currency to protect their position. For the king, it was easier to keep order over a specified number of men and locations, the better to oversee the quality of the coinage, and potentially to extract seigniorage from the minting process.

The historical and economic setting of the middle of the eighth century and after therefore accords well with the emergence of a small network of comparatively large mints. Other arrangements – such as distribution of dies from a main centre to smaller subsidiary minting-places or the movement of peripatetic moneyers – have also been proposed.[21] But comparisons from the mint-signed and carefully studied late Anglo-Saxon coinage reveal that patterns of die-supply even at this time were rarely very stable for minor mints, which had to look to various suppliers and sometimes fell back on their own resources.[22] If smaller mints were active two centuries earlier the stability with which they related to the

---

[18] Cf. *T&S* I, 22 (though here Metcalf qualifies the argument as 'one *wic* – one coinage', meaning that most but not all Anglo-Saxon kingdoms were home to just one mint).

[19] E. Pirie, 'Contrasts and Continuity within the Coinage of Northumbria *c.* 670–876', in *Coinage and History*, ed. Cook and Williams, pp. 211–39, at 224–5.

[20] Blackburn, 'Alfred's Coinage Reforms', pp. 205–8, and 'Mints, Burhs and the Grately Code'.

[21] Cf. *MEC*, p. 273. For the possibility of smaller mints under Offa, see Metcalf, 'Betwixt Sceattas and Offa's Pence', pp. 3–4; though cf. Naismith, 'Coinage of Offa Revisited', pp. 78–80.

[22] M. Blackburn and C. S. S. Lyon, 'Regional Die-Production in Cnut's *Quatrefoil* Issue', in *Anglo-Saxon Monetary History*, ed. Blackburn, pp. 223–72, esp. 223–6.

main centres of die-production was quite exceptional. Likewise some moneyers were peripatetic in the late tenth and eleventh centuries in that they produced coins at multiple mints. However, their movements tended to be from a main, larger mint to others in the vicinity: work at widely scattered mints was much less common,[23] and there were harsh punishments for tenth-century moneyers who worked outside the public forum of a *burh* or *port*.[24] There was, in short, a strong bond between urban status and minting;[25] at least, urban status as defined by the Anglo-Saxons. Not every place labelled a *burh* or *port* supported minting, even in the tenth and eleventh centuries, and providing a centre of trade, production and (possibly) population was only one element of their role.[26] Administrative and especially military needs loomed just as large: both *burh* and *port* were standard terms for defensive structures of military purpose,[27] and fortification was a defining characteristic of urban identity across early medieval Europe.[28]

MONEYERS AND DIE-CUTTERS

Although minting seems to have been associated with towns from at least the time of Offa onwards, Anglo-Saxon towns contained no single mint building. Speaking of 'the mint of London' is therefore misleading. Rather, the basis of coin production within Anglo-Saxon towns was the moneyer: a man who oversaw the processes of minting and exchange, and who took responsibility for the finished product by placing his name on the coin.[29] The 'mint' of a town must be understood as the agglomeration of all moneyers active therein, each of whom probably operated his own separate workshop. How this devolved system of minting probably worked is indicated by the twelfth-century document known as the Winton Domesday, which contains material going back to the time of Edward the Confessor.[30] At this stage, Winchester's moneyers possessed

---

[23] Freeman, *Moneyer and the Mint* I, 46–53.
[24] Cf. II Æthelstan c. 14 and IV Æthelred c. 5 (ed. Liebermann I, 158 and 234).
[25] II Æthelstan c. 14 (ed. Liebermann I, 158). Cf. D. M. Metcalf, 'The Ranking of Boroughs: Numismatic Evidence from the Reign of Æthelred II', in *Ethelred the Unready: Papers from the Millenary Conference*, ed. D. H. Hill (Oxford, 1978), pp. 159–212, at 160–1.
[26] H. Loyn, 'Boroughs and Mints', in *Anglo-Saxon Coins*, ed. Dolley, pp. 122–35; M. Biddle, 'Towns', in *The Archaeology of Anglo-Saxon England*, ed. D. M. Wilson (London, 1976), pp. 99–150, at 99–100.
[27] A. H. Smith, *English Place-Name Elements* I, 58–62 and II, 70–1.
[28] C. Wickham, 'Bounding the City: Concepts of Urban–Rural Difference in the West in the Early Middle Ages', *Settimane* 56 (2009), 61–80, at pp. 64–5.
[29] J. D. Brand, *Periodic Change of Type in the Anglo-Saxon and Norman Periods* (Rochester, 1984), pp. 45–50.
[30] M. Biddle and D. Keene, 'Winchester in the Eleventh and Twelfth Centuries', in *Winchester in the Early Middle Ages: An Edition and Discussion of the Winton Domesday*, ed. M. Biddle (Oxford, 1976),

individual houses and separate forges or workshops (*monete*) clustered together on the high street, and several of them also worked as gold-smiths.[31] Occasional inter-moneyer die-links among Winchester coins from this time suggest that moneyers or their dies could sometimes go from one workshop to another, or that one workshop could serve multiple moneyers.[32]

Winchester's evidence of dispersed production in (probably) the 1050s need not reflect the situation at all other English mint-towns throughout the Anglo-Saxon period.[33] At York in the tenth century, for example, minting was sometimes concentrated in the hands of a single prolific moneyer,[34] who may or may not have had subordinates. A high degree of inter-moneyer die-linking in the pre-viking Northumbrian coinage also suggests shared premises for some moneyers.[35] But the rarity of inter-moneyer die-links in the south in the eighth and ninth centuries strongly suggests that a system similar to that of eleventh-century Winchester was already in operation in southern England. Each moneyer was in an important sense his own mint, and as far as Anglo-Saxon law-codes were concerned in the tenth century, legislation of minting was largely a matter of the interaction of moneyers and their king.[36] Organization on a larger level was of secondary concern.

This is not to deny broader structural elements. In particular, the number of moneyers active within a town at any point seems to have been relatively stable, suggesting limitations on how many moneyers could work at any one time. The assumption is that, as in the tenth century, kings stipulated how many moneyers could work in each town. In both the ninth and the tenth centuries, however, a certain amount of flexibility applied in the implementation of these rules.[37] In the absence

pp. 241–448, at 396–422; D. M. Metcalf, 'Were Ealdormen Exercising Independent Control over the Coinage in Mid-Tenth-Century England?', *BNJ* 57 (1987), 24–33.

[31] Gannon, *Iconography*, p. 15; D. J. Symons, 'Aspects of the Anglo-Saxon and Norman Mint of Worcester, 975–1158' (unpublished Ph.D. thesis, University of Birmingham, 2003), pp. 169–70.

[32] Y. Harvey *et al.*, *The Winchester Mint and Coins and Related Finds from the Excavations of 1961–71* (Oxford, forthcoming).

[33] Cf. Biddle and Keene, 'Winchester', p. 422 n. 6; Symons, 'Anglo-Saxon and Norman Mint', pp. 172 and 178.

[34] M. Blackburn, 'The Coinage of Scandinavian York', in *Aspects of Anglo-Scandinavian York*, ed. R. A. Hall *et al.* (York, 2004), pp. 325–49, pp. 341–2; C. E. Blunt, 'The Coinage of Athelstan, King of England 924–939', *BNJ* 42 (1974), 35–158, at pp. 88–93. However, finds of minting paraphernalia from the Coppergate excavations might suggest that this location was more of an area than a single building: Blackburn, 'Scandinavian York', pp. 331–2 and 340–1; cf. C. S. S. Lyon and I. Stewart, 'The Northumbrian Viking Coins in the Cuerdale Hoard', in *Anglo-Saxon Coins*, ed. Dolley, pp. 96–121, at 98–9.

[35] E. Pirie, *Coins of the Kingdom of Northumbria, c. 700–867, in the Yorkshire Collections* (Llanfyllin, 1996), pp. 32–3 and 50–64.

[36] Screen, 'Anglo-Saxon Law', pp. 164–70. [37] Blackburn, 'Mints, Burhs', pp. 167–72.

of written sources for the earlier period, assigning any relevance to fluctuations in the number of moneyers hinges on the correct attribution of moneyers and on all moneyers being represented by at least one surviving coin. Generally speaking, the lack of new moneyers among new finds, especially among coins minted from 796 onwards, suggests that the complement known to modern numismatists is fairly complete. Under Offa, however, there is less certainty, both on the attribution of individuals and on the completeness of the surviving sample.

Canterbury was generally home to the greatest number of moneyers. There was a trend for four or five royal and two or three archiepiscopal moneyers to remain in office between phases of minting, strongest between the end of the eighth century and the 830s (Figures 5.1 and 5.2). Variation thereafter should probably be attributed to new administrative policies on the part of the West Saxon kings.[38] However, the earlier set-up may have made a lasting impression: four moneyers is the number accorded to the king in the Grately code, alongside one for the abbot of St Augustine's (conceivably the fifth 'royal' moneyer in the ninth century) and two for the archbishop.

The Grately pattern also applied at Rochester (Figure 5.5), where three moneyers were allowed (two for the king, one for the bishop), and it was normal for two or three moneyers to survive between phases earlier in the ninth century. There was probably some increase in complement in the 840s, when up to six moneyers are recorded in relatively short phases,[39] and it becomes impossible to follow the different fortunes of Canterbury and Rochester after the 850s.

London occasionally supported up to seven moneyers continuing between some of the phases before *c.* 800, but probably never possessed the eight moneyers mentioned in the Grately code (Figure 5.6). In general London also displayed much less regularity than the other mints in the number of moneyers continuing from one phase into another, especially after *c.* 800 – presumably a feature of its precipitous decline and recovery over the course of the ninth century.[40]

No East Anglian mint is mentioned in the Grately code. However, there is some consistency shown between different phases in late eighth- and ninth-century Ipswich, with three, four or five moneyers being the standard continuing complement for much of the period, putting it behind Canterbury but ahead of Rochester (Figure 5.7).

It is impossible to break down the products of the West Saxon mint into short phases, so the number of moneyers working there at any

---

[38] Above, pp. 106–12 and below p. 142. [39] Pagan, 'Coinage in Southern England', pp. 54–6.
[40] Below, pp. 196–8.

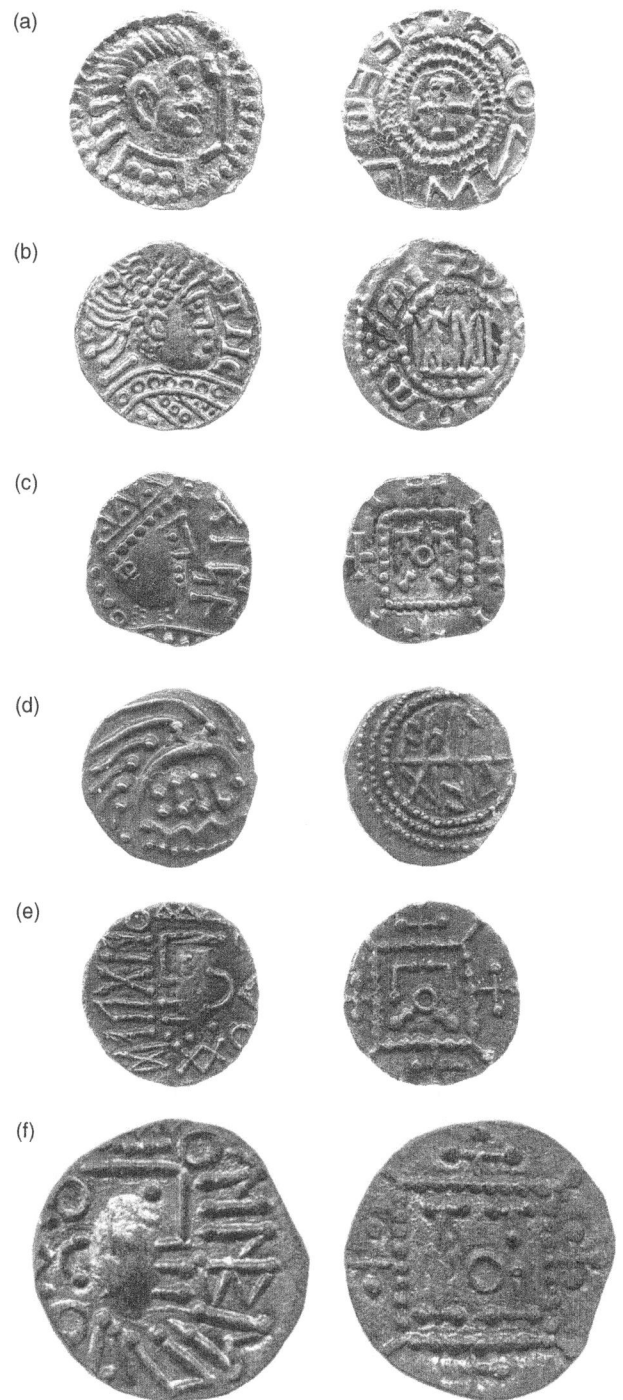

Figure 5.1 *Thrymsas* and *sceattas* in the names of probable moneyers.

(a)

(b)

Figure 5.2 Specimens of the royal and archiepiscopal Anonymous coinage.

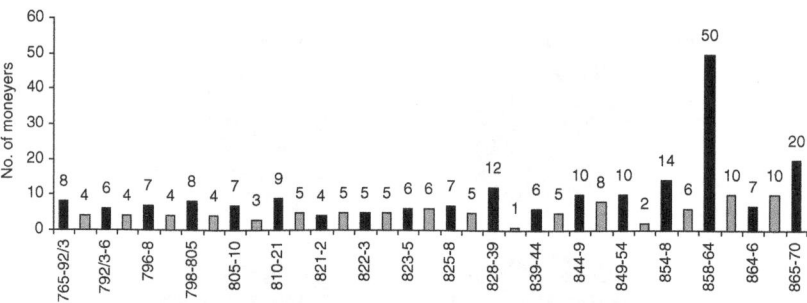

Figure 5.3 Royal moneyer continuity at Canterbury. Here, and in Figures 5.4–8, dark bars represent the number of moneyers in a phase; light bars the number of moneyers persisting into the next phase.

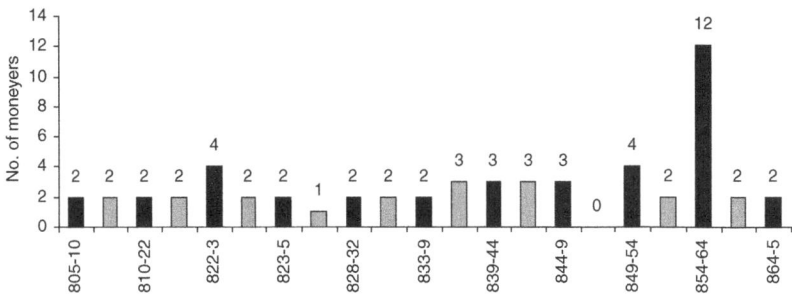

Figure 5.4 Archiepiscopal moneyer continuity at Canterbury.

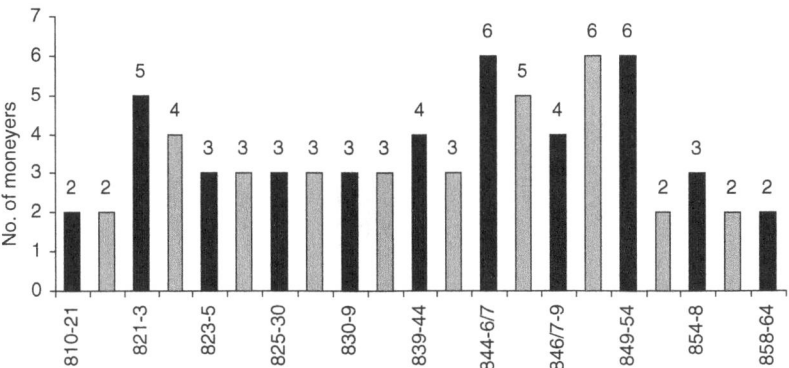

Figure 5.5 Moneyer continuity at Rochester.

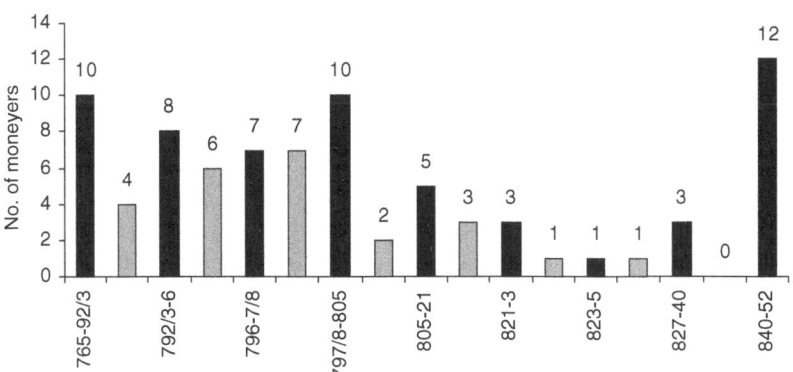

Figure 5.6 Moneyer continuity at London.

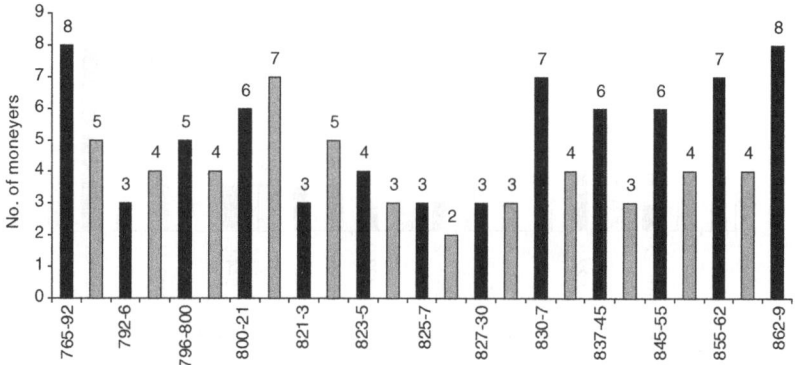

Figure 5.7 Moneyer continuity at Ipswich.

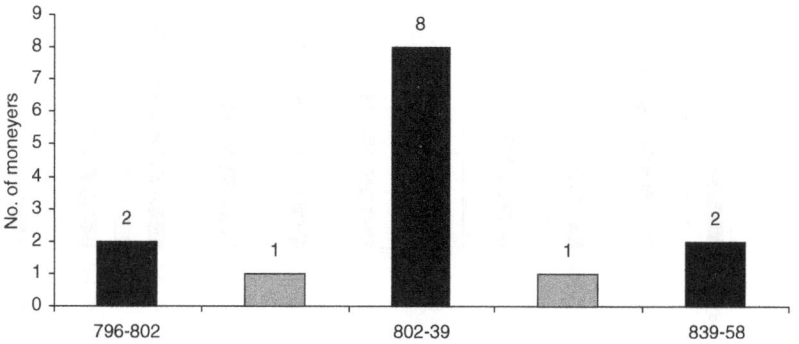

Figure 5.8 Moneyer continuity at Southampton/Winchester.

one time remains unclear, although it was potentially as low as one (Figure 5.8).

These restrictions within each mint-town were complemented by the gradual emergence of at least one element of moneyer co-operation: use of common die-cutters. How and by whom dies were designed and made in Anglo-Saxon England is generally quite obscure. Fast, reliable and high-quality die-cutting required specialized tools and skills which cannot have been very widely available, and were presumably associated with moneyers and with the highly regarded work of smiths.[41] One might compare the evidence of the recent finds from the Thames Exchange site in London, which has unveiled what may have been an eleventh-century

---

[41] M. D. O'Hara *et al.*, 'An Iron Reverse Die of the Reign of Cnut', in *The Reign of Cnut, King of England, Denmark and Norway*, ed. A. R. Rumble (Leicester, 1994), pp. 231–71, at 239–53. On smiths see C. R. Dodwell, *Anglo-Saxon Art*, pp. 72–5; Gannon, *Iconography*, p. 15.

die-making centre where equipment was made or repaired and then distributed to the rest of the kingdom, as mentioned in Domesday Book.[42] But centralized die-production of this sort was unusual before the tenth century, and more commonly dies were made within each town. This seems to have been the norm in the eighth and ninth centuries, although it did not emerge suddenly or achieve instant stability.

In Offa's reign, and especially during the earlier (pre-792/3) phase of his coinage, patterns of die-production were extremely complicated. There were probably multiple sources of dies within Canterbury and London, some of which were closely related in terms of preferred dialectal and epigraphic forms or other elements of design, implying relationships between various die-cutters. The ways in which moneyers worked with these die-cutters varied. One moneyer might spend his whole career receiving dies of a consistent and distinctive type; others drew on multiple sources at different times. The London moneyer Ealhmund, for instance, called on the services of one die-cutter who tended towards the orthographic forms **ALHMVND** and **EALHMVND**, and on another who favoured **EALMVND**.[43] Some moneyers temporarily shared types from a single die-cutter with a small group of others. Interestingly, there were also certain moneyers – Eoba in particular – who were associated with Canterbury but clearly drew some dies from London (though never vice versa).[44] There is a sense about the whole Light coinage of a system in flux, and it is likely that several different arrangements for die-production and distribution were essayed over its course. Certain moneyers may have made their own dies some or all of the time, while the existence of fluctuating workshops of multiple individuals who collaborated sporadically might explain the complex arrangements within mints. Movement of dies between mints was presumably a result of the flexibility built into the system, as well as the freedom and – perhaps – special privileges accorded to certain moneyers.

In Offa's Heavy coinage and after, the making and distribution of dies became more settled, essentially focusing on a single workshop within each mint-town. There were sometimes outlying moneyers who did not fit into this basic scheme. For instance, in the reign of Æthelstan of East Anglia the moneyer Regenhere produced coins of distinctive and generally much poorer style, suggesting that he drew on the services of a separate die-cutter either within the main mint or possibly at a subsidiary mint. This ceased to be the case in the reign of Æthelstan's successor,

---

[42] O'Hara *et al.*, 'Iron Reverse Die'; M. Archibald, J. Lang and G. Milne, 'Four Early Medieval Coin Dies from the London Waterfront', *NC* 155 (1995), 163–200.

[43] Chick 35–50. See above p. 78.

[44] See further Naismith, 'Coinage of Offa Revisited', pp. 85–6.

Æthelweard, however.[45] London after *c.* 800 and the West Saxon mint throughout its existence seem to have been less stable in die-production than the other probable mints of the period. Both were characterized by a multiplicity of diverse die-cutting styles over a relatively short period, suggesting a number of interconnected sources. But a number of sources does not necessarily mean a number of mints. Complex systems of die-production could be a result of these places' smaller-scale and consequently more ad hoc mechanisms of supply and production.

General unity of die-cutting within each mint-town did not erase all possibilities of individuality among the moneyers. Sometimes it is apparent that the same die-cutting workshop was making dies of varied design at the same time expressly for different moneyers or groups of moneyers.[46] Some letter forms (on both obverse and reverse dies) were particular to certain moneyers, even when the die-cutter responsible was probably supplying a number of others simultaneously. Early in Coenwulf's reign at Canterbury, for example, the general rule was for the round and lozenge-shaped O on the Tribrach coinage to be used interchangeably in the obverse inscription. Yet in the case of one moneyer, Eoba, there is only one die out of twelve which carries a lozenge-shaped O and has a legend beginning at 6 instead of 12 o'clock; certainly rare enough to imply a deliberate effort, for whatever reason, to give Eoba obverse dies of a consistent form, on the part of a die-cutter who was comfortable with alternate letter forms.[47] Legends were not the only feature of coinage susceptible to such manipulation. A few years later at Canterbury, the prolific late coinage of Coenwulf (*c.* 810–21) reveals great consistency in the design and style of the obverse and the inscriptions, but a curious mix of reverse designs. A few were common to multiple moneyers – typically four – but were used alongside a selection of other designs particular to individual moneyers. The significance of this arrangement can only be guessed at. At Ipswich in the reigns of Coenwulf and Ceolwulf I the interaction between moneyers and die-cutters was even more complex. There were very few cases of multiple moneyers sharing the same reverse design or, even more surprisingly, the same exact form of obverse. The design of the bust seems to have been deliberately varied, often quite subtly: under Ceolwulf I, for example, busts on pennies of Eadgar carry a double-lined jewelled diadem which required a slightly different rendering of the ear, while Werbald's busts never had a jewelled diadem.[48] Other moneyers' busts had different styles of drapery, or varied in how

---

[45] Naismith E39.1–6, E46 and E51.
[46] For a mid-ninth-century Northumbrian parallel see the work of the moneyer Leofthegn: Pirie, 'Contrasts and Continuity', p. 224.
[47] Naismith C14.1–2.   [48] Naismith E16 and E18.

they were arranged relative to the inscription. These differences suggest that although there was often only one die-cutter or die-cutting centre supplying the moneyers of a town, a conscious effort was at times made to distinguish the dies for each moneyer – presumably to prevent them from being interchangeable and thus reinforce the individual basis on which the moneyers worked.

Movement of dies between mints and the growth of larger networks of distribution are difficult to trace thanks to the lack of mint-signatures on most coins. The most that can be said is that inter-mint sharing of dies was rare and linked with very specific episodes. In the reign of Coenwulf, isolated instances can be found of dies moving between Canterbury and London, possibly Canterbury and Ipswich and from Canterbury and London to Rochester, probably at the outset of the latter's activity when technical support may have been needed from neighbouring mints.[49] More sustained periods of inter-mint die-distribution occurred in the reign of Offa, when certain Canterbury moneyers enjoyed access to high-quality portrait dies from London, and in the late 840s, when London under Berhtwulf received both dies and, it seems, a moneyer (Brid) from contemporary Rochester. This short but intriguing case of co-operation between mints – mints which, it should be stressed, lay under the authority of different kings – has justifiably received considerable attention.[50] Debate has centred on the possible political ramifications, and certainly it would have been surprising had this occurred at a time of open hostility between the kingdoms. Yet monetary collaboration during a period of cordial relations between Wessex and Mercia does not necessarily mean that the exchange was initiated or directly stimulated by Berhtwulf or Æthelwulf. It was confined to the initial years of London's re-establishment as a mint: before long a distinctive local die-cutter emerged to serve the London moneyers. Also, importantly, the collusion of Rochester and London did not result in any coins bearing designs or titulature outside customary norms. Except for the fact that the London coins were made in the style of the Rochester die-cutter and in one case in the name of a Rochester moneyer, they are in no way exceptional. For this reason historians and numismatists should be wary of seeing too strong a political motive in the Rochester–London link of the 840s. Doubtless the kings of Mercia and Wessex did not oppose it, but the connection was of a very technical nature, and accordingly the suspicion must be that the initiative was

[49] Naismith L19.1c, R1.1 and R2.7a.
[50] Booth, 'Monetary Alliance'; *MEC*, pp. 292–3; Keynes, 'King Alfred and the Mercians', p. 6; Lyon, 'Historical Problems (2)', pp. 228–9; Pagan, 'Coinage in Southern England', pp. 55–6.

taken at a level below that of the king – quite possibly by the moneyers and die-cutters themselves.

Altogether different was the last major coinage of Wessex in this period: the Inscribed Cross issue of *c.* 854–64. This historically important coinage saw steps taken towards the system of currency management that would prevail throughout the ninth and even the tenth century. One of these was the centralization of die-production for the mints of Canterbury and Rochester at some point *c.* 854×858, with Canterbury taking it over for both. Rochester moneyers can no longer be traced with certainty, and it is likely that the mint petered out during the course of this coinage; it did not revive until the tenth century.[51]

This survey of the network of moneyers, die-cutters and mint-towns has necessarily been laboured, as these obscure men and structures were the basic building blocks of the minting system in Anglo-Saxon England: it was through them that kings interacted with the coinage. They did so in several ways. The number of places which could strike coins was apparently quite strictly limited, as – with somewhat more flexibility – was the number of moneyers who could issue coins within each town. There was a strong bond between urban or burghal status and minting in law-codes from the time of Æthelstan and after, which probably had its roots in the limitation of eighth- and ninth-century coin production to the mints which survived the mid-eighth-century monetary decline and coincided with the leading urban or proto-urban settlements of the day.

The tendency of royal interaction with minting organization was generally towards maintenance rather than manipulation. New mints, or substantial alterations of arrangements within mints, were rare. A high degree of initiative was therefore left to the institutions below the king, and central among these were the moneyers. Their position lay at the heart of Anglo-Saxon coinage. In this respect the way in which Offa, Æthelwulf and other rulers of this period oversaw the coinage was not in qualitative terms any different from that which prevailed in tenth-century written legislation on minting in Anglo-Saxon England. The focus was above all on the relationship between king and moneyer.

THE MONEYERS OF ANGLO-SAXON ENGLAND

Origins and parallels

Tracing the origins of the moneyers' role in Anglo-Saxon coinage before the middle of the eighth century is in many ways just as problematic as

---

[51] Pagan, 'Coinage in Southern England', pp. 55 and 61; *MEC*, p. 310. Also above p. 129–30.

tracing that of the king or the Church. The same difficulties apply, most notably the lack of inscriptions on most early coins. Moneyers – men who organized and supervised the work of minting and (probably) the exchange of other coins and bullion – must have existed in some form as long as coins had been made in England; the question is for how long they had formed the basis of production, as they seem to have done from Offa's reforms onwards.

It is possible that the great diversity of designs among the *scillingas* and early pennies struck before *c.* 750 reflects the output of a network of small, single-moneyer mints, though some of the larger types and series fit less well into such a system and suggest that groups of moneyers could have shared the services of a common die-cutter using a single design, or that there could have been extreme disparities in moneyers' shares of output.[52] More secure evidence comes from a small number of inscribed issues which name individuals not identifiable with known kings, members of the secular elite or clergy (Figure 5.1a–f). These individuals were probably moneyers,[53] whose names were intended as a point of reference and authentication by coin-users. Towards the end of the early pennies, in the case of the East Anglian Series R, it appears that the moneyer's name became slightly more institutionalized as a pair of them, Wigræd and Tilbeorht, simultaneously placed their names on coins of similar design. The background to this was marked by spiralling debasement and falling output; a combination which may have prompted greater wariness of new coins among users and thus generated a sharper focus on their issuing authority.[54] This was the immediate background from which the introduction of moneyers' names in other mid-eighth-century coinages stemmed, though the earlier cases of probable moneyer-signed coins show that it did not spring *ex nihilo*.

The origins of this personally based system of production probably go back to the introduction of coinage into Anglo-Saxon England in the early seventh century, when the minting of gold *scillingas* began *c.* 620/30, modelled closely on practices in contemporary Merovingian Gaul. There, the norm was for coins to name only the moneyer and the mint, and vast numbers of both are known: more than 1,500 moneyers and 800 mint-places are named on the Frankish coinage of *c.* 570/80–670.[55] These moneyers seem to have been relatively independent operatives, with only infrequent traces of wider organization.[56] Coins in the

---

[52] Above, pp. 94–5 and below pp. 192–4.
[53] For some of the more contentious examples see *MEC*, pp. 166 and 176; *T&S* I, 120.
[54] Naismith, 'Kings, Crisis and Coinage Reforms'.
[55] *MEC*, p. 118.   [56] *Ibid.*, pp. 97–102. Cf. Dieudonné, 'Monétaires'.

name of the king existed, but were rare. Moneyers could work either on their own account, or in the name of the king or a church, sometimes switching allegiance multiple times. Such regulation as existed was primarily focused on the occasional enforcement of common weight and metal standards, and the introduction of silver *denarii* may have been instituted by royal or mayoral decree in the 660s or 670s.[57] Up to a point, therefore, the Merovingian coinage can be characterized as a private enterprise undertaken with only slight and sporadic involvement on the part of the king.[58]

The crucial point is that the coinage from which the earliest Anglo-Saxon issues took their cue was the Merovingian currency. From this the Anglo-Saxons inherited the principle of moneyer-based production, although it was adopted into a context where one of the key fiscal props of minting and circulation – Roman-style taxation of land – was absent, and royal power was in general still quite limited. Consequently Anglo-Saxon coinage developed along different lines in terms of its political and administrative role, yet retained – indeed, probably expanded upon – the central role of the moneyer.

By the time this system emerged more clearly in the middle of the eighth century it had few parallels across early medieval Europe. In the Byzantine world minting remained closely linked to the imperial palace and the fiscal administration, as it had been in the later Roman empire.[59] In Lombard Italy mints as a rule remained under strict royal control, and were usually located in specific buildings associated with the Roman forum of the mint-town, as at Milan, Pavia and Verona. By the tenth century, the mints of Milan and Pavia were operated by, respectively, four and nine *magistri monetari*.[60] A fiscal role and relatively strong royal grasp

---

[57] *MEC*, pp. 94–5.

[58] Hendy, 'Public to Private', pp. 59–70; D. M. Metcalf, 'The Premises of Early Medieval Mints: The Case of Eleventh-Century Winchester', in *I luoghi della moneta: le sedi delle zecche dell'antichità all'età moderna: atti del convegno internazionale 22–23 Ottobre 1999, Milano*, ed. R. La Guardia (Milan, 2001), pp. 59–67, at 64–5.

[59] M. Hendy, *Studies*, pp. 371–447, 'Aspects of Coin Production and Fiscal Administration in the Late Roman and Early Byzantine Period', *NC* 12 (1972), 117–39, 'On the Administrative Basis of the Byzantine Coinage *c.* 400–*c.* 900 and the Reforms of Heraclius', *University of Birmingham Historical Journal* 12 (1970), 129–54; C. Morrisson, 'Moneta, Kharagè, Zecca: les ateliers byzantins et le palais impérial', in *I luoghi della moneta*, ed. La Guardia, pp. 49–58, and 'Byzantine Money: Its Production and Circulation', in *The Economic History of Byzantium*, ed. A. E. Laiou, 3 vols. (Washington, DC, 2002) III, 909–66, at pp. 911–17.

[60] *Honorantie civitatis Papie* (ed. Brühl and Violante, lines 76–94). L. Travaini, 'Sedi di zecca nell'Italia medievale', in *I luoghi della moneta*, ed. La Guardia, pp. 69–85, at 71; R. S. Lopez, 'An Aristocracy of Money in the Early Middle Ages', *Speculum* 28 (1953), 1–43, at p. 30. For wider governmental context see F. Bougard, 'Public Power and Authority', in *Italy in the Early Middle Ages*, ed. C. La Rocca (Oxford, 2002), pp. 34–58.

of minting have also been discerned in Visigothic Spain, despite a comparatively decentralized minting network.[61]

The most pertinent comparison is with Frankish coinage under the Carolingians, the format of which directly influenced the new broad pennies of England. Yet despite this overt borrowing in physical form and design, the administration which had emerged behind Carolingian coinage at this time was not emulated in England. From soon after 751 Carolingian coinage replaced the moneyer's name with the king's, but retained the mint-name. This was not merely a cosmetic change: capitularies from the ninth century repeatedly highlight the *moneta publica* as the basis of minting, located in a *civitas* and placed under the authority of a *comes* or (later and less commonly) a bishop.[62] Like other areas of Carolingian government, minting was subject to the inspection and intervention of royal *missi*, but on a day-to-day basis the count was the key figure in organizing and overseeing the production of coinage. Thus a fragmentary capitulary on coinage of *c.* 820 decrees 'civitatis illius moneta publice sub custodia comitis fiat'.[63] In a small minority of cases personal names occur on very early Carolingian coins in place of the mint-name, but without the common earlier label of *monetarius*. As several among them can probably be identified with known magnates, it is likely that these names now represent *comites* rather than moneyers.[64] Carolingian moneyers faded into the background except as subordinates of the *comes* linked to the *moneta publica* and were only occasionally called upon for technical purposes; comital authority and guarantee henceforth took precedence over the moneyer's responsibility. It should be stressed that there were no coins in the names of non-royal secular magnates in England before a brief spell in the reign of Stephen (1135–54), and no firm evidence survives for a substantial role in organization of minting ever accruing to ealdormen.[65]

---

[61] *MEC*, pp. 49–54; Hendy, 'Public to Private', pp. 49–59; Pliego, *Moneda Visigoda* I, 187–98 and 215–30.

[62] J. Lafaurie, 'La surveillance des ateliers monétaires au IXe siècle', *Francia* 9 (1980), 486–96, at pp. 495–6; de Barthélemy, 'Note'.

[63] 'The public mint of that city should be under the protection of the count.' MGH Capit. I, no. 147, c. 1, p. 299. Cf. capitularies of Louis the Pious from the 820s (MGH Capit. I, no. 150, c. 20, p. 306) and 829 (MGH Capit. II, no. 192, c. 8, pp. 15–16) and Charles the Bald's Edict of Pîtres (MGH Capit. II, no. 273, cc. 13–15, pp. 315–16).

[64] J. Stiennon, 'Le denier de Charlemagne au nom de Roland', *Cahiers de la civilisation médiévale* 3 (1960), 87–95; A. Engel and R. Serrure, *Traité de numismatique du moyen âge*, 3 vols. (Paris, 1891–1905) I, 202–3 and 210–11; Lafaurie, 'Des Mérovingiens aux Carolingiens', pp. 41–2; Grierson, 'Money and Coinage', pp. 512–13; Coupland, 'Charlemagne's Coinage', p. 213; Lopez, 'Continuità', pp. 86–114.

[65] K. Jonsson, *The New Era: The Reformation of the Late Anglo-Saxon Coinage* (Stockholm, 1986), pp. 65–8, 'The Pre-Reform Coinage of Edgar – the Legacy of the Anglo-Saxon Kingdoms', in *Coinage and History*, ed. Cook and Williams, pp. 325–46; Metcalf, 'Were Ealdormen'.

Connections and positions

The emphasis on moneyers rather than mints and the apparent prominence accorded to those moneyers were central features of the Anglo-Saxon coinage as it developed over several centuries. These moneyers are, unfortunately, enigmatic in many important respects.[66] They presumably had to possess a working knowledge of precious metals and their handling, and consequently must often have been identical or closely associated with goldsmiths and silversmiths. This technical expertise was not common, and so in itself must have narrowed the pool of potential moneyers considerably. Other criteria for appointment may have been more personal, and based on connections rather than merit or skill. Families of moneyers with other interests in and around their home towns might be tentatively postulated from patterns of alliteration and common name-elements within mints.[67] At London, for example, one might speculate that Ceolheard was connected with Ceolbald; they might both have been related to the *praefectus* Ceolmund who gave his name to a *haga* in London mentioned in 857.[68] Other possibly familial groups among eighth- and ninth-century moneyers include: Eanbald, Eanmund and Eanred at London; Eadberht, Eadgar, Eadmund, Eadnoth and Eadwald at Ipswich; Sigeberht and Sigestef at Canterbury; and Ecghard and Ecgred at the West Saxon mint. A minority of moneyers may also have called on family or other social connections in attracting business from distant parts of the country,[69] and there is evidence from the twelfth century that moneyers could sometimes exchange their products at markets outside their home town.[70] It should further be noted that only a negligible proportion of the *c.* 210 moneyers active in southern England between 757 and 865 possessed a non-native name. The sole cases of names among southern moneyers strongly suggesting a continental Germanic background seem to be Ludoman at London in the 790s and Regenhere at Ipswich in the 830s and 840s. The position of moneyer thus seems to

[66] See in general Stewart, 'English and Norman', pp. 68–75.
[67] Families of moneyers are proposed in *MEC*, p. 100; P. Nightingale, 'Some London Moneyers and Reflections on the Organization of English Mints in the Eleventh and Twelfth Centuries', *NC* 142 (1982), 34–50; R. H. M. Dolley, 'More Thoughts on the Winchester Mint under William II', *Seaby's Coin and Medal Bulletin* (1969), 11–15, at p. 15; Symons, 'Anglo-Saxon and Norman Mint', pp. 180–2. On this use of names and how far it can be pushed, see R. Naismith, 'The Origins of the Line of Ecgberht, King of the West Saxons 802–39', *EHR* 126 (2011), 1–16, at pp. 10–11.
[68] S 208 (BCS 492).
[69] Below, pp. 220–24.
[70] In the 1120s moneyers from Stamford operated exchanges at Oundle and Peterborough, for which they owed 20s. per annum to the abbey of Peterborough: ed. Stapleton, *Chronicon Petroburgense*, p. 166.

have been relatively exclusive, was dominated by native Anglo-Saxons and may sometimes have been cornered by familial groups.

This assumes, of course, that the position of moneyer was a desirable one, for which men may have competed or petitioned.[71] It brought duties, dangers and expenses as well as potential remuneration. This last was not necessarily large or constant, and depended entirely on the pace of minting for each moneyer, which could be highly variable. That said, moneyers were sometimes successful individuals, at least when they are recorded in documents from early medieval Italy and the late Anglo-Saxon period.[72] Underlings might be employed, presumably to do the more gruelling tasks,[73] and one moneyer at Winchester in the tenth century was mentioned in Lantfred's *Translatio et miracula S. Swithuni* as a wealthy man who could put up a pilgrim for several months and who possessed a substantial household and an ornate sword sheath adorned with gold and silver.[74]

The prosperity that moneyers enjoyed was, with a few important exceptions, not derived directly from the high political establishment. Their position was not normally under threat when a new king came to the throne, even if he came from a different dynasty or was a conqueror from a rival kingdom. The moneyers remained in splendid isolation from most of the political vicissitudes around them, and in some cases could see up to half a dozen rulers come and go. An apparent by-product of this relatively apolitical status is that moneyers can only rarely be traced in surviving documentation: they simply seem to have moved in different circles from the magnates, thegns and clergy who gathered at royal meetings. An exhaustive search through all contemporary charters produces a number of names also known for moneyers, but very few of these identifications can be asserted with any confidence.[75] One of the more persuasive (though still far from certain) cases is that of Dunn, a moneyer active for several decades in Rochester down to the late 840s. A charter from Rochester cathedral records how, in 855, King Æthelwulf issued a plot of land in Rochester with various appurtenances to Dunn,

---

[71] Symons, 'Anglo-Saxon and Norman Mint', pp. 171–2.

[72] R. S. Lopez, 'Continuità e adattamento nel medio evo: un millennio di storia delle associazioni di monetieri nell'Europa meridionale', in *Studi in onore di Gino Luzzatto*, 4 vols. (Milan, 1949–50) II, 74–117; also above, p. 144.

[73] IV Æthelred c. 9.1 (ed. Liebermann I, 236). On this problematic composite document, the date of which remains uncertain, see Wormald, *Making of English Law*, pp. 322 and 325–6; Lawson, *Cnut*, pp. 186–7; D. Keene, 'Text, Visualisation and Politics: London 1150–1250', *TRHS* 18 (2008), 69–99, at pp. 93–4.

[74] Lantfred, *Translatio et miracula S. Swithuni* c. 2 (ed. and trans. Lapidge, pp. 266–75).

[75] This search builds on the conclusions in I. Stewart, '*Ministri* and *Monetarii*', *Revue numismatique* 30 (1988), 166–75, and makes use of the invaluable resources of PASE.

minister meus, which Dunn later bequeathed to his wife in his will.[76] He – and perhaps two of his counterparts at the Rochester mint, Æthelhere and Beagmund – may also have witnessed a charter in 858 granting land to another royal *minister*.[77] 'Dunn' is not a common name,[78] and the date and the connection with Rochester suggest that this is indeed the moneyer. If so, however, there must have been a hiatus of several years between his last known minting and the 855 grant, and Dunn was surely an elderly man at this stage after working as a moneyer since the time of Coenwulf.

In Kent in the mid ninth century, at a time when witness lists to charters were comparatively long and broad in composition, several more possible royal moneyers can be picked out: Æthelmod at Rochester,[79] and Hunred, Osmund, Æthelred and Coenweald at Canterbury.[80] These are never references to moneyers in their own right, but to moneyers who also held another position: all are described as *ministri* or *milites*,[81] and there is not a single case of a moneyer being named as such in any Anglo-Saxon document before the eleventh century. It is possible that in a sense all moneyers were royal thegns, for until approximately the tenth century the primary determinant of the title was service, especially to the king, rather than social class or landholding.[82] But these few coincidences between moneyers and thegns are not enough to confirm more than occasional crossover between them.[83]

Archiepiscopal moneyers are also possibly represented in documents from around the same time, and may have included members of the clergy. For example, one of the most prolific archiepiscopal moneyers in the earlier part of Archbishop Ceolnoth's coinage was Wynhere. This is a rare name, attested in only one other case in pre-Conquest England: an ecclesiastic at St Augustine's, Canterbury, who was deacon and subsequently abbot in the 840s, but was probably dead by around 850, and who thus matches the chronology of the moneyer very closely.[84] In 863

---

[76] S 315 and 1514.   [77] S 328.

[78] See the relevant entries in PASE, many of which relate to this moneyer working under different rulers.

[79] S 293, 296, 316 and 319.

[80] S 319, 332, 338 and 1196.

[81] For two more *ministri* possibly identifiable with moneyers in the late ninth and late tenth centuries, see Stewart, 'Ministri and Monetarii', pp. 168–72.

[82] S. Keynes, 'Thegn', in *BEASE*, pp. 443–4; Chadwick, *Studies*, pp. 76–114 and 308–54; Pratt, *Political Thought*, pp. 28–43; Loyn, 'Gesiths and Thegns', pp. 540–9, and *Anglo-Saxon England*, pp. 223–7.

[83] Symons, 'Anglo-Saxon and Norman Mint', pp. 176–7.

[84] He appears in S 296–7 and 1198 (845 and *c.* 850) but is assigned the abbatial dates 864–6 in the later medieval list of abbots of St Augustine's (probably mistakenly: Kelly, *St Augustine's*, pp. 80–1 and 210).

a man named Biarnulf (Beornwulf) appeared in a witness list as part of the Canterbury religious community associated with Archbishop Ceolnoth, described as *presbyter abbas*.[85] A moneyer using the identical Kentish spelling of the name was active in the contemporary Inscribed Cross issue of Ceolnoth.

In the areas around the mints outside Kent, charters and other documents are so rare that the chances of identifying moneyers are almost non-existent, unless they occupied a relatively exalted position such as ealdorman or bishop.[86] One such identification has been suggested: that of Weohthun, one of two moneyers recorded for Beorhtric of Wessex, with a contemporary bishop of Selsey by the same name (787×789–805×811).[87] The dates of the moneyer and bishop are entirely compatible, and the name is very rare; furthermore, at the outset of a new coinage at a peripheral mint such as that of Southampton or Winchester, there was perhaps more scope for unusual circumstances of production. But two finds of this moneyer from 2008 have cast doubt on the link between the coins of Weohthun and the bishop of Selsey. Both the new coins were struck under Ecgberht, not Beorhtric, which suggests that his position was not as exceptional as it previously seemed.[88] There is also the important point that no evidence exists to suggest that Sussex was in the political orbit of Wessex rather than Mercia at any point around this time. Weohthun, for instance, does not appear in either surviving charter witness list of Beorhtric.[89]

Very little is known about the moneyers as individuals, and in most cases they will remain nothing more than names on coins around which a few tentative dates of activity may be reconstructed. Yet as a group they stand out in a number of respects. They enjoyed a relatively direct relationship with the king, at least with regard to minting, but were not dependent upon the position of a specific ruler or dynasty. Rather, their affiliations were local, and probably for the most part artisanal or mercantile, although a moneyer could also be wealthy and perhaps function as a thegn. Some could have been clerics, but it is unlikely that bishops or ealdormen numbered among them. Beyond this all conclusions are dependent solely on the coins themselves and their context. Nonetheless, these have important insights to offer about the ways in which moneyers and their links to higher authority might work in practice.

---

[85] S 332.
[86] For a seventh-century Merovingian parallel of a moneyer and metalworker later becoming a bishop, see J. Lafaurie, 'Eligius Monetarius', *Revue numismatique* 19 (1977), 111–51.
[87] Stewart, '*Ministri* and *Monetarii*', pp. 173–5.
[88] Naismith, 'New Moneyer'.   [89] S 268–9.

CASE STUDIES IN THE ROLE OF MONEYERS I:
FAVOURED MONEYERS

Not all moneyers were created equal. Some appeared and disappeared in the course of just a year or two; others held on for up to fifty or sixty years.[90] Even among moneyers with careers of comparable duration there could be major discrepancies in output, suggesting that some may – for whatever reason – have issued far more coins than others. In a few cases it also appears that specific moneyers had privileged access to the custom of certain regions.[91]

None of these trends should come as a surprise given the probably quite dispersed nature of minting within the towns of eighth- and ninth-century England. However, there are a few outstanding examples of moneyers whose positions, and especially whose ties to the crown, merit special consideration. The two clearest examples both occurred relatively early in the period, during the reign of Offa, when the regularity of the coinage was still being established and the individuality of moneyers was most pronounced: Eoba, a moneyer active at Canterbury in the period *c.* 765–805×810; and Lul, an East Anglian moneyer of *c.* 785/90–*c.* 810.

Eoba's long career began at the inception of the broad penny coinage in southeast England in the 760s. He was responsible for the one surviving penny of Heaberht, king of Kent, and was also the sole moneyer to strike Offa's earliest Kentish coins.[92] Eoba thus took a leading role in the establishment of the broad penny coinage, and consolidated this status during the rest of Offa's Light coinage (struck down to 792/3). He stood out from his fellow moneyers at London and Canterbury in three main respects. One of these is quite simply the scale on which he worked. At the peak of his activity, Eoba probably accounted for some 40 per cent of all the coins produced at Canterbury, at a point when it was home to at least three or four other moneyers. His average of more than ten pairs of dies per annum (in the period down to 792/3) is probably four times that of the next most productive Canterbury moneyer of the time.[93] Why Eoba attracted such a disproportionate share of minting at Canterbury is not clear, though it may well be connected with the other two unusual features of his coins, which relate to their form rather than their volume. One of these is the source of his dies. Despite being based in Canterbury, Eoba was (along with Ealred) the recipient of portrait dies of very fine

---

[90] Cf. Freeman, *Moneyer and the Mint* I, 27–40.   [91] For details see pp. 220–3.
[92] Chick 84, 86 and 102–3. For dates and context see Naismith, 'Coinage of Offa Revisited', pp. 88–95.
[93] Below, p. 192–4.

style which were made in London. This conduit was not reliable or plentiful. Eoba's non-portrait issues for Offa, for example, mostly seem to have been struck from local dies, and some of the coarser portrait dies used for Offa and Cynethryth pennies by Eoba should likewise be seen as locally made substitutes from periods when his London source failed him.[94] It could be that Eoba's unusual inter-mint die supply reveals a temporary transfer from Canterbury to London. Yet there is no obvious lacuna in his Canterbury issues, and thus the likelihood is that Eoba and Ealred had special interests or privileges which gave them access to diverse sources of minting equipment.

Perhaps the most outstanding feature of Eoba is that he was the sole moneyer responsible for the coinage of Cynethryth, Offa's queen.[95] This issue probably began around the time of the introduction of the substantive Light coinage in *c.* 785, and at the time constituted a major issue of currency: some forty-three specimens survive representing thirty-two obverse and reverse dies. The exact status of this coinage has already been discussed, and it should probably be seen as a specially commissioned variant of the royal coinage, not as a formal grant of Eoba's services to the queen. Either way, Eoba must have been a man of special prominence to be singled out for its exclusive production. In the same way, at London Offa or a figure from his immediate circle influenced iconography and titulature in the Light coinage through the work of individual moneyers, suggesting a pattern of specific patronage.[96]

Eoba's position during the first three decades of Offa's coinage was therefore exceptional on a number of levels. He enjoyed a monopoly during the very early and rare coinages of the 760s, and managed to transfer this into a uniquely prolific and privileged output during the subsequent phase of the coinage. But it is telling that Eoba's prominence did not outlast the Light coinage, which was a formative stage characterized by several experimental practices. He went on to work in Offa's Heavy coinage and then in the first two Canterbury coinages of Coenwulf (Tribrach and Cross-and-Wedges, *c.* 798–805 and *c.* 805–10 respectively), although at this time neither the appearance nor the volume of his output was in any way exceptional. The only hint of Eoba's previous special status is his absence from the coinage of Eadberht 'Præn' immediately after Offa's death, which might be a result of his unusually close ties with the Mercian kingdom.

A comparable case from East Anglia is the moneyer Lul. His coinage began with Offa's Light coinage, and he worked until some point

---

[94] Naismith, 'Coinage of Offa Revisited', pp. 85–6.
[95] Chick 138–48.　[96] Above, pp. 84–6.

around the middle of Coenwulf's reign. This included two interludes during which he issued coins for East Anglian claimants to the throne: Æthelberht II and Eadwald. The starting date of Lul's career and the scale of his coinage were not unusual, though he was always among the better represented moneyers of Ipswich. But just as Eoba was the sole moneyer responsible for Cynethryth's coinage, so Lul is the only moneyer known for Æthelberht II.[97] Specific patronage of moneyers again seems to have been the custom, and in this case it implies that Æthelberht's control was either tenuous and partial or held (at least for a time) with Offa's permission in a manner analogous to Cynethryth's coinage.[98] It should be noted that the events leading up to Æthelberht's execution at Offa's command are highly mysterious, and may not always have been characterized by rebellion and hostility, especially if there is any merit to the claims of later *vitae* that Æthelberht sought the hand of one of Offa's daughters.[99] But Æthelberht's relationship with Offa certainly ended badly, and it is in these circumstances that Lul's coinage seems to have maintained the unusual wolf and twins reverse design with an obverse die naming Offa. Unlike the coins of Æthelberht, which placed the word **REX** on the reverse and the moneyer's name (immediately preceding the king's) on the obverse, those issued under Offa moved over to the standard arrangement of the moneyer's name on the reverse. These dies were, in other words, made specifically for use under Offa and abandoned the unusual layout of Æthelberht's coinage. This suggests that Offa's penny was produced after Æthelberht's coinage had come to an end, but retained the same unusual reverse design. The dynastic significance of this motif has been challenged,[100] but whatever its associations it was found only on these two issues. After Æthelberht's death it perhaps served the interests of either the king himself or the die-cutter and moneyer to signal Offa's assumption of the earlier ruler's position.

Eoba and Lul highlight the directness with which kings could at times take a hand in minting, but also that this role might be mediated through specific moneyers. The moneyer thus stood at the centre of the minting process and was the key conduit through which rulers interacted with the coinage. This was, admittedly, strongest in the period before 792/3, when Offa's third major reform seems to have regularized many of the

---

[97] Chick 186.

[98] Cf. Burghart, 'Mercian Polity', p. 165. Another possibility would be that Lul alone worked at a separate minting location: Naismith, 'Coinage of Offa Revisited', p. 79.

[99] Stenton, *Anglo-Saxon England*, p. 210. *Vitae* of Æthelberht survive (M. R. James, 'Two Lives of St Ethelbert, King and Martyr', *EHR* 32 (1917), 214–44), though their value is unclear and probably limited.

[100] Gannon, *Iconography*, pp. 144–7.

more obvious unevennesses in the coinage. Thereafter common die-cutting and (sometimes) types within mints became more common. The moneyers, nevertheless, remained a force to be reckoned with, even if it was now more often as a group that they interacted with the king.

CASE–STUDIES IN THE ROLE OF MONEYERS II:
THE ANONYMOUS COINAGE

The most vivid illustration of the moneyers' collective power came in the early 820s, during the troubled reign of Ceolwulf I and its aftermath. Although Ceolwulf's reign saw the establishment of two new designs encompassing multiple mints, the Canterbury moneyers seem to have been lukewarm towards him from an early stage, as coins in his name are remarkably rare from that mint and several well-known moneyers are not represented among them at a time when production at Rochester and East Anglia was buoyant.[101] At Canterbury, instead of regular royal and archiepiscopal coins one finds the 'Anonymous' royal and archiepiscopal series, which bear the names of moneyer and mint, but omit any reference to Ceolwulf I or Wulfred (Figure 5.2a–b). These coins suggest that the moneyers' own authority was guarantee enough for minting to continue without verbal reference to king or archbishop. They were made, used and hoarded in exactly the same way as other royal and archiepiscopal pennies. The profile and facing busts characteristic of earlier royal and archiepiscopal series were retained as a visual reference to the authorities under whom the system had grown up, but clearly the moneyers were not dependent on recognition of a king or archbishop for minting to take place.

A particularly surprising feature of the Anonymous coinage is that it included the archiepiscopal as well as royal moneyers. There is nothing to suggest that Archbishop Wulfred's position was in any way under threat during the few years when this coinage was produced, or that he ever spent any length of time away from Canterbury, in contrast with the precarious nature of Ceolwulf I's royal power at the same time.[102] Wulfred was responsible for the coronation of Ceolwulf in 822,[103] though only after substantial payment, and there is no hint that he was on particularly poor terms with the secular rulers of Mercia. There is apparently no reason why Wulfred's coinage should have been changed except to keep in step with the Anonymous coinage of the royal moneyers. In effect, group

[101] Blunt, Lyon and Stewart, 'Coinage', p. 41. See also above pp. 104–6.
[102] Brooks, *Early History*, pp. 135–6; Keynes, 'Control of Kent', pp. 119–20.
[103] S 186.

solidarity of the moneyers prevailed, despite the presence of one of the ruling authorities within the city. Only a well-organized association of moneyers in ninth-century Canterbury could, one assumes, lie behind this move. Such associations were an important part of the formation and social make-up of emergent towns in Anglo-Saxon England,[104] though rulers were generally wary of allowing *coniurationes* and similar bodies to become too established or formalized.[105] The moneyers may have been one such group.

KINGS, MINTS AND MONEYERS

Anglo-Saxon coinage in the late eighth and ninth centuries was, and always had been, a shared enterprise. In earlier times it had accommodated a wide range of independent moneyers and patrons of various stripes. Only after the onset of deep monetary decline in the middle of the eighth century did the kings of southern England and its neighbours take on a larger and more overt role in management of the coinage. But they succeeded in doing so only by entering into partnership with the agencies responsible for handling the work of minting on a local level. In the Frankish kingdom this task was transferred into the hands of the secular aristocracy. The southern English kingdoms instead followed and refined the ultimately Merovingian model of mint organization, which was based on the relatively independent status of each moneyer. It was thus with the moneyers that Offa and subsequent kings of Southumbrian kingdoms had to work. Sometimes, especially in the formative stages of the new coinage, the relationship between the king and certain individual moneyers seems to have been extremely close. From the end of Offa's reign onwards some of these unevennesses began to be ironed out. Design and die-distribution became more unified within each mint-town, probably as a result of the maturation of the system rather than thanks to intervention from above. Kings always continued to work with the moneyers, albeit with greater local cohesion allowing more scope for dealing with them as a group.

But it must be reiterated that the scale and nature of royal interaction with the coinage worked on two very different levels. There was a foundation of stability which depended on effective enforcement of penalties

---

[104] Astill, 'Community, Identity'; A. G. Rosser, 'Anglo-Saxon Gilds', in *Minsters and Parish Churches: The Local Church in Transition, 950–1200*, ed. J. Blair (Oxford, 1988), pp. 31–3; Brooks, *Early History*, pp. 27–9. Cf. Wickham, 'Bounding the City'; Lopez, 'Aristocracy of Money' and 'Continuità'.

[105] Goetz, 'Social and Military', pp. 477–8; M. Rouche, 'Marchés et marchands en Gaule du Ve au Xe siècle', *Settimane* 40 (1992), 395–434, at pp. 427–30; G. Althoff, *Family, Friends and Followers: Political and Social Bonds in Early Medieval Europe*, trans. C. Carroll (Cambridge, 2004), pp. 95–101.

for monetary infractions. Numbers of mints and (to a lesser extent) moneyers were limited, and weight and metal standards generally remained uniform, even across mints and kingdoms. These supported another cornerstone of the Southumbrian monetary economy: the exclusion and reminting of Carolingian and other foreign silver currencies. Maintenance of these policies required the co-operation of moneyers and die-cutters as well as kings and their agents, and served the interests of both these parties as well as those of coin-users at large.

Beyond this baseline of royal supervision in collaboration with the moneyers there lurked a second level of royal manipulation of the coinage, which was characterized by a plethora of different practices and priorities. Coinage was only royal to a degree, and rulers handled coinages under their authority in extremely different ways. Regularization of titulature, design and die-distribution all fluctuated from reign to reign and even within some reigns. Important details of the projection of royal power were often decided on a local level, presumably without the supervision of the king. Sustained changes in the relationship between kings and coinage only began to emerge at the end of this period, in the 850s and 860s, when typology and later die-distribution were centralized within West Saxon Kent, the number of moneyers expanded dramatically and the first *renovationes* for some sixty years were put in place. Soon this was to be followed by typological unification between Mercia and Wessex, and by the opening of new mints and the imposition of a new weight standard. The old order, established under Offa and preserved for almost a century, passed, but left an important legacy in the partnership between king and moneyers; a union which would remain at the heart of Anglo-Saxon coinage until 1066 and in the English coinage long after.

Chapter 6

VALUE JUDGEMENTS: WEIGHT
AND FINENESS

Early medieval coinage was fundamentally different from most modern currencies in that its value and acceptability were grounded in its precious-metal content. For this reason the amount of silver or gold in the coinage was usually controlled by the minting authorities and carefully scrutinized by coin-users.[1] There were two factors which determined the quantity of precious metal in a coin: its weight and the purity of the precious metal from which it was struck. These were intimately associated with one another in the early Middle Ages, and together constituted a vital part of the general estimation of the coinage. For Isidore of Seville, weight and fineness – *pondus et metallum* – were just as important as design (*figura*) in giving a coin its acceptable status.[2] Standardization and reliability were the underlying concerns and were an important end in themselves for early medieval rulers.[3] Respect for these essential features of the currency was repeatedly demonstrated in early medieval legislation against defective coin. Charlemagne laid down large fines in 794 for anyone who rejected *denarii* that carried the king's name and 'are of sound silver and full weight' (*mero sunt argento, pleniter pensantes*); an injunction that was repeated several times in later Carolingian capitularies.[4] Late Anglo-Saxon law-codes made an explicit link between good coinage and the spiritual wellbeing of society as a whole. The 'maintenance of the coinage' (*feos bot*), in the words of the Wulfstanian law-codes V and VI Æthelred and II Cnut, was an integral feature of the 'maintenance of peace' (*friðes*

---

[1] On the processes of medieval minting, see Grierson, *Numismatics*, pp. 94–123; D. Sellwood, 'Medieval Minting Techniques', *BNJ* 31 (1962), 57–65.

[2] Isidore, *Etymologiae*, XVI.xviii.12 (ed. Lindsay, II, 214).

[3] K. Hart, 'Heads or Tails? Two Sides of the Coin', *Man* 21 (1986), 637–56, at p. 650. For the pedigree of the symbolic importance of monetary purity, see D. R. Walker, *The Metrology of the Roman Silver Coinage*, 3 vols. (Oxford, 1976–8) III, 106–10. See also above p. 89 and below, p. 180.

[4] MGH Capit. I, no. 28, cc. 4–5, p. 74. Cf. MGH Capit. I, no. 63, c. 7, p. 152; MGH Capit. II, no. 273, cc. 8 and 10, pp. 314–15.

bot), on a par with the performance of military service and the avoidance of sins such as murder, fraud, adultery and sacrilege.[5] As far as one can tell from these documents, reliable coinage was seen as a vital ingredient of a healthy society, and a reliable coinage was one which looked and weighed the part and contained as much silver as it was supposed to.[6]

To understand early medieval coinage in its proper setting, therefore, it is necessary to examine these features of weight and fineness as they metamorphosed over time. Quality and consistency were the primary aims, and by and large both were achieved fairly successfully; hence the generally extensive use of coinage in southern England in this period, even outside its kingdom of origin. But standards could change or slip, reflecting fluctuations in the supply of silver or exploitation of the currency. Who changed standards and why is not always easy to determine, and neither is it always possible to know the economic causes and consequences of such fluctuations, at least on a short-term basis. Yet the matter of how much silver contemporary coinage contained was evidently important to early medieval observers and represented an integral part of its relationship with contemporary society and power.

METAL STANDARDS

Silver sources

Knowledge of the make-up of ancient and medieval coins can only partially be gauged from their appearance. Other methods – touchstones (at least in the case of gold), the ring of a coin when dropped on a hard surface, biting or even taste and smell – could be used to provide a broad indication of metallic content, but most early medieval coin-users had limited means at their disposal for ascertaining how much of any particular metal was contained within a coin. They had good reason to be cautious of their money, as impurities could be substantial and were an inherent part of the medieval minting process. Small (2–10 per cent) additions of copper or other metals were made to silver to harden it before minting throughout the eighth and ninth centuries. Lead and gold were also present in trace quantities, as they were extremely difficult to separate completely from silver and can for practical purposes be counted as part of the silver content of a coin.[7] The quantity of gold relative

---

[5] V Æthelred, c. 26 (ed. Liebermann I, 242); VI Æthelred, cc. 28 and 31–2 (ed. Liebermann I, 254); II Cnut cc. 8–9 (ed. Liebermann I, 314).

[6] Cf. Screen, 'Anglo-Saxon Law and Numismatics', p. 156.

[7] D. M. Metcalf and P. Northover, 'Debasement of the Coinage in Southern England in the Age of King Alfred', *NC* 145 (1985), 150–76, at p. 152.

to silver remains constant across multiple meltings, and can provide an important clue to the ultimate origin of a batch of silver, as can minute quantities of other trace elements like bismuth.[8]

Details such as these can be determined very precisely using modern scientific techniques: electron pulse microanalysis, x-ray fluorescence or neutron activation analysis, among others.[9] Although potentially highly informative, the application of these processes is far from straightforward. Multiple analyses from different parts of a coin might be needed to confirm the make-up of its metal, and chemical leaching in the soil can lead to surface enrichment. Accurate results therefore depend on cutting through the outer layer to analyse the inner part of the coin. For this reason curators and collectors are often hesitant about metallurgical analysis, and not all coins are sound enough to withstand the process. Internal corrosion may also render coins unsuitable, and constraints of finance and security can limit the number and sources of coins available for analysis. For all these reasons, it should be stressed that there are major gaps in the record of early medieval metal standards. One is forced to deal in generalities and round numbers, even though occasional instances of more thoroughly analysed series (such as the coinage of Beonna) show how much complexity there could be in detail.[10] The points made here should be taken only as indicative: the full story of numismatic metallurgy in the early Middle Ages is yet to be determined.

The beginning of that story lies in the sources of silver which were tapped for the purposes of minting. Silver came in two basic forms: 'primary' or fresh silver extracted from argentiferous lead ore; and 'secondary' silver made from melting coins or other worked objects. The bullion required for a substantial mint could run into tonnes, and even a period of light production still required a steady flow of silver, especially in southern England, where general recoinages of the local supply were rare.[11] Mining of silver-bearing lead ore in Anglo-Saxon England is not attested on a large scale, and the mints of the eighth and ninth centuries were distant from possible sources of silver in the Mendips, Derbyshire and more tentatively Northumbria.[12] The location of the Southumbrian

[8] S. E. Kruse, 'Metallurgical Evidence of Silver Sources in the Irish Sea Province', in *Viking Treasure from the North West: The Cuerdale Hoard in Its Context*, ed. J. Graham-Campbell (Liverpool, 1992), pp. 73–88, at 76–82.

[9] G. Sarah, 'Caractérisation de la composition et de la structure des alliages argent-cuivre par ICP-MS avec prélèvement par ablation laser. Application au monnayage carolingien', 2 vols. (unpublished Ph.D. dissertation, Université d'Orléans, 2008) I, 21–172.

[10] *T&S* III, 617–20.   [11] Below, pp. 181–4.

[12] For lead in Wessex, see Lupus of Ferrières, MGH Epist. VI, no. 12, p. 22 (trans. *EHD*, pp. 878–9); K. Elkington, 'The Mendip Lead Industry', in *The Roman West Country: Classical Culture and Celtic Society*, ed. K. Branigan and P. J. Fowler (Newton Abbot, 1976), pp. 183–97. For Derbyshire, see

mints, as well as some elements of the metallurgical record, hint that a major source of silver was incoming Frankish currency. While this doubtless remained significant, there are inconsistencies (not least changes in the trace gold content of Canterbury pennies) which suggest that, by the mid ninth century, Carolingian *denarii* are less likely to have been the principal origin of English silver.[13] It would be misleading, however, to speak of the Carolingian empire as awash with consistent and distinctive sources of bullion: just as large a question-mark hangs over the background of the silver that went into Carolingian coinage.[14] Movement back and forth across the North Sea could have accounted for a large amount of minting on both sides, but within the Carolingian empire there was no single native source of fresh silver which could have supplied all the metal needed for the coinage (let alone other purposes). Scrutiny of trace elements and lead isotopes in surviving coins suggests that even the major mines at Melle, for example, only partially supplied the local mints of western France, and are thus unlikely to have been capable of fulfilling the needs of the whole empire.[15] This conundrum has not been satisfactorily solved, but one potential explanation is the importation of silver into the west from the Byzantine and Muslim worlds. This may have come in considerable volume; probably much greater than surviving western finds of eastern coins would suggest.[16] The trace elements of certain Viking-Age Scandinavian silver objects, for instance, suggest manufacture from melted dirhams.[17] Some of the ore which went into these dirhams was mined at Panjhir, Afghanistan, and was distinctive for its low gold and high bismuth trace contents,[18] but there were also other sources of both fresh and recycled silver in the Islamic world.[19] These

---

S 1624; Maddicott, 'Trade, Industry', p. 46. On Northumbria see J. R. Maddicott, 'Two Frontier States: Northumbria and Wessex, *c.* 650–750', in *The Medieval State: Essays Presented to James Campbell*, ed. J. R. Maddicott and D. M. Palliser (London, 2000), pp. 25–45, at 31–2.

[13] Below, n. 31.

[14] For the most up-to-date discussion see G. Sarah, M. Bompaire, M. McCormick, A. Rovelli and C. Guerrot, 'Analyses élémentaires de monnaies de Charlemagne et Louis le Pieux du Cabinet de Médailles: l'Italie carolingienne et Venise', *Revue numismatique* 164 (2009), 355–406, at pp. 357–9.

[15] *Ibid.*, p. 387 (for other possible mines in the Alps). On Melle, see F. Téreygeol, S. Hoelzl and P. Horn, 'Le monnayage de Melle au haut moyen âge: état de la recherche', *Bulletin de l'Association des Archéologues de Poitou-Charentes* 34 (2005), 49–56; F. Téreygeol, 'Production and Circulation of Silver and Secondary Products (Lead and Glass) from Frankish Royal Silver Mines at Melle (Eighth to Tenth Century)', in *Post-Roman Towns*, ed. Henning, I, 123–34; Sarah, 'Caractérisation' I, 370–401.

[16] McCormick, *Origins*, pp. 343–84.

[17] B. Hårdh, *Wikingerzeitliche Depotfunde aus Südschweden. Probleme und Analysen* (Bonn and Lund, 1976), pp. 110–27.

[18] N. Lowick, 'Silver from the Panjhir Mines', in *Metallurgy in Numismatics*, ed. W. A. Oddy (London, 1988) II, 65–74.

[19] For analyses of Arabic silver, see Sarah, 'Caractérisation' I, 429–41; L. Ilisch *et al., Dirham und Rappenpfennig: mittelalterliche Münzprägung in Bergbauregionen. Analysenreihen* (Bonn, 2003),

were numerous, and can be traced through the substantially different trace elements of coins from various Islamic mints in the Umayyad and early Abbasid periods.[20] Important gold and silver mines existed in the Arabian peninsula, Transoxania and north Africa, and the first caliphs also inherited and recycled the very large silver currency of the Sassanian empire.[21] Byzantine silver *miliaresia* of the eighth and ninth centuries probably exploited some native silver sources, but included a significant component made from reminted Islamic dirhams.[22]

Two possible routes provided a pathway for eastern silver to western Europe: one fairly directly across the Mediterranean, via emerging entrepôts such as Venice;[23] the other via Russia and Scandinavia.[24] The latter route was only beginning to open up *c*. 800, and did not provide large quantities of silver to western Scandinavia until *c*. 850.[25] As for the Mediterranean route, the most that can be said is that the trace elements of dirhams and *miliaresia* are diverse and not incompatible with the (similarly variable) trace elements of English and Carolingian silver coins.

Other possibilities should also be kept in mind for early medieval silver sources, not least dethesaurization: the recycling of bullion in other forms. Sudden demands such as viking tribute payments, or changes in value or taste, could have major effects on the apparent coin supply by opening up stores of bullion in the form of plate.[26] But a clear understanding of how far eastern or western silver filled Anglo-Saxon or Carolingian melting

pp. 62–115; N. Lowick, 'An Early Tenth-Century Hoard from Isfahan', *NC* 15 (1975), 110–54, at pp. 123–4. On possible treatment of Islamic silver before being reminted in tenth-century England, see H. McKerrell and R. B. K. Stevenson, 'Some Analyses of Anglo-Saxon and Associated Oriental Silver Coinage', in *Methods of Chemical and Metallurgical Investigation of Ancient Coinage*, ed. D. M. Metcalf and E. T. Hall (London, 1972), pp. 195–210, at 200–3.

[20] A. A. Gordus, 'Neutron Activation of Coins and Coin Streaks', in *Methods*, ed. Hall and Metcalf, pp. 127–48, at 138–48. It should be noted that the 'streak' method of analysis is substantially affected by surface enrichment of a coin, and may not always be reliable: G. R. Gilmore, 'The Application of Activation Analysis', in *A Survey of Numismatic Research 1978–1984*, ed. M. Price *et al.*, 3 vols. (London, 1986) II, 1004–21, at pp. 1008–9.

[21] G. W. Heck, 'First Century Islamic Currency: Mastering the Message from the Money', in *Money, Power and Politics in Early Islamic Syria*, ed. J. Haldon (Aldershot, 2010), pp. 97–123, at 105–7; E. Savage and A. A. Goldus, 'Dirhams for the Empire', in *Genèse de la ville islamique en al-Andalus et au Maghreb occidental*, ed. P. Cressier and M. García-Arenal (Madrid, 1998), pp. 377–402, at 381–9.

[22] A. A. Gordus and D. M. Metcalf, 'The Alloy of the Byzantine *Miliaresion* and the Question of the Reminting of Islamic Silver', *Hamburger Beiträge zur Numismatik* 24/26 (1970/2), 9–36.

[23] *Ibid.*, pp. 384–90.

[24] *Ibid.*, pp. 384–5.

[25] M. Blackburn, 'The Coin-Finds', in *Means of Exchange. Dealing with Silver in the Viking Age*, ed. D. Skre (Århus, 2007), pp. 29–74, at 52; C. Kilger, 'Kaupang from Afar: Aspects of the Interpretation of Dirham Finds in Northern and Eastern Europe between the Late 8th and Early 10th Centuries', in *Means of Exchange*, ed. Skre, pp. 199–252, at 214–28.

[26] *MEC*, pp. 96–7.

pots awaits further investigation. What is needed is a wide-ranging and carefully scrutinized array of metallurgical analyses, not only of English and Frankish coins but also encompassing Roman, Islamic and Byzantine issues, as well as surviving silver objects.

Fineness

Fluctuations in the composition of the silver coinage in the century 757–865 were just one episode in a much longer history of cycles of debasement which played out several times in the early Middle Ages.[27] These affected the Frankish as well as the Anglo-Saxon lands, although at times there were important divergences among the various mints and kingdoms, and links to other neighbouring regions. The first of these cycles took place in the seventh century and affected the gold currency, which became more and more debased with silver until issues emerged on both sides of the Channel which were effectively pure silver *c.* 675 – the so-called *sceattas* of England and Frisia and *denarii* of Francia. At first these new coinages remained largely unadulterated, but by approximately 730 they had begun to go the same way as the gold. In Francia the decline was never too deep and varied from region to region.[28] In England the proportion of silver in each coin declined substantially from over 90–95 per cent to as little as 10 per cent or less, this time coinciding with a (not necessarily directly proportionate) fall in weight and mint-output.[29] Beginning *c.* 740, new coinages were instituted in different kingdoms using an improved standard. In Northumbria and East Anglia, the coinages of Eadberht and Beonna did not return to the highest silver content achieved in the Primary (pre-*c.* 710) phase of the *sceattas*, but to possibly *c.* 65% initially and later *c.* 50% in the case of the former. An early standard of *c.* 75%, later reduced to *c.* 50% and subsequently *c.* 25%, prevailed in Beonna's coinage.[30]

The earliest coinages of Offa and the Kentish kings did not follow the pattern set in East Anglia and Northumbria, but rather that of Pippin III. His new coinage appears to have been based on a consistently high standard of *c.* 90–95 per cent silver, with a relatively high trace content

---

[27] Blackburn, 'Money and Coinage', pp. 539–51; and *T&S* III, 611–12.

[28] D. M. Metcalf, 'Interpreting the Alloy of the Merovingian Silver Coinage', in *Studies in Numismatic Method Presented to Philip Grierson*, ed. C. N. L. Brooke *et al.* (Cambridge, 1983), pp. 113–25; J. Lafaurie, 'Monnaies épiscopales de Paris à l'époque mérovingienne', *Cahiers de la Rotonde* 20 (1998), 61–99, at pp. 62–4.

[29] *T&S* III, 660–79.

[30] Archibald, 'Coinage of Beonna', pp. 42–8; and *T&S* III, 617–20 and 623–9. Note that slightly different results for Northumbria were reached in M. Archibald and M. R. Cowell, 'The Fineness of Northumbrian Sceattas', in *Metallurgy in Numismatics*, ed. Oddy, II, 55–64.

of gold.[31] By the reign of Charlemagne gold content had fallen considerably, and the fineness of *denarii* was generally high but apparently more variable, especially in Italy.[32] A high standard comparable to that of Pippin's coinage was adopted at the southern English mints under Offa (including Ipswich), which produced coins of *c.* 94–96 per cent silver.[33] Trace contents of gold were generally very low in Offa's coinage, indicating that these were not made from reminted *sceattas*,[34] although it must be noted that none of the very early specimens of the reign has been subjected to metallurgical analysis. On present evidence, the silver used to produce southern English currency from Offa's reign onwards was similar to that used for Charlemagne's coinage, probably indicating the main source of bullion.[35]

Only a few outliers of lower fineness can be identified from the whole of the period *c.* 765–*c.* 840, at least on the basis of the available results. These were generally alloyed with a higher proportion of copper than was normal, and still never fell below 86 per cent silver.[36] One interesting pair of coins minted at very slightly below the customary standard of silver (92 per cent and 93 per cent) both belong to the moneyer Deormod in the latter part of Coenwulf's reign:[37] they may indicate that moneyers oversaw the refinement of silver on an individual level, as was sometimes done in the late Anglo-Saxon period.[38] A larger sample from the period would confirm how representative the case of Deormod might be. In general, however, there was close uniformity among all the southern mints for approximately seven decades, and changes to the metallurgical profile of the southern English coinage were, at this stage, relatively minor. At some point in the early 820s the quantity of zinc rose in southern English pennies,[39] possibly as a result of adding brass rather than pure copper or a heterogeneous mix of copper alloys to the silver. This could

---

[31] Sarah, 'Caractérisation' I, 309–12; D. M. Metcalf and P. Northover, 'Coinage Alloys from the Time of Offa and Charlemagne to *c.* 864', *NC* 149 (1989), 101–20, at pp. 107 and 120.

[32] Sarah, 'Caractérisation' I, 312–18; Sarah *et al.*, 'Analyses élémentaires', pp. 373–81. Sarah *et al.* found a general improvement in alloy later in Charlemagne's reign and early in that of Louis the Pious, followed by decline. Low fineness of 38–65 per cent silver was also recorded for four early (pre-793/4) *denarii* of Charlemagne in M. Bompaire and G. Depierre, 'Le trésor carolingien de Dijon, rue du Chapeau Rouge', *BSFN* 44 (1989), 577–81.

[33] All analyses of southern English coins minted 757–865 (excluding pennies of Burgred) are assembled in Chick, *Coinage of Offa*, p. 187; Naismith, *Coinage of Southern England* I, 145–6.

[34] Metcalf and Northover, 'Coinage Alloys', pp. 105–6.

[35] *Ibid.*

[36] For this least fine specimen see Naismith C30.1a.

[37] Naismith C39.2b and one more specimen of the same moneyer.

[38] D. M. Metcalf and P. Northover, 'Interpreting the Alloy of the Later Anglo-Saxon Coinage', *BNJ* 56 (1986), 35–63, at p. 40.

[39] To above 0.5 per cent, sometimes rising to 2–3 per cent: Metcalf and Northover, 'Coinage Alloys', p. 107.

have resulted from reuse of Roman brass coins or other old brass objects, or from trade with the Rhineland, where zinc was probably still being extracted from Roman-era facilities in the form of calamine.[40] Use of brass did not, however, affect the precious-metal content of the coinage, just its trace elements. Significant changes to the actual silver content did not occur in southern England until approximately 840.[41] Knowledge of the chronology of the coinage at this period is imperfect, and metallurgical analyses few, for which reasons the exact details of the beginning of ninth-century debasement remain obscure. As in the seventh and eighth centuries, the beginning of the process in southern England roughly coincided with developments in Francia. In the latter, debasement of the silver coinage had already begun in the *Christiana religio* coinage of Louis the Pious (*c.* 822–40) and became much more marked in the issues of the 840s.[42] It continued across the empire into the 860s, but dating individual issues is problematic and there was probably no uniformity between, or even within, the kingdoms which emerged after 843.[43]

Patchy though it is, English evidence suffices to show that the southern mints did not simply follow the progress of contemporary continental coinages.[44] The picture is clearest in the case of Canterbury. The moneyers there began to reduce the silver content of their pennies in the first phase of Æthelwulf's and Archbishop Ceolnoth's coinage (tentatively dated 839–*c.* 844), during which the silver content of the royal and archiepiscopal pennies dropped to *c.* 80–90%. In the subsequent phase of the coinage (*c.* 844–*c.* 849) the precious-metal content slipped still further, to *c.* 60–65% silver. Developments at other mints are less clear. Æthelstan's coinage from Ipswich remained at *c.* 92% pure or higher until the last part of his coinage (probably minted *c.* 837/8–*c.* 845), when it adopted the fineness of *c.* 90% current at contemporary Canterbury. Only a few specimens each from contemporary London (*c.* 846/7–52) and Rochester (*c.* 844–*c.* 846/7) have been analysed; they were found to cluster around *c.* 70–75% silver. No great weight can be placed on a conclusion based on such sparse figures, but as far as these results go they reflect a close correlation between London and Rochester, as observed in other aspects of the coinage.[45]

---

[40] J. Day, 'Brass and Zinc in Europe from the Middle Ages until the 19th Century', in *2000 Years of Zinc and Brass*, ed. P. T. Craddock (London, 1990), pp. 123–50, at 123–5. On the mixed nature of copper alloys in early medieval Britain, see J. Bayley, 'The Production of Brass in Antiquity with Particular Reference to Roman Britain', in *2000 Years of Zinc and Brass*, ed. Craddock, pp. 7–27, at 22.

[41] Metcalf and Northover, 'Coinage Alloys', pp. 109–12.

[42] *Ibid.*, pp. 108–9; Sarah, 'Caractérisation' I, 328–48; Sarah *et al.*, 'Analyses élémentaires', pp. 373–8.

[43] Metcalf and Northover, 'Coinage Alloys', pp. 114–20.

[44] *Ibid.*, p. 120.   [45] Below, p. 164.

Following the metallic content of the coinage after the 840s is again hampered by the sparseness of available data. One coin of the DORB/CANT type of *c.* 849–54 contained 62% silver, implying a continuation of the fineness of the preceding coinage.[46] Only the Inscribed Cross coinage from Canterbury and Rochester (minted *c.* 854–*c.* 864) is known in any detail, from seventeen analysed coins. These suggest that, at the beginning of the coinage, there may have been an attempt at restoration of the standard current until *c.* 840, represented by one Canterbury penny from early in the phase with a silver content of 95%.[47] Another relatively early penny of Archbishop Ceolnoth contained 89% silver.[48] This policy seems not to have extended to Rochester, where coins of local style probably associated with the earlier stages of the coinage contained 48% and 33% silver.[49] Among the later bulk of the coinage two possible clusters of fineness can be distinguished: one of *c.* 40–50% fine and one of *c.* 30% fine. The latter was apparently characteristic of Æthelberht's Inscribed Cross coinage at Canterbury, though a single new analysis of a Floreate Cross penny shows it to have had a fineness of 84%.[50] This restoration suggests that, despite its brevity and rarity in modern finds, Floreate Cross was indeed intended as a recoinage.[51]

Rochester under Æthelberht is known from only one analysed specimen by the moneyer Manning, which contains 74% silver.[52] Despite coming to share dies, in metallic content Rochester and Canterbury did not march perfectly in step. Neither, it should be added, did the other mints of the time, Ipswich and London. At Ipswich, two pennies of Æthelweard contained *c.* 85% silver, declining very slightly from the fineness current at the end of Æthelstan's reign. Four analyses of pennies of Edmund of East Anglia reveal that, after temporarily resuming the older standard of *c.* 90% silver, his coinage gave way to a lower fineness of *c.* 65%, which seems to have persisted until his death. London, which revived as a mint on a small scale with just one moneyer until approximately the early 860s, seems, surprisingly, to have returned to the high level of fineness characteristic until *c.* 840 (93% silver),[53] while the so-called 'six-dot' group produced by four moneyers around the same time as the Floreate Cross coinage (*c.* 864–5) appears to have been based on a standard of approximately 75% silver.[54] This is close to the one result from a Rochester penny struck under Æthelberht, indicating that it and London perhaps maintained the links that went back to the 840s.

[46] Naismith C131f.   [47] Naismith C144a.   [48] Naismith C150a.
[49] Naismith R38b and R41.1a.   [50] Naismith C212b.   [51] Below, p. 182.
[52] Naismith R43a.   [53] *BMC* 386.
[54] Metcalf and Northover, 'Debasement', pp. 155–6.

The course of debasement later in the reign of Burgred is known in comparatively rich detail thanks to the studies of Michael Metcalf and Peter Northover.[55] In the early 870s a nadir was reached with Lunettes pennies which contained as little as 10–15% silver, after which the new Cross-and-Lozenge coinage of Alfred the Great and Ceolwulf II was inaugurated, based on a composition of *c.* 95–97% silver.[56] This mirrored the revived standard of the *Gratia Dei rex* coinage of Charles the Bald, which came in with the Edict of Pîtres in summer 864.[57]

As already noted, this survey of ups and downs in metal standards over the century 757–865 barely scratches the surface of many of the finer points of the phenomenon. Differences between mint-towns (especially outside Canterbury) can only be sketched, but it seems to have been on this level that metallic composition was determined. Kings did not always succeed in standardizing silver contents at all mints under their control: Canterbury and Rochester, for example, seem to have differed in the 840s and after. Based on available evidence there was usually general standardization within each mint-town, with slight divergences occurring in the work of individual moneyers from time to time.

Answers of only the most tentative nature can therefore be offered for questions concerning the causes and effects of debasement; much more tentative than has often been admitted in the past. These questions can only be approached with primary reference to the coins. Inferences from other sources or comparisons should be anchored closely to the numismatic and monetary details, not vice versa. These indicate, first, that at least until the 860s debased coins continued to circulate alongside older currency with a higher silver content. Hoards from the 840s onwards such as Middle Temple, Sevington, Dorking and Croydon (*c.* 1906) were very mixed. There were also periods, such as the early 860s, when the silver content of pennies minted in the same place fluctuated considerably over a short period. Assuming that the value of silver remained relatively stable and the coins were not actually being minted at a loss,[58] these points suggest that pennies continued to be used at face value, not their uneven intrinsic value. Both valuations are recorded during other episodes of debasement in ancient and medieval Europe,[59] sometimes

[55] *Ibid.*   [56] *Ibid.*, pp. 163–5.
[57] Sarah, 'Caractérisation' I, 348–50; D. M. Metcalf and P. Northover, 'Carolingian and Viking Coins from the Cuerdale Hoard: An Interpretation of and Comparison of Their Metal Contents', *NC* 148 (1988), 97–116, at pp. 98–106.
[58] Cf. Walker, *Metrology* III, 139–40.
[59] Compare J. D. Gould, *The Great Debasement: Currency and the Economy in Mid-Tudor England* (Oxford, 1970), pp. 16–17; A. J. Rolnick, F. R. Velde and W. E. Weber, 'The Debasement Puzzle: An Essay on Medieval Monetary History', *JEcH* 56 (1996), 789–808, at pp. 800–1. For a thirteenth-century account of one aggrieved Icelander's reaction to being paid by tale with debased coins

coexisting for different denominations or metals.[60] Maintenance of face value in southern England presupposes a relatively high degree of confidence in the currency, and possibly limited awareness of the extent of debasement. Users of Inscribed Cross pennies in particular, which varied between 95 per cent and 25 per cent silver, would have been faced with visually identical coins of wildly different intrinsic value, and one assumes that ascertaining the silver content of each coin at every transaction was prohibitive.[61] Of course, no substantive indicators of practices or prices in the mid ninth century have survived to confirm whether different coins were treated differently, or if the onset of debasement had an inflationary effect. The general rarity of coin-losses in the period of debasement might reflect widespread wariness of currency and its declining intrinsic value but static face value: a manifestation of the perennial weakness of the link between an ultimately commodity-based money and abstract units of account.[62] Yet this downturn had begun before debasement set in, and available hoards indicate that circulation continued as before on at least some level.

Three main explanations have been offered for ancient and medieval monetary debasements: falling supply of bullion; rising scale of minting; and the impact of taxation and other fiscal dues. The first assumes that declining silver content reflects wider scarcity of bullion. Debasement was one way of eking out these supplies and might be combined with reductions in weight and output. Monetary historians have attributed numerous reductions in fineness and minting to 'bullion famines', not least those of northwest Europe in the seventh, eighth and ninth (and eleventh and fourteenth) centuries, or of the Islamic world in the late tenth and eleventh centuries.[63] Differences in the valuation of precious metals could lead canny traders to take money from one kingdom to

---

by Haraldr Harðráði (1045–66) (which his more compliant Norwegian companions accepted) see K. Skaare, *Coins and Coinage in Viking-Age Norway: The Establishment of a National Coinage in Norway in the XI Century, with a Survey of the Preceding Currency History* (Oslo, 1976), pp. 9–10 and 79–85.

[60] Rolnick, Velde and Weber, 'Debasement Puzzle', p. 801; A. Motomura, 'The Best and Worst of Currencies: Seigniorage and Currency Policy in Spain, 1597–1650', *JEcH* 54 (1994), 104–27, at pp. 104–5.

[61] For limited awareness of debasement, Gould, *Great Debasement*, pp. 13–16; C. Kaplanis, 'The Debasement of the "Dollar of the Middle Ages"', *JEcH* 63 (2003), 768–801, at p. 787; N. Sussman, 'Debasements, Royal Revenues, and Inflation in France during the Hundred Years' War, 1415–1422', *JEcH* 53 (1993), 44–70, at pp. 53–4. However, Rolnick, Velde and Weber, 'Debasement Puzzle', pp. 802–4, note that in some cases prices adjusted almost instantly to debasement, demonstrating keen awareness of intrinsic content, at least among well-connected merchants.

[62] G. Ingham, 'Further Reflections on the Ontology of Money: Responses to Lapavitsas and Dodd', *Economy and Society* 35 (2006), 259–78, esp. pp. 263–9; also below, pp. 252–3.

[63] See A. M. Watson, 'Back to Gold – and Silver', *EcHR* 20 (1967), 1–34, at pp. 2–4; Blackburn, '"Productive" Sites', pp. 34–5; Spufford, *Money*, pp. 339–62.

another on a large scale, eventually having an impact on the local currency.[64] Other monetary explanations for debasement emphasize increasing production and use of coinage as a driving force behind adulteration
of the currency.[65] Fiscal explanations, on the other hand, postulate that
the authorities responsible for minting eroded the intrinsic value of the
coinage for gain. Transforming one penny into two or three, but keeping
the face value the same, allowed the ruler to make a handsome profit,
and periods of extensive debasement in the later Middle Ages normally
coincided with hikes in the rate of seigniorage taken by the authorities.
Demonetization of earlier coinages for some or all purposes coerced
owners of cash to bring their money in for reminting, and at times there
may have been other incentives. By such means a ruler could multiply
the normally small income from minting many times over and turn it
into a major source of revenue to sustain finances at a time when large
expenditures were needed.[66] Thus at certain times during the Hundred
Years War, French kings derived 70–90 per cent of their income from
the coinage, and even in the midst of the dissolution of the monasteries
in the 1540s, a quarter of Henry VIII's revenue came from manipulation of the currency.[67] These methods were not sustainable in the long
run, and stretching the differential between face value and intrinsic value
too far risked damaging trust in the currency and forcing acceptance
of coin only at intrinsic value (as may have happened in ninth-century
Northumbria),[68] or encouraging the extraction and possibly export of
purer currency.[69] It should also be noted that profit could be gained by
altering other features of the coinage. Complex chronological and geographical variations in coin-weight in late Anglo-Saxon England have
been explained as a method of extracting revenue from the currency,
assuming that pennies circulated at face value.[70] Outright revaluation of
certain issues was also possible, particularly when there was a large difference in intrinsic value between intermingling coinages.[71]

---

[64] P. Grierson, 'The Monetary Reforms of 'Abd al-Malik: Their Metrological Basis and Their Financial Repercussions', *Journal of Economic and Social History of the Orient* 3 (1960), 241–64, at pp. 260–4; C. M. Cipolla, 'Sans Mahomet, Charlemagne est inconcevable', *Annales. Économies, Sociétés, Civilisations* 17 (1962), 130–6; Watson, 'Back to Gold', pp. 30–4.

[65] C. M. Cipolla, 'Depreciation in Medieval Europe', *EcHR* 15 (1963), 413–22, at pp. 417–18; C. Morrisson, 'La dévaluation de la monnaie byzantine au XIe siècle: essai d'interprétation', *Travaux et Mémoires* 6 (1976), 6–48, at pp. 29–30.

[66] Watson, 'Back to Gold', p. 31; for a case study, Kaplanis, 'Debasement', pp. 784–9.

[67] Rolnick, Velde and Weber, 'Debasement Puzzle', pp. 796–8.

[68] Below, pp. 246–9.

[69] Gould, *Great Debasement*, pp. 24 and 53–5; Sussman, 'Debasements', pp. 57–8; Kaplanis, 'Debasement', pp. 793–4.

[70] Petersson, *Anglo-Saxon Currency*, pp. 96–101.

[71] Gould, *Great Debasement*, pp. 7–9 and 56.

The dearth of sources and the scarcity of metallurgical data from the era of Æthelwulf are such that no certainty is possible on why the currency was debased in southern England at this time. What should be stressed, however, is that these basic motivations for debasement were not mutually exclusive, and could interact with each other and with other developments. The most reasonable hypothesis for the context of ninth-century debasement relies on such a cocktail of causes and effects, some clearer than others. Relatively stable mint-output combined with declining use of currency in the mid ninth century militates against a monetary motivation for debasement at this time. The near-simultaneous beginning of the process in the Frankish empire and southern England suggests that, initially at least, reduced precious-metal content in incoming Frankish coinage was probably an important factor, while the limited scale of the practice and the absence of other changes in minting practice at this time does not point (at least initially) towards substantial fiscal exploitation. In other words, falling bullion supplies probably precipitated the mid-ninth-century cycle of debasement, although its intensification may be connected to fiscal manipulation beginning in the second half of the 850s. Southern English debasement after this time went much further than that of contemporary Francia, where it may have been more a failure of regulation than a concerted policy.[72] In England it also coincided with swift and substantial change in the nature of minting organization that saw the complement of moneyers expand dramatically. This has been interpreted as another attempt to exploit the coinage, assuming that fees were paid on a per-moneyer basis. These policies began when the kingdom of Wessex was split and the rulers of the eastern portion may have been forced to turn to auxiliary sources of revenue. Like other debasements, it was a stopgap measure associated with a time of crisis when Æthelwulf's power was challenged and subsequent rulers were faced with serious viking attacks. How far it solved their problems, or created new ones for the populace, is largely unknowable.

WEIGHT STANDARDS

Coinage bears a uniquely heavy burden of evidence with regard to early medieval weight standards, as it is the only medium surviving in relatively large quantity and intact condition which was made to a closely controlled weight standard. If the correspondence between coins and written accounts of weight systems can be ascertained, many other important

---

[72] Cf. S. Coupland, 'The Early Coinage of Charles the Bald, 840–64', *NC* 151 (1991), 121–58, at pp. 151–2 and 154–5.

measurements become clear. Assessments of the Carolingian pound, for example, have been based primarily on calculations derived from the coinage.[73] Different pounds may have existed in different circumstances, just as with other weights and measures: by account (i.e., by number of coins) or by weight, perhaps based for the purposes of minting on a slightly heavier pound than in other contexts, to allow for the extraction of the king's and makers' dues.[74] Although their reconstruction is at best problematic and at worst little more than speculative, weights and measures were a matter of deep significance for day-to-day existence at all levels in the early Middle Ages: it was in pounds, sesters, *modii* and related measures of weight and volume that basic foodstuffs, for example, were reckoned. Understanding of weights and measures is fundamental for unlocking many quantitative aspects of Anglo-Saxon and Carolingian economic life.[75]

However, a major gulf separates modern metrological analysis from the methods by which people in the eighth and ninth centuries understood weights. The fundamental components of medieval and ancient weight standards were seeds – typically carob seeds (c. 0.19g) and wheat (c. 0.045g) or barley grains (c. 0.06g) in the early medieval period.[76] Any attempt to map actual coins onto these standards faces many hurdles. Some 1,685 surviving southern English pennies of 757–865 are sufficiently well preserved and recorded for their weights to be taken as a likely reflection of the original production weight. Even so, weight standards always built in a certain amount of tolerance for variation in production, and a common tendency to extract the heaviest coins for hoarding means that in practice underweight coins are often more common, and that the target weight is frequently found towards the top of the modal distribution on a frequency table.[77] This is particularly clear for later medieval England, when

[73] For example, H. Miskimin, 'Two Reforms of Charlemagne? Weights and Measures in the Middle Ages', *EcHR* 20 (1967), 35–52; D. M. Metcalf and H. Miskimin, 'The Carolingian Pound: A Discussion', *Numismatic Circular* 76 (1968), 296–8 and 333–4; J.-P. Devroey, 'Units of Measurement in the Early Medieval Economy: The Example of Carolingian Food Rations', *French History* 1 (1987), 68–92; H. Witthöft, *Münzfuss, Kleingewichte, 'pondus Caroli' und die Grundlegung des nordeuropäischen Mass- und Gewichtswesens in fränkischer Zeit* (Ostfildern, 1984); K. F. Morrison, 'Numismatics and Carolingian Trade: A Critique of the Evidence', *Speculum* 38 (1963), 403–32, at pp. 412–24.

[74] Morrison, 'Numismatics', p. 416.

[75] L. Kula, *Measures and Men*, trans. R. Szreter (Princeton, NJ, 1986).

[76] See in general *ibid.*, esp. pp. 18–81 and 102–19; C. S. S. Lyon, 'Historical Problems of the Anglo-Saxon Coinage (3): Denominations and Weights', *BNJ* 38 (1969), 204–22; *MEC*, p. 14; R. D. Connor, *The Weights and Measures of England* (London, 1987), pp. 100–48.

[77] Grierson, *Numismatics*, p. 148. Cf. R. Duncan-Jones, *Money and Government in the Roman Empire* (Cambridge, 1994), p. 219 n. 28; J. M. Keynes, 'Keynes and Ancient Currencies', in *The Collected Writings of John Maynard Keynes*, vol. XXVII, *Social, Political and Literary Writings*, ed. E. Johnson and D. Moggridge (Cambridge, 1984), pp. 223–94, at 250–2.

numerous hoards of very well-preserved coins are available to provide good samples, and documentary evidence for the mints' target weights and tolerances is also available.[78]

The average weight of a sample can also be affected by the subsequent circulation and preservation of the coins: a particular problem for eighth- and ninth-century southern English pennies. These are not known from any large, well-preserved hoards, and instead derive from heterogeneous hoards and single-finds from all over the country. Even excluding coins which are obviously chipped, damaged or corroded, it remains likely that the effects of wear and especially of chemical leaching in certain types of soil will have reduced the weight of apparently sound coins, while soil adhesion and other processes may sometimes increase it.[79] For these reasons it is necessary to take a flexible approach and resist the temptation to fasten on to too specific a figure for the likely original standard. In approaching the most probable estimate of this figure one must take account both of averages (especially the median) and of frequency table distributions.[80]

Despite these caveats, there is strong evidence for the internal consistency of weights among the sample selected from the surviving corpus: whatever standard was being aimed at was being adhered to quite closely.[81] At all mints, there was a general tendency towards homogeneity within any given phase, and 50 per cent of the well-preserved coins across the century 757–865 lie within 0.10g of others from the same phase of minting. Another useful gauge of consistency is presented by die-duplicates of good condition. These offer some idea of how much variation was tolerated at the same point in production, and show that, overall, the large majority (*c.* 80 per cent) of coins differed in weight by less than 0.20g (*c.* 15 per cent) from their duplicate(s).[82] This again indicates effective quality control at the time of minting.[83]

---

[78] Mayhew, 'Regional to Central', pp. 126–7; M. Allen, 'The Weight Standard of the English Coinage, 1158–1279', *NC* 165 (2005), 227–33, at p. 229; M. Archibald, 'The Mayfield (Sussex) 1968 Hoard of English Pence and French Gros, *c.* 1307', in *Mints, Dies and Currency: Essays Dedicated to the Memory of Albert Baldwin*, ed. R. A. G. Carson (London, 1971), pp. 151–9, at 154–6.

[79] F. Delamare, *Le frai et ses lois, ou De l'évolution des espèces* (Paris, 1994), pp. 155–64; P. Grierson, 'Coin Wear and the Frequency Table', *NC* 3 (1963), i–xvi.

[80] The median is the preferred method of reckoning the average, as it is less affected by extreme values than the mean, while a frequency table allows secondary peaks to be detected (C. E. Blunt, I. Stewart and C. S. S. Lyon, *Coinage in Tenth-Century England from Edward the Elder to Edgar's Reform* (Oxford, 1989), p. 235; Grierson, *Numismatics*, pp. 146–9).

[81] Cf. P. Grierson, 'Weight and Coinage', *NC* 4 (1964), i–xvii, at pp. xiv–xv.

[82] Naismith, *Coinage of Southern England*.

[83] For similar tolerance levels in later Anglo-Saxon England see C. S. S. Lyon, 'Some Problems in Interpreting Anglo-Saxon Coinage', *ASE* 5 (1976), 173–224, at pp. 209 and 216–17, and 'Historical Problems (3)', p. 206. Lyon also notes that most Anglo-Saxon coins fall within the tolerance limits of thirteenth-century English minting (cf. *De Moneta*, ed. Johnson, pp. 57 and 76).

It is over a longer period that ascertaining standards becomes problematic, particularly if deliberate changes in standard are to be distinguished successfully from chance variation among surviving coins, or unauthorized drifting away from the officially intended weight. In the Carolingian empire weight standards frequently diverged from the norm established by Charlemagne in 793/4 (*c.* 1.70g): coins of Louis the Pious' class II coinage (minted 818–22) seem to have been based on a slightly higher standard of *c.* 1.80g;[84] a lower weight standard of *c.* 1.55g–1.60g was used at Toulouse under Pippin II;[85] and several different standards were apparently followed by various mints under Lothar I[86] and in the pre-864 coinage of Charles the Bald.[87] Still greater complexity has been observed in the late Anglo-Saxon coinage: each recoinage would see a new pattern of greater or lesser local variation in weight standards, often becoming more marked as each type went on. At the same time, all coins of current type within England could circulate together, implying that for most users the face value remained identical regardless of weight.[88]

Offa's weight standards

Within England, the sharpest break in weight standards occurred around 792/3, and is associated with a general reform late in the reign of Offa, king of the Mercians, that brought Canterbury, London and Ipswich over from the 'Light' to the 'Heavy' coinage. This reign was an important formative phase of southern English metrology: the imposition of the same weights at all southern mints created a standard which was followed more or less closely everywhere until the 870s, and survived in viking-controlled areas until the 950s. Study of weight standards in this period has consequently been most intense in the context of Offa's reforms, though the exact target weights and their relationships with contemporary Carolingian coinage remain elusive.

---

[84] S. Coupland, 'Money and Coinage under Louis the Pious', *Francia* 1 (1990), 23–48, at p. 29; K. F. Morrison and H. Grunthal, *Carolingian Coinage* (New York, 1967), pp. 40–56; but *MEC*, pp. 215–16.

[85] S. Coupland, 'The Coinages of Pippin I and II of Aquitaine', *Revue numismatique* 31 (1989), 194–222, at p. 216.

[86] S. Coupland, 'The Coinage of Lothar I (840–55)', *NC* 161 (2001), 157–98, at pp. 167–8; Morrison and Grunthal, *Carolingian Coinage*, p. 57.

[87] Coupland, 'Early Coinage of Charles', p. 153.

[88] Lyon, 'Variations in Currency', pp. 101–10; D. M. Metcalf, *An Atlas of Anglo-Saxon and Norman Coin Finds, c. 973–1086* (London, 1998), pp. 56–69; Petersson, *Anglo-Saxon Currency*, pp. 92–101, 'Coins and Weights. Late Anglo-Saxon Pennies and Mints c. 973–1066', in *Studies in Late Anglo-Saxon Coinage in Memory of Bror Emil Hildebrand*, ed. K. Jonsson (Stockholm, 1990), pp. 207–434, at 219–34; Blackburn and Lyon, 'Regional Die-Production', pp. 253–6.

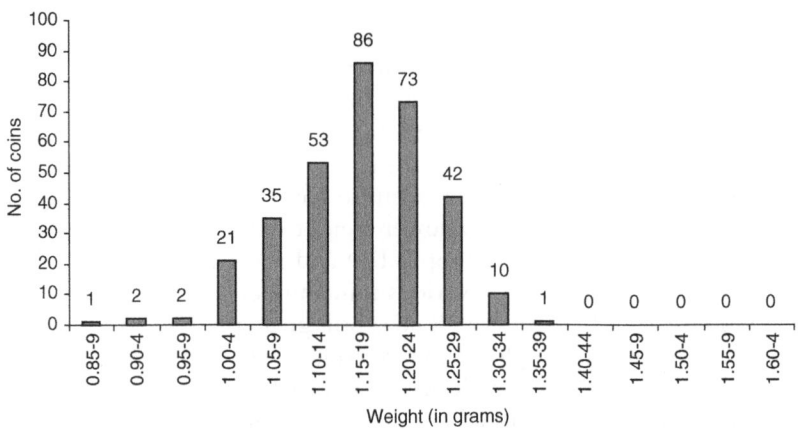

Figure 6.1 Weights of all Offa's Light coinage.

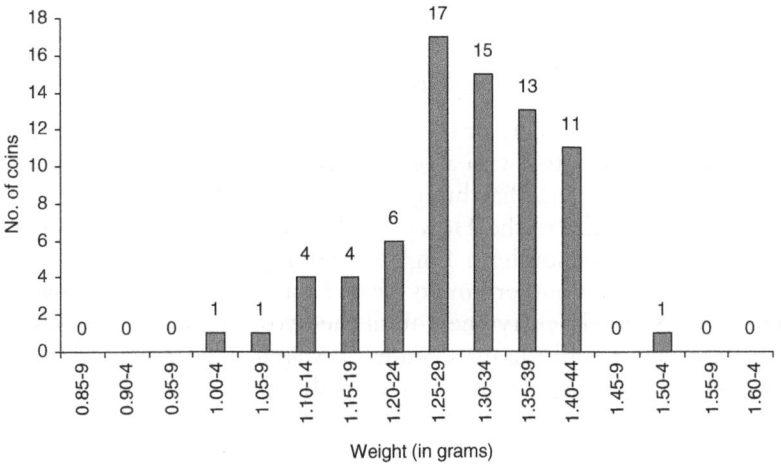

Figure 6.2 Weights of all Offa's Heavy coinage.

Estimates of Offa's weight standards have included 1.30g, 1.23g or 1.17g for the Light coinage,[89] and for the Heavy coinage 'distinctly over 20 grains' (1.36g) or 1.45g.[90] The data provided by Derek Chick's catalogue do not show as neat a distribution as contemporary Carolingian coins: the modal weight band of the Light coinage is 1.15g–1.19g (Figure 6.1) and 1.25g–1.29g for the Heavy coinage (Figure 6.2). In

[89] *MEC*, p. 278; Blunt, 'Coinage of Offa', p. 54.
[90] *MEC*, p. 280; Blunt, 'Coinage of Offa', p. 54.

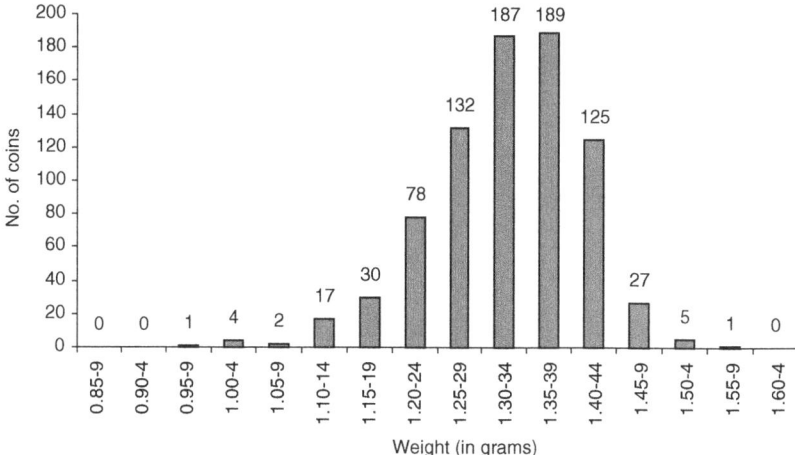

Figure 6.3 Weights of all coins struck 792/3–*c*. 840 (to Offa's Heavy standard).

both coinages the mean (1.17g and 1.30g), mode (1.17g and 1.30g) and median (1.17g and 1.30g) fall close together within these bands, and one might expect the target weight to have been somewhat higher.[91] These target weights could have been as high as *c*. 1.30g for the Light coinage and *c*. 1.40g–1.45g for the Heavy coinage.

In the case of the Heavy coinage it is possible to expand the sample substantially, as there is no evidence that a different target weight was adopted at any of the southern mints for the rest of the period in question, although there was somewhat less consistency in the coinages of Canterbury, London and Rochester struck after *c*. 840. Survey of the weights of 789 specimens probably struck to this standard at all mints before then produces the histogram shown in Figure 6.3, the trend of which is repeated by the data for individual mints.

On the basis of these histograms, the modal group is 1.35g–1.39g, and the 789 pre-840 coins give a median of 1.33g and a mean of 1.32g. Using the method advocated by Philip Grierson of averaging the coins within the modal group to ascertain the standard produces the figure of 1.37g, while taking into account the coins in both top bands produces 1.34g. Grouping the weights in different bands would produce yet another different result. Applying the same process to Offa's Light coinage is even more uncertain because of the distribution of the data, with more coins lying above the modal weight band. The average of this band is 1.17g;

91 Grierson, *Numismatics*, p. 148.

taking into account the next highest band as well gives 1.19g; and this band alone (1.20g–1.24g) 1.22g.

Flexibility remains the best course of action on the weight standards instituted under Offa: 1.15g–1.30g for the Light coinage and 1.30g–1.45g for the Heavy coinage. These might reflect 23–6 wheat grains or 18–20 barley grains for the Light coinage and 26–9 wheat grains or 20–2 barley grains for the Heavy coinage. In the case of the Light coinage, however, although pinning down the exact target weight remains problematic, it was almost certainly based on the same standard as early Carolingian coins, for which a target weight of about 1.30g has been proposed.[92] Although only about 38 per cent of undamaged Light pennies of Offa lie within 0.10g of 1.30g, they include some of the earliest coins of the Light period;[93] in addition, the proportion of early Carolingian coins approximating the same target weight is not substantially higher (47 per cent) and includes many more specimens from hoards. These figures are derived from a sample of 479 pre-793/4 Carolingian coin-weights listed by Karl Morrison and Henry Grunthal, which provides a mean, median and mode almost identical to those of Offa's Light coinage: 1.18g. This excludes coins specifically said to be damaged, but the catalogue does not always make it clear which weights belong to such coins. For this reason 109 coins of the same period listed and illustrated in the Chwartz collection, Fitzwilliam Museum, British Museum and Bibliothèque nationale have also been tabulated as a control group to correct any distortion in the sometimes unreliable data offered by Morrison and Grunthal.[94] These give extremely similar results: a mean of 1.19g and a median of 1.20g. The curve of a histogram of these coins, and the modal bands within the histogram, also compare closely with those for contemporary southern England (Figure 6.4).

It therefore seems extremely probable that Offa's Light coinage was based on the same weight standard as contemporary Frankish coinage. This was apparently not, it should be noted, true of the other reformed English coinages of the mid eighth century struck under Beonna and Eadberht,[95] although the standard *c.* 1.30g had been current since

[92] Grierson, 'Money and Coinage', p. 513; *MEC*, pp. 204 and 278 (*c.* 1.24g); Blunt, 'Coinage of Offa', p. 54. Proposed standards for pre-793/4 Carolingian issues include Morrison, 'Numismatics', pp. 416–17 (*c.* 1.30g); Miskimin, 'Two Reforms', pp. 51–2 (*c.* 1.38g); Lyon, 'Some Problems', p. 184 (*c.* 1.33g).

[93] Chick 6a, 102f, 103a, b and d and 160a–b.

[94] Chwartz collection (Alde sale, Paris, 18 June 2009), M. Prou, *Les monnaies carolingiennes. Catalogue des monnaies françaises da la Bibliothèque nationale* (Paris, 1896); *MEC*; R. H. M. Dolley and K. F. Morrison, *The Carolingian Coins in the British Museum* (London, 1966).

[95] Archibald, 'Coinage of Beonna', pp. 25–7 (*c.* 1.00g for Beonna's coinage); Booth, 'Sceattas', p. 78; *MEC*, p. 173; *T&S* III, 580 (*c.* 1.00g–1.10g for Eadberht's coinage). See also Naismith, 'Kings, Crisis and Coinage Reform'.

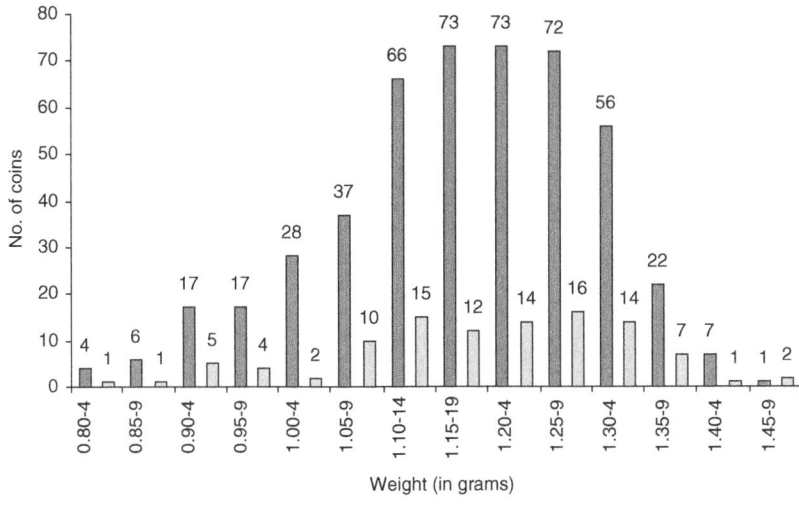

Figure 6.4 Weights of Carolingian *denarii* of Pippin II, Carloman
and Charlemagne, struck *c.* 755–93/4.

Merovingian times and appears to have been used for *thrymsas* and primary *sceattas* in England.[96]

Offa, Charlemagne and the coin reforms of 792–4

A bigger puzzle is what the connection was between the reforms of Offa and Charlemagne in the early 790s. Both raised the weight of their coinage, but the new weights did not coincide. The exact dates of the reforms are also unclear. On current evidence Offa's Heavy coinage seemingly came first. Its introduction was probably associated with the year between the death of Archbishop Iænberht (12 August 792) and the appointment of Archbishop Æthelheard (elected 792, consecrated 21 July 793).[97] Charlemagne's reform is thought to be represented in the provisions for *novi denarii* in the decrees of the council of Frankfurt in June 794, which implies either a recent change or one soon to be enacted.[98]

---

[96] P. Grierson, 'La fonction sociale de la monnaie en Angleterre aux VIIe–VIIIe siècles', *Settimane* 8 (1961), 341–62, at pp. 351–2; Morrison, 'Numismatics', p. 416; *MEC*, pp. 168–9; *T&S* I, 86–7, 100–1, 118 and 123.

[97] Blunt, 'Coinage of Offa', pp. 48 and 53. The PONTIFEX coins of Æthelheard (Chick 240–6) should probably not be seen as his earliest issue (*MEC*, p. 280).

[98] MGH Capit. I, no. 28, c. 5, p. 74.

Standardization of weights and measures in 789,[99] and the composition of the Ilanz hoard provided some support for dating this coin reform to *c.* 790,[100] though 793/4 is now most widely accepted.[101]

Commentators have generally assumed that the two reforms were linked in some way, although deducing the nature of the relationship between the specific weights is fraught with problems, and any errors in divining the standard of the coins run the risk of being magnified when calculating other units. The English weights provide a median of 1.33g (or 1.30g based solely on Offa's Heavy coinage) and a possible target weight of about 1.40g–1.45g. Based on 323 post-793/4 *denarii* of Charlemagne listed by Morrison and Grunthal, a median of 1.60g and mean of 1.56g appear to have applied to post-793/4 Carolingian coinage. A sample of fifty-five coins of the same period in the Chwartz collection, Fitzwilliam Museum, British Museum and Bibliothèque nationale gives a median of 1.63g and a mean of 1.60g (Figure 6.5).[102] Based on these relationships, and theoretical target weights of 1.40g–1.45g and 1.70g respectively, one might suggest a basic metrological exchange rate of six to five – or ten Carolingian *denarii* turning into twelve Offan pennies. One might further speculate that two of these twelve could have been retained for the king and moneyer, resulting in an exact numerical exchange, but until more evidence surfaces the exact mechanics of cross-Channel monetary exchange will remain enigmatic.

There is thus a need for flexibility and acknowledgement that creating a stable monetary exchange rate may not have been the only, or even the primary, motive in reform for either Offa or Charlemagne. One effect of increasing the weight of the coinage would, for example, have been to augment the intrinsic value of any payments made to the king and other members of the elite at a fixed numerical quantity. Manipulation of the coinage for fiscal profit is generally difficult to discern, but the early 790s was a time when supplementary resources would surely have been welcome. Famine gripped both Francia and England in the years 792–3, and in Francia this was compounded by a revolt of Charlemagne's

---

[99] MGH Capit. I, no. 22, c. 74, p. 60.

[100] S. Suchodolski, 'La date de la grande réforme monétaire de Charlemagne', *Quaderni ticinesi di numismatica e antichità classiche* 10 (1981), 399–409; P. Grierson, 'Cronologia delle riforme monetarie di Carlo Magno', *Rivista italiana di numismatica* 56 (1954), 65–79; Story, *Carolingian Connections*, p. 194.

[101] Grierson, 'Money and Coinage', pp. 507–11 and 528–30; *MEC*, p. 208; S. Coupland, 'Charlemagne's Coinage: Ideology and Economy', in *Charlemagne: Empire and Society*, ed. J. Story (Manchester, 2005), pp. 211–29, at p. 218; Nelson, 'Carolingian Contacts', p. 132.

[102] Grierson, 'Money and Coinage', pp. 527–8; S. Suchodolski, 'Le poids des monnaies de Charlemagne émises après la réforme: contribution à la métrologie numismatique', in *Dona numismatica: Walter Hävernick zum 23. Januar 1965 dargebracht*, ed. P. Berghaus and G. Hatz (Hamburg, 1965), pp. 43–50.

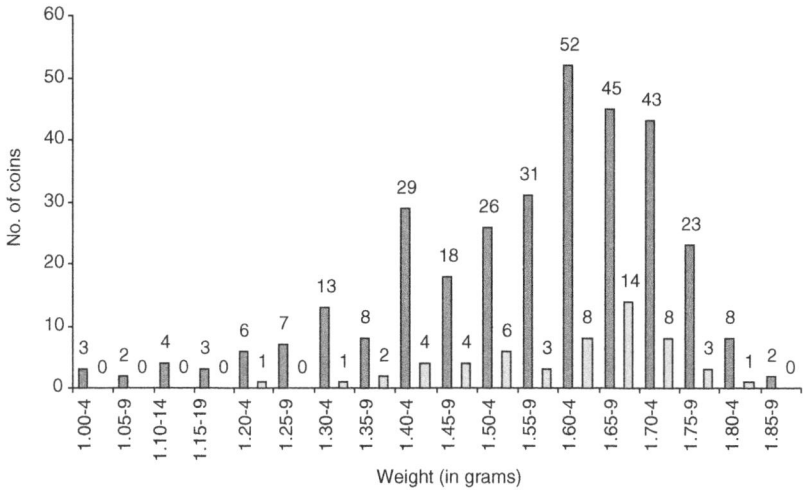

Figure 6.5 Weights of Carolingian *denarii* of Charlemagne, struck 793/4–814.

son Pippin in 792 and another among the Saxons in 794.[103] The combination of famine and (in Francia) political and military disturbances was not unprecedented – famines are also recorded in 778–9 and 805–6, for example, reactions to which were first and foremost religious in nature[104] – and so may only have been one factor which drove Offa and Charlemagne to turn to auxiliary sources of revenue. Other, less profit-driven aims were also in play. In Francia, a general changeover in 793/4 from a wheat-grain standard to a barley-grain standard may have had a significant impact on monetary policy.[105] The difficulty and significance of this move, executed on such a massive scale, can hardly be overestimated: it was surely sufficient to drive coinage reform even in the absence of other incentives.[106] The increase in coin-weight of about

[103] MGH Capit. I, no. 28, c. 4, p. 74; *ASC* s.a. 793. Cf. Hammer, '"Pipinus rex"';Verhulst, *Carolingian Economy*, pp. 117–18, 'Karolingische Agrarpolitik. Das Capitulare de Villis und die Hungersnöte von 792/3 und 805/6', *Zeitschrift für Agrargeschichte und Agrarsoziologie* 13 (1965), 175–89; F.-L. Ganshof, 'Observations sur le synode de Francfort de 794', in *Miscellanea historica in honorem Alberti de Meyer*, 2 vols. (Louvain, 1946) I, 306–18.

[104] H. Mordek, 'Karls des Großen zweites Kapitular von Herstal und die Hungersnot der Jahre 778/779', *Deutsches Archiv für Erforschung des Mittelalters* 61 (2005), 1–52; C. Jörg, 'Die Besänftigung göttlichen Zorns in karolingischer Zeit. Kaiserliche Vorgaben zu Fasten, Gebet und Buße im Umfeld der Hungersnot von 805/06', *Das Mittelalter* 15 (2010), 38–51.

[105] Grierson, 'Money and Coinage', pp. 528–30; and *MEC*, p. 206.

[106] H. Witthöft, '"Denarius novus", "Modius publicus" und "Libra panis" im Frankfurter Kapitulare: Elemente und Struktur einer materiellen Ordnung im fränkischer Zeit', in *Das Frankfurter Konzil von 794. Kristallisationspunkt karolingischer Kultur. Akten zweier Symposien (vom 23. bis 27. Februar und*

a quarter before and after Charlemagne's reform mirrors the difference in weight between the wheat grain and the barley grain: the number of grains per coin theoretically remained the same. Offa's reform does not line up so neatly, implying that this change was not mirrored in England. Taking the greatest possible extremes in weight standard of 1.17g–1.30g for the Light coinage and 1.35g–1.50g for the Heavy would make the old coinage anywhere from 78% to 96% the weight of the new, with 90% or 93% the most probable differentials (based on target weights of 1.30g and 1.40g–1.45g). What Offa sought to achieve by reforming the coinage and changing its weight is unclear, but profit is unlikely to be the sole explanation.

Metrology after 792/3

In the period after Offa's reign there was relative consistency in obser- vance of the target weight established in 792/3. In the case of the East Anglian mint, in fact, this consistency was very strong indeed: the median never dropped below 1.30g at any point in the ninth century and remained identical (at 1.30g) under all three independent East Anglian kings *c.* 827–869, while the modal weight band was uniformly 1.30g– 1.34g or 1.35g–1.39g.[107] This consistently high weight of East Anglian coinage coincided with relatively stable metal content.

The mints of Canterbury, Rochester and London showed a simi- lar pattern in the decades after Offa's reform: median weights mostly remained at 1.30g or higher, and the modal weight band was 1.30g–1.34g or 1.35g–1.39g.[108] There were some temporary and minor local variations. At Canterbury *c.* 810–*c.* 825 the median was often somewhat higher at 1.36g or similar, while at London *c.* 805–*c.* 830 the mean and median could be as high as 1.40g or more. Rochester ran to a high median of 1.36g under Coenwulf and Ceolwulf I, but only 1.26g under Baldred. In some cases, however, these conclusions are based on a relatively small number of coins.

There was a trend towards lighter coinage displayed at all three of the southeastern mints in the 840s and 850s, which coincides closely with the onset of debasement in the southern English coinage. A fall in weight often accompanied a decline in fineness, as was vividly demonstrated

---

vom 13. bis 15. Oktober 1994) anläßlich der 1200-Jahrfeier der Stadt Frankfurt am Main, ed. R. Berndt, 2 vols. (Mainz, 1997) I, 219–52.

[107] Naismith, *Coinage of Southern England.*

[108] *Ibid.* The medians and modal weight bands are lower at Rochester in the 820s, but these are dependent on a very small sample.

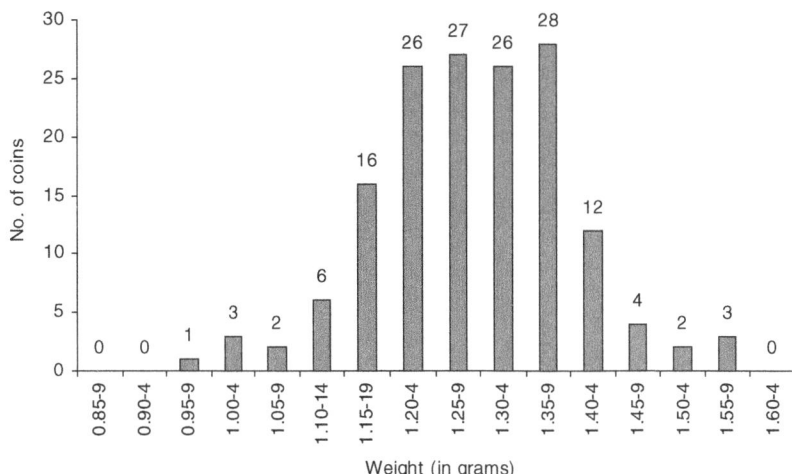

Figure 6.6 Weights of the Inscribed Cross coinage *c.* 854–*c.* 864.

when both fineness and weight collapsed in England in the early 870s,[109] and in the first part of the tenth century leading up to Edgar's reform of *c.* 973.[110] The beginnings of this process in ninth-century England occurred in the 840s. At Canterbury, in the second phase of Æthelwulf's coinage (struck *c.* 844–9), during which debasement first became substantial, the median fell as low as 1.26g and the modal weight band to 1.25g–1.29g (based on sixty-six coins). In the DORB/CANT coinage (*c.* 849–54) the median was 1.24g and the modal band 1.20g–1.24g, though this is on the basis of a small sample of coins (twenty-eight). After this, however, the weights of Canterbury coins picked up again, and in the Inscribed Cross coinage the median rose back to 1.29g and the modal weight band was the same as that of most of the coinages struck after 792/3 (1.35g–1.39g) (Figure 6.6). There is a wider distribution of coins across the three weight bands below the modal than is common in the ninth century, and further metallurgical analyses would show if the lighter coins tend to be more debased.

At Rochester the median and modal weight band fell to around 1.25g–1.29g after *c.* 840, and likewise recovered in the Inscribed Cross phase. London's coinage under Berhtwulf showed a downturn in weight, with a median of 1.25g and a modal band of 1.25g–1.29g. The rare early Lunettes pennies of Burgred, like the Inscribed Cross coins struck

[109] Blackburn, 'Alfred's Coinage Reforms', p. 205.
[110] Blunt, Stewart and Lyon, *Coinage*, pp. 235–47.

contemporaneously at Canterbury and Rochester, seem to have returned to the earlier modal values of over 1.30g.[111]

Declining weight standards and fineness are often seen as symptoms of incipient breakdown in organization, but in the 840s and after, other features including design and internal consistency of weights within a phase do not lend support to a similar conclusion. Gradual, controlled reduction of weight and of fineness appear to have been a reaction to dwindling bullion supply.[112] These seem to have been temporary and limited measures, however, suggesting that the same theoretical weight standards remained in use throughout the period after 792/3.

A well-known biblical passage often quoted in the context of standards and their observance emphasized the divine associations of fixed and consistent reckonings:[113] 'but Thou hast ordered all things in measure, number and weight' (*sed omnia mensura et numero et pondere disposuisti*).[114] For the men and women of early medieval Europe, stable measures and weights were part of the very bedrock of Christian society, enshrined by laws of man and God. Preserving these more or less effectively – in minting and in other areas – was an important duty, one which was generally fulfilled in the eighth and ninth centuries, sometimes in the face of considerable monetary and political duress.

---

[111] For a sample of specimens, see E. Pirie, *Coins in Yorkshire Collections: The Yorkshire Museum, York; the City Museum, Leeds; the University of Leeds*, Sylloge of Coins of the British Isles 21 (London, 1975), no. 960 (1.36g); *BMC*, nos. 251 and 386–7 (1.41g, 1.33g and 1.37g).

[112] Above, pp. 161–8.

[113] I. Peri, 'Omnia mensura et numero et pondere disposuisti. Die Auslegung von Weish 11, 20 in der lateinischen Patristik', in *Mensura, Maß, Zahl, Zahlensymbolik im Mittelalter, Teil 1*, ed. A. Zimmermann (Berlin, 1983), pp. 1–21.

[114] Wisd. 11:(20)21.

Chapter 7

PRODUCTION OF COINAGE

COINAGE AND RECOINAGE

Among the many provisions of the Edict of Pîtres laid down in June 864 was one in which Charles the Bald stipulated 'ut ab ipsa missa sancti Martini per omne regnum nostrum non nisi istius nostrae novae monetae meri et bene pensantes denarii accipiantur'.[1] This has been connected by numismatists with a major reform of the currency which swept away the earlier coinages of diverse design and inconsistent metallic quality in favour of the *Gratia Dei rex* issue.[2] Just as Charles commanded, west Frankish hoards from 864 onwards quickly came to be dominated by the new coinage. His measure, so it seemed, had been a success.

What Charles implemented in 864 is the classic example of what numismatists have called a *renovatio monetae*:[3] a reform of the coinage in which the old currency was demonetized in favour of a new one. The roots of the policy go back to ancient times, and it can be traced in various proclamations of late Roman and Byzantine emperors.[4] In the context of a precious-metal coinage this meant melting down the old coins and having them restruck throughout the kingdom. Charles the Bald's 864 recoinage was not the only one to work along these lines, but it is among the best-recorded. It combines a clear monetary impact with relatively detailed documentation, and its provisions have been tentatively assumed to apply to many other times and places in the early Middle Ages.

[1] 'That from the feast of St Martin no coins should be accepted anywhere in my kingdom except for those of the new coinage which are of good alloy and weight.' MGH Capit. II, no. 273, c. 10, p. 315.
[2] P. Grierson, 'The "*Gratia dei rex*" Coinage of Charles the Bald', in *Charles the Bald*, ed. Gibson and Nelson, pp. 52–64; cf. Coupland, 'Early Coinage'.
[3] Although this term was not current before the late eleventh century: P. Grierson, 'Numismatics and the Historian', *NC* 2 (1962), i–xiv, at p. x.
[4] Hendy, *Studies*, p. 319.

181

In eighth- and ninth-century England, however, *renovationes* such as this were unusual. More common were what might simply be called 'type changes': alterations in the design of the coinage which were not accompanied by general reminting of the currency. Distinguishing these on the basis of little written and hoard evidence is problematic, but some *renovationes* probably did occur in eighth- and ninth-century Anglo-Saxon England.[5] In Northumbria *c.* 740, for instance, Eadberht's new inscribed coinage apparently swept away the later *sceattas* and totally dominated the currency from the Sancton productive site.[6] Offa's substantive Light coinage, which began in the 780s, seems to have put an end to circulation of *sceattas* and foreign coins. His Heavy coinage, instituted in 792/3, was probably also a recoinage, as although no hoards from the period of its currency are preserved, only Heavy coins survived to be included in later hoards. The next recoinage – this time restricted to Wessex – probably did not come until the 850s, when the Inscribed Cross issue of Kent expanded in scale part-way through its period of production.[7] If it was intended as a *renovatio*, its impact and effectiveness were limited.[8] Another *renovatio* may have been attempted with the rare Floreate Cross coinage of the last years of Æthelberht, as its restored metallic quality and a recently discovered hoard from near York appear to indicate. This practice of *renovatio* persisted into the later 860s and after with the new Lunettes coinage of Wessex and Mercia, and subsequently the Cross-and-Lozenge and Two-Line coinages of Alfred the Great.[9]

The capacity of Anglo-Saxon governments to bring about successful recoinages, even as early as the first half of the eighth century, must not be downplayed. It may not have been a regular system, but it was an effective one. When a recoinage was brought into force it undoubtedly had a major effect on the currency and minting, resulting in short periods of intense activity as coin-users flocked to the moneyers to change their money, followed by a substantial drop-off as business refocused on other, probably smaller sources of silver. But the rarity of recoinages in England also calls attention to the long period of about sixty years after 792/3 when, it seems, there were no general recoinages but only type-changes.

[5] Blackburn, 'Alfred's Coinage Reforms', pp. 202–3.

[6] Naismith, 'Kings, Crisis and Coin Reforms'.

[7] R. H. M. Dolley and D. M. Metcalf, 'The Reform of the English Coinage under Eadgar', in *Anglo-Saxon Coins*, ed. Dolley, pp. 136–68, at 156; R. H. M. Dolley, 'Ælfred the Great's Abandonment of the Concept of Periodic Recoinage', in *Studies in Numismatic Method*, ed. Brooke *et al.*, pp. 153–60, at 153; Pagan, 'Coinage in Southern England', pp. 58–60.

[8] *MEC*, pp. 307–8. See also above, pp. 109–12.

[9] Dolley, 'Ælfred the Great's Abandonment'; Blackburn, 'Alfred's Coinage Reforms', pp. 199–205.

Such is made clear by the hoards of the period. Just 39 per cent of the Delgany hoard of *c.* 830 had been struck within the preceding decade, and even the most recent specimens included a mix from all the southern English mints active at the time in three separate kingdoms. Similarly the Middle Temple hoard, deposited *c.* 840, contained only about 57 per cent of coins struck in the 830s and after, and in the case of the Dorking hoard of *c.* 863 only 68 per cent of the coins belonged to the 850s or 860s. In geographical origin these hoards as well as the contemporary single-finds are highly mixed.[10]

It might fairly be asked what the purpose was of changing the design of the coinage if it was accompanied by no general *renovatio*, especially when this took place in the middle of a reign. Fear of forgery was a common concern for early medieval rulers,[11] and relatively frequent changes in the appearance of coinage may have been intended to discourage such fraudulent activities. This was the most common concern reported in Carolingian and late Anglo-Saxon legislation on minting.[12] Another answer might lie in requiring the use of current coinage only for restricted purposes, such as payments made directly to the king or to his agents. This could have been supported by offering a more favourable rate of exchange for the current or outgoing type of coin.[13] In the 850s and 860s increasing awareness of debasement in new coin may have encouraged the withdrawal of older currency from circulation.[14] Yet continued adherence to common weight and (until *c.* 840) metal standards at all mints suggests there was no serious attempt to introduce a coinage which would be incompatible with others of the day: an assumption of mixed circulation seems to have prevailed in southern England from 792/3 until at least the 850s.

From the point of view of production, minting in eighth- and ninth-century England must therefore be treated quite differently from minting in late tenth- and early eleventh-century England, when there were quite effective recoinages every few years.[15] These earlier issues were probably produced more evenly over the period of manufacture, with less of an initial peak. They were probably not for the most part struck from older English coins, but from other sources of silver, not least foreign coin. Thus they contributed to a currency of diverse dates and origins. At the same time this currency was constantly being depleted by various

---

[10] Below, pp. 199–209.   [11] Hendy, *Studies*, pp. 320–8, for the origins of this.
[12] Screen, 'Anglo-Saxon Law and Numismatics', pp. 164–70.
[13] Cf. Hendy, *Studies*, p. 319.   [14] *MEC*, pp. 308–9 (but see above, pp. 168–71).
[15] Dolley and Metcalf, 'Reform of the English Coinage', pp. 156–8; cf. Stewart, 'Coinage and Recoinage'.

pressures, so that despite its heterogeneity there was, on the evidence of surviving hoards, always a high proportion of coins from within the last decade or so.[16] These aspects of the coinage are essential to a full appreciation of the way and scale on which it was produced.

THE SCALE OF MINTING

For all that it now comprises many thousands of coins, there can be no question that the sample of early medieval currency which was lost and went unrecovered until modern times represents 'only a tiny fraction of what was once produced.[17] The rub lies in determining how representative this fraction might be: how far it can be used to give an impression of the original scale of the coinage. The potential value of such data to economic history can hardly be exaggerated. In the context of later medieval England, for example, when extensive mint records survive for how much money was coined at particular times and places, it is possible to follow the peaks and troughs of mint-output very closely. In general the waxing and waning of the coinage was related to wider trends in population and agricultural productivity, though it was also affected by the flow of bullion.[18] In addition, it is possible to see that the coinage was a major resource, the silver portion of it amounting to approximately £30,000–80,000 in circulation in 1158, £500,000 in 1247 and over £1,000,000 by 1290, greasing the wheels of monetary exchange at all levels of society.[19]

There are, unfortunately, no mint records surviving from England before the Norman Conquest; nor would even the most optimistic estimate rate the Anglo-Saxon currency as comparable in volume to that of the late thirteenth century. Yet this is not to say that assessment of it is impossible: it should not be assumed to have been negligible in

---

[16] Above, p. 182–3 and below pp. 224–9.

[17] Annual rate of loss in modern times can vary enormously depending on the size and value of a coin, typically from 2 per cent up to 40 per cent (E. Goldin, 'Statistical Analysis of Coins Lost in Circulation', *Journal of Business and Economic Statistics* 3 (1985), 36–42). Because of the higher value of most ancient and medieval coins a rate on the lower side of this (typically 2 per cent or less) is often used (K. Hopkins, 'Rome, Taxes, Rents and Trade', in *The Ancient Economy*, ed. W. Scheidel and S. von Reden (Edinburgh, 2002), pp. 190–232, at 213), though even this is highly speculative.

[18] See, for example, N. Mayhew, 'Modelling Medieval Monetisation', in *A Commercialising Economy: England 1086 to c. 1300*, ed. R. Britnell and M. Campbell (Manchester, 1995), pp. 55–77, 'Money and Prices in England from Henry II to Edward III', *Agricultural History Review* 35 (1987), pp. 121–32, and 'Population, Money Supply and the Velocity of Circulation in England, 1300–1700', *EcHR* 48 (1995), 238–57.

[19] J. Bolton, 'What Is Money? What Is a Money Economy? When Did a Money Economy Emerge in Medieval England?', in *Medieval Money Matters*, ed. D. Wood (Oxford, 2004), pp. 1–15; M. Allen, 'The English Currency and the Commercialization of England before the Black Death', in *Medieval Money Matters*, ed. Wood, pp. 31–50, at 38–9.

quantity or impact. Numerous die-studies of the late Anglo-Saxon currency have hinted at manufacture on a large scale, while recent metal-
detected finds of the early pennies or *sceattas* have become extremely
numerous, enough to suggest a truly vibrant monetary economy in the
early eighth century.[20] Complete corpora and die-studies of the coinage issued in southern England 757–865 now allow these matters to be
approached with more confidence than has ever before been possible for
a large swathe of pre-viking Anglo-Saxon coinage.

Access to the totality of the evidence permits cautious use of methods
of estimating productivity developed by numismatists and statisticians
since the 1960s. It was at this time that calculations based on the numbers
of obverse and reverse dies behind the surviving sample of a coinage first
began to be used to estimate its original scale.[21] In theory, if the surviving
remnants of a coinage were struck from a small number of dies, then the
original output was probably not especially large. But if the coins were
struck from a large number of dies which are duplicated only rarely, then
there is a good chance that the coinage was large – perhaps in spite of the
rate of survival. Much more uncertain is moving from the approximate
number of dies making up a coinage to the actual number of coins those
dies produced.[22] Hard evidence for how many coins could be struck
from dies is only forthcoming in the thirteenth century and after, and
even then shows that some (obverse) dies broke immediately while the
bulk produced between 23,000 and 69,000 coins each.[23] Moreover, the
hardened-steel cap which actually came into contact with the coin could
be detached from a worn-out shaft and refitted to another if necessary,

[20] Blackburn, '"Productive" Sites', pp. 28–35.
[21] Dolley, *Anglo-Saxon Coins*, p. 109; I. Stewart, 'Medieval Die-Output for English Mints in the Fourteenth Century', *NC* 3 (1963), 97–106, and 'Second Thoughts on Medieval Die-Output', *NC* 4 (1964), 293–303; F. de Callataÿ, 'Statistique et numismatique: les limites d'un apport', *Revue des archéologues et historiens d'art de Louvain* 20 (1987), 76–95; G. Carter, 'Comparison of Methods for Calculating the Total Number of Dies from Die-Link Statistics', in *Statistics and Numismatics*, ed. C. Carcassonne and T. Hackens (Strasbourg, 1981), pp. 204–13; W. Esty, 'Estimation of the Size of a Coinage: A Survey and Comparison of Methods', *NC* 146 (1986), 185–215.
[22] T. V. Buttrey, 'Calculating Ancient Coin Production I: Facts and Fantasies', *NC* 153 (1993), 335–51, and 'Calculating Ancient Coin Production II: Why It Cannot Be Done,' *NC* 154 (1994), 341–52; N. Brooks, 'Epilogue', in *Coinage in Ninth-Century Northumbria*, ed. Metcalf, pp. 397–401, at 398–9. The coinage of Offa was one of the first coinages to be debated in these terms: D. M. Metcalf, 'Offa's Pence Reconsidered', pp. 44–7, 'English Monetary History in the Time of Offa: A Reply', *Numismatic Circular* 71 (1963), 165–7, 'How Large Was the Anglo-Saxon Currency?', *EcHR* 18 (1965), 475–82, and 'The Prosperity of North-Western Europe in the Eighth and Ninth Centuries', *EcHR* 20 (1967), 344–57, at pp. 352–5; P. Grierson, 'Mint Output in the Time of Offa', *Numismatic Circular* 71 (1963), 114–15, 'Some Aspects of the Coinage of Offa', *Numismatic Circular* 71 (1963), 223–5, and 'The Volume of Anglo-Saxon Coinage', *EcHR* 20 (1967), 153–60.
[23] M. Allen, 'Medieval English Die-Output', *BNJ* 74 (2004), 39–49; building on M. Mate, 'Coin Dies under Edward I and II', *NC* 9 (1969), 207–18.

prolonging a die's life considerably and without any outward clue to its longevity.[24]

Despite this variability, later medieval averages of die-output have often been carried back into the early medieval or ancient period, typically of 10,000–30,000 coins being produced per reverse die.[25] The uncertainties plaguing this back-projection of later medieval averages are legion. There can be no telling how closely Anglo-Saxon minting technology and expertise generally compared to that of the large, industrialized mints of thirteenth- and fourteenth-century England.[26] Here, assessment of eighth- and ninth-century minting will be based on the probable numbers of dies contributing to each coinage. Even this must be undertaken with caution. Inherent in these calculations is the assumption that the average output from a given number of dies was broadly comparable at different times and places in eighth- and ninth-century England. Certainly the coins themselves were of broadly comparable shape, size and metal. Yet one must be wary of practices that could offset the general correlation of die-output and coin-output. At smaller mints, for example, dies may not have been used to capacity, and may have suffered from poorer technological expertise than was available at bigger centres. For these reasons it must be accepted that the results of die-estimation need to be used with extreme care.

Fortunately it is normally possible to get an impression of the reliability of an estimate from the data itself. The corpus should ideally be drawn from a random sample and avoid hoards which contain an unusually high proportion of die-linked coins.[27] This is generally the case with the southern English coinage of the eighth and ninth centuries, which includes a high proportion of coins from single-finds and excavations.[28] Hoards of this period are also heterogeneous in their composition.[29] The size of the sample is another important factor, since there must be enough information to enable the process: the more coins that are available, and the more die-links noticeable among them, the more secure the conclusions.[30] François de Callataÿ has pointed out that once the

---

[24] O'Hara *et al.*, 'Iron Reverse Die', pp. 248–50.

[25] Buttrey, 'Why It Cannot', pp. 350–1; Metcalf, 'Offa's Pence Reconsidered', p. 44.

[26] Grierson, 'Mint Output', pp. 2–3. For general discussion of the emergence of large-scale, industrialized minting in later medieval England, see Mayhew, 'Regional to Central'.

[27] Grierson, *Numismatics*, p. 131.

[28] On the advantages of these sources see Metcalf, *Atlas*, pp. 14–17.

[29] There are few die-links among the Inscribed Cross pennies from the Dorking hoard, for example. On the other hand, the many Rochester die-duplicates of Æthelwulf in the Middle Temple hoard taint its evidence for the currency of that mint.

[30] Thus the preference in many studies for longer-lasting obverse dies: F. de Callataÿ, 'Calculating Ancient Coin Production: Seeking a Balance', *NC* 155 (1995), 289–311, at p. 294.

overall ratio of coins to dies has equalled or surpassed three to one then most equations will arrive at similar results – but below this figure, and especially if the number of dies comes close to the number of coins, the results of different calculations deviate more substantially.[31] For this reason, in the context of eighth- and ninth-century Anglo-Saxon silver pennies, preference here has been given to the obverse die figures rather than the reverse: as die-links and die-duplicates are comparatively rare in general, sticking only to reverse figures would have produced figures of lower reliability, despite any advantages that estimates based on reverse dies might offer.[32]

Also of paramount importance is the type of calculation used to analyse this information. The formulae used here are those devised by Warren Esty, which rely on comparing the number of surviving coins, the number of dies represented within that sample and the number of those dies which are represented by just one surviving coin (singletons). A major advantage of these formulae in comparison with some older methods is the estimation of the coverage of a sample (a term first used in this context by Stewart Lyon):[33] how likely it is that a new coin will reveal a known die, essentially giving an impression of how representative the sample probably is.[34] There are a number of eighth- and ninth-century coinages which have coverages of 0.6 or over, which present comparatively sound evidence for the original scale of production. Many cluster between about 0.4 and 0.6, and there are also several which fall below this scale. The coverage is used to create not only a single best estimate, but also a spread showing the upper and lower 95 per cent confidence intervals. The distance between these estimates is again dependent on the degree of die-linking in the surviving sample, and can be very large indeed when the coverage is low. Taking the Canterbury Cross-and-Wedges coinage of *c.* 805–10 as an example, the obverse coverage is 0.56 based on 112 coins struck from 72 dies, of which 49 are known from only one coin. This produces a best estimate of *c.* 170 original dies, with a lower estimate of *c.* 125 dies and an upper estimate of *c.* 240 dies. A decrease in the coverage results in a wider

---

[31] *Ibid.*, pp. 294–6.

[32] D. M. Metcalf in I. Stewart, 'CVNNETTI Reconsidered', in *Coinage in Ninth-Century Northumbria*, ed. Metcalf, pp. 345–54, at 350–2. Reverse dies generally present slightly higher estimates because they were worn out more quickly: they would thus need to be replaced on a more frequent basis than obverse dies.

[33] H. R. Mossop, R. H. M. Dolley and C. S. S. Lyon, 'Analysis of the Material', in *The Lincoln Mint c. 890–1279*, ed. V. Smart (Newcastle upon Tyne, 1970), pp. 11–19, at 16 and 19.

[34] W. Esty, 'Estimation', and 'How to Estimate the Original Number of Dies and the Coverage of a Sample', *NC* 166 (2006), 359–64; T. Crafter, 'A Die-Study of the *Cross-and-Crosslets* Type of the Ipswich Mint, *c.* 1161/2–1180', *NC* 162 (2002), 237–51, at pp. 239–41.

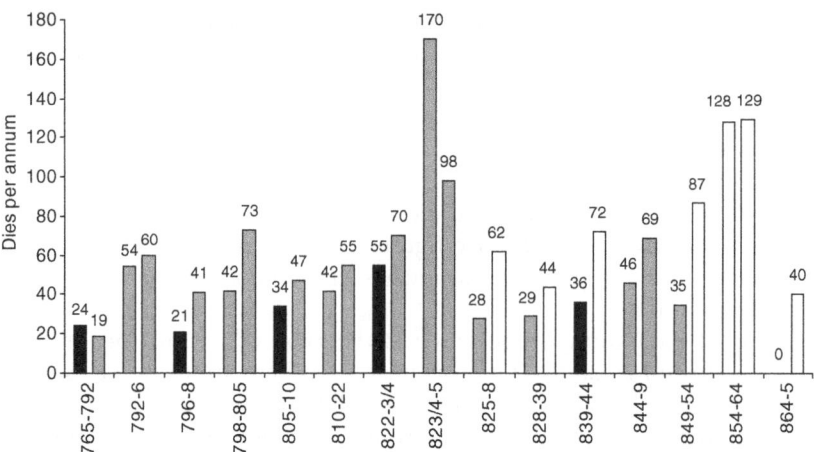

Figure 7.1 Estimated output in dies per annum at Canterbury.

margin of error. Thus the coinage of Berhtwulf – 93 coins struck from 81 obverse dies, 72 known from one coin – produces a coverage of only 0.23, and a correspondingly uncertain estimate of *c.* 520 dies with a low endpoint of the 95 per cent confidence interval of *c.* 285 and a high endpoint of *c.* 1,000 dies.

It should be noted that in the case of the West Saxon mint and most of the coinage of Rochester, specimens are too scarce and the estimates too uncertain to provide reliable results of this kind. Moreover, there were almost certainly internal rhythms of production within the numbers presented here, most of which are impossible to ascertain. Typological study of Offa's Light coinage indicates an early phase of very low productivity before minting picked up steam in the portrait and related coinages, probably in the 780s. On an even smaller scale, later records reveal that the intensity of output of the same coinage could vary substantially year to year, and even seasonally within a year.[35]

Figures 7.1–7.4 display the rate of output for the southern English mints, based on the probable number of obverse and reverse dies used per year in each phase of minting. All should be used with reference to the original data, as these figures are derived from the estimate of output derived by the probable duration of the phase, and some of the variation within them is attributable to the quality of data rather than any real change in production. The shades of columns give some impression

[35] Stahl, *Zecca*, pp. 369–71.

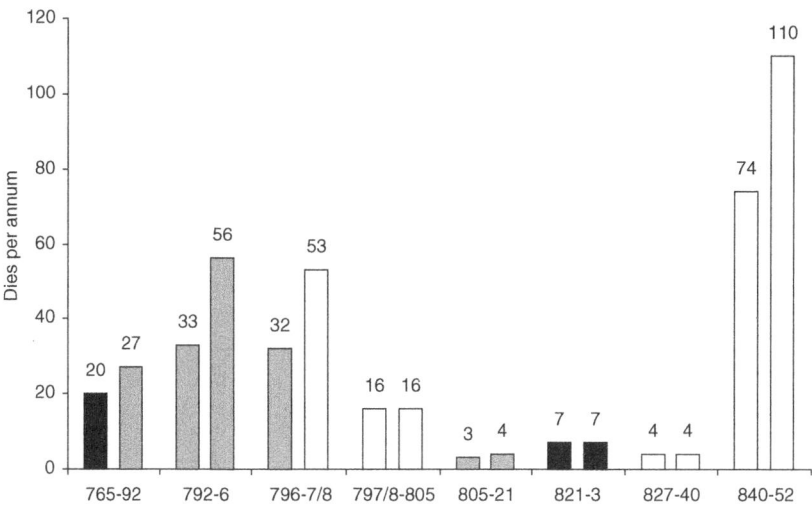

Figure 7.2 Estimated output in dies per annum at London.

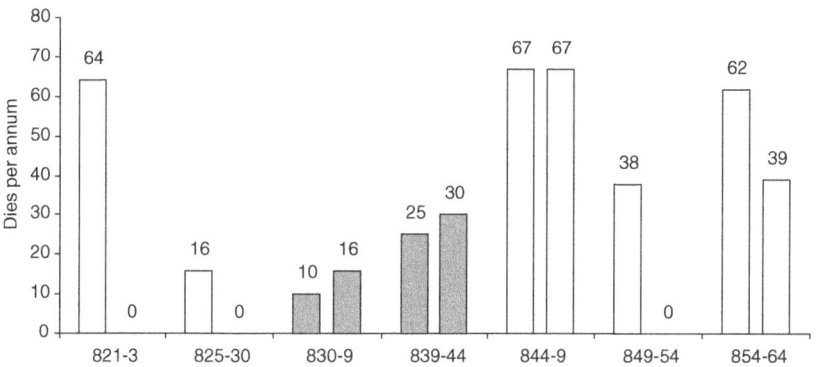

Figure 7.3 Estimated output in dies per annum at Rochester.

of their reliability: black columns indicate figures based on a relatively high estimated coverage of 0.5 or higher; grey columns indicate figures based on a middling estimated coverage of 0.31–0.49; and white columns indicate figures based on a poor estimated coverage of below 0.3. The latter in particular must be treated with extreme caution. It should also be noted that the data are simply not available for some mints in some periods, and not at all from Southampton. Finally, the output for the 860s was probably considerably larger than appears to be the case here, as no production data are yet available for the Mercian coinage

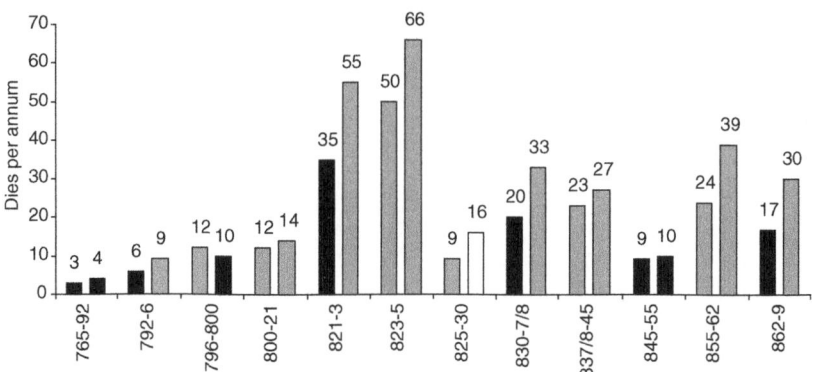

Figure 7.4 Estimated output in dies per annum at Ipswich.

of Burgred, though it probably did not become substantial in quantity until the late 860s.[36]

There are many features to be teased out from these results. Overall, the 790s and 840s–50s stand out as periods of generally substantial productivity, while the 820s were also marked by buoyant output at Canterbury and the East Anglian mint. The later 860s probably also saw extensive production at Canterbury and London for Æthelred I and Burgred respectively. The prominence of the 790s can be explained by the activity of two very productive mints in a major recoinage, one of which was to go into swift decline at the end of the decade. In the 840s and 850s Canterbury retained a constant and relatively high level of productivity, but it was the resurgence of the London mint under Berhtwulf combined with the increased output of the East Anglian mint that made those years so exceptional. It should be added, however, that the reliability of estimates from this later period is often very low; actual numbers of dies used may have been substantially smaller

Within this general picture of national trends different developments can be traced for each of the five known mints. The keynote at Canterbury seems to have been relative stability and high output across the century. Many of the most reliable estimates cluster at twenty to thirty obverse and thirty-five to seventy reverse dies per annum throughout the period from the late eighth century until the 850s. The Inscribed Cross coinage of *c.* 854–*c.* 864 appears to have been produced on a somewhat larger scale, although the coverage of surviving coins is low and the

---

[36] Pagan, 'Southern England', p. 61; *MEC*, p. 310. The contemporary coinage of Æthelred I of Wessex has been incorporated into Figure 7.1 on the basis of the data in A. Lyons and W. MacKay, 'The Coinage of Æthelred I (865–871)', *BNJ* 77 (2007), 71–118.

estimate correspondingly uncertain. The exact dating of the coinage is also approximate, and it is possible that some of the many new moneyers of this coinage who have been assigned to Canterbury were in fact active at Rochester or elsewhere. In addition, a brief surge in production associated with a probable recoinage part-way through the coinage would not be detectable from these results.

Production at Ipswich seems to have begun at a very low rate under Offa, Eadwald and Coenwulf. A major increase in productivity came in the early ninth century, most clearly visible in the reigns of Ceolwulf I and Beornwulf. This temporary boom in output came to an end with the reign of Æthelstan, although production remained more substantial than it had been before *c.* 820. Another resurgence came in the reign of Edmund, when Ipswich followed Canterbury in an upsurge. In the case of Canterbury this has in the past been associated with a *renovatio monetae*, but there is no clear evidence for such a reform in East Anglia, suggesting that other forces may have been at work. Despite these vicissitudes, for most of the forty years after *c.* 825 Ipswich displaced London as the most productive mint of southern England after Canterbury, remaining stable at approximately half the output of Canterbury.

London's story was almost the opposite of Ipswich's: it initially experienced a high rate of productivity, on a par with Canterbury at some twenty to thirty obverse dies per year in the 780s–90s, which declined over the time of Coenwulf to ten or fewer. Estimates of output combined with the surviving numbers of coins and moneyers suggest that the mint took a sudden nosedive at some point during the course of the Tribrach coinage (797/8–*c.* 805). It is tempting to associate this swift decline with the two fires which are recorded as ravaging London in 798 and 801.[37] Vivid illustrations of this change can be seen in other aspects of the coinage. For example, just a few years prior to its decline London seems to have been the mint of origin for the influential Tribrach design, which spread and was taken up by all other southern English mints. This presumably suggests either a notional adherence to the coin-type of London, or alternatively to the coin-type of the politically dominant Mercian king, who had traditionally commanded the lion's share of minting in southern England. Either way, London was still very much at the heart of the minting network of southern England. But in the 800s, after the decline had set in, the famous gold mancus of Coenwulf was struck from Canterbury-made dies but with the mint-signature of London – presumably because local dies were unavailable or thought unsuitable for a prestigious coinage such as this.[38]

---

[37] *Historia regum* 798 and 801 (ed. Arnold II, 59 and 66; trans. *EHD*, pp. 275–6).
[38] Above, pp. 114–17.

Minting at London slowed still further in the first quarter of the ninth century and perhaps stopped altogether in the time of Beornwulf and Ludica, the later reign of Wiglaf and the early 840s. It was probably for this reason that support was sought from Rochester when minting restarted in earnest in the later 840s, using the services of a new clutch of twelve moneyers. On the (admittedly imprecise) evidence of their surviving coins it looks as if London in the late 840s and early 850s experienced a brief but impressive restoration of minting. The background of Berhtwulf's reign is highly obscure,[39] and this resurgence may or may not have been the result of royal initiative. The burst of productivity under Berhtwulf was followed by another trough in the first half of the reign of Burgred, when minting of the Lunettes type began at a very low rate using the services of just one moneyer, Tatel, who had first appeared under Berhtwulf.[40]

It is dangerous to speculate on how Rochester and the West Saxon mint fit into these patterns on the basis of only a few very uncertain die-estimates. When the data available from Rochester are at their best, in the 840s, its productivity usually appears to have been about two-thirds that of contemporary Canterbury (less in the Inscribed Cross coinage). However, it should be noted that this last decade of discernible coinage at Rochester was also marked by a temporary increase in the complement of moneyers (*c.* 844) from two or three to five or six: this may well have been a time of generally higher productivity at Rochester. In the case of Southampton, the three attributable coins from the reign of Beorhtric are too few for a reliable estimate, though their scarcity implies a very small issue. The obverse and reverse coverage for Ecgberht's West Saxon pence is extremely low (0.13), and indicates something in the region of 350 dies for the whole coinage. But since new evidence indicates that this coinage probably spanned the whole of Ecgberht's long reign,[41] it appears that productivity was generally low compared to other southern mints.

The productivity of moneyers

To a certain extent estimating the output of the mint-towns in this period is misleading, since there is no evidence of a single minting establishment ever existing in these places.[42] It is therefore also important to analyse

[39] On the events of Berhtwulf's reign see Keynes, 'King Alfred and the Mercians', pp. 2–6; J. Booth, 'Monetary Alliance or Technical Co-operation? The Coinage of Berhtwulf of Mercia (840–52)', in *Kings, Currency and Alliances*, ed. Blackburn and Dumville, pp. 63–103, at 63–7.

[40] Booth, 'Monetary Alliance', p. 79; Pagan, 'Coinage in Southern England', pp. 57–8; *MEC*, p. 310.

[41] Naismith, 'New Moneyer'. [42] Above, pp. 126 and 132–3.

Table 7.1 *Output of individual moneyers*

Name	Years of service	No. of coins	No. of dies	No. of single-tons	Cover-age (%)	Point estimate	95% confidence intervals	Estimated dies per year
Canterbury								
Eoba	35–40	163	Obv. 116	88	46	350	255–480	9–10
	(770s–800s)		Rev. 118	91	44	370	265–515	9–11
Babba	27–35	32	Obv. 28	18	44	85	45–180	2–3
	(770s–800s)		Rev. 30	21	34	120	60–285	3–4
Swefherd	22–31	81	Obv. 54	39	52	140	95–210	5–6
	(800s–840s)		Rev. 55	40	51	150	100–225	5–7
Sæberht	17–26	66	Obv. 42	25	62	73	50–105	3–5
	(800s–820s)		Rev. 47	32	51	142	85–235	5–7
Osmund	20–26	43	Obv. 33	24	44	100	55–190	4–5
	(820s–840s)		Rev. 35	30	30	165	85–365	6–8
Werheard	23–41	72	Obv. 47	34	53	120	80–185	3–5
	(790s–830s)		Rev. 53	41	43	170	105–280	4–7
London								
Alhmund	3–16	65	Obv. 46	34	48	130	85–215	8–44
	(770s–790s)		Rev. 50	39	40	175	105–300	11–58
Æthelweald	5?–12	53	Obv. 28	15	72	50	35–70	4–10
	(770s–790s)		Rev. 36	27	49	100	60–170	8–20
East Anglia								
Eadnoth	6–25	17	Obv. 8	5	71	15	10–25	1–3
	(780s–800s)		Rev. 8	5	71	15	10–25	1–3
Lul	9–41	59	Obv. 37	23	61	80	55–120	2–9
	(780s–820s)		Rev. 42	31	47	120	75–200	3–13
Wodel	21–27	46	Obv. 31	21	54	75	45–130	3–4
	(790s–820s)		Rev. 29	18	61	60	40–100	2–3
Monna	3–20	54	Obv. 36	24	56	85	55–140	4–29
	(820s–840s)		Rev. 43	36	42	185	100–360	9–61
Wihtred	31–53	55	Obv. 42	32	42	140	80–250	3–4
	(780s–820s)		Rev. 45	36	35	180	100–355	3–6

the surviving output of individual moneyers. Almost no moneyers of this period are represented by enough coins to permit such calculations within any one phase, although amalgamating the products of all phases in which a moneyer was active can provide a much sounder basis for die-estimation. Only a few moneyers are known from enough coins to make this a worthwhile exercise, and all are listed in Table 7.1.

It should be noted that these moneyers are not necessarily representative of their profession: the mere fact that so many coins survive in their names indicates that they were more active and long-lived. They also tend to cluster in the early and middle parts of the period, when the continuity of moneyers was strongest and the number of specimens highest. What the comparative output of other, less well-known money-ers was remains an unknown quantity. Also, if a moneyer began or ended his career in a long phase, or during one of the more obscure phases of the coinage, there can be considerable uncertainty as to how long his career lasted. Finally, it must be remembered that the output of long-lived moneyers was susceptible to more general fluctuations in demand, debasement, availability of bullion and suchlike. For this reason the esti-mated output per year must be taken with a pinch of salt, and read in comparison with the estimated general output of each mint.

Nevertheless, the key point is that there were major differences in the scale of operations undertaken by different moneyers. The 'average' output of a well-established moneyer usually seems to have been around five pairs of dies per annum. Under Offa in particular there was a ten-dency for some moneyers to be notably more productive. Æthelwald and Alhmund from London are conspicuous for their unusually high levels of productivity, as is Eoba at Canterbury, who stands out for a number of reasons.[43] These moneyers may have used at least ten sets of dies each year. What brought them to their position of prominence is unclear: they may have been wealthier, better connected, more commercially astute or in a more elevated social position.[44]

Contexts and comparisons

Extreme variation in the output of different mints and moneyers was not a phenomenon restricted to the eighth and ninth centuries. Informative comparisons can be made with some of the better-studied mint-towns later in the Anglo-Saxon period. Mark Blackburn has provided calcula-tions for the Anglo-Scandinavian mint at York in the tenth century which show a similar scale of production to Canterbury and (at times) the East Anglian mint in the eighth and ninth centuries: that is, the equivalent of some twenty to thirty obverse dies per annum.[45] Sometimes tenth-century York was probably significantly less productive than its southern counterparts of the previous century. Moving into the later tenth and eleventh centuries, Lincoln, Winchester and York – three of the top four mints in the kingdom – have all been the focus of general die-studies.[46]

[43] Above, pp. 150–7.   [44] Above, pp. 146–9.
[45] Blackburn, 'Scandinavian York', pp. 342–4.
[46] Mossop *et al.*, *Lincoln Mint*, esp. Appendix, table 4; Harvey *et al.*, *Winchester Mint*.

To take the Crux type of Æthelred II as an example (probably current *c.* 991–7), these three mints all produce remarkably similar estimates of obverse die-output: 182, 180 and 173 respectively. The reverse estimates are somewhat less homogeneous: 260, 283 and 430. It must be emphasized that this somewhat artificial comparison is based on mints which worked in fundamentally different ways from those of the eighth and ninth centuries: much of the output of Lincoln, Winchester and York in this period would probably have come in the early stages of a type as coin-owners brought in their currency to be reminted, with a substantial drop-off thereafter. It should also be noted that although these (along with London) were the largest mints, there were dozens of others active simultaneously,[47] compared with the probable total of six for the whole of England in the ninth century. Nonetheless, even assuming a relatively equal output in each year of production, these three leading late Anglo-Saxon mints appear comparable to Canterbury and (at times) Ipswich in the late eighth and ninth centuries, with approximately thirty obverse and forty-five reverse dies being used per annum.

The origins of variation at the level of moneyer as well as mint hence go back at least to the inception of moneyer-signed coinage in eighth-century Southumbrian England. Pursuing detailed comparisons of output beyond these bounds is not yet possible, and there are two particularly urgent desiderata which would serve to flesh out the context of English minting 757–865. The first of these is more die-studies of early pennies of the period *c.* 675–*c.* 750. These would provide a more secure impression of how output under Offa and his successors measured up to earlier times, and possibly of what authority is most likely to have been behind various earlier coin-issues. The second is how Canterbury, London and the other English mints compare with their contemporary counterparts elsewhere in Europe. Carolingian coins do not carry moneyers' names, leaving it unclear how many moneyers could have been working at any one mint or even if production was organized in this way. There may have been significant differences between major coastal or frontier mints such as Dorestad and Quentovic, which (like the English mints) handled the heavy business of incoming foreign money,[48] and smaller inland mints, which may only have been substantially active at times of coinage reform. Some of these mints may have been comparable in scale and output to the workshop of a single moneyer in southern England:

[47] D. M. Metcalf, 'Continuity and Change in English Monetary History *c.* 973–1086. Part II', *BNJ* 51 (1981), 52–90, at pp. 78–85.

[48] S. Coupland, 'Trading Places: Quentovic and Dorestad Reassessed', *EME* 7 (1998), 85–114.

a conclusion tentatively suggested by die-studies of the mints of Dinant and Trier.[49] But more thorough study of Carolingian coinage is needed before this question can be approached in any detail. Information about single-finds and productive sites will help offset the potential bias of hoard data, and would very effectively complement any future die-studies.

CONCLUSION

In sum, the mints whose moneyers answered to Offa, Coenwulf and Æthelwulf included some which must be counted as substantial enterprises, comparable in scale to even the largest late Anglo-Saxon mints. This was of course less true of the smaller mints, Rochester and Southampton/Winchester. It should also be stated that these mints followed their own distinct path in many respects. At all of them, recoinages of the type familiar from the last century of Anglo-Saxon England were rare. Their products should probably be seen as the remains of a more constant process of reminting, based on a currency that was relatively open to issues from elsewhere in southern England, whatever their date or origin. Each mint also had its own unique history. London started out strong, but soon entered a swift decline to almost nothing in the decades after *c.* 800, save for a temporary and West Saxon-supported resurgence in the late 840s. Ipswich grew quickly in the ninth century from small beginnings in the eighth, eventually becoming the second most productive mint south of the Humber. In contrast Rochester and especially the West Saxon mint retained more stable if substantially lower rates of activity. Canterbury was the largest mint overall, and shows signs of unusually intense activity in the 820s and 850s–60s.

In most instances it is difficult to relate these progressions to other events in the course of a mint's history except on a very general level, but a striking exception is the case of London.[50] Here there is a remarkably close fit of the numismatic, archaeological and historical records from the same period. Excavations within the 'Strand settlement' known as *Lundenwic* have shown that in the early ninth century defences were constructed through earlier habitations at a time when the activity and

---

[49] C. Meert, 'Les monnaies carolingiennes de l'atelier de Dinant', *Revue belge de numismatique* 108 (1962), 153–72; R. Weiller, *Die Münzen von Trier. Erster Teil: Erster Abschnitt. Beschreibung der Münzen: 6. Jahrhundert–1307* (Düsseldorf, 1988), pp. 266–80.

[50] Stewart, 'English and Norman', p. 27; D. M. Metcalf, 'The Monetary Economy of Ninth-Century England South of the Humber: A Topographical Analysis', in *Kings, Currency and Alliances*, ed. Blackburn and Dumville, pp. 167–97, at 184. For comments on the archaeology and history of the other towns, see pp. 32–5, 128–30 and 235–8.

organization of the settlement were in decline.[51] Fires were reported in 798 and 801, coinciding closely with the major downturn in mint-output.[52] After *c.* 820 the coins suggest that London's decline only deepened. Although it was certainly not the preferred haunt of Mercian rulers, London was still favoured by Coenwulf, and was also seat of a bishop and occasionally host to Church councils.[53] Explicit evidence of its continued prominence in the 830s and 840s is lacking, though so are all substantial written records from the Mercian kingdom at this time. There is limited evidence for interest in commercial activity there again in the 840s, coinciding with the sudden re-expansion of the mint under Berhtwulf.[54] By the 860s, however, the bishop of London had moved into the political orbit of the West Saxon kingdom.[55]

These events probably reflect important changes in London's economic status, which may have included a change in the preferred route of foreign traders bringing silver towards England. This could partly explain the establishment of a second mint in Kent in the middle of Coenwulf's reign (at Rochester) and the growth of Ipswich's output: they may have picked up the slack from London, and thereby contributed to its ongoing decline.

London's fall contrasts not only with Ipswich's prosperity and Rochester's establishment, but also with received views of the early ninth century which accord London a prominent role in the Mercian regime – certainly more so than Canterbury.[56] Kent was an often unwilling appanage of the Mercian kingdom, and it is perhaps surprising that most of the realm's monetary activity came to be focused on its southeastern tip; a corner of the kingdom dominated by an assertive archbishop of Canterbury and which in many ways remained several steps removed from royal movements and policies.[57] Coenwulf, king of the Mercians during the crucial part of this process, was presumably either unable or unwilling to halt the shift of monetary production in the direction of

---

[51] G. Malcolm, D. Bowsher and R. Cowie, *Middle Saxon London: Excavations at the Royal Opera House, 1989–99* (London, 2003), pp. 118–20.

[52] However, neither war nor fire put a dent in the activities of mints elsewhere: Rochester was apparently unaffected by a viking attack in 842, and Canterbury bounced back swiftly after a fire in 798: Brooks, *Early History*, pp. 121–4.

[53] The Coenwulf 'mancus' (Naismith G2a) is important evidence for London's changing status (cf. above, pp. 119–20), as are the charters S 168 and 170. For councils, see Cubitt, *Church Councils*, pp. 27–31.

[54] S 88. Cf. Booth, 'Monetary Alliance', p. 65.

[55] Keynes, 'Control of Kent', pp. 128–30, and 'King Alfred and the Mercians', p. 8.

[56] Cf. the letter to Coenwulf on the proposition that Canterbury's metropolitan status be transferred to London (MGH Epist. IV, no. 127, pp. 187–9; trans. *EHD*, pp. 861–2) and S 170 and 1436.

[57] Keynes, 'Control of Kent', esp. pp. 113–15; Crick, 'Church, Land'; Brooks, *Early History*, pp. 111–206. See also above pp. 19–20.

Kent and East Anglia. If other indications of limited Mercian interests in Kent are correct, then this provides a further vivid illustration of the small part management of minting generally played in the purview of Anglo-Saxon rulers, and of their powerlessness to manipulate the trends of commerce and production in any meaningful way. Control of coinage simply did not entail control over the general movement of bullion and trade.

Chapter 8

THE CIRCULATION OF COINAGE

The scale of minting in southern England in the eighth and ninth centuries prompts a number of questions, above all what became of these pennies after leaving the mint. It is at this point that numismatics gives way to monetary history. England's plentiful find-data allow this to be pursued in great detail, on the basis of the material recorded for several decades in the pages of Coin Hoards and the Coin Register, and latterly in the electronic Corpus of Early Medieval Coin Finds and Portable Antiquities Scheme.

Making the most of this information depends on the contributions different types of coin-find have to offer. Hoards of multiple coins, on the one hand, represent agglomerations of currency hidden or lost, and not recovered until modern times. They might be the savings of an individual or community put together painstakingly over many years, including a wide array of coins added at different times; alternatively, they might have been drawn *en bloc* from the circulating currency, with or without prejudice in favour of coins of specific design or weight. Dangerous times – war, civil and political unrest, plague and similar – could have a significant effect on the rate at which coins were deposited and not recovered. Both savings and currency hoards are a fundamental source for determining the chronology of a coinage, and also give some insight into which issues were acceptable in use at a specific place and time.[1]

Single-finds, on the other hand, are a very different phenomenon. Some may have been deposited deliberately for economic, religious or other reasons, but the assumption is that most single-finds from either an excavated or a metal-detected context were lost accidentally. That is to say, each single-find represents a separate and unintentional loss. There are now almost 1,300 single-finds (*c.* 1,000 local pennies and *c.* 300 foreign coins) with a more or less precise find-provenance recorded from England south of the

---

[1] Grierson, *Numismatics*, pp. 124–5 and 130–6.

Humber in the period 757–865. This large sample is enough to rewrite the much more limited testimony of contemporary hoards, and has only become available since the 1970s thanks to the spread of metal-detecting as a hobby, the increased use of metal-detectors in an archaeological context and, above all, the establishment of databases for the preservation of find information.[2] The corpus has crystallized into two broad categories of single-find: the true single-find or stray-find, which turns up in an isolated context without any other contemporary finds in the vicinity; and those from 'hot spots' of metallic finds which have been termed 'productive sites' by numismatists. The nature of these sites remains controversial,[3] but the volume and importance of the material they present does not. Some have now produced over a thousand early medieval objects, with their own distinctive chronological and geographical profiles which must be borne in mind in relation to other sites and finds. For the purposes of assessing circulation, the key point is that each find from either a productive site or an isolated context very probably reflects a random loss.

Although they are the single greatest resource available for understanding the early medieval currency, single-finds cannot be used uncritically, and are subject to certain important caveats. In the first place, there is normally no indication of when loss occurred. Loss of a coin eventually recovered as a single-find could have occurred moments after minting, or many decades later. Contemporary hoards provide a partial blueprint of the currency and its wastage rate, which can be used to give a proportional breakdown of how long coins remained in circulation. There may also be reason to query whether a single-find was originally lost where it was found. Many coins from excavated contexts such as Southampton turned up in spoil heaps and other areas of refuse-dumping, suggesting that they were inadvertently lost, perhaps within a household, and thrown away with other refuse. Coins found in fields far from any known habitation may likewise have been lost in rubbish and spread out for fertilization only later.[4] There is nothing beyond guesswork to aid modern numismatists and archaeologists in determining if, how and from where coins may have been spread in waste, though it is unlikely that such movements, at least in the early Middle Ages, took them far.[5]

---

[2] Blackburn, '"Productive" Sites', pp. 20–1; for a Byzantine perspective see C. Morrisson, 'Byzantine Money: Its Production and Circulation', in *Economic History of Byzantium*, ed. Laiou, III, 909–66', at pp. 936–40.

[3] See below, pp. 238–9 and 279–80.

[4] M. Blackburn, 'What Factors Govern the Number of Coins Found on an Archaeological Site?', in *Coins and Archaeology: Medieval Archaeology Research Group, Proceedings of the First Meeting at Isegran, Norway 1988*, ed. H. Clarke and E. Schia, BAR International Series 556 (Oxford, 1989), pp. 15–24, at 17–18.

[5] Naismith, 'Money of the Saints'.

A more subtle criticism sometimes levelled against single-finds is that of the effect modern methods of recovery might have on the value of their testimony. The bulk of single-finds now occur as the fruit of amateur searching with the aid of a metal-detector. It would be naïve to assume that the reported total of this material constitutes the entirety of what is unearthed every year.[6] Coins of the late eighth and ninth centuries are sufficiently rare, famous and valuable that, if brought to light, they stand little chance of being overlooked as common and not worth reporting; but an unknown proportion of finds is never reported, either through negligence or criminality. Trawls of commercial catalogues help bring some of these errant specimens to light, albeit often without any details of when and where they were uncovered. Nevertheless, there must be many new finds which slip through the net completely every year, and the proportion of finds which is properly reported is believed to vary from region to region. Norfolk, for example, has for decades been noted for especially good and close relations between detectorists, archaeologists and museum staff.[7] Its large volume of recorded finds reflects not only the rich resources of the area but also the diligence and dutiful record-keeping of its modern investigators.[8] In contrast, the area of modern London stands out as a relative blank on distribution maps because of the obvious difficulties of metal-detecting in a heavily urbanized area, while an exodus of detectorists from the capital means that finds from the environs are plentiful, and tend to be concentrated along the routes of modern motorways.[9]

Local trends of this kind do not negate the conclusions of a broader regional or national study, though factors of modern recovery have been invoked to criticize interpretation of the find-record on a larger scale. For example, a perennial tendency of coin distribution from the Roman period to the later Middle Ages is for finds to cluster in eastern and southern England: essentially the area from Yorkshire southwest to Dorset, with gaps in the Weald and the East Anglian fens. To a large extent this is simply a result of the long-term concentration of population, trade and wealth in these regions,[10] but it has also been proposed that it reflects the distribution

---

[6] Cf. Metcalf, *Atlas*, pp. 14–17.

[7] For a critique of the interpretation of early Anglo-Saxon detector-finds from Norfolk, see M. Chester-Kadwell, *Early Anglo-Saxon Communities in the Landscape of Norfolk*, BAR British Series 481 (Oxford, 2009), esp. pp. 62–90.

[8] J. Richards, J. Naylor and C. Holas-Clark, 'Anglo-Saxon Landscape and Economy: Using Portable Antiquities to Study Anglo-Saxon and Viking England', *Internet Archaeology* 25 (2009), §§ 2.4.1 and 2.4.2.4 (http://intarch.ac.uk/journal/issue25/richards_index.html).

[9] *Ibid.*, § 2.4.2.5. On the importance of knowing which areas have not been subjected to search by metal-detectorists, see Chester-Kadwell, *Early Anglo-Saxon Communities*, pp. 85–8.

[10] Bolton, 'What Is Money?', p. 5; Metcalf, *Atlas*, pp. 33–4.

of modern metal-detector activity. The increasingly plentiful data offered by the Portable Antiquities Scheme and other databases have alleviated this concern, however, by building up a broader portfolio of finds from across the country. The find-spots of these do not always coincide with modern centres of settlement, and can be related to rivers, Roman roads, prehistoric routeways and known ancient centres of population.[11] At a local level one can thus have confidence in a high proportion of the data, and more broadly there are now many patterns among detector finds which do not adhere to an easterly distribution, as one would expect for all categories of object if the key factor was the bias of modern searching. Roman gold coins, for example, are now known from over 700 single-finds in England (along with 122 hoards): compared to other Roman coins recorded on the Portable Antiquities Scheme database, they show a noticeably stronger distribution in northern England and Wales and a weaker concentration in the south and east. This pattern has been linked with the different and especially military uses of gold coinage.[12]

In sum, single-finds have risen in recent decades to be both numerous and representative. The *c.* 1,300 recorded single-finds from southern England from Offa to Æthelberht need to be handled with care in some respects, but provide the key to a uniquely detailed view of circulation and coin-use. They will be at the heart of this chapter on the nature of the monetary economy of Southumbrian England, which focuses on the chronological and regional breakdown of coin-finds. For these purposes the whole of modern England has been divided up into ten regions (Map 8.1). These are based on the modern geography of pre-1974 counties, but are intended to approximate known Anglo-Saxon geographical entities including Wessex, Mercia, East Anglia, Northumbria and Lindsey. The imposition of any such units will of necessity be somewhat speculative: Anglo-Saxon boundaries and territories can rarely be traced in detail and were often unstable. Thus, for instance, although the Thames has been used here as the boundary between Mercia and Wessex, for much of the late eighth and ninth centuries the land to the immediate south was debatable territory.[13] Nevertheless, using larger units based on approximations of known early medieval political divisions clarifies broader trends in the material, and is a useful complement to the methods previously used by Michael Metcalf and others to survey the currency.[14]

[11] Richards, Naylor and Holas-Clark, 'Anglo-Saxon Landscape and Economy', § 2.4.2.5.
[12] R. Bland, 'Roman Gold Coins in Britain', *International Committee of Money and Banking Museums e-Proceedings 3* (Utrecht, 2008), pp. 31–43, at 40 (www.icomon.org.).
[13] Yorke, *Wessex*, pp. 61–4 and 94–6.
[14] See, for examples of these methods, D. M. Metcalf, 'Monetary Economy' and 'Determining the Mint-Attribution of East Anglian *Sceattas* through Regression Analysis', *BNJ* 70 (2000), 1–11; Chick, *Coinage of Offa*, pp. 17–29.

Map 8.1 Monetary regions of England.

ENGLISH MONEY, FOREIGN MONEY

Perhaps the most arresting feature of the English currency in the late eighth and ninth centuries was its homogeneity. No denominations other than the silver penny were struck regularly by any southern English moneyer in this period. Gold coins were made occasionally, but these belong to a different and relatively well-defined context of high-value use. The first known English round halfpennies belong to the 870s.[15] This model largely held true for England's immediate cross-Channel neighbour – the

---

[15] EMC 2004.0009 (a Cross-and-Lozenge halfpenny of Ceolwulf II).

Frankish empire. Essentially the same currency prevailed across southern England and northwest continental Europe, stretching down into Italy after the 780s.

Theoretically, coin-users in Southumbrian England could have come into contact with a wide variety of coins, including those from various southern English kingdoms, Northumbria, the Frankish empire and occasionally even further afield. Late eighth- and ninth-century England was not, however, a monetary free-for-all: coin-users clearly felt able to accept some types of currency and not others. In the absence of written reference to the acceptability of different coinages one must rely on the evidence of hoards and single-finds alone. What these show is that coins from all five southern English mints could safely be used across southern England – regardless of whether they lay within Mercian, West Saxon or East Anglian control. In particular, the determining factor in whether the majority of finds from Mercia or Wessex came from 'friendly' mints (i.e., those working in the name of the king of Mercia or Wessex) was who controlled Kent and its two substantial towns of Canterbury and Rochester. This is summarized in Table 8.1, while the regional breakdown based on mint rather than kingdom will be examined further below.[16]

In other words, except for periods when one kingdom happened to dominate all functioning mints of the period (as was the case with Mercia in most of the period before 796), and with the possible and partial exception of Wessex after the late 850s,[17] there was always an appreciable proportion of non-local English currency circulating within any given kingdom. When none of the leading mints – which (after *c.* 800) is to say those of Kent and East Anglia – lay within the control of a kingdom only a small proportion of its finds came from 'friendly' mints.

The dominance of one mint or another in different regions of the country was thus a function of economics rather than politics: there was apparently no systematic attempt to exclude coins from other southern English kingdoms.[18] Use of general weight and metal standards was probably what drove this common market. Intrinsically, pennies from Mercia, Wessex, Kent and East Anglia were normally quite closely comparable and consequently interchangeable.[19] This was not, however, true of non-English silver coinage, at least after Charlemagne's and Offa's reforms in

---

[16] For these purposes, 'Mercia' comprises the regions of western Mercia, eastern Mercia and Lincolnshire, and 'Wessex' consists of east and west Wessex.

[17] Above, p. 109–12.   [18] Cf. Metcalf, 'Monetary Economy', pp. 179–83.

[19] A possible exception can be seen in the near-total absence of recent Mercian issues in the Dorking hoard of *c.* 862–4, which were made using a much finer standard of silver than their West Saxon contemporaries: see above, p. 109–12 and 164–5.

Table 8.1 *Representation of local or friendly mints within independent kingdoms 757–865, based on date of production*

Area	Date	Mints under control/total no. of active mints	Total number of finds	Number of finds from controlled mints	Percentage local coinage	Percentage non-local coinage
Mercia	757–96	3/3 (London, Canterbury, East Anglia)	130	129	*99*	*1*
	796–825	4/5 (London, Canterbury, East Anglia, Rochester)	137	122	*89*	*11*
	825–52	1/5 (London)	45	4	*9*	*91*
Wessex	760–96	0/3	43	0	*0*	*100*
	796–825	1/5 (Wessex)	71	3	*4*	*96*
	825–65	3/5 (Canterbury, Rochester, Wessex)	40	31	*78*	*22*
East Anglia	825–69	1/5 (East Anglia)	70	50	*71*	*29*

the 790s. Prior to this, the same weight standard of *c.* 1.30g had apparently prevailed on both sides of the Channel; thereafter, southern English pennies used a standard of *c.* 1.40g–1.45g, Carolingian *denarii* one of *c.* 1.70g.

This change in weight standard contributed to a significant shift in the way in which Carolingian silver coins circulated in southern England (Table 8.2). Prior to 793/4 the distribution of Carolingian silver roughly mirrors (though in much smaller volume) the distribution of native coinage. Among these early Carolingian finds there is a preponderance of *denarii* of Pippin III (seven out of eleven), produced in 768. This is not the pattern seen in estimates of output or volume of finds from the Carolingian empire itself, where coins of the period *c.* 771 (and especially 793/4) until 840 tend to be most prevalent.[20] Michael Metcalf has interpreted this pattern as a remnant of quite widespread and unrestricted use of Carolingian coinage in the decades around Offa's first reform, before the expansion of his substantive Light coinage *c.* 785: that is to say, Carolingian coins were used in England more extensively at a time when native pennies were still scarce.[21] Estimating based on the numbers of known finds, and allowing for some which may have been lost at a

[20] Coupland, 'Carolingian Single-Finds', and 'Trading Places', pp. 213 and 222–5.
[21] Metcalf, 'Betwixt Sceattas and Offa's Pence', pp. 17–18.

Table 8.2 *Finds of Carolingian and related silver coins in England 751–c. 864, based on date of production*

	Before 793/4		793/4–840		840–64	
	No.	%	No.	%	No.	%
Kent	2	*18*	3	*19*	0	*0*
Essex	0	*0*	0	*0*	3	*15*
Sussex	1	*9*	0	*0*	2	*10*
East Anglia	1	*9*	9	*56*	7	*35*
East Mercia	3	*27*	1	*6*	1	*5*
West Mercia	1	*9*	1	*6*	2	*10*
East Wessex	2	*18*	1	*6*	2	*10*
West Wessex	1	*9*	1	*6*	3	*15*
Lincolnshire	0	*0*	0	*0*	0	*0*
Northumbria	0	*0*	0	*0*	0	*0*
TOTAL	11		16		20	

later date, some 71% of the southern English currency c. 750/60–85 was locally produced, 24% was Carolingian and 5% Northumbrian.[22]

The early decades of Offa's reign were in many ways the heyday of Carolingian silver coinage in pre-viking England.[23] A crackdown on foreign currency apparently came c. 785. Some 369 single-finds are known of pennies minted from then until 796, alongside perhaps 3 Carolingian *denarii* and 1 Northumbrian coin of the same period: in other words, approximately 99 per cent of the currency was now made up of native coinage.[24] Similar proportions prevailed early in the ninth century: approximately 11 Carolingian and 18 Northumbrian losses in southern England in the period from 796 down to c. 830 correspond with some 432 native finds: together the Carolingian and Northumbrian coins made up around 7 per cent of the currency. Later, from c. 830 to c. 865, the proportion of Carolingian coins is slightly higher – 10 per cent – as

[22] A generous count of single-finds of pennies of Offa probably minted before c. 785 amounts to twenty-seven coins. There are also two Northumbrian coins minted 758–c. 785 with a Southumbrian find-spot. This produces a total of thirty-eight finds probably lost before c. 785, including nine Carolingian.

[23] On Carolingian coins in ninth-century England see Metcalf, 'Monetary Economy', pp. 175–9; Story, *Carolingian Connections*, pp. 243–55.

[24] It should be noted that all these figures are based on the date of production of coins: the date of loss is more difficult to define (see below, pp. 224–9). However, Offa's Heavy coinage probably constituted a *renovatio*, sweeping away older currency: the large majority of Light coin losses therefore probably occurred before 792/3.

Table 8.3 *Southern English finds of Northumbrian coins,
based on date of production*

	757–96		796–840		840–67	
	No.	%	No.	%	No.	%
Kent	1	33	4	25	5	3
Essex	0	0	0	0	5	3
Sussex	0	0	2	13	1	1
East Anglia	0	0	4	25	39	23
East Mercia	0	0	0	0	7	4
West Mercia	1	33	0	0	15	9
East Wessex	0	0	0	0	2	1
West Wessex	0	0	0	0	2	1
Lincolnshire	1	33	6	38	97	56
Northumbria	—	—	—	—	—	—
TOTAL	3		16		173	

the number of native finds declines to about 196. However, it is probable that a high proportion of the Carolingian single-finds minted in this period, and indeed even some of those from earlier in the ninth century, represent later losses from the Viking Era (i.e., the late ninth or early tenth century).[25] Moreover, there emerges a relatively strong concentration of Carolingian silver finds in East Anglia. The majority of these probably represent Viking-Age losses from after the kingdom's conquest in 869, though the possibility cannot be excluded that some of the losses might have occurred earlier.

Northumbrian coins can be treated in a similar way to Carolingian *denarii* until approximately the death of Eanred (*c.* 840). Towards the end of his reign, debasement became more severe, and the coinage effectively ceased to have a meaningful silver content.[26] It was at approximately this time that the volume and spread of Northumbrian coins in the south increased substantially (Table 8.3). The distribution of Northumbrian finds before *c.* 840, like that of Carolingian coins, seems to have been dictated by the wider patterns of circulation: areas which were rich in finds of local coin were also relatively rich in finds of foreign coin. These foreign losses represent the few strays which slipped through the net and entered the general currency. The same phenomenon can be observed in

---

[25] Carolingian *denarii* from the time of Louis the Pious onwards have been found extensively in Viking-Age contexts such as the Cuerdale hoard.

[26] Below, pp. 246–9.

hoards from the period,[27] and indeed with English coins in contemporary continental hoards.[28] But the volume of Northumbrian coins circulating in the south took off *c.* 840. These became so numerous, and occur in so many contexts (archaeological and otherwise), that they simply cannot be dismissed as predominantly modern or peripheral losses.[29] They penetrated all the country to some degree, but were numerous only in Lincolnshire and (to a lesser extent) East Anglia. The latter's strong showing of Northumbrian finds can probably be put down to its relatively high level of monetization and effective recording of finds. Lincolnshire, on the other hand, has an obvious advantage of proximity, which means a relatively high volume of Northumbrian finds is known from the eighth century onwards. It is also home to a number of sites rich in *stycas* which have been thoroughly excavated and surveyed by metal-detectorists in recent years, such as Torksey and Flixborough.[30] Within Lincolnshire the monetary situation of the mid ninth century must have been complex, as silver pennies from the south circulated alongside debased Northumbrian coins.[31] There especially, and to a much more limited extent elsewhere in Southumbrian England, *stycas* became an acceptable form of fractional or low-value currency, fulfilling an important monetary role even if for only a few decades.[32]

On the whole, foreign silver coinage was very effectively shut out of circulation in Southumbrian England during the late eighth and ninth centuries. This is not to say that foreign coins simply ceased entering the country; on the contrary, metallurgical analyses suggest that continental bullion remained an important source for English minting from Offa's reign onwards.[33] But a short time after the establishment of the broad penny Offa's kingdom experienced a monetary dislocation of long-term significance when foreign silver coin was effectively banned from circulation. One need only compare the quantity of finds of Frisian *sceattas* from England before *c.* 750 – which may have constituted as much as a third of all known finds of that period – to appreciate the magnitude of this step and of the efforts that must have been taken to

---

[27] One papal coin was in the Delgany hoard (*c.* 830), one Carolingian coin in the Middle Temple hoard (*c.* 840) and one Carolingian coin in the Dorking hoard (*c.* 863).

[28] Cf. the three Anglo-Saxon and two Arabic coins in the Ilanz hoard (*c.* 794), the uncertain number of papal coins in the Biebrich hoard (*c.* 800) and the one Anglo-Saxon and one papal coin in the Roermond hoard (*c.* 855): for details see H. H. Völckers, *Karolingische Münzfunde der Frühzeit (751–800)* (Göttingen, 1965), nos. xxiv and xlii; C. M. Haertle, *Karolingische Münzfunde aus dem 9. Jahrhundert*, 2 vols. (Cologne, 1997), no. 50.

[29] Metcalf, 'Monetary Economy', pp. 177–9.

[30] It should be noted that Torksey is associated primarily with viking activity in the 870s, however.

[31] M. Blackburn, 'Coin Finds and Coin Circulation in Lindsey, *c.* 600–900', in *Pre-Viking Lindsey*, ed. A. Vince (Lincoln, 1993), pp. 80–9, at 81–2.

[32] Below, pp. 284–90.   [33] Above, pp. 157–61.

implement it.[34] Presumably a strict rule of reminting was enforced at ports of entry, while elsewhere in the kingdom decrees and penalties along the lines of those laid down by Charles the Bald and Æthelstan were promulgated to foster the exclusion of unacceptable coin.

Yet the definition of acceptable coin remained quite flexible, and pennies minted in different English kingdoms were manifestly not excluded in the same way as coins from overseas. Rulers, moneyers and coin-users in Kent, Mercia, Wessex and East Anglia observed a monetary *entente cordiale* which can be traced back to the rule of all three main mints by Offa in the period down to 796, when the weight and metal standards that would prevail for many decades thereafter were first laid down. Firm recognition of the de facto interchangeability of coins from different southern English kingdoms did not come until the introduction of the Lunettes type to Wessex *c.* 865.

GLOBAL TRENDS WITHIN SOUTHERN ENGLAND: 'MONETARY
RECESSION, WITHOUT GEOGRAPHICAL RETREAT'[35]

In the reign of Offa, a currency emerged in England south of the Humber which was by and large local in origin: continental and Northumbrian issues served largely as sources of bullion rather than coinage as such. This currency was far from static in its make-up and movement, however. It came from up to five mints which all played different roles, and over time the direction and volume of circulation from these mints across Southumbrian England changed substantially.

There are now a little over 1,000 provenanced English single-finds of silver pennies (from around 600 locations) known from the century 757–865. In determining the general trends within this large sample it is helpful to break it down into three roughly equal chronological phases: the age of Offa (*c.* 760–96);[36] the age of Coenwulf (796–*c.* 830);[37] and the rise of Wessex (*c.* 830–*c.* 865).[38]

---

[34] D. M. Metcalf and W. Op den Velde, 'Series E Reconsidered', in *Studies in Early Medieval Coinage* 2, ed. Abramson, pp. 104–10.

[35] Metcalf, 'Monetary Economy', p. 173.

[36] This phase includes everything in Chick, *Coinage of Offa*, as well as sixty-three finds of this period listed in Naismith, 'Coinage of Offa Revisited', pp. 97–106; it covers the years *c.* 760–96.

[37] This phase includes the coinages of Coenwulf, Ceolwulf I, Beornwulf and Ludica of the Mercians; Eadberht 'Præn', Cuthred and Baldred of Kent; the Anonymous coinage of *c.* 822–3; Eadwald of East Anglia; Archbishop Æthelheard's independent coinage and issues with Coenwulf; Archbishop Wulfred's coinage (except for the DOROB-C type); Beorhtric of Wessex; and the first coinages of Ecgberht of Wessex from Canterbury and Rochester.

[38] This phase includes the coinages of Wiglaf and Berhtwulf of Mercia; Æthelstan, Æthelweard and Edmund of East Anglia; the last type of Archbishop Wulfred and all coins (save those of Lunettes type) of Archbishop Ceolnoth; the second coinages of Ecgberht of Wessex from Canterbury

These divisions are based in the first instance on events in political history, but they also reflect numismatic periodizations more or less neatly, and in the case of the division at *c.* 830 coincide with an important change in the way in which coins were used. This is brought home most immediately by the dramatic fall in the number of finds: while the first two periods are very well covered, with 396 and 432 finds respectively, the years after *c.* 830 are represented by only 196 known finds. The reasons for this sudden dip in coin-loss will be discussed in due course, along with the data which suggest a change *c.* 830.

Northumbria stands out as a near blank for southern English pennies. Just as Northumbrian coins seem to have been treated as foreign currency or small change in southern England, so southern coins did not penetrate in large numbers into Northumbria. Those which have turned up beyond the Humber should not be viewed in the same light as those found to the south: they were foreign, and apparently excluded from general use. Only fourteen such single-finds are known from the whole century 757–*c.* 865, along with two small hoards of southern coins. Some or all of these could have belonged to special contexts, such as the several coins found in the excavations of York Minster, which may have been deposited in a religious (possibly votive) context.[39]

Despite the slump in actual number of losses in the middle of the ninth century, the proportional spread of these finds by region stayed much the same across the period. Most striking of all is the general concentration of finds in eastern and southern England (Table 8.4). More western areas – western Wessex and Mercia – have fewest coin-finds, and those which are known come predominantly from their eastern and southern portions (Dorset, Wiltshire, Oxfordshire, Gloucestershire and Warwickshire). Within southern and eastern England the share of finds in different regions varied substantially. Sussex fares relatively poorly, especially in comparison to the neighbouring regions of Kent and eastern Wessex. This is probably due to Sussex's isolated position, which is apparent in other cultural and economic respects.[40] Kent declined from 23 per cent of all finds of pennies minted in Offa's reign to just 13 per cent of those minted *c.* 830–65; the proportion represented by Essex likewise halved over the course of the period. Yet on the whole the shape of monetary circulation in southern England proved highly resilient, weathering several ups and downs. Monetary recession did not mean geographical retreat.

and Rochester, and all his West Saxon and London issues; and all the coins of Æthelwulf and Æthelberht of Wessex.

[39] See in general E. Pirie, *Thrymsas, Sceattas and Stycas of Northumbria: An Inventory of Finds Recorded to 1997* (Llanfyllin, 2000), pp. 20–4, and 'Contrasts and Continuity', pp. 222–3 and 227–8.

[40] S. Kelly, 'Sussex', in *BEASE*, pp. 431–2.

Table 8.4 *Number and percentage of finds per region per period*

Area	c. 760–96		796–c. 830		c. 830–c. 865	
	No.	%	No.	%	No.	%
Kent	91	23	60	14	24	13
Essex	61	15	30	7	13	7
Sussex	14	4	13	3	5	3
East Anglia	55	14	109	26	65	36
Middle Anglia	62	16	73	17	17	9
Mercia	32	8	43	10	9	5
East Wessex	30	8	47	11	23	13
West Wessex	13	3	24	6	8	4
Lincolnshire	36	9	27	6	19	10
Northumbria	3	1	5	1	6	3

A TALE OF TWO MINTS: CANTERBURY
AND IPSWICH COMPARED

A particularly important feature which emerges from the find-data is the rise of East Anglia as apparently the most highly monetized area of southern England. It grew from providing 14 per cent of all finds from Offa's reign to 36 per cent of all those from the period *c.* 830–65. This mirrors the rise to prominence, especially local prominence, of the East Anglian mint, probably located at Ipswich.

Figures 8.1 and 8.2 highlight the close bond between the region of East Anglia and the mint of Ipswich. Figure 8.1 shows the regional distribution of finds of pennies from the latter mint. It emphasizes how Ipswich began with a high representation among the finds from East Anglia even though these did not yet form a large proportion of all finds nationally. But it went from strength to strength over the period, accounting for over 60 per cent of all finds from East Anglia by the period *c.* 830–*c.* 865.

Pennies from Ipswich did of course circulate elsewhere: they found their way all over southern England, albeit in smaller quantity. Figure 8.2 takes a different approach, showing how various mints of origin were represented among the finds from East Anglia. The purpose of this is to show how Ipswich slowly overtook the other Southumbrian mints in the find-record from East Anglia. Canterbury, the leading competitor, enjoyed the lion's share of finds from East Anglia until 796, but was slightly overtaken by Ipswich in the period down to *c.* 830. Thereafter

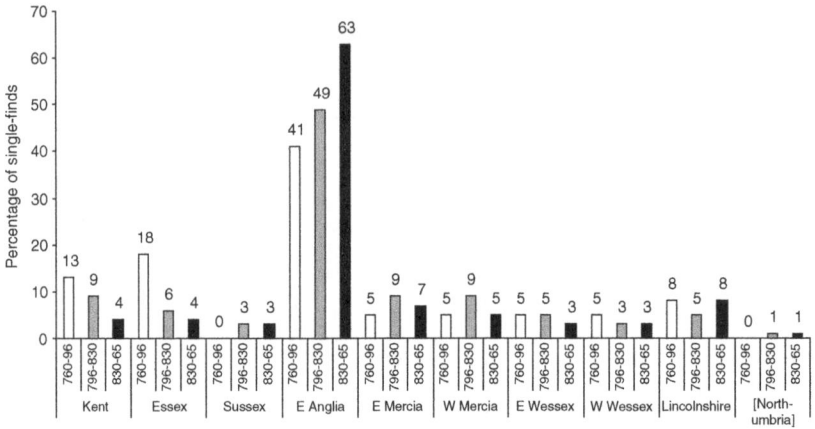

Figure 8.1 Regional representation of finds of pennies minted at Ipswich.

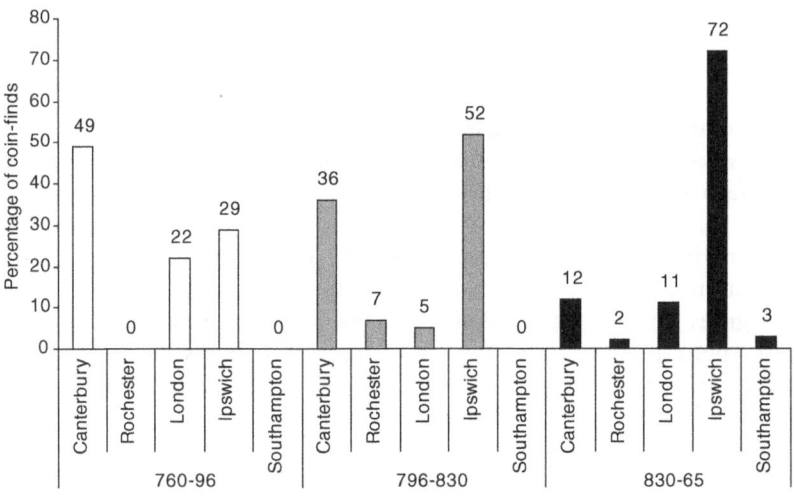

Figure 8.2 Representation of different mints within all finds from East Anglia.

Ipswich's dominance was much more substantial,[41] and indeed helped buoy the regional monetary economy through the lean years of the mid ninth century. East Anglia accounts for 65 of 183 Southumbrian finds (36 per cent): more than twice as much as any other region at that time. The bulk of these East Anglian finds were Ipswich-minted pennies. So, although circulation of southeastern coin had declined dramatically

[41] Metcalf, 'Monetary Economy', pp. 175–9.

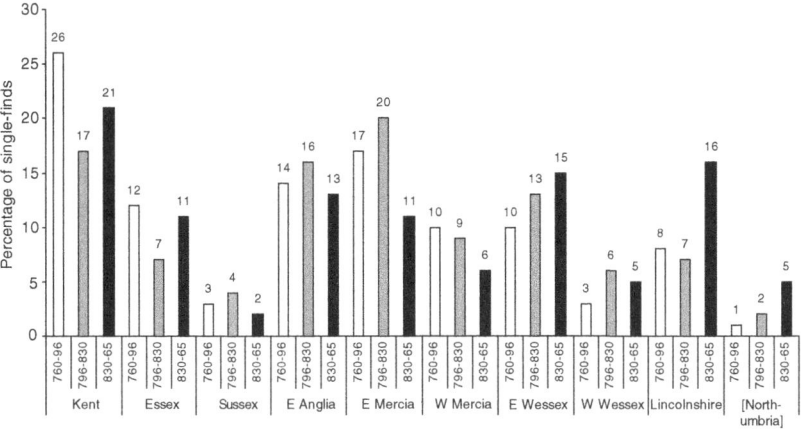

Figure 8.3 Regional representation of finds of pennies minted at Canterbury.

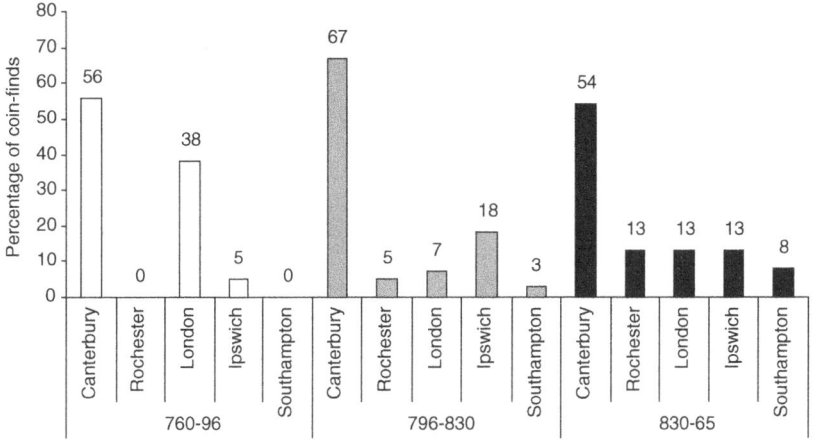

Figure 8.4 Representation of different mints within all finds from Kent.

in East Anglia as elsewhere, it seems clear that the circulation of local currency was still as vibrant as it had been in the preceding decades – uniquely so in southern England.

Canterbury contrasts with Ipswich in several important ways. Most striking is the fact that the home region of Kent was never outstandingly rich in coins of the Canterbury mint (Figure 8.4). It enjoyed a slight lead over most areas in the time of Offa, but thereafter it was comparable to others such as East Anglia, eastern Mercia and eastern Wessex. On the other hand, Canterbury's productivity was such that although its output was spread much more evenly (Figure 8.3), it still often represented over 50 per cent of all known finds from most regions.

Not only were Canterbury's products widely dispersed, but the level of dispersal seems to have remained relatively stable over the century, with a few notable exceptions. Eastern Mercia's share fell considerably in the last period, in contrast with Lincolnshire, which became noticeably more prominent among Canterbury finds from the same period. It is unclear whether there is any connection between these two changes, and it should be noted that the actual number of finds from Lincolnshire remained largely consistent (twelve from 796–*c*. 830, nine from *c*. 830–*c*. 865): Lincolnshire may simply have been more stable at this time than regions to the south.

Canterbury therefore did not serve Kent any more thoroughly than it served a very broad swathe of Southumbrian England. It functioned as a monetary entrepôt, a national-level centre of production and an important node in long-distance networks of exchange. If anything Canterbury became even more prominent in this role in the ninth century than it had been in the eighth century. Canterbury and Ipswich thus provide distinct but complementary models of large-scale monetary development over the course of the eighth and ninth centuries.

LONDON

Despite its nosedive in productivity around 800, London had not always functioned on such a small scale. In the time of Offa it was a serious competitor to Canterbury in output,[42] although Canterbury held the advantage in number of finds: 191 to 156 losses of broad pennies struck before 796. London was slightly better represented among foreign finds of Offa's time, perhaps suggesting that a higher proportion of its output was being removed from England.[43]

London's prominence in both productivity and number of losses persisted even in the years immediately after Offa's death, until the Tribrach coinage (797/8–805). Thereafter its decline only deepened with time: it is likely that minting was sporadic and limited, probably ceasing altogether for a time in the mid 820s, and among pennies minted 796–*c*. 830 London provided only thirty-five single-finds, or 8 per cent of the total from

---

[42] There are also some moneyers of Offa who cannot be attributed conclusively to either London or Canterbury.

[43] Of seventeen provenanced single-finds of Offa's pennies found outside England (mostly from Italy) eight come from London, seven from Canterbury and two from East Anglia. Among foreign hoards Ilanz contained one coin of London and two of Canterbury, whereas the Aiskew hoard contained nine coins of London to five of Canterbury.

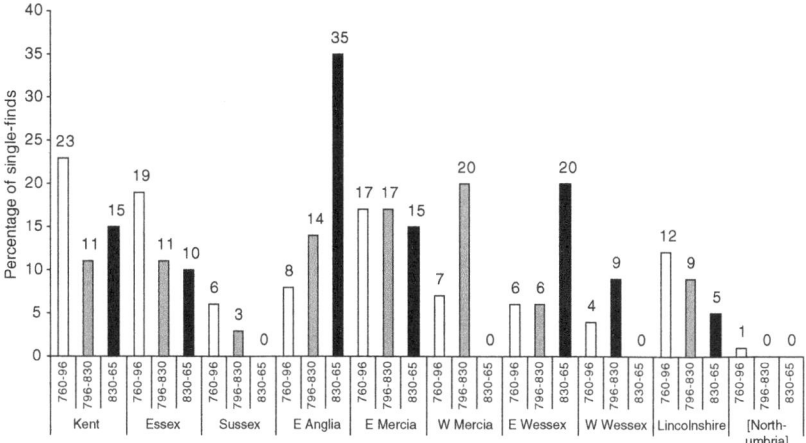

Figure 8.5 Regional representation of finds of pennies minted at London.

Southumbrian England. In relative if not absolute terms London recovered slightly in the 830s and especially the 840s, when twenty known single-finds of London pennies represent 11 per cent of the all southern English finds from that time.

Yet in spite of contraction in output and in contribution to the currency, the distribution of London-struck pennies remained relatively stable. It was essentially similar to Canterbury in that it did not primarily serve the home region, but a much larger territory extending across southern and eastern England. Essex, the home region of London, did not fare any better than Kent did among finds from Canterbury. It enjoyed a slightly higher representation in the period of Offa's coinage, although already more pennies from London were being lost in Kent than in Essex.

Figure 8.5 highlights this relatively broad circulation, which persisted across the ninth century. Whatever factors had caused the mint to shrink in output and contribution to the currency had evidently not altered its basic economic function as a well-connected monetary entrepôt. East Anglia, east and west Mercia, east Wessex and Lincolnshire all stand out among finds of London coins at least as effectively, as do the southeastern regions of Kent and Essex. There are also divergences from the Canterbury distribution: in the poor representation of eastern Wessex before *c.* 830,[44] and in the high proportion of finds from East Anglia

---

[44] Metcalf, 'Monetary Economy', p. 187, took this to signify that Canterbury enjoyed a larger share of circulation south of the Thames, although it should be noticed that London's late eighth-century representation among finds from Kent and Sussex was more appreciable.

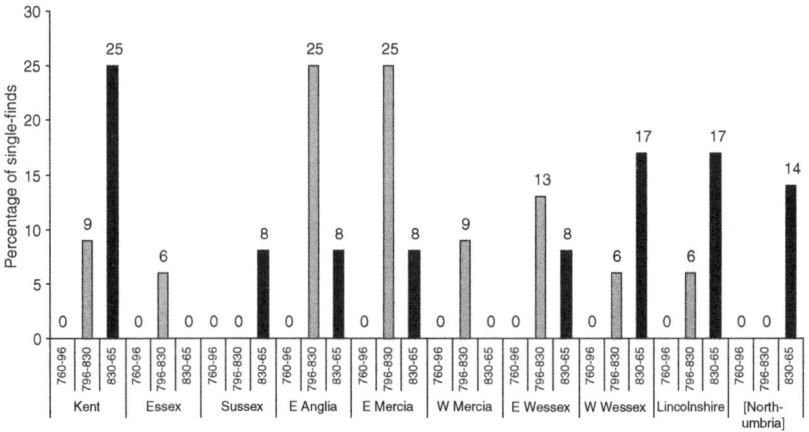

Figure 8.6 Regional representation of finds of pennies minted at Rochester.

minted in London after *c.* 830 (though this is based on a small sample of data). These two regions both claimed a larger and larger share of finds as the ninth century wore on, for reasons which will be discussed below. On the other hand, despite being the sole mint under Mercian political control from 825, Mercia itself was not particularly better represented than other areas among finds of London-mint pennies. Indeed, specimens from Ipswich and Canterbury were more plentiful from east and west Mercia throughout the period after 796.

ROCHESTER AND SOUTHAMPTON: THE MINOR MINTS

For these mints, as for London after 796, it is difficult to reach any very secure conclusions, as the number of known finds available for analysis is simply too small. Nevertheless, they are suggestive of how these two smaller mints functioned. On the one hand Rochester comes across as fulfilling the same role as Canterbury and London: a centre focused on long- and middle-distance coin-circulation. This was true from the beginning of Rochester's activity *c.* 810. In the two decades following its opening Kent provides no more finds of Rochester pennies than East Anglia, east Mercia or east Wessex. After *c.* 830 Kent has a higher proportion of Rochester finds than other areas – 25 per cent. However, this is based on only twelve known single-finds from southern England (Figure 8.6).

Southampton, on the other hand, is the most poorly represented mint of all in southern England (Figure 8.7). Only forty coins survive in total,

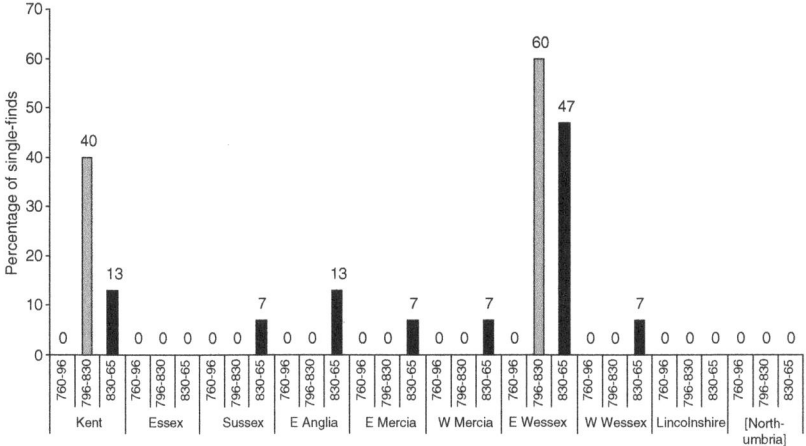

Figure 8.7 Regional representation of finds of pennies minted at
Southampton/Winchester.

twenty of them with known single-find provenances. Some of these
made it to Kent, East Anglia and other distant regions, but a high proportion come from eastern Wessex, the region in which the coins were
produced. Southampton was not active before (probably) 797/8 and of
the losses of coins from then down to *c.* 830, 60 per cent are from the
home region, and 47 per cent in the subsequent period.

There was clearly a strong tendency for this mint to cater primarily
to local needs, as it had done in the early eighth century.[45] But it never
did so with any great success, as coins from the West Saxon mint at no
point constituted more than 26 per cent of the finds from within eastern
Wessex. More coins from the Canterbury mint alone were found in eastern Wessex than of the local mint throughout the period.[46]

This proliferation of coins in eastern Wessex was an important feature
of the whole period, and it may have been burgeoning circulation that
encouraged the mint at (probably) Southampton to reopen, in combination with royal interest in establishing the trappings of kingship.[47] In the
time of Offa, eastern Wessex yielded thirty finds, forty-seven in 796–*c.*

---

[45] *T&S* III, 321–32.
[46] It should be noted that the West Saxon mint is more problematic to divide chronologically at *c.*
830, as its products seem to have spanned the whole of Ecgberht's reign and cannot confidently
be broken down into phases on either side of this date. Since it is not possible to split the coins,
they have been allotted to the later period, but it is likely that some of them were minted and lost
before *c.* 830.
[47] Above, pp. 120.

830 and twenty-three in *c.* 830–65, which represented 8%, 11% and 13% of all English finds respectively. A crucial motor which accounts for a high proportion of these coin-finds is Southampton, a declining but still very significant commercial centre in the late eighth and early ninth centuries, which is especially notable for the quality and quantity of finds it has produced. It has produced thirty-seven English coin-finds dating to approximately 757–865, along with a hoard and five Carolingian coins.[48] These account for about a third of all finds from eastern Wessex. Although it would remain an area of significant circulation without Southampton, eastern Wessex in general came to be a very well-represented and presumably very well-monetized area – significantly more so than the western part of Wessex.[49]

COIN-CIRCULATION AND KINGS,
MONEYERS AND CLERGY

The basic pattern of monetary circulation seems to have been that coins from the southeastern mints spread fairly evenly – and, in the case of Canterbury, thickly – across the country, whereas those from Ipswich and Southampton had a greater tendency to remain close to home, though the latter operated on only a very small scale.[50] Nevertheless, coins from all five mints reached all areas south of the Humber in at least some quantity, suggesting a monetary economy that was not noticeably encumbered by political or geographical boundaries (except at the coasts and at the Humber), and which was driven by long- and middle-distance circulation.

These general trends ultimately represent the traces of extensive interpersonal contacts and relationships. Bonds between men of all levels were at the heart of early medieval exchange, administration and society. Anglo-Saxon coinage bearing the names of king and moneyer from the mid-eighth century onwards was nothing if not personal, and it is worth scrutinizing the find-record in more detail to determine if these personal ties exerted any influence on distribution. Did the fact that a penny was produced by a specific king or moneyer, or by an archbishop, have any impact on its chances of reaching a specific part of the country?

In general this may be answered in the negative: most permutations of moneyer and ruler do not show a strong pattern different from that of their mint's general distribution at that time. This is especially true of coins of rulers like Offa and Coenwulf of Mercia, Ecgberht and Æthelwulf of Wessex and the independent East Anglian rulers, for all of whom

[48] Metcalf, 'Coins', pp. 54–5.   [49] Yorke, *Wessex*, pp. 299–309.
[50] Metcalf, 'Monetary Economy', pp. 185–95.

Table 8.5 *Finds of the coinage of*
Cynethryth arranged by region

Area	Finds of Cynethryth	
	No.	%
Kent	5	20
Essex	4	16
Sussex	3	12
East Anglia	2	8
Middle Anglia	4	16
Mercia	4	16
East Wessex	3	12
West Wessex	0	0
Lincolnshire	0	0
Northumbria	0	0

significant numbers of finds are known. Minor royal coinages are problematic, in that although they theoretically present more probability of
being struck under unusual conditions and therefore perhaps for special
purposes with limited circulation, they survive in such small numbers that
secure conclusions are difficult to reach.[51] The three surviving coins of
Beorhtric of Wessex, for example, include two found in Surrey (Sunbury
and Guildford). But there is no evidence that Beorhtric had any power over
Surrey – indeed, it was apparently ruled by the kings of the Mercians.[52]
If Beorhtric did have any special connection with Surrey, it is impossible
to divine. Similarly the independent rulers of Kent (Heaberht, Ecgberht
II and Eadberht 'Præn') produced relatively small coinages. In eight cases
coins of Ecgberht II have occurred as single-finds, which include three
from Kent and one from Surrey; others come from Worcestershire, Essex
and two from Greater London (north of the Thames).[53] Some thirteen
coins of Eadberht 'Præn' have known find-provenances: three from Kent,
five from Norfolk and one each from Bedfordshire, Buckinghamshire,
Lincolnshire, Northamptonshire and Wiltshire. Both spreads of coins are,
for the number of finds in question, entirely consistent with the general
pattern of finds from the Canterbury mint at the time, with a significant
number ending up quite close to home, but a majority travelling to distant
locations. The same is true of the coinage of Cynethryth, struck solely by
the moneyer Eoba at Canterbury (Table 8.5).

---

[51] Above, pp. 117–27.
[52] J. Blair, *Early Medieval Surrey: Landholding, Church and Settlement before 1300* (Stroud, 1991), pp. 103–4.
[53] Cf. Metcalf, 'Betwixt Sceattas and Offa's Pence', pp. 27–8.

Among the coins of King Eadwald of East Anglia there is (not surprisingly) a concentration in East Anglia itself, especially Norfolk (seven finds, as opposed to four from Suffolk). Beyond this, however, there is a scatter of finds from Kent, Essex and Northamptonshire (one find each) and a surprising cluster of six finds from western Mercia (three from Warwickshire, two from Nottinghamshire and one from Oxfordshire).

Of these six west Mercian finds, five are of one moneyer: Eadnoth. The three Warwickshire finds all stem from the same productive site at Bidford-on-Avon, which was close to the major salt-manufacturing area of the diocese of Worcester.[54] A further two finds (from Chiseldon, Wiltshire, and Hinton Waldrist, Oxfordshire) both lie in the Thames valley, arguably representing residue of the trade that flowed along this major route from London to the heart of Wessex and Mercia. The other Mercian find of Eadnoth (from Newark-upon-Trent, Nottinghamshire) is harder to fit into this same context, though the connection may again be riverine if the Trent provided an alternative route for travel into Mercia.[55] This unusually high concentration of Mercian finds – 29 per cent of all known finds of this moneyer – suggests that Eadnoth had some sort of connection with individuals or groups engaged in trade with Mercia. It was moneyer rather than king that lay behind this unusual distribution pattern, and it was the moneyers who generally provided the more striking examples of targeted circulation.[56]

Certain reservations must be expressed concerning conclusions derived from such figures. In particular, the sixteen moneyers named in Table 8.6 stand out for the relatively large volume of their coinage and their consequent prominence among surviving finds: the majority of moneyers from this period are simply known from too few provenanced coins to inspire confidence in interpretation of their distribution. There may have been several moneyers with special interests which are simply not detectable from the surviving sample. The chronological distribution of these sixteen moneyers is also largely dictated by the higher number of finds recorded in the period before *c.* 830 and the greater tendency for moneyers at this time to enjoy long careers: none of them began to work after *c.* 830, and only four of them persisted into the 830s or after.

---

[54] Maddicott, 'London and Droitwich', pp. 44–7.

[55] B. Palmer, 'The Hinterlands of Three Southern English *Emporia*: Some Common Themes', in *Markets*, ed. Pestell and Ulmschneider, pp. 48–60, at 51–2; D. Hooke, 'Uses of Waterways in Anglo-Saxon England', in *Waterways and Canal-Building in Medieval England*, ed. J. Blair (Oxford, 2007), pp. 37–54.

[56] For a similar investigation see D. M. Metcalf, 'The Ninth-Century Moneyer Werheard, and the Problem of Local Connections', *Wiltshire Archaeological Magazine* 72–3 (1980 for 1977–8), 195–8. However, the representation of this moneyer in the southwest is no longer as striking as it was in the 1970s.

Table 8.6 *Regional distribution of finds of coins of certain moneyers*

CANTERBURY

	Eoba		Babba		Duda		Wihtred		Sæberht		Oba		Swefherd		Tidberht	
	No.	%	No.	%	No.	%	No.	%	No.	%	No.	%	No.	%	No.	%
Kent	15	22	4	19	5	14	4	18	3	13	3	15	6	27	4	17
Essex	9	13	3	14	3	9	0	0	2	8	1	5	0	0	0	0
Sussex	2	3	1	5	0	0	0	0	0	0	1	5	0	0	1	4
East Anglia	9	13	5	24	8	23	3	14	2	8	4	20	2	9	4	17
Middle Anglia	12	18	4	19	11	31	2	9	8	33	3	15	2	9	5	22
Mercia	7	10	1	5	1	3	2	9	2	8	3	15	4	18	2	9
East Wessex	5	7	2	10	4	11	4	18	4	17	4	20	2	9	1	4
West Wessex	4	6	0	0	3	9	4	18	0	0	0	0	1	5	1	4
Lincolnshire	4	6	1	5	0	0	1	5	3	13	1	5	3	14	3	13
Northumbria	1	1	0	0	0	0	1	5	0	0	0	0	2	9	2	9
TOTAL	68		21		35		22		24		20		22		23	

Table 8.6 (cont.)

| | LONDON | | | | | | | | | | IPSWICH | | | | | |
| | Æthelwald | | Dud | | Ealhmund | | Wihtred | | Lul | | Eadnoth | | Wodel | | Monna | |
	No.	%	No.	%	No.	%	No.	%	No.	%	No.	%	No.	%	No.	%
Kent	8	35	9	39	8	27	3	11	6	22	0	0	2	11	2	13
Essex	5	22	4	17	6	20	5	19	3	11	1	6	0	0	1	6
Sussex	0	0	1	4	1	3	0	0	1	4	0	0	0	0	2	13
East Anglia	1	4	1	4	2	7	11	41	12	44	8	50	9	50	7	44
Middle Anglia	4	17	3	13	6	20	2	7	1	4	0	0	2	11	3	19
Mercia	2	9	2	9	3	10	2	7	2	7	5	31	1	6	0	0
East Wessex	0	0	0	0	3	10	0	0	1	4	0	0	0	0	0	0
West Wessex	0	0	1	4	1	3	2	7	0	0	1	6	2	11	0	0
Lincolnshire	3	13	2	9	0	0	2	7	0	0	1	6	2	11	1	6
Northumbria	0	0	0	0	0	0	0	0	1	4	0	0	0	0	0	0
TOTAL	23		23		30		27		27		16		18		16	

Rochester and Southampton are known from too few coins in general for any individual moneyers to be examined.

Nonetheless, Eadnoth has already provided one probable case of a moneyer who did have a high number of customers plying a particular route for commercial or other reasons, and a few other moneyers' profiles of finds contain similar 'blips'. Both Babba and Duda from Canterbury are unusually well represented among East Anglian finds: 24% and 23% respectively, which compares with about 15% from Canterbury as a whole before *c.* 830. The East Anglian moneyer Lul is known from six Kentish finds, 22% of all known finds of his coins, which is significantly more than the whole mint's proportion of Kentish finds (13% before 796, 9% from 796–*c.* 830). Particularly outstanding is Dud, a probable London moneyer in the time of Offa who is known from nine Kentish finds (39% of his total), which compares with 23% of London finds as a whole coming from Kent. Not all moneyers provide a hint of particular connections with specific areas of the country, however. Finds in the name of Eoba, the best-represented single moneyer from the whole century after the introduction of the broad penny, do not stand out from the pattern of contemporary Canterbury. Most other moneyers' find-totals mirror in more or less detail those of their home-mint's general circulation at that time. The bulk of moneyers, it seems, did not cater to any geographically specific clientele, at least not to such an extent that they differed from the wider distribution of all coins from their mint-town.

The final special agency to consider is the Church. The scale of its involvement in minting before the advent of Offa's pence is debatable, and certainly its role in the time after the reform was, although significant, very much secondary to that of the king, and in the same way operated through individual moneyers.[57] Recent study of the circulation of ecclesiastical *sceattas* and pennies, and of the finds of coins made at sites of ecclesiastical institutions, strongly suggests that there was no special ecclesiastical sphere of circulation: ecclesiastical issues mingled with the rest of the currency and were used in the same way as other coins.[58] For the most part the data from the late eighth and ninth centuries corroborate this impression. The find-spots of coins of the four archbishops of Canterbury and one bishop of London known to have issued coins in this period are in line with the distribution of regular king- and moneyer-signed coins from the same mints (Table 8.7).

There is one notable exception to this tendency. Among the finds of Archbishop Iænberht of Canterbury there is a disproportionately large number of coins from eastern Wessex: seven of eighteen known finds, or

[57] Naismith, 'Money of the Saints'.   [58] *Ibid.*

Table 8.7 *Regional distribution of finds of ecclesiastical coins*

	Eadberht		Iænberht		Æthelheard				Wulfred		Ceolnoth	
					To 796		After 796					
Area	No.	%	No.	%	No.	%	No.	%	No.	%	No.	%
Kent	2	22	4	22	4	19	6	32	6	24	2	11
Essex	2	22	1	6	1	5	3	16	3	12	1	11
Sussex	1	11	0	0	0	0	3	16	4	16	0	0
East Anglia	0	0	0	0	7	33	1	5	2	8	1	11
Middle Anglia	1	11	1	6	6	29	1	5	1	4	3	22
Mercia	0	0	2	22	0	0	1	5	3	12	2	22
East Wessex	1	14	7	39	0	0	3	16	3	12	2	11
West Wessex	0	0	1	6	1	5	1	5	1	4	1	11
Lincolnshire	2	22	1	6	2	10	0	0	2	8	1	0
Northumbria	0	0	1	6	0	0	0	0	0	0	0	0
TOTAL	9		18		21		19		25		12	

39 per cent, mostly clustered around Winchester.[59] This is considerably higher than the overall proportion of Canterbury coins from eastern Wessex in the same period (10 per cent), and suggests that some sort of special relationship may have been at work. What the nature of this link may have been is less clear. Winchester was an episcopal seat,[60] and a gift of money sent from Archbishop Iænberht to the bishop of Winchester is entirely possible. Parcels of archiepiscopal coinage may also have been sent in connection with estates or other rights possessed by the archbishop in this area, but if so little trace of them has survived.[61] Other motivations could also have been in play, including the connections of the archiepiscopal moneyer rather than the archbishop himself.

THE RATE OF LOSS: MONETIZATION AND PRODUCTION COMPARED

Such was the general chronological and geographical picture of circulation in late eighth- and ninth-century Southumbria. But this leaves

[59] Metcalf, 'Betwixt Sceattas and Offa's Pence', pp. 28–9.
[60] M. Biddle, 'Winchester: The Development of an Early Capital', in *Vor- und Frühformen der europäischen Stadt im Mittelalter*, ed. H. Jankuhn, W. Schlesinger and H. Steuer, 2 vols. (Göttingen, 1975) I, 229–61; Dolley, 'Location'.
[61] On one minster in Berkshire controlled by Canterbury (Cookham) see Brooks, *Early History*, pp. 103–4. Cf. D. M. Metcalf, 'Financial Support for Outlying Churches? A Perspective on the Uses of Money in Eighth-Century Northumbria', *BNJ* 72 (2002), 167–9.

to one side an important dimension of the single-find evidence, which is how much it can reveal about the general scale and fluctuations of monetization. There have been many debates over the nature and extent of coin-use in the early Middle Ages.[62] Until recently, however, it has been difficult to found these arguments on the evidence of a substantial, random and representative body of finds: reliance solely on chance discoveries of hoards and strays risked presenting a very imprecise, even misleading, view of the early medieval currency. Here the view is taken that single-finds achieve this goal and hence offer a much firmer impression of the changing size and make-up of the currency.

An immediate statistical disclaimer must be made, that with all these calculations and estimates the numbers in question are not always large. Consequently their evidence must be handled with care, and the resultant conclusions vary in reliability. One major unknown quantity is the time likely to have expired between the striking of a coin and its loss.[63] In theory eighth- and ninth-century pennies could stay in circulation for a long time, as only occasionally was there systematic reminting of older coinage. As well as attritional loss from circulation, currency probably drained out of southern England in various directions and was replenished by reminting incoming silver.[64] However, by the early 870s West Saxon coins from before the Inscribed Cross phase seem to have disappeared from circulation, implying a greater emphasis on the current circulating type.[65] Assessing the likely gap between production and loss before this time is more problematic as only a few hoards from southern England are known from 757–865, some of them (especially the larger hoards) probably representing savings accumulated over time. But even these still tend to be made up of coins struck within the decade or two before concealment, and small hoards present a more homogeneous profile favouring recent types (see Table 8.9).

Approximately 1,000 of the 3,500 surviving southern English pennies have a non-hoard provenance attached to them. Their chronological distribution is shown in Table 8.8.

The implications of these figures are thrown into relief when the duration of various phases of the coinage is taken into account. Qualifications apply about the uncertain length of some phases of minting, but on the whole the margins of variation are not sufficient to upset the general trends of the evidence. The global trajectory is best displayed by

---

[62] Below, pp. 252–92.
[63] Cf. M. Blackburn, 'Coin-Finds', in *Means of Exchange*, ed. Skre, pp. 29–74, at 34–45, and 'What Factors', pp. 19–21.
[64] Above, pp. 157–61.   [65] See Pagan, 'Coinage in Southern England', p. 58.

Table 8.8 *Totals of single- and stray-finds*

Canterbury	No. of finds	London	No. of finds	Rochester	No. of finds	East Anglia	No. of finds	Wessex	No. of finds
765–92/3	136	765–92/3	126	810–21	7	765–92/3	30	796–802	5
792/3–6	65	792/3–6	30	821–3	10	792/3–6	9	802–39	15
796–8	15	796–7	11	823–5	6	796–800	24		
798–805	80	797–805	16	825–30	9	800–21	52		
805–10	38	805–21	6	830–9	7	821–3	16		
810–22	68	821–3	2	839–44	3	823–5	17		
822–3	11	827–40	5	846/7–9	1	825–7	2		
823–5	20	840–52	15	849–54	2	827–30	6		
825–8	8			854–64	1	830–7/8	24		
828–39	27					837/8–45	15		
839–44	13					845–55	8		
844–9	8					855–62	22		
849–54	2					862–9	7		
854–64	13								
864–5	2								

amalgamating the figures for each mint and breaking them down proportionally by decade (Figure 8.8).

An improvement on this is to build in some estimate of the probable time-lag between production and loss. On the basis of surviving hoards, one might allow that 45–60 per cent of coins were lost within a decade of their production, and the rest over the subsequent decades, the proportion decreasing as time went on. Effective reforms in 792/3 and again in the 860s created bottlenecks across which few, if any, coins survived in circulation (Table 8.9). Figure 8.9 shows the corrected estimates of losses per annum allowing for these factors.[66]

At present, the basic story seems to be that the rate of coin-use began at a mediocre level with Offa's reforms in the 760s, when Carolingian and Northumbrian coinage still circulated freely and made up an appreciable proportion of the currency. But the 780s brought major changes: foreign money was more effectively forced out of circulation, and the volume of native coinage in circulation increased many times over. A similar rate of loss persisted for approximately the next five decades, with the high-water mark of circulation falling in the 790s. In approximately the 830s a decline

---

[66] Both histograms also make allowance (in the 860s) for probable losses of Lunettes pennies of Æthelred I and Burgred recorded on EMC. It should be noted that this is not a complete record of losses, but undoubtedly includes the large majority.

Table 8.9 *Estimated rate of loss after production*

		Decade of production										
		760s	770s	780s	790s	800s	810s	820s	830s	840s	850s	860s
Estimated	760s	40										
percentage	770s	40	45									
lost per	780s	20	35	66								
decade	790s		20	34	40							
	800s				30	40						
	810s				20	30	40					
	820s				10	20	30	40				
	830s					10	20	30	55			
	840s						10	20	30	55		
	850s							10	10	30	55	
	860s								5	10	40	50

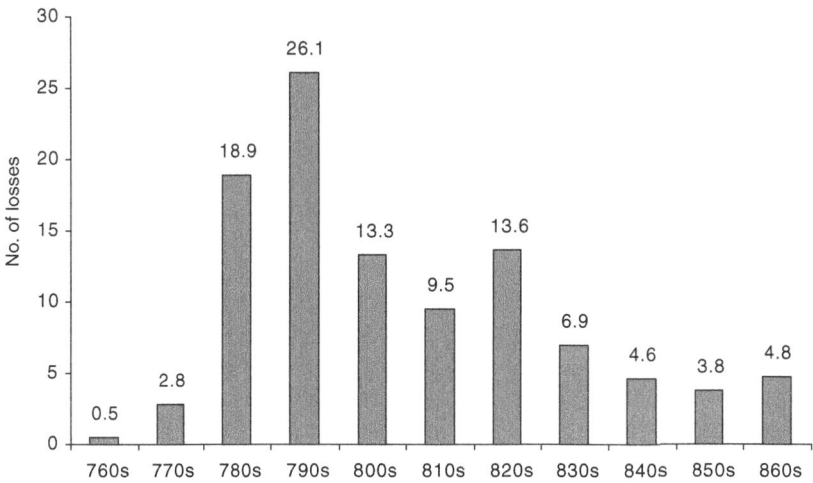

Figure 8.8 Losses per annum based on date of production.

in the rate of loss seems to have set in; a decline which accelerated in subsequent decades. By the 860s, less than half as many pennies were being lost per annum as in the 830s. A similar general pattern in the rate of loss has previously been noticed, especially when viewed in the context of productive sites that had been in existence since the time of the *sceattas*,[67] while

[67] M. Blackburn, 'Coin Circulation in Germany during the Early Middle Ages: The Evidence of Single-Finds', in *Fernhandel und Geldwirtschaft. Beiträge zum deutschen Münzwesen in sächsischer*

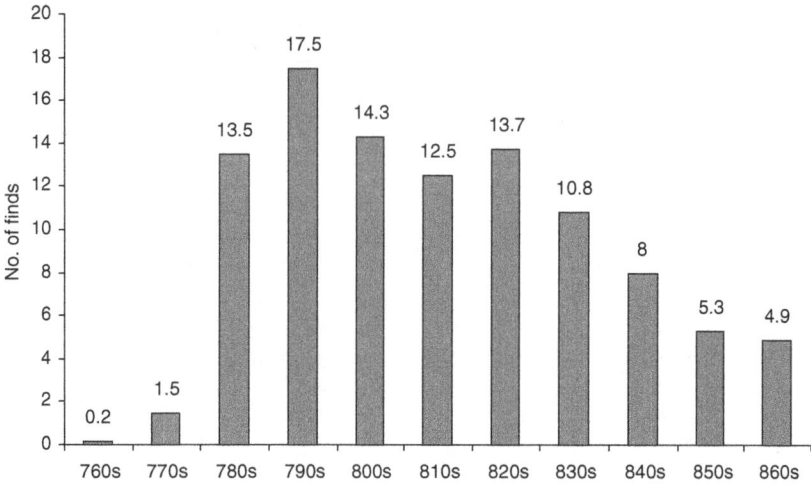

Figure 8.9 Single-finds per annum adjusted for probable time in circulation.

in the Carolingian empire the 820s and 830s similarly stand out as a time of vibrant circulation before decline began.[68] To a large extent this pattern is also repeated in the finds from each individual English mint (Table 8.8), with a high rate of losses per year in the reign of Offa and into approximately the 820s or 830s. Thereafter the rate tends to fall off, sometimes dramatically. The decline is most marked at Canterbury, the best-represented and most productive mint in Southumbrian England. London's rate of loss began to fall even earlier than elsewhere, at the end of the eighth century, coinciding closely with the city's decline in productivity; a partial and temporary recovery came with the coinage of Berhtwulf in the late 840s. The East Anglian mint's rise to significance in productivity began in earnest only around 800, and its rate of loss under Offa was correspondingly low. It rose quickly with the coinage of Eadwald, levelled out and temporarily declined *c.* 825, though it revived somewhat compared to other southern English mints in the period after *c.* 830.

One might expect a certain correspondence between phases of high productivity and phases of extensive loss, but this is not exactly the case. Comparison of Figures 7.1–7.4 and 8.9 gives an impression of the changing disparity between the rates of loss and die-output per annum. What they show is that the apparent decline in coin-use in the 830s and after

---

und salischer Zeit: Ergebnisse des Dannenberg-Kolloquiums 1990, ed. B. Kluge (Sigmaringen, 1993), pp. 37–54, at 44, and '"Productive" Sites'.
[68] Coupland, 'Carolingian Single Finds'.

did not coincide with a drop-off in mint-output. Rather, the major change seems to have been related to the rate of survival, which began to be apparent from even the 820s. In other words, just as many coins carried on being produced even though fewer and fewer of them turn up as single-finds. What had changed in where they went, or the uses to which they were put, cannot be teased out of numbers alone and requires deeper contextualization.[69]

THE FORCES BEHIND CIRCULATION

The monetary economy of southern England

The leap from where coins have been found and in what numbers to identifying the forces responsible for their movement is not a straightforward one, and there were surely many different answers that applied to different people, times and places in the first century of the broad penny coinage. It should first be stated, however, that coinage was not a wholly independent entity lacking any meaningful link to the pulse of exchange. On the one hand, bullion supply was probably the leading variable which could affect minting and money supply. But episodes of debasement and depressed production brought on by shortfalls in bullion supply, sometimes in combination with other factors, can be defined and diagnosed as exceptions;[70] at other times, the extent and spread of coin-use was considerable, and variations within it that do not coincide with changes in minting practice or output should probably be related to the waxing and waning of coinage's role in exchanges of various kinds. At the heart of this was a well-integrated monetary economy was based on a unified Southumbrian currency. Changes in the political affiliation of mints had no discernible effect on their coins' circulation. Neither did regions such as western Wessex and western Mercia – those which contained high concentrations of royal lands and where the bulk of kings' time was spent – attract a higher volume of coinage. Single-finds remain concentrated in the east. Eastern England has further evidence of greater economic diversification,[71] some of which allows modern scholars to trace other networks.[72] Minting was thus closely linked to the inflow of silver and, indirectly, other goods from overseas and to the flow of domestic circulation. Kings apparently had very limited control over the directions this took, and their benefit came in a portion of the profits of production and in the less tangible statements of symbolic authority bound up with coinage.

---

[69] Metcalf, 'Monetary Economy', pp. 171–4.   [70] Above, pp. 161–5.
[71] Faith, 'Forces and Relations', p. 35.   [72] Below, pp. 239–44.

Within the southern English monetary zone the five mint-towns played different roles. London, Rochester and, above all, Canterbury worked as nationally focused engines of production, catering to coin-use throughout Southumbrian England without any special focus on particular regions, including the hinterland of the mints. These mint-ports were part of a small number of hubs of long-distance trade from which coins and other items were dispersed across northern Europe.[73] Earlier *sceattas*, especially of Series K and L, show that London and Canterbury had played a similar role since at least the early eighth century.[74]

East Anglia was a special case. On one level this localized monetary economy was not completely divorced from the broader network of Southumbrian circulation. Neither was there any consistent difference between the trace elements of East Anglian and southeastern pennies, implying that they used largely the same refining techniques and sources of silver.[75] However, an unusually high proportion of pennies from Ipswich remained close to home: this was a proportion that only increased as time went by and the productivity of the East Anglian mint increased. In the ninth century especially, East Anglia was a uniquely dynamic monetary region, which maintained a much higher level of circulation than the rest of the country in the decades after *c.* 830, almost solely on the basis of local issues. Although this development reached its zenith under the independent East Anglian rulers, it had roots that went back to the preferential use of local issues of *sceattas* of Series R and Q in the early eighth century.[76] It is unlikely, however, that any of the rulers of late eighth- and ninth-century East Anglia were operating a deliberate policy of excluding or deterring non-local issues. The local mint's dominance was not driven by political fiat, but by economic conditions within East Anglia. There probably was, quite simply, enough trade and demand for cash within East Anglia to dominate circulation of the products of the local mint to an exceptional degree – perhaps a regional balance of trade which was export-heavy but light on imports and an unusually close integration between the hinterland and Ipswich.[77]

East Anglia does not properly emerge into written history until the tenth century, and as the documentary evidence mounts it becomes

---

[73] Sindbæk, 'Small World' and 'Networks'; building on Hodges, *Dark Age Economics*, p. 25.
[74] *T&S* III, 368–415.
[75] Metcalf and Northover, 'Coinage Alloys', pp. 109–10. Metcalf and Northover state that higher proportions of zinc and tin are characteristic of East Anglian coins, though other issues of the same period from the southeast (e.g., their nos. 49–52) also include *c.* 3 per cent or more of zinc and, in one case, 0.78 per cent tin.
[76] *T&S* III, 483–523, and Metcalf, 'Determining'.   [77] *FEMA*, p. 810.

apparent that Norfolk and Suffolk were among the richest, most densely populated areas of England,[78] dominated by a high proportion of free peasants and organized under highly idiosyncratic social and economic structures.[79] How far back these characteristics can be projected is debatable, and many of East Anglia's distinguishing features have been attributed to the influence of Scandinavian settlement in the late ninth century.[80] However, a case can also be made for earlier origins,[81] and the evidence presented by the late eighth- and ninth-century coinage of East Anglia may be a valuable shred of evidence for the origins of East Anglia's economic prominence.[82]

Changes in the monetary economy

The complex system which tied the minting and circulation of pennies together in southern England was far from monolithic. There were major differences by region, both in the overall quantity of finds and in the origins of those finds, which underscore general strengths or weaknesses of exchange within that region and hint at differences in the rate of monetization. There were also chronological ups and downs which touched on the whole of the monetary economy – not, it should be stressed, usually altering its basic form, as the proportions of finds from different parts of the country did not change dramatically, but with important ramifications for its scale.

The first of these which should be remarked upon was the resounding up which followed the languid coin-circulation of the period *c.* 740/50–80 in Southumbrian England. Offa's substantive Light coinage built on the more modest quantitative revival of the 770s to reintroduce a penny coinage of considerable volume; one which approached

---

[78] Cf. D. Hill, *Atlas*, p. 19.

[79] D. C. Douglas, *Social Structure of Medieval East Anglia* (Oxford, 1927); T. Williamson, *The Origins of Norfolk* (Manchester, 1993), pp. 83–104; J. Campbell, 'Hundreds and Leets: A Survey with Suggestions', in *Medieval East Anglia*, ed. C. Harper-Bill (Woodbridge, 2005), pp. 153–67; Loyn, *Anglo-Saxon England*, pp. 321 and 354.

[80] As in, for instance, B. Dodwell, 'Holdings and Inheritance in Medieval East Anglia', *EcHR* 20 (1967), 53–66, at p. 53.

[81] R. H. C. Davis, 'East Anglia and the Danelaw', *TRHS* 5 (1955), 23–39; G. C. Homans, 'The Frisians in East Anglia', *EcHR* 10 (1957), 189–206, and 'The Explanation of English Regional Differences', *P&P* 42 (1969), 18–34, who presents an extreme view. Cf. R. Faith, 'Peasant Families and Inheritance Customs in Medieval England', *Agricultural History Review* 14 (1966), 77–95, at pp. 78–9; Rippon, *Beyond the Medieval Village*, pp. 138–201.

[82] *FEMA*, pp. 808–13. Note, however, that the later prosperity of East Anglia can equally be explained by a collapse of lordship which fostered the prosperity of free peasants (Faith, 'Peasant Families', pp. 84–5; J. Campbell, 'Hundreds and Leets', p. 164).

that of the early pennies or *sceattas* of the earlier eighth century in its economic vitality.[83] Exactly how this new coinage was achieved is still obscure: doubtless it built significantly on new sources of silver, probably stemming in part from the Frankish world, but the details remain to be fleshed out. To some extent it is more instructive to view the period *c.* 740/50–80 as an aberration, when silver supplies contracted across northwest Europe and brought on related reforms in several kingdoms.

Rates of loss, and presumably therefore of coin-use, remained comparable to those of the 780s for several decades thereafter, constituting an Indian summer of monetary activity for pre-viking England. A decisive end came at approximately the end of the first third of the ninth century: rates of loss probably remained buoyant into the 830s, although a discrepancy between mint-output and rate of loss had been growing for some time by that point. Certainly some significant change was underway across southern England by *c.* 830 and gained in momentum thereafter. Its effects were impressive but its causes and context are difficult to define and deserving of more extended comment. They are best characterized as a change in how coinage was being used which, at least eventually, affected all of southern England. Its impact can be traced through the global totals of finds, but is also apparent at many individual sites south of the Humber, so there is little chance that major caches of single-finds of mid-ninth-century pennies are waiting to come to light.[84]

New developments which could have resulted in this effect are several, and some defy quantification. Among these unknown factors is the possibility, for example, that although the numbers of dies used at the various mints remained high, suggesting substantial output, the quantity of coins which they made for some reason began to decrease. But it is difficult to imagine that chronic inefficiency on this level prevailed for thirty years or more at five different mints. Much more probable is a change in what people were doing with their pennies, which worked against using them as a means of exchange. This leads to the question of whether other functions of coinage saw a corresponding upsurge: did minted silver come to represent more of a store of value, to be hidden in a safe place for recovery at a later time?[85] If so, there may have been some sort of impact on the quantity of hoard material known from ninth-century England. On the whole this is simply not the case: during the years around *c.* 830 and

---

[83] The rate of loss of the *sceattas* can only be determined imprecisely, as dating is problematic and it is likely that a smaller proportion of finds is recorded. As of August 2010 the Corpus of Early Medieval Coin Finds and the Portable Antiquities Scheme had recorded 2,829 single-finds; assuming that these were produced and used *c.* 675–745, the rate of loss was thus approximately 40 coins per annum.

[84] Blackburn, '"Productive" Sites'.   [85] On these uses of coinage, see below, p. 251–2.

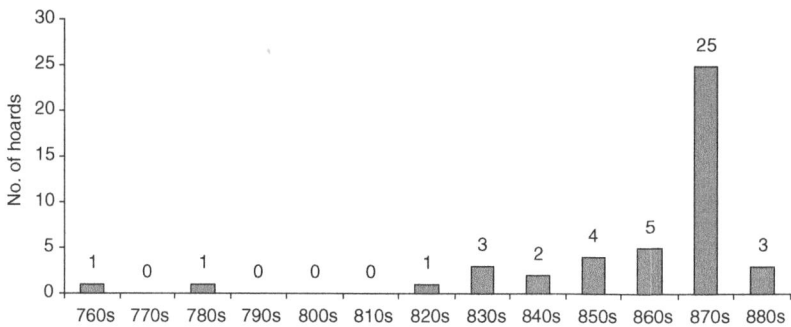

Figure 8.10 Approximate number of known southern English hoards per decade.

thereafter there is only a slight rise in the number of hoards surviving from England, mirrored in contemporary Francia.[86]

This is far from an ideal measure of the extent to which coins were being used as a store of value, and a rise in hoards surviving until modern times reflects one or both of two things: more hoards being concealed and fewer hoards being recovered. The former would have most effect on the circulating medium, but the latter is usually taken to be the cause of more hoards surviving down to the present. Both phenomena could explain why so many hoards have survived from the 870s, for example, when viking invasions were at their most severe and presumably resulted in widespread death and disorder (Figure 8.10) – although it should be noted that not all viking assaults had such an effect.[87] But if there was no compelling reason why hoards should go unrecovered then presumably even a substantial increase in use of coin as a store of value might leave relatively little impact. For the early ninth century the material is simply too scarce to allow a conclusion one way or the other: a slight increase in hoarding *c.* 830 is apparent, but its significance must remain uncertain.

The other obvious explanation for why coins continued to be minted but not lost is that they were being used in such a way that most of them ended up somewhere they could not be found and in most cases were destroyed – that is to say, somewhere outside England. Again, this raises major methodological problems, as areas where English coins would not have been universally reminted – such as Ireland, Scotland and Scandinavia – have thrown up relatively few finds of this

---

[86] S. Armstrong, 'Carolingian Coin Hoards and the Impact of the Viking Raids in the Ninth Century', *NC* 158 (1998), 131–64, at p. 136.
[87] *Ibid.*, pp. 136–8.

period.[88] Attempts to hunt exported English silver bullion supply through metallurgical analysis are hampered by the fact that Anglo-Saxon moneyers probably made most of their coins from incoming Carolingian silver, and at many locations in northwest Europe it was common to mix metals of different origins, masking any trace elements that might diagnose their source(s).[89] Mass exportation of silver from England after *c.* 830 hence is possible, but again cannot be confirmed on present evidence.

If either or both of these developments did take place, something must have changed in the period beginning *c.* 820/30 to make hiding or exporting coin more attractive propositions. Military activity, and the disturbance it caused for the rest of society, is one possible culprit. It was in the 830s that the viking raids on southern England picked up after an apparent hiatus of several decades,[90] at the same time as viking ravagers intensified their attacks and made their first winter camps in Ireland.[91] These depredations have often been cited as catalysts for economic catastrophe in the ninth century,[92] though despite the destruction and mayhem the vikings are known to have caused in some quarters,[93] there has been a revisionary trend to recast them not as raiders but as traders and settlers,[94] valued if volatile customers at North Sea trading centres such as Dorestad.[95] They could serve to galvanize native reactions to an impressive degree, resulting in fortification, monetary payments, mobilization

---

[88] D. M. Metcalf, 'Viking-Age Numismatics 2: Coinage in the Northern Lands in Merovingian and Carolingian Times', *NC* 156 (1996), 399–428, at pp. 409–28; M. Bogucki, 'Two Northumbrian Stycas of Eanred and Æthelred II from Early Medieval Truso in Poland', *BNJ* 79 (2009), 34–42; M. Blackburn, 'Coin Finds', pp. 56–8, and 'Currency under the Vikings. Part 3: Ireland, Wales, Isle of Man and Scotland in the Ninth and Tenth Centuries', *BNJ* 77 (2007), 119–49, at pp. 122–6.

[89] Kruse, 'Metallurgical Evidence', p. 82.

[90] S. Keynes, 'The Vikings in England, *c.* 790–1016', in *The Oxford Illustrated History of the Vikings*, ed. P. Sawyer (Oxford, 1997), pp. 48–82, at p. 52.

[91] C. Downham, *Viking Kings of Britain and Ireland: The Dynasty of Ívarr to AD 1014* (Edinburgh, 2007), pp. 11–12; D. Ó Corráin, 'Ireland, Wales, Man, and the Hebrides', in *History of the Vikings*, ed. Sawyer, pp. 83–109, at 85–8. For contemporary attacks on northwest Francia, see J. L. Nelson, 'The Frankish Empire', in *History of the Vikings*, ed. Sawyer, pp. 19–47, at 23–4.

[92] For example, Booth, 'Sceattas', p. 86

[93] Sawyer, *From Roman Britain*, p. 226; Loyn, *Anglo-Saxon England*, pp. 50–4; Spufford, *Money*, pp. 53–5; N. Brooks, 'England in the Ninth Century: The Crucible of Defeat', *TRHS* 29 (1979), 1–20; G. Halsall, 'Playing by Whose Rules? A Further Look at Viking Atrocity in the Ninth Century', *Medieval History* 2.2 (1992), 2–12; S. Coupland, 'The Vikings in Francia and Anglo-Saxon England to 911', in *NCMH* II, pp. 190–201. A balanced approach is J. L. Nelson, 'England and the Continent in the Ninth Century: II, the Vikings and Others', *TRHS* 13 (2003), 1–28.

[94] P. Sawyer, 'Two Viking Ages' and *Kings and Vikings. Scandinavia and Europe AD 700–1100* (London, 1982); a range of surveys developing out of this theme can be found in Sawyer, *History of the Vikings*.

[95] S. Coupland, 'The Rod of God's Wrath or the People of God's Wrath? The Carolingians' Theology of the Viking Invasions', *Journal of Ecclesiastical History* 42 (1991), 535–54.

of arms and prayers for deliverance.[96] But the monetary effects of these policies on the ground are debated,[97] and more importantly it is difficult to make a case for the severity of viking raids having such a debilitating and widespread effect so early in the ninth century. Some of the same effects – disorder, uncertainty and death – could have been inflicted by native warfare, such as the West Saxon campaigns against Mercia 825–30 and the accompanying unrest within Mercia.[98] But the Anglo-Saxon Chronicle and other sources, written and archaeological, are reticent about the effects these battles and conquests had on the populace. Other episodes of warfare, such as Coenwulf's reconquest of Kent in 798, had no discernible effect on production or circulation of coin whatsoever, and as far as the moneyers were concerned, at least, it was very much business as usual. As far as can be seen from the Anglo-Saxon Chronicle and associated sources, the period after *c.* 830 was generally more settled, at least between English kingdoms, with no apparent recovery in the rate of loss.

If warfare is unlikely to have provided the sole driving force behind changes in the extent and nature of coin-use, a stronger case might be made for wider changes in economic life, above all those which affected the nodal points of circulation – the mints – and their connections with the rest of England and the Continent. The early ninth century was, for several English minting-towns, clearly a troubled time. At London the area excavated under the Royal Opera House was bisected by a possibly defensive ditch, perhaps implying contraction of the settlement.[99] Comparable developments can also be traced at Southampton.[100] Dorestad, too, was in the final phase of its prosperity in the 820s and 830s, and would eventually be surpassed in importance by Quentovic.[101]

There is a danger of circularity in defining and especially in dating the decline of some of these settlements, as they often depend heavily on the closely datable and quantifiable evidence of coin-finds.[102] A wider,

[96] Hill and Rumble, *Defence of Wessex*; Coupland, 'Rod of God's Wrath'; Pratt, *Political Thought*, pp. 93–111; Brooks, 'England', pp. 16–18.

[97] Coupland, 'Frankish Tribute Payments'; R. Hodges, 'Trade and Market Origins in the Ninth Century: Relations between England and the Continent', in *Charles the Bald*, ed. Gibson and Nelson, pp. 203–23, at 214–15; Sawyer, 'Coins and Commerce', p. 285; Spufford, *Money*, pp. 61–4; Grierson, '*Gratia dei rex*'; Verhulst, *Carolingian Economy*, pp. 119–20.

[98] Stenton, *Anglo-Saxon England*, pp. 231–3; Keynes, 'Mercia and Wessex', pp. 314–23, and 'England, 700–900', pp. 38–40.

[99] Keene, 'Alfred and London', esp. pp. 235–9; Malcolm, Bowsher and Cowie, *Middle Saxon London*, pp. 128–9 and 278–84; J. Leary and G. Brown, *Tatberht's Lundenwic: Archaeological Excavations in Middle Saxon London* (London, 2004), pp. 143–5.

[100] Metcalf, 'Coins', esp. p. 22.   [101] Coupland, 'Trading Places', pp. 218–20.

[102] Several of the phases identified by Richard Hodges (*Towns and Trade in the Age of Charlemagne* (London, 2000), pp. 76–9) rest implicitly or explicitly on coin-find evidence.

independent process of contracting coin-use could therefore present a misleading impression of general urban decline. Low points in coin-use and/or mint-output at other times did not coincide with the abandonment of towns. Southampton, for example, was at its peak *c.* 750–75: a nadir in terms of coinage.[103] In a number of cases, however, there is corroborating evidence from other sources for a downturn in urban activity in the early ninth century, as provided by dendrochronology at Dorestad or by carefully defined stratigraphy at Ribe.[104] It is therefore likely that the early ninth century was a troubled time at the North Sea *wic*,[105] but it is more difficult to link these problems very specifically with the general southern English monetary decline beginning *c.* 830. Sometimes quite different tendencies can be detected. At York, for example, the decline of the Fishergate settlement began about 800, though occupation continued on a reduced scale for another half-century.[106] Decline here is roughly in inverse proportion to the scale of mint-output at York, which reached a peak in the middle of the ninth century.

There were also important cases of towns which bucked the trend of decline in the early ninth century. Some inland urban sites in the Frankish empire reached their peak of coin-loss in the middle decades of the ninth century,[107] and at the same time other towns were beginning to crystallize around important churches or secular estate centres.[108] Even in England the ninth century could be a time of continuity or expansion, especially in the cases of Canterbury, Ipswich and (possibly) Rochester. Ceramic production from the former two centres was substantial in the ninth century, and progressed seamlessly into the late Anglo-Saxon period.[109] Ipswich was unique among the *wic* in occupying the same site

---

[103] A. D. Morton, ed., *Excavations at Hamwic*, vol. I (London, 1992), pp. 53–4 and 70–6; Andrews and Metcalf, 'Coinage', p. 175.

[104] R. Hodges, *Goodbye to the Vikings* (London, 2006), p. 158; S. Coupland, 'Dorestad in the Ninth Century: The Numismatic Evidence', *Jaarboek voor Munt- en Penningkunde* 75 (1988), 5–26, at pp. 7–8, and 'Trading Places', pp. 220–6; C. Feveile, 'The Coins from 8th–9th Centuries Ribe – Survey and Status 2001', *Nordisk Numismatisk Årsskrift 2000–2002: Nordic Numismatic Journal. 6th Nordic Numismatic Symposium: Single Finds: The Nordic Perspective* (2006), 149–62, at pp. 152–7.

[105] Hall, 'Decline of the Wic'; Hodges, 'Trade and Market', esp. pp. 214–17; J. Cherry and R. Hodges, 'The Dating of *Hamwih*: Saxon Southampton Reconsidered', *Antiquaries Journal* 58 (1978), 299–309; Hodges, *Dark Age Economics*, p. 156; G. G. Astill, 'General Survey 600–1300', in *Cambridge Urban History*, ed. Palliser, pp. 27–50, at 33–5; Hinton, 'Large Towns', pp. 220–1.

[106] Russo, *Town Origins*, pp. 153–5; Hinton, 'Large Towns', pp. 221 and 225. For York see R. L. Kemp, *Anglian Settlement at 46–54 Fishergate* (York, 1996); D. Tweddle, J. Moulden and E. Logan, *Anglian York: A Survey of the Evidence* (York, 1999).

[107] Blackburn, 'Coin Circulation', pp. 39–42; Coupland, 'Trading Places'; *FEMA*, pp. 801–5.

[108] A. Verhulst, 'Roman Cities, *Emporia* and New Towns (Sixth–Ninth Centuries)', in *Long Eighth Century*, ed. Hansen and Wickham, pp. 105–20, at 113–20, and *Rise of Cities*, pp. 44–67.

[109] L. Blackmore, 'Pottery: Trade and Tradition', in *Wics*, ed. Hill and Cowie, pp. 22–42, at 34.

all the way through the Anglo-Saxon period,[110] and only experienced a partial decline *c.* 900.[111]

Canterbury and Rochester have received comparatively little notice in studies of urban and economic history. In the case of Rochester this is understandable given its obscurity: besides the establishment of a mint there *c.* 810 little evidence survives for its status as a port or urban centre.[112] Canterbury, however, is in many ways the best-attested urban settlement anywhere in England at this time. It is brought into sharp focus by a series of local charters which flesh out the evidence of coins and archaeological excavation. These charters show a vibrant and densely settled town with emerging gilds and high property values all the way through the ninth century.[113] Excavations have shed further light on the course of development. One intramural site stood largely inactive over the eighth and early ninth centuries but began to develop in the middle of the ninth century, while pottery production in and around Canterbury only took off late in the eighth century.[114] The emphasis of some mint-signed coins on their production in the *civitas* of Canterbury implies that minting took place within the walled Roman city,[115] but metal-detecting and archaeological excavations have shown that there were a number of 'productive sites' around the town, among them Fordwich, Sandwich and Sarre.[116] These could all have functioned as miniature *emporia* for Canterbury, in a more dispersed arrangement than at other such centres.[117] Although these productive sites follow the usual pattern of tailing off in coin-finds over the ninth century, Canterbury seems to have been especially insulated from the troubled times, and the output of the mint remained vigorous throughout the eighth and ninth centuries. Minting is in this case only the tip of an iceberg. It was just one part of the extensive economic and administrative continuity Canterbury enjoyed over much of the eighth and ninth centuries.[118] Monetary history was closely but not inextricably

---

[110] Hodges, *Anglo-Saxon Achievement*, pp. 97–101; Scull, 'Urban Centres', pp. 277–8; Wade, 'Ipswich' and 'Gipeswic'.

[111] Wade, 'Urbanisation', p. 150. [112] Above, pp. 83, 123 and 129–30.

[113] Brooks, *Early History*, pp. 22–33; Russo, *Town Origins*, pp. 199–200.

[114] K. Blockley *et al.*, *Excavations in the Marlowe Car Park and Surrounding Areas*, 3 vols., Archaeology of Canterbury 5 (Canterbury, 1995) I, 21 and 895–6.

[115] J. Campbell, 'Bede's Words', pp. 99–100 and 105. The same may also have been true at ninth-century London: Keene, 'Alfred and London', pp. 240–1.

[116] S 29. D. Hill, 'Appendix 2. Gazetteer of Possible Anglo-Saxon *Wics*', in *Wics*, ed. Hill and Cowie, pp. 95–103; Russo, *Town Origins*, pp. 146–8; Hodges, *Anglo-Saxon Achievement*, pp. 92–4.

[117] Clarke and Ambrosiani, *Towns*, p. 23; Tatton-Brown, 'Towns of Kent', pp. 213–21.

[118] Canterbury's mint-output declined suddenly and dramatically in the 890s (C. S. S. Lyon, 'The Coinage of Edward the Elder', in *Edward the Elder, 899–924*, ed. N. Higham and D. Hill (London, 2001), pp. 67–78, at 75; Blunt, Stewart and Lyon, *Coinage*, p. 21); whether this was accompanied by more general difficulties is unclear.

bound to the fates of towns,[119] and a one-to-one relationship between successful towns, mint-output and coin-finds cannot be assumed.

A change in the sources and volume of southern England's bullion flow does not necessarily depend on general urban malaise. Redirection rather than decline could have produced the same result of a change in the balance of trade. Specifically, Frankish trade from Dorestad and other northern ports may have turned more towards northern Germany and Scandinavia at this time.[120] This presupposes a strong link between coinage and foreign trade, especially foreign trade concentrated at the ports of entry which also served as mints. Silver in itself could have been moved as a commodity, as it sometimes was later in the Middle Ages,[121] but if it is correct that most of the bullion used to mint English currency entered the country in the form of foreign coin and was subsequently reminted, then it probably came as an adjunct to the transport of other goods.[122] An increase in English imports, if exports remained stable or declined, could have had the net effect of draining silver out of England into Francia and Frisia:[123] an ever wider gulf would have resulted between mint-output, which could have remained considerable, and the proportion of that output which was quite soon afterwards taken back to the Continent in payment for imports. Historians are, however, in no position to calculate the GDP of any kingdom in early medieval Europe, or even to follow the identity and quantity of most of the products of international trade. Wool and textile products, which dominated English exports later in the Middle Ages, may already have been prominent among exports from Anglo-Saxon England.[124] Goods known to have come as imports from Francia include pottery (and presumably its contents, among them wine) and quernstones,[125] but the perishability of most commodities and the lack of detailed references in contemporary texts are enough to imperil

---

[119] Blackburn, '"Productive" Sites', pp. 31–4; Metcalf, 'Coins'; P. Stott, 'Saxon and Norman Coins from London', in *Aspects of Saxo-Norman London*, vol. II, *Finds and Environmental Evidence*, ed. A. Vince (London, 1991), pp. 279–325, at 285–6.

[120] A. Verhulst, 'Les origines urbaines dans le Nord-Ouest de l'Europe: essai de synthèse', *Francia* 14 (1986), 57–81, at pp. 69–70; U. Näsman, 'Exchange and Politics: The Eighth–Early Ninth Century in Denmark', in *Long Eighth Century*, ed. Hansen and Wickham, pp. 35–68; *FEMA*, p. 801; in general H. Steuer, 'Der Handel der Wikingerzeit zwischen Nord- und Westeuropa aufgrund archäologischer Zeugnisse', in *Der Handel der Karolinger- und Wikingerzeit*, ed. K. Düwel *et al.* (Göttingen, 1987), pp. 113–97.

[121] Hermann of Laon, *De miraculis S. Mariae Laudunensis* ii.4 (*PL* 156, cols. 975C–977A).

[122] Middleton, 'Early Medieval Port Customs', p. 351.

[123] For declining Anglo-Carolingian trade from *c.* 830 see Hodges, 'Trade and Market', pp. 214–17.

[124] P. J. Crabtree, 'The Wool Trade and the Rise of Urbanism in Middle Saxon England', in *Craft Specialization and Social Evolution in Memory of V. Gordon Childe*, ed. B. Wailes (Philadelphia, PA, 1996), pp. 99–105; Spufford, *Money*, p. 31; Loyn, *Anglo-Saxon England*, p. 103; Sawyer, *From Roman Britain*, p. 233.

[125] Below, pp. 239–41 and 244–6.

all attempts at quantifying the cargoes which were ferried across the Channel in conjunction with the movement of silver.

To conclude, the monetary decline of southern England in the middle third of the ninth century is best set in the local context of a string of adverse developments rather than a monocausal crisis: mounting violence from native and Scandinavian hands alike; widespread if not general urban decline; and possible adjustment of international trade and trade-routes. It was this barrage which, in approximately the 830s, began to inflict a major blow on the monetary economy of Southumbrian England. There may well also have been other, less visible contributions to the cocktail, and it is by turning to parallel developments in other areas – material and geographical – that the monetary and economic condition of late eighth- and ninth-century England can be better understood.

Contexts of circulation: pottery and metalwork

Early medieval coins bear an especially heavy burden among material sources in that, broadly speaking, they survive in substantial quantity from across a period of often scant written sources, and have the near-unique advantage of being closely attributable to a known date and origin. For these reasons, and also thanks to long-established disciplinary boundaries, coins often end up being examined in isolation from other important categories of material: to name just a few, these include pottery, non-numismatic metalwork, textiles and architectural remains. The testimony of all these items complements the picture offered by the coinage, enriching and sometimes challenging the conclusions derived from numismatic evidence alone.

Just a few of these comparisons will be pursued here, but particularly important among them are ceramics. These were made and used across medieval Europe and survive in massive bulk, dwarfing even the number of surviving coins. About 46,000 pieces of early medieval pottery were found in Southampton alone.[126] Unlike metallic objects – and especially precious-metal objects such as coins – pottery was not particularly valuable in itself. Finds therefore indicate a different kind of activity from that of most coin-finds, and often belong to a domestic setting. They can potentially give an impression of how a very broad swathe of society interacted with networks of exchange, and are the index of choice in Chris Wickham's general overviews of the early medieval economy.[127] In

---

[126] Blackmore,'Pottery', p. 23; J. Timby,'The Middle Saxon Pottery', in *Coins and Pottery from Hamwic*, ed. Andrews, pp. 73–122.

[127] C. Wickham,'Rethinking the Structure of the Early Medieval Economy', in *The Long Morning of Early Medieval Europe: New Directions in Early Medieval Studies*, ed. J. R. Davis and M. McCormick (Aldershot, 2008), pp. 19–31, at 24–6, and *FEMA*, pp. 700–6.

the same way as coins, however, ceramics must be understood on their own terms.[128] There may be difficulties in assigning an exact date, and in distinguishing some Middle-Anglo-Saxon ceramics from Early when the context is problematic.[129] Pottery is also not actively sought out in the same way as metallic objects, and so its distribution is dependent on the results of archaeological excavations and field-walking campaigns – both now, admittedly, very numerous. Above all, despite the fact that pottery can be argued to present the best overall picture of exchange in the early Middle Ages, it still constitutes only one portion of the archaeological residue of production and exchange. The dominance exercised by ceramic evidence must not be accepted blindly, and needs to be taken in association with coins and other materials, and especially of now lost products like wood, textiles and consumables.[130]

Within studies of pottery and the economy of Middle Saxon England, Ipswich ware tends to take centre stage, as it was the first wheel-thrown pottery manufactured and distributed on a large scale in Anglo-Saxon England. It was essentially a phenomenon of eastern England, most plentiful within East Anglia itself.[131] But there were other important wares available, for instance two varieties of Maxey ware. These enjoyed quite widespread and plentiful distribution across the midlands and East Anglia, stretching up into Lincolnshire and Yorkshire.[132] Elsewhere, old-fashioned local wares often persisted, which can be hard to distinguish from earlier pottery.[133] In some parts of the country basic forms of sand- and grass-tempered ware were probably made domestically,[134] but in Southampton, Canterbury and possibly London there was production of gritty and shell-tempered wares on a large enough scale to support circulation across southern England.[135] In contrast with the numismatic record, these industries only really expanded in the mid and late eighth century, and largely at the expense of Ipswich ware.[136] There was also an important and well-established element of cross-Channel exchange in pottery (and presumably any products the pots once

[128] L. Blackmore, 'La céramique du Vème au Xème siècle à Londres et dans la région londonienne', in *La céramique du Vème au Xème siècle dans l'Europe du Nord-Ouest*, ed. D. Piton (Arras, 1993), pp. 129–50, and 'Pottery'; Hamerow, 'Pottery'; J. Hurst, 'The Pottery', in *Archaeology of Anglo-Saxon England*, ed. Wilson, pp. 283–348, esp. 299–313; for methodological comparison J. W. Hayes, *Late Roman Pottery* (London, 1972).

[129] A. Vince, 'Ceramic Petrology and the Study of Anglo-Saxon and Later Medieval Ceramics', *Medieval Archaeology* 49 (2005), 219–45, at pp. 226–8.

[130] Faith, 'Forces and Relations', p. 34.

[131] Blinkhorn, 'Of Cabbages'; *FEMA*, pp. 812–13.

[132] P. V. Addyman, 'A Dark-Age Settlement at Maxey, Northants', *Medieval Archaeology* 8 (1964), 20–73, at pp. 47–58; Vince, 'Ceramic Petrology', p. 227.

[133] A. J. Mainman, *Pottery from 46–54 Fishergate* (London, 1993), p. 579–80.

[134] *Ibid.*   [135] Blackmore, 'Pottery', pp. 26–7.   [136] *Ibid.*, p. 27.

carried).[137] These international wares are most prominent at the sites of *wic* such as Ipswich, Southampton, London and York,[138] where they constitute up to a third of all finds.[139] Rhenish wares were prominent among these imports and can be compared with the extensive importation of Mayen lava quernstones from the same area.[140] It is now apparent, however, that Rhenish dominance was not total and that a large quantity of pottery came to England from the north and west of France as well.[141]

The scale of international trade in bulk goods which these pots evince might be suspected on the basis of the coins, but is impossible to verify. In addition, what metal-detectorists have revealed for coin-circulation, field-walking and ongoing, excavations have revealed for pottery; that is, that ceramics made at major centres could penetrate into the countryside and did not remain the preserve of towns and elite settlements.[142] In the case of Ipswich ware this was true only within East Anglia,[143] and here and elsewhere there could be substantial disparities between the ceramic records of relatively nearby sites, showing very different sets of connections.[144]

The distribution networks of pottery share important points with those of coinage. The general buoyancy of production and exchange are clearly apparent, and might be associated with increasing stability and the expansion of markets;[145] in particular, the dominance of eastern and southern England is very strongly emphasized. But just as important are the divergences of numismatic and ceramic evidence. Chronologically they took different courses. There was, for example, no general collapse in the making and movement of pots *c.* 740–70 such as there was with coins. Geographically, it should be noted that the long-distance circulation of Ipswich ware was not matched by the circulation of coins probably struck at Ipswich, or at least not to the same extent as coins from the southeastern mints, which generally circulated much more widely.

[137] G. C. Dunning, 'Trade Relations between England and the Continent in the Late Anglo-Saxon Period', in *Dark Age Britain*, ed. D. B. Harden (London, 1956), pp. 218–33.
[138] Vince, 'Ceramic Petrology', p. 227.
[139] Blackmore, 'Pottery', p. 23; Mainman, *Pottery*, p. 570.
[140] J. Parkhouse, 'The Distribution and Exchange of Mayen Lava Quernstones in Early Medieval Northwest Europe', in *Exchange and Trade in Medieval Europe*, ed. G. De Boe and F. Verhaeghe (Zellik, 1997), pp. 97–106.
[141] Hurst, 'Pottery', pp. 311–13; Blackmore, 'Pottery', pp. 27–32.
[142] Vince, 'Ceramic Petrology', p. 220; Moreland, 'Significance of Production', pp. 87–96.
[143] Blackmore, 'Pottery', pp. 36–8.
[144] J. Newman, '*Sceattas* in East Anglia: An Archaeological Perspective', in *Two Decades of Discovery*, ed. T. Abramson (Woodbridge, 2008), pp. 17–22, at 20–1; Hurst, 'Pottery', pp. 307–8 (on Castor, with much Ipswich ware, and Maxey, with none); H. Hamerow, 'Angles, Saxons and Anglo-Saxons: Rural Centres, Trade and Production', *Studien zur Sachsenforschung* 13 (1999), 189–206, at pp. 197–200 (with important continental comparisons).
[145] McCormick, *Origins*, pp. 656–63.

There is also more interaction with Northumbria observable through the ceramic record than is the case with coins.[146]

Another instructive case is that of ornamental metalwork, which differs from coins and ceramics in the nature of both its manufacture and distribution. Metalwork presents substantial methodological problems in that date, origin and representativeness can be difficult to define.[147] Archaeological evidence suggests that most Anglo-Saxon metalworking in this period was concentrated at towns and specialized rural settlements of ecclesiastical or aristocratic nature.[148] This holds true for both precious and non-precious metals: the important ironworking site at Ramsbury, for example, was probably associated with a royal estate.[149] The distribution of decorative metalwork suggests complex and distinct networks of exchange which share only limited similarities with pottery and coinage. Lindsey, for example, has produced finds of ornamental metalwork from both Northumbria and the south, which matches its mix of coins from both areas.[150] On the other hand, finds of 'Mercian-style' ornamental metalwork are concentrated between the Thames and the Humber, but include a strong element of western finds, with a number occurring in the areas of the upper Trent and Severn valleys – exactly where coin-finds are fewest.[151]

The obvious question is where and under what circumstances ornamental metalwork was made and distributed. It is often found at the same 'productive sites' as coins – indeed, metalwork normally constitutes 50–90 per cent of the known metallic material from these sites[152] – and does not always show the same decline in volume in the later ninth and tenth centuries.[153] Lichfield and Peterborough have both been advanced as possible metalwork and sculpture workshops, though other possibilities

---

[146] Mainman, *Pottery*, pp. 564–83.

[147] G. Thomas, 'Silver Wire Strap-Ends from East Anglia', *ASSAH* 9 (1996), 81–100, '"Brightness in a Time of Dark": The Production of Secular Ornamental Metalwork in 9th-Century Northumbria', in *De Re Metallica: The Uses of Metal in the Middle Ages*, ed. R. Bork (Aldershot, 2005), pp. 31–48, and 'Strap-Ends and the Identification of Regional Patterns in the Production and Circulation of Ornamental Metalwork in Late Anglo-Saxon and Viking-Age Britain', in *Pattern and Purpose in Insular Art. Proceedings of the Fourth International Conference on Insular Art Held at the National Museum and Gallery, Cardiff 3–6 September 1998*, ed. M. Redknap et al. (Oxford, 2001), pp. 39–49.

[148] Hamerow, 'Angles, Saxons', p. 200.

[149] J. Haslam, 'A Middle Saxon Iron Smelting Site at Ramsbury, Wiltshire', *Medieval Archaeology* 24 (1980), 1–68.

[150] G. Thomas, 'Strap-Ends', pp. 40–2.

[151] L. Webster, 'Metalwork of the Mercian Supremacy', in *Mercia*, ed. Brown and Farr, pp. 263–77, at 269–74.

[152] Richards, Naylor and Holas-Clark, 'Anglo-Saxon Landscape and Economy', § 4.5.

[153] Blackburn, '"Productive" Sites', p. 32.

exist.[154] Presumably Kent, Sussex and Wessex were not devoid of metal-workers at this time, and may have seen the continuation of earlier styles as well as (in the early ninth century) the emergence of the so-called Trewhiddle style.[155] The lack of finds of Mercian-style metalwork in Kent is especially striking, given the close and usually subordinate relationship it had with Mercia, which is observable in coin-circulation as well as through manuscript art and (possibly) dialectal influence.[156] A quite different network of distribution applied to the Mercian kingdom, focused on the midlands rather than the south or east. One category of decorative metalwork from this period – strap-ends decorated with silver wire – seems to be associated with East Anglia and a small number of coastal sites elsewhere in the country,[157] and there are other groups that can be attributed by similar means. Prestigious and attractive metalwork probably belonged to a context of high-status movement and interaction and may have often changed hands as gift or tribute.[158] As a result, the distribution of finds of ornamental metalwork shows a stronger relationship with political geography and, in Mercia, the royal itinerary.[159]

Coins cannot be viewed in isolation: they were not the only objects which travelled or which allow an insight into modes and measures of exchange. Pottery and metalwork provide valuable correctives showing quite different networks of distribution. However, any conclusion which relies too heavily on one category of material risks presenting a warped picture. Exchanges worked at a number of levels and went in a number of directions. Coins, in comparison to other sources, were marked out by their consistently widespread distribution within a large segment of Southumbrian England, most intense and most closely related to a local mint-town in East Anglia, otherwise depending on the trio of mint-towns around the Thames estuary. Exactly who used these pennies and for what is discussed in due course, but unlike pottery and metalwork coins were not in all respects a commodity in and of themselves; rather, they illustrate the general movements of bulk and

---

[154] Brown, 'Lichfield Angel'; Plunkett, 'Mercian Perspective', p. 211; R. N. Bailey, 'The Gandersheim Casket and Anglo-Saxon Stone Sculpture', in *Das Gandersheimer Runenkästchen. Internationales Kolloquium Braunschweig, 24.–26. März 1999*, ed. R. Marth (Braunschweig, 2000), pp. 43–52.

[155] Webster, 'Metalwork', pp. 274–5.

[156] M. Brown, 'Mercian Manuscripts? The "Tiberius" Group and Its Historical Context', in *Mercia*, ed. Brown and Farr, pp. 278–90, esp. 285–9; T. E. Toon, *The Politics of Early Old English Sound Change* (New York, 1983).

[157] G. Thomas, 'Silver Wire'; Newman, '*Sceattas*', p. 20.

[158] Innes, 'Framing', pp. 47–8; Brookes, *Economics*, pp. 20–2; R. Le Jan, 'Frankish Giving of Arms and Rituals of Power: Continuity and Change', in *Rituals of Power. From Late Antiquity to the Early Middle Ages*, ed. F. Theuws and J. L. Nelson (Leiden, 2000), pp. 377–99.

[159] Webster, 'Metalwork', p. 274.

mid- to high-value commodities and their exchange. Their production and possibly part of their circulation were closely bound to international trade, and initial stages of their movement within England may have been linked to a relatively small body of merchants, travellers and members of the elite who moved between the centres of commerce and of ecclesiastical and political power.[160] Thereafter, however, coinage was dispersed and used among a broad swathe of society across eastern England, apparently on a much more localized level. Eighth- and ninth-century coins, in other words, do not tell the whole story, but they do provide a qualified overview.

Contexts of circulation: Francia, Northumbria and Italy

England is one of relatively few substantial areas in Europe for which a large volume of data on the nature and extent of coin-circulation is available. Elsewhere, conclusions depend on hoards and on a smaller quantity of stray- and excavation-finds. The different conditions these suggest must thus be read with caution, but the evidence still allows some measure of comparison to be undertaken and for the question to be asked of how representative southern England was of wider developments in eighth- and ninth-century Europe.

The Frankish empire presents the most obvious comparison to southern England. Currency in the two areas seems to have been closely related. Adoption of silver instead of gold occurred almost simultaneously on both sides of the Channel *c.* 675, and there was probably a link between Pippin III's coinage reform of the early 750s and those of Northumbria and East Anglia. Similarly, the onset of debasement in the 840s occurred at roughly the same time in both areas, albeit with different future developments. Southern England and Francia thus shared coinages of very similar format and development. These were not produced using quite the same administrative mechanisms, and they could not always circulate interchangeably, but nevertheless there is good evidence for regular and substantial exchange of ideas and silver between the two realms.[161] Thanks to this basic monetary similarity, one may tentatively accept that what can be learned of coin-use from Frankish capitularies and saints' lives also applied in southern England. In the latter, a dearth of written sources contrasts with plentiful single-finds, evincing circulation on the level Frankish texts imply; conversely, relatively few single-finds have

---

[160] Cf. W. Davies, *Small Worlds: The Village Community of Early Medieval Brittany* (London, 1988), pp. 105–33; alongside Sindbæk, 'Small World' and 'Networks'.
[161] Above, pp. 3–7 and 161–5.

been recorded in France, Belgium and Germany to confirm the testimony of other sources.[162] It is only by combining resources from the two areas that a full view can be reached.

Documents permitting a comparatively detailed view of how and by whom coins were used in the Carolingian world are discussed in Chapter 9, but knowledge of monetary circulation within the Frankish empire has perforce had to proceed primarily on the basis of hoard evidence.[163] Be that as it may, the tendencies of coin-circulation within the hoards of the Frankish empire have been closely traced.[164] The relatively high number of mints active at any one time – never fewer than a dozen, and over 150 are known in total – has provided the main variable.[165] Broadly speaking there were two tiers among them: some, such as Paris, Rouen, Orleans, Quentovic and Dorestad, were very large and productive, and their products travelled across Francia to be included in many hoards; the second tier consisted of smaller mints whose products tended to circulate more locally. This was a pattern which can be traced back into the Merovingian era,[166] and which was not without further nuance. Even for some larger mints, localized distribution was still dominant and wider circulation was concentrated on specific axes, such as the northern coast and certain rivers. Political divisions could also be significant: Aquitaine in particular was largely separate from the circulation of the rest of the kingdom and contained a number of 'cells' of very localized distribution. Some regions were in addition much more highly monetized than others, and both finds and documents reveal that certain parts of the Frankish empire – such as Brittany and the lands beyond the Rhine – were relatively little touched by coin-circulation.[167] In general, the richest area of coin-circulation was that between the Rhine and the Loire.

---

[162] Single-finds from before Pippin's reign are gathered in J. Lafaurie and J. Pilet-Lemière, *Monnaies du haut moyen âge découvertes en France (Ve–VIIIe siècle)* (Paris 2003). Later finds have also been gathered for certain regions, as in Coupland, 'Carolingian Single Finds'; Blackburn, 'Coin Circulation'; J. C. Moesgaard, 'Stray Finds of Carolingian Coins in Upper Normandy, France', in *Studia Numismatica: Festschrift, Arkadi Molvõgin 65*, ed. I. Leimus (Tallinn, 1995), pp. 87–102; O. Jeanne-Rose, 'Trouvailles isolées de monnaies carolingiennes en Poitou: inventaire provisoire', *Revue numismatique* 151 (1996), 241–83.

[163] For the crucial publications of Carolingian hoards see above, n. 28.

[164] Especially in Bruand, *Voyageurs et marchandises*, pp. 155–84; D. M. Metcalf, 'A Sketch of the Currency in the Time of Charles the Bald', in *Charles the Bald*, ed. Gibson and Nelson, pp. 65–97. Cf. A. Rovelli, 'Coins and Trade in Early Medieval Italy', *EME* 17 (2009), 45–76; Coupland, 'Carolingian Single Finds'.

[165] *MEC*, p. 196.

[166] J. Lafaurie, 'Les routes commerciales indiquées par les trésors et trouvailles monétaires mérovingiens', *Settimane* 8 (1961), 231–78, at pp. 248–9, 250–1 and 268–9.

[167] W. Davies, *Small Worlds*, pp. 58–60 and 98–9; C. I. Hammer, 'Land Sales in Eighth- and Ninth-Century Bavaria: Legal, Economic and Social Aspects', *EME* 6 (1997), 47–76, at pp. 63–5 (on Bavaria); Blackburn, 'Coin Circulation'.

Just like England, therefore, Francia had some regions which enjoyed much more extensive coin-circulation than others and a substantial band of territory where coins and the commodities with which they were associated were comparatively plentiful. These two swathes of coin-rich lands in England and Francia faced each other and in many respects can be read as a single monetary supra-region. Points of divergence include the number and nature of mints, which in Francia included a large number of often very small institutions, and the regionalization of Aquitaine, which was a result of other economic and political developments.[168]

Southern England and Francia – or more specifically the eastern and southern part of Southumbrian England and northwest Francia – might be thought of as presenting the norm of western European currency, but they were surrounded by regions which made little or no use of coinage in the case of areas such as Wales, Ireland and parts of Germany. Other regions had their own coinages of very different form and function. More extensive comparison with Scandinavia or the Muslim and Byzantine worlds would highlight significant differences, as would a detailed comparison with England earlier or later in the Middle Ages. To any well-travelled observer of the eighth or ninth century, it would not necessarily have been obvious that the broad, thin silver coins of northwest Europe were to be the preferred currency for several centuries to come. Northumbria and Italy offer important contemporary contrasts which throw the distinctive strengths and weaknesses of southern England and northern Francia into sharper relief. Both regions would have been known to traders and travellers from southern England in the eighth and ninth centuries, and there is direct evidence for this in both cases thanks to coin-finds.[169]

In the case of Northumbria, there is the advantage of a strong evidential base, finds from here being covered by the Corpus of Early Medieval Coin Finds and the Portable Antiquities Scheme. But the obscurity of the kingdom from the point of view of other sources – particularly documentation which might give some insight into the social and economic repercussions of monetary developments – is such that it remains essentially an enigma. Even the royal chronology is uncertain and has been challenged on the basis of numismatic data.[170] What is clear is that in the century after Eadberht's reform and institution of a signed royal coinage *c.* 740, Northumbria maintained a coinage based on the small, thick

---

[168] M. Rouche, *L'Aquitaine des Wisigoths aux Arabes, 418–781* (Paris, 1979); Bruand, *Voyageurs et marchandises*, pp. 102–6.

[169] C. E. Blunt, 'Anglo-Saxon Coins Found in Italy', in *Anglo-Saxon Monetary History*, ed. Blackburn, pp. 159–69.

[170] Lyon, 'Ninth-Century Northumbrian Chronology'; H. Pagan, 'Northumbrian Numismatic Chronology in the Ninth Century', *BNJ* 38 (1969), 1–15.

model of the *sceattas*. This was struck in small numbers for three decades after the death of Eadberht in 758, but in greater volume from the second reign of Æthelred I (788/9–96).[171]

The best-known feature of the ninth-century Northumbrian coinage was its debasement, which led eventually to the first substantial base-metal coinage in the post-Roman West. The quantity of silver in the coinage did not decline in a straightforward way, but by the reign of Eanred it was certainly very low; two phases of his coinage can be identified, the second being the first to contain coins with almost no precious-metal content.[172] By the end of his reign the coinage was formed of brass, which, although inferior to silver, was perhaps still a metal of some value.[173] No evidence survives for how contemporaries reacted to the declining fineness of the coinage. On some level debasement must have been related to shortage in the supply of bullion, though it should be noted that ornamental silver metalwork continued to be produced in Northumbria, implying that not all silver was handled in the same way.[174]

Whatever the intention behind it, one probable result of debasement was a fall in value. The implementation of a closed currency system would have bolstered the kingdom against inflation to some extent,[175] but it is very likely that Northumbria in the ninth century suffered from rising prices. In the long term this was not necessarily an economic disaster, as an important side-effect would have been to render the coinage more versatile for day-to-day purchases than was the case earlier in Northumbria or in contemporary southern England. The extent of Northumbrian inflation is impossible to quantify, and one would have to demonstrate a large-scale increase in both production and circulation even to approach a conclusion.[176] The tendency towards bulk in surviving hoards is suggestive, but no statistical data have yet been produced from which original production can be estimated.[177] It is therefore necessary

---

[171] *MEC*, pp. 296–303; Booth, '*Sceattas*'; J. Naylor, 'The Circulation of Early-Medieval European Coinage: A Case Study from Yorkshire, *c.* 650–*c.* 867', *Medieval Archaeology* 51 (2007), 41–61; Pirie, 'Contrasts'.

[172] C. S. S. Lyon, 'A Reappraisal of the *Sceatta* and *Styca* Coinage of Northumbria', *BNJ* 28 (1955–7), 227–42, at pp. 232–3.

[173] J. Gilmore, 'Metal Analysis of the Northumbrian *Stycas*: Review and Suggestions', in *Coinage in Ninth-Century Northumbria*, ed. Metcalf, pp. 159–73, at 169; C. Smith, 'A Barbarised Coinage? Copper Alloy in Pre-Viking Northumbrian Coinage', *Quaestio Insularis* 3 (2002), 59–75.

[174] G. Thomas, 'Strap-Ends', p. 43.

[175] D. M. Metcalf, 'A Topographical Commentary on the Coin Finds from Ninth-Century Northumbria (*c.* 780–*c.* 870)', in *Coinage in Ninth-Century Northumbria*, ed. Metcalf, pp. 361–82, at 367.

[176] For sketches of Northumbrian monetary history, see Metcalf, 'Topographical Commentary'; Naylor, 'Circulation'.

[177] For the period before *c.* 788, see D. M. Metcalf, 'Estimation of the Volume of the Northumbrian Coinage, *c.* 738–88', in *Sceattas*, ed. Hill and Metcalf, pp. 113–16.

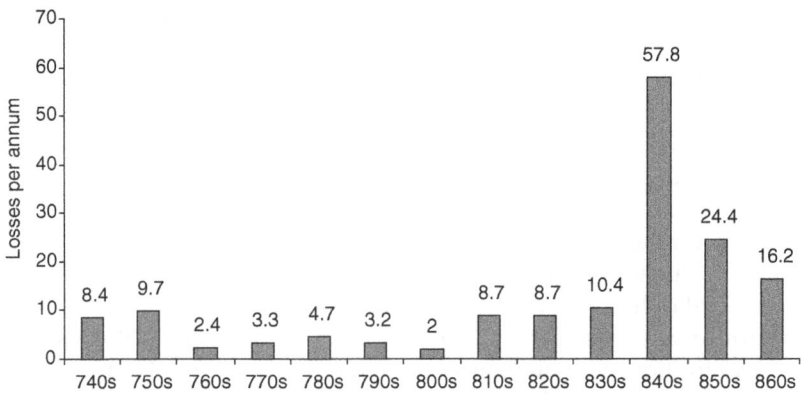

Figure 8.11 Loss rate of single-finds of Northumbrian coins.

to turn to the single-finds. Some 1,600 of these have been recorded on the Corpus of Early Medieval Coin Finds and the Portable Antiquities Scheme (Figure 8.11); other sources would augment these totals, and the coins are so common that a significant proportion of finds probably goes unrecorded.

This figure illustrates available evidence for the rate of loss of coins from the Northumbrian mint based on date of production, which was comparable to that of any of the major southern mints down to *c.* 840. The level of coin-use – the volume of currency and the intensity with which it was used – was therefore probably not significantly greater than that which applied to the products of contemporary southern mints. An upsurge in the apparent rate of loss came in the reigns of Eanred and especially Æthelred II (and the usurper Rædwulf). Theoretical loss rates of almost sixty coins per year represent a great velocity of use and, probably, volume of production, while a fall in value may have reduced the incentive to retrieve lost coins.

The full implications of these figures for Northumbria are beyond the scope of the present study. In brief, however, Northumbria's currency and circulation seem to have been comparable to those of the south in most respects until approximately the 830s, when the precious-metal content of the coinage declined to almost nil, but the quantity in circulation and the intensity of its use probably increased substantially. For a few decades around the middle of the ninth century Northumbria effectively had a base-metal coinage. A certain quantity of these *stycas* made it into circulation south of the Humber, but in general the precedent set by Northumbria was not followed elsewhere in western Europe. The kingdom's viking conquerors abandoned the earlier model after taking over around 867,[178] and when a new currency was established in the 890s it was based on the silver pennies of southern England and the Carolingian empire.

In many ways early medieval Italy was the exact opposite of Northumbria. The peninsula's political fragmentation was reflected in its coinages: there were significant differences between those of the northern Lombard kingdom; the Byzantine exarchate which survived, centred on Ravenna, until 751; Rome and its hinterland; and the Byzantine and Lombard realms of southern Italy. In Rome and the lands to the north, prior to Charlemagne's monetary reform of 781, there still remained a currency of debased gold coins, with occasional issues of silver and bronze.[179] After that time, as in Francia and England, a single silver denomination became current for most practical purposes and gradually gained ground in the south in the ninth century.[180]

The coinage of early medieval Italy is problematic in that the written sources appear to tell quite a different story from that of the coin-finds. Relatively plentiful references in documents from central and northern Italy suggest that silver was widely used and that gold coinage from external sources remained a substantial component of the currency, at least for high-value transactions;[181] but both gold and, more strikingly, silver coins are extremely scarce among actual finds, indicating a limited role in day-to-day use.[182] Extensive excavations in major cities like Milan, Brescia and

---

[178] On the transition see M. Blackburn, 'Currency under the Vikings, Part 1: Guthrum and the Earliest Danelaw Coinages', *BNJ* 75 (2005), 18–43, at p. 23.

[179] Rovelli, 'Coins and Trade', pp. 48–55; W. R. Day, 'The Monetary Reforms of Charlemagne and the Circulation of Money in Early Medieval Campania', *EME* 6 (1997), 25–45. The exact date of the end of formal Byzantine coinage in Rome is unclear: *MEC*, p. 638; Grierson, *Byzantine Coins*, pp. 169–70.

[180] A. Rovelli, 'Some Considerations on the Coinage of Lombard and Carolingian Italy', in *Long Eighth Century*, ed. Hansen and Wickham, pp. 195–223, at 209–10; P. Toubert, 'Il sistema curtense: la produzione e lo scambio interno in Italia nei secoli VIII, IX e X', in *Storia d'Italia: Annali VI. Economia naturale, economia monetaria*, ed. R. Romano and U. Tucci (Turin, 1983), pp. 3–63, at 54.

[181] Toubert, *Europe*, p. 197; E. Bernareggi, *Moneta Langobardorum* (Lugano, 1989), pp. 89–91.

[182] A feature highlighted in several publications by Alessia Rovelli: for a selection see 'Some Considerations', 'La moneta nella documentazione altomedievale di Roma e del Lazio', in *La storia di Roma nell'alto medioevo alla luce dei recenti scavi archeologici*, ed. P. Delogu and L. Paroli (Florence, 1993), pp. 333–52, 'La funzione della moneta tra l'VIII e X secolo. Un'analisi della documentazione archeologica', in *La storia dell'alto medioevo italiano (VI–X sec.) alla luce dell'archeologia. Atti del Convegno internazionale di Siena, 2–6 dicembre 1992*, ed. R. Francovich and G. Noyé (Florence, 1994), pp. 521–38, 'Circolazione monetaria e formulari notarili nell'Italia altomedievale', *Bulletino dell'istituto storico italiano per il medio evo e archivio Muratoriano* 98 (1992), 109–44, 'I tesori monetali', in *Tesori. Forme di accumulazione della ricchezza nell'alto medioevo (secoli V–XI)*, ed. S. Gelichi and C. La Rocca (Rome, 2004), pp. 241–56, and 'Coins and Trade'. See also C. Wickham, 'Economic and Social Institutions in Northern Tuscany in the Eighth Century', in *Istituzione ecclesiastiche della Toscana medievale*, ed. C. Wickham *et al.* (Galatina, 1980), pp. 7–34, at 27–34; W. R. Day, 'Monetary Reforms'.

Rome have produced negligible coin-finds of the Carolingian period, in contrast with numerous coins of other periods and other early medieval artefacts. Even trading centres like Torcello, Aosta and Luni have produced only a tiny number of Carolingian-period coins.[183] Private metal-detector-use in Italy is illegal, and so this picture is dictated in large part by the presence or absence of excavations.[184] Further, die-studies of coins from Carolingian-era Italy have been scarce and so the scale of production is much less clear. But there can be little doubt that currency in eighth- and ninth-century Italy was at a low ebb. In the case of the Lombard principality of Benevento die-analysis indicates that the silver *denarii* of the ninth century were struck in significantly smaller quantity than the *solidi* and *tremisses* of earlier times.[185]

It does not follow that Italy was a poverty-stricken backwater, however. Ceramics and other sources can be used to track relative prosperity, and for Rome in particular the late eighth and ninth centuries were a period of incipient economic revival.[186] Neither were gold and silver as bullion noticeably rare. The amount of both metals which successive kings and emperors lavished on Rome, as recorded in the *Liber pontificalis*, is truly staggering. Over the eighth and ninth centuries, the total rose to some 4,480 pounds of gold and 45,867 pounds of silver, most given between 772 and 816.[187] In Italy, it appears, silver currency simply never achieved the volume and penetration of society that seem to have applied in southern England and northern Francia. *Denarii* instead remained the preserve of higher-value and higher-status transactions, perhaps functioning more as a store of wealth, influenced by the practice applied to earlier gold coinage. Chris Wickham, Jean-Pierre Devroey and Alessia Rovelli have also suggested that the relative lack of inter-regional bulk exchange in Italy might explain the small scale of coin-use, in contrast to what can be observed in northern Francia and England at the same time.[188]

---

[183] Rovelli, 'Some Considerations', pp. 208–9, and 'Funzione', pp. 524–9.

[184] Rovelli, 'Some Considerations', p. 211 n. 51.

[185] E. A. Arslan, 'Sequenze dei conii e valutazioni quantitative delle monetazioni argentea ed aurea di Benevento longobarda', in *Rythmes de la production monétaire de l'antiquité à nos jours*, ed. G. Depeyrot, T. Hackens and G. Moucharte (Louvain-la-Neuve, 1987), pp. 387–409; Rovelli, 'Some Considerations', pp. 218–20.

[186] *FEMA*, pp. 735–6, and C. Wickham, 'Overview: Production, Distribution and Demand', in *Long Eighth Century*, ed. Hansen and Wickham, pp. 345–77, at 361–3.

[187] P. Delogu, 'Oro e argento in Roma tra il VII e il IX secolo', in *Cultura e società nell'Italia medievale. Studi per P. Brezzi* (Rome, 1988), pp. 273–93; Noble, 'Topography, Celebration', pp. 54–5.

[188] Rovelli, 'Coins and Trade', pp. 57–69; J.-P. Devroey, 'Courants et réseaux d'échange dans l'économie franque entre Loire et Rhin', *Settimane* 40 (1993), 327–90; Wickham, 'Rethinking', pp. 27–8 (though see above, pp. 223 and 229).

CONCLUSION

Patterns of minting and especially of coin-circulation were not simplistically dictated by any one influence. This was not a command economy, in which the demands of the state governed production, distribution and exchange. Indeed, the influence of the king was relatively restricted. The strongest card he had to play was in relation to the legal status of coinage: where and possibly by whom coins could be issued; which coins could and could not be used; and what standards were to be acceptable. But the actual circulation of coinage did not follow the same paths as royal itineraries and landholding or even, in so far as they can be traced, the patterns of large-scale elite or ecclesiastical landholding. If the royal, ecclesiastical and aristocratic elements of society did drive circulation, they did so largely without any direct effect on coin distribution. Their contribution was to provide stable anchors of wealth and patronage, the economic orbits of which remained flexible and fissile. What remains to be considered is who was behind this diversified circulation and for what purposes they used coins.

Chapter 9

THE NATURE OF COIN-USE IN
THE EARLY MIDDLE AGES

Even after 1,200 years, voluminous finds have occurred of coins lost in eighth- and ninth-century England, and examination of these in the two previous chapters leads to the central conclusion that they bear witness to vibrant minting and monetary circulation. It will never be possible to pin down exactly how many coins safely changed hands for each one that was lost or concealed in a hoard, though given the relatively high value of even one silver penny at this time, they cannot have been lost lightly.[1]

The finds which metal-detectorists and archaeologists bring to light therefore are very much the tip of the iceberg in terms of evidence for monetary circulation; they are all the more impressive for their quantity and all the more exigent of further investigation. External forces such as warfare and bullion supply had significant effects on coin-use and production, but questions such as who used these coins, how often and for what purposes – the small-scale, grass-roots level of coin-use – are easily side-stepped. Yet they are integral to establishing what part coinage played in the early medieval economy. Refinement is both possible and necessary on the important question of what coin-use meant in the context of the society and economy of the early Middle Ages.

BACKGROUND: MAUSS, PIRENNE,
GRIERSON AND AFTER

Money, as defined by a distinguished line of economists and philosophers beginning with Aristotle and Plato, serves a number of purposes: these have traditionally been summarized as means of exchange (sometimes

---

[1] Modern assessments of wastage rates (i.e., rate of loss) provide only the vaguest of guides, as modern coins are much lower in value and were not necessarily used in the same ways or in comparable settings. See above, p. 184; and below, pp. 287–8, for prices.

with a sub-division of means of payment for fines and taxes), store of value and unit of account; all ultimately depend on this last, on an abstract measure of value relationship which endows other objects or commodities with monetary qualities.[2] Money thus reflects broad consensus on value and derives from binding and mutual relationships within society.[3] Coined metallic money was a particularly successful and persistent form of money which served all of these related uses in Anglo-Saxon England, though it was not the only means available. Here, the emphasis will be on the extent to which coined currency functioned as a means of exchange and payment: how and by whom it was used in transactions. Other forms of money probably existed (though are very difficult to identify),[4] and other purposes for coins can also be traced. Hoarding, for example, presupposes an important role as a store of value (which may have fluctuated in scale and often been limited),[5] while the sums recorded in written sources highlight links between the coinage and units of account. These uses should not be forgotten, even if the non-exchange functions of coinage are difficult to perceive and resistant to quantification.

Leaving other media of exchange and other roles for coinage temporarily to one side, coins as a means of exchange have in themselves generated a great deal of debate. The ways in which coins changed hands – as gifts, payments or in some other form – have long been considered by early medieval numismatists and historians. Enquiry into this subject has been subject to many practical problems and changes in historiographical direction, and as a result views on how important coinage was to the early medieval economy have varied. Until approximately 1959 the tendency among early medievalists was to assume fairly uncritically that, in a similar way to modern currency, Anglo-Saxon, Frankish and other coins betokened trade, often specifically the presence and movements of merchants.[6] A dearth of coin-use was indicative of a dearth of trade in general. In that year, however, Philip Grierson published a landmark paper in which he took to pieces this simplistic view of coin-finds as an indicator of commerce.[7] Grierson showed, particularly with reference to gold coinage of the seventh century and before, that there was considerable

---

[2] J. A. Schumpeter, *History of Economic Analysis* (London, 1955), pp. 59–61; K. Polanyi, *The Livelihood of Man* (New York, 1977), pp. 97–121; P. Grierson, *The Origins of Money* (London, 1977).

[3] G. Ingham, *The Nature of Money* (Cambridge, 2004), esp. pp. 69–85; S. von Reden, *Money in Classical Antiquity* (Cambridge, 2010), pp. 1–6; K. Hart, 'Money: One Anthropologist's View', in *A Handbook of Economic Anthropology*, ed. J. Carrier (Cheltenham, 2005), pp. 160–75, at 161–5.

[4] Below, pp. 289–90.   [5] Above, pp. 232–3.

[6] For example, H. Pirenne, *Mohammed and Charlemagne*, trans. B. Miall (London, 1939), pp. 116 and 244. For an early contrary view, see Dopsch, *Economic and Social Foundations*, pp. 373–83.

[7] P. Grierson, 'Commerce in the Dark Ages: A Critique of the Evidence', *TRHS* 9 (1959), 123–40.

evidence for other uses of money which militated against a simple relationship between coins and mercantile trade. Payments of fines, tribute and even symbolic gifts to the dead all needed to be factored in as well, and collectively outweighed what he saw as relatively small-scale employment of coins for commercial purposes. In emphasizing alternative uses of coinage Grierson drew inspiration from work in the social sciences, particularly Marcel Mauss' now well-known 'Essai sur le don' ('Essay on the gift').[8] Mauss drew attention to the cycles of reciprocity that gift-giving established as a mechanism for structuring social and economic relationships. Although based on practices in parts of the modern world like Polynesia and the northwest coast of North America, Mauss' study offered many comparisons from ancient and medieval Europe – including a stanza of the Old Norse poem *Hávamál* as an epigraph – and was of patent relevance for Grierson and other medievalists, especially given prevailing interpretations of the early medieval economy as a whole.

Grierson's famous and deeply influential critique of the early medieval monetary economy took as its second point of departure the so-called 'Pirenne thesis', first formulated in the early twentieth century by Henri Pirenne and still the subject of debate a century later.[9] According to the Pirenne thesis, there was substantial economic and cultural continuity after the fall of the Roman empire in much of the west (despite political takeover by barbarian invaders) until the Islamic conquests of the seventh century. These effectively ended trade between east and west and brought about the real beginning of the Dark Ages from the point of view of Francia and other western kingdoms. Pirenne and other economic historians saw the impact of these conquests extending into the eighth and ninth centuries, when they forced a reorientation and reimagining of power in northern Europe that led to the Carolingian renaissance and the reforms of Charlemagne's reign. In Pirenne's famous summation, 'sans Mohamet, Charlemagne est inconcevable' ('Charlemagne, without Mohammad, would be inconceivable').[10] As far as economic life was concerned, the late seventh, eighth and ninth centuries were thus seen

---

[8] Cited here in English translation as M. Mauss, *Gift: The Form and Reason for Exchange in Archaic Societies*, trans. W. D. Halls, with foreword by M. Douglas (London, 1990).

[9] Developed particularly in Pirenne, *Medieval Cities*, pp. 24–5, and *Mohammed and Charlemagne*, pp. 107–17. There are many good summaries of Pirenne's work and its subsequent development, among them B. Lyon, *Henri Pirenne: A Biographical and Intellectual Study* (Ghent, 1974), esp. pp. 441–56; Hodges, *Dark Age Economics*, pp. 6–28; P. Delogu, 'Reading Pirenne Again', in *The Sixth Century: Production, Distribution and Demand*, ed. R. Hodges and W. Bowman (Leiden, 1998), pp. 15–40; A. Verhulst, *Carolingian Economy*, pp. 1–8, 'Marchés, marchands et commerce au haut moyen âge dans l'historiographie récente', *Settimane* 40 (1992), 23–43; Bruand, *Voyageurs et marchandises*, pp. 16–38; J. Moreland, 'Concepts of the Early Medieval Economy', in *Long Eighth Century*, ed. Hansen and Wickham, pp. 1–34; Morrison, 'Numismatics and Carolingian Trade', pp. 404–7.

[10] Pirenne, *Medieval Cities*, p. 18.

essentially as dark times, during which manorial estates were closed to external exchange and, despite increasingly strict control over production, still struggled to maintain themselves at a subsistence level.[11] Hence, according to most mid-twentieth-century interpretations of the early medieval economy on which Grierson and other numismatists drew, there simply was no substantial context for commercial coin-use, and few outlets for any kind of circulation except for a few occasional and formalized payments. Merovingian- and Carolingian-era coinage was viewed as economically marginal.

These two lines of investigation – pro- and contra-Pirenne, and drawing on anthropological studies – continue to exert a strong influence on views of the early medieval economy. East–west trade has been reassessed, for example, and found never to have ended completely, or even to have fallen anywhere near the level suggested by Pirenne.[12] Yet the minimalist views on coinage laid down by Grierson are still widely current, despite important developments affecting many of the factors which led him to these conclusions.[13] Prime among them is the sheer volume of coin-finds now known: a feature which has been highlighted since the 1960s by Michael Metcalf,[14] and corroborated by the explosion of new finds thrown up by metal-detectorists since approximately 1970.[15] Details of these are only available in large and representative quantity from England and the Netherlands, where metal-detector-use is permitted and systems are in place for logging new finds.[16] Some 4,000 single-finds of silver pennies issued *c.* 675–*c.* 865 have now been recorded in England. In the case of the coinage of Offa, some 50 per cent of all known coins have surfaced only since 1971, including the large majority of those with a known find-provenance.[17] Even the quantity of sixth- and seventh-century gold finds has increased substantially, now totalling some 140 single-finds from England.[18] Many of these coin-finds came to light at locations far from

---

[11] For example, F. Carli, *Storia del Commercio Italiano I: il mercato nell'alto Medio Evo* (Padua, 1934), pp. 277–82, 287–8, 302–3 and 306–7 (an early view); R. Doehaard, *Le haut moyen âge occidental. Économies et sociétés* (Paris, 1971), pp. 319–45; R. Fossier, 'Les tendances de l'économie: stagnation ou croissance?', *Settimane* 27 (1981), 261–74.

[12] McCormick, *Origins*, esp. pp. 784–96.

[13] For minimalist and maximalist positions on coin-circulation, see Blackburn, 'Money and Coinage', p. 539.

[14] For example, Metcalf, 'Prosperity', 'Monetary Expansion', pp. 230–1, 'Sketch', 'Coins' and 'Monetary Economy'.

[15] Blackburn, '"Productive" Sites'.

[16] In England these records consist of the Corpus of Early Medieval Coin Finds (EMC), the Portable Antiquities Scheme (PAS) and, in the Netherlands, the Numismatic Information System (NUMIS).

[17] Chick, *Coinage of Offa*, p. 186.

[18] R. Abdy and G. Williams, 'A Catalogue of Hoards and Single Finds from the British Isles, *c.* AD 410–675', in *Coinage and History*, ed. Cook and Williams, pp. 11–74 (with additions from EMC

known towns, elite settlements or Roman roads; neither should their general rarity among finds from actual rural settlement sites be seen as an impediment to wide and general use.[19] The exact circumstances behind any specific single-find are rarely retrievable. Nevertheless, it is becoming difficult to sustain the belief that all these coins were lost in the proverbial back of beyond by merchants, clergy and aristocrats engaged in the exchange of economically marginal luxury items.

Put boldly, the volume of new finds is sufficient to establish that whatever people were doing with coinage, they were doing it on a substantial scale. A glance at wider Anglo-Saxon monetary history is enough to offer some quantification of 'substantial'.[20] The background to the minting and use of gold coinage is especially obscure; certainly it was on a much smaller scale than later silver issues. The fiscal role of Merovingian gold did not apply in England, yet there may have been a symbolic motivation associated with the transition from paganism to the full trappings of contemporary Christian civilization, which need not have been restricted only to kings and bishops.[21] Ongoing and increasingly irregular debasement in the Merovingian coinage in the first decades of the seventh century perhaps also created an economic impetus for local minting in England rather than continued reliance on Frankish imports.[22] In general a range of uses for gold *scillingas* probably prevailed: fines and gifts may have been among them, although the dominance of these has been called into question in favour of a more diverse range of uses, including high-level commerce.[23]

In the context of medieval England there can be little disputing a high point of coin-use during the age of the *sceattas*, with a brief

to 2010). In addition to these 140 Merovingian and Anglo-Saxon gold finds there have also been some 40 finds of pierced or mounted Merovingian, English and other issues of *c.* 580 and after. Although these coins ended up playing a non-monetary role, they may well have circulated as currency in England at an earlier time (G. Williams, 'Circulation and Function', pp. 162–4).

[19] L. de Ligt, 'Demand, Supply, Distribution. The Roman Peasantry between Town and Countryside: Rural Monetization and Peasant Demand', *Münstersche Beiträge zur antiken Handelsgeschichte* 9 (1990), 24–56, at pp. 39–41; K. Greene, *The Archaeology of the Roman Economy* (London, 1986), p. 60.

[20] See also below, pp. 284–90.

[21] G. Williams, 'Circulation and Function', pp. 186–8.

[22] *T&S* I, 39–40 and 52–5. However, cf. *MEC*, pp. 108–10.

[23] D. M. Metcalf, 'The Availability and Uses of Gold Coinage in England, *c.* 670: Kentish Primacy Reconsidered', *Numismatiska Meddelanden* 37 (1989), 267–74; G. Williams, 'Circulation and Function', esp. pp. 188–90; F. Kloss, *Goldvorrat und Geldverkehr im Merowingerreich* (Baden, 1929), pp. 65–93; Banaji, *Agrarian Change*, pp. 66–87; D. Claude, 'Zu Fragen der merowingischen Geldgeschichte', *Vierteljahrschrift für Sozial- und Wirtschaftsgeschichte* 48 (1961), 236–50, and (for a similar view of Visigothic gold coinage) 'Zur Funktion des Münzgeldes im hispanischen Westgotenreich', *Münstersche Beiträge zur antiken Handelsgeschichte* 8.2 (1989), 32–51; but cf. I. Stewart, 'Anglo-Saxon Gold Coins', in *Scripta Nummaria Romana: Essays Presented to Humphrey Sutherland*, ed. R. A. G. Carson and C. M. Kraay (London, 1978), pp. 143–72, at 144; Grierson, 'Commerce in the Dark Ages'.

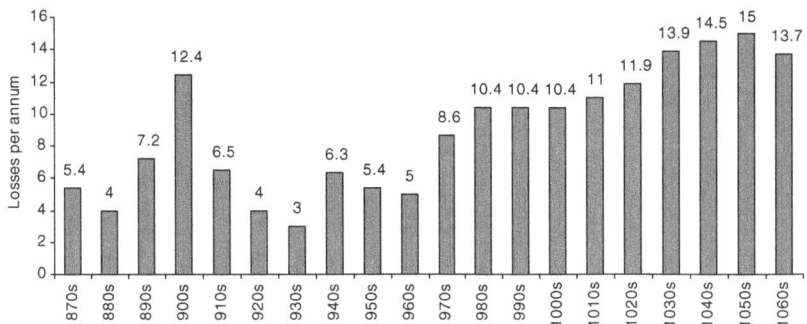

Figure 9.1 Rate of loss per decade in later Anglo-Saxon England.

resurgence in the heyday of the broad silver penny *c.* 780–*c.* 830. It was not until approximately the eleventh century that the apparent losses per annum of silver pennies would again reach the levels seen in the early ninth century (Figure 9.1), and the volume of losses of *sceattas* was probably only matched in the late twelfth century and after.[24] In relative terms the years *c.* 675–830 thus stand out as the peak period in coin-use in England between the fall of the Roman empire and the age of the Plantagenets.

This expansion in the volume of data available to monetary historians has taken place alongside ongoing debate and review of other aspects of the early medieval economy. Of particular importance for inform-ing views of coin-use are revised readings of agrarian life and of towns and trade. Indeed, for much of the twentieth century it was common for studies on these topics to proceed in isolation from each other: a division which in part originated with the Pirenne thesis, when agricul-tural production came to be seen as the only viable way of looking at the economy.[25] Because of the richer source material available concern-ing Frankish estates, these are somewhat better understood than their English counterparts in this period and lie at the heart of new readings of the Carolingian economy.[26] Agricultural surpluses produced at this time could, theoretically, be very considerable, providing much more than

---

[24] Blackburn, '"Productive" Sites', pp. 34–5.
[25] Wickham, 'Rethinking', pp. 19–21.
[26] General overviews include Verhulst, *Carolingian Economy*; J.-P. Devroey and C. Zoller, 'Villes, cam-pagnes, croissance agraire dans le pays mosan avant l'an mil: vingt ans après', in *Villes et cam-pagnes au moyen âge. Mélanges Georges Despy*, ed. J.-M. Devosquel and A. Dierckens (Liège, 1991), pp. 223–60; Devroey, *Puissants et misérables*, esp. pp. 359–68, and *Économie rurale*; C. Loveluck, 'Rural Settlement Hierarchy in the Age of Charlemagne', in *Charlemagne*, ed. Story, pp. 230–58; Toubert, *Europe*. A summation of work on aspects of the Carolingian economy since approximately 1950 can be found in Bruand, *Voyageurs et marchandises*, pp. 23–38.

subsistence.[27] These contrast with the insular, hand-to-mouth existence envisaged at one time: now the emphasis is on widespread (albeit slow and faltering) demographic expansion, as manifested in the clearance of forest to provide new land, and the production of surplus crops and other goods which could be transferred around the holdings of a major landowner, or sold at one of many developing markets.[28] Many of the same developments can be traced in outline in England, where major ecclesiastical landowners like Archbishop Wulfred consolidated their landholdings across the eighth and ninth centuries, and, perhaps as a result of such enterprises, large, fortified estate centres appeared at rural locations such as Goltho and Flixborough in the course of the ninth century.[29]

This more dynamic view of the agrarian economy has arisen alongside impressive discoveries in urban archaeology, especially in the second half of the twentieth century around the rim of the North Sea. Dorestad and Southampton, and later Ribe, York, Ipswich and London – to list only some of the most famous sites of this kind – have all been the targets of substantial excavations.[30] These places grew to be settlements of very considerable size, with a high concentration of artefacts (not least pottery and coins) which suggest long-distance trade on a large scale during a heyday that stretched from the late seventh century through to the early ninth: exactly the time when economic life was at a low ebb according to the original form of the Pirenne thesis.[31] Expansion in field-walking as well as metal-detecting has broadened the impact ascribed to these products by revealing their widespread circulation outside the towns, particularly in coastal areas.[32]

These elements of the eighth- and ninth-century economic landscape will be revisited in due course; but the basic point is that the preconditions

[27] R. Delatouche, 'Regards sur l'agriculture aux temps carolingiens', *Journal des savants* 2 (1977), 73–100; Devroey, *Économie rurale*, pp. 115–19; Hamerow, *Early Medieval Settlements*, pp. 137–9 and 147–55.

[28] Toubert, *Europe*, pp. 101–8. See also below, pp. 276–84.

[29] On Wulfred see Brooks, *Early History*, pp. 137–9; more generally *FEMA*, pp. 347–9. Goltho (Lincolnshire) was a manor established around the middle of the ninth century: G. Beresford and J. Geddes, *Goltho: The Development of an Early Medieval Manor, c. 850–1150* (London, 1987). Flixborough (Lincolnshire) may have been at different times a monastery and a secular estate: C. Loveluck, 'A High-Status Anglo-Saxon Settlement at Flixborough, Lincolnshire', *Antiquity* 72 (1998), 146–61, and 'Wealth, Waste and Conspicuous Consumption: Flixborough and Its Importance for Middle and Late Saxon Rural Settlement Studies', in *Image and Power in the Archaeology of Early Medieval Britain. Essays in Honour of Rosemary Cramp*, ed. H. Hamerow and A. MacGregor (Oxford, 2001), pp. 78–130. Cf. above, p. 29–32 and below pp. 285–6.

[30] For further discussion see above, pp. 32–6 and 235–7.

[31] Surveys include Verhulst, *Rise of Cities*; Clarke and Ambrosiani, *Towns in the Viking Age*.

[32] Blackmore, 'Pottery'. For the important case of Ipswich ware, see Blinkhorn, 'Of Cabbages'. The integration of towns into the surrounding countryside is surveyed in Moreland, 'Significance of Production'; Scull, 'Urban Centres'. Also below n. 162.

for views of minimal coin-circulation have changed considerably. Above all, Grierson and his contemporaries had to work in the general absence of direct evidence for coin-circulation, save for a relatively small number of chance finds. Now there is plentiful evidence for the volume and direction of monetary circulation in England and some neighbouring kingdoms. The crucial question is, quite simply, *cui bono*: who made use of these coins and for what purposes?

COINS AND COMMERCE?

Following Mauss and Grierson, it has often been asserted that the prevailing use of early medieval currency was non-commercial: gift-exchange and the payment of fines were seen as the driving forces, leading to the conclusion that whatever commerce there was, coinage had little part in it.[33] When coinage was used, it was as part of a closed and tightly controlled redistributive network; an interpretation which was lent vigour by the research of Richard Hodges, who associated this use of coins with the royally founded *emporia*.[34] Much of the conceptual framework and terminology he used came from the important work of Karl Polanyi, who stressed the 'embeddedness' of the economy in social interactions and set market exchange alongside elite-focused gift-giving motivated by the demands of reciprocity, and, most pertinently, redistribution: the concentration and controlled reallocation of goods and services, often at central places or carefully monitored ports of trade.[35] In this way, elites endowed goods with value by restricting access to specialist skills and long-distance trade.[36] Pre-modern societies, Polanyi and Hodges stressed, could see considerable circulation of men and material wealth without recourse to a commercial economy.

This reading built originally on the realization among anthropologists, sociologists and eventually historians, in the early and mid twentieth century, of a stronger sense of the 'Other' — of the gulf separating them from early and non-western cultures.[37] Attention focused on what distinguished them from western, capitalistic civilization of the twentieth century; a tendency with the potential to be just as distorting as the

---

[33] For recent statements to this effect see *FEMA*, p. 702 n. 16, and Wickham, *Inheritance*, pp. 226–7. For criticism of the opposite extreme see Moreland, 'Concepts', pp. 12–13.

[34] Hodges, *Dark Age Economics*, pp. 104–17.

[35] Polanyi, *Livelihood of Man*, pp. 35–43 and 225–51, *Primitive, Archaic and Modern Economies*, pp. 139–74 and 238–60. For general discussion see *FEMA*, pp. 694–700; A. E. Laiou, 'Economic and Noneconomic Exchange', in *Economic History of Byzantium*, ed. Laiou, II, 681–96, at pp. 681–9.

[36] Cf. M. Helms, *Craft and the Kingly Ideal: Art, Trade, and Power* (Austin, TX, 1993), esp. pp. 160–70.

[37] Moreland, 'Concepts', p. 2; C. Kilger, 'Wholeness and Holiness: Counting, Weighing and Valuing Silver in the Early Viking Period', in *Means of Exchange*, ed. Skre, pp. 253–326, at pp. 256–8.

search for glimmers of proto-modernism, in mechanisms of exchange or elsewhere. In the eyes of some scholars such as Mauss and Georg Simmel this difference meant highlighting what were seen as failings in their own societies.[38] In particular, men and women in Britain, France, Germany, the United States and elsewhere were believed to see the price of everything but the value of nothing. The concern was that monetary exchange had come to over-dominate day-to-day life, to the detriment of the human relationships on which gift-exchange was based. Gift-exchange was thus set up as the opposite to money-driven economic life: the former was implicitly assumed to be a foundation of non-western cultures,[39] and the latter to be incompatible with societies based on extensive social obligations.[40]

Gifts and coins

Any claim that coinage, at least in its role as a medium of market-based exchange, constituted a significant force in early medieval society was impossible to sustain on the basis of this interpretation: such was Grierson's conclusion, fuelled by Mauss' insight. It has stood the test of time impressively and been developed in a number of respects. The importance of interpersonal ties in the early Middle Ages – of kinship, lordship and bonds of other forms – has been discussed repeatedly by subsequent scholars as an eminently suitable background for gift-exchange, and coins, like other precious objects, were presumably involved.[41] Texts attesting to gifts in Anglo-Saxon England and its neighbours naturally tend to be concerned with the elite and associated prestige goods, and it is on them that most studies have focused.[42] *Beowulf* has been a favourite point of departure. The characters of this poem took part in frequent presentations of glittering treasures from men to lords and vice versa,

[38] Mauss, *Gift*, pp. 65–83; G. Simmel, *The Philosophy of Money*, trans. T. Bottomore and D. Frisby (London, 1978), pp. 389–94.

[39] J. Parry and M. Bloch, 'Introduction: Money and the Morality of Exchange', in *Money and the Morality of Exchange*, ed. J. Parry and M. Bloch (Cambridge, 1989), pp. 1–32, at 7–8.

[40] Wilk and Cliggett, *Economies and Cultures*, pp. 158–60; N. Thomas, *Entangled Objects: Exchange, Material Culture, and Colonialism in the Pacific* (Cambridge, MA, 1991), pp. 9–10; D. Graeber, *Toward an Anthropological Theory of Value: The False Coin of Our Own Dreams* (New York, 2001), pp. 151–63; Y. Yan, 'The Gift and Gift Economy', in *Handbook*, ed. Carrier, pp. 246–61. Cf. P. Geary, 'Gift Exchange and Social Science Modelling: The Limitations of a Construct', in *Negotiating the Gift. Pre-Modern Figurations of Exchange*, ed. G. Algazi, V. Groebner and B. Jussen (Göttingen, 2003), pp. 129–40; Moreland, 'Concepts', pp. 22–31.

[41] For example, J. Smith, *Europe after Rome*, pp. 183–214; A.-J. Bijsterveld, *Do ut des: Gift Giving, Memoria, and Conflict Management in the Medieval Low Countries* (Hilversum, 2007), pp. 17–50; J. Hennig, '*Ars donandi*. Zur Ökonomie des Schenkens im früheren Mittelalter', in *Armut, Liebe, Ehre: Studien zur historischen Kulturforschung*, ed. R. van Dülmen (Frankfurt, 1988), pp. 11–27.

[42] Cf. Moreland, 'Concepts', pp. 19–20.

which clearly functioned as a means of establishing and expressing relationships. Buying, selling, markets and traders are entirely absent, but gifts permeate the language and thought of *Beowulf* to an impressive degree. A king could be described as a *syncgifa* ('treasure-giver'), his throne as a *gifstol* ('gift-throne'), his hall as a *gifhealle* ('gift-hall'): the distribution of treasure was a hallmark of civilized society, and that treasure consisted overwhelmingly of gold and war-gear.[43] This is one of several features to betray the ahistorical setting of the poem, which was in many respects divorced from what is known of life in Anglo-Saxon England.[44] It evoked an idealized and archaizing heroic milieu focused on a warrior elite, within which exchange as well as other facets of material culture were founded on a blend of nostalgia and imagination with aristocratic practice.[45]

Life, even as refracted through the opaque lens of early medieval documents and narratives, was much more complex. In Merovingian-era Frankish texts such as Gregory of Tours' *Historiae* there was often a sharp edge to elite gift-giving. Reciprocity of gifts was only partially related to value and could be manipulated on a number of levels.[46] One more personable form of gift-giving is revealed by letters between various ecclesiastical correspondents in England, Francia and elsewhere in the eighth and ninth centuries. To give just one example, a letter sent to St Boniface during his mission in Frisia *c.* 720 by an English nun named Bugga closes with mention of the exchange of books and prayers, and lastly with an offer of gifts: 'et per eundem portitorem tibi transmitto nunc quinquaginta solidos et pallium altaris; quia maiora munuscula minime potui adipiscere. Sed tamen haec sunt cum maxima caritate directa, licet sint parva in speciae.'[47] Here, however, the interest is not so much in the need for a suitable counter-gift, or – at least theoretically – in the value of what was given. Humble devaluation of *munuscula* which were sent as

---

[43] Gold is mentioned (either alone or as part of a compound) some sixty times over the course of the poem; silver is not mentioned explicitly at all. Cf. C. Hills, '*Beowulf* and Archaeology', in *A Beowulf Handbook*, ed. R. E. Bjork and J. D. Niles (Exeter, 1996), pp. 291–310, at 306.

[44] D. Dumville, '*Beowulf* and the Celtic World: The Uses of Evidence', *Traditio* 37 (1981), 109–60; J. D. Niles, 'Myth and History', in *Beowulf Handbook*, ed. Bjork and Niles, pp. 213–32.

[45] J. Bazelmans, 'Beyond Power. Ceremonial Exchanges in *Beowulf*', in *Rituals of Power*, ed. Theuws and Nelson, pp. 311–75, and *By Weapons Made Worthy: Lords, Retainers and Their Relationship in Beowulf* (Amsterdam, 1999); J. M. Hill, 'Social Milieu', in *Beowulf Handbook*, ed. Bjork and Niles, pp. 255–69, at 259–60, 'Beowulf and the Danish Succession: Gift Giving as an Occasion for Complex Gesture', *Medievalia et humanistica* 11 (1982), 177–97, and *The Cultural World in Beowulf* (Toronto, 1995), pp. 85–107.

[46] C. Wickham, 'Conclusion', in *The Languages of Gift in the Early Middle Ages*, ed. W. Davies and P. Fouracre (Cambridge, 2010), pp. 238–61, at 254–9.

[47] 'And by the same messenger I am now sending you fifty *solidi* and an altar-cover, since I have been unable to obtain greater gifts. But though small in value these are sent with the greatest of goodwill.' MGH Epp. sel. 1, no. 15, p. 28.

tokens of piety and affection rather than economic resources was a standard topos, even when the value of those gifts was made quite explicit.[48]

Economic value and social meaning as transmitted through gifts were always highly flexible. This spectrum was reflected by a wide and finely honed vocabulary for different acts of giving.[49] In the context of Frankish manorial documents a range of terms was used to emphasize the status of different parties and their notionally voluntary gifts to the landlord: thus one might *solvere* ('pay off/discharge') a monetary payment or *reddere* ('give back') from the land, both of which reiterated the landowner's underlying authority.[50] Other terms such as *donum* and *munus* belonged much more to the world of symbolic aristocratic gifts and to religious contexts.[51] *Munera* (and the diminutive *munuscula*) were offerings that magnified the giver rather than the given object: *munera* given to holy men were expected to be redistributed to the poor, and any counter-gift they elicited was a symbolic token of acceptance, while *remuneratio* was a general recognition of the giver's good works, not a specific counter-gift as such.[52] Gifts, in other words, wore many masks and served many purposes: the temptation to homogenize and generalize based on modern categorizations should be resisted.

There can be no denying that gifts of many sorts changed hands in the early Middle Ages or that, especially among the elite, they were an important part of gaining and keeping favour.[53] What is more problematic is establishing how far these dominated exchange as a whole; how far they could be relied on for 'serving a function analogous to that of commerce in securing the distribution of goods and services',[54] and replaced markets, commerce and other mechanisms for the circulation of coinage and of other goods.[55] The dominance of gifting in the early medieval economy has come under sustained fire from several directions. In particular the characteristics of literary, high-value gifts such as those of *Beowulf* and Gregory of Tours' *Historiae* did not always transfer to

---

[48] J.-H. Clay, 'Gift-Giving and Books in the Letters of St Boniface and Lul', *Journal of Medieval History* 35 (2009), 313–25.

[49] Wickham, 'Conclusion', in *The Languages of Gift*, ed. Davies and Fouracre, pp. 246–7.

[50] L. Kuchenbuch, 'Porcus donativus: Language Use and Gifting in Seigniorial Records between the Eighth and the Twelfth Centuries', in *Negotiating the Gift*, ed. Algazi, Groebner and Jussen, pp. 193–246, at 199–209.

[51] *Ibid.*, p. 212.

[52] Curta, 'Merovingian and Carolingian Gift Giving', pp. 678–81; B. Jussen, 'Religious Discourses of the Gift in the Middle Ages: Semantic Evidences (Second to Twelfth Centuries)', in *Negotiating the Gift*, ed. Algazi, Groebner and Jussen, pp. 173–92, at 187–92. Cf. N. Thomas, *Entangled Objects*, p. 63 for a parallel in modern Fiji.

[53] Above, pp. 23–5.   [54] Grierson, 'Commerce in the Dark Ages', p. 137.

[55] Wickham, 'Conclusion', in *The Languages of Gift*, ed. Davies and Fouracre, p. 246; Laiou, 'Economic and Noneconomic Exchange', pp. 684–5.

other forms of gift-exchange.[56] Neither were they necessarily as socially important outside the elite. Gifts from tenants to landlords in Carolingian Francia were concentrated among *ministri* rather than tenants in general and were carefully differentiated from actual rents; they consisted of perishable foods and token quantities of cash rather than long-term supplies in any quantity.[57] Even within the elite, the sequence of gift and countergift was not always reliable in scale or time span,[58] and many other factors besides reciprocity and economic value could come into play. Thus the items of clothing which passed between ecclesiastical correspondents probably reflect obedience to Christ's command to clothe the naked.[59] The size of Offa's annual gift of gold to the papacy was of 'quantos dies annus habuerit, tantos mancusas'.[60] Similarly, horses given to the king on a probably annual basis in the Carolingian empire were a demonstration of free status on the part of the giver.[61]

Expressions of status and symbolic relationships were among the key *raisons d'être* of gifts, and early medieval gift-exchange was not always the unifying, stabilizing force characterized by Mauss; it could also be used to awe, dominate or exploit.[62] Many of the classic studies of gift-exchange have side-stepped questions of inequality and power relations:[63] these could turn the giving of gifts into a draining or antagonistic arena, which potential participants may have deliberately avoided. Ceolfrith, abbot of Monkwearmouth-Jarrow (d. 716), kept secret his plans to go to Rome so that, according to Bede, 'nec pecunia daretur illi a quibusdam, quam retribuere pro tempore nequiret'.[64] In the words of one recent analysis, 'gift-giving was primarily about politics, not economics, although the

[56] N. Thomas, *Entangled Objects*, pp. 65–9.
[57] Kuchenbuck, 'Porcus donativus', pp. 212–14; Devroey, *Puissants et misérables*, pp. 503–5. It should nevertheless be noted (Devroey, *Puissants et misérables*, p. 230) that tenant 'gifts' became more regularized, essentially turning into supplementary rents.
[58] Cf. P. Bourdieu, *Outline of a Theory of Practice*, trans. R. Nice (Cambridge, 1977), pp. 6–7 and 14–15; N. Thomas, *Entangled Objects*, p. 17; J. Carrier, 'Gifts, Commodities, and Social Relations: A Maussian View of Exchange', *Sociological Forum* 6 (1991), 119–36, at pp. 123–5.
[59] Clay, 'Gift-Giving and Books', p. 320.
[60] 'As many mancuses as the year has days.' MGH Epist. IV, no. 127, pp. 188–9.
[61] J. L. Nelson, 'Settings of the Gift in the Reign of Charlemagne', in *Languages of Gift*, ed. Davies and Fouracre, pp. 116–48, at 134–40; Curta, 'Merovingian and Carolingian Gift Giving', pp. 687–8 and 698.
[62] Curta, 'Merovingian and Carolingian Gift Giving', pp. 697–8; Parry and Bloch, 'Introduction', pp. 9–10; Samson, 'Economic Anthropology and Vikings', pp. 92–6. For further socially charged transactions in a Scandinavian context, see W. I. Miller, 'Gift, Sale, Payment, Raid: Case Studies in the Negotiation and Classification of Exchange in Medieval Iceland', *Speculum* 61 (1986), 18–50.
[63] Wickham, 'Conclusion', in *The Languages of Gift*, ed. Davies and Fouracre, pp. 258–9; N. Thomas, *Entangled Objects*, pp. 56–7.
[64] 'No money could be given to him by anyone which he would not be able to pay back for the time being'. Bede, *Historia abbatum*, c. 17 (ed. Plummer I, 381). For discussion see I. N. Wood, 'The Gifts of Wearmouth and Jarrow', in *Languages of Gift*, ed. Davies and Fouracre, pp. 89–115, at 107.

two spheres of activity were not completely separate'.[65] This economic component must not be forgotten: although they may not have been a reliable source of income, or indeed more than a token from the point of view of kings, aristocrats and high clergy, gifts could be very precious. They could easily shade into bribes or purchases of favour or service when value came to the fore.[66] It is this which has been seen as characterizing barter of commodities rather than exchange of personalized gifts.[67] In charters, payments for land or privilege straddled an ambiguous divide between gifts associated with general loyalty and purchases of specific estates, and were often listed in precise detail; the better, it seems, to affirm the new owner's hold over the land.[68] Sometimes, then, value did matter, especially in contexts when it was substantial and intended to sway the recipient, while the hesitation to express a personal relationship in monetary terms felt in modern western society should not be assumed for the early Middle Ages.[69] But gift-giving in Anglo-Saxon England and its immediate neighbours probably did not amount to an entire economy based on gift-exchange. It is better characterized as a symbolically charged complement to the distribution of goods or the gathering of wealth, rather than the primary motor of circulation.

Coins as such are difficult to trace in references to early medieval gifts. In part this is a reflection of the nature of the gifts in question and of the status of the givers: gold and silver were important but not dominant, and often came explicitly in the form of other items – liturgical plate, dining dishes and the like[70] – which were prestige objects naturally to be associated with the elite.[71] The presence of coin is also obscured by terminological ambiguities. A rich Latin and Old English vocabulary covered units of account in Anglo-Saxon England and was closely related to that of coins, weights and measures of volume. Silver coins were normally known as *denarii* or *pæningas*, and there was a multitude of larger units available for different purposes. These were inherited from a range of backgrounds. The Bible and biblical exegesis were one important source for the use of monetary terminology and perpetuated units such as the obol (*obolus*) and the shekel (*siclus*). What these actually denoted

---

[65] Curta, 'Merovingian and Carolingian Gift Giving', pp. 698–9.

[66] Samson, 'Economic Anthropology and Vikings', p. 94; C. Wickham, 'Compulsory Gift Exchange in Lombard Italy, 650–1150', in *Languages of Gift*, ed. Davies and Fouracre, pp. 193–216, at 211.

[67] C. Gregory, *Gifts and Commodities* (London, 1982), esp. p. 12.

[68] Below, pp. 273–9; W. Davies, 'When Gift Is Sale: Reciprocities and Commodities in Tenth-Century Christian Iberia', in *Languages of Gift*, ed. Davies and Fouracre, pp. 217–37; and S. Weinberger, 'Donations-ventes ou ventes-donations? Confusion ou système dans la Provence du XIème siècle', *Le moyen âge* 105 (1999), 667–80.

[69] Parry and Bloch, 'Introduction', esp. pp. 8–12.

[70] Hardt, *Gold und Herrschaft*, pp. 56–122.   [71] Moreland, 'Concepts', pp. 18–22.

in weight or value when recycled in the early Middle Ages is not always easy to determine. *Obolus* became the standard description for a half-*denarius* despite beginning as a unit of weight, twenty of which made up a shekel. Isidore of Seville recognized that the shekel had different values depending on whether it was being used in a Hebrew (one ounce) or Latin (quarter ounce) context,[72] which explains why in some cases the obol was reckoned as two *denarii*.[73] In the Anglo-Saxon context, it looks as though *sicli* may have been used even more vaguely, and in some circumstances they seem to have been synonymous with *solidi*.[74]

Other usages came from native, Frankish and Roman tradition. *Scilling* was especially versatile. In the seventh-century Kentish law-codes it probably referred to the Merovingian and Merovingian-inspired gold *tremisses* current at the time. These were each divisible into twenty *sceattas*, which must have originated as small weights of gold but may later have also been equated with silver coins.[75] In Ine's law-code *scilling* is also used, combined for the first time with *pæningas*. However, the *scilling* by this time seems to have been equated with four pennies, not twenty *sceattas*. To add further complication, a five-penny *scilling* emerges in Wessex in the late ninth or early tenth century, and the twelve-penny *scilling* familiar from pre-decimal British currency and already long current in the Frankish kingdoms was used in England by the late tenth century. *Scilling* was generally equated with *solidus* in Latin, despite its origins referring to one third of a late antique gold *solidus*. The intricacies of early medieval monetary terminology will not be approached in detail here:[76] the key point, however, is that terminology was vibrant and malleable, and the same words could be used to signify coins, units of account and weights. The bond between units of account and currency was thus far from straightforward.[77] Despite the ambiguity this multiple usage creates in surviving texts, it was by no means inconvenient for early medieval users, and has survived into modern times with, for example, the pound. This was already a standard measure in the seventh century

---

[72] Isidore, *Etymologiae*, XVI.xxv.18 (ed. Lindsay II, 222).

[73] See, for example, Bischoff, *Anecdota Novissima*, p. 169.

[74] For example, S 1201.

[75] *MEC*, p. 157; P. Grierson, 'La fonction sociale de la monnaie en Angleterre aux VIIe–VIIIe siècles', *Settimane* 8 (1961), 341–62, at pp. 344–52; J. Hines, 'Units of Account in Gold and Silver in Seventh-Century England: *Scillingas*, *Sceattas* and *Pæningas*', *Antiquaries Journal* 90 (2010), 153–73, at pp. 154–61.

[76] For monetary terminology, see Hines, 'Units of Account'; Chadwick, *Studies*, pp. 1–63; B. Bischoff and M. Lapidge, ed., *Biblical Commentaries from the Canterbury School of Theodore and Hadrian* (Cambridge, 1994), pp. 213–14, 262–3 and 275–95; Lyon, 'Historical Problems (3)'.

[77] J. Melitz, 'The Polanyi School of Anthropology on Money: An Economist's View', *American Anthropologist* 72 (1970), 1020–40, at pp. 1026–30.

and remained prevalent for larger sums or weights thereafter. Although divided into different numbers of *solidi/scillingas*, the pound of 240 pence was apparently current in England by at least the mid ninth century and possibly already in the time of Ine.[78] Similarly, *solidi/scillingas*, *mancosi* and other terms sometimes associated with coins could also be used freely as weights or as abstract units of account for other materials. In the will of King Eadred (946–55), for instance, it was famously ordered that 'nime man twentig hund mancusa goldes and gemynetige to mancusan'.[79] Units of account, coins and bullion always remained closely related, as was common with any form of money substantially supported wholly or to a large extent by precious-metal value, and a great deal of gold and silver in non-numismatic form circulated in early medieval Europe.[80] In England, gold and especially silver objects have been found at the same 'productive sites' and in the same hoards as coins and may have changed hands as the equivalent of high-value currency regulated by weight.[81]

In many documents, when there is no hint of what was meant by *mancus*, *solidus* or *libra*, it is simply impossible to tell exactly what was intended. The fifty *solidi* sent to Boniface by Bugga could have been silver coins, Byzantine or Roman gold pieces or uncoined gold or silver; they might be compared with the arm-ring received by the eponymous poet in the Old English poem *Widsith*, which was 'gescyred sceatta scillingrime'.[82] It is this difficulty which plagues the interpretation of coin-use in several sources: the sums stated in charters; the occasional tributes levied to pay off vikings and other marauders;[83] the tolls which were exacted at borders and ports;[84] and the fines which were stipulated

---

[78] S 208. In Ine's law-code (c. 74) a slave's wergild is sixty *scillingas*, which may be commensurate with the rate of a pound current in later times (see, e.g., II Æthelred, c. 5 (ed. Liebermann, I, 222)).

[79] 'Two thousand mancuses of gold are to be taken and minted into mancuses.' S 1515 (ed. Miller, *New Minster, Winchester*, no. 17).

[80] Cf. Kilger, 'Wholeness and Holiness', pp. 298–301; H. Steuer, 'Gewichtsgeldwirtschaften im frühgeschichtlichen Europa: Feinwaagen und Gewichte als Quellen zur Währungsgeschichte', in *Der Handel der Karolinger- und Wikingerzeit*, ed. Düwel *et al.*, pp. 405–527, esp. 431–516.

[81] Blackburn, '"Productive" Sites', p. 32; and above p. 242. Among pre-viking hoards with English coins, non-numismatic bullion occurred in those from Ilanz, Sevington, Trewhiddle and Gravesend.

[82] 'Reckoned by the tally of *sceattas* and *scillingas*.' *Widsith*, lines 90–2 (*ASPR* III, 152).

[83] On the scale and nature of English tribute payments to the vikings in the late tenth and early eleventh centuries, see M. K. Lawson, 'The Collection of Danegeld and Heregeld in the Reigns of Aethelred II and Cnut', *EHR* 99 (1984), 721–38, '"Those Stories Look True": Levels of Taxation in the Reigns of Aethelred II and Cnut', *EHR* 104 (1989), 385–406, 'Danegeld and Heregeld Once More', *EHR* 105 (1990), 951–61, and *Cnut: England's Viking King* (Stroud, 2004), pp. 179–88; J. Gillingham, '"The Most Precious Jewel in the English Crown": Levels of Danegeld and Heregeld in the Early Eleventh Century', *EHR* 104 (1989), 373–84, and 'Chronicles and Coins as Evidence for Levels of Tribute and Taxation in Late Tenth- and Early Eleventh-Century England', *EHR* 105 (1990), 939–50. Cf. Grierson, 'Volume', pp. 159–60.

[84] Above, p. 34.

in legal texts. In early Anglo-Saxon law-codes, exactly the same terms as those in *Widsith* dominate: *scilling* and *sceat*, joined only later by *pæning*. Grierson suggested that the payment of these fines could have accounted for a substantial proportion of coin-use.[85] But it is clear that non-numismatic payments were also anticipated.[86] *Sceat* and *scilling* were ambiguous, and even *pæning/pending* ('penny') did not automatically sig- nify a coined penny in the law-codes. Alfred the Great's law-code twice stipulates payment of a third part of a penny, which, in the absence of any surviving third-penny pieces, must indicate a penny by weight or goods to the value of one third of a penny.[87] The question of the general applicability of the law-codes may be a moot point, as their relation to actual suits is notoriously obscure, and so how fines were paid in prac- tice cannot be known.[88] But if nothing else the laws must be used with extreme caution as evidence for coin-use, and with still greater caution as evidence for the primary arena in which coins – even gold coins struck before *c.* 675 – were used.

Case study: payments in Anglo-Saxon charters

An important illustration of the complex interaction of coin, bullion and different forms of high-value exchange comes from charters, which con- stitute the only source of documentation in England to discuss transactions involving precious metal in any quantity.[89] These stem from a substantial number of occasions on which lands or rights over land were bought and sold, or other arrangements were made for the expenditure of precious metal. Approximately 109 charters mentioning coin or precious metal in some form have survived from England before *c.* 900.[90] There are also sev- eral which mention payments explicitly reckoned in agricultural products

---

[85] P. Grierson, 'Fonction sociale', and 'The Purpose of the Sutton Hoo Coins', *Antiquity* 44 (1970), 14–18, at p. 15.

[86] Cf. *Dunsætan* c. 7 (ed. Liebermann I, 378–9).

[87] Alfred's law-code, cc. 3, 47 and 71 (ed. Liebermann, I, 50, 80 and 86). For an attempt to identify third-pennies of Alfred, see P. Grierson, 'Halfpennies and Third-Pennies of King Alfred', *BNJ* 28 (1955–7), 477–93; shot down by R. H. M. Dolley and C. E. Blunt, 'The Chronology of the Coins of Alfred the Great', in *Anglo-Saxon Coins*, ed. Dolley, pp. 77–95, at 89.

[88] P. Wormald, *Making of English Law*, pp. 143–61, and 'A Handlist of Anglo-Saxon Lawsuits', *ASE* 17 (1988), 247–81; A. Kennedy, 'Disputes about *Bocland*: The Forum for Their Adjudication', *ASE* 14 (1985), 175–95.

[89] For general background see F. M. Stenton, *Latin Charters of the Anglo-Saxon Period* (Oxford, 1955).

[90] At least seven of these charters allegedly concerning sales have been condemned as forgeries (S 67, 79, 82, 107, 189, 200 and 318) while eleven others (S 119, 124, 133, 149, 166, 167, 183, 192, 193, 197 and 359) are seriously suspect.

rather than precious metal,[91] while one famous charter issued in the late seventh century in favour of Abbot Hædda of Peterborough states that the abbot paid the king 500 *solidi* for an estate. It immediately goes on to explain that these *solidi* came in the form of twelve well-appointed mattresses along with two servants, an ornate gold brooch and two horses.[92] In terms of coverage these charters are not evenly distributed across England or the whole period before *c.* 900. There are more from the ninth century than the eighth, and the archives of Kent (Rochester and the two Canterbury houses) and Worcester dominate the surviving total. East Anglia and Northumbria are almost virtually a blank, and the east midlands almost so. Despite these flaws the charters remain the most detailed written source available and provide a rich insight into how money and goods changed hands in one particular setting.[93]

The 109 pertinent documents cover a multitude of situations. A few are leases or wills,[94] but the large majority concern transfer of landed possessions. Some of these (including a high proportion of non-royal charters) seem to relate to straightforward purchase of land and rights to it, as signalled by context or with dispositive verbs such as *emere* or *vendere*.[95] Others relate to the purchase of both land and, apparently on the same occasion (possibly) with a separate payment, of rights over that land, probably those which defined it as bookland.[96] One particularly clear example written in Old English describes how Forthred the king's thegn 'salde to lond ceape xxx mancessan [and] nigen hund scill[ingas] wið ðaem londe him in ece erfe'.[97] Occasionally only the bookland status of

---

[91] S 106, 122, 154, 347 and 354. Agricultural products feature alongside precious metal in S 183, 190, 193 (if genuine), 212, 345 and 1440.

[92] S 1804 (ed. Kelly, *Peterborough Abbey*, no. 4).

[93] Masterfully surveyed in J. Campbell, 'The Sale of Land and the Economics of Power in Early England: Problems and Possibilities', *Haskins Society Journal* 1 (1989), 23–37.

[94] Leases include S 199, 215, 218, 1270, 1278, 1412 and 1440. Wills and other documents include: S 44, 1187, 1195, 1200 and 1436.

[95] These include S 44, 169, 319, 354, 359, 1193, 1196, 1199, 1445, 1203, 1204, 1205, 1256–7, 1268, 1276, 1410 (?), 1439, 1625 and 1785.

[96] These include S 9, 39–41, 54, 58 (?), 59, 61, 63 (?), 105, 122, 124 (?), 149 (?), 154 (?), 155, 157, 161, 164, 166, 168, 177, 178, 183 (?), 186, 187, 192 (?), 196 (?), 208, 210, 212 (?), 214, 268 (?), 269, 279, 282, 286a, 287, 296–7, 327, 330, 332, 337 (?), 344 (?), 345 (?), 350, 1177 (?), 1201 (?) and 1789 (?). The exact nature of bookland (*bocland*) is still debated: its core meaning was land held by virtue of a *boc* or charter, which conferred greater liberty of bequest and possibly exemption from certain royal exactions. For selected discussion see A. Williams, 'Land Tenure', in *BEASE*, pp. 277–8; S. Baxter and J. Blair, 'Land Tenure and Royal Patronage in the Early English Kingdom: A Model and a Case Study', *Anglo-Norman Studies* 28 (2005), 19–46; S. Reynolds, 'Bookland, Folkland and Fiefs', *Anglo-Norman Studies* 14 (1992), 211–27; P. Wormald, 'On *þa Wæpnedhealfe*: Kingship and Royal Property from Æthelwulf to Edward the Elder', in *Edward the Elder, 899–924*, ed. N. Higham and D. Hill (London, 2001), pp. 264–79; T. Charles-Edwards, 'Anglo-Saxon Kinship Revisited', in *The Anglo-Saxons*, ed. Hines, pp. 171–204, at 192–7.

[97] 'Gave in land-purchase thirty mancuses and 900 shillings for that land's eternal possession.' S 204 (BCS 452).

an estate was bought – that is to say, the purchaser seems to have already held the land or rights to it under other conditions.[98] Thus one (unfortunately problematic) charter of Offa states that a *minister* acquired the 'amplitudinem viginti mansis estimatam quam omnis sua cognatio habebat ante eum in provincia Mediterraneorum Saxonum', in return for payment of 100 mancuses in the form of an *armilla*.[99]

The bulk of the surviving payment charters are, however, somewhat ambiguous, and are couched in exactly the same terms as other charters granting land outright, save that they mention the handover of a *praetium* or some *pecunia*. This might be put side by side with the religious motivation for a grant, presumably implying that the payment was not the sole incentive which led to the grant being made, as in the case of a charter from Worcester issued 764×774, by which Uhtred, sub-king of the Hwicce, gave land to the bishop for the foundation of a monastery. The charter explains the motivation for the grant as follows: 'insuper atque placabili pecunia ab eo suscepta pro amore cælestis patriæ et pro stabilitate regni mei, hanc donationis terram concedens donabo ad æcclesiam'.[100] In some slightly later charters it is stated that the money was not given for the land as such, but rather as a gift to the king as a general reflection of loyalty and generosity;[101] likewise the land received by a lay beneficiary was frequently said to have been given in recognition of prior service.[102] Generosity on both sides greased the wheels of medieval aristocratic society, and an eventual grant of land kept the recipient in the king's debt.[103] This is made very explicit in one charter of Edmund issued for a royal thegn, Ælfsige, in 943, which states that the grant was made 'pro ejus amabili obedientia ejusque placabili pecunia quam michi in suæ devotionis obsequio detulit'.[104]

---

[98] These include S 70 (?), 87 (?), 119, 133 (?), 190, 193–4, 197–8, 204 (?), 206–7, 218, 221 (?), 1172 and 1186a.

[99] 'Increase in land rated at twenty hides which all his family owned before him in Middlesex.' S 119 (ed. Gelling, *Thames Valley*, no. 203).

[100] 'And so, having also received satisfactory payment from him, for love of the heavenly realm and for the security of my kingdom, I permit and grant this donation of land to the church.' S 61 (BCS 205) (uncertain authenticity but cf. 554 and 155 among others).

[101] J. Campbell, 'Sale of Land', pp. 229–32. Theoretically non-specific *remuneratio* finds parallels in contemporary religious terminology: above, n. 52.

[102] For the problematic relationship of land and service see S. D. White, 'Service for Fiefs or Fiefs for Service: The Politics of Reciprocity', in *Negotiating the Gift*, ed. Algazi, Groebner and Jussen, pp. 63–98, esp. 63–70; P. Fouracre, 'The Use of the Term *beneficium* in Frankish Sources: A Society Based on Favours', in *Languages of Gift*, ed. Davies and Fouracre, pp. 62–88.

[103] For a modern parallel see A. Strathern, *Rope of Moka: Big-Men and Ceremonial Exchange in Mount Hagen, New Guinea* (Cambridge, 1971), pp. 10–14.

[104] 'For his amiable deference and for the satisfactory payment, which he has offered me out of the obedience of his devotion.' S 486 (BCS 788). Cf. S 440.

Ælfsige may or may not have known that his *pecunia* would bring a grant of land, and parallels can be drawn with occasional references in letters and other sources to the wheeling, dealing and gift-giving which took place as a prelude to the granting of Carolingian sovereign charters,[105] or to the resolution of legal disputes in tenth-century England.[106] These were not payments as such: the boundary between gifts and purchases was often blurred in Anglo-Saxon charters, and documents from elsewhere in contemporary western Europe present similar problems of classification.[107] Behind this lies the difficulty raised by the restrictive formats and terminology of documentary production, which forced all transactions – regardless of their complexity, or the ways in which different parties interpreted them – to be shoehorned into one of two categories,[108] or, in England, often only one. These transactions were the culmination of all sorts of politicking, which simply did not always fit the basic moulds of gift or sale; indeed, different parties could construe them in different ways depending on what worked to their advantage.[109] In Anglo-Saxon England in particular there may have been a certain amount of ambiguity concerning the status of presentations which were theoretically spontaneous gifts but which combined with long-standing loyalty and goodwill to result in the bestowal of land and privilege, sharing similarities with the 'instrumental gifts' of modern China and Japan which occupy a position mid-way between the sales and gifts of western tradition.[110] If nothing else these payments highlight that forms of

---

[105] E. Screen, 'The Reign of Lothar I (795–855), Emperor of the Franks, through the Charter Evidence' (unpublished Ph.D. dissertation, University of Cambridge, 1998), pp. 176–91; Mersiowsky, 'Towards a Reappraisal', pp. 22–4.

[106] For example, S 1483 (ed. Whitelock, *Wills*, no. 2) and 1497 (ed. Whitelock, *Will of Æthelgifu*).

[107] For selected discussion see W. Davies, *Acts of Giving. Individual, Community and Church in Tenth-Century Christian Spain* (Oxford, 2007), pp. 135–8 and 156–60; T. Reuter, 'Property, Transactions and Social Relations between Rulers, Bishops and Nobles in Early Eleventh-Century Saxony: The Evidence of the *Vita Meinwerci*', in *Property and Power in Early Medieval Europe*, ed. W. Davies and P. Fouracre (Cambridge, 1995), pp. 165–98, at 181–3; E. Z. Tabuteau, *Transfers of Property in Eleventh-Century Norman Law* (Chapel Hill, NC, and London, 1988), pp. 14–30; B. Rosenwein, *To Be the Neighbor of Saint Peter: The Social Meaning of Cluny's Property, 909–1049* (Ithaca, NY, and London, 1989), pp. 85–108; C. B. Bouchard, *Holy Entrepreneurs: Cistercians, Knights and Economic Exchange in Twelfth-Century Burgundy* (Ithaca, NY, and London, 1991), pp. 61–5 and 75–9; Innes, *State and Society*, pp. 103–4; J. F. Lemarignier, 'Les actes de droit privé de Saint-Bertin en haut moyen âge: survivances et déclin du droit romain dans la pratique franque', *Mélanges Fernand de Visscher: Revue internationale des droits de l'antiquité* 4 (1950), 35–72, at pp. 53–8; H. Siems, *Handel und Wucher im Spiegel frühmittelalterlicher Rechtsquellen* (Hannover, 1992), pp. 384–94; Hammer, 'Land Sales', pp. 63–8; W. Davies, 'Sale Price and Valuation in Galicia and Castile-León in the Tenth Century', *EME* 11 (2002), 149–74, at pp. 156–70.

[108] W. Davies, 'When Gift Is Sale', pp. 227–37.   [109] *Ibid.*

[110] A. Offner, 'Between the Gift and the Market: The Economy of Regard', *EcHR* 50 (1997), 450–76; T. Reuter, 'Gifts and Simony', in *Medieval Transformations: Texts, Power and Gifts in Context*, ed. E. Cohen and M. de Jong (Leiden, 2000), pp. 157–68. On the tendency to misrepresent transactions

exchange were highly flexible in categorization and carefully described by contemporaries.

One way to build on the charters as a window onto the interaction of gifts and sales would be to consider the extent to which they reflect a market of land. Unfortunately, attempts to identify market prices in these (and other early medieval) charters have been unsuccessful.[111] The amount paid per hide seems to have varied case by case. Land, as the most basic and important economic resource and a crucial component of elite status, may simply not have been marketable in the same way as other goods.[112] It retained a special tie to previous owners and was frequently transferred only as part of ongoing links between different families or institutions.[113] The final price could also be affected by the variable quality of land in different areas or by the relationship between buyer and seller.[114] The main purpose in recording payments nevertheless seems relatively clear: to forestall any suspicions about how the beneficiary acquired the land. This explains why in a number of Anglo-Saxon charters the payment is added only as an afterthought at the end of the charter, or even on the dorse of the original document, sometimes explicitly by the beneficiary him- or herself.[115]

The charters of England at this time are therefore an important resource, albeit one that must be used with caution concerning exchange, coin-use and other economic activity as a whole. They provide an important sample of symbolically charged transactions dominated by the elite, in which many of the considerations that apply to gift-exchange come to the fore. From the point of view of coinage and the monetary economy, it is still of great interest that precious metal features so prominently among them. The 109 relevant charters include some 139 references to

---

between parties of different status, see Bourdieu, *Outline*, pp. 176–7; and for 'instrumental gifts' Yan, 'Gift and Gift Economy', p. 256.

[111] For a classic discussion of this, see C. Violante, *La società Milanese nell'età precomunale* (Bari, 1953), pp. 99–110.

[112] L. Feller, 'Enrichissement, accumulation et circulation des biens: quelques problèmes liés au marché de la terre', in *Le marché de la terre au moyen âge*, ed. L. Feller and C. Wickham (Rome, 2005), pp. 3–28.

[113] Silber, 'Gift-Giving'; Bourdieu, *Outline*, pp. 182–4.

[114] Wickham, *Land and Power*, pp. 257–74.

[115] For example, S 282, with the beneficiary's note at the foot of the charter (albeit on an eleventh-century single sheet, probably transmitting an essentially genuine charter of *c.* 830: H. Edwards, *The Charters of the Early West Saxon Kingdom* (Oxford, 1988), pp. 273–5). In S 178 Archbishop Wulfred added a postscript pointing out that he paid Coenwulf a ring of twenty-three mancuses. In S 190 a note at the foot of the charter mentions payment of land, whilst payment of gold shillings is stated in an endorsement. S 1186a is an endorsement to an earlier charter, declaring the buyer's legitimate purchase of the same plot of land. The tenth-century S 535 contains the payment in a completely separate clause clearly added after the main text of the grant had been written.

means of payment which included or could have included some precious metal. About a quarter of the charters (twenty-six) refer only vaguely to the fact that some *pecunia* or a *praetium* was handed over, and are of no further use in this context. Among the references to precious metal there are some fifty-eight to silver in some form. Of these, nine are to sums or objects of both gold and silver. Most of the remaining references are to sums of pounds, *solidi/scillingas*, shekels or *argentei*: thirty-five altogether, including three which explicitly refer to silver objects. Many of these denominations could be applied to sums of coin, and it is entirely possible that many of them do indeed signify sums of pennies. Yet explicit references to coins – *denarii/peningas* – appear only ten times.[116] They refer either to annual payments or, surprisingly, to very large numbers of pennies – 270, 600, 800 or even 3,000.[117] These large sums could easily have been broken down into pounds, *solidi/scillingas* or other larger denominations if so desired. The fact that they were not hints that it may have been relatively unusual to make payments for land in silver coin.

Another arresting feature of these charters is the frequency with which gold rather than silver appears in them as the medium for land transactions. A total of fifty-eight appearances of units normally associated with silver contrast with sixty-four of those associated with gold (again including nine references to both gold and silver). By far the most common unit of measurement among the latter is the mancus, a term which probably originated in Italy around the 770s to refer to Arabic gold dinars and which was current in England a decade later.[118] *Mancosi* occur thirty-eight times among these charters. In seven cases they are used to refer to the weight of an object, and eleven times they are specifically of *coctum* ('refined') or *bonum* ('good') gold. Emphasis on the quality of the gold may have reflected biblical precedent or been intended to discourage payment in debased gold, such as the imitations of *solidi* of Louis the Pious which circulated in large quantity in England in the ninth century.[119]

Throughout the Middle Ages gold coins are much more commonly encountered as references in documents than among actual finds.[120]

---

[116] Several of them (S 1193, 1196, 1199 and 1204) come in a cluster from mid-ninth-century Canterbury: Kelly, *St Augustine's*, p. 93.

[117] S 41, 1193, 1196, 1199 and 1204 record payments for land in pence; annual renders or bequests in pence are recorded in S 208, 1195, 1414, 1482 and 1508.

[118] On the origins and spread of this term, see above, p. 113.

[119] Blackburn, 'Gold in England', p. 57.

[120] P. Grierson, 'Muslim Coins in Thirteenth-Century England', in *Near Eastern Numismatics, Iconography and History. Studies in Honor of George C. Miles*, ed. D. Kouymjian (Beirut, 1974), pp. 387–91, at 391; B. Cook, 'The Bezant in Angevin England', *NC* 159 (1999), 255–75, and 'Foreign Coins in Medieval England', in *Moneta locale, moneta straniera: Italia ed Europa, XI–XV secolo (Local Coins, Foreign Coins: Italy and Europe 11th–15th Centuries)*, ed. L. Travaini (Milan, 1999), pp. 231–84, at 255–60.

Their value and the context of their use militated strongly against casual loss.[121] The total number of known late eighth- and ninth-century gold coins from England thus stands out as comparatively high: approximately thirty-five. This is more than for any other century between the seventh and thirteenth. Gold was about ten or twelve times as valuable as silver in this period,[122] and so all the difficulties which pertain to the question of how extensively silver was used apply even more acutely in the case of gold. The volume of finds is best interpreted simply as evidence of a comparatively plentiful gold currency, one which was certainly not used universally, but which did enjoy a prominent role in high-value transactions. Cut halves and quarters suggest use as currency rather than always as bullion,[123] though the link between gold coin and gold objects always remained stronger than that between silver coin and silver objects.

Use of gold was, in short, substantial, as both the charters and the finds demonstrate. But it was surely concentrated to a large extent among the elite, while the charters suggest the opposite may have been true of silver currency. A maximal reading of the charters and of other evidence for gift-giving and other high-value, non-commercial transfers of wealth would lead to the conclusion that pennies were used on a limited scale among the elite, and not commonly for 'special' purposes and contexts such as land purchases – in other words, that they were primarily a currency for more mundane purposes concentrated below the elite.

Coinage and exchange in context

Addressing the question of coin-use in gifts and other non-commercial contexts from a culturally specific perspective is in keeping with current trends in anthropological studies: broad comparisons across many times and places relating to just one sphere of society run the risk of missing vital elements of local background.[124] Conclusions reached through study of Pacific Islanders, native American Indians or other societies should not necessarily be mapped wholesale onto each other or onto Anglo-Saxon

---

[121] Thus just one gold coin was recorded as having been found in the context of excavations of later medieval rural villages: C. Dyer, 'Peasants and Coins: The Uses of Money in the Middle Ages', *BNJ* 67 (1997), 31–47, at pp. 39–40.

[122] *MEC*, p. 327. See MGH Capit. II, no. 273, c. 24, p. 320, which lays down a gold:silver relationship of 12:1.

[123] Naismith, 'Six English Finds', pp. 222–3. It is not clear when these coins were cut, as imitative *solidi* continued to be made and used into the viking period. However, there was a precedent for native Anglo-Saxon cutting of gold coins, recently highlighted by a pair of cut seventh-century *scillingas*: EMC 2005.0228 and 2007.0305.

[124] Cf. B. Rosenwein, 'Francia and Polynesia: Rethinking Anthropological Approaches', in *Negotiating the Gift*, ed. Algazi, Groebner and Jussen, pp. 361–79.

England. Many of the conditions in these societies which led to the emergence of their economic and social structures were highly localized: they were engendered by features such as the strong dominance of kin-groups, often as a result of hostile or geographically isolating physical conditions.[125] European colonialism also wrought major direct and indirect changes, which can easily be mistaken for local tradition.[126] These could bring networks of gift-exchange into being as a replacement for more violent transfers of wealth and lead to the idealization of local customs as a reaction to encroaching westernization.[127]

Furthermore, the danger of creating a simplified dichotomy of mutually exclusive types of economy based on gifts or commodities has been addressed, above all with regard to the nature of the social connections which led to and developed out of a particular exchange.[128] Especially influential has been the work of Marshall Sahlins, who associated different degrees of reciprocity with different levels and types of relationship, noting that the less close and permanent the connection between parties in exchange, the more care is taken to see that a fair and immediate trade is made: barter and purchase therefore prevail in 'neutral' settings when a trading partner is neither friend nor foe, while less immediate and exact recompense is expected from family and trusted acquaintances.[129] Sahlins has been just one among many to observe that societies – especially complex societies in which individuals have many connections and affiliations – embrace a range of different types of exchange, sometimes strongly associated with particular contexts, commodities or forms of currency.[130] Gift-exchange continues to be an important phenomenon in western capitalist societies, while pre-modern and other societies can witness extensive commodity exchange. In all cultures there were intermediary forms between these extremes and strong bonds linking them inextricably together in society.[131] Objects did not remain monolithic in their status or value as they moved between different individuals and

---

[125] Samson, 'Economic Anthropology and Vikings', pp. 87–8.
[126] C. Gregory, *Savage Money: The Anthropology and Politics of Commodity Exchange* (Amsterdam, 1997), p. 43; N. Thomas, *Entangled Objects*, pp. 83–184.
[127] N. Thomas, *Entangled Objects*, pp. 202–4.
[128] A. Appadurai, 'Introduction: Commodities and the Politics of Value', in *The Social Life of Things: Commodities in Cultural Perspective*, ed. A. Appadurai (Cambridge, 1986), pp. 3–63, at 11–12. On the distinction between gifts and commodities see Gregory, *Gifts and Commodities*, pp. 10–24.
[129] M. Sahlins, *Stone-Age Economics* (Chicago, IL, 1972), pp. 185–204.
[130] Classic statements include P. Bohannon, 'Some Principles of Exchange and Investment among the Tiv', *American Anthropologist* 57 (1955), 60–9; J. M. Keynes, 'Keynes and Ancient Currencies', pp. 256–60. Cf. Kilger, 'Wholeness and Holiness', pp. 258–61.
[131] N. Thomas, *Entangled Objects*, esp. pp. 17–21 and 33–4; D. Cheal, *Gift Economy* (London, 1988), esp. pp. 3–19; J. Carrier, *Gifts and Commodities: Exchange and Western Capitalism since 1700* (London, 1995); Yan, 'Gift and Gift Economy', pp. 230–7.

settings. One man's ancestral treasure to be kept or reserved for gifts of particular magnitude – an 'inalienable' possession – was another man's junk or commodity, to be got rid of for the best exchange possible.[132] This was as true of precious metals, including early medieval coins,[133] as it was of other things, although these can and have been seen as a particularly flexible case. Gold and silver were of little direct use except for the fact of their consistency and desirability, the ultimate in commodities or alienable possessions.[134]

It was the universality of money which troubled Mauss and Simmel, but even this was not always as total or as threatening as they feared. The existence of money has always been as grounded in social custom and acceptance as in state imposition and exploitation.[135] Jonathan Parry and Maurice Bloch have stressed that money's negative connotations belong to a late medieval and modern western tradition: in other societies the simultaneous employment of money for commerce, gifting and other uses is seen as in no way invidious.[136] Viviana Zelizer has highlighted that nineteenth-century America – a cradle of modern capitalism – still saw the theoretically universal dollar being put to all manner of uses which belied fears of its destabilization of society.[137] Monies from different sources were treated differently, and with the application of a little special treatment or contextualization could be used effectively for the giving of gifts and other expressions of relationships. Even modern currency has never achieved total fungibility in practice,[138] and fictional figures like Ebenezer Scrooge and Charles Foster Kane who reduce their fellow men to monetary abstractions are still targets of vilification.[139] Monetary transactions at levels high and low can remain strongly embedded within society.[140]

In conclusion, comparisons from Polynesia and other pre-modern societies do not in themselves confirm gifts and other forms of

---

[132] Appadurai, 'Commodities', pp. 6–56; A. B. Weiner, *Inalienable Possessions. The Paradox of Keeping-While-Giving* (Berkeley, CA, and Oxford, 1992), esp. pp. 1–43. On how this can fit into different strata of exchange see Gregory, *Savage Money*, pp. 8–13 and 52–5; Parry and Bloch, 'Introduction'.

[133] Gregory, *Savage Money*, pp. 246–52.

[134] M. Godelier, *The Enigma of the Gift*, trans. N. Scott (Cambridge, 1999), pp. 161–7; N. Thomas, *Entangled Objects*, p. 28; Kilger, 'Wholeness and Holiness', p. 262; Brookes, *Economics*, pp. 130–4.

[135] K. Hart, 'Money', pp. 170–1.

[136] Parry and Bloch, 'Introduction'; M. Bloch, 'The Symbolism of Money in Imerina', in *Money and the Morality of Exchange*, ed. Bloch and Parry, pp. 165–90, at 165–74; K. Hart, 'Money', pp. 163–8.

[137] V. Zelizer, *The Social Meaning of Money* (New York, 1994), esp. pp. 1–30.

[138] Cf. Melitz, 'Polanyi School of Anthropology', pp. 1020–6.

[139] Gregory, *Savage Money*, p. 8.

[140] M. Granovetter, 'Economic Action and Social Structure: The Problem of Embeddedness', *American Journal of Sociology* 91 (1985), 481–510.

non-commercial exchange as the backbone of the economy in Anglo-Saxon England. Examination of more specific local sources suggests that although gifts were exchanged, and sometimes on a large scale, it is problematic to see these as the defining element of exchanges as a whole and also difficult to confirm a major role for coinage in such transactions. The sheer volume of coins now found and estimated to have been produced sits ill with a partial role in occasional gift-giving dominated by the political and ideological concerns of the elite. A more successful approach is to build on the fluidity between different roles for currency – commerce, gift-giving, means of payment, store of value and others – and on the coexistence of several varieties of exchange encompassing all levels of society.[141]

COINAGE, MARKETS AND PEASANTS

Early medieval observers were certainly aware of the potential diversity of different kinds of transaction that could take place, and also, more importantly, of the close connections between market, alms, rent, purchase, gift and so forth. Coins sometimes explicitly featured in narratives illustrating that fact. One example is the *vita* of St Anskar, written at Hamburg around 870. At one point in this text, a woman named Catla brings a purse of silver coins left by her recently deceased mother Frideburg from Birka in Sweden to Dorestad, in order to give alms to needy souls. Some of the coins from this purse were distributed to the poor, after which Catla and her companions indulged in four *denarii* of wine from the remainder to help them recuperate from their work. Then the rest of the coins were given out, and the women went to bed exhausted. The next morning, they miraculously found the purse full up again – except for the four *denarii* they had spent on themselves. On asking the local priests what this meant, they were told that the miraculous money was a divine gift to be spent as they wished. But 'ea quae in usus tuos acceperas ipse tibi reddere noluit, quia ea tantum sua benignitate retribuit, quae pro eius amore in pauperes illius distributa fuerint'.[142]

Catla the Swedish almsgiver and her friends came from a wealthy but not royal family, and the money they gave out went to *indigentes*. They bring us into an important but generally much less visible dimension of coin-use outside the elite. A basic axiom for medievalists is that the surviving written sources stem from, and for the most part deal with,

---

[141] Cf. Grierson, *Numismatics*, pp. 5–8. For role of coinage as a store of value, see above, pp. 238–9 and 258–9.

[142] 'That which you have taken and used for your own purposes He would not restore, for in His kindness He gave back only that which had been distributed amongst the poor out of love for Him.' Rimbert, *Vita Anskarii*, c. 20 (ed. Waitz, p. 45).

the spiritual and secular rulers of society: those further down the social ladder who underpinned the prosperity of their lords and clergy are largely consigned to historical oblivion.[143] Hence references to how they interacted with coinage are few and far between, and only the broadest conclusions can be reached about how often they used coin, for what and how these tendencies changed over time. What is possible, however, is to present the occasional but important glimpses of detail which surface at various times and places. Collectively these cast light on the traces of what must have been a quite considerable foundation of coin-use that embraced all levels of society and a wide range of purposes.[144]

Most of these references derive from the context of interactions with the elite, especially the Church. A classic and oft-cited example of this kind is the evidence preserved in Carolingian-period estate surveys – polyptychs – from the Frankish empire. These documents list the responsibilities of tenants to pay their landlords various quantities of money, produce and service.[145] The length and level of detail offered depended on the specific polyptych, and also (presumably) on factors such as the local availability of coin and the arrangement of estates: more distant holdings might have paid more in cash or service than in kind because of the difficulty in gathering their produce,[146] and in some cases tenants had the option of paying in cash or kind.[147] The result is a series of disconnected snapshots of the agrarian economy at diverse times and places across the Carolingian empire.[148] Thus, for example, one finds that in a polyptych of 893 the abbey of Prüm in east Francia (Germany) received only 1,500 *denarii* from 2,000 *mansi* in the Low Countries. Conversely, the lands of St-Germain-des-Prés in the rich, densely settled and relatively coin-rich Paris basin during the time of Abbot Irminon (806–29) produced 3 per cent of all revenue from servile *mansi*, and 24 per cent of revenue in cash from free *mansi* in cash. Many of these payments probably represented a commutation of earlier services owed to the landlord.[149]

---

[143] For a recent survey of peasant society in early medieval Europe, see *FEMA*, pp. 383–588.

[144] Comparative analysis of peasant society in modern central India finds a prominent place for markets and monetary exchange: Gregory, *Savage Money*, pp. 58–63.

[145] Spufford, *Money*, pp. 60–1.

[146] J. Morimoto, 'Considérations nouvelles sur les "villes et campagnes" dans le domaine de Prüm au haut moyen âge', in *Villes et campagnes au moyen âge*, ed. Duvosquel and Dierkens, pp. 515–31, at 522–3.

[147] Toubert, *Europe*, p. 205; A. Dopsch, *Die Wirtschaftsentwicklung der Karolingerzeit vornehmlich in Deutschland*, 3rd edn, 2 vols. (Darmstadt, 1962) II, 263–9.

[148] Bruand, *Voyageurs et marchandises*, pp. 162–4; R. Latouche, *The Birth of Western Economy: Economic Aspects of the Dark Ages*, 2nd edn (London, 1967), pp. 190–202.

[149] Spufford, *Money*, pp. 47 and 60; A. Verhulst, 'Economic Organisation', in *NCMH* II, pp. 481–509, at 482. On Prüm see K. Petry, 'Die Geldzinse im Prümer Urbar von 893. Bemerkungen zum spätkarolingischen Geldumlauf des Rhein-, Maas- und Moselraumes im 9. Jahrhunderts',

Movement towards payment in cash rather than kind or service has been charted all over Europe from antiquity onwards.[150] Often it was seen as desirable by both tenants and landlords, offering a perception of greater freedom to the former and more versatility in expenditure to the latter.[151] The close link between coin- and grain-weights may even have acted as a perennial reminder of the concatenation of harvest, bread, rent and coin.[152] Specific evidence for this aspect of coin-use in England is slight. No estate surveys survive from Anglo-Saxon England before at the earliest the tenth century,[153] though given the similarity of the Carolingian and southern English currencies in many important respects it is reasonable to work on the basis that coins were being used for similar purposes in England. A few rare and smaller-scale survivals from England provide important hints that some rents were being paid in cash. From the late eighth century a lease survives from the archive of Peterborough, by which an ealdorman promised an annual payment to Peterborough abbey of one night's provisions and thirty shekels; a sum which could represent cash payments from the estate in question.[154]

Paying rents probably accounted for a significant proportion of rural coin-circulation, but the ability to pay them depended on the availability of means with which to exchange agricultural surpluses for silver coin-age. In other words, the development of a network of markets at which agricultural surpluses and secondary products of peasant labour could be sold in return for cash would have been an important force behind rural coin-use.[155] 'Market' should not automatically be taken to signify a large, permanent or static entity. In the early Middle Ages – as at all other

Rheinische Vierteljahrsblätter 52 (1988), 16–42, and 'Die Münz- und Geldgeschichte der Abtei Prüm im Spiegel der Münzfunde und der schriftlichen Überlieferung', in *Das Prümer Urbar als Geschichtsquelle und seine Bedeutung für das Bitburger und Luxemburger Land*, ed. E. Erpelding (Bitburg, 1993), pp. 27–46.

[150] On the Roman period see L. de Ligt, 'Demand, Supply, Distribution', pp. 34–5, and *Fairs and Markets in the Roman Empire: Economic and Social Aspects of Periodic Trade in a Pre-Industrial Society* (Amsterdam, 1993), p. 21.

[151] C. Dyer, *Making a Living in the Middle Ages. The People of Britain 850–1520* (New Haven, CT, and London, 2002), pp. 26–35; C. Wickham, *The Mountains and the City: The Tuscan Appennines in the Early Middle Ages* (Oxford, 1988), pp. 69–70, 76–82 and 167, and 'Economic and Social', pp. 17–18; Devroey, 'Courants et réseaux', pp. 343–52; Toubert, 'Sistema curtense', pp. 43–59, and *Europe*, pp. 91–2 and 204–6; R. Britnell, *The Commercialisation of English Society, 1000–1500*, 2nd edn (Manchester, 1996), pp. 43–7; L. Kuchenbuch, 'Probleme der Rententwicklung in den klösterlichen Grundherrschaften des frühen Mittelalters', in *Benedictine Culture 750–1050*, ed. W. Lourdeaux and D.Verhelst (Leuven, 1983), pp. 130–72.

[152] Kilger, 'Wholeness and Holiness', pp. 270–5.

[153] One list of renders attached to a charter of Edward the Elder dated to 900 (S 359) was probably added to the document in the eleventh century. For differing views see H. Finberg, *Lucerna: Studies of Some Problems in the Early History of England* (London, 1964), pp. 131–43; Maitland, *Domesday Book*, pp. 330–1.

[154] S 1412.   [155] Cf. Gregory, *Savage Money*, pp. 125–6.

times and places in history – markets could be large or small, specialized or diverse, permanent or temporary; in essence, a market can be defined as any place where people come together for the purpose of buying and selling commodities and services.[156] At the apex of the early medieval hierarchy were a few large, high-profile coastal centres which provided the foci for long-distance inter-regional exchange, among them Dorestad, London, Hedeby and Venice.[157] Although often seen as the archetypes of planned and coherent royal management of trade, recent research has re-evaluated the extent of royal and other magnate control over the formation and running of these centres, and over associated phenomena such as minting, contending that it was far from monopolistic.[158] Major trading settlements could come into being independently of kings' actions, and it is likely that the strongest manifestation of royal interest in many centres was the extraction of tolls on pre-existing trade.[159]

These well-known nodes of international trade were only the high points of what must have been a far more deep-rooted system of capillary markets and central places extending out into the countryside.[160] In England the earliest witnesses to their development are possibly the 'productive sites' which appeared in the seventh century and after. The most recent discussions of these sites have suggested that they may often have been connected with secular or ecclesiastical estate centres,[161] but include a wide range of sizes and profiles when subjected to excavation or other survey techniques.[162] Their associated landowners would have

---

[156] Lie, 'Sociology of Markets'; K. Applbaum, 'The Anthropology of Markets', in *Handbook*, ed. Carrier, pp. 275–89. For pre-industrial markets in general see de Ligt, *Fairs and Markets*, pp. 1–32.

[157] Above, pp. 128–32 and 235–8.

[158] Above, pp. 33–4.

[159] D. Skre, 'Post-Substantivist Towns and Trade AD 600–1000', in *Means of Exchange*, ed. Skre, pp. 327–42, at 338–40; R. Fleming, 'Elites, Boats and Foreigners: Rethinking the Birth of English Towns', *Settimane* 56 (2009), 393–426, at pp. 410–20, and *Britain after Rome*, pp. 183–212; C. Loveluck and D. Tys, 'Coastal Societies, Exchange and Identity along the Channel and Southern North Sea Shores of Europe, AD 600–1000', *Journal of Maritime Archaeology* 1 (2006), 140–69, at pp. 146–7 and 152–3.

[160] Skre, 'Post-Substantivist Towns and Trade', p. 338; Fleming, 'Elites, Boats and Foreigners', pp. 417–20. On the impact of transport costs in such systems see S. R. H. Jones, 'Transaction Costs, Institutional Change and the Emergence of a Market Economy in Later Anglo-Saxon England', *EcHR* 46 (1993), 658–78, at p. 662.

[161] K. Ulmschneider, *Markets, Minsters and Metal Detectors: The Archaeology of Middle Saxon Lincolnshire and Hampshire Compared*, BAR British Series 307 (Oxford, 2000), pp. 81–100; J. Naylor, *An Archaeology of Trade in Middle Saxon England*, BAR British Series 376 (Oxford, 2004), pp. 116–34 (which both favour identification as ecclesiastical centres); A. R. J. Hutcheson, 'The Origins of King's Lynn? Control of Wealth on the Wash Prior to the Norman Conquest', *Medieval Archaeology* 50 (2006), 71–104, esp. pp. 79–92.

[162] G. Davies, 'Early Medieval "Rural Centres" and West Norfolk: A Growing Picture of Diversity, Complexity and Changing Lifestyles', *Medieval Archaeology* 54 (2010), 89–122. For comparative discussion of elite residential sites, C. Loveluck, 'The Dynamics of Elite Lifestyles in the "Rural World", AD 600–1150: Archaeological Perspectives from North West Europe', in *La culture du*

been the takers of cash as well as rents in kind, and there were strong Roman precedents for the institution of domanial markets.[163] Such links between long-distance trade, specialist crafts and centres of religious and ideological power find many parallels in other pre-industrial societies.[164] However, the exact nature of most productive sites remains contentious when there is little context to draw on.[165] Sites in close proximity to each other are less likely to represent estate centres, and a flexible interpretation of varied statuses and functions encompassing some degree of exchange is probably preferable.[166] Less archaeological evidence for similar sites is forthcoming from Gaul (perhaps not surprisingly given French restrictions on metal-detecting),[167] where there is richer written evidence for market centres which were associated with major churches, saints' days and surviving Roman cities.[168] In 744 the Mayor of the Palace Pippin singled out the bishops as responsible for guaranteeing a market (*forus*) somewhere within their diocese.[169] Markets can, however, be traced in more quantity and detail in Carolingian documentation,[170] and it was assumed that a regular feature of such markets, as well as of *civitates* and *vici*, would be vendors offering a *denarius*-worth of bread, wine or cooked meat.[171]

---

haut moyen âge: une question d'élites?, ed. F. Bougard, R. Le Jan and R. McKitterick (Turnhout, 2009), pp. 139–70.

[163] De Ligt, *Fairs and Markets*, pp. 155–98.

[164] Helms, *Craft and the Kingly Ideal*, p. 119.

[165] On the nature of 'productive sites', see Hutcheson, 'Origins of King's Lynn'; for an alternative view J. Richards, 'What's So Special about "Productive" Sites? Middle Saxon Settlements in Northumbria', *ASSAH* 10 (1999), 71–80.

[166] Richards, Naylor and Holas-Clark, 'Anglo-Saxon Landscape and Economy', § 4.5.

[167] Hodges, *Dark Age Economics*, pp. 50–2; but see now Coupland 'Carolingian Single-Finds'.

[168] D. Claude, 'Aspekte des Binnenhandels im Merowingerreich auf Grund der Schriftquellen', in *Der Handel des frühen Mittelalters. Bericht über die Kolloquien der Kommission für Altertumskunde Mittel- und Nordeuropas in den Jahren 1980–1983*, ed. K. Düwel et al. (Göttingen, 1985), pp. 9–99, at 48–54; F. Theuws, 'Exchange, Religion, Identity and Central Places in the Early Middle Ages', *Archaeological Dialogues* 10 (2004), 121–38; Y. Hen, *Culture and Religion in Merovingian Gaul, A.D. 481–751* (Leiden, 1995), pp. 231–4; (on the urban role) *FEMA*, pp. 674–81. There has been much debate on the survival of Roman fairs and markets into the early Middle Ages: see, e.g., A. Lombard-Jourdan, 'Foires gauloises et origines urbaines', *Archéocivilisation* 11–13 (1974), 46–86; M. Mitterauer, 'La continuité des foires et la naissance des villes', *Annales* 28 (1973), 711–34.

[169] MGH Capit. I, no. 12, c. 6, p. 30.

[170] Above, n. 28, and also Latouche, *Birth of Western Economy*, pp. 240–67; Wickham, *Inheritance*, pp. 534–5; J. Durliat, 'La vigne et le vin dans la région parisienne au début du IXe siècle, d'après le Polyptyque d'Irmion', *Le moyen âge* 74 (1968), 387–419; G. Despy, 'Villes et campagnes aux IXe et Xe siècles: l'exemple du pays mosan', *Revue du Nord* 50 (1968), 145–68; Devroey and Zoller, 'Villes, campagnes, croissance agraire'; Mitterauer, *Markt und Stadt*; F. Irsigler, 'Grundherrschaft, Handel und Märkte zwischen Maas und Rhein im frühen und hohen Mittelalter', in *Grundherrschaft und Stadtentstehung am Niederrhein*, ed. K. Flink and W. Janssen (Kleve, 1989), pp. 52–78; Toubert, *Europe*, pp. 108–15.

[171] MGH Capit. II, no. 273, c. 20, p. 319.

Merchants and members of the elite – the latter often acting through dependent merchants – are well known to have patronized markets large and small, but were not alone in doing so.[172] Peasants going to market with surplus agricultural goods or items of secondary production to sell for money,[173] or with a few coins needed to buy other necessary items, were a recurring motif in Carolingian-era hagiographical texts.[174] Just one example need be offered here,[175] drawn from the *Translatio et miracula sancti Adelphi Mettensis*, a text probably written in the middle of the ninth century. According to one of the miracles here:

Mulier quaedam paupercula de villa quae Hoffelden dicitur duos denarios per quendam vicinum suum misit, ut sibi necessaria compararet. Quos cum ille per negligentiam perdidisset et ideo infecto negocio cum ingenti tristicia rediret, praecipue cum mulieri fere nihil amplius reliquerit, nec ipse per quod dampnum restituere posset habuerit, sicque quidnam agere deberet animo revolveret, ad quoddam venit pratum ibique genibus fixis, Dei et sancti Adelphi misericordiam et solatium super hac re postulavit statimque deorsum respiciens in herba nummos quos perdiderat reperit; quos etiam ad sancti Adelphi ecclesiam portavit.[176]

What became of the poor woman and her shopping is left unexplained.

Anecdotes from saints' lives are not always to be taken at face value, and episodes such as this are to some extent heirs to biblical parables on the interaction of the poor with coinage, such as Mark 12:42 and

---

[172] McCormick, *Origins*, pp. 12–15 and 614–17; Siems, *Handel und Wucher*, pp. 110–38; E. Sabbe, 'Quelques types de marchands des IXe et Xe siècles', *Revue belge de philologie et d'histoire* 13 (1934), 176–87; Kelly, 'Trading Privileges', pp. 13–16; Scull, 'Urban Centres', pp. 299–300; Devroey, *Économie rurale*, pp. 154–5, and 'Courants et réseaux', pp. 376–81; Verhulst, 'Marchés, marchands', pp. 38–9, and 'Economic Organisation', pp. 505–6 and 508–9. Frisians and Jews were particularly prominent as merchants: see Lebecq, *Marchands et navigateurs*; P. Johanek, 'Der fränkische Handel der Karolingerzeit im Spiegel der Schriftquellen', in *Der Handel der Karolinger- und Wikingerzeit*, ed. Düwel *et al.*, pp. 7–68, at 55–60.

[173] For peasant crafts and use of markets, see de Ligt, *Fairs and Markets*, pp. 131–4.

[174] For discussion see G. Duby, *The Early Growth of the European Economy: Warriors and Peasants from the Seventh to the Twelfth Century*, trans. H. B. Clarke (London, 1974), pp. 91–9; Nelson, *Charles the Bald*, pp. 24–6; Verhulst, *Carolingian Economy*, pp. 120–3; Bruand, *Voyageurs et marchandises*, pp. 155–68; Spufford, *Money*, pp. 46–9.

[175] For another example see *Miracula S. Benedicti*, c. 35 (ed. Holder-Egger, p. 496). Cf. W. Davies, *Small Worlds*, pp. 53–8 and 168–9.

[176] 'A certain poor woman from a village called Hochfelden sent off two pennies in the hands of one of her neighbours, so that he might buy things that she needed. But having lost the pennies through negligence and thus not completed his errand he was coming home in great distress, particularly since almost nothing more remained to the woman, and he did not have the means to make restitution for the loss. As he was racking his brains over what he should do he came to a certain field and there, with his knees fixed on the ground, he asked for mercy and comfort on the matter from God and St Adelphus, and as soon as he looked down he found in the grass the coins which he had lost. These he brought to the church of St Adelphus.' *Translatio et miracula S. Adelphi Mettensis*, c. 12 (ed. de Heinemann, pp. 295–6).

Luke 15:8. But miracle stories concerning peasants and coins should not be dismissed as pious fantasy. They use different settings and vocabulary from the biblical precedents and recur often enough that they must have drawn on an awareness that such things formed a regular part of life for denizens of Carolingian-period Europe. Further corroboration comes from occasional recognition in Frankish capitularies and Alfred the Great's law-code that even peasants and slaves should have access to markets in order to make purchases (although the use of coin is not always made explicit).[177]

Markets, these scattered but significant references suggest, should not be left out of all debate on the extent and nature of early medieval exchange: they existed in substantial quantity and varied forms and were patronized by everyone from peasants up to wealthy merchants and even aristocrats. And it was not only the occasional enterprising peasants of hagiographical anecdotes who associated the getting and spending of money with markets. In the minds of Carolingian and late Anglo-Saxon legislators the bond between minting, towns and markets was self-evident,[178] and charters granting Frankish bishops and monasteries the right to establish or control mints were prompted (at least allegedly) by the scarcity of coin and were coupled with control over a market and toll-station.[179]

Access to markets and coinage at an even lower level is implied by another use to which coinage was sometimes put in the eighth and ninth centuries: the distribution of alms. Here commercial use of coins is presumed as an adjunct to the distribution of Christian charity, but as a non-reciprocal act almsgiving was grounded in a milieu quite different from that of the gifts most closely studied by anthropologists and has therefore attracted less attention from this perpective. Moreover, recent analyses of late antique and early medieval almsgiving have concluded that its economic impact on individuals was probably slight and varied substantially depending on the status of particular paupers.[180] Orphans and widows, for example, could expect sustained assistance from the Church and were preferred recipients of alms. This state of precarious dependence was what defined medieval *pauperi* – not poverty in itself.[181] The intention of

---

[177] Below, p. 288–9; Alfred, *Laws*, c. 43 (ed. Liebermann I, 78; trans. Keynes and Lapidge, *Alfred the Great*, p. 170).

[178] As was the case with II Æthelstan, IV Æthelred and the Edict of Pîtres: see above, pp. 132 and 145.

[179] For example, W. Jesse, *Quellenbuch zur Münz- und Geldgeschichte des Mittelalters* (Halle, 1929), nos. 44–6 and 141–2.

[180] C. Sotinel, 'Le don chrétien et ses retombées sur l'économie dans l'antiquité tardive', *Antiquité tardive* 14 (2006), 105–16, at pp. 113–16. For the late Roman context see R. Finn, *Almsgiving in the Later Roman Empire: Christian Promotion and Practice* (Oxford, 2008), esp. pp. 67–89; for Merovingian parallels Kloss, *Goldvorrat und Geldverkehr*, pp. 82–4; T. Sternberg, *Orientalium more secutus. Räume und Institutionen der Caritas des 5. bis 7. Jahrhunderts in Gallien* (Münster, 1991).

[181] Sternberg, *Orientalium more secutus*, pp. 48–51; Devroey, *Puissants et misérables*, pp. 317–51.

alms was always to support the poor, not help them change their status. To this end the sums that each individual received were small and given out in conjunction with parcels of food.[182] Yet the manner of distribution should not detract from the large scale on which alms could be given. Spiritual benefits to the donor of alms were every bit as important as the material assistance received by the destitute,[183] and as such the overall bequests from which alms were drawn could be very large and were quantified by the number of individuals who benefited from them: their gradual dispersal represented a major transfer of wealth. These bequests could extend to thousands of individuals and were sufficient to attract crowds of paupers to congregate at major churches and in cities. Frideburg, the wealthy Swede mentioned in the *vita* of St Anskar who wished to distribute some of her money to the poor, told her daughter Catla that the number of indigent people in Birka did not warrant such an outlay, and that to find a sufficiently large *indigentium multitudo* ('crowd of needy people'), it was necessary to go to Dorestad.[184]

The distribution of alms – which was a perennial element of Christian religious life – guaranteed that the poor could occasionally receive direct access to cash with which they were expected to purchase food or clothing, presumably from vendors situated in the vicinity. In one rare and important survival from early ninth-century England, a will left by the Canterbury priest Werhard (which also covers the bequests made by his much more famous kinsman, Archbishop Wulfred) gives specific instructions for how one such batch of alms was to be distributed:

Apud Hergan quinque paupers; apud Otteford quinque; apud Clive ii; apud Gravenea ii; apud Oesuualun vii; in civitate Dorobernia sex; unicuique detur cotidie ad manducandum quod convenienter sit satis, et per annum cuique pauperi ad vestitum xxvi denarii. Cotidie quoque præcepit missam celebrari pro anima sua [et] pro animabus supra memoratorum; in anniversario suo precepit dari mille cc pauperibus ad manducandum cuique panem unum [et] caseum aut lardum et denarium unum.[185]

---

[182] Alms of food alone are stipulated in S 1188, for example.

[183] Finn, *Almsgiving*, pp. 177–97; E. Stanley, 'Did the Anglo-Saxons Have a Social Conscience Like Us?', *Anglia* 121(2003) 238–64; P. Jobert, *La notion de donation: convergences, 630–750* (Paris, 1977); A. Angenendt, T. Braucks, R. Busch and H. Lutterbach, 'Counting Piety in the Early and High Middle Ages', in *Ordering Medieval Society. Perspectives on Intellectual and Practical Modes of Shaping Social Relations*, ed. B. Jussen (Philadelphia, PA, 2001), pp. 15–54, esp. 16–20 and 33–8.

[184] Above, n. 142.

[185] 'To five paupers at Harrow, five at Otford, two at Cliffe, two at Graveney, seven at Easole and six in the city of Canterbury let enough to eat be given each day as is convenient, and over the year let each pauper be given twenty-six pence for clothing. [Werhard] also commanded that a mass be celebrated for his soul every day, and for the souls of those mentioned above he commanded that on his anniversary 1,200 paupers should each be given for food a loaf of bread, some cheese or butter and one penny.' S 1414 (BCS 402). Another mid-ninth-century Kentish will enjoined

A very few coins inscribed **ELIMOSINA** or similar survive, which were specifically intended for distribution as alms to churches or the poor.[186] Among them are the so-called 'offering pieces' of Alfred the Great. Weighing approximately six times as much as a normal penny, these may have had a special use as alms to be sent abroad – perhaps to Rome.[187] But coins with this inscription are extremely rare, and if any specific types of coinage – such as, for example, the ecclesiastical coinages of the archbishops of Canterbury and York or any of the few inscribed ecclesiastical types of *sceat* – were used for almsgiving, this was not done on a large enough scale to affect the pattern of loss.[188] Either other coins were used for alms, or the scale of their distribution and the nature of their expenditure led them to blend immediately back into the general pool of currency.

The underlying point is that money was available to all members of early medieval society, and was closely related to use in a market setting. This is not to say, however, that England in the ninth century should be characterized as a market economy, let alone a monetized economy; rather, it was a society in which there were many interwoven strata of exchange, of which markets were only one and money was used only in part. Rents, fines and tolls could be taken by kings, churches and the landowning elite in coin or other media; alms and gifts could be given; and both gold and silver could be melted down into other forms to perform still more uses. It should be stressed how closely these various kinds of exchange coexisted. A gift of alms could be spent that same day at a market in a commercial setting, then used shortly afterwards to pay rent or toll and perhaps later given as part of a gift between members of the elite. All were interdependent, and all can be traced in England and its neighbours in the eighth and ninth centuries.

THE PROBLEM OF SMALL CHANGE

Successful though the early medieval denarial coinage was, it still had a major limitation: by and large there was only one denomination in circulation. Gold coins existed, but were relatively few and high in value; thus they were concentrated in the hands of the elite for special, prestigious

---

that possession of a certain estate was conditional on an annual 100 pence gift of alms to Christ Church, Canterbury (S 1195). The early tenth-century text known as 'Almsgiving' or 'Æthelstan's Charity Ordinance' (which was transmitted with the Latin text of I Æthelstan) contains similar stipulations (ed. Liebermann I, 148–9).

[186] For an early Carolingian example see Morrison and Grunthal, *Carolingian Coinage*, no. 53.

[187] Only two 'offering pieces' survive (one from the Goldsborough hoard and another found near Poole, Dorset): Dolley and Blunt, 'Chronology of the Coins', pp. 77–8; *MEC*, p. 314.

[188] Above, pp. 223–4.

transactions. For practical purposes, the large majority of the population had to work around having only silver pennies available. These left much to be desired when small transactions had to be made. For denizens of the Roman, Byzantine and Muslim empires, base-metal currency was produced in bulk for such purposes, and it was the only coinage which would be encountered on a day-to-day basis: silver and especially gold were too valuable and in some cases too closely associated with special uses (such as payment of taxes and the army) for other purposes.[189] The volume of these base-metal coinages and the extent to which they permeated daily life could be staggering, and they bring us to an altogether different level of monetization. The thousands of single-finds of Anglo-Saxon gold *scillingas*, early pennies/*sceattas* and of broad pennies appear quite paltry when compared to over 100,000 recorded English single-finds of Roman base-metal coins from a period of similar length recorded by the Portable Antiquities Scheme; many times that number have probably been found in total.[190] This body of material was unquestionably linked (at least in some parts of the province) to a relatively high level of monetization, extending to the lowest in society and the smallest of transactions. One bronze coin could buy a loaf of bread or a litre of wine.[191] This level of monetization was replicated at various times in the Byzantine and Muslim worlds, and eventually in later medieval Europe,[192] as well as in pre-Roman Britain, from which some 14,300 single-finds (9,500 of them base metal) have been recorded.[193] It is figures such as these which are essential for keeping the monetization of the eighth and ninth centuries in perspective. Substantial it may have been, but total or even large by the yardstick of ancient or modern monetary systems it was not.

Analogy with the pre-industrial contexts of the contemporary developing world and early modern Europe indicates that even the presence of a plentiful low-value medium of exchange does not always translate into a high overall proportion of transactions being carried out with cash. There could be substantial social, chronological and geographical variation within a single polity. In the Roman empire, for example, coin-use in the countryside was substantial but less so than in cities and with more

---

[189] Above, pp. 37–8 and 201–2.

[190] Based on figures of August 2010.

[191] See A. Burnett, *Coinage in the Roman World* (London, 1987), pp. 95–7; C. Howgego, 'The Supply and Use of Money in the Roman World 200 B.C. to A.D. 300', *Journal of Roman Studies* 82 (1992), 1–31, at pp. 16–29. For the limitations of the late Roman bronze coinage, see *MEC*, pp. 9–10.

[192] C. Morrisson, 'Byzantine Money', pp. 950–4; Spufford, *Money*, pp. 319–38.

[193] These figures are derived from the *Celtic Coin Index* (http://web.arch.ox.ac.uk/coins/ccindex. htm), as of August 2010. The coins would have been made and used over a period of approximately a century and a half.

seasonal fluctuations.[194] Taking such variables into account, the overall rate of monetization (taken as money supply relative to GDP) in France *c.* 1800 was still only about 40%, and at the time of setting up an independent currency in Mali in 1962 it was 17%.[195] In India in the 1950s only some 60% of rural transactions and 90% of those in the cities made use of currency.[196] Estimates of the proportion of monetized exchanges in the Byzantine world (at times when bronze coinage was extensively available) have been put at 15–30% for different areas, with an optimistic maximum for the twelfth-century economic heyday of 46%.[197]

In Anglo-Saxon England and its neighbours in the early medieval West, on the other hand, there was no low-value base-metal coinage. Bronze coin-issues had effectively ended in the post-Roman west by the sixth century, and there was a general dearth of silver coin in the Mediterranean from the early fifth century onwards.[198] Gold currency probably survived in large part because of its increasingly close links to the fiscal mechanisms of the empire, and consequently the authority which accrued to its production and use.[199] Hence the emphasis on *solidi* and *scillingas* in post-Roman law-codes even when the coins themselves could be substituted in kind or had completely gone out of use. By the seventh century, currency in western Europe was essentially monometallic, and to a large extent even monodenominational, as the dominant coin in circulation in England, Francia, Spain and Lombard Italy was the gold *tremissis* (one third of a *solidus*).[200]

On some level the end of the elaborate currency system of the late Roman empire must betoken a fall in economic complexity, as well as the reorientation and downsizing of minting operations.[201] Low-value currency had always been the least economically viable of coinages to produce, as minting it required comparable time and expertise to the

---

[194] Howgego, 'Supply and Use of Money', pp. 20–2.

[195] C. Morrisson, 'Monnaie et finances dans l'empire byzantine: Xe–XIVe siècles', in *Hommes et richesses dans l'empire byzantine*, ed. C. Abadie-Reynal, 3 vols. (Paris, 1989–91) II, 291–315, at pp. 294–5.

[196] A. G. Chandavarkar, 'Money and Credit (1858–1947)', in *The Cambridge Economic History of India II, c. 1757–c. 1970*, ed. D. Kumar (Cambridge, 1983), pp. 762–803, at 764.

[197] C. Morrisson, 'Byzantine Money', pp. 946–50. Documents from tenth- and eleventh-century Italy also indicate a limited use of coin, though are subject to many of the same qualifications as Anglo-Saxon charters: D. Herlihy, 'Treasure Hoards in the Italian Economy, 960–1139', *EcHR* 10 (1957), 1–14.

[198] On the decline of base-metal coinage in the early medieval west, see Spufford, *Money*, pp. 8–11.

[199] For the importance of (at least theoretically) monetized taxation and legal fees, see above, pp. 253–6 and 266–7.

[200] Some *solidi* were still being produced and used, though in small numbers. In England, both the Crondall and Sutton Hoo hoards contained no coins besides *tremisses*.

[201] Ward-Perkins, *Fall of Rome*, pp. 110–17.

much more valuable gold and silver. Shortages were common even in the ancient world,[202] and it was associated with the beneficence of the imperial government towards its poorer subjects.[203] Its disappearance as mints multiplied and declined in size was therefore entirely to be expected.

The end of base-metal currency meant that the lowest levels of coin-use in the west were no longer catered for. The silver pennies introduced in England and Gaul in the 670s were an improvement on the very high-value gold coinage of earlier times,[204] yet remained too valuable for use in small-scale transactions.[205] Reliable prices from the early Middle Ages are few but nonetheless clear in this respect. Examples include the four *denarii* paid by a group of women in ninth-century Dorestad for wine,[206] and the compensations required in the Anglo-Saxon law-code VI Æthelstan for various animals: thirty pence for an ox, twenty for a cow, ten for a pig and five for a sheep.[207] More helpful are the details from Francia in the famine-stricken year 794, when Charlemagne legislated at the council of Frankfurt that no one was to sell a *modius* of oats for more than one *denarius*, a *modius* of barley for more than two, a *modius* of rye for more than three or a *modius* of wheat for more than four. In terms of bread, this translated into prices per *denarius* of twelve two-pound wheat loaves, fifteen rye loaves, twenty barley loaves or twenty-five oat loaves.[208] These were maximum prices intended to apply *tempore abundantiae sive tempore caritatis* ('in time of abundance and in time of charity'), and reduced prices were offered for supplies taken from the royal supply in case of emergency. Market prices were thus dictated by demand rather than monolithic perceptions of value, and the prevalent concern was of people charging more (or less) than was currently acceptable when they could get away with it, not the fact that prices were set by current demand.[209] Inflation might be detectable in Frankish grain prices of the ninth century, though on the whole the rise of prices was (short-term fluctuations notwithstanding)

[202] Von Reden, *Money in Classical Antiquity*, pp. 26–8.
[203] C. M. Cipolla, *Money, Prices, and Civilization in the Mediterranean World, Fifth to Seventeenth Century* (Princeton, NJ, 1956), pp. 27–37. For the economic significance of small change, see Bolton, 'What Is Money?'.
[204] Cf. Spufford, *Money*, p. 8.
[205] R. S. Lopez, 'Monete e monetieri nell'Italia barbarica', *Settimane* 8 (1961), 57–88, at p. 81; P. Riché, *Daily Life in the World of Charlemagne*, trans. J. A. McNamara (Liverpool, 1978), pp. 118–21; Wickham, 'Rethinking', p. 25; Toubert, 'Sistema', p. 53.
[206] Above, pp. 165–7 and 276, and the table in Riché, *Daily Life*, pp. 118–19.
[207] VI Æthelstan, c. 6.2 (ed. Liebermann I, 176; trans. *EHD*, p. 424).
[208] MGH Capit. I, no. 28, c. 4, p. 74.
[209] MGH Capit. II, no. 287, c. 13, p. 375; and MGH Conc. II, no. 50, c. 52, p. 645. On the 'just price', see D. Wood, *Medieval Economic Thought* (Cambridge, 2002), pp. 132–58.

probably very slow,[210] at least if the continuity seen in England between the tenth and late twelfth centuries is any guide.[211]

Yet the rarity of reliable quotations of prices or wages from England before the twelfth century, or even from the Carolingian realms, makes it impossible to pursue their development with any degree of confidence. It is likewise extremely dangerous to try to pin down the modern equivalents of these prices. The effects of supply, demand and incidental costs of production and transportation were probably quite different from those of modern times and cannot be traced in any detail. At best, it seems safe to accept that a silver penny or *denarius* had the buying power of a substantial number of modern US dollars, euros or pounds sterling. Certainly it was a lot more than was needed for one loaf of bread or one litre of wine.

The coinage of Anglo-Saxon England or any of its neighbours was thus of limited usefulness, and leads one to ask how people went about paying smaller transactions. The problem may not have been as glaring to eighth- and ninth-century coin-users as it is to modern society, as there is no way of determining how commonly small change may actually have been needed. The bulk of the early medieval population (i.e., peasants) lived in relatively close-knit rural communities where most needs could be met internally.[212] The ideal was for peasants to produce at least enough food to live on independently;[213] the proportion of the population that lived largely or entirely off the fruits of others' cultivation was probably relatively small. Recourse could also be made to networks of trust and casual barter of goods and favours which flourish most effectively in such small, intimate societies.[214] Retail credit (although notionally anathema to the Church) would have been a further option for smaller-scale purchases when there was an ongoing relationship between buyer and seller.[215]

Nonetheless, there were things which peasants and others could not find or make at home and which had to be sought out at market,[216]

---

[210] Johanek, 'Der fränkische Handel', pp. 30–1.

[211] D. Farmer, 'Prices and Wages', in *The Agrarian History of England and Wales*, vol. II, *1042–1350*, ed. H. Hallam (Cambridge, 1988), pp. 716–817, at 716–17. Cf. Latouche, *Birth of Western Economy*, pp. 157–60.

[212] W. Davies, *Small Worlds*, pp. 105–33.

[213] See, for example, Devroey, *Puissants et misérables*, pp. 558–9, building ultimately on the work of Alexander Chayanov.

[214] C. Humphrey and S. Hugh-Jones, 'Introduction: Barter, Exchange and Value', in *Barter, Exchange and Value: An Anthropological Approach*, ed. C. Humphrey and S. Hugh-Jones (Cambridge, 1992), pp. 1–20, at 5–6; P. Heady, 'Barter', in *Handbook*, ed. Carrier, pp. 262–74; Grierson, *Numismatics*, pp. 6–7; Sahlins, *Stone-Age Economics*, pp. 193–204.

[215] Devroey, *Économie rurale*, pp. 156–7; Humphrey and Hugh-Jones, 'Introduction', pp. 5–6.

[216] De Ligt, *Fairs and Markets*, p. 140, and 'Demand, Supply, Distribution', pp. 47–51.

while in lean years a higher proportion of the population must have had to resort to purchasing supplies in order to ward off starvation.[217] These purchases might often have been bought in bulk, as the prices laid down by Charlemagne at the council of Frankfurt suggest was the norm.[218] Gregory of Tours and Merovingian hagiographers have left several anecdotes regarding sixth- and seventh-century use of gold coins for such purchases at one extreme,[219] while lower-value alternatives to pennies also existed. *Oboli* (halfpennies) were issued under the Merovingians in the Carolingian world from the mid-eighth century and in England from the 870s, though never in large volume.[220] At times Roman bronze coins could have been pressed back into service as low-value currency, though distinguishing eighth- and ninth-century use is extremely difficult, and it was probably never substantial.[221] In parts of mid-ninth-century England there was another option available in the form of Northumbrian *stycas*: small, thick, base-metal coins which were made and used in massive quantities north of the Humber.[222] Within Lincolnshire and East Anglia, where finds of *stycas* are relatively numerous, they probably circulated as a fractional coinage alongside southern silver pennies for a few decades in the middle of the ninth century.[223]

Coins were not the only possible form of money in the early Middle Ages. They served a useful purpose in being durable and of relatively consistent value in a medium – precious metal – which was desired by all, even if not practically usable save in exchange for something else.[224] Its use was also sanctioned by long-established custom and by an entrenched place in the ideology of rulership and other social interactions.[225] Some at least of these features could be duplicated by other items. Livestock

---

[217] De Ligt, *Fairs and Markets*, pp. 110–11 and 131.

[218] Cf. Spufford, *Money*, pp. 10–11, for the tendency of country-dwellers towards larger purchases.

[219] Kloss, *Goldvorrat und Geldverkehr*, pp. 88–90.

[220] English finds of Carolingian *oboli* include EMC 1986.0346, 1999.0062, 2001.0195, 1994.0175, 1997.0103, 1029.1080 and 1029.1103.

[221] Roman bronzes have been found in the context of eighth- and ninth-century sites at Middle Harling (Archibald, 'Coinage of Beonna', p. 17), the 'near Royston' productive site (EMC 1986.00001–2), West Stow, Southampton (Andrews, ed., *Coins and Pottery*, nos. 151–87), Burrow Hill (V. Fenwick *et al.*, 'Insula de Burgh: Excavations at Burrow Hill, Butley, Suffolk 1978–1981', *ASSAH* 3 (1984), 43–54, at p. 50) and possibly at one location in London (anon. note in *NC* 2 (1837–8), 109). They may also have served as weights, amulets or scrap-metal. For medieval reuse of Roman bronzes in Italy, see G. P. Bognetti, 'Il problema monetario dell'economia longobarda e il "panis" e la "scutella de cambio"', in *Storia dell'economia italiana*, ed. C. M. Cipolla (Turin, 1959), pp. 51–60, at 54 n. 2; in Gaul, see Spufford, *Money*, p. 10.

[222] Above, pp. 246–9.   [223] Above, pp. 206–8.

[224] Ingham, *Nature of Money*, pp. 97–101; Godelier, *Enigma of the Gift*, pp. 163–6; Kilger, 'Wholeness and Holiness', p. 262. Cf. Grierson, *Origins of Money*; Simmel, *Philosophy of Money*, pp. 79–81 and 119–30.

[225] On the special aura of gold in particular, see above, pp. 37–40.

(especially cattle and slaves) were used as units of account and means of payment in early Ireland,[226] while silver objects and gold provided an upper stratum of exchange, especially for the elite. For transactions of value comparable to or lower than a silver penny there were a number of possibilities. Barter pure and simple of one commodity for another was perhaps the most basic, and could have been very common. Neither did its prevalence preclude close interaction with monetary exchanges: there are many parallels for barter and currency working side by side in rural as well as urban communities.[227] Exchanges carried out by barter were regulated by late Anglo-Saxon law in exactly the same way as those involving currency.[228] In addition, there could also have been one or more substitute monies: objects which fulfilled some of the roles of coinage when it was unavailable or inappropriate. Coins were measured in weight standards based on seeds, for example,[229] and Christoph Kilger has recently proposed that behind this lies an extremely close relationship between grain and coinage, to the extent that crops could be exchanged as currency.[230] Although wheat, rye, oats and other grains were ubiquitous and universally useful as the staple food-source of the early medieval period, they must have presented problems in day-to-day use as currency, in that they were perishable unless carefully stored and, in small quantities, inconvenient to handle. Yet the very existence of 'substitute' monies – which can be difficult to distinguish from common commodities exchanged in sale or barter – is debatable, at least in the early medieval context.[231] If they were used, then the items that were accepted as substitute monies are obscure. Scholars of early medieval Italy have postulated that *panes* and *scutellae de cambio* ('loaves of bread and containers for them') recorded in the eleventh century may have presented one lower-value money,[232] as may sticks akin to later English tally sticks.[233] There is also a tantalizing mention of leather coins (*corii solidi*) being handed out by Constantine V (741–75) during the siege of Constantinople in 743, with the promise of their being redeemed once the city was taken.[234] But barring the discovery of fresh evidence, the nature and extent of non-monetary exchange is likely to remain an unknown quantity of considerable potential importance.

[226] F. Kelly, *Early Irish Farming*, rev. edn (Dublin, 2000), pp. 587–99.

[227] De Ligt, 'Demand, Supply, Distribution', pp. 37–9.

[228] I Æthelræd, c. 3 (ed. Liebermann I, 220); cf. Loyn, *Anglo-Saxon England*, pp. 120–1.

[229] Cf. *MEC*, pp. 14–15; Kilger, 'Wholeness and Holiness', pp. 264–7.

[230] Kilger, 'Wholeness and Holiness', pp. 269–71. For the limited mechanics of such a practice in Ptolemaic Egypt, see von Reden, *Money in Classical Antiquity*, p. 27.

[231] C. Morrisson, 'Byzantine Money', p. 943.

[232] Bognetti, 'Problema', pp. 56–60.   [233] Rovelli, 'Funzione', p. 532.

[234] *Gesta episcoporum Neapolitanorum*, c. 39 (ed. Waitz, p. 423).

CONCLUSION: COINAGE IN THE ECONOMY

No amount of special pleading will transform Anglo-Saxon England into a fully monetized economy. The coins in circulation were too valuable and not sufficiently diverse to cater for all purposes. Both the elite and the very poor would have had alternatives enough to permit them to turn elsewhere, to other forms of wealth and other types of exchange.

Yet although Anglo-Saxon England may not have been a monetized economy, there was a substantial monetary component to the economy.[235] At any one time coinage must have accounted for only a limited proportion of all transactions that took place in society;[236] how limited is unknowable, though comparisons from the developing world and early modern Europe might suggest something well under 50 per cent (though perhaps more by value).[237] Even this rate surely fluctuated. It must have been substantially lower at all times in western England, and presumably dwindled almost to nothing everywhere in the 750s and 760s and again in the middle of the ninth century; conversely, relatively plentiful supply did not fundamentally alter the nature of coin-use or exchange as a whole. Coins, to put it bluntly, were not indispensable. They were a convenience, not a necessity, and their absence could be sustained by the economy.

Conveniences, nonetheless, can be extremely important, and it is clear that throughout the eighth and ninth centuries there was always a strong impetus to make and use currency which was dictated by the needs of several levels of exchange, not by regnal fiat.[238] Episodes of coinlessness or near-coinlessness were the exception, and could be the result of effectively independent and uncontrollable factors such as bullion supply. Having a substantial circulating stock of currency was the norm, and it presumably fulfilled a constant and considerable demand for coin. This demand is most apparent not in any surviving written sources, but from the large quantity in which coinage was originally produced and in which it percolated out from a small number of mints to hundreds of urban and rural locations in the eastern half of England. It is highly unlikely that all the travelling and transactions needed to produce this volume of loss can be put down to gift-exchange and the movement of luxuries dominated by the elite and a small number of merchants.

---

[235] Devroey, *Économie rurale*, pp. 148–54; M. Aymard, 'Autoconsommation et marchés: Chayanov, Labrousse ou Le Loy Ladurie', *Annales d'histoire sociale et économique* 38 (1983), 1392–410, at p. 1392.

[236] De Ligt, 'Demand, Supply, Distribution', p. 40; for a classic statement to this effect M. Bloch, *Feudal Society*, 2nd edn, 2 vols., trans. L. A. Manyon (London, 1962) I, 65–9.

[237] Above, pp. 285–6.   [238] Above, pp. 154–5, 229–31 and 276–84.

A range of sources can be brought to bear showing a substantially broader clientele and a much more diverse range of socially embedded uses. Coinage was not associated purely with gifts, markets, fines or hoarding: rather, it served all these roles and more for different people at different times. The closeness of these contexts is worth re-emphasizing; all could be found simultaneously, working hand-in-glove across society. Assigning priority to any particular use of coinage is much more problematic, as extant sources are rarely susceptible to quantification. However, the balance of the surviving written and material evidence suggests that the association of coins with markets and commercial use was much more prominent than has been allowed in some recent literature and could have played an important integrative role in exchanges and society as a whole.[239] This use lay at the heart of a rich, well-supplied and varied sphere of monetary exchange.

[239] Laiou, 'Economic and Noneconomic Exchange', p. 688; M. de Cecco, 'Monetary Theory and Roman History', *JEcH* 45 (1985), 809–22, at p. 819.

Chapter 10

CONCLUSION

There is much that simply is not and cannot be known about the coinage of southern England in the years 757–865. Aspects of how it fitted into contemporary government and was used in society remain unclear, as does the (probably large) proportion of exchanges which went on without it. But it does not stand alone. The coinage bears comparison with the English currency minted before and after this period, as well as that of contemporary kingdoms elsewhere in western Europe. Other sources, written and archaeological, are likewise essential to its interpretation. By comparison and careful analysis it yields unique testimony to the historian of early medieval Europe; testimony which could not be gleaned from elsewhere. Above all, access to the totality of surviving material (as Michael Dolley used to put it) brings home just how much coinage there was in late eighth- and early ninth-century England: how much was being minted and how much it was being used. There were of course significant variations – chronological, geographical and practical – but in relation to the rest of Britain and Europe in the early Middle Ages, the eastern part of England (especially in the years *c.* 780–830) still emerges as a place of significant monetary expansion, circulation and dynamism. The coinage at this time was, in short, a major economic resource which could in principle be a great source of power and income to whoever controlled it.

However, 'control' is not a word to be taken without qualification, and in the case of early medieval currency, 'control' meant a cacophony of separate relationships and interests. The intensity of this control – usually taken as the degree to which kings micro-managed and profited from the currency – was not necessarily commensurate with the scale of the monetary economy, except in so far as the ruler took responsibility for the existence and standards of a circulating coinage. Important elements of the coinage such as the scale of production and the general flow of currency and bullion lay well outside the remit of the king's role.

Rather, the economic logic of profit and maximum exploitation was only one of the motivations which governed the interaction of power and resources, as has long been realized in other branches of early medieval history: kings and others were guided as much, and often more, by social and ideological concerns. Their policy towards coinage was no exception. Standardization, reliability and general recognition of kingly authority were the key features which came in with the expanded royal role in the mid eighth century. More diverse or sophisticated expressions of kingship depended partly on the initiative of individual rulers, and partly on that of other agencies with a say in minting. These other agencies were, in England, a tight-knit community of moneyers and die-cutters based in a relatively small number of towns on or near the coast. Ealdormen and most abbots and bishops apparently had no role to play in minting, in contrast to their Carolingian counterparts, but this did not make the resultant English pennies straightforwardly and consistently 'royal'. At all times royal interests were refracted through the lens of more localized interests, which could accrue a surprising degree of independence, extending to the design of coinage and even hesitation in recognizing the ruling authorities. The moneyers and die-cutters behind the coinage were a long-established body, but from at least the middle of the eighth century they provided a direct if unevenly utilized conduit through which the king could oversee and potentially manipulate the coinage. Taken as a whole, the development of 'control' over the coinage can be summed up as the history of interaction between the king and local minting agencies, and any assessment must take full account of the roles and responsibilities of both groups and the changing dynamic that existed between them. Coinage was thus a considerable source of symbolic and economic power, but not one which was exploited straightforwardly or monopolistically.

It ought to be noted that these points can be fully brought out only with reference to the neighbours and heirs of England in the period 757–865. To a greater or lesser extent the same conclusion that 'royal coinage' was a grey area therefore applies at other times and places as well: to the contemporary realms mentioned in the chapters above, as well as to their successors in England and on the Continent. The development in the relationship between coinage and power was not identical across Europe, but in very few cases can it be said to have been simple. In the later Carolingian empire and its successors, for example, the portion of the currency struck under or in the name of the current king shrank in favour of immobilized and 'feudal' issues in the names of various potentates. These remain a striking indicator of the growth of the power of secular and ecclesiastical magnates at the expense of the king's in the late ninth and the tenth century.[1] This rarely amounted to wholesale rejection of the king, but rather to gradual modification of the relationship between him and his subordinates, as manifested through various other rights and powers.

In England, on the other hand, coinage remained very much the preserve of kings and moneyers, albeit tending towards a much broader role for minting within royal government as the late ninth and early tenth centuries wore on. This built ultimately on the stronger royal involvement in the relationship with the moneyers which emerged in Wessex in the aftermath of 856, and also, from the time of Alfred onwards, on an extension of the geographically restricted minting network to new locations.[2] The moneyers never faded into insignificance, but their heyday as relatively independent agents working at a safe distance from the centres of royal power ended in the second half of the ninth century.

---

[1] J. Lafaurie, 'Numismatique: des Carolingiens aux Capétiens', *Cahiers de civilisation médiévale* 13 (1970), 117–37; F. Dumas, 'Le début de l'époque féodale en France d'après les monnaies', *Bulletin du Cercle d'études numismatiques* (1973), 65–77.

[2] Dolley and Metcalf, 'Reform'; Blackburn, 'Mints, Burhs and the Grateley Code'.

BIBLIOGRAPHY

PRINTED PRIMARY SOURCES

Æthelweard, *Chronicon*, ed. A. Campbell, *The Chronicle of Æthelweard* (London, 1962)

Alcuin, *Epistolae*, ed. E. Duemmler, MGH *Epistolae* IV (Berlin, 1895), 1–493

Versus de patribus, regibus et sanctis Euboricensis ecclesiae, ed. P. Godman, *The Bishops, Saints and Kings of York* (Oxford, 1982)

Aldhelm, *De virginitate*, ed. R. Ehwald, MGH *Auctores antiquissimi* XV (Berlin, 1919), 211–471

trans. M. Herren and M. Lapidge, *Aldhelm: The Prose Works* (Ipswich, 1979)

Annales Bertiniani, ed. F. Grat, J.Vielliard and S. Clémencet (Paris, 1964)

trans. J. L. Nelson, *The Annals of St-Bertin* (Manchester, 1991)

Anglo-Saxon Chronicle, ed. C. Plummer, *Two of the Saxon Chronicles Parallel*, 2 vols. (Oxford, 1892–9)

trans. D. Whitelock, D. C. Douglas and S. I. Tucker, *The Anglo-Saxon Chronicle: A Revised Translation* (London, 1961)

Asser, *Life of King Alfred*, ed. W. H. Stevenson, *Asser's Life of King Alfred, Together with the Annals of St Neots, Erroneously Ascribed to Asser*, new imp. (Oxford, 1959)

Bede, *De templo expositio*, ed. D. Hurst, *Baedae Venerabilis opera exegetica*, CCSL 119A (Turnhout, 1969)

Historia abbatum, ed. C. Plummer, *Venerabilis Baedae Opera historica*, 2 vols. (Oxford, 1896) I, 364–87

Historia ecclesiastica gentis Anglorum, ed. B. Colgrave and R. A. B. Mynors, *Bede's Ecclesiastical History of the English People* (Oxford, 1969)

In libros regum quaestiones xxx, PL **91**, cols. 715A–736C

Birch, W. de G. (ed.), *Cartilarium Saxonicum: A Collection of Charters Relating to Anglo-Saxon History*, 3 vols. (London, 1885–99)

Bischoff, B. and Lapidge, M. (eds.), *Biblical Commentaries from the Canterbury School of Theodore and Hadrian* (Cambridge, 1994)

Boethius/Alfred, *De consolatione philosophiae/Froferboc*, ed. and trans. M. Godden and S. Irvine, *The Old English Boethius: An Edition of the Old English Versions of Boethius's Consolation of Philosophy*, 2 vols. (Oxford, 2009)

Boniface, *Epistolae*, ed. M. Tangl, MGH *Epistolae selectae* I (Berlin, 1916)

Campbell, A. (ed.), *Charters of Rochester* (London, 1973)

Bibliography

Capitularia regum Francorum, ed. A. Boretius and V. Krause, MGH *Legum sectio* II, 2 vols. (Hanover, 1883–97)

Charlemagne, *Epistolae*, ed. E. Dümmler, MGH *Epistolae* IV (*Epistolae Merowingici et Karolini aevi* II) (Berlin, 1895)

Codex Carolinus, ed. W. Gundlach, MGH *Epistolae* III (*Epistolae Merowingici et Karolini aevi* I) (Berlin, 1892)

Codex Theodosianus, ed. T. Mommsen and P. Meyer, *Theodosiani libri XVI cum constitutionibus Sirmondianis et leges novellae ad Theodosianum pertinentes*, 2 vols. (Berlin, 1905)

Concilium Chalcedonense, ed. E. Schwartz, *Acta conciliorum oecumenicorum 2: concilium universale Chalcedonense*, 6 vols. (Berlin, 1917–32)

Constitutum Constantini, ed. H. Fuhrmann, MGH *Fontes iuris Germanici antique in usum scholarum* X (Hanover, 1968)

Einhard, *Vita Karoli*, ed. O. Holder-Egger, MGH *Scriptores rerum Germanicarum in usum scholarum* XXV (Hanover, 1911)

Erchempert, *Historia Langobardorum Beneventanorum*, ed. G. Waitz, MGH *Scriptores rerum Langobardicarum et Italicarum* I (Hanover, 1878), 231–64

Ermoldus Nigellus, *In honorem Hludowici carmen*, ed. E. Duemmler, MGH *Poetae latini aevi Carolini* II (Berlin, 1884), 1–91

Eusebius/Rufinus, *Historia ecclesiastica*, ed. E. Schwartz and T. Mommsen, *Die Kirchengeschichte*, 2 vols. (Berlin, 1903–8)

Felix, *Vita sancti Guthlaci*, ed. B. Colgrave, *Felix's Life of St Guthlac* (Cambridge, 1956)

Gelling, M. (ed.), *Early Charters of the Thames Valley* (Leicester, 1979)

Gesta episcoporum Neapolitanorum, ed. G. Waitz, MGH *Scriptores rerum Langobardicarum et Italicarum* I (Hanover, 1878), 398–466

Gesta sanctorum patrum Fontanellensis coenobii, ed. F. Lohier and J. Laporte (Rouen, 1936)

Hermann of Laon, *De miraculis S. Mariae Laudunensis*, PL **156**, cols. 961B–1018A

Historia Augusta, ed. S. Ballou, H. Peter and D. Magie, *Scriptores historiae Augustae*, 3 vols. (London, 1921–32)

Historia regum, ed. T. Arnold, *Symeonis monachi opera omnia*, 2 vols. (London, 1882)

Honorantie civitatis Papie, ed. C. Brühl and C. Violante, *Die Honorantie civitatis Papie: Transkription, Edition, Kommentar* (Cologne, 1983)

Isidore, *Etymologiae*, ed. W. M. Lindsay, 2 vols. (Oxford, 1911)

Johnson, C. (ed. and trans.), *The De Moneta of Nicholas Oresme and English Mint Documents* (London, 1956)

Kelly, S. (ed.), *Charters of Abingdon Abbey*, 2 vols. (Oxford, 2000–1)
  Charters of Peterborough Abbey (Oxford, 2009)
  Charters of St Augustine's Abbey, Canterbury, and Minster-in-Thanet (Oxford, 1995)
  Charters of Selsey (Oxford, 1998)

Keynes, S. and Lapidge, M., *Alfred the Great: Asser's Life of King Alfred and Other Contemporary Sources* (London, 1983)

Krapp, G. P. and van K. Dobbie, E. (eds.), *The Anglo-Saxon Poetic Records*, 6 vols. (New York, 1931–42)

Lantfred, *Translatio et miracula S. Swithuni*, ed. and trans. M. Lapidge, *The Cult of St Swithun*, Winchester Studies 4.ii (Oxford, 2003), pp. 252–333

Liebermann, F. (ed.), *Die Gesetze der Angelsachsen*, 3 vols. (Halle, 1903–16)

Bibliography

Life of St Æthelberht, ed. M. R. James, 'Two Lives of St Ethelbert, King and Martyr', *EHR* **32** (1917), 214–44

Lupus of Ferri ères, *Epistolae*, ed. E. Dümmler, MGH *Epistolae* VI (*Epistolae Merowingici et Karolini aevi* IV) (Berlin, 1925), 1–126

Migne, J. P. (ed.), *Patrologiae cursus completus. Series (Latina) prima*, 221 vols. (Paris, 1844–64)

Miller, S. (ed.), *Charters of the New Minster, Winchester* (Oxford, 2001)

Miracula S. Benedicti, ed. O. Holder-Egger, MGH *Scriptores* XV.i (Stuttgart, 1887), 474–97

Napier, A. S. (ed.), *Old English Glosses, Chiefly Unpublished* (Oxford, 1900)

Procopius, *History of the Wars*, ed. H. B. Dewing, 5 vols. (London, 1914–28)

Pseudo-Cyprian, *De duodecim abusivis saeculi*, ed. S. Hellmann, *Texte und Untersuchungen zur geschichte der Altchristlichen Literatur* **34** (I) (Leipzig, 1910), 1–61

Rimbert, *Vita Anskarii*, ed. G. Waitz, MGH *Scriptores rerum Germanicarum in usum scholarum separatim editi* LV (Hanover, 1884)

Shippey, T. (ed. and trans.), *Poems of Wisdom and Learning in Old English* (Cambridge, 1976)

Stapleton, T. (ed.), *Chronicon Petroburgense* (London, 1849)

Tangl, M. (ed.), *Die Briefe des Heiligen Bonifatius und Lullus*, MGH *Epistolae selectae* I (Berlin, 1916)

Translatio et miracula S. Adelphi Mettensis, ed. L. de Heinemann, MGH *Scriptores* XV.i (Stuttgart, 1887), 294–6

Whitelock, D. (ed.), *Anglo-Saxon Wills* (Cambridge, 1930)

Whitelock, D. (ed. and trans.), *The Will of Æthelgifu* (Oxford, 1968)

PRINTED SECONDARY WORKS

Abdy, R. and Williams, G., 'A Catalogue of Hoards and Single Finds from the British Isles, *c.* AD 410–675', in *Coinage and History*, ed. Cook and Williams, pp. 11–74

Abels, R. *Lordship and Military Obligation in Anglo-Saxon England* (Berkeley, CA, 1988)

Abramson, T. (ed.), *Studies in Early Medieval Coinage 2: New Perspectives* (Woodbridge, 2011)

Addyman, P. V., 'A Dark-Age Settlement at Maxey, Northants', *Medieval Archaeology* 8 (1964), 20–73

Airlie, S., 'The Aristocracy in the Service of the State in the Carolingian Period', in *Staat im frühen Mittelalter*, ed. Airlie, Pohl and Reimitz, pp. 93–111

Airlie, S., Pohl, W. and Reimitz, H. (eds.), *Staat im frühen Mittelalter* (Vienna, 2006)

Algazi, G., Groebner, V. and Jussen, B. (eds.), *Negotiating the Gift. Pre-Modern Figurations of Exchange* (Göttingen, 2003)

Allen, D. F., *A Catalogue of English Coins in the British Museum: The Cross-and-Crosslets ('Tealby') Type of Henry II* (London, 1951)

Allen, M., *The Durham Mint* (London, 2003)

'The English Currency and the Commercialization of England before the Black Death', in *Medieval Money Matters*, ed. Wood, pp. 31–50

'Medieval English Die-Output', *BNJ* **74** (2004), 39–49

'The Weight Standard of the English Coinage, 1158–1279', *NC* **165** (2005), 227–33

Bibliography

Althoff, G., *Family, Friends and Followers: Political and Social Bonds in Early Medieval Europe*, trans. C. Carroll (Cambridge, 2004)

Otto III, trans. P. G. Jestice (University Park, PA, 2003)

Die Ottonen. Königsherrschaft ohne Staat, 2nd edn (Stuttgart, 2005)

Anderson, E. R., *Cynewulf: Structure, Style and Theme in His Poetry* (Rutherford, NJ, and London, 1983)

Anderton, M. (ed.), *Anglo-Saxon Trading Centres: Beyond the Emporia* (Glasgow, 1999)

Andrews, P. (ed.), *The Coins and Pottery from Hamwic*, Southampton Finds 1 (Southampton, 1988)

Andrews, P. and Metcalf, D. M., 'A Coinage for King Cynewulf of Wessex?', in *Sceattas*, ed. Hill and Metcalf (Oxford, 1984), pp. 175–9

Angenendt, A., Braucks, T., Busch, R. and Lutterbach, H., 'Counting Piety in the Early and High Middle Ages', in *Ordering Medieval Society. Perspectives on Intellectual and Practical Modes of Shaping Social Relations*, ed. B. Jussen (Philadelphia, PA, 2001), pp. 15–54

Anton, H., *Fürstenspiegel und Herrscherethos in der Karolingerzeit*, Bonner Historische Forschungen **32** (Bonn, 1968)

'Pseudo-Cyprian: *De duodecimo abusivis saeculi* und sein Einfluß auf den Kontinent, insbesondere auf die karolingischen Fürstenspiegel', in *Die Iren und Europa im früheren Mittelalter*, ed. H. Lowe, 2 vols. (Stuttgart, 1982) II, 568–617

Appadurai, A., 'Introduction: Commodities and the Politics of Value', in *The Social Life of Things: Commodities in Cultural Perspective*, ed. A. Appadurai (Cambridge, 1986), pp. 3–63

Applbaum, K., 'The Anthropology of Markets', in *Handbook*, ed. Carrier, pp. 275–89

Archibald, M., 'The Coinage of Beonna in the Light of the Middle Harling Hoard', *BNJ* **55** (1985), 10–54

'The Mayfield (Sussex) 1968 Hoard of English Pence and French Gros, *c.* 1307', in *Mints, Dies and Currency: Essays Dedicated to the Memory of Albert Baldwin*, ed. R. A. G. Carson (London, 1971), pp. 151–9

'A Sceat of Ethelbert I of East Anglia and Recent Finds of Coins of Beonna', *BNJ* **65** (1995), 1–19

'A Ship Type of Athelstan I of East Anglia', *BNJ* **52** (1982), 34–40

Archibald, M., Brown, M. and Webster, L., 'The Heirs of Rome: The Shaping of Britain A.D. 400–900', in *The Transformation of the Roman World, A.D. 400–900*, ed. L. Webster and M. Brown (London, 1997), pp. 208–48

Archibald, M. and Cowell, M. R., 'The Fineness of Northumbrian Sceattas', in *Metallurgy in Numismatics*, ed. Oddy, II, 55–64

Archibald, M., Lang, J. and Milne, G., 'Four Early Medieval Coin Dies from the London Waterfront', *NC* **155** (1995), 163–200

Armstrong, S., 'Carolingian Coin Hoards and the Impact of the Viking Raids in the Ninth Century', *NC* **158** (1998), 131–64

Arnold, C. and Wardle, P., 'Early Medieval Settlement Patterns in England', *Medieval Archaeology* **25** (1981), 145–9

Arslan, E. A., 'Emissioni monetarie e segni del potere', *Settimane* **39** (1992), 791–854

'Sequenze dei conii e valutazioni quantitative delle monetazioni argentea ed aurea di Benevento longobarda', in *Rythmes de la production monétaire de l'Antiquité à*

Bibliography

nos jours, ed. G. Depeyrot, T. Hackens and G. Moucharte (Louvain-la-Neuve, 1987), pp. 387–409

Astill, G. G., 'Archaeology, Economics and Early Medieval Europe', *Oxford Journal of Archaeology* **4** (1985), 215–31

'Community, Identity and the Later Anglo-Saxon Town: The Case of Southern England', in *People and Space in the Middle Ages*, ed. A. Reynolds, W. Davies and G. Halsall (Turnhout, 2006), pp. 233–54

'General Survey 600–1300', in *Cambridge Urban History*, ed. Palliser, pp. 27–50

Aymard, M., 'Autoconsommation et marchés: Chayanov, Labrousse ou Le Loy Ladurie', *Annales d'histoire sociale et économique* **38** (1983), 1392–410

Bachrach, B., *Early Carolingian Warfare: Prelude to Empire* (Philadelphia, PA, 2000)

Bailey, R. N., 'The Gandersheim Casket and Anglo-Saxon Stone Sculpture', in *Das Gandersheimer Runenkästchen. Internationales Kolloquium Braunschweig, 24.–26. März 1999*, ed. R. Marth (Braunschweig, 2000), pp. 43–52

Bak, J. M., 'Medieval Symbology of the State: Percy E. Schramm's Contribution', *Viator* **4** (1973), 33–64

Balzaretti, R. and Nelson, J. L., 'Trade, Industry and the Wealth of King Alfred', *P&P* **135** (1992), 142–63

Banaji, J., *Agrarian Change in Late Antiquity: Gold, Labour, and Aristocratic Dominance*, 2nd edn (Oxford, 2007)

Banton, N., 'Ealdormen and Earls in England from the Reign of King Alfred to the Reign of King Æthelred II' (unpublished D.Phil. thesis, University of Oxford, 1981)

Barlow, F., *Edward the Confessor*, 2nd edn (New Haven, CT, and London, 1997)

Barnish, S., Lee, A. D. and Whitby, M., 'Government and Administration', in *NCAH* XIV, pp. 164–206

Bartlett, R., *England under the Norman and Angevin Kings* (Oxford, 2000)

Bassett, S., 'Divide and Rule? The Military Infrastructure of Eighth- and Ninth-Century Mercia', *EME* **15** (2007), 53–85

Bassett, S. (ed.), *The Origins of Anglo-Saxon Kingdoms* (Leicester, 1989)

Bastien, P., *Le buste monétaire des empereurs romains*, 3 vols. (Wetteren, 1992)

Bately, J., 'Did King Alfred Actually Translate Anything? The Integrity of the Alfredian Canon Revisited', *Medium Aevum* **78** (2009), 189–215

Bates, D., 'England and the "Feudal Revolution"', *Settimane* **61** (2000), 1–49

Bautier, R. H., 'La chancellerie et les actes royaux dans les royaumes carolingiens', *Bibliothèque de l'École des chartes* **142** (1984), 5–80

Baxter, S., *The Earls of Mercia. Lordship and Power in Late Anglo-Saxon England* (Oxford, 2007)

Baxter, S. and Blair, J., 'Land Tenure and Royal Patronage in the Early English Kingdom: A Model and a Case Study', *Anglo-Norman Studies* **28** (2005), 19–46

Bayley, J., 'The Production of Brass in Antiquity with Particular Reference to Roman Britain', in *2000 Years of Zinc and Brass*, ed. Craddock, pp. 7–27

Bazelmans, J., 'Beyond Power. Ceremonial Exchanges in *Beowulf*', in *Rituals of Power*, ed. Theuws and Nelson, pp. 311–75

By Weapons Made Worthy: Lords, Retainers and Their Relationship in Beowulf (Amsterdam, 1999)

Bedos Rezak, B., 'The King Enthroned: A New Theme in Anglo-Saxon Royal Iconography. The Seal of Edward the Confessor and Its Political Implications', in *Kings and Kingship*, ed. J. Rosenthal (Binghampton, NY, 1986), pp. 53–88

Bibliography

Beresford, G. and Geddes, J., *Goltho: The Development of an Early Medieval Manor, c. 850–1150* (London, 1987)

Bernareggi, E., *Moneta Langobardorum* (Lugano, 1989)

Bianchi Bandinelli, R., *Rome, the Late Empire. Roman Art, A.D. 200–400*, trans. P. Green (London, 1971)

Biddle, M., 'Towns', in *Archaeology of Anglo-Saxon England*, ed. Wilson, pp. 99–150
  'Winchester: The Development of an Early Capital', in *Vor- und Frühformen der europäischen Stadt im Mittelalter*, ed. H. Jankuhn, W. Schlesinger and H. Steuer, 2 vols. (Göttingen, 1975) I, 229–61

Biddle, M. and Keene, D., 'Winchester in the Eleventh and Twelfth Centuries', in *Winchester in the Early Middle Ages: An Edition and Discussion of the Winton Domesday*, ed. M. Biddle (Oxford, 1976), pp. 241–448

Biddle, M. and Kjølbye-Biddle, B., 'The Repton Stone', *ASE* 14 (1985), 233–92

Bijsterveld, A.-J., *Do ut des: Gift Giving, Memoria, and Conflict Management in the Medieval Low Countries* (Hilversum, 2007)

Bischoff, B., *Anecdota novissima: Texte des vierten bis sechzehnten Jahrhunderts* (Stuttgart, 1984)
  Latin Palaeography: Antiquity and the Middle Ages, trans. D. Ó Cróinín and D. Ganz (Cambridge, 1990)

Bisson, T. N., *Conservation of Coinage: Monetary Exploitation and Its Restraint in France, Catalonia and Aragon (c. 1000–c. 1125)* (Oxford, 1979)

Bjork, R. E. and Niles, J. D. (eds.), *A Beowulf Handbook* (Exeter, 1996)

Blackburn, M., 'Alfred's Coinage Reforms in Context', in *Alfred the Great*, ed. Reuter, pp. 199–217
  'Coin Circulation in Germany during the Early Middle Ages: The Evidence of Single-Finds', in *Fernhandel und Geldwirtschaft. Beiträge zum deutschen Münzwesen in sächsischer und salischer Zeit: Ergebnisse des Dannenberg-Kolloquiums 1990*, ed. B. Kluge (Sigmaringen, 1993), pp. 37–54
  'The Coin-Finds', in *Means of Exchange*, ed. Skre, pp. 29–74
  'Coin Finds and Coin Circulation in Lindsey, c. 600–900', in *Pre-Viking Lindsey*, ed. A. Vince (Lincoln, 1993), pp. 80–9
  'The Coinage of Scandinavian York', in *Aspects of Anglo-Scandinavian York*, ed. R. A. Hall *et al.* (York, 2004), pp. 325–49
  'Currency under the Vikings, Part 1: Guthrum and the Earliest Danelaw Coinages', *BNJ* 75 (2005), 18–43
  'Currency under the Vikings. Part 3: Ireland, Wales, Isle of Man and Scotland in the Ninth and Tenth Centuries', *BNJ* 77 (2007), 119–49
  'Gold in England during the "Age of Silver" (Eighth–Eleventh Centuries)', in *Silver Economy in the Viking Age*, ed. J. Graham-Campbell and G. Williams (Walnut Creek, CA, 2007), pp. 55–98
  'The London Mint in the Reign of Alfred', in *Kings, Currency and Alliances*, ed. Blackburn and Dumville, pp. 105–23
  'Mints, Burhs and the Grateley Code, cap. 14.2', in *The Defence of Wessex: The Burghal Hidage and Anglo-Saxon Fortifications*, ed. D. H. Hill and A. R. Rumble (Manchester, 1996), pp. 160–75
  'Money and Coinage', in *NCMH* II, pp. 538–59
  '"Productive Sites" and the Pattern of Coin Loss in England, 600–1180', in *Markets*, ed. Pestell and Ulmschneider, pp. 20–36

Bibliography

'Stenton and Anglo-Saxon Numismatics', in *Anglo-Saxon England Fifty Years On*, ed. D. Matthew (Reading, 1994), pp. 61–81

'A Survey of Anglo-Saxon and Frisian Coins with Runic Inscriptions', in *Old English Runes and Their Continental Background*, ed. A. Bammesberger (Heidelberg, 1991), pp. 137–89

'Two New Types of Anglo-Saxon Gold Shillings', in *Coinage and History*, ed. Cook and Williams, pp. 127–40

What Factors Govern the Number of Coins Found on an Archaeological Site?', in *Coins and Archaeology: Medieval Archaeology Research Group, Proceedings of the First Meeting at Isegran, Norway 1988*, ed. H. Clarke and E. Schia, BAR International Series 556 (Oxford, 1989), pp. 15–24

Blackburn, M. (ed.), *Anglo-Saxon Monetary History* (Leicester, 1986)

Blackburn, M. and Dumville, D. (eds.), *Kings, Currency and Alliances: History and Coinage of Southern England in the Ninth Century* (Woodbridge, 1998)

Blackburn, M. and Lyon, C. S. S., 'Regional Die-Production in Cnut's *Quatrefoil* Issue', in *Anglo-Saxon Monetary History*, ed. Blackburn, pp. 223–72

Blackmore, L., 'La céramique du Vème au Xème siècle à Londres et dans la région londonienne', in *La céramique du Vème au Xème siècle dans l'Europe du Nord-Ouest*, ed. D. Piton (Arras, 1993), pp. 129–50

'Pottery: Trade and Tradition', in *Wics*, ed. Hill and Cowie, pp. 22–42

Blair, J., *The Church in Anglo-Saxon Society* (Oxford, 2005)

Early Medieval Surrey: Landholding, Church and Settlement before 1300 (Stroud, 1991)

Bland, R., 'Roman Gold Coins in Britain', *International Committee of Money and Banking Museums e-Proceedings* 3 (Utrecht, 2008), pp. 31–43

Blattmann, M., '"Ein Unglück für sein Volk". Der Zusammenhang zwischen Fehlverhalten des Königs und Volkswohl in Quellen des 7.–12. Jahrhunderts', *Frühmittelalterliche Studien* 30 (1996), 80–102

Blinkhorn, P., 'Of Cabbages and Kings: Production, Trade and Consumption in Middle-Saxon England', in *Anglo-Saxon Trading Centres*, ed. Anderton, pp. 4–23

Bloch, M., *Feudal Society*, 2nd edn, 2 vols., trans. L. A. Manyon (London, 1962)

'The Symbolism of Money in Imerina', in *Money and the Morality of Exchange*, ed. Parry and Bloch, pp. 165–90

Blockley, K., Blockley, M., Blockley, P., Frere, S. S. and Stow, S., *Excavations in the Marlowe Car Park and Surrounding Areas*, 3 vols., Archaeology of Canterbury 5 (Canterbury, 1995)

Blunt, C. E., 'The Anglo-Saxon Coinage and the Historian', *Medieval Archaeology* 4 (1960), 1–15

'Anglo-Saxon Coins Found in Italy', in *Anglo-Saxon Monetary History*, ed. Blackburn, pp. 159–69

'The Coinage of Athelstan, King of England 924–939', *BNJ* 42 (1974), 35–158

'The Coinage of Offa', in *Anglo-Saxon Coins*, ed. Dolley, pp. 39–62

Blunt, C. E., Lyon, C. S. S. and Stewart, I., 'The Coinage of Southern England, 796–840', *BNJ* 32 (1963), 1–74

Blunt, C. E., Stewart, I. and Lyon, C. S. S., *Coinage in Tenth-Century England from Edward the Elder to Edgar's Reform* (Oxford, 1989)

Bognetti, G. P., 'Il problema monetario dell'economia longobarda e il "panis" e la "scutella de cambio"', in *Storia dell'economia italiana*, ed. C. M. Cipolla (Turin, 1959), pp. 51–60

Bibliography

Bogucki, M., 'Two Northumbrian Stycas of Eanred and Æthelred II from Early Medieval Truso in Poland', *BNJ* **79** (2009), 34–42

Bohannon, P., 'Some Principles of Exchange and Investment among the Tiv', *American Anthropologist* **57** (1955), 60–9

Bolton, J., 'What Is Money? What Is a Money Economy? When Did a Money Economy Emerge in Medieval England?', in *Medieval Money Matters*, ed. Wood, pp. 1–15

Bompaire, M. and Depierre, G., 'Le trésor carolingien de Dijon, rue du Chapeau Rouge', *BSFN* **44** (1989), 577–81

Booth, J., 'Monetary Alliance or Technical Co-operation? The Coinage of Berhtwulf of Mercia (840–52)', in *Kings, Currency and Alliances*, ed. Blackburn and Dumville, pp. 63–103

'Northumbrian Coinage and the Productive Site at South Newbald ("Sancton")', *ASSAH* **11** (2000), 83–97

'*Sceattas* in Northumbria', in *Sceattas*, ed. Hill and Metcalf, pp. 71–111

Bouchard, C. B., *Holy Entrepreneurs: Cistercians, Knights and Economic Exchange in Twelfth-Century Burgundy* (Ithaca, NY, and London, 1991)

Bougard, F., 'Public Power and Authority', in *Italy in the Early Middle Ages*, ed. C. La Rocca (Oxford, 2002), pp. 34–58

Bourdieu, P., *Distinction. A Social Critique of the Judgement of Taste*, trans. R. Nice (London, 1984)

The Logic of Practice, trans. R. Nice (Cambridge, 1990)

Outline of a Theory of Practice, trans. R. Nice (Cambridge, 1977)

Bourdillon, J., 'The Animal Provisioning of Saxon Southampton', in *Environment and Economy in Anglo-Saxon England*, ed. J. Rackham (York, 1994), pp. 120–5

Brand, J. D., *Periodic Change of Type in the Anglo-Saxon and Norman Periods* (Rochester, 1984)

Britnell, R., *The Commercialisation of English Society, 1000–1500*, 2nd edn (Manchester, 1996)

Brooke, C. N. L., Stewart, B. H. I. H., Pollard, J. G. and Volk, T. R. (eds.), *Studies in Numismatic Method Presented to Philip Grierson* (Cambridge, 1983)

Brookes, S., *Economics and Social Change in Anglo-Saxon Kent AD 400–900: Landscapes, Communities and Exchange*, BAR British Series **431** (Oxford, 2007)

Brooks, N., 'Alfredian Government', in *Alfred the Great*, ed. Reuter, pp. 153–73

Bede and the English (Jarrow, 1999)

Church, State and Access to Resources in Early Anglo-Saxon England, Brixworth Lecture, second series, 2 (Brixworth, 2003)

'The Development of Military Obligations in Eighth- and Ninth-Century England', in *England before the Conquest: Studies in Primary Sources Presented to Dorothy Whitelock*, ed. P. Clemoes and K. Hughes (Cambridge, 1971), pp. 69–84

The Early History of the Church of Canterbury. Christ Church from 597 to 1066 (Leicester, 1984)

'England in the Ninth Century: The Crucible of Defeat', *TRHS* **29** (1979), 1–20

'English Identity from Bede to the Millennium', *Haskins Society Journal* **14** (2005), 33–51

'Epilogue', in *Coinage in Ninth-Century Northumbria*, ed. Metcalf, pp. 397–401

'Rochester Bridge, A.D. 43–1381', in *Traffic and Politics: The Construction and Management of Rochester Bridge, A.D. 43–1993*, ed. N. Yates and J. M. Gibson (Woodbridge, 1994), pp. 3–40

Bibliography

Brown, M., *The Book of Cerne: Prayer, Patronage and Power in Ninth-Century England* (London, 1996)

'The Lichfield Angel and the Middle Saxon Context: Lichfield as a Centre for Insular Art', *Journal of the British Archaeological Association* **160** (2007), 8–19

The Lindisfarne Gospels: Society, Spirituality and the Scribe (London, 2003)

'Mercian Manuscripts? The "Tiberius" Group and Its Historical Context', in *Mercia*, ed. Brown and Farr, pp. 278–90

Brown, M. and Farr, C. (eds.), *Mercia: An Anglo-Saxon Kingdom in Europe* (London, 2001)

Bruand, O., *Voyageurs et marchandises aux temps carolingiens* (Brussels, 2002)

Bullough, D., '*Imagines regum* and Their Significance in the Early Medieval West', in *Carolingian Renewal: Sources and Heritage* (Manchester, 1991), pp. 39–96

Burghart, M. A., 'The Mercian Polity, 716–918' (unpublished Ph.D. dissertation, King's College London, 2007)

Burnett, A., *Coinage in the Roman World* (London, 1987)

Buttrey, T. V. 'Calculating Ancient Coin Production I: Facts and Fantasies', *NC* **153** (1993), 335–51

'Calculating Ancient Coin Production II: Why It Cannot Be Done,' *NC* **154** (1994), 341–52

Cabrol, F. (ed.), *Dictionnaire de l'archéologie chrétienne et de liturgie*, 15 vols. (Paris, 1907–53)

Cameron, A. (ed.), *The Byzantine and Early Islamic Near East 3: States, Resources and Armies* (Princeton, NJ, 1995)

Cameron, A., Ward-Perkins, B. and Whitby, M. (eds.), *The New Cambridge Ancient History XIV: Late Antiquity: Empire and Successors, A.D. 425–600* (Cambridge, 2000)

Campbell, A., *Old English Grammar* (Oxford, 1959)

Campbell, J., 'Bede's Words for Places', in *Names, Words and Graves: Early Medieval Settlement*, ed. P. H. Sawyer (Leeds, 1979), pp. 34–54

'Hundreds and Leets: A Survey with Suggestions', in *Medieval East Anglia*, ed. C. Harper-Bill (Woodbridge, 2005), pp. 153–67

'The Late Anglo-Saxon State: A Maximum View', *Proceedings of the British Academy* **87** (1995), 39–65

'The Sale of Land and the Economics of Power in Early England: Problems and Possibilities', *Haskins Society Journal* **1** (1989), 23–37

'The United Kingdom of England: The Anglo-Saxon Achievement', in *Uniting the Kingdom? The Making of British History*, ed. A. Grant and K. Stringer (London, 1995), pp. 31–47

Carli, F., *Storia del Commercio Italiano I: il mercato nell'alto Medio Evo* (Padua, 1934)

Carrié, J.-M., 'L'état à la recherche de nouveaux modes de financement des armées (Rome et Byzance, IVe–VIIIe siècles)', in *Byzantine and Early Near East*, ed. Cameron, pp. 27–60

Carrier, J., 'Gifts, Commodities, and Social Relations: A Maussian View of Exchange', *Sociological Forum* **6** (1991), 119–36

Gifts and Commodities: Exchange and Western Capitalism since 1700 (London, 1995)

Carrier, J. (ed.), *A Handbook of Economic Anthropology* (Cheltenham, 2005)

Carter, G., 'Comparison of Methods for Calculating the Total Number of Dies from Die-Link Statistics', in *Statistics and Numismatics*, ed. C. Carcassonne and T. Hackens (Strasbourg, 1981), pp. 204–13

Bibliography

Cerati, A., *Caractère annonaire et assiette de l'impôt foncier au Bas-Empire* (Paris, 1975)

Chadwick, H. M., *Studies on Anglo-Saxon Institutions* (Cambridge, 1905)

Challis, C. (ed.), *A New History of the Royal Mint* (Cambridge, 1992)

Chandavarkar, A. G., 'Money and Credit (1858–1947)', in *The Cambridge Economic History of India II, c. 1757–c. 1970*, ed. D. Kumar (Cambridge, 1983), pp. 762–803

Chaplais, P., 'The Anglo-Saxon Chancery: from the Diploma to the Writ', *Journal of the Society of Archivists* **3.4** (1966), 160–76

'The Origin and Authenticity of the Royal Anglo-Saxon Diploma', *Journal of the Society of Archivists* **3.2** (1965), 48–61

Charles-Edwards, T., 'Anglo-Saxon Kinship Revisited', in *The Anglo-Saxons*, ed. Hines, pp. 171–204

'Kinship, Status and the Origin of the Hide', *P&P* **56** (1972), 3–33

Chazelle, C., *The Crucified God in the Carolingian Era. Theology and Art of Christ's Passion* (Cambridge, 2001)

Cheal, D., *Gift Economy* (London, 1988)

Cherry, J. and Hodges, R., 'The Dating of *Hamwih*: Saxon Southampton Reconsidered', *Antiquaries Journal* **58** (1978), 299–309

Chester-Kadwell, *Early Anglo-Saxon Communities in the Landscape of Norfolk*, BAR British Series **481** (Oxford, 2009)

Chick, D., *The Coinage of Offa and His Contemporaries* (London, 2010)

Cipolla, C. M., 'Depreciation in Medieval Europe', *EcHR* **15** (1963), 413–22

Money, Prices, and Civilization in the Mediterranean World, Fifth to Seventeenth Century (Princeton, NJ, 1956)

'Sans Mahomet, Charlemagne est inconcevable', *Annales. Économies, Sociétés, Civilisations* **17** (1962), 130–6

Clarke, H. and Ambrosiani, B., *Towns in the Viking Age* (Leicester, 1991)

Clarke, P. A., *The English Nobility under Edward the Confessor* (Oxford, 1994)

Claude, D., 'Aspekte des Binnenhandels im Merowingerreich auf Grund der Schriftquellen', in *Der Handel des frühen Mittelalters. Bericht über die Kolloquien der Kommission für Altertumskunde Mittel- und Nordeuropas in den Jahren 1980–1983*, ed. K. Düwel *et al.* (Göttingen, 1985), pp. 9–99

'Zu Fragen der merowingischen Geldgeschichte', *Vierteljahrschrift für Sozial- und Wirtschaftsgeschichte* **48** (1961), 236–50

'Zur Funktion des Münzgeldes im hispanischen Westgotenreich', *Münsterische Beiträge zur antiken Handelsgeschichte* **8.2** (1989), 32–51

Clay, J.-H., 'Gift-Giving and Books in the Letters of St Boniface and Lul', *Journal of Medieval History* **35** (2009), 313–25

Cohen, E. and de Jong, M. (eds.), *Medieval Transformations: Texts, Power and Gifts in Context* (Leiden, 2000)

Collins, R., *Charlemagne* (Basingstoke, 1998)

'Theodebert I: *Rex Magnus Francorum*', in *Ideal and Reality*, ed. Wormald, Bullough and Collins, pp. 7–33

Connor, R. D., *The Weights and Measures of England* (London, 1987)

Cook, B., 'The Bezant in Angevin England', *NC* **159** (1999), 255–75

'Foreign Coins in Medieval England', in *Moneta locale, moneta straniera: Italia ed Europa, XI–XV secolo (Local Coins, Foreign Coins: Italy and Europe 11th–15th Centuries)*, ed. L. Travaini (Milan, 1999), pp. 231–84

Bibliography

Cook, B. and Williams, G. (eds.), *Coinage and History in the North Sea World c. 500–1250. Essays in Honour of Marion Archibald* (Leiden and Boston, MA, 2006)

Coupland, S., 'Carolingian Single Finds and the Economy of the Early Ninth Century', *NC* **170** (2010), 287–319

'Charlemagne's Coinage: Ideology and Economy', in *Charlemagne: Empire and Society*, ed. J. Story (Manchester, 2005), pp. 211–29

'The Coinage of Lothar I (840–55)', *NC* **161** (2001), 157–98

'The Coinages of Pippin I and II of Aquitaine', *Revue numismatique* **31** (1989), 194–222

'Dorestad in the Ninth Century: The Numismatic Evidence', *Jaarboek voor Munt- en Penningkunde* **75** (1988), 5–26

'The Early Coinage of Charles the Bald, 840–64', *NC* **151** (1991), 121–58

'Money and Coinage under Louis the Pious', *Francia* **1** (1990), 23–48

'The Rod of God's Wrath or the People of God's Wrath? The Carolingians' Theology of the Viking Invasions', *Journal of Ecclesiastical History* **42** (1991), 535–54

'Trading Places: Quentovic and Dorestad Reassessed', *EME* **7** (1998), 85–114

'The Vikings in Francia and Anglo-Saxon England to 911', in *NCMH* II, pp. 190–201

Cowie, R., 'The Evidence for Royal Sites in Middle Anglo-Saxon London', *Medieval Archaeology* **48** (2004), 201–9

'Mercian London', in *Mercia*, ed. Brown and Farr, pp. 194–209

Crabtree, P. J., 'The Wool Trade and the Rise of Urbanism in Middle Saxon England', in *Craft Specialization and Social Evolution in Memory of V. Gordon Childe*, ed. B. Wailes (Philadelphia, PA, 1996), pp. 99–105

Craddock, P. T. (ed.), *2000 Years of Zinc and Brass* (London, 1990)

Crafter, T., 'A Die-Study of the *Cross-and-Crosslets* Type of the Ipswich Mint, c. 1161/2–1180', *NC* **162** (2002), 237–51

Crick, J., 'Church, Land and Local Nobility in Early Ninth-Century Kent: The Case of Ealdorman Oswulf', *Bulletin of the Institute of Historical Research* **61** (1988), 251–69

Cubitt, C., *Anglo-Saxon Church Councils c. 650–c. 850* (London, 1995)

'"As the Lawbook Teaches": Reeves, Lawbooks and Urban Life in the Anonymous Old English Legend of the Seven Sleepers', *EHR* **124** (2009), 1021–49

'Finding the Forger: An Alleged Decree of the 679 Council of Hatfield', *EHR* **114** (1999), 1217–48

Curta, F., 'Merovingian and Carolingian Gift Giving', *Speculum* **81** (2006), 671–99

Dabbs, J. A., *Dei gratia in Royal Titles* (The Hague, 1971)

Davies, G., 'Early Medieval "Rural Centres" and West Norfolk: A Growing Picture of Diversity, Complexity and Changing Lifestyles', *Medieval Archaeology* **54** (2010), 89–122

Davies, R., 'The Medieval State: The Tyranny of a Concept?', *Journal of Historical Sociology* **16** (2003), 280–300

Davies, W., *Acts of Giving. Individual, Community and Church in Tenth-Century Christian Spain* (Oxford, 2007)

'Sale Price and Valuation in Galicia and Castile-León in the Tenth Century', *EME* **11** (2002), 149–74

Small Worlds: The Village Community of Early Medieval Brittany (London, 1988)

Bibliography

'When Gift Is Sale: Reciprocities and Commodities in Tenth-Century Christian Iberia', in *Languages of Gift*, ed. Davies and Fouracre, pp. 217–37

Davies, W. and Fouracre, P. (eds.), *The Languages of Gift in the Early Middle Ages* (Cambridge, 2010)

Davis, R. H. C., 'East Anglia and the Danelaw', *TRHS* 5 (1955), 23–39

Day, J., 'Brass and Zinc in Europe from the Middle Ages until the 19th Century', in *2000 Years of Zinc and Brass*, ed. Craddock, pp. 123–50

Day, W. R., 'The Monetary Reforms of Charlemagne and the Circulation of Money in Early Medieval Campania', *EME* 6 (1997), 25–45

de Barthélemy, A., 'Note sur la classification des monnaies carolingiens', *Revue numismatique* 13 (1895), 79–87

de Benedittis, G. and Lafaurie, J., 'Trésor de monnaies carolingiennes du VIIIe siècle trouvé à Larino (Italie, Molise): les monnaies de Louis, roi d'Aquitaine (781–94)', *Revue numismatique* 153 (1998), 217–43

de Callataÿ, F., 'Calculating Ancient Coin Production: Seeking a Balance', *NC* 155 (1995), 289–311

'Statistique et numismatique: les limites d'un apport', *Revue des archéologues et historiens d'art de Louvain* 20 (1987), 76–95

de Cecco, M., 'Monetary Theory and Roman History', *Journal of Economic History* 45 (1985), 809–22

de Jong, M., 'Ecclesia and the Early Medieval Polity', in *Staat im frühen Mittelalter*, ed. Airlie, Pohl and Reimitz, pp. 113–32

The Penitential State. Authority and Atonement in the Age of Louis the Pious, 814–840 (Cambridge, 2009)

'The State of the Church: Ecclesia and Early Medieval State Formation', in *Der frühmittelalterliche Staat*, ed. Pöhl and Wieser, pp. 241–54

Delamare, F., *Le frai et ses lois, ou De l'évolution des espèces* (Paris, 1994)

Delatouche, R., 'Regards sur l'agriculture aux temps carolingiens', *Journal des savants* 2 (1977), 73–100

de Ligt, L., 'Demand, Supply, Distribution. The Roman Peasantry between Town and Countryside: Rural Monetization and Peasant Demand', *Münstersche Beiträge zur Antiken Handelsgeschichte* 9 (1990), 24–56

Fairs and Markets in the Roman Empire: Economic and Social Aspects of Periodic Trade in a Pre-Industrial Society (Amsterdam, 1993)

Delogu, P., 'Il mancuso è ancora un mito', in *774: ipotesi su una transizione. Atti del seminario di Poggibonsi, 16–18 febbraio 2006*, ed. S. Gasparri (Turnhout, 2008), pp. 141–59

'Oro e argento in Roma tra il VII e il IX secolo', in *Cultura e società nell'Italia medievale. Studi per P. Brezzi* (Rome, 1988), pp. 273–93

'Reading Pirenne Again', in *The Sixth Century: Production, Distribution and Demand*, ed. R. Hodges and W. Bowman (Leiden, 1998), pp. 15–40

Derolez, R., 'Runic Literacy among the Anglo-Saxons', in *Britain 400–600: Language and History*, ed. A. Bammesberger and A. Wollmann (Heidelberg, 1990), pp. 397–436

Deschamps, P., 'Étude sur la paléographie des inscriptions lapidaires de la fin de l'époque mérovingienne aux dernières années du XIIe siècle', *Bulletin monumental* 88 (1929), 5–86

Deshman, R., '*Christus rex et magi reges*: Kingship and Christology in Ottonian and Anglo-Saxon Art', *Frühmittelalterliche Studien* 10 (1976), 367–406

Despy, G., 'Villes et campagnes aux IXe et Xe siècles: l'exemple du pays mosan', *Revue du Nord* **50** (1968), 145–68

Devosquel, J.-M. and Dierckens, A. (eds.), *Villes et campagnes au moyen âge. Mélanges Georges Despy* (Liège, 1991)

Devroey, J.-P., 'Courants et réseaux d'échange dans l'économie franque entre Loire et Rhin', *Settimane di studio del centro italiano di studi sull'alto medioevo* **40** (1993), 327–90

Économie rurale et société dans l'Europe franque (VIe–IXe siècles), vol. I, Fondements matériels, échanges et lien social (Paris, 2003)

Études sur le grand domaine carolingien (Aldershot, 1993)

Puissants et misérables. Système social et monde paysan dans l'Europe des Francs (VIe–IXe siècles) (Brussels, 2006)

'Réflections sur l'économie des premiers temps carolingiens (768–877): grands domaines et action politique entre Seine et Rhin', *Francia* **13** (1986), 475–88

'Units of Measurement in the Early Medieval Economy: The Example of Carolingian Food Rations', *French History* **1** (1987), 68–92

Devroey, J.-P. and Zoller, C., *Dictionary of Old English*, Centre for Medieval Studies, University of Toronto (www.doe.utoronto.ca/)

'Villes, campagnes, croissance agraire dans le pays mosan avant l'an mil: vingt ans après', in *Villes et campagnes au moyen âge*, ed. Devosquel and Dierckens, pp. 223–60

Diebold, W., *Word and Image: An Introduction to Early Medieval Art* (Boulder, CO, and Oxford, 2000)

Dieudonné, A., 'Les monétaires mérovingiens', *Bibliothèque de l'École des chartes* **103** (1942), 20–51

Dinkler, E. and Dinkler-von Schubert, E., 'Kreuz', in *Lexikon*, ed. Kirschbaum, II, 562–90

Dodwell, B., 'Holdings and Inheritance in Medieval East Anglia', *EcHR* **20** (1967), 53–66

Dodwell, C. R., *Anglo-Saxon Art: A New Perspective* (Manchester, 1982)

Doehaard, R., *Le haut moyen âge occidental. Économies et sociétés* (Paris, 1971)

Dolley, R. H. M., 'Ælfred the Great's Abandonment of the Concept of Periodic Recoinage', in *Studies in Numismatic Method*, ed. Brooke *et al.*, pp. 153–60

Anglo-Saxon Pennies (London, 1964)

'The Location of the Pre-Ælfredian Mint(s) of Wessex', *Proceedings of the Hampshire Field Club and Archaeology Society* **27** (1970), 57–61

'More Thoughts on the Winchester Mint under William II', *Seaby's Coin and Medal Bulletin* (1969), 11–15

Dolley, R. H. M. (ed.), *Anglo-Saxon Coins: Studies Presented to Sir Frank Stenton on the Occasion of his 80th Birthday* (London, 1961)

Dolley, R. H. M. and Blunt, C. E., 'The Chronology of the Coins of Alfred the Great', in *Anglo-Saxon Coins*, ed. Dolley, pp. 77–95

Dolley, R. H. M. and Metcalf, D. M., 'The Reform of the English Coinage under Eadgar', in *Anglo-Saxon Coins*, ed. Dolley, pp. 136–68

Dolley, R. H. M. and Morrison, K. F., *The Carolingian Coins in the British Museum* (London, 1966)

Dopsch, A., *The Economic and Social Foundations of European Civilization*, trans. M. G. Beard and N. Marshall (London, 1937)

Die Wirtschaftsentwicklung der Karolingerzeit vornehmlich in Deutschland, 3rd edn, 2 vols. (Darmstadt, 1962)

Douglas, D. C., *Social Structure of Medieval East Anglia* (Oxford, 1927)

Downham, C., *Viking Kings of Britain and Ireland: The Dynasty of Ívarr to AD 1014* (Edinburgh, 2007)

Drögereit, R., 'Kaiseridee und Kaisertitel bei den Angelsachsen', *Zeitschrift der Savigny-Stiftung für Rechtsgeschichte: Germanistische Abteilung* **69** (1952), 24–73

Duby, G., *The Early Growth of the European Economy: Warriors and Peasants from the Seventh to the Twelfth Century*, trans. H. B. Clarke (London, 1974)

Dumas, F., 'Le début de l'époque féodale en France d'après les monnaies', *Bulletin du Cercle d'études numismatiques* (1973), 65–77

'La monnaie au Xe siècle', *Settimane* **38** (1991), 565–609

Dumville, D. N., 'The Ætheling: A Study in Anglo-Saxon Constitutional History', *ASE* **8** (1979), 1–33

'*Beowulf* and the Celtic World: The Uses of Evidence', *Traditio* **37** (1981), 109–60

'Essex, Middle Anglia and the Expansion of Mercia in the South-East Midlands', in *Britons and Anglo-Saxons in the Early Middle Ages* (Aldershot, 1993), no. IX

'Terminology of Overkingship in Early Anglo-Saxon England', in *The Anglo-Saxons*, ed. Hines, pp. 345–65

'Textual Archaeology and Northumbrian History Subsequent to Bede', in *Coinage in Ninth-Century Northumbria*, ed. Metcalf, pp. 43–55

'The Tribal Hidage: An Introduction to Its Texts and Their History', in *Origins*, ed. Bassett, pp. 225–30

Wessex and England from Alfred to Edgar (Woodbridge, 1992)

Duncan-Jones, R., *Money and Government in the Roman Empire* (Cambridge, 1994)

Dunning, G. C., 'Trade Relations between England and the Continent in the Late Anglo-Saxon Period', in *Dark Age Britain*, ed. D. B. Harden (London, 1956), pp. 218–33

Durliat, J., *Les finances publiques de Dioclétian aux Carolingiens (284–889)* (Sigmaringen, 1990)

'La vigne et le vin dans la région parisienne au début du IXe siècle, d'après le Polyptyque d'Irmion', *Le moyen âge* **74** (1968), 387–419

Düwel, K., Jankuhn, H., Siems, H. and Timpe, D. (eds.), *Der Handel der Karolinger- und Wikingerzeit* (Göttingen, 1987)

Dyer, C., *Making a Living in the Middle Ages. The People of Britain 850–1520* (New Haven, CT, and London, 2002)

'Peasants and Coins: The Uses of Money in the Middle Ages', *BNJ* **67** (1997), 31–47

Dyson, T. and Schofield, J., 'Saxon London', in *Anglo-Saxon Towns in Southern England*, ed. J. Haslam (Chichester, 1984), pp. 285–313

Edwards, H., *The Charters of the Early West Saxon Kingdom*, BAR British Series **198** (Oxford, 1988)

Ekwall, E., *Old English Wīc in Place-Names*, Acta Universitatis Upsaliensis: Nomina Germanica **13** (Uppsala, 1964)

Elkington, K., 'The Mendip Lead Industry', in *The Roman West Country: Classical Culture and Celtic Society*, ed. K. Branigan and P. J. Fowler (Newton Abbot, 1976), pp. 183–97

Elsner, J., *Imperial Rome and Christian Triumph: The Art of the Roman Empire A.D. 100–450* (Oxford, 1998)

Bibliography

Engel, A. and Serrure, R., *Traité de numismatique du moyen âge*, 3 vols. (Paris, 1891–1905)

Enright, M., 'Charles the Bald and Æthelwulf of Wessex', *Journal of Medieval History* 5 (1979), 291–302

Erdmann, C., *Forschungen zur politischen Ideenwelt des Frühmittelalters* (Berlin, 1951)

Esty, W., 'Estimation of the Size of a Coinage: A Survey and Comparison of Methods', *NC* **146** (1986), 185–215

'How to Estimate the Original Number of Dies and the Coverage of a Sample', *NC* **166** (2006), 359–64

Everett, N., *Literacy in Lombard Italy, c. 568–774* (Cambridge, 2003)

Ewig, E., 'Das Bild Constantins des Großen in den ersten Jahrhunderten des abend-ländischen Mittelalters', *Historisches Jahrbuch* **75** (1956), 1–46

Faith, R., *The English Peasantry and the Growth of Lordship* (Leicester, 1997)

'Forces and Relations of Production in Early Medieval England', *Journal of Agrarian Change* **9** (2009), 23–41

'Peasant Families and Inheritance Customs in Medieval England', *Agricultural History Review* **14** (1966), 77–95

Fanning, S., 'Bede, *Imperium* and the Bretwaldas', *Speculum* **66** (1991), 1–26

Farmer, D., 'Prices and Wages', in *The Agrarian History of England and Wales*, vol. II, *1042–1350*, ed. H. Hallam (Cambridge, 1988), pp. 716–817

Favreau, R., 'Les commanditaires dans les inscriptions du haut moyen âge occiden-tal', *Settimane* **39** (1992), 681–722

Feller, L., 'Enrichissement, accumulation et circulation des biens: quelques problèmes liés au marché de la terre', in *Le marché de la terre au moyen âge*, ed. L. Feller and C. Wickham (Rome, 2005), pp. 3–28

Fenwick, V. *et al.*, 'Insula de Burgh: Excavations at Burrow Hill, Butley, Suffolk 1978–1981', *ASSAH* **3** (1984), 43–54

Ferrari, M., *Il 'Liber sanctae crucis' di Rabano Mauro: testo, immagine, contesto* (Berne and New York, 1999)

Feveile, C., 'The Coins from 8th–9th Centuries Ribe – Survey and Status 2001', *Nordisk Numismatisk Årsskrift 2000–2002: Nordic Numismatic Journal. 6th Nordic Numismatic Symposium: Single Finds: The Nordic Perspective* (2006), 149–62

Finberg, H., *The Early Charters of Wessex* (Leicester, 1964)

The Early Charters of the West Midlands (Leicester, 1961)

Lucerna: Studies of Some Problems in the Early History of England (London, 1964)

Finley, M., *The Ancient Economy*, 2nd edn (Berkeley, CA, 1999)

Finn, R., *Almsgiving in the Later Roman Empire: Christian Promotion and Practice* (Oxford, 2008)

Fleming, R., *Britain after Rome. The Fall and Rise, 400 to 1070* (London, 2010)

'Elites, Boats and Foreigners: Rethinking the Birth of English Towns', *Settimane* **56** (2009), 393–426

Flemming, J., 'Baum, Baüme', in *Lexikon*, ed. Kirschbaum, I, 258–68

Folz, R., *The Concept of Empire in Western Europe from the Vth to the XIVth Century*, trans. S. A. Ogilvie (London, 1969)

Foot, S., 'The Making of *Angelcynn*: English Identity before the Norman Conquest', *TRHS* **6** (1996), 25–49

'The Role of the Minster in Earlier Anglo-Saxon Society', in *Monasteries and Society in Medieval Britain*, ed. B. Thompson (Stamford, 1999), pp. 35–58

Bibliography

Fossier, R., 'Les tendances de l'économie: stagnation ou croissance?', *Settimane* **27** (1981), 261–74

Fouracre, P., 'Carolingian Justice: The Rhetoric of Improvement and Contexts of Abuse', *Settimane* **42** (1995), 771–803

'Comparing the Resources of the Merovingian and Carolingian States: Problems and Perspectives', in *Der frühmittelalterliche Staat*, ed. Pöhl and Wieser, pp. 287–98

'The Use of the Term *beneficium* in Frankish Sources: A Society Based on Favours', in *Languages of Gift*, ed. Davies and Fouracre, pp. 62–88

Fouracre, P. (ed.), *The New Cambridge Medieval History I c. 500–c. 700* (Cambridge, 2005)

Fouracre, P. and Gerberding, R. A., *Late Merovingian France: History and Historiography, 640–720* (Manchester, 1996)

Freeman, A., *The Moneyer and the Mint in the Reign of Edward the Confessor, 1042–1066*, 2 vols., BAR British Series **145** (Oxford, 1985)

Fried, J., *Donation of Constantine and Constitutum Constantini: The Misinterpretation of a Fiction and Its Original Meaning* (Berlin, 2007)

'Das karolingische Herrschaftsverband im 9. Jh. zwischen "Kirche" und "Köngishaus"', *Historische Zeitschrift* **235** (1982), 1–43

Fuhrmann, H., 'Das frühmittelalterliche Papsttum und die Konstantinische Schenkung', *Settimane* **20** (1973), 257–92

Gannon, A., *The Iconography of Early Anglo-Saxon Coinage: Sixth to Eighth Centuries* (Oxford, 2003)

Ganshof, F.-L., 'À propos du tonlieu à l'époque carolingienne', *Settimane* **6** (1959), 485–508

Frankish Institutions under Charlemagne, trans. B. and M. Lyon (Providence, RI, 1968)

'Observations sur le synode de Francfort de 794', in *Miscellanea historica in honorem Alberti de Meyer*, 2 vols. (Louvain, 1946) I, 306–18

Garipzanov, I., 'The Coinage of Tours in the Merovingian Period and the Pirenne Thesis', *Revue belge de numismatique et de sigillographie* **147** (2001), 79–118

'Communication of Authority in Carolingian Titles', *Viator* **36** (2005), 41–82

'David, *imperator augustus, gratia dei rex*: Communication and Propaganda in Carolingian Royal Iconography', in *Monotheistic Kingship: The Medieval Variants*, ed. A. Al-Azmeh and J. M. Bak (Budapest and New York, 2005), pp. 89–117

'The Image of Authority in Carolingian Coinage: The Image of a Ruler and Roman Imperial Tradition', *EME* **8** (1999), 197–218

'Metamorphoses of the Early Medieval *signum* of a Ruler in the Carolingian World', *EME* **14** (2006), 419–64

The Symbolic Language of Authority in the Carolingian World (c. 751–877) (Leiden and Boston, MA, 2008)

Geary, P., 'Gift Exchange and Social Science Modelling: The Limitations of a Construct', in *Negotiating the Gift*, ed. Algazi, Groebner and Jussen, pp. 129–40

Gibson, M. and Nelson, J. L. (eds.), *Charles the Bald: Court and Kingdom*, 2nd edn (Aldershot, 1990)

Gillingham, J., 'Chronicles and Coins as Evidence for Levels of Tribute and Taxation in Late Tenth- and Early Eleventh-Century England', *EHR* **105** (1990), 939–50

'"The Most Precious Jewel in the English Crown": Levels of Danegeld and Heregeld in the Early Eleventh Century', *EHR* **104** (1989), 373–84

Bibliography

Gilmore, G. R., 'The Application of Activation Analysis', in *A Survey of Numismatic Research 1978–1984*, ed. M. Price, E. Besly, D. MacDowall, M. Jones and A. Oddy, 3 vols. (London, 1986) II, 1004–21

Gilmore, J., 'Metal Analysis of the Northumbrian *Stycas*: Review and Suggestions', in *Coinage in Ninth-Century Northumbria*, ed. Metcalf, pp. 159–73

Godden, M., 'The Alfredian Project and Its Aftermath: Rethinking the Literary History of the Ninth and Tenth Centuries', *Proceedings of the British Academy* **162** (2009), 93–122

'Did King Alfred Write Anything?', *Medium Aevum* **76** (2007), 1–23

'Money, Power and Morality in Late Anglo-Saxon England', *ASE* **19** (1990), 41–65

Godelier, M., *The Enigma of the Gift*, trans. N. Scott (Cambridge, 1999)

Goetz, H.-W., 'Social and Military Institutions', in *NCMH* II, pp. 451–80

'Die Wahrnehmung von "Staat" und "Herrschaft" im frühen Mittelalter', in *Staat im frühen Mittelalter*, ed. Airlie, Pohl and Reimitz, pp. 39–58

Goffart, W., *Barbarians and Romans A.D. 418–584: The Techniques of Accommodation* (Princeton, NJ, 1980)

'Old and New in Merovingian Taxation', *P&P* **96** (1982), 3–21

Goldberg, E., *Struggle for Empire: Kingship and Conflict under Louis the German, 817–876* (Ithaca, NY, and London, 2006)

Goldin, E., 'Statistical Analysis of Coins Lost in Circulation', *Journal of Business and Economic Statistics* **3** (1985), 36–42

Goodson, C. L. and Nelson, J. L., 'The Roman Contexts of the "Donation of Constantine"', *EME* **18** (2010), 446–67

Gordus, A. A., 'Neutron Activation of Coins and Coin Streaks', in *Methods of Chemical*, ed. Metcalf and Hall, pp. 127–48

Gordus, A. A. and Metcalf, D. M., 'The Alloy of the Byzantine *Miliaresion* and the Question of the Reminting of Islamic Silver', *Hamburger Beiträge zur Numismatik* **24/26** (1970/2), 9–36

Gould, J. D., *The Great Debasement: Currency and the Economy in Mid-Tudor England* (Oxford, 1970)

Graeber, N., *Toward an Anthropological Theory of Value: The False Coin of Our Own Dreams* (New York, 2001)

Granovetter, M., 'Economic Action and Social Structure: The Problem of Embeddedness', *American Journal of Sociology* **91** (1985), 481–510

Grassi, J. L., 'The Lands and Revenues of Edward the Confessor', *EHR* **117** (2002), 251–83

Gray, N., *A History of Lettering. Creative Experiment and Letter Identity* (Oxford, 1986)

'The Palaeography of Latin Inscriptions in the Eighth, Ninth and Tenth Centuries in Italy', *Papers of the British School at Rome* **16** (1948), 38–171

Greene, K., *The Archaeology of the Roman Economy* (London, 1986)

Gregory, C., *Gifts and Commodities* (London, 1982)

Savage Money: The Anthropology and Politics of Commodity Exchange (Amsterdam, 1997)

Gregson, N., 'The Multiple Estate Model: Some Critical Questions', *Journal of Historical Geography* **11** (1985), 339–51

Gretsch, M., *Intellectual Foundations of the English Benedictine Reform* (Cambridge, 1999)

Bibliography

Grierson, P., '*Byzantine Coins* (London, 1982)

'Coin Wear and the Frequency Table', *NC* **3** (1963), i–xvi

Coins of Medieval Europe (London, 1991)

'Commerce in the Dark Ages: A Critique of the Evidence', *TRHS* **9** (1959), 123–40

'Cronologia delle riforme monetarie di Carlo Magno', *Rivista italiana di numismatica* **56** (1954), 65–79

'Domesday Book, the *Geld de moneta* and *Monetagium*: A Forgotten Minting Reform', *BNJ* **55** (1985), 84–94

'La fonction sociale de la monnaie en Angleterre aux VIIe–VIIIe siècles', *Settimane* **8** (1961), 341–62

The Gold Solidus of Louis the Pious and Its Imitations', *Jaarboek voor Munt- en Penningkunde* **38** (1951), 1–41

'The "*Gratia dei rex*" Coinage of Charles the Bald', in *Charles the Bald*, ed. Gibson and Nelson, pp. 52–64

'Halfpennies and Third-Pennies of King Alfred', *BNJ* **28** (1955–7), 477–93

'Mint Output in the Time of Offa', *Numismatic Circular* **71** (1963), 114–15

'The Monetary Reforms of 'Abd al-Malik: Their Metrological Basis and Their Financial Repercussions', *Journal of Economic and Social History of the Orient* **3** (1960), 241–64

'Money and Coinage under Charlemagne', in *Karl der Grosse. Lebenswerk und Nachleben*, ed. W. Braunfels, 2 vols. (Düsseldorf, 1965) I, 501–36

'Muslim Coins in Thirteenth-Century England', in *Near Eastern Numismatics, Iconography and History. Studies in Honor of George C. Miles*, ed. D. Kouymjian (Beirut, 1974), pp. 387–91

Numismatics (Oxford, 1975)

'Numismatics and the Historian', *NC* **2** (1962), i–xiv

The Origins of Money (London, 1977)

'The Purpose of the Sutton Hoo Coins', *Antiquity* **44** (1970), 14–18

'Some Aspects of the Coinage of Offa', *Numismatic Circular* **71** (1963), 223–5

'Symbolism in Early Medieval Charters and Coins', *Settimane* **23** (1976), 601–40

'The Volume of Anglo-Saxon Coinage', *EcHR* **20** (1967), 153–60

'Weight and Coinage', *NC* **4** (1964), i–xvii

Grierson, P. and Blackburn, M., *Medieval European Coinage I: The Early Middle Ages (5th–10th Centuries)* (Cambridge, 1986)

Grierson, P. and Hendy, M., *Byzantine Coins in the Dumbarton Oaks Collection and in the Whittemore Collection*, 5 vols. in 9 (Washington, DC, 1966–99)

Haertle, C. M., *Karolingische Münzfunde aus dem 9. Jahrhundert*, 2 vols. (Cologne, 1997)

Hall, R., 'The Decline of the *Wic?*', in *Towns in Decline AD 100–1600*, ed. T. R. Slater (Aldershot, 2000), pp. 120–36

Halsall, G., 'Playing by Whose Rules? A Further Look at Viking Atrocity in the Ninth Century', *Medieval History* **2.2** (1992), 2–12

Warfare and Society in the Barbarian West, 450–900 (London, 2003)

Hamerow, H., 'Agrarian Production and the *Emporia* of Mid Saxon England, ca. AD 650–850', in *Post-Roman Towns*, ed. Henning, I, 219–32

'Angles, Saxons and Anglo-Saxons: Rural Centres, Trade and Production', *Studien zur Sachsenforschung* **13** (1999), 189–206

Bibliography

Early Medieval Settlements: The Archaeology of Rural Communities in Northwest Europe, 400–900 (Oxford, 2002)

Hammer, C. I., 'Land Sales in Eighth- and Ninth-Century Bavaria: Legal, Economic and Social Aspects', *EME* **6** (1997), 47–76

"Pipinus rex": Pippin's Plot of 792 and Bavaria', *Traditio* **63** (2008), 235–72

Handley, M., *Death, Society, and Culture. Inscriptions and Epitaphs in Gaul and Spain, AD 300–750*, BAR International Series 1135 (Oxford, 2003)

Hannig, J., '*Ars donandi*. Zur Ökonomie des Schenkens im früheren Mittelalter', in *Armut, Liebe, Ehre: Studien zur historischen Kulturforschung*, ed. R. van Dülmen (Frankfurt, 1988), pp. 11–27

Hansen, I. L. and Wickham, C. (eds.), *The Long Eighth Century* (Leiden and Boston, MA, 2000)

Hårdh, B., *Wikingerzeitliche Depotfunde aus Südschweden. Probleme und Analysen* (Bonn and Lund, 1976)

Hardt, M., *Gold und Herrschaft. Die Schätze europäischer Könige und Fürsten im ersten Jahrtausend* (Berlin, 2004)

'Royal Treasures and Representation in the Early Middle Ages', in *Strategies of Distinction: The Construction of Ethnic Communities, 300–800*, ed. W. Pohl and H. Reimitz (Leiden, 1998), pp. 255–80

Harmer, F. (ed.), *Select English Historical Documents of the Ninth and Tenth Centuries* (Cambridge, 1914)

Harrison, D., 'Structures and Resources of Power in Early Medieval Europe', in *The Construction of Communities in the Early Middle Ages: Texts, Resources and Artefacts*, ed. R. Corradini, M. Diesenberger and H. Reimitz (Leiden, 2003), pp. 17–37

Hart, C., 'The Kingdom of Mercia', in *Mercian Studies*, ed. A. Dornier (Leicester, 1977), pp. 43–61

Hart, K., 'Heads or Tails? Two Sides of the Coin', *Man* **21** (1986), 637–56

'Money: One Anthropologist's View', in *Handbook*, ed. Carrier, pp. 160–75

Harvey, Y. et al., *The Winchester Mint and Coins and Related Finds from the Excavations of 1961–71*, ed. M. Biddle (Oxford, forthcoming)

Haslam, J., 'A Middle Saxon Iron Smelting Site at Ramsbury, Wiltshire', *Medieval Archaeology* **24** (1980), 1–68

Hawkes, J., 'The Legacy of Constantine in Anglo-Saxon England', in *Constantine the Great: York's Roman Emperor*, ed. E. Hartley, J. Hawkes, M. Henig and F. Mee (York, 2006), pp. 104–14

Hawkins, E., *The Silver Coins of England Arranged and Described with Remarks on British Money Previous to the Saxon Dynasties* (London, 1841)

Hayes, J. W., *Late Roman Pottery* (London, 1972)

Heady, P., 'Barter', in *Handbook*, ed. Carrier, pp. 262–74

Heck, G. W., 'First Century Islamic Currency: Mastering the Message from the Money', in *Money, Power and Politics in Early Islamic Syria*, ed. J. Haldon (Aldershot, 2010), pp. 97–123

Helms, M., *Craft and the Kingly Ideal: Art, Trade, and Power* (Austin, TX, 1993)

Hen, Y., *Culture and Religion in Merovingian Gaul, A.D. 481–751* (Leiden, 1995)

Henderson, I., 'The "David Cycle" in Pictish Art', in *Early Medieval Sculpture in Britain and Ireland*, ed. J. Higgitt (Oxford, 1986), pp. 87–123

"'*Primus inter pares*": The St Andrews Sarcophagus and Pictish Sculpture', in *The St Andrews Sarcophagus: A Pictish Masterpiece and Its International Connection*, ed. S. M. Foster (Dublin, 1998), pp. 97–167

Hendy, M., 'Aspects of Coin Production and Fiscal Administration in the Late Roman and Early Byzantine Period', *NC* 12 (1972), 117–39

'East and West: Divergent Models of Coinage and Its Use', *Settimane* 38 (1991), 637–74

'From Public to Private: The Western Barbarian Coinages as a Mirror of the Disintegration of late Roman State Structure', *Viator* 19 (1988), 29–78

'On the Administrative Basis of the Byzantine Coinage *c.* 400–*c.* 900 and the Reforms of Heraclius', *University of Birmingham Historical Journal* 12 (1970), 129–54

Studies in the Byzantine Monetary Economy c. 300–1450 (Cambridge, 1985)

Henning, J., 'Early European Towns: The Way of the Economy in the Frankish Area between Dynamism and Deceleration 500–1000 AD', in *Post-Roman Towns*, ed. Henning, I, 3–40

Henning, J. (ed.), *Post-Roman Towns. Trade and Settlement in Europe and Byzantium*, 2 vols. (Berlin and New York, 2007)

Herlihy, D., 'Treasure Hoards in the Italian Economy, 960–1139', *EcHR* 10 (1957), 1–14

Higgitt, J., 'The Dedication Inscription at Jarrow and Its Context', *Antiquaries Journal* 59 (1979), 343–74

'The Display Script of the Book of Kells and the Tradition of Insular Decorative Capitals', in *The Book of Kells: Proceedings of a Conference at Trinity College, Dublin 6–9 September 1992*, ed. F. O'Mahony (Aldershot, 1994), pp. 209–33

'*Legentes quoque vel audientes*. Early Medieval Inscriptions in Britain and Ireland and Their Audiences', in *The Worm, the Germ and the Thorn. Pictish and Related Studies Presented to Isabel Henderson*, ed. D. Henry (Balgavies, 1997), pp. 67–78

'The Pictish Latin Inscription at Tarbat in Ross-shire', *Proceedings of the Society of Antiquaries of Scotland* 112 (1982), 300–21

'The Stone-Cutter and the Scriptorium: Early Medieval Inscriptions in Britain and Ireland', in *Epigraphik 1988: Fachtagung für mittelalterliche und neuzeitliche Epigraphik, Graz, 10.–14. Mai 1988: Referate und Round-Table-Gespräche*, ed. W. Koch (Vienna, 1990), pp. 149–62

Hill, D., 'Appendix 2. Gazetteer of Possible Anglo-Saxon *Wics*', in *Wics*, ed. Hill and Cowie, pp. 95–103

An Atlas of Anglo-Saxon England (Oxford, 1981)

Hill, D. and Cowie, R. (eds.), *Wics. The Early Medieval Trading Centres of Northern Europe* (Sheffield, 2001)

Hill, D. and Metcalf, D. M. (eds.), *Sceattas in England and on the Continent*, BAR British Series 128 (Oxford, 1984)

Hill, D. and Rumble, A. (eds.), *The Defence of Wessex: The Burghal Hidage and Anglo-Saxon Fortifications* (Manchester, 1996)

Hill, D. and Worthington, M., *Offa's Dyke: History and Guide* (Stroud, 2003)

Hill, D. and Worthington, M. (eds.), *Æthelbald and Offa: Two Eighth-Century Kings of Mercia*, BAR British Series 383 (Oxford, 2005)

Hill, J. M., 'Beowulf and the Danish Succession: Gift Giving as an Occasion for Complex Gesture', *Medievalia et humanistica* 11 (1982), 177–97

The Cultural World in Beowulf (Toronto, 1995)

'Social Milieu', in *Beowulf Handbook*, ed. Bjork and Niles, pp. 255–69

Hill, T. D., 'The Falling Leaf and Buried Treasure: Two Notes on the Imagery of *Solomon and Saturn*', *Neuphilologische Mitteilungen* **71** (1970), 571–6

Hills, C., '*Beowulf* and Archaeology', in *Beowulf Handbook*, ed. Bjork and Niles, pp. 291–310

Hines, J., 'Units of Account in Gold and Silver in Seventh-Century England: *Scillingas, Sceattas* and *Pæningas*', *Antiquaries Journal* **90** (2010), 153–73

Hines, J. (ed.), *The Anglo-Saxons from the Migration Period to the Eighth Century: An Ethnographic Perspective* (Woodbridge, 1997)

Hinton, D., 'Coins and Commercial Centres in Anglo-Saxon England', in *Anglo-Saxon Monetary History*, ed. Blackburn, pp. 11–26

'The Large Towns, 600–1300', in *Cambridge Urban History*, ed. Palliser, pp. 217–43

Southampton Finds, vol. II, *The Gold, Silver and Other Non-Ferrous Alloy Objects from Hamwic, and the Non-Ferrous Metalworking Evidence* (Stroud, 1996)

Hodges, R., *The Anglo-Saxon Achievement* (London, 1989)

Dark Age Economics: The Origins of Towns and Trade A.D. 600–1000, 2nd edn (London, 1989)

Goodbye to the Vikings (London, 2006)

'Society, Power and the First English Industrial Revolution', *Settimane* **38** (1991), 125–50

Towns and Trade in the Age of Charlemagne (London, 2000)

'Trade and Market Origins in the Ninth Century: Relations between England and the Continent', in *Charles the Bald*, ed. Gibson and Nelson, pp. 203–23

Hodges, R. and Whitehouse, D., *Mohammed, Charlemagne and the Origins of Europe: Archaeology and the Pirenne Thesis* (London, 1983)

Homans, G. C., 'The Explanation of English Regional Differences', *P&P* **42** (1969), 18–34

'The Frisians in East Anglia', *EcHR* **10** (1957), 189–206

Hooke, D., 'The Droitwich Salt Industry: The West Midlands Charter Evidence', *ASSAH* **2** (1981), 123–69

'Uses of Waterways in Anglo-Saxon England', in *Waterways and Canal-Building in Medieval England*, ed. J. Blair (Oxford, 2007), pp. 37–54

Hopkins, K., 'Rome, Taxes, Rents and Trade', in *The Ancient Economy*, ed. W. Scheidel and S. von Reden (Edinburgh, 2002), pp. 190–232

Howgego, C., 'The Supply and Use of Money in the Roman World 200 B.C. to A.D. 300', *Journal of Roman Studies* **82** (1992), 1–31

Humphrey, C. and Hugh-Jones, S., 'Introduction: Barter, Exchange and Value', in *Barter, Exchange and Value: An Anthropological Approach*, ed. C. Humphrey and S. Hugh-Jones (Cambridge, 1992), pp. 1–20

Hurst, J., 'The Pottery', in *Archaeology of Anglo-Saxon England*, ed. Wilson, pp. 283–348

Hutcheson, A. R. J., 'The Origins of King's Lynn? Control of Wealth on the Wash Prior to the Norman Conquest', *Medieval Archaeology* **50** (2006), 71–104

Ilisch, L., Lorenz, S., Stern, W. B. and Steuer, H., *Dirham und Rappenpfennig: mittelalterliche Münzprägung in Bergbauregionen. Analysenreihen* (Bonn, 2003)

Ingham, G., 'Further Reflections on the Ontology of Money: Responses to Lapavitsas and Dodd', *Economy and Society* **35** (2006), 259–78

The Nature of Money (Cambridge, 2004)

Innes, M., 'Framing the Carolingian Economy', *Journal of Agrarian Change* **9** (2009), 42–58

State and Society in the Early Middle Ages: The Middle Rhine Valley, 400–1000 (Cambridge, 2000)

Irsigler, F., 'Grundherrschaft, Handel und Märkte zwischen Maas und Rhein im frühen und hohen Mittelalter', in *Grundherrschaft und Stadtentstehung am Niederrhein*, ed. K. Flink and W. Janssen (Kleve, 1989), pp. 52–78

Jeanne-Rose, O., 'Trouvailles isolées de monnaies carolingiennes en Poitou: inventaire provisoire', *Revue numismatique* **151** (1996), 241–83

Jesse, W., *Quellenbuch zur Münz- und Geldgeschichte des Mittelalters* (Halle, 1929)

Jewell, R., 'The Anglo-Saxon Friezes at Breedon-on-the-Hill, Leicestershire', *Archaeologia* **108** (1986), 95–115

'Classicism of Southumbrian Sculpture', in *Mercia*, ed. Brown and Farr, pp. 246–62

Jobert, P., *La notion de donation: convergences, 630–750* (Paris, 1977)

Johanek, P., 'Der fränkische Handel der Karolingerzeit im Spiegel der Schriftquellen', in *Der Handel der Karolinger- und Wikingerzeit*, ed. Düwel *et al.*, pp. 7–68

John, E., *Orbis Britanniae and Other Studies* (Leicester, 1966)

Jolly, K. L., Karkov, C. and Keefer, S. L. (eds.), *Cross and Culture in Anglo-Saxon England: Studies in Honor of George Hardin Brown* (Morgantown, WV, 2008)

Jones, G., 'Multiple Estates and Early Settlement', in *Medieval Settlement: Continuity and Change*, ed. P. H. Sawyer (London, 1976), pp. 15–40

Jones, S. R. H., 'Transaction Costs, Institutional Change and the Emergence of a Market Economy in Later Anglo-Saxon England', *EcHR* **46** (1993), 658–78

Jonsson, K., *The New Era: The Reformation of the Late Anglo-Saxon Coinage* (Stockholm, 1986)

'The Pre-Reform Coinage of Edgar – the Legacy of the Anglo-Saxon Kingdoms', in *Coinage and History*, ed. Cook and Williams, pp. 325–46

Jonsson, K. (ed.), *Studies in Late Anglo-Saxon Coinage in Memory of Bror Emil Hildebrand* (Stockholm, 1990)

Jörg, C., 'Die Besänftigung göttlichen Zorns in karolingischer Zeit. Kaiserliche Vorgaben zu Fasten, Gebet und Buße im Umfeld der Hungersnot von 805/06', *Das Mittelalter* **15** (2010), 38–51

Jussen, B., 'Religious Discourses of the Gift in the Middle Ages: Semantic Evidences (Second to Twelfth Centuries)', in *Negotiating the Gift*, ed. Algazi, Groebner and Jussen, pp. 173–92

Kamp, N., *Moneta regis: Königliche Münzstätten und königliche Münzpolitik in der Stauferzeit* (Hanover, 2006)

Kaplanis, C., 'The Debasement of the "Dollar of the Middle Ages"', *JEcH* **63** (2003), 768–801

Karkov, C., *The Ruler Portraits of Anglo-Saxon England* (Woodbridge, 2003)

Keary, C. F. and Grueber, H. A., *A Catalogue of English Coins in the British Museum. Anglo-Saxon Series*, 2 vols. (London, 1887–93)

Keene, D., 'Alfred and London', in *Alfred the Great*, ed. Reuter, pp. 235–49

'Text, Visualisation and Politics: London 1150–1250', *TRHS* **18** (2008), 69–99

Keller, H., 'Grundlagen ottonischer Königsherrschaft', in *Reich und Kirche vor dem Investiturstreit*, ed. K. Schmid (Sigmaringen, 1985), pp. 17–34

Bibliography

Ottonische Königsherrschaft. Organisation und Legitimation königlicher Macht (Darmstadt, 2002)

Kelly, F., *Early Irish Farming*, rev. edn (Dublin, 2000)

Kelly, S., 'Early Anglo-Saxon Society and the Written Word', in *Uses of Literacy*, ed. McKitterick, pp. 36–62

'King Æthelwulf's Decimations', *Anglo-Saxon* I (2007), 285–317

'Sussex', in *BEASE*, pp. 431–2

'Trading Privileges from Eighth-Century England', *EME* I (1992), 3–28

Kemp, R. L., *Anglian Settlement at 46–54 Fishergate* (York, 1996)

Kennedy, A., 'Disputes about *Bocland*: The Forum for Their Adjudication', *ASE* 14 (1985), 175–95

Keynes, J. M., 'Keynes and Ancient Currencies', in *The Collected Writings of John Maynard Keynes*, vol. XXVIII, *Social, Political and Literary Writings*, ed. E. Johnson and D. Moggridge (Cambridge, 1984), pp. 223–94

Keynes, S., 'Angelsächsische Urkunden (7.–9. Jahrhundert)/Anglo-Saxon Charters (7th–9th Century)', in *Mensch und Schrift im frühen Mittelalter*, ed. P. Erhart and L. Hollenstein (St Gallen, 2006), pp. 97–109

'Anglo-Saxon Entries in the *Liber Vitae* of Brescia', in *Alfred the Wise. Studies in Honour of Janet Bately on the Occasion of Her Sixty-Fifth Birthday*, ed. M. Godden, J. Robert and J. L. Nelson (Cambridge, 1997), pp. 99–119

An Atlas of Attestations in Anglo-Saxon Charters, c. 670–1066 (Cambridge, 2002)

'The Control of Kent in the Ninth Century', *EME* 2 (1993), 111–31

The Councils of Clofesho (Leicester, 1993)

The Diplomas of King Æthelred 'the Unready' 978–1016: A Study in Their Use as Historical Evidence (Cambridge, 1980)

'Edgar, *rex admirabilis*', in *Edgar, King of the English*, ed. Scragg, pp. 3–59

'England, 700–900', in *NCMH* II, pp. 18–42

'England, 900–1016', in *NCMH* III, pp. 456–84

'King Æthelred's Charter for Eynsham Abbey (1005)', in *Early Medieval Studies in Memory of Patrick Wormald*, ed. S. Baxter, C. Karkov, J. L. Nelson and D. Pelteret (Aldershot, 2009), pp. 451–73

'King Alfred and the Mercians', in *Kings, Currency and Alliances*, ed. Blackburn and Dumville, pp. 1–45

'King Athelstan's Books', in *Learning and Literature in Anglo-Saxon England*, ed. M. Lapidge and H. Gneuss (Cambridge, 1985), pp. 143–201

'The Kingdom of the Mercians in the Eighth Century', in *Æthelbald and Offa: Two Eighth-Century Kings of Mercia*, ed. D. Hill and M. Worthington (Oxford, 2005), pp. 1–26

'Mercia and Wessex in the Ninth Century', in *Mercia*, ed. Brown and Farr, pp. 310–28

'The Power of the Written Word: Alfredian England 871–899', in *Alfred the Great*, pp. 175–97

'Rædwald the *Bretwalda*', in *Voyage to the Other World: The Legacy of Sutton Hoo*, ed. C. B. Kendall and P. S. Wells (Minneapolis, MN, 1992), pp. 103–23

'The Reconstruction of a Burnt Cottonian Manuscript: The Case of Cotton MS. Otho A. I', *British Library Journal* 22 (1996), 113–60;

'Thegn', in *BEASE*, pp. 443–4

'The Vikings in England, c. 790–1016', in *History of the Vikings*, ed. Sawyer, pp. 48–82

Bibliography

'The West Saxon Charters of King Æthelwulf and His Sons', *EHR* **109** (1994), 1109–49

Kilger, C., 'Kaupang from Afar: Aspects of the Interpretation of Dirham Finds in Northern and Eastern Europe between the Late 8th and Early 10th Centuries', in *Means of Exchange*, ed. Skre, pp. 199–252

'Wholeness and Holiness: Counting, Weighing and Valuing Silver in the Early Viking Period', in *Means of Exchange*, ed. Skre, pp. 253–326

Kirby, D., *The Earliest English Kings*, 2nd edn (London, 2000)

Kirschbaum, E. (ed.), *Lexikon der christlichen Ikonographie*, 8 vols. (Freiburg, 1968–76)

Kirschner, J., *Die Bezeichnungen für Kranz und Krone im Altenglischen* (Munich, 1975)

Kloss, F., *Goldvorrat und Geldverkehr im Merowingerreich* (Baden, 1929)

Kluge, B., 'Nomen imperatoris und *Christiana religio*', in *Kunst und Kultur*, ed. Stiegemann and Wemhoff, III, 82–90

Koch, W., *Inschriftenpaläographie des abendländischen Mittelalters und der frühen Neuzeit. Teil 1: Früh- und Hochmittelalter* (Munich, 2006)

Körntgen, L., *Köngisherrschaft und Gottes Gnade: zu Kontext und Funktion sakraler Vorstellungen in Historiographie und Bildzeugnissen der ottonisch-frühsalischen Zeit* (Berlin, 2001)

Kozodoy, R., 'The Reculver Cross', *Archaeologia* **108** (1986), 67–94

Kruse, S. E., 'Metallurgical Evidence of Silver Sources in the Irish Sea Province', in *Viking Treasure from the North West: The Cuerdale Hoard in Its Context*, ed. J. Graham-Campbell (Liverpool, 1992), pp. 73–88

Kuchenbuch, L., 'Porcus donativus: Language Use and Gifting in Seigniorial Records between the Eighth and the Twelfth Centuries', in *Negotiating the Gift*, ed. Algazi, Groebner and Jussen, pp. 193–246

'Probleme der Rententwicklung in den klösterlichen Grundherrschaften des frühen Mittelalters', in *Benedictine Culture 750–1050*, ed. W. Lourdeaux and D. Verhelst (Leuven, 1983), pp. 130–72

Kula, L., *Measures and Men*, trans. R. Szreter (Princeton, NJ, 1986)

Lafaurie, J., 'Des Mérovingiens aux Carolingiens. Les monnaies de Pépin le Bref', *Francia* **2** (1974), 26–48

'Eligius Monetarius', *Revue numismatique* **19** (1977), 111–51

'Monnaies épiscopales de Paris à l'époque mérovingienne', *Cahiers de la Rotonde* **20** (1998), 61–99

'Les monnaies impériales de Charlemagne', *Comptes-rendus de l'académie des inscriptions et belles-lettres* (1978), 154–72

'Numismatique: des Carolingiens aux Capétiens', *Cahiers de civilisation médiévale* **13** (1970), 117–37

'Les routes commerciales indiquées par les trésors et trouvailles monétaires mérovingiens', *Settimane* **8** (1961), 231–78

'La surveillance des ateliers monétaires au IXe siècle', *Francia* **9** (1980), 486–96

Lafaurie, J. and Pilet-Lemière, J., *Monnaies du haut moyen âge découvertes en France (Ve–VIIIe siècle)* (Paris, 2003)

La Guardia, R. (ed.), *I luoghi della moneta: le sedi delle zecche dell'antichità all'età moderna: atti del convegno internazionale 22–23 Ottobre 1999, Milano* (Milan, 2001)

Laiou, A. E., 'Economic and Noneconomic Exchange', in *Economic History of Byzantium*, ed. Laiou, II, 681–96

Bibliography

Laiou, A. E. (ed.), *The Economic History of Byzantium*, 3 vols. (Washington, DC, 2002)

Langefeld, B., '*Regula canonicorum* or *Regula monasterialis uitae*? The Rule of Chrodegang and Archbishop Wulfred's Reforms at Canterbury', *ASE* **25** (1996), 21–36

Lapidge, M., *Anglo-Latin Literature 600–899* (London and Rio Grande, OH, 1996) 'Artistic and Literary Patronage in Anglo-Saxon England', *Settimane* **39** (1992), 137–91

Lapidge, M., Blair, J., Keynes, S. and Scragg, D. (eds.), *The Blackwell Encyclopaedia of Anglo-Saxon England* (Oxford, 1999)

Lammers, W., 'Ein karolingisches Bildprogramm in der Aula Regia von Ingelheim', in *Festschrift für Hermann Heimpel*, 3 vols. (Göttingen, 1971–2) III, 226–89

Latouche, R., *The Birth of Western Economy: Economic Aspects of the Dark Ages*, 2nd edn (London, 1967)

Lawson, M. K., *Cnut: England's Viking King* (Stroud, 2004) 'The Collection of Danegeld and Heregeld in the Reigns of Aethelred II and Cnut', *EHR* **99** (1984), 721–38 'Danegeld and Heregeld Once More', *EHR* **105** (1990), 951–61 '"Those Stories Look True": Levels of Taxation in the Reigns of Aethelred II and Cnut', *EHR* **104** (1989), 385–406

Leahy, K., 'Anglo-Saxon Coin Brooches', in *Coinage and History*, ed. Cook and Williams, pp. 267–85

Leary, J. and Brown, G., *Tatberht's Lundenwic: Archaeological Excavations in Middle Saxon London* (London, 2004)

Lebecq, S., *Marchands et navigateurs frisons du haut moyen âge*, 2 vols. (Lille, 1983)

Le Blant, E., 'Paléographie des inscriptions latines du IIIe siècle à la fin du VIIIe', *Revue archéologique* **29** (1896), 177–97, 345–55; 30 (1897), 30–40, 171–84; 31 (1897), 172–84

Le Jan, R., 'Frankish Giving of Arms and Rituals of Power: Continuity and Change', in *Rituals of Power*, ed. Theuws and Nelson, pp. 377–99

Lemarignier, J. F., 'Les actes de droit privé de Saint-Bertin en haut moyen âge: survivances et déclin du droit romain dans la pratique franque', *Mélanges Fernand de Visscher: Revue internationale des droits de l'antiquité* **4** (1950), 35–72

Levison, W., *England and the Continent in the Eighth Century* (Oxford, 1946) 'The Inscription on the Jarrow Cross', *Archaeologia Aeliana* **21** (1943), 121–6

Leyser, K., 'Early Medieval Warfare', in *The Battle of Maldon: Fiction and Fact*, ed. J. Cooper (London, 1993), pp. 87–108

Lie, J., 'Sociology of Markets', *Annual Review of Sociology* **23** (1997), 341–60

Lockett, R. C., 'The Coinage of Offa', *NC* **20** (1920), 57–89

Lombard-Jourdan, A., 'Foires gauloises et origines urbaines', *Archéocivilisation* **11–13** (1974), 46–86

Lopez, R. S., 'An Aristocracy of Money in the Early Middle Ages', *Speculum* **28** (1953), 1–43 'Continuità e adattamento nel medio evo: un millennio di storia delle associazioni di monetieri nell'Europa meridionale', in *Studi in onore di Gino Luzzatto*, 4 vols. (Milan, 1949–50) II, 74–117 'Monete e monetieri nell'Italia barbarica', *Settimane* **8** (1961), 57–88

L'Orange, H. P., 'Le Néron constitutionnel et le Néron apothéosé', *Collections of the Ny Carlsberg Glyptothek* **3** (1942), 247–67

320

Bibliography

Lorans, E., 'Les élites et l'espace urbain: approches archéologique et morphologique (France du Nord et Angleterre, VIIe–Xe siècles', in *Les élites et leurs espaces: mobilité, rayonnement, domination (VIe–XIe s.)*, ed. P. Depreux, F.Bougard and R. Le Jan (Turnhout, 2007), pp. 67–97

Loveluck, C., 'The Dynamics of Elite Lifestyles in the "Rural World", AD 600–1150: Archaeological Perspectives from North West Europe', in *La culture du haut moyen âge: une question d'élites?*, ed. F. Bougard, R. Le Jan and R. McKitterick (Turnhout, 2009), pp. 139–70

'A High-Status Anglo-Saxon Settlement at Flixborough, Lincolnshire', *Antiquity* **72** (1998), 146–61

'Rural Settlement Hierarchy in the Age of Charlemagne', in *Charlemagne*, ed. Story, pp. 230–58

'Wealth, Waste and Conspicuous Consumption: Flixborough and Its Importance for Middle and Late Saxon Rural Settlement Studies', in *Image and Power in the Archaeology of Early Medieval Britain. Essays in Honour of Rosemary Cramp*, ed. H. Hamerow and A. MacGregor (Oxford, 2001), pp. 78–130

Loveluck, C. and Tys, D., 'Coastal Societies, Exchange and Identity along the Channel and Southern North Sea Shores of Europe, AD 600–1000', *Journal of Maritime Archaeology* **1** (2006), 140–69

Lowe, E. A., *Palaeographical Papers, 1907–1965*, 2 vols. (Oxford, 1972)

Lowe, K., 'Lay Literacy in Anglo-Saxon England and the Development of the Chirograph', in *Anglo-Saxon Manuscripts and Their Heritage*, ed. P. Pulsiano and E. M. Treharne (Aldershot, 1998), pp. 161–204

Lowick, N., 'An Early Tenth-Century Hoard from Isfahan', *NC* **15** (1975), 110–54

'Silver from the Panjhir Mines', in *Metallurgy in Numismatics*, ed. Oddy, II, 65–74

Loyn, H., *Anglo-Saxon England and the Norman Conquest*, 2nd edn (London, 1991)

'Boroughs and Mints', in *Anglo-Saxon Coins*, ed. Dolley, pp. 122–35

'Currency and Freedom: Some Problems in the Social History of the Early Middle Ages', in *Studies in Medieval History Presented to R. H. C. Davis*, ed. H. Mayr-Harting and R. I. Moore (1985), pp. 7–19

'Gesiths and Thegns in Anglo-Saxon England from the Seventh to the Tenth Century', *EHR* **70** (1955), 529–49

The Governance of Anglo-Saxon England, 500–1087 (Stanford, CA, 1984)

Lyon, B., *Henri Pirenne: A Biographical and Intellectual Study* (Ghent, 1974)

Lyon, C. S. S., 'The Coinage of Edward the Elder', in *Edward the Elder, 899–924*, ed. N. Higham and D. Hill (London, 2001), pp. 67–78

'Historical Problems of the Anglo-Saxon Coinage (2): The Ninth Century – Offa to Alfred', *BNJ* **37** (1968), 216–38

'Historical Problems of the Anglo-Saxon Coinage (3): Denominations and Weights', *BNJ* **38** (1969), 204–22

'Ninth-Century Northumbrian Chronology', in *Coinage in Ninth-Century Northumbria*, ed. Metcalf, pp. 27–41

'A Reappraisal of the *Sceatta* and *Styca* Coinage of Northumbria', *BNJ* **28** (1955–7), 227–42

'Some Problems in Interpreting Anglo-Saxon Coinage', *ASE* **5** (1976), 173–224

'Variations in Currency in Late Anglo-Saxon England', in *Mints, Dies and Currency: Essays Dedicated to the Memory of Albert Baldwin*, ed. R. Carson (London, 1971), pp. 101–20

Bibliography

Lyon, C. S. S. and Stewart, I., 'The Northumbrian Viking Coins in the Cuerdale Hoard', in *Anglo-Saxon Coins*, ed. Dolley, pp. 96–121

Lyons, A. and MacKay, W. A., 'The Coinage of Æthelred I (865–871)', *BNJ* **77** (2007), 71–118

Maddicott, J. R., 'London and Droitwich, *c.* 650–750: Trade, Industry and the Rise of Mercia', *ASE* **34** (2005), 7–58

'Prosperity and Power in the Age of Bede and Beowulf', *Proceedings of the British Academy* **117** (2002), 49–71

'Trade, Industry and the Wealth of King Alfred', *P&P* **123** (1989), 3–51

'Trade, Industry and the Wealth of King Alfred: A Reply', *P&P* **125** (1991), 164–88

'Two Frontier States: Northumbria and Wessex, *c.* 650–750', in *The Medieval State: Essays Presented to James Campbell*, ed. J. R. Maddicott and D. M. Palliser (London, 2000), pp. 25–45

Maguire, H., 'Magic and Money in the Early Middle Ages', *Speculum* **72** (1997), 1037–54

Mainman, A. J., *Pottery from 46–54 Fishergate* (London, 1993)

Maitland, F. W., *Domesday Book and Beyond: Three Essays in the Early History of England* (Cambridge, 1897)

Malcolm, G., Bowsher, D. and Cowie, R., *Middle Saxon London: Excavations at the Royal Opera House, 1989–99* (London, 2003)

Martin, P.-H., 'Eine Goldmünze Karls des Großen', in *Karl der Große in Ingelheim, Bauherr der Pfalz und europäischer Staatsmann*, ed. K. H. Henn and E. Kähler (Ingelheim, 1998), pp. 37–47

Mate, M., 'Coin Dies under Edward I and II', *NC* **9** (1969), 207–18

Mathews, T. F., *The Clash of Gods: A Reinterpretation of Early Christian Art*, 2nd edn (Princeton, NJ, and Chichester, 1999)

Matthews, S., 'Good King Offa: Legends of a Pious King', *Transactions of the Lancashire and Cheshire Antiquarian Society* **98** (2002), 1–14

Mauss, M., *Gift: The Form and Reason for Exchange in Archaic Societies*, trans. W. D. Halls, with foreword by M. Douglas (London, 1990)

Mayhew, N. J., 'From Regional to Central Minting, 1158–1464', in *History of the Royal Mint*, ed. Challis, pp. 83–178

'Modelling Medieval Monetisation', in *A Commercialising Economy: England 1086 to c. 1300*, ed. R. H. Britnell and B. M. S. Campbell (Manchester, 1995), pp. 55–77

'Money and Prices in England from Henry II to Edward III', *Agricultural History Review* **35** (1987), 121–32

'Population, Money Supply, and the Velocity of Circulation in England 1300–1700', *EcHR* **48** (1995), 238–57

Mayr-Harting, H., 'Charlemagne as a Patron of Art', *Studies in Church History* **28** (1992), 43–77

'Charlemagne, the Saxons and the Imperial Coronation of 800', *EHR* **111** (1996), 1113–33

The Coming of Christianity to Anglo-Saxon England, 3rd edn (London, 1991)

'Herrschaftsrepräsentation der ottonischen Familie', in *Otto der Grosse. Magdeburg und Europa*, ed. M. Puhle, 2 vols. (Mainz, 2001) I, 133–48

Ottonian Book Illumination: An Historical Survey, 2nd edn, 2 vols. (London, 1999)

Bibliography

McCormick, M., *Origins of the European Economy: Communications and Commerce A.D. 300–900* (Cambridge, 2001)

'Textes, images et iconoclasme dans le cadre des relations entre Byzance et l'occident carolingien', *Settimane* **41** (1994), 95–158

'Um 808. Was der frühmittelalterliche König mit der Wirtschaft zu tun hatte', in *Die Macht des Königs. Herrschaft in Europa vom Frühmittelalter bis in die Neuzeit*, ed. B. Jussen (Konstanz, 2005), pp. 55–71

McKerrell, H. and Stevenson, R. B. K., 'Some Analyses of Anglo-Saxon and Associated Oriental Silver Coinage', in *Methods of Chemical*, ed. Metcalf and Hall, pp. 195–210

McKitterick, R., *The Carolingians and the Written Word* (Cambridge, 1989)

Charlemagne: The Formation of a European Identity (Cambridge, 2008)

The Frankish Kingdoms under the Carolingians, 751–987 (London, 1983)

Frankish Kings and Culture in the Early Middle Ages (Aldershot, 1995)

History and Memory in the Carolingian World (Cambridge, 2004)

'Royal Patronage of Culture in the Frankish Kingdoms under the Carolingians: Motives and Consequences', *Settimane* **39** (1992), 93–129

'Text and Image in the Carolingian World', in *Uses of Literacy*, ed. McKitterick, pp. 297–318

McKitterick, R. (ed.), *The New Cambridge Medieval History II c. 700–c. 900* (Cambridge, 1995)

The Uses of Literacy in Early Mediaeval Europe (Cambridge, 1990)

Meens, R., 'Politics, Mirrors of Princes and the Bible: Sins, Kings and the Well-Being of the Kingdom', *EME* **7** (1998), 345–57

Meert, C., 'Les monnaies carolingiennes de l'atelier de Dinant', *Revue belge de numismatique* **108** (1962), 153–72

Melitz, J., 'The Polanyi School of Anthropology on Money: An Economist's View', *American Anthropologist* **72** (1970), 1020–40

Mersiowsky, M., 'Towards a Reappraisal of Carolingian Sovereign Charters', in *Charters and the Use of the Written Word in Medieval Society*, ed. K. Heidecker (Turnhout, 2000), pp. 15–25

Metcalf, D. M., *An Atlas of Anglo-Saxon and Norman Coin Finds, c. 973–1086* (London, 1998)

'The Availability and Uses of Gold Coinage in England, c. 670: Kentish Primacy Reconsidered', *Numismatiska Meddelanden* **37** (1989), 267–74

'Betwixt Sceattas and Offa's Pence. Mint Attributions, and the Chronology of a Recession', *BNJ* **79** (2009), 1–33

'The "Bird and Branch" Sceattas in the Light of a Find from Abingdon', *Oxoniensia* **37** (1972), 51–65

'The Coinage of King Aldfrith of Northumbria (685–704) and Some Contemporary Imitations', *BNJ* **76** (2006), 147–58

'The Coins', in *The Coins and Pottery from Hamwic*, ed. P. Andrews (Southampton, 1988), pp. 17–59

'Continuity and Change in English Monetary History c. 973–1086. Part I', *BNJ* **50** (1980), 20–49

'Continuity and Change in English Monetary History c. 973–1086. Part II', *BNJ* **51** (1981), 52–90

Bibliography

'Determining the Mint-Attribution of East Anglian *Sceattas* through Regression Analysis', *BNJ* **70** (2000), 1–11

'English Monetary History in the Time of Offa: A Reply', *Numismatic Circular* **71** (1963), 165–7

'Estimation of the Volume of the Northumbrian Coinage, *c.* 738–88', in *Sceattas*, ed. Hill and Metcalf, pp. 113–16

'Financial Support for Outlying Churches? A Perspective on the Uses of Money in Eighth-Century Northumbria', *BNJ* **72** (2002), 167–9

'Geographical Patterns of Minting in Medieval England', *Seaby's Coin and Medal Bulletin* (1977), 314–17, 353–7 and 390–1

'How Large Was the Anglo-Saxon Currency?', *EcHR* **18** (1965), 475–82

'Interpreting the Alloy of the Merovingian Silver Coinage', in *Studies in Numismatic Method*, ed. Brooke *et al.*, pp. 113–25

'Monetary Affairs in Mercia in the Time of Æthelbald (716–57)', in *Mercian Studies*, ed. A. Dornier (Leicester, 1977), pp. 87–106

'The Monetary Economy of Ninth-Century England South of the Humber: A Topographical Analysis', in *Kings, Currency and Alliances*, ed. Blackburn and Dumville, pp. 167–97

'Monetary Expansion and Recession: Interpreting the Distribution-Patterns of Seventh- and Eighth-Century Coins', in *Coins and the Archaeologist*, ed. J. Casey and R. Reece, 2nd edn (London, 1988), pp. 230–53

'The Ninth-Century Moneyer Werheard, and the Problem of Local Connections', *Wiltshire Archaeological Magazine* **72–3** (1980 for 1977–8), 195–8

'Offa's Pence Reconsidered', *Cunobelin* **9** (1963), 37–52

'The Premises of Early Medieval Mints: The Case of Eleventh-Century Winchester', in *I luoghi della moneta*, ed. La Guardia, pp. 59–67

'The Prosperity of North-Western Europe in the Eighth and Ninth Centuries', *EcHR* **20** (1967), 344–57

'The Ranking of Boroughs: Numismatic Evidence from the Reign of Æthelred II', in *Ethelred the Unready: Papers from the Millenary Conference*, ed. D. H. Hill (Oxford, 1978), pp. 159–212

'Runes and Literacy: Pondering the Evidence of Anglo-Saxon Coins of the Eighth and Ninth Centuries', in *Runeninschriften als Quellen interdisziplinärer Forschung*, ed. K. Düwel (Berlin and New York, 1998), pp. 434–8

'A *Sceat* of Series K Minted by Archbishop Berhtwald of Canterbury (693–731)', *BNJ* **58** (1988), 124–6

'A Sketch of the Currency in the Time of Charles the Bald', in *Charles the Bald*, ed. Gibson and Nelson, pp. 65–97

'The Taxation of Moneyers under Edward the Confessor and in 1086', in *Domesday Studies: Papers Read at the Novocentenary Conference of the Royal Historical Society and the Institute of British Geographers*, ed. J. C. Holt (Woodbridge, 1987), pp. 279–93

Thrymsas and Sceattas in the Ashmolean Museum, Oxford, 3 vols. (London, 1993–4)

'A Topographical Commentary on the Coin Finds from Ninth-Century Northumbria (*c.* 780–*c.* 870)', in *Coinage in Ninth-Century Northumbria*, ed. Metcalf, pp. 361–82

'Variations in the Composition of the Currency at Different Places in England', in *Markets*, ed. Pestell and Ulmschneider, pp. 37–47

Bibliography

'Viking-Age Numismatics 2: Coinage in the Northern Lands in Merovingian and Carolingian Times', *NC* **156** (1996), 399–428

'Were Ealdormen Exercising Independent Control over the Coinage in Mid-Tenth-Century England?', *BNJ* **57** (1987), 24–33

Metcalf, D. M. (ed.), *Coinage in Ninth-Century Northumbria*, BAR British Series **180** (Oxford, 1987)

Metcalf, D. M. and Hall, E. T. (eds.), *Methods of Chemical and Metallurgical Investigation of Ancient Coinage* (London, 1972)

Metcalf, D. M. and Miskimin, H., 'The Carolingian Pound: A Discussion', *Numismatic Circular* **76** (1968), 296–8 and 333–4

Metcalf, D. M. and Northover, P., 'Debasement of the Coinage in Southern England in the Age of King Alfred', *NC* **145** (1985), 150–76

'Carolingian and Viking Coins from the Cuerdale Hoard: An Interpretation of and Comparison of Their Metal Contents', *NC* **148** (1988), 97–116

'Coinage Alloys from the Time of Offa and Charlemagne to *c.* 864', *NC* **149** (1989), 101–20

'Interpreting the Alloy of the Later Anglo-Saxon Coinage', *BNJ* **56** (1986), 35–63

Metcalf, D. M. and Op Den Velde, W., 'The Monetary Economy of the Netherlands, *c.* 690–*c.* 715 and the Trade with England: A Study of the *Sceattas* of Series D', *Jaarboek vor Munt en Penningkunde* **90** (2007 for 2003), 1–211

'Series E Reconsidered', in *Studies in Early Medieval Coinage 2*, ed. Abramson, pp. 104–10

Meyvaert, P., 'Bede, Cassiodorus and the Codex Amiatinus', *Speculum* **71** (1996), 827–83

Middleton, N., 'Early Medieval Port Customs, Tolls and Controls on Foreign Trade', *EME* **13** (2005), 313–58

Miller, W. I., 'Gift, Sale, Payment, Raid: Case Studies in the Negotiation and Classification of Exchange in Medieval Iceland', *Speculum* **61** (1986), 18–50

Milne, G., *The Port of Medieval London* (Stroud, 2003)

Miskimin, H., 'Two Reforms of Charlemagne? Weights and Measures in the Middle Ages', *EcHR* **20** (1967), 35–52

Mitterauer, M., 'La continuité des foires et la naissance des villes', *Annales* **28** (1973), 711–34

Markt und Stadt im Mittelalter. Beiträge zur historischen Zentralitätsforschung (Stuttgart, 1980)

Moesgaard, J. C., 'Stray Finds of Carolingian Coins in Upper Normandy, France', in *Studia Numismatica: Festschrift, Arkadi Molvõgin 65*, ed. I. Leimus (Tallinn, 1995), pp. 87–102

Mordek, H., 'Karls des Großen zweites Kapitular von Herstal und die Hungersnot der Jahre 778/779', *Deutsches Archiv für Erforschung des Mittelalters* **61** (2005), 1–52

Morehart, M. J., 'Anglo-Saxon Art and the "Archer" *Sceat*', in *Sceattas*, ed. Hill and Metcalf, pp. 181–92

'Female Centaur or Sphinx? On Naming *Sceat* Types: The Case of *BMC* Type 47', *BNJ* **55** (1985), 1–9

Moreland, J., 'Concepts of the Early Medieval Economy', in *Long Eighth Century*, ed. Hansen and Wickham, pp. 1–34

Bibliography

'The Significance of Production in Eighth-Century England', in *Long Eighth Century*, ed. Hansen and Wickham, pp. 69–104

Morimoto,Y., 'Considérations nouvelles sur les "villes et campagnes" dans le domaine de Prüm au haut moyen âge', in *Villes et campagnes au moyen âge*, ed. Duvosquel and Dierkens, pp. 515–31

Morison, S., *Politics and Script: Aspects of Authority and Freedom in the Development of Graeco-Latin Script from the Sixth Century B.C. to the Twentieth Century A.D.* (Oxford, 1972)

Morrish, J., 'King Alfred's Letter as a Source on Learning in England in the Ninth Century', in *Studies in Earlier Old English Prose*, ed. P. Szarmach (Albany, NY, 1986), pp. 87–107

Morrison, K. F., 'Numismatics and Carolingian Trade: A Critique of the Evidence', *Speculum* **38** (1963), 403–32

Morrison, K. F. and Grunthal, H., *Carolingian Coinage* (New York, 1967)

Morrisson, C., 'Byzantine Money: Its Production and Circulation', in *Economic History of Byzantium*, ed. Laiou, III, 909–66

'La dévaluation de la monnaie byzantine au XIe siècle: essai d'interprétation', *Travaux et Mémoires* **6** (1976), 6–48

'Moneta, Kharagè, Zecca: les ateliers byzantins et le palais impérial', in *I luoghi della moneta*, ed. La Guardia, pp. 49–58

'Monnaie et finances dans l'empire byzantine: Xe–XIVe siècles', in *Hommes et richesses dans l'empire byzantine*, ed. C. Abadie-Reynal, 3 vols. (Paris, 1989–91) II, 291–315

Morton, A. D. (ed.), *Excavations at Hamwic*, vol. I (London, 1992)

Mossop, H. R., Dolley, R. H. M and Lyon, C. S. S. 'Analysis of the Material', in *The Lincoln Mint c. 890–1279*, ed. V. Smart (Newcastle upon Tyne, 1970), pp. 11–19

Motomura, A., 'The Best and Worst of Currencies: Seigniorage and Currency Policy in Spain, 1597–1650', *JEcH* **54** (1994), 104–27

Naismith, R., 'The Coinage of Offa Revisited', *BNJ* **80** (2010), 76–106

The Coinage of Southern England 796–865 (London, 2011)

'Kings, Crisis and Coinage Reforms in Northwest Europe c. 740–70', *EME* (forthcoming)

'Kingship and Learning on the Broad Penny Coinage of the "Mercian Supremacy"', in *Studies in Early Medieval Coinage 2*, ed. Abramson, pp. 70–87

'Money of the Saints: Church and Coinage in Early Anglo-Saxon England', *Anglo-Saxon* **2** (forthcoming)

'A New Moneyer for Ecgberht of Wessex's West Saxon Mint', *Numismatic Circular* **106** (2008), 192–4

'An Offa You Can't Refuse? Eighth-Century Mercian Titulature on Coins and in Charters', *Quaestio Insularis* **7** (2006), 71–10

'The Origins of the Line of Ecgberht, King of the West Saxons 802–39', *EHR* **126** (2011), 1–16

'Six English Finds of Carolingian-Era Gold Coins', *NC* **170** (2010), 215–25

'Tribrach Pennies of Eadberht "Præn" and Eadwald', *BNJ* **78** (2008), 216–22

Näsman, U., 'Exchange and Politics: The Eighth–Early Ninth Century in Denmark', in *Long Eighth Century*, ed. Hansen and Wickham, pp. 35–68

Naylor, J., 'Access to International Trade in Middle Saxon England: A Case of Urban Over-Emphasis?', in *Close Encounters: Sea- and Riverborne Trade, Ports and*

Hinterlands, Ship Construction and Navigation in Antiquity, the Middle Ages and in Modern Time, ed. M. Pasquinucci and T. Weski, BAR International Series 1283 (Oxford, 2004), pp. 139–48

An Archaeology of Trade in Middle Saxon England, BAR British Series **376** (Oxford, 2004)

'The Circulation of Early-Medieval European Coinage: A Case Study from Yorkshire, *c. 650–c.* 867', *Medieval Archaeology* **51** (2007), 41–61

Nelson, J. L., 'Carolingian Contacts', in *Mercia*, ed. Brown and Farr, pp. 126–43

Charles the Bald (London and New York, 1992)

'England and the Continent in the Ninth Century: II, the Vikings and Others', *TRHS* **13** (2003), 1–28

'England and the Continent in the Ninth Century: III, Rights and Rituals', *TRHS* **14** (2004), 1–24

'The Frankish Empire', in *History of the Vikings*, ed. Sawyer, pp. 19–47

'Inauguration Rituals', in *Early Medieval Kingship*, ed. P. H. Sawyer and I. N. Wood (Leeds, 1977), pp. 50–71

'Kingship and Empire in the Carolingian World', in *Carolingian Culture: Emulation and Innovation*, ed. R. McKitterick (Cambridge, 1994), pp. 52–87

'Kingship and Royal Government', in *NCMH* II, pp. 383–430

'The Lord's Anointed and the People's Choice: Carolingian Royal Ritual', in *Rituals of Royalty: Power and Ceremonial in Traditional Societies*, ed. D. Cannadine and S. Price (Cambridge, 1987), pp. 137–80

'The Problematic in the Private', *Social History* **15** (1990), 355–64

'Settings of the Gift in the Reign of Charlemagne', in *Languages of Gift*, ed. Davies and Fouracre, pp. 116–48

'Translating Images of Authority: The Christian Roman Emperors in the Carolingian World', in *Images of Authority. Papers Presented to Joyce Reynolds on the Occasion of Her 70th Birthday*, ed. M. M. Mackenzie and C. Roueché (Cambridge, 1989), pp. 194–205

'West Frankia and Wessex in the Ninth Century Compared', in *Der frühmittelalterliche Staat*, ed. Pöhl and Wieser, pp. 99–112

Newman, J., '*Sceattas* in East Anglia: An Archaeological Perspective', in *Two Decades of Discovery*, ed. T. Abramson (Woodbridge, 2008), pp. 17–22

'*Wics*, Trade and the Hinterlands – the Ipswich Region', in *Anglo-Saxon Trading Centres*, ed. Anderton, pp. 32–47

Nightingale, P., 'Some London Moneyers and Reflections on the Organization of English Mints in the Eleventh and Twelfth Centuries', *NC* **142** (1982), 34–50

Niles, J. D., 'Myth and History', in *Beowulf Handbook*, ed. Bjork and Niles, pp. 213–32

Noble, T. F. X., *Images, Iconoclasm, and the Carolingians* (Philadelphia, PA, 2009)

The Republic of St Peter: The Birth of the Papal State, 680–825 (Philadelphia, PA, 1984)

'Secular Sanctity: Forging an Ethos for the Carolingian Nobility', in *Lay Intellectuals*, ed. Wormald and Nelson, pp. 8–36

'Topography, Celebration, and Power: The Making of a Papal Rome in the Eighth and Ninth Centuries', in *Topographies of Power in the Early Middle Ages*, ed. M. de Jong and F. Theuws (Leiden and Boston, MA, 2001), pp. 45–91

Norberg, D., *Manuel pratique de latin médiéval* (Paris, 1968)

Novelli, S. C., 'Scritture e immagini Insulari', *Settimane* **41** (1994), 463–504

Ó Corráin, D., 'Ireland, Wales, Man, and the Hebrides', in *History of the Vikings*, ed. Sawyer, pp. 83–109

Oddy, W. A. (ed.), *Metallurgy in Numismatics*, vol. II (London, 1988)

Offner, A., 'Between the Gift and the Market: The Economy of Regard', *EcHR* **50** (1997), 450–76

O'Hara, M. D., Pirie, E. and Thornton-Pett, V, 'An Iron Reverse Die of the Reign of Cnut', in *The Reign of Cnut, King of England, Denmark and Norway*, ed. A. R. Rumble (Leicester, 1994), pp. 231–71

Okasha, E., 'The Non-Runic Scripts of Anglo-Saxon Inscriptions', *Transactions of the Cambridge Bibliographical Society* **4** (1968), 321–38

    'Script-Mixing in Anglo-Saxon Inscriptions', in *Writing and Texts in Anglo-Saxon England*, ed. A. R. Rumble (Woodbridge, 2006), pp. 62–70

Pagan, H., 'Coinage in Southern England, 796–874', in *Anglo-Saxon Monetary History*, ed. Blackburn, pp. 45–66

    'Northumbrian Numismatic Chronology in the Ninth Century', *BNJ* **38** (1969), 1–15

Page, R., *An Introduction to English Runes*, 2nd edn (Woodbridge, 1999)

Palliser, D. M. (ed.), *The Cambridge Urban History of Britain I, 600–1540* (Cambridge, 2000)

Palmer, B., 'The Hinterlands of Three Southern English *Emporia*: Some Common Themes', in *Markets*, ed. Pestell and Ulmschneider, pp. 48–60

Parkhouse, J., 'The Distribution and Exchange of Mayen Lava Quernstones in Early Medieval Northwest Europe', in *Exchange and Trade in Medieval Europe*, ed. G. De Boe and F. Verhaeghe (Zellik, 1997), pp. 97–106

Parry, J. and Bloch, M., 'Introduction: Money and the Morality of Exchange', in *Money and the Morality of Exchange*, ed. Parry and Bloch, pp. 1–32

Parry, J. and Bloch, M. (eds.), *Money and the Morality of Exchange* (Cambridge, 1989)

Patzold, S., *Episcopus. Wissen über Bischöfe im Frankenreich des späten 8. bis 10. Jahrhunderts* (Ostfildern, 2008)

Peers, G., *Subtle Bodies: Representing Angels in Byzantium* (Berkeley, CA, and London, 2001)

Peri, I., 'Omnia mensura et numero et pondere disposuisti. Die Auslegung von Weish 11,20 in der lateinischen Patristik', in *Mensura, Maß, Zahl, Zahlensymbolik im Mittelalter, Teil 1*, ed. A. Zimmermann (Berlin, 1983) pp. 1–21

Pestell, T. and Ulmschneider, K. (eds.), *Markets in Early Medieval Europe: Trading and 'Productive' Sites, 650–850* (Macclesfield, 2003)

Petersson, H. B. A., *Anglo-Saxon Currency* (Lund, 1969)

    'Coins and Weights. Late Anglo-Saxon Pennies and Mints c. 973–1066', in *Late Anglo-Saxon Coinage*, ed. Jonsson, pp. 207–434

Petry, K., 'Die Geldzinse im Prümer Urbar von 893. Bemerkungen zum spätkarolingischen Geldumlauf des Rhein-, Maas- und Moselraumes im 9. Jahrhunderts', *Rheinische Vierteljahrsblätter* **52** (1988), 16–42

    'Die Münz- und Geldgeschichte der Abtei Prüm im Spiegel der Münzfunde und der schriftlichen Überlieferung', in *Das Prümer Urbar als Geschichtsquelle und seine Bedeutung für das Bitburger und Luxemburger Land*, ed. E. Erpelding (Bitburg, 1993), pp. 27–46

Bibliography

Pirenne, H., *Medieval Cities: Their Origin and the Revival of Trade*, trans. F. D. Halsey (Princeton, NJ, 1925)

Mohammed and Charlemagne, trans. B. Miall (London, 1939)

Pirie, E., *Coins in Yorkshire Collections: The Yorkshire Museum, York; the City Museum, Leeds; the University of Leeds*, Sylloge of Coins of the British Isles **21** (London, 1975)

Coins of the Kingdom of Northumbria, c. 700–867, in the Yorkshire Collections (Llanfyllin, 1996)

'Contrasts and Continuity within the Coinage of Northumbria *c*. 670–876', in *Coinage and History*, ed. Cook and Williams, pp. 211–39

'Eanred's Penny: A Northumbrian Enigma', *Yorkshire Numismatist* **3** (1997), 65–8

Thrymsas, Sceattas and Stycas of Northumbria: An Inventory of Finds Recorded to 1997 (Llanfyllin, 2000)

Pliego, R., *La Moneda Visigoda*, 2 vols. (Seville, 2009)

Plunkett, S. J., 'The Mercian Perspective', in *The St Andrews Sarcophagus: A Pictish Masterpiece and Its International Connection*, ed. S. Foster (Dublin, 1998), pp. 202–26

Pohl, W., 'Ethnic Names and Identities in the British Isles: A Comparative Perspective', in *The Anglo-Saxons*, ed. Hines, pp. 7–32

Pohl, W. and Wieser, V. (eds.), *Der frühmittelalterliche Staat: europäische Perspektiven* (Vienna, 2009)

Polanyi, K., *The Great Transformation* (Boston, MA, 1957)

The Livelihood of Man (New York, 1977)

Primitive, Archaic and Modern Economies: The Essays of Karl Polanyi, ed. G. Dalton (New York, 1968)

Pössel, C., 'Authors and Recipients of Carolingian Capitularies, 779–829', in *Texts and Identities in the Early Middle Ages*, ed. R. Corradini, R. Meens, C. Pössel and P. Shaw (Vienna, 2006), pp. 253 –74

Poupardin, R., 'Études sur la diplomatique des princes Lombards de Bénévent, de Capoue et de Salerne', *Mélanges d'histoire et d'archéologie. École française de Rome* **21** (1901), 117–80

Pratt, D., 'The Illnesses of King Alfred the Great', *ASE* **30** (2001), 39–90

'Persuasion and Invention at the Court of King Alfred', in *Court Culture in the Early Middle Ages. Proceedings of the First Alcuin Conference*, ed. C. Cubitt (Turnhout, 2003), pp. 189–221

The Political Thought of King Alfred the Great (Cambridge, 2007)

'Problems of Authorship and Audience in the Writings of King Alfred the Great', in *Lay Intellectuals*, ed. Wormald and Nelson, pp. 162–91

Prou, M., *Les monnaies carolingiennes. Catalogue des monnaies françaises da la Bibliothèque nationale* (Paris, 1896)

Ramsay, J., *History of the Revenues of the Kings of England, 1066–1399*, 2 vols. (Oxford, 1925)

Redin, M. A., *Studies on Uncompounded Personal Names in Old English* (Uppsala, 1919)

Reuter, T., 'Gifts and Simony', in *Medieval Transformations*, ed. Cohen and de Jong, pp. 157–68

'Plunder and Tribute in the Carolingian Empire', *TRHS* **35** (1985), 75–94

'Property, Transactions and Social Relations between Rulers, Bishops and Nobles in Early Eleventh-Century Saxony: The Evidence of the *Vita Meinwerci*', in

Bibliography

Property and Power in Early Medieval Europe, ed. W. Davies and P. Fouracre (Cambridge, 1995), pp. 165–98

'The Recruitment of Armies in the Early Middle Ages: What Can We Know?', in *Military Aspects of Scandinavian Society in a European Perspective, A. D. 1–1300*, ed. A. Nørgård Jørgensen and B. L. Clausen (Copenhagen, 1997), pp. 32–7

'"You Can't Take It with You": Testaments, Hoards and Moveable Wealth in Europe 600–1100', in *Treasure in the Medieval West*, ed. E. M. Tyler (York, 2000), pp. 11–24

Reuter, T. (ed.), *Alfred the Great. Papers from the Eleventh-Centenary Conferences* (Aldershot, 2003)

The New Cambridge Medieval History III c. 900–c. 1024 (Cambridge, 1999)

Reynolds, S., 'Bookland, Folkland and Fiefs', *Anglo-Norman Studies* **14** (1992), 211–27

'Compulsory Purchase in the Earlier Middle Ages', in *Frankland. The Franks and the World of the Early Middle Ages. Essays in Honour of Dame Jinty Nelson*, ed. P. Fouracre and D. Ganz (Manchester, 2008), pp. 28–43

'The Historiography of the Medieval State', in *Companion to Historiography*, ed. M. Bentley (London, 1997), pp. 117–38

Richards, J., 'What's So Special about "Productive Sites"? Middle Saxon Settlements in Northumbria', *ASSAH* **10** (1999), 71–80

Richards, J., Naylor, J. and Holas-Clark, C., 'Anglo-Saxon Landscape and Economy: Using Portable Antiquities to Study Anglo-Saxon and Viking England', *Internet Archaeology* **25** (2009) (www.intarch.ac.uk/)

Riché, P., *Daily Life in the World of Charlemagne*, trans. J. A. McNamara (Liverpool, 1978)

Richter, M., 'Bede's *Angli*: Angles or English?', *Peritia* **3** (1984), 99–114

Rippon, S., *Beyond the Medieval Village: The Diversification of Landscape Character in Southern Britain* (Oxford, 2008)

Robben, A., *Sons of the Sea Goddess: Economic Practice and Discursive Conflict in Brazil* (New York, 1989)

Rollason, D. W., *Northumbria, 500–1100: Creation and Destruction of a Kingdom* (Cambridge, 2003)

Rolnick, A. J., Velde, F. R. and Weber, W. E., 'The Debasement Puzzle: An Essay on Medieval Monetary History', *JEcH* **56** (1996), 789–808

Roscoe, P. B., 'Practice and Political Centralisation. A New Approach to Political Evolution', *Current Anthropology* **34** (1993), 111–40

Rosenwein, B., 'Francia and Polynesia: Rethinking Anthropological Approaches', in *Negotiating the Gift*, ed. Algazi, Groebner and Jussen, pp. 361–79

Negotiating Space: Power, Restraint, and Privileges of Immunity in Early Medieval Europe (Manchester, 1999)

To Be the Neighbor of Saint Peter: The Social Meaning of Cluny's Property, 909–1049 (Ithaca, NY, and London, 1989)

Rosser, A. G., 'Anglo-Saxon Gilds', in *Minsters and Parish Churches: The Local Church in Transition, 950–1200*, ed. J. Blair (Oxford, 1988), pp. 31–3

Rouche, M., *L'Aquitaine des Wisigoths aux Arabes, 418–781* (Paris, 1979)

'Marchés et marchands en Gaule du Ve au Xe siècle', *Settimane* **40** (1992), 395–434

Bibliography

Rovelli, A., 'Circolazione monetaria e formulari notarili nell'Italia altomedievale', *Bulletino dell'istituto storico italiano per il medio evo e archivo Muratoriano* **98** (1992), 109–44

'Coins and Trade in Early Medieval Italy', *EME* **17** (2009), 45–76

'Emissione e uso della moneta: le testimonianze scritte e archeollogiche', *Settimane* **48** (2001), 821–52

'La funzione della moneta tra l'VIII e X secolo. Un'analisi della documentazione archeologica', in *La storia dell'alto medioevo italiano (VI–X sec.) alla luce dell'archeologia. Atti del Convegno internazionale di Siena, 2–6 dicembre 1992*, ed. R. Francovich and G. Noyé (Florence, 1994), pp. 521–38

'La moneta nella documentazione altomedievale di Roma e del Lazio', in *La storia di Roma nell'alto medioevo alla luce dei recenti scavi archeologici*, ed. P. Delogu and L. Paroli (Florence, 1993), pp. 333–52

'Some Considerations on the Coinage of Lombard and Carolingian Italy', in *Long Eighth Century*, ed. Hansen and Wickham, pp. 195–223

'I tesori monetali', in *Tesori. Forme di accumulazione della ricchezza nell'alto medioevo (secoli V–XI)*, ed. S. Gelichi and C. La Rocca (Rome, 2004), pp. 241–56

Rumble, A., 'HAMTVN alias HAMWIC (Saxon Southampton): The Place-Name Traditions and Their Significance', in *Excavations at Melbourne Street, Southampton, 1971–6*, ed. P. Holdsworth (London, 1980), pp. 7–20

'Notes on the Linguistic and Onomastic Characteristics of Old English *wic*', in *Wics*, ed. Hill and Cowie, pp. 1–2

Russo, D., *Town Origins and Development in Early England, c. 450–950 A.D.* (Westport, CT, and London, 1998)

Sabbe, E., 'Quelques types de marchands des IXe et Xe siècles', *Revue belge de philologie et d'histoire* **13** (1934), 176–87

Sahlins, M., *Stone Age Economics* (Chicago, IL, 1972)

Samson, R., 'Economic Anthropology and Vikings', in *Social Approaches*, ed. Samson, pp. 87–96

'Fighting with Silver: Re-thinking Trading, Raiding and Hoarding', in *Social Approaches*, ed. Samson, pp. 123–33

Samson, R. (ed.), *Social Approaches to Viking Studies* (Glasgow, 1991)

Sarah, G., 'Caractérisation de la composition et de la structure des alliages argent-cuivre par ICP-MS avec prélèvement par ablation laser. Application au monnayage carolingian' (unpublished Ph.D. dissertation, Université d'Orléans, 2008)

Sarah, G., Bompaire, M., McCormick, M., Rovelli, A. and Guerrot, C., 'Analyses élémentaires de monnaies de Charlemagne et Louis le Pieux du Cabinet de Médailles: l'Italie carolingienne et Venise', *Revue numismatique* **164** (2009), 355–406

Savage, E. and Goldus, A.A., 'Dirhams for the Empire', in *Genèse de la ville islamique en al-Andalus et au Maghreb occidental*, ed. P. Cressier and M. García-Arenal (Madrid, 1998), pp. 377–402

Sawyer, P., *Anglo-Saxon Charters: An Annotated List and Bibliography* (London, 1968)

'Coins and Commerce', in *Sigtuna Papers. Proceedings of the Sigtuna Symposium on Viking Age Coinage 1–4 June 1989*, ed. K. Jonsson and B. Malmer (Stockholm, 1990), pp. 283–8

From Roman Britain to Norman England, 2nd edn (London, 1998)

Bibliography

'Kings and Merchants', in *Early Medieval Kingship*, ed. P. H. Sawyer and I. N. Wood (Leeds, 1977), pp. 139–58

Kings and Vikings. Scandinavia and Europe AD 700–1100 (London, 1982)

'The Two Viking Ages of Britain', *Mediaeval Scandinavia* **2** (1969), 163–207

Sawyer, P. (ed.), *The Oxford Illustrated History of the Vikings* (Oxford, 1997)

Scharer, A., *Die angelsächsische Königsurkunde im 7. und 8. Jahrhundert* (Cologne and Vienna, 1982)

'Duke Tassilo of Bavaria and the Origins of the Rupertus Cross', in *Belief and Culture in the Middle Ages: Studies Presented to Henry Mayr-Harting*, ed. R. Gameson and H. Leyser (Oxford, 2001), pp. 69–75

'Die Intitulationes der angelsächsischen Könige im 7. und 8. Jahrhundert', in *Intitulatio III. Lateinische Herrschertitel und Herrschertitulaturen vom 7. bis zum 13. Jahrhundert*, ed. H. Wolfram and A. Scharer (Vienna, Cologne and Graz, 1988), pp. 9–74

Schmitz, K., *Ursprung und Geschichte der Devotionsformeln bis zu ihrer Aufnahme in die fränkische Königsurkunde* (Amsterdam, 1965)

Schramm, P. E., *Die deutschen Kaiser und Könige in Bildern ihrer Zeit: I. Teil, bis zur Mitte des 12. Jahrhunderts (751–1152)*, 2 vols. (Leipzig, 1928)

Herrschaftszeichen und Staatssymbolik: Beiträge zu ihrer Geschichte vom dritten bis zum sechzehnten Jahrhundert, 3 vols. (Stuttgart, 1954–6)

Schumpeter, J. A., *History of Economic Analysis* (London, 1955)

Scragg, D. (ed.), *Edgar, King of the English, 959–975: New Interpretations* (Woodbridge, 2007)

Screen, E., 'Anglo-Saxon Law and Numismatics: A Reassessment in the Light of Patrick Wormald's *The Making of English Law*', *BNJ* **77** (2007), 148–72

'The Reign of Lothar I (795–855), Emperor of the Franks, through the Charter Evidence' (unpublished Ph.D. dissertation, University of Cambridge, 1998)

Scull, C., 'Ipswich: Development and Contexts of an Urban Precursor in the Seventh Century', in *Central Places in the Migration and the Merovingian Periods. Papers from the 52nd Sachsensymposium, Lund, August 2001*, ed. B. Hårdh and L. Larsson (Stockholm, 2002), pp. 303–16

'Urban Centres in Pre-Viking England?', in *The Anglo-Saxons*, ed. Hines, pp. 269–98

Sellwood, D., 'Medieval Minting Techniques', *BNJ* **31** (1962), 57–65

Siems, H., *Handel und Wucher im Spiegel frühmittelalterlicher Rechtsquellen* (Hannover, 1992)

Silber, I. F., 'Gift-Giving in the Great Traditions: The Case of Donations to Monasteries in the Medieval West', *European Journal of Sociology* **36** (1995), 209–43

Simmel, G., *The Philosophy of Money*, trans. T. Bottomore and D. Frisby (London, 1978)

Sims-Williams, P., *Religion and Literature in Western England, 600–800* (Cambridge, 1990)

Sindbæk, S., 'Networks and Nodal Points: The Emergence of Towns in Early Viking Age Scandinavia', *Antiquity* **81** (2007), 119–32

'The Small World of the Vikings: Networks in Early Medieval Communication and Exchange', *Norwegian Archaeological Review* **40** (2007), 59–74

Skaare, K., *Coins and Coinage in Viking-Age Norway: The Establishment of a National Coinage in Norway in the XI Century, with a Survey of the Preceding Currency History* (Oslo, 1976)

Bibliography

Skre, D., 'Post-Substantivist Towns and Trade AD 600–1000', in *Means of Exchange*, ed. Skre, pp. 327–42

Skre, D. (ed.), *Means of Exchange. Dealing with Silver in the Viking Age*, Kaupang Excavation Project Publication Series **2** (Århus, 2007)

Smith, A. H., *English Place-Name Elements*, 2 vols. (Cambridge, 1956)

Smith, C., 'A Barbarised Coinage? Copper Alloy in Pre-Viking Northumbrian Coinage', *Quaestio Insularis* **3** (2002), 59–75

Smith, J., *Europe after Rome: A New Cultural History 500–1000* (Oxford, 2005)

Smyth, A., *King Alfred the Great* (Oxford, 1995)

Sotinel, C., 'Le don chrétien et ses retombées sur l'économie dans l'antiquité tardive', *Antiquité tardive* **14** (2006), 105–16

Speake, G., *Anglo-Saxon Animal Art and Its Germanic Background* (Oxford, 1980)

Spufford, P., *Money and Its Use in Medieval Europe* (Cambridge, 1987)

Stafford, P., 'Charles the Bald, Judith and England', in *Charles the Bald*, ed. Gibson and Nelson, pp. 139–53

'Historical Implications of the Regional Production of Dies under Æthelred II', *BNJ* **48** (1978), 35–51

'Political Women in Mercia, Eighth to Early Tenth Centuries', in *Mercia*, ed. Brown and Farr, pp. 35–49

'Reeve', in *BEASE*, pp. 386–7

Unification and Conquest: A Political and Social History of England in the Tenth and Eleventh Centuries (London, 1989)

Stahl, A., *The Merovingian Coinage of the Region of Metz* (Louvain-la-neuve, 1982)

Zecca: The Mint of Venice in the Middle Ages (Baltimore, MD, 2000)

Stanley, E., 'Did the Anglo-Saxons Have a Social Conscience Like Us?', *Anglia* 121 (2003), 238–64

Staubach, N., *Herrscherbild Karls des Kahlen: Formen und Funktionen monarchischer Repräsentation im früheren Mittelalter* (Münster, 1982)

Rex christianus: Hofkultur und Herrschaftspropaganda im Reich Karls des Kahlen (Cologne, 1993)

Steger, H., *David Rex et Propheta: König David als vorbildliche Verkörperung des Herrschers und Dichters im Mittelalter, nach Bilddarstellungen des achten bis zwölften Jahrhunderts* (Nuremberg, 1961)

Stengel, E., *Abhandlungen und Untersuchungen zur Geschichte des Kaisergedankens im Mittelalter* (Cologne and Graz, 1965)

Stenton, F. M., *Anglo-Saxon England*, 3rd edn (Oxford, 1971)

Latin Charters of the Anglo-Saxon Period (Oxford, 1955)

Preparatory to Anglo-Saxon England, ed. D. M. Stenton (Oxford, 1970)

Sternberg, T., *'Orientalium more secutus'. Räume und Institutionen der Caritas des 5. bis 7. Jahrhunderts in Gallien* (Münster, 1991)

Steuer, H., 'Gewichtsgeldwirtschaften im frühgeschichtlichen Europa – Feinwaagen und Gewichte als Quellen zur Währungsgeschichte', in *Der Handel der Karolinger- und Wikingerzeit*, ed. Düwel *et al.*, pp. 405–527

'Der Handel der Wikingerzeit zwischen Nord- und Westeuropa aufgrund archäologischer Zeugnisse', in *Der Handel der Karolinger- und Wikingerzeit*, ed. Düwel *et al.*, pp. 113–97

Stevenson, W. H., '*Trinoda necessitas*', *EHR* **29** (1914), 689–703

Bibliography

Stewart, I., 'Anglo-Saxon Gold Coins', in *Scripta Nummaria Romana: Essays Presented to Humphrey Sutherland*, ed. R. A. G. Carson and C. M. Kraay (London, 1978), pp. 143–72

'Coinage and Recoinage after Edgar's Reform', in *Late Anglo-Saxon Coinage*, ed. Jonsson, pp. 455–85

'CVNNETTI Reconsidered', in *Coinage in Ninth-Century Northumbria*, ed. Metcalf, pp. 345–54

'The English and Norman Mints, *c.* 600–1158', in *History of the Royal Mint*, ed. Challis, pp. 1–82

'Medieval Die-Output for English Mints in the Fourteenth Century', *NC* 3 (1963), 97–106

'*Ministri* and *Monetarii*', *Revue numismatique* 30 (1988), 166–75

'Second Thoughts on Medieval Die-Output', *NC* 4 (1964), 293–303

Stiegemann, C. and Wemhoff, M. (eds.), *799: Kunst und Kultur der Karolingerzeit: Karl der Grosse und Papst Leo III. in Paderborn: Katalog der Ausstellung, Paderborn 1999*, 3 vols. (Mainz, 1999)

Stiennon, J., 'Le denier de Charlemagne au nom de Roland', *Cahiers de civilisation médiévale* 3 (1960), 87–95

Stoclet, J., '*Immunes ab omni teloneo*': *étude de diplomatique, de philologie et d'histoire sur l'exemption de tonlieux au haut moyen âge et spécialement sur la 'Praeceptio de navibus'* (Brussels, 1999)

Story, J., *Carolingian Connections: Anglo-Saxon England and Carolingian Francia, c. 750–870* (Aldershot, 2003)

Story, J. (ed.), *Charlemagne: Empire and Society* (Manchester, 2005)

Story, J. *et al.*, 'Charlemagne's Black Marble: The Origins of the Epitaph of Pope Hadrian I', *Papers of the British School at Rome* 73 (2005), 157–90

Stott, P., 'Saxon and Norman Coins from London', in *Aspects of Saxo-Norman London*, vol. II, *Finds and Environmental Evidence*, ed. A. Vince (London, 1991), pp. 279–325

Strathern, A., *Rope of Moka: Big-Men and Ceremonial Exchange in Mount Hagen, New Guinea* (Cambridge, 1971)

Suchodolski, S., 'La date de la grande réforme monétaire de Charlemagne', *Quaderni ticinesi di numismatica e antichità classiche* 10 (1981), 399–409

'Le poids des monnaies de Charlemagne émises après la réforme: contribution à la métrologie numismatique', in *Dona numismatica: Walter Hävernick zum 23. Januar 1965 dargebracht*, ed. P. Berghaus and G. Hatz (Hamburg, 1965), pp. 43–50

Sussman, N., 'Debasements, Royal Revenues, and Inflation in France during the Hundred Years' War, 1415–1422', *JEcH* 53 (1993), 44–70

Symons, D. J., 'Aspects of the Anglo-Saxon and Norman Mint of Worcester, 975–1158' (unpublished Ph.D. thesis, University of Birmingham, 2003)

Tabuteau, E. Z., *Transfers of Property in Eleventh-Century Norman Law* (Chapel Hill, NC, and London, 1988)

Tatton-Brown, T., 'The Towns of Kent', in *Anglo-Saxon Towns in Southern England*, ed. J. Haslam (Chichester, 1984), pp. 1–36

Téreygeol, F., 'Production and Circulation of Silver and Secondary Products (Lead and Glass) from Frankish Royal Silver Mines at Melle (Eighth to Tenth Century)', in *Post-Roman Towns*, ed. Henning, I, 123–34

Téreygeol, F., Hoelzl, S. and Horn, P., 'Le monnayage de Melle au haut moyen âge: état de la recherche', *Bulletin de l'Association des Archéologues de Poitou-Charentes* **34** (2005), 49–56

Tessier, G., *Diplomatique royale française* (Paris, 1962)

Thacker, A., 'Some Terms for Noblemen in Anglo-Saxon England, *c.* 650–900', *ASSAH* **2** (1981), 201–36

Theuws, F., 'Exchange, Religion, Identity and Central Places in the Early Middle Ages', *Archaeological Dialogues* **10** (2004), 121–38

Theuws, F. and Nelson, J. L. (eds.), *Rituals of Power. From Late Antiquity to the Early Middle Ages* (Leiden, 2000)

Thomas, G., '"Brightness in a Time of Dark": The Production of Secular Ornamental Metalwork in 9th-Century Northumbria', in *De Re Metallica: The Uses of Metal in the Middle Ages*, ed. R. Bork (Aldershot, 2005), pp. 31–48

'Silver Wire Strap-Ends from East Anglia', *ASSAH* **9** (1996), 81–100

'Strap-Ends and the Identification of Regional Patterns in the Production and Circulation of Ornamental Metalwork in Late Anglo-Saxon and Viking-Age Britain', in *Pattern and Purpose in Insular Art. Proceedings of the Fourth International Conference on Insular Art held at the National Museum and Gallery, Cardiff 3–6 September 1998*, ed. M. Redknap, N. Edwards, S. Youngs, A. Lane and J. Knight (Oxford, 2001), pp. 39–49

Thomas, N., *Entangled Objects: Exchange, Material Culture, and Colonialism in the Pacific* (Cambridge, MA, 1991)

Timby, J., 'The Middle Saxon Pottery', in *Coins and Pottery from Hamwic*, ed. Andrews, pp. 73–122

Toon, T. E., *The Politics of Early Old English Sound Change* (New York, 1983)

Toubert, P., *L'Europe dans sa première croissance: de Charlemagne à l'an mil* (Paris, 2004)

'Il sistema curtense: la produzione e lo scambio interno in Italia nei secoli VIII, IX e X', in *Storia d'Italia: Annali VI. Economia naturale, economia monetaria*, ed. R. Romano and U. Tucci (Turin, 1983), pp. 3–63

Travaini, L., 'Sedi di zecca nell'Italia medievale', in *I luoghi della moneta*, ed. La Guardia, pp. 69–85

Treffort, C., *Mémoires carolingiennes. L'épitaphe entre celebration mémorielle, genre littéraire et manifeste politique: milieu VIIIe–début XIe siècle* (Rennes, 2007)

Tweddle, D., Moulden, J. and Logan, E., *Anglian York: A Survey of the Evidence* (York, 1999)

Tyler, D., 'Orchestrated Violence and the "Supremacy" of the Mercian Kings', in *Æthelbald and Offa*, ed. Hill and Worthington, pp. 27–33

Ulmschneider, K., *Markets, Minsters and Metal Detectors: The Archaeology of Middle Saxon Lincolnshire and Hampshire Compared*, BAR British Series **307** (Oxford, 2000)

Verhulst, A., *The Carolingian Economy* (Cambridge, 2002)

'Economic Organisation', in *NCMH* II, pp. 481–509

'Karolingische Agrarpolitik. Das Capitulare de Villis und die Hungersnöte von 792/3 und 805/6', *Zeitschrift für Agrargeschichte und Agrarsoziologie* **13** (1965), 175–89

'Marchés, marchands et commerce au haut moyen âge dans l'historiographie récente', *Settimane* **40** (1992), 23–43

Bibliography

'Les origines urbaines dans le Nord-Ouest de l'Europe: essai de synthèse', *Francia* **14** (1986), 57–81

The Rise of Cities in North-West Europe (Cambridge, 1999)

'Roman Cities, *Emporia* and New Towns (Sixth–Ninth Centuries)', in *Long Eighth Century*, ed. Hansen and Wickham, pp. 105–20

Vince, A., 'Ceramic Petrology and the Study of Anglo-Saxon and Later medieval Ceramics', *Medieval Archaeology* **49** (2005), 219–45

Violante, C., *La società Milanese nell'età precomunale* (Bari, 1953)

Völckers, H. H., *Karolingische Münzfunde der Frühzeit (751–800)* (Göttingen, 1965)

Vollrath-Reichelt, H., *Königsgedanke und Königtum bei den Angelsachsen bis zur Mitte des 9. Jahrhunderts* (Cologne, 1971)

von Reden, S., *Money in Classical Antiquity* (Cambridge, 2010)

Wade, K., 'Gipeswic – East Anglia's First Economic Capital', in *Ipswich from the First to the Third Millennium*, ed. N. Salmon and R. Malster (Ipswich, 2001), pp. 1–6

'Ipswich', in *The Rebirth of the Town in the West, AD 700–1050*, ed. R. Hodges and B. Hobley (London, 1988), pp. 93–100

'The Urbanisation of East Anglia: The Ipswich Perspective', in *Flatlands and Wetlands: Current Themes in East Anglian Archaeology*, ed. J. Gardiner (Norwich, 1993), pp. 142–51

Walker, D. R., *The Metrology of the Roman Silver Coinage*, 3 vols. (Oxford, 1976–8)

Wallace-Hadrill, J. M., *Bede's Ecclesiastical History of the English People: A Historical Commentary* (Oxford, 1988)

Early Germanic Kingship in England and on the Continent: The Ford Lectures Delivered in the University of Oxford in Hilary Term 1970 (Oxford, 1971)

Early Medieval History (Oxford, 1975)

Ward-Perkins, B., *The Fall of Rome and the End of Civilization* (Oxford, 2005)

Watson, A. M., 'Back to Gold – and Silver', *EcHR* **20** (1967), 1–34

Weber, M., *Economy and Society: An Outline of Interpretive Sociology*, trans. G. Roth and C. Wittich, 2 vols. (Berkeley, CA, and London, 1979)

Webster, L., '*Ædificia nova*: Treasures of Alfred's Reign', in *Alfred the Great*, ed. Reuter, pp. 79–103

'Metalwork of the Mercian Supremacy', in *Mercia*, ed. Brown and Farr, pp. 263–77

Webster, L. and Backhouse, J., *The Making of England: Anglo-Saxon Art and Culture A.D. 600–900* (London, 1991)

Weiller, R., *Die Münzen von Trier. Erster Teil: Erster Abschnitt. Beschreibung der Münzen: 6. Jahrhundert–1307* (Düsseldorf, 1988)

Weinberger, S., 'Donations-ventes ou ventes-donations? Confusion ou système dans la Provence du XIème siècle', *Le moyen âge* **105** (1999), 667–80

Weiner, A. B., *Inalienable Possessions. The Paradox of Keeping-While-Giving* (Berkeley, CA, and Oxford, 1992)

Werner, K.-F., '"Hludowicus Augustus". Gouverner l'empire chrétien: idées et réalités', in *Charlemagne's Heir: New Perspectives on the Reign of Louis the Pious, 814–840*, ed. P. Godman and R. Collins (Oxford, 1990), pp. 3–123

Werner, K.-F. '*Missus – Marchio – Comes*: entre l'administration centrale et l'administration locale de l'empire carolingienne', in *Vom Frankenreich zur Entfaltung Deutschlands und Frankreichs: Ursprünge, Strukturen, Beziehungen: ausgewählte Beiträge: Festgabe zu seinem sechzigsten Geburtstag* (Sigmaringen, 1984), pp. 121–61

Bibliography

Werner, M., 'The Cross-Carpet Page in the Book of Durrow: The Cult of the True Cross, Adomnan and Iona', *Art Bulletin* **72** (1990), 174–223

White, S. D., 'Service for Fiefs or Fiefs for Service: The Politics of Reciprocity', in *Negotiating the Gift*, ed. Algazi, Groebner and Jussen, pp. 63–98

Whitelock, D., *Some Anglo-Saxon Bishops of London* (London, 1975)

Whitelock, D. (trans.), *English Historical Documents*, vol. I, *c. 500–1042*, 2nd edn (London, 1979)

Wickham, C., 'Bounding the City: Concepts of Urban–Rural Difference in the West in the Early Middle Ages', *Settimane* **56** (2009), 61–80

'Compulsory Gift Exchange in Lombard Italy, 650–1150', in *Languages of Gift*, ed. Davies and Fouracre, pp. 193–216

'Conclusion', in *Byzantine and Early Islamic Near East*, ed. Cameron, pp. 461–8

'Conclusion', in *Languages of Gift*, ed. Davies and Fouracre, pp. 238–61

'Economic and Social Institutions in Northern Tuscany in the Eighth Century', in *Istituzione ecclesiastiche della Toscana medievale*, ed. C. Wickham, M. Ronzani, Y. Milo and A. Spicciani (Galatina, 1980), pp. 7–34

'The Fall of Rome Will Not Take Place', in *Debating the Middle Ages: Issues and Readings*, ed. B. H. Rosenwein and L. K. Little (Oxford, 1998), pp. 45–57

Framing the Early Middle Ages: Europe and the Mediterranean 400–800 (Oxford, 2005)

The Inheritance of Rome. A History of Europe from 400 to 1000 (London, 2009)

Land and Power: Studies in Italian and European Social History 400–1200 (London, 1994)

The Mountains and the City: The Tuscan Appennines in the Early Middle Ages (Oxford, 1988)

'Overview: Production, Distribution and Demand', in *Long Eighth Century*, ed. Hansen and Wickham, pp. 345–77

'Rethinking the Structure of the Early Medieval Economy', in *The Long Morning of Early Medieval Europe: New Directions in Early Medieval Studies*, ed. J. R. Davis and M. McCormick (Aldershot, 2008), pp. 19–31

Wilk, R. and Cliggett, L., *Economies and Cultures: Foundations of Economic Anthropology*, 2nd edn (Boulder, CO, and London, 2007)

Williams, A., '*Kingship and Government in Pre-Conquest England, c. 500–1066* (Basingstoke, 1999)

'Land Tenure', in *BEASE*, pp. 277–8

'Some Notes and Considerations on Problems Connected with the English Royal Succession, 860–1066', *Anglo-Norman Studies* **1** (1979), 144–67 and 225–33

Williams, G., 'The Circulation and Function of Coinage in Conversion-Period England, *c.* AD 580–675', in *Coinage and History*, ed. Cook and Williams, pp. 145–92

Early Anglo-Saxon Coins (Oxford, 2008)

'The Influence of Dorestad Coinage on Coin Design in England and Scandinavia', in *Dorestad in an International Framework. New Research on Centres of Trade and Coinage in Carolingian Times*, ed. A. Willemsen and H. Kik (Turnhout, 2010), pp. 105–11

'Mercian Coinage and Authority', in *Mercia*, ed. Brown and Farr, pp. 210–28

'Military Obligations and Mercian Supremacy in the Eighth Century', in *Æthelbald and Offa*, ed. Hill and Worthington, pp. 103–9

Bibliography

Williamson, T., *The Origins of Norfolk* (Manchester, 1993)

Wilson, D. M., *Anglo-Saxon Ornamental Metalwork 700–1100 in the British Museum* (London, 1964)

Wilson, D. M. (ed.), *The Archaeology of Anglo-Saxon England* (London, 1976)

Wilson, D. M. and Blunt, C. E., 'The Trewhiddle Hoard', *Archaeologia* **98** (1961), 75–122

Witthöft, H., '"Denarius novus", "Modius publicus" und "Libra panis" im Frankfurter Kapitulare: Elemente und Struktur einer materiellen Ordnung im fränkischer Zeit', in *Das Frankfurter Konzil von 794. Kristallisationspunkt karolingischer Kultur. Akten zweier Symposium (vom 23. bis 27. Februar und vom 13. bis 15. Oktober 1994) anläßlich der 1200-Jahrfeier der Stadt Frankfurt am Main*, ed. R. Berndt, 2 vols. (Mainz, 1997) I, 219–52

Münzfuß, Kleingewichte, 'pondus Caroli' und die Grundlegung des nordeuropäischen Maß- und Gewichtswesens in fränkischer Zeit (Ostfildern, 1984)

Wolfram, H., *Intitulatio I: Lateinische Königs- und Fürstentitel bis zum Ende des 8. Jahrhunderts* (Graz, 1967)

'Lateinische Herrschertitel im neunten und zehnten Jahrhundert', in *Intitulatio II: Lateinische Herrscher- und Fürstentitel im neunten und zehnten Jahrhundert*, ed. H. Wolfram (Graz, 1973), pp. 19–178

Wood, D., *Medieval Economic Thought* (Cambridge, 2002)

Wood, D. (ed.), *Medieval Money Matters* (Oxford, 2004)

Wood, I. N., 'The Gifts of Wearmouth and Jarrow', in *Languages of Gift*, ed. Davies and Fouracre, pp. 89–115

The Merovingian Kingdoms 450–751 (Harlow, 1994)

Wormald, P., 'The Age of Offa and Alcuin', in *The Anglo-Saxons*, ed. J. Campbell (London, 1982), pp. 101–28

'Bede, *Beowulf* and the Conversion of the Anglo-Saxon Aristocracy', in *Bede and Anglo-Saxon England: Papers in Honour of the 1300th Anniversary of the Birth of Bede*, ed. R. T. Farrell (Oxford, 1978), pp. 32–95

'Bede, the *Bretwaldas* and the Origins of the *Gens Anglorum*', in *Ideal and Reality in Frankish and Anglo-Saxon Society: Studies Presented to J. M. Wallace-Hadrill*, ed. P. Wormald, with D. Bullough and R. Collins (Oxford, 1983), pp. 99–129

'The Emergence of Anglo-Saxon Kingdoms', in *The Making of Britain: The Dark Ages*, ed. L. M. Smith (Basingstoke, 1984), pp. 49–62

'A Handlist of Anglo-Saxon Lawsuits', *ASE* **17** (1988), 247–81

'In Search of King Offa's "Law-Code"', in *People and Places in Northern Europe, 500–1600: Studies Presented to P. H. Sawyer*, ed. I. Wood and N. Lund (Woodbridge, 1991), pp. 25–45

The Making of English Law: King Alfred to the Twelfth Century, vol. I, *Legislation and Its Limits* (Oxford, 1999)

'Pre-Modern "State" and "Nation": Definite or Indefinite?', in *Staat im frühen Mittelalter*, ed. Airlie, Pohl and Reimitz, pp. 179–89

'The Uses of Literacy in Anglo-Saxon England and Its Neighbours', *TRHS* **27** (1977), 95–114

Wormald, P., Bullough, D. and Collins, R. (eds.), *Ideal and Reality in Frankish and Anglo-Saxon Society: Studies Presented to J. M. Wallace-Hadrill* (Oxford, 1983)

Wormald, P. and Nelson, J. L. (eds.), *Lay Intellectuals in the Carolingian World* (Cambridge, 2007)

Bibliography

Yan, Y., 'The Gift and Gift Economy', in *Handbook*, ed. Carrier, pp. 246–61

Yorke, B., 'The Anglo-Saxon Kingdoms 600–900 and the Beginnings of the Old English State', in *Der frühmittelalterliche Staat*, ed. Pöhl and Wieser, pp. 73–86

'Joint Kingship in Kent *c.* 560 to 785', *Archaeologia Cantiana* **99** (1983), 1–19

'The Kingdom of the East Saxons', *ASE* **14** (1985), 1–36

Kings and Kingdoms of Early Anglo-Saxon England (London, 1990)

'The Vocabulary of Anglo-Saxon Overkingship', *ASSAH* **2** (1981), 171–200

Wessex in the Early Middle Ages (Leicester, 1995)

Zahnd, U., 'Novus David – Νεος Δαυιδ. Zur Frage nach byzantinische Vorläuren eines abendlandischen Topos', *Frühmittelalterliche Studien* **42** (2008), 71–88

Zelizer, V., *The Social Meaning of Money* (New York, 1994)

Zipperer, S., 'Coins and Currency – Offa of Mercia and His Frankish Neighbours', in *Völker an Nord- und Ostsee und die Franken: Akten des 48. Sachsensymposiums in Mannheim vom 7. bis 11. September 1997*, ed. U. von Freeden, U. Koch and A. Wieczorek (Bonn, 1999), pp. 121–7

INDEX

Ælfsige, thegn, 269, 270

Ælfwald, king of the East Angles (713–49), 84

Æthelbald, king of the Mercians (716–57), 9, 20, 34, 36, 54, 91
titulature, 80

Æthelbald, West Saxon king (855–60), 109, 110, 125

Æthelberht I, king of Kent (d. 616), 58, 61, 115

Æthelberht II, king of the East Angles (d. 794), 85, 117, 120, 152
coinage of, 118–20

Æthelberht, West Saxon king (858–65), 11, 53, 202
coinage of, 61, 65, 66, 110, 111, 112, 115, 125, 152, 164, 182

Æthelflæd, wife of Ealdorman Æthelred, 121

Æthelheard, archbishop of Canterbury, 175

Æthelhere, moneyer, 148

Æthelmod, moneyer, 148

Æthelred I, king of the Northumbrians (788/9–96), 247

Æthelred I, West Saxon king (865–71), 11, 110, 190
coinage of, 110

Æthelred II the Unready, king of the English (978–1016), 195
coinage of, 88

Æthelred II, king of the Northumbrians (840/1–4844–8), 248

Æthelred, ealdorman of the Mercians, 121

Æthelred, moneyer, 148

Æthelstan, king of the East Angles (c. 825–45), 139
coinage of, 85, 164, 191

Æthelstan, king of the English (924/5–39), 50, 51, 131, 142, 209

Æthelwald, moneyer, 194

Æthelweald, bishop of Dunwich, 70

Æthelweard, king of the East Angles (c. 845–55), 140
coinage of, 164

Æthelwulf, West Saxon king (839–58), 27, 42, 47, 53, 123, 125, 141, 142, 168, 196, 218
coinage of, 65, 66, 84, 106, 107–12, 125
decimation of lands, 109
pilgrimage to Rome (854–6), 109–10

Africa, north, 41, 160

agrarian change, 257–58

Aiskew hoard (1990s), 214

Alcuin, 10, 61, 76

Aldfrith, king of the Northumbrians (685–704)
coinage of, 91, 97

Aldhelm of Malmesbury, 60

Alfred the Great, king of the Anglo-Saxons (871–99), 9, 11, 18, 21, 23, 24, 27, 32, 36, 61, 121, 126, 129, 131, 282, 295
coinage of, 165, 182
'offering pieces', 284
law-code, 267
objects associated with, 51–52

alms and almsgiving, 262, 282–84
economic impact, 282; see also gifts and gift-giving; pauperes

alpha and omega, 70–71, 73, 84; see also iconography, christian

Althoff, Gerd, 16

Andrew, St, 123, 128

Angles, Saxons and Jutes, see ethnic identity

Anglo-Saxon Chronicle, 9, 11, 47, 235

Anskar, St, 276, 283

anthropology, 25

Aosta, Italy, 250

Aquitaine, 17, 121

Arabian peninsula, 160

Arichis II, prince of Benevento, 13

Aristotle, 252

Asser, 9, 23, 24, 51, 110, 125

autarky, 288

Index

Babba, moneyer, 223
Baldred, king of Kent (*c.* 823–5), 125
  coinage of, 69, 83
Bardney, Lincolnshire, 61
barter, 264, 274, 288, 290
  regulation of, 290
Bath, 115
Bavaria, 17
Beaduheard, reeve, 35
Beagmund, moneyer, 148
Bede, 6, 23, 47, 55, 61, 263
  Historia ecclesiastica gentis Anglorum, 61
Bedfordshire, 219
Belgium, 245
Benevento, principality of, 250
Beonna, king of the East Angles (*c.* 749–60),
  6, 97
  coinage of, 99, 158, 161, 174
Beorhtric, West Saxon king (786–802), 35,
  117, 120
  coinage of, 70, 103, 106, 120, 149, 192, 219
Beornmod, bishop of Rochester, 123
Beornwulf, king of the Mercians (823–5),
  107, 125
  coinage of, 191, 192
Beornwulf, moneyer, 149
Beowulf, 24, 262
  portrayal of gift-giving, 260–61
Berhtwulf, king of the Mercians (840–52), 141,
  192, 197
  coinage of, 83, 141–42, 188, 190, 192, 228
Bertha, Frankish princess, 61
Bexley, Kent, 116
Bibliothéque Nationale, Paris, 174, 176
Bidford-on-Avon, Warwickshire, 220
Biebrich hoard (1921), 208
bird and branch, motif, 92
Birka, Sweden, 276, 283
Blackburn, Mark, 114, 194
Bloch, Maurice, 275
Boethius, Old English version of *De consolatione
  philosophiae* of, 23
Boniface, St, 261, 266
Bourdieu, Pierre, 23
brass, 162–63, 247
brassage, 43; *see also* mints and minting, profits
  of; seigniorage
Breedon on the Hill, Leicestershire, 57
Brescia, 249
bretwalda, 80; *see also imperium* and imperial
  ideas of rule; titulature
Brid, moneyer, 141
Britain, pre-Roman, 285
British Museum, 116, 174, 176
British Numismatic Society, 1
Brittany, 17

brooches, nummular, 49; *see also* metalwork
Buckinghamshire, 219
Bugga, nun, 261, 266
Burgred, king of the Mercians (852–74), 11
  coinage of, 165, 179, 190, 192
Burrow Hill, Suffolk, 289
Byzantine empire, 55, 69, 246
  coinage of, 68, 90, 181, 285
  Italian exarchate, 249
  mints, 144
  source of silver, 159, 160

caliphate, 90, 98, 166, 246, 285
  conquest of, 254
  source of silver, 159
Callataÿ, François de, 186
Campbell, James, 87
Canterbury, 35, 77, 78, 115, 116, 204, 236, 237–38,
  240, 268, 272, 283
  archbishopric of, 7, 62, 68, 77, 121–23, 128,
  134, 197, 223, 284
  coinage of, 54, 64, 65, 68, 71, 73, 75, 77,
  82, 95, 104, 105, 106, 107, 109, 114,
  118, 140, 165, 173, 178–80, 187, 190–91,
  211, 214, 215, 216, 217, 218, 219, 223,
  224, 228
  mint and moneyers of, 7, 63, 64, 78, 100, 102,
  103, 104, 110, 124, 125, 128, 131, 134, 139,
  140, 141, 142, 146, 148, 150, 153, 154, 171,
  194, 195, 196, 197–98, 214, 216, 219, 223,
  230, 237
capitularies, 15, 43, 90, 145, 244; *see also* law
Carolingian kingdom and empire, 7, 17, 28, 31,
  36, 40, 72, 74, 76, 79, 86, 87, 97, 168, 238,
  241, 254, 262, 277, 287, 288, 294–95
  coinage of, 204, 233, 250
  mints, 145, 154
  renaissance, 254
  silver supply, 161
  urbanization, 236
Catla, Swedish almsgiver, 276, 283
central places, 259
Ceolbald, moneyer, 146
Ceolfrith, abbot, 263
Ceolheard, moneyer, 146
Ceolmund, *praefectus,* 146
Ceolnoth, archbishop of Canterbury,
  69, 149
  coinage of, 67, 69, 73, 164
Ceolwulf I, king of the Mercians (821–3), 20,
  53, 123, 140, 153–54
  coinage of, 64, 65, 66, 75, 78, 83, 104–06,
  128, 191
Ceolwulf II, king of the Mercians (874–9)
  coinage of, 165
Chalcedon, Council of (451), 58

Charlemagne, Frankish king and emperor,
13–14, 15, 17, 27, 28, 29, 36–37, 59, 76,
116, 121, 156, 204, 254, 287, 289
coinage of, 54, 65, 116, 162, 171, 249
metrology, 175–78
Charles the Bald, West Frankish king and
emperor, 40, 51, 109, 209
coinage of, 165, 171, 181
charters, 2, 14, 15, 18, 21–22, 49, 73, 80, 82, 83,
115, 127, 149, 264, 282
ambiguity of transactions, 269–71
Canterbury, 237
Carolingian, 270
coinage and, 267–73
'decimation', 109
moneyers in, 147–49
precious metal references, 271–72
production of, 80; *see also* land; titulature
Chayanov, Alexander, 288
Chester, 121
Chick, Derek, 172
China, 270
Chindaswinth, Visigothic king, 81
Chiseldon, Wiltshire, 220
Christianity and Christian teaching, 16–17, 85
christogram, 73; *see also* iconography, christian
Church councils, 197; *see also* synods
Chwartz, coin collection, 174, 176
circulation, coin, 89, 203–32, 243, 252, 259, 293
and elites, 251
Canterbury, 213–14, 215, 219, 223
East Anglia, 230–31
ecclesiastical, 223–24
effects of debasement, 165–66
foreign within southern England, 204–09, 226
Carolingian, 205–07
Northumbrian, 207–08
gold, 256, 272–73
in Carolingian empire, 228, 244–46
influence of moneyers, 220–23
Inscribed Cross, 225
Ipswich, 211–13
kings and, 218–20
London, 214–16
Northumbria, 247–48
regions, 202
Rochester, 216
social and administrative influences, 218–24
Southampton/Winchester, 216–18
southern coins within Northumbria, 210
unified across Southumbria, 204, 229;
see also monetization; trade and exchange
Coenweald, moneyer, 148
Coenwulf, king of the Mercians (796–821), 9,
12, 18, 19, 20, 47, 51, 53, 117, 140, 141,
148, 196, 197, 209, 218, 235, 271

coinage of, 64, 65, 66, 68, 75, 77, 102, 104, 120,
124–25, 140, 151, 152, 191
gold, 114–16, 117, 128
titulature of, 82–83
Coin Hoards, 199
Coin Register, 199
coinage
base-metal, 39, 247, 248, 249, 285, 286–87, 289
control over, 2, 3, 27, 85–86, 87–127, 142,
152–53, 154–55, 170, 197–98, 204, 229,
251, 291, 295
definition of control, 88–89
establishment of control, 96–100
exportation, 233–34
foreign (in England), 155
gold, 8, 39–40, 47, 156, 157, 244, 249, 250, 253,
255, 263, 264, 284, 285, 286, 287
Anglo-Saxon, 4–5, 53, 67, 112–17, 143–44,
203, 256, 267, 285
Arabic, 113–14
Byzantine, 266
Carolingian, 116, 249, 272
Coenwulf mancus, 114–16, 128, 191
Lombard, 13–14
Merovingian, 5, 37, 39–40, 256
Offa dinar, 113–14
prevalence in charters, 272–73
Roman, 202, 266
tremissis, 286
manipulation, 157
reforms in 740s–70s, 98–100
silver, 39, 41, 156, 160, 244, 246, 249, 255, 256,
264, 285, 286, 287
Carolingian, 65, 86, 163, 165, 168, 195, 204,
228, 249, 294–95
Merovingian, 5, 144, 161
symbolic importance of, 39–40, 45–46,
47–50, 114, 116, 117–21, 229, 256, 294
terminology, 264–67, 271–72
ambiguity, 266–67
argenteus, 272
mancus, 113–14, 266, 272
obolus, 264–65, 289
sceat, 265, 267
shekel, 264–65, 272, 278
solidus/scilling, 265, 267, 268, 272, 286
use of, 37–39, 168, 224–29, 232–33, 236,
243–44, 252–92, 293
biblical, 281–82
decline *c.* 830, 226–28, 232–33, 234,
236, 239
gold, 114, 289
Northumbria, 247
peasants, 276–84, 288
small change, 284–90; *see also* money;
penny

colonialism, 274
coniurationes, 154
Constantine I the Great, emperor, 40, 55, 69
  representation of, 58–62
  reputation of, 61–62
Constantine V, emperor, 290
Constantine VI, emperor, 63
Constantinople, 39, 290
conversion, 256
Cornwall, 36
corrosion, 158
credit, 288
Crondall hoard (1882), 286
cross, 60, 69, 83, 93, 105
  and Constantine I the Great, 59–60;
    see also iconography, Christian
Croydon hoard (*c.* 1906), 111, 165
Cuerdale hoard (1840), 207
Cunincpert, Lombard king, 81
Cuthred, king of Kent (798–807), 53, 117
  coinage of, 64, 68, 83, 124–25
cynehelm, 91; *see also* headgear, royal
Cynethryth, queen of the Mercians, 62–64, 124
  coinage of, 151, 219
Cynewulf, poet, 60

David, biblical king, 57–58
debasement, *see* fineness
Delgany hoard (1874), 183, 208
demography, 258
Deormod, moneyer, 162
Desiderius, king of the Lombards, 13
Devroey, Jean-Pierre, 250
dialects, Old English, 243
  West Saxon, 78
die-cutters, 2, 7, 55, 62, 64, 72, 76, 77–78, 81, 83,
    86, 100, 101, 114, 127, 138–42, 143, 155,
    294; *see also* mints and minting
dies and die-studies, 2, 43, 44, 68, 77, 78, 94, 101,
    118, 138–42, 185–88
  distribution, 89, 94, 110, 114–15, 131, 150–51,
    155, 191
  Italy, 250
  late Anglo-Saxon, 185
  output per die, 185–86
  production, 78, 94–95, 100, 104; *see also* mints
    and minting
Dinant, Belgium, 196
Dolley, Michael, 293
Domesday Book, 42, 43, 44, 139
  Winton Domesday, 132
'Donation of Constantine', 60
Dorestad, 195, 234, 235, 236, 238, 245, 258, 276,
    279, 283
Dorking hoard (1817), 112, 165, 183, 186, 204, 208
Dorset, 201, 210

Dream of the Rood, 70
Droitwich, 34
Dud, moneyer, 58, 223
Duda, moneyer, 223
Dunn, moneyer, 147–48
Durham, 45
Durrow, Book of, 70

Eadbald, king of Kent (616–40)
  coinage of, 91
Eadberht 'Præn', Kentish king (796–8), 124
  coinage of, 102, 103, 151, 219
Eadberht, bishop of London, 62, 77, 123, 128
Eadberht, king of the Northumbrians
    (737–58), 6
  coinage of, 97, 161, 182, 246
  metrology, 174
Eadberht, moneyer, 146
Eadgar, moneyer, 140, 146
Eadmund, moneyer, 146
Eadnoth, moneyer, 146, 220
Eadwald, king of the East Angles (*c.* 796–800)
  coinage of, 102, 103, 104, 152, 191, 220, 228
Eadwald, moneyer, 146
Eadwig, king of the English (955–9), 121
ealdormen, 20, 21, 22, 23, 294
Ealhmund, moneyer, 78, 139, 194
Ealred, moneyer, 150
Eanbald, moneyer, 146
Eanmund, moneyer, 146
Eanred, king of the Northumbrians (*c.* 810–41),
    117, 207, 247, 248
  coinage of, 118
Eanred, moneyer, 146
East Anglia, 7, 11, 19, 35, 84, 85, 96, 104, 119, 198,
    201, 202, 204, 207, 208, 209, 211, 213,
    215, 216, 217, 218, 223, 230, 240, 241, 243,
    244, 268
  mint and moneyers of, 7, 64, 75, 77, 82, 103,
    106, 112, 128, 134, 140, 141, 146, 152,
    153, 162, 164, 171, 190, 191, 196, 204,
    211–13, 214, 216, 218, 228, 230–31;
    see also Ipswich
ecclesiastical coinage, 7, 89, 90, 91, 121–23,
    148–49
  circulation, 223–24, 284
  iconography, 92–94
Ecgberht II, Kentish king (*c.* 764–79), 219
Ecgberht, West Saxon king (802–39), 9, 12, 21,
    22, 112, 121, 123, 192, 218
  coinage of, 48, 69, 73, 78, 83, 106–07, 128,
    149, 217
Ecgfrith, king of the Mercians (796), 121, 124
Ecghard, moneyer, 146
Ecgred, moneyer, 146
economic change, 257–59

Edgar, king of the English (959–75), 18, 51, 121
  coin reform, 87, 88, 179
Edmund, king of the English (939–46), 269
Edmund, St, king of the East Angles (855–69),
    11, 84
  coinage of, 164, 191
Edward the Confessor, king of the English
    (1042–66), 44, 45, 132
Edward the Elder, king of the Anglo-Saxons
    (899–924), 278
Egil, legendary hero, 92
Egypt, 290
electron pulse microanalysis, 158
Elene, 60
Eligius, St, 149
elites, 17, 26, 27, 29, 33, 34, 35, 37, 114, 147, 149,
    241, 242, 256, 258, 259, 260, 269, 271,
    276–77, 281, 284, 291, 294
  coinage and, 251
  exchanges among, 262–64
  residences, 279
  use of gold, 273; *see also* ealdormen
Eoba, moneyer, 95, 140, 150–51, 194, 219, 223
Erchempert, chronicler, 13
Ermoldus Nigellus, 60
Essex, 19, 106, 210, 215, 219
estate-centres, 29–31, 35, 110, 115, 224, 241, 255,
    256, 268, 269, 277, 278, 279, 280
  Carolingian, 257
  documentation, 262
  fortified, 258
  iron production, 242
  role in urbanization, 236
  urban, 115–16; *see also* land; elites
Esty, Warren, 187
exchange, *see* gifts and gift-giving; trade and
    exchange
ethnic identity, 79, 80, 82, 84

famine, 176, 177
Faustina, wife of Antoninus Pius, 64
Faversham, Kent, 19
fineness, 42, 47, 89, 90, 94, 111, 155, 156, 158,
    161–68, 230
  Carolingian, 161, 162, 163, 165, 168
  Cross and Lozenge coinage, 165
  debasement, 161, 163–65, 178, 183, 229,
    244, 256
    Canterbury, 163, 164
    causes, 166–68
    cycles of, 161
    effect on coin-use, 165–66, 247–48
    fiscal, 167, 168
    Ipswich, 163, 164
    London, 163, 164
    Northumbria, 167, 207, 247

    Rochester, 163, 164
    DORB/CANT coinage, 164
    early/*sceattas*, 161
    Floreate Cross coinage, 164
    gold, 161
    Inscribed Cross coinage, 164, 166
    Lunettes coinage, 165
    Merovingian, 161
    trace elements, 157–58, 159, 161, 162, 208,
      230, 234
    under Offa, 161–62
fines, *see* payments
Fitzwilliam Museum, Cambridge, 174, 176
Flixborough, Lincolnshire, 208, 258
Fordwich, Kent, 237
forest, 258
forgery, 183
Forthred, thegn, 268
France, 87, 245, 260, 286
Frankfurt, Council of (794), 175, 287, 289
Frideburg, Swedish almsgiver, 276, 283
Frisia and Frisians, 5, 238, 281
  coinage of, 208

Gannon, Anna, 55
Germany, 87, 238, 245, 246, 260
gifts and gift-giving, 26–27, 253, 254, 259–76,
    282, 291
  anthropological context, 273–74
  books, 261
  clothing, 263
  coinage and, 264–67
  counter-gifts, 261, 262, 263
  economic role, 262–64
  elite, 259, 262–64
  horses, 263
  'instrumental gifts', 270
  to obtain charters, 270
  as opposite of monetary exchange, 259–60
  to papacy, 113, 250, 263, 284
  relation to sales of land, 269–71
  social context, 260, 274–75
  symbolic, 263
  from tenants to landlords, 263
  value, 264
  vocabulary of, 262; *see also* trade and
    exchange
Gloucester, 121
Gloucestershire, 210
goldsmiths, 133, 146
Goltho, Lincolnshire, 258
Gravesend hoard (1838), 266
Gregory of Tours, 261, 262, 289
Grierson, Philip, 173, 253–54, 255, 259, 260, 267
Grimoald III, prince of Benevento, 13–14, 37
Grunthal, Henry, 174, 176

Index

Hadrian I, pope, 28, 67, 76
Hædda, abbot, 268
hagiography, 276, 281–82, 289
halfpennies, 203
Hamburg, 276
Haraldr Harðráði, king of Norway, 166
Harold II, king of the English (1066), 121
Hávamál, 254
Heaberht, Kentish king (*fl. c.* 765), 7, 117, 150, 219
  coinage of, 98, 118
headgear, royal, 55–56
Heavenfield, battle of (634), 61
Hedeby, 279
Helena, mother of Constantine I the Great, 60, 64
Hendy, Michael, 41
Henry II, 45
Henry VIII, 123, 167
'heptarchy', 10, 11
Hereford, 42
Hinton Waldrist, Oxfordshire, 220
Historia Augusta, 39
hoards, 166, 169, 174, 186, 199, 200, 208, 225, 244, 245, 253
  Continental, 208
  economic impact of, 232–33
  Frankish, 233; *see also* single-finds
Hodges, Richard, 32, 259
Hohenstaufen dynasty, 45
household, royal, 16; *see also* kingship; itineraries, royal
Humber, 19, 218, 242
Hundred Years War, 167
Hunred, moneyer, 148
hunting, 31
Hwicce, 20, 36, 269
Hygeberht, archbishop of Lichfield, 123

Iænberht, archbishop of Canterbury, 175
  coinage of, 223–24
Ibba, moneyer, 58
iconography, 5–6, 89, 112, 114, 117, 119–20
  Carolingian, 57, 86
  Christian, 69–71, 92–94
  manuscript, 40, 49, 50–51, 54, 60, 70, 72, 243
  Merovingian, 59
  Northumbrian, 91
  numismatic, 47–71, 91–94, 141, 151, 153, 155, 156
  Roman, 8, 39, 40, 48, 52, 53, 54, 55–57, 59, 85
  royal, 91–92
  sculpture, 50, 51
  serpents, 85; *see also* alpha and omega; cross; portraits; inscriptions
Ilanz hoard (1904), 176, 208, 214, 266

imperium and imperial ideas of rule, 80; *see also* kingship; titulature
India, 277, 286
Ine, West Saxon king (688–726), 29, 266
Ingelheim, palace of, 60
Innes, Matthew, 16
inscriptions, 72–84
  numismatic, 91, 114; *see also* script forms
Ipswich, 35, 64, 75, 103, 106, 128, 129, 131, 140, 141, 146, 152, 162, 171, 191, 196, 211–13, 216, 218, 230, 236, 241, 258; *see also* East Anglia, mint and moneyers of
Ireland, 233, 234, 246, 290
Irene, empress, 63
Irminon, abbot, 277
Isidore of Seville, 156, 265
Islam, *see* caliphate
Italy, 17, 36, 41, 73, 74, 246, 286
  Anglo-Saxon coin-finds, 214
  coin fineness, 162
  coinage in, 9, 204, 249–50, 289, 290
    documentation, 249
    rarity of finds, 249–50
  moneyers in, 144, 147
  pottery, 250
itineraries, royal, 36, 229, 243, 251

Japan, 270
Jerusalem, 60
Jouarre, abbey, 76
Judith, wife of Æthelwulf and Æthelbald, 109
Jutland, 5, 8

Kent, 7, 32, 75, 83, 84, 96, 104, 106, 120, 148, 149, 182, 197–98, 204, 209, 210, 213, 214, 215, 216, 217, 219, 223, 243, 268
  coinage of, 161
  under Mercian rule, 19, 20, 35
  under West Saxon rule, 107, 155; *see also* Canterbury; Rochester
Kilger, Christoph, 290
kin-groups, 274
kingship, 16–46, 293, 294
  and coinage, 2, 11, 14–15, 41–46, 50–52, 85–86, 87–127, 131, 133, 142, 151, 152–53, 154–55, 198, 218, 251, 291, 295
    Carolingian empire, 145
    establishment of control, 96–100
    comparison between England and elsewhere, 17–18
    ecclesiastical conception of, 29
    economic resources of, 23–37, 110, 111
    generosity, 261, 269
    Mercian, 19–20
    representation of, 49–52, 85, 91–92

kingship (*cont.*)
  and towns, 32–36
  West Saxon, 21–22
Kingston, council of (838), 69

land, 16, 251, 262, 263, 267
  bookland, 268
  economic importance of, 23, 26–27, 29–31,
    271
  market for, 271
  reasons for granting/selling, 269–71
  sales of, 267–73; *see also* charters
landholding, 148
Lantfred, 147
Lateran palace, 60
Latin, 49, 78, 264
law, 2, 61, 90, 115, 127, 286, 287, 290
  access to markets, 282
  concerning coinage, 42, 90, 133, 156, 183, 209
  law-codes
    I Æthelstan, 284
    Grately code (II Æthelstan), 123, 131, 132,
      134–38, 282
    VI Æthelstan, 284
    II Æthelred, 266
    IV Æthelred, 132, 147, 282
    V Æthelred, 157
    VI Æthelred, 157
    Alfred the Great, 267
    II Cnut, 157
    Hlothhere and Eadric, 115
    Ine, 266
  monetary terminology, 267;
    see also Frankfurt, Council of (794);
    Pîtres, Edict of (864); Theodosian Code
Leo III, pope, 113
letters and letter-writing, 261
Levison, Wilhelm, 4
Liber pontificalis, 250
Lichfield, 20, 242
  archbishopric of, 62, 123
Lincoln, 194, 195
Lincolnshire, 208, 214, 215, 219, 240
Lindisfarne Gospels, 57
Lindsey, 20, 202, 242
literacy, 48, 49, 75, 76–79
Lombards, 13, 76, 98, 249
  coinage of, 81, 90
  mints, 144
London, 7, 20, 34, 35, 43, 115–16, 146, 201, 219,
    220, 235, 240, 241, 258, 279, 289
  bishopric of, 197, 223
  coinage of, 48, 54, 65, 71, 75, 82, 83, 103, 104,
    105, 106, 118, 173, 178–80, 190, 191–92,
    195, 214–16, 223, 228
  fires, 191, 197

Lundenwic, 196
mint and moneyers of, 7, 58, 62, 64, 82, 95,
    100, 102, 104, 121, 128, 131, 134, 139, 140,
    141, 146, 151, 171, 194, 195, 196–97, 214,
    216, 230
  relationship with Rochester in 840s, 109,
    141–42, 163
  Thames Exchange site, 138
Lothar I, Frankish emperor, 171
Louis the Pious, Frankish emperor, 16, 29,
    54, 60
  coinage of, 65, 86, 116, 121, 162, 163, 171,
    207, 272
Ludica, king of the Mercians (825–7), 192
Ludoman, moneyer, 146
Lul, moneyer, 118, 151–52, 223
Luni, Italy, 250
Lyon, Stewart, 187

Magonsætan, 20
Mali, 286
mancus, *see* coinage, terminology
Marcian, emperor, 58
Marcus Aurelius, emperor, 60
markets, 1, 33–34, 146, 241, 258, 259, 260, 261,
    262, 277, 278–82, 284, 288, 292
  definition, 278–79
  Frankish, 280
  price setting, 287
  role in economy, 284
  Roman, 280
  rural, 279–81; *see also* estate-centres;
    'productive sites'; towns; trade and
    exchange
Mauss, Marcel, 254, 260, 263, 275
Maxims, Old English, 24
Melle, 159
Mendips, 158
merchants, 26, 28, 33, 35, 149, 197, 253, 256, 281,
    291
  Jewish, 281; *see also* trade and exchange
Mercia, 7, 9, 10, 11, 15, 22, 36, 79, 96, 106, 120,
    126, 128, 131, 141, 155, 197, 202, 204,
    209, 210, 213, 214, 215, 216, 220, 229,
    235, 243
  coinage of, 112
  development of royal coinage, 100–06
  military prowess, 32
Merovingian kingdoms, 37, 38, 39–40, 41
metal-detectors, 200, 201–02, 237, 241, 250, 280;
    see also single-finds; 'productive sites'
metallurgy, *see* fineness
metalwork, 51, 70, 72, 161, 239, 240, 242–43,
    268, 273, 290
  distribution, 242–43, 266
  gifts of, 264

'Mercian-style', 242, 243
Northumbria, 247
relationship to coinage, 266
silver, 272
strap-ends, 243
Trewhiddle style, 243
Metcalf, Michael, 94, 130, 165, 202, 205, 255
metrology, 42, 47, 89, 90, 94, 98, 106, 155, 156,
     168–80, 199, 205, 264, 265, 278
  under Baldred, 178
  basis in seeds, 169
  Carolingian, 171, 174, 175–78
  under Ceolwulf I, 178
  under Coenwulf, 178
  DORB/CANT coinage, 179
  East Anglia, 178
  effects of wear, 170
  Inscribed Cross coinage, 179
  late Anglo-Saxon, 171
  manipulation for fiscal purposes, 176–78
  methodology, 169–70
  non-numismatic, 266
  under Offa, 101, 171–78
  pound, 265–66
  scillingas and early pennies, 175
  tolerance limits, 170; *see also* weights and
     measures
Middle Angles, 20
Middle Harling, Norfolk, 289
Middle Temple hoard (1893), 165, 183, 186, 208
midlands, east, 268
Milan, 144, 249
military services, 31
Milvian Bridge, battle of the (312), 58, 61
mines and mining, 158
  Derbyshire, 158
  lead and silver, 158–59
  Melle, 159
  Mendips, 158
  Muslim, 160
  Northumbria, 158; *see also* silver, sources of
minsters, 93
mints and minting, 2, 38, 44, 77, 100, 128–32,
     204, 235, 237, 286, 287, 291, 294
  Anglo-Saxon, 7, 117, 126
  Carolingian, 145, 245, 294
  Frankish, 39–40
  link to markets, 282
  Merovingian, 143–44
  profits, 41–46, 165, 167
     debasement, 167
  scale of production, 94–95, 111, 168, 184–96,
     229, 232, 238, 247, 252, 291, 293
     Frankish, 195–96
     late Anglo-Saxon, 194–95
     later medieval, 184

methods of estimating, 186–88
moneyers, 192–94
short-term fluctuations, 188
type changes, 182–83; *see also* moneyers;
     renovatio monetae; *and names of individual
     mints*
Mohammad, 254
monasteries and monasticism, 26, 68, 269
monetization, 208, 231, 252–92
  Byzantine, 286
  single-finds as evidence for, 224–29;
     see also coinage, use of
money, 275
  definitions of, 252–53, 289
  economic role, 291–92
  effects on society, 259–60
  flexible role, 275–76
  functions of, 3, 252–53
     store of wealth, 232–33, 250
     unit of account, 253, 264–67
  non-numismatic, 8, 253, 267
     bread, 290
     grain, 290
     leather, 290
     livestock, 289
     sticks, 290
  substitute, 289–90
moneyers, 2, 5, 7, 40, 42, 44, 62, 63, 64, 68, 75,
     77, 84, 86, 90, 95, 96, 106, 107, 111, 125,
     128, 132–38, 140–41, 145, 150–54, 155,
     195, 214, 295
  and coin circulation, 220–23
  and gold coinage, 116
  control over, 133–34
  emergence in England, 142–44
  in written sources, 147–49
  individual output, 192–94
  peripatetic, 131
  position and responsibilities, 146–49;
     see also mints and minting; *and names of
     individual moneyers*
Monkwearmouth-Jarrow, 60, 61
monograms, 72–73
Montecassino, 13
Morrison, Karl, 174, 176
Muslim world, *see* caliphate

names and name-elements, 146
Netherlands, 255
neutron activation, 158
New Guinea, 26
Newark-upon-Trent, Nottinghamshire, 220
Norfolk, 201, 219, 231
North America, 254
Northamptonshire, 219
Northover, Peter, 165

347

Northumbria, kingdom of, 2, 7, 10, 11, 96, 97, 202, 244, 268
  coinage of, 6, 8, 75, 97, 133, 182, 204, 207–08, 236, 246–49, 289
  debasement, 167
  metalwork, 242
  southern coinage in, 210

Offa, king of the Mercians (757–96), 7, 9, 12, 13, 18, 19, 20, 27, 28, 36–37, 47, 53, 86, 115, 118, 120, 124, 131, 132, 134, 141, 142, 150, 155, 196, 202, 204, 206, 208, 209, 211, 213, 214, 215, 217, 218, 223, 228, 263, 269
  coinage of, 54–64, 75, 77, 78, 85, 86, 100–2, 114, 126, 139, 150–51, 152, 188, 191, 194, 206, 231, 255
    gold dinar, 113–14
    metrology, 171–78
    reforms, 7, 40, 91, 94, 96, 98–100, 182, 205, 223, 226
  dyke associated with, 32
  titulature, 80, 83
Old English, 49, 264
Orléans, 245
Osmund, moneyer, 148
Oswald, St, 61, 69
Otto III, emperor, 51
Oundle, Northamptonshire, 146
Oxford, 121
Oxfordshire, 210

Pacific ocean, 273
Panjhir, Afghanistan, 159
Paris, 245
Paris basin, 17
Parry, Jonathan, 275
pauperes, 28, 282–83, 291
Pavia, 144
payments, 39, 42, 43, 44, 111, 176, 183, 253, 254, 255, 262, 269
  fines, 44, 254, 259, 267, 284
  land, 264
  tribute, 160, 234, 254, 266; *see also* tolls; trade and exchange
peasants, 28, 37
penny, 203, 249, 255, 256, 264, 267, 272, 285, 287
  'broad', 4, 8, 11
  Anonymous coinage, 53, 64, 95, 153–54
  Cross-and-Lozenge, 165, 182
  Cross-and-Wedges, 64, 65, 114, 124, 151, 187
  Crux, 195
  DORB/CANT, 73, 109, 110–11, 164, 179
  DOROB-C, 107
  Floreate Cross, 65, 69, 70, 164, 182

Inscribed Cross, 65, 69, 78, 109, 110–12, 125, 142, 149, 164, 166, 179, 182, 186, 190, 192, 225
  Large Portrait, 75
  London Monogram, 66
  Lunettes, 11, 69, 112, 164, 165, 179, 182, 192, 209, 226
  Tribrach, 70, 83, 102–04, 120, 124, 140, 151, 191, 214
  Two Emperors, 66
  Two Line, 182
  early/*sceattas*, 5–6, 55, 59, 70, 97, 106, 123, 143–44, 161, 162, 185, 195, 223, 227, 232, 256, 285
    control of production, 90–96
    ecclesiastical, 91
    Frisian, 208
    Series H, 94
    Series K, 123, 230
    Series L, 230
    Series Q, 230
    Series R, 95, 97, 143, 230
    Series U, 91
    Series X, 94
  late Anglo-Saxon, 88, 89
  rarity in charters, 272; *see also* coinage, silver; money
Perctarit, Lombard king, 81
Peterborough, 146, 242, 268, 278
Pippin I, king of Aquitaine, 121
Pippin II, king of Aquitaine, 171
Pippin III, Frankish king, 6, 43, 97
  coinage of, 161, 205, 244
  as Mayor of the Palace, 280
  titulature of, 81
Pippin the hunchback, son of Charlemagne, 177
Pirenne, Henri, 254–55, 257, 258
Pîtres, Edict of (864), 40, 165, 181, 282
Plato, 252
Polanyi, Karl, 33, 259
Polynesia, 254
polyptychs, 277
Portland, Dorset, 35
portraits, 39, 45, 52, 53–69, 83, 153
  archiepiscopal, 67–69
  Carolingian, 65
  female, 62–64
  hair, 57
  Offa, king of the Mercians (757–96), 54–64
  post-Offa, 64–66
  Roman, 64; *see also* iconography
pottery, 239–42, 243
  Canterbury, 237
  comparison with coins, 241–42
  evidential value, 239

imported, 238, 240
Ipswich ware, 240, 241
Italy, 250
limitations as source, 239–40
Maxey ware, 240
prices, 165, 166, 252, 287–88
  inflation, 166, 247–48, 287
  land, 271
  precious metal, 273; *see also* coinage, use of;
    monetization; trade and exchange
Procopius, 39
'productive sites', 200, 237, 279–80, 289
  metalwork found at, 266
  non-numismatic metalwork, 242;
    see also metal-detectors
propaganda, coinage as, 48, 112, 117;
    see also iconography
Prüm, abbey, 277
pseudo-Cyprian, *De duodecim abusivis saeculi*,
    17, 28
public and private spheres, 41

Quentovic, 195, 235, 245
quernstones, 238
  Mayen lava, 241

Rædwulf, king of the Northumbrians (844),
    248
Rainham, Kent, 19
Ramsbury, Wiltshire, 242
rate of survival, 229
rationality, economic, 24–27, 111, 156, 269, 294
  'embeddedness', 259
Ravenna, 249
Reculver Cross, 57
reeves, 21, 22, 30, 35
refuse and waste, 200
Regenhere, moneyer, 139, 146
regiones, 18–19
relationships, social, 16, 17, 23, 25, 26, 27, 218,
    224, 253, 259, 262, 269, 270, 274–75, 288
  context for gift-exchange, 260
  effects on prices, 271
  inequality, 263
  kinship, 229
  money and, 259–60, 275–76
  reciprocity, 254, 259, 261, 263, 274;
    see also gifts and gift-giving
renovatio monetae, 111, 155, 181–83, 191, 196, 206,
    226; *see also* mints and minting, type
    changes
rents, 29–31, 37–39, 263, 277–78, 284
  cash, 30, 42, 278
  in kind, 29–30; *see also* states and statehood;
    taxation
Repton Stone, 54, 56

Rhine, 17
Rhineland, 163, 241
Ribe, Denmark, 94, 236, 258
Rochester, 116, 129, 204, 236, 237, 268
  bishopric of, 128, 134
  coinage of, 73, 75, 82, 83, 84, 104, 106, 107,
    109, 118, 153, 173, 178–80, 188, 189, 192,
    216
  mint and moneyers of, 7, 64, 78, 104, 111, 125,
    128, 129–30, 134, 141, 142, 147–48, 191,
    196, 197, 223, 230, 237
  relationship with London in 840s, 109,
    141–42, 163, 192
Roermond hoard (1968), 208
Roman empire, 15, 36, 37–39, 40–41, 119, 254,
    257
  coinage of, 5, 49, 53, 54, 55, 85, 181, 201, 285,
    286, 289
  mints, 144
  roads, 202, 256
Rome, 68, 109, 113, 121, 249, 250, 263, 284
  prosperity in eighth and ninth
    centuries, 250
Romuald, son of Arichis II, 13
Rouen, 245
Rovelli, Alessia, 250
Royal Opera House, 235
runes, 75, 77
Rupertus Cross, 70
Russia, 160

Sahlins, Marshall, 274
St Augustine's abbey, Canterbury, 139, 148
St-Germain-des-Prés, abbey, 277
saints' lives, 244
Sandwich, 237
Sarah, Guillaume, 162
Sarre, Kent, 237
Sassanian empire, 160
Sawyer, Peter, 11
Saxon revolt against Charlemagne, 177
Scandinavia, 160, 233, 238
  coin-finds, 159
sceat(tas), *see* coinage, terminology; penny,
    early/*sceattas*
Scotland, 233
script forms, 73–76
  abbreviations, 77
  capitals, 73, 76
  Insular half-uncial, 73
  ligatures, 77
  'mixed' majuscules, 73
  runic, 75, 77
  uncial, 73; *see also* inscriptions
sculpture, 70, 92
seals, 51, 54, 116

seigniorage, 43, 89, 167; *see also* brassage; mints
  and minting, profits
Selsey, 80
  bishopric of, 149
Severn, 242
Sevington hoard (1834), 165, 266
Sigeberht, moneyer, 64, 146
Sigestef, moneyer, 146
silver
  sources of, 157–61, 165, 168, 182, 183, 184,
    208, 225, 229, 230, 234, 238, 252, 291
    'bullion famines', 166–67
    Carolingian empire, 158–59
    dethesaurization, 160
    eastern, 160
    mining, 158–59
    primary and secondary, 158
  supply of, 6, 7, 95, 97, 117, 155, 157
    Northumbria, 247; *see also* mines and
      mining; fineness
silversmiths, 146
Simmel, Georg, 260, 275
single-finds, 166, 170, 199–202, 209–18, 229,
    252, 255, 285
  date of loss, 200
  evidential value, 201–02
  Northumbria, 247–48
  rarity from rural settlements, 256
  rate of loss, 224–29, 257
  Roman, 202
  significance for monetary history, 255–57
  in towns, 235; *see also* metal-detectors
Southampton, 35, 83, 94, 106, 107, 115, 120, 128,
    129, 149, 189, 196, 200, 223, 235, 236,
    239, 240, 241, 258, 289
  coin-finds, 218; *see also* Wessex, mint and
    moneyers of
Stamford, Lincolnshire, 146
standardization
  coinage, 48, 82, 83, 84, 85–86, 87, 90, 92, 104,
    106, 107, 112, 156, 157, 165, 170, 294;
    see also kingship, control over coinage
State Museum, Berlin, 116
states and statehood, 16–22, 251
staurogram, 73; *see also* iconography, christian
Stenton, Sir Frank, 1
Stephen, king of the English (1135–54), 145
styles, royal, *see* titulature
Suffolk, 231
surpluses, agricultural, 257; *see also* agrarian
  change
Surrey, 19, 106, 219
Sussex, 19, 32, 36, 80, 106, 243
  coin-finds from, 210
  under Mercian rule, 149
Sutton Hoo hoard (1939), 286

Sylvester, St, 60
synods, 35; *see also* Church councils

Tamworth, 20
Tatel, moneyer, 192
taxation, 37–38, 144, 256, 285; *see also* kingship,
  economic resources of; payments; rents;
  states and statehood
Thames, 19, 202, 219, 220, 242, 243
thegns, 148, 149
Theodosian Code, 40
Theudebert I, Frankish king, 39
Tilbeorht, moneyer, 95
Tilberht, moneyer, 143
titulature, 79–84, 89
  in charters, 80, 82, 83
  on coins, 39, 48, 52, 75, 80–84, 89, 97, 103,
    104, 105, 112, 117, 141, 155, 156
  East Anglian, 84
  Kentish, 83
  West Saxon, 83–84
tolls, 27, 34–35, 266, 279, 284
Torcello, Italy, 250
Torksey, Lincolnshire, 208
touchstones, 157
Toulouse, 171
towns, 235–39, 241, 242, 256, 258, 282, 294
  association with coin-use, 285
  control, 279
  'emporia', 32–34, 196, 236, 237, 259, 279
  Frankish, 280
  minting and, 128–32, 142
  ninth-century decline, 235–36
  ports, 209, 230, 259
  and royal power, 32–36; *see also* Wessex,
    burghal system
trade and exchange, 5, 36–37, 117, 130, 163, 215,
    229, 230, 231, 235–39, 240, 243, 253, 255
  balance of, 230
  bulk goods, 241, 250, 289
  commercial, 259, 260, 261, 292
  east-west, 160, 255
  and gift-giving, 274
  high-value, 249, 256, 273, 291
  long-distance, 33, 230, 258
  networks, 34, 214, 218, 229, 239
  redirection, 238–39
  riverine, 220, 245
  role of coinage, 243–44
  role of markets, 284
  role of relationships, 218
  silver, 233–34, 238, 244
  status of goods, 274
  wool and textiles, 238, 239; *see also* gifts and
    gift-giving; merchants
Translatio et miracula S. Adelphi Mettensis, 281

Index

Translatio et miracula S. Swithuni, 147
Transoxania, 160
Trent, 220, 242
Trewhiddle hoard (1774), 266
Tribal Hidage, 20
tribute, *see* payments
Trier, 196

Uhtred, sub-king of the Hwicce, 269

Valentinian I, emperor, 38
Venice, 45, 160, 279
Verberie, dép. Oise, 109
Veroli Casket, 58
Verona, 144
vicus, 115; *see also wic*; towns, 'emporia'
vikings, 4, 10–11, 207, 234–35, 239
  coinage, 248
  conquests, 11, 101, 171
  economic impact, 234
  effects of, 111
  invasions, 233
  raids, 10–11, 168
  settlement, 231
  tribute, 234, 266
violence, 239
Visigothic kingdom, 38, 81
  coinage of, 74, 81, 90, 98
  mints, 145
volume, measures of, 264; *see also* weights and
  measures

Wales, 32, 36, 246
warfare, 31–32, 199, 252, 261
  effect on coinage, 234–35; *see also* vikings;
    violence
Warwickshire, 210, 220
Weald, 201
wealth, 23
weights and measures
  barley grain, 169
  basis in seeds, 169
  carob seed, 169
  importance of, 180
  modius, 169
  pound, 169, 265–66
  sester, 169
  wheat seed, 169; *see also* metrology; coinage,
    terminology
Weohthun, moneyer, 149

Werbald, moneyer, 140
Werhard, priest, 283
Wessex 7, 10, 11, 22, 32, 36, 83–84, 96, 109, 120,
  131, 141, 155, 168, 182, 202, 204, 209, 210,
  213, 215, 216, 217, 218, 220, 224, 229, 235,
  243, 295
  burghal system, 32
  development of royal coinage, 106–12
  mint and moneyers of, 7, 71, 83, 103, 106,
    107, 110, 120, 128, 129, 140, 146,
    149, 188, 189, 192, 196, 216–18, 223;
    see also Southampton; Winchester
West Stow, Suffolk, 289
wic, 115; *see also* towns, 'emporia'
Wickham, Chris, 239, 250
Widsith, 266
Wiglaf, king of the Mercians (829–40)
  coinage of, 192
Wigmund, archbishop of York, 67
Wigræd, moneyer, 95, 143
Wiltshire, 210, 219
Winchester, 35, 83, 120, 128, 132, 133, 147, 149,
  194, 195, 196
  bishopric of, 224; *see also* Wessex, mint and
    moneyers of
wine, 238
wolf and twins, 119
Worcester, 20, 61, 80, 82, 268
  bishopric of, 220
Worcestershire, 219
Wuffingas, 120
Wulfred, archbishop of Canterbury, 104, 107,
  153–54, 258, 271, 283
  coinage of, 67, 68, 69, 71, 73, 77
Wulfstan, archbishop of York, 156
Wynhere, moneyer, 148

x-ray fluorescence, 158

York, 133, 182, 236, 241, 258
  archbishopric of, 7, 116, 123, 284
  coinage of, 194, 195
    under viking rule, 194
  Coppergate, 133
  Fishergate, 236
  mint and moneyers of, 7
Yorkshire, 201, 240

Zelizer, Viviana, 275
zinc, 162–63

Lightning Source UK Ltd.
Milton Keynes UK
UKOW06f0618080415

249286UK00010B/578/P